THROUGH MANY EYES

KERSHAW COUNTY DURING THE CONFEDERATE WAR YEARS AND BEYOND

Compiled by
WILLIAM GUERRY FELDER

Copyright © 2020 William Guerry Felder
All rights reserved. No part(s) of this book may be reproduced, distributed or transmitted in any form, or by any means, or stored in a database or retrieval systems without prior expressed written permission of the author of this book.

ISBN: 978-1-5356-1768-0

About the Cover

THE FLAG ON THE FRONT cover is the Kirkwood Ranger's flag, located at the Camden Archives and Museum in Camden, South Carolina. The flag is thirty inches long from the top to the bottom of the flag, and forty-three to forty-five inches across in width.

The inscription of the flag on a piece of paper that came with the flag said that the flag was presented to the Kirkwood Rangers by the ladies of Camden in 1861. The material was a dress given by Mrs. Pickens, our war governor's wife. It was made by the nuns of Columbia, South Carolina, who had the central medallion blessed by the Pope. On the rear of the flag is another symbol like the front, which was an arched banner or motto in Latin, and centered underneath is a cross of stars numbering thirteen for the states of the Confederacy. The Latin phrase means "In this sign victory."

This flag was given to the John D. Kennedy Chapter of the United Daughters of the Confederacy by Mr. John Boykin, son of Colonel Edward M. Boykin.

The paper was signed by;
Captain Wm. M. Shannon
Captain James Doby
Captain Edward M. Boykin
Lieutenants Zack Cantey
Lieutenants Robert Johnson
Lieutenants Usher Bonney
Lieutenants James G. Jones
Lieutenants James D. Matheson
Entered into service — 118 men
Surrendered — 33 men

The flag was restored by the Museum of Early Southern Decorative Arts in May 1983. The case was built by Benjamin Covington, a furniture maker from Columbia, South Carolina. Funds were provided by the City of Camden, with the case being funded by interested individuals, especially those in the Joseph B. Kershaw Camp #82, Sons of Confederate Veterans, Camden, South Carolina.

Introduction

CAMDEN IS THE OLDEST INLAND town in South Carolina. Originally it was called Fredericksburg in the 1700s. During the military periods leading up to today, in the Camden area and surrounding vicinity, the citizens were patriotic and willing to serve. From the Revolutionary War, people in this area saw fourteen engagements with a radius of thirty miles of Camden, and six within the present confines of Kershaw County today. Those battles took place near Camden on July 20, 1780, near Flat Rock, on August 15, 1780 at Wateree Ferry near Camden, on December 4, 1780, at Rugeley's Mill, on March 6, 1781, at Radcliff's Bridge on Lynches Creek, and on April 25, 1781, at Hobkirk Hill. The Battle of Camden took place eight miles north of Camden, near Gum Swamp above Sander's Creek with 900 killed and 1000 taken prisoner by Cornwallis. The War of 1812 had two companies from the area, Captain Chapman Levy's riflemen and Captain Francis Blair's company, leaving October 6, 1814. In the Seminole or Florida War, Colonel John Chesnut's company of seventy-six men saw little service, but Captain Chesnut died a few months later. The Mexican War of 1846 had eighty-six people on the roll, and forty-eight men died on their return July 12, 1848. Some of those losing their lives were James Polk Dickinson and Willis Cantey. James Cantey went to Mexico as second lieutenant and Joseph B. Kershaw as a first lieutenant. This book will explore the period referred as the War Between the States in Camden, Kershaw County, South Carolina. Included will be events leading up to this confrontation with the North, what happened in Camden and the surrounding vicinity during 1860-1865, information pertaining to Camden and its Confederate Heritage afterwards, and soldiers from the area and those that left before and after this war. Though the effort to document all the soldiers has taken place, some may have been left out due to no information of serving in the war, lost records, and the possibility exists the names used may not have been correct due to misspelling. Enjoy this book and travel back in time to those days long, long ago.

Contents

About the Cover iii

Introduction iv

On to Camden 3

1861: The Beginning of the War 7

The Southern Cross 25

1862 27

1863 51

1864 73

1865 101

The White Arabian: Jefferson Davis's Horse 139

The State Survivor's Association 145

The Kershaw County Survivors' Association 151

The Ladies Aid Society 167

1904 Confederate Reunion at Camden, South Carolina 187

1914 Confederate Reunion in Bethune, South Carolina 191

Kershaw Counties Six Brigadier Generals 197

The Southern Commission Claims of Kershaw County 237

Church Records 243

A Look Back at Sherman's Visit in Camden through the Eyes of Miss. A.E. Davis 247

The Story of the Cockade 251

Camden's Spy - Josephine Noel By Elizabeth P. Hough 255

The Body Servants from Kershaw County 259

- Soldiers of the War Between the States Buried in Quaker and Beth-El Cemeteries in Camden. ...267
- Stories from the War by Camden Confederates, Camden People, and Kershaw County Descendants. ...271
- Camden During February 1865 ...273
- The Capture of Joseph Brevard Kershaw ...277
- A Reminiscence of the War ...283
- Recollections of a Southern Girl ...285
- An Account of the Experiences of the Family of the Reverend and Mrs. Trapier During and After the War Between the States. ...299
- Liberty Hill ...311
- The Bloody Battle for Carolinians ...313
- General Sherman Feasted in Kershaw County Home ...317
- Camden Man Relates Stirring Incidents in His Life As A Scout During War Between the States. ...319
- Marcus Baum Died with General Jenkins ...323
- Thrilling Experiences as Told by Captain C. C. Haile ...327
- Dr. George Rodgers Clark Todd ...331
- What Makes a Hero? ...333
- Battle Of Ream's Station ...337
- I Saw Sherman's Army ...341
- Memories of Mrs. U. N. Myers, Sr. 1938 ...343
- Some Diaries and Letters of Soldiers ...347
- Persons Captured at Lynches Creek ...359
- Understanding the makeup of how units began and how during attrition came together ...361
- The Role of Pensions in Kershaw County ...367
- Kershaw County Pension Records ...369
- Persons Exempt from Military Service in Kershaw County ...399
- More Confederate Reunion Pictures ...401
- Our Confederates Can't Speak Anymore ...407

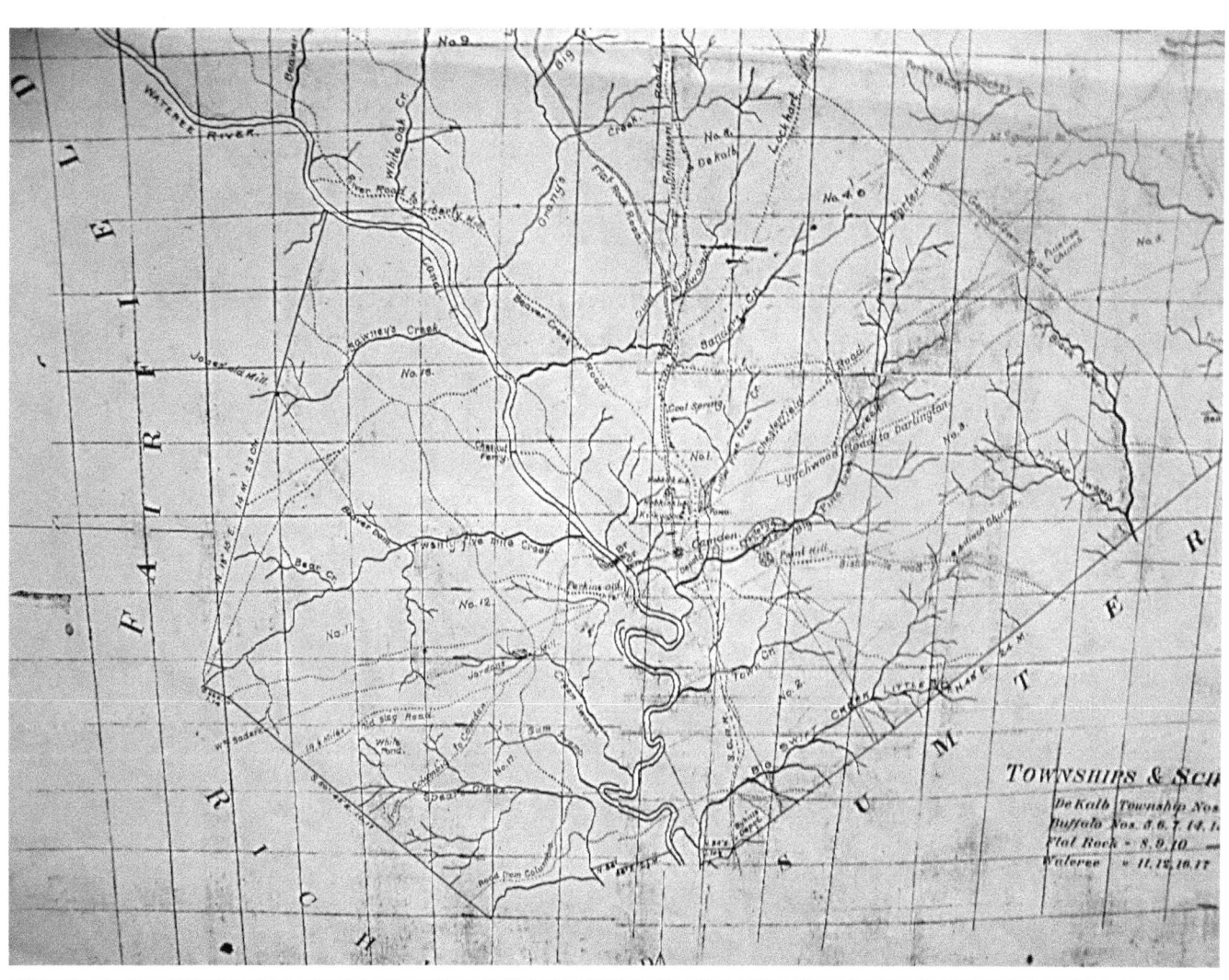

C.C. Haile Map of 1894
Courtesy of Camden Archives and Museum.

On to Camden

JOHN WILLIAM SHIVER WAS A planter, a blacksmith, an overseer, and many things on his farm near the Pisgah-Spring Hill area. In those days, one had to be equipped to deal with the rigors of country living. Eighteen-sixty had arrived, and October had come. Time for a trip to Camden, South Carolina, which was about twelve miles away. Only two routes could be used to travel, those being by Boykin, South Carolina or by Spring Hill. John Shiver usually took the Boykin route and, by wagon, would take a day to go and come back. On this day, the whole family would go. His wife, Emma, and their children, Elizabeth Emma (now Hatfield), John Jr., James William, and Martha Cornelia. John was well-respected and had become a pillar of his community. His farm had a brick kiln, a blacksmith shop, grapevines, assorted berry bushes, one smokehouse for meat and one storehouse for vegetables, hogs, horses, mules, and open farmland to grow vegetables and various crops.

When John and his family arrived in Camden, he parked his mules and wagon at the designated parking for horses and wagons on the lower end of Broad Street on the right as he came in. He gave his mules some water from the nearby trough after he and his sons cooled down the mules.

Off to shopping the family went. Emma and her daughters went looking for clothes and groceries, and John and his sons looked at farming implements and shopped at Eli Bonney's. While walking on the street, a commotion was ahead on the left, at the town hall, now the galleria of today. As they approached, a gentleman of distinction was seen. That person was Joseph Brevard Kershaw, five feet eleven, dark blue eyes, blondish-looking hair, and a mustache which flowed around his mouth. A mob followed him inside.

"Hello, ladies and gentlemen of Camden and surrounding areas! I am here to inform you of the goings on within this state and that of the northern states. I was alerted to the fact that once this election of 1860 became official, we must have in place a group to defend this town and surrounding areas. If Lincoln wins, then this nation will be in turmoil and disarray. It will be up to each one of us to plan, organize, and implement to be successful in dealing with this situation," said Kershaw.

"We need to select certain positions to be in charge. Those being captain, first lieutenant, second lieutenant, and third lieutenant. Do we have any nominations from the gathering?" asked Kershaw.

"Yes, I do," said Eli Bonney, a noted merchant, banker, and respected citizen of Camden. "I wish to nominate you, Joseph Kershaw, to lead us as captain." The crowd got excited as nods of approval and shouts for Kershaw began.

"Any others to be considered?" said Kershaw.

The word "no" came back from the crowd.

"All those in favor of electing me as captain, please say yes."

Almost in unison, the crowd shouted an overwhelming "yes."

"I guess I can't refuse the fine people of Camden with such a fine position. I accept humbly and with God's leadership and spirit," said Kershaw.

By the time the proceedings were over, the first lieutenant would be William Shannon, T.J. Ancrum, second lieutenant, and Sheriff Elijah E. Sill would be third lieutenant.[1] The organization would be called the Minutemen of Kershaw County, and just like their namesakes in Revolutionary War times, they would spring into action to protect and preserve the area of Camden. At the end of this session, one hundred-twenty had signed up to be involved.[2] Adopted was a blue rosette measuring two and a half inches with a military like button in the center, and it was meant to be worn on the side of their hats.[3] One can only imagine what it must have been like for these enlistees to become the first to enlist for the War Between the States in 1861.

Eli came by and said to John, "What do you think of this, John?"

"Being from Sumter County, I hope that this will happen there. You have a great leader in Kershaw, and he will make it work right," said John Shiver.

"Eli! I came into town to see if you had something. Are you going back to the store?" asked John.

Eli commented that he would be at the store in an hour, so John turned to his sons and told them that they had better go find the rest of the family and see what they are doing.

"On the way, we will stop by the blacksmith shop and talk to Lazarus Shiver, my brother."

After he did a few errands, John said he would meet him there then.

As John got closer, he motioned to his sons to stay. He walked in and asked if the owner was in because he would like to see him. He was from out of town and needed his help. The owner came out from behind a wall.

"John, you are not a traveler in need, you know everything about blacksmithing. You taught me and Samuel (Shiver)." They both burst out laughing.

In the western part of the district, another meeting was taking place at the Beaver Dam Church. The purpose of this meeting will be to organize and act as an auxiliary unit of the Minutemen Association in the Kershaw District.[4] The man behind this effort of organizing this company is the eloquent, masterful, and persuasive speaker Colonel W. Z. Leitner. Forty men signed up, and the words that swayed the crowd to come forward were "Southern Constitutional Equality in the Union, or failing that, to establish our independence out of it."[5]

When the meeting was over, Dr. James G. Jones was elected captain; Dr. John A. Glenn, first lieutenant; J. L. Logan, second lieutenant; and Captain E. Parker, ensign[6]. By the end of November into early December, the Kershaw District had four others:

1　The Charleston Mercury, Charleston, South Carolina, October 18, 1860.
2　Ibid.
3　The Evening Star, Washington, DC, October 18, 1860.
4　*The Charleston Courier*, Charleston, South Carolina, October 25, 1860.
5　Ibid.
6　Ibid.

Lynches Creek Minutemen — Organized December 1, fifty men signed up; Colonel B. Jones, Captain; Major C.C. Haile, First Lieutenant; Captain S.D. Jones, Second Lieutenant; James M. Kirkley, Ensign.

Troy Minutemen — Sixty-five men signed up. A.J. Haile, Captain; James T. Cauthen, First Lieutenant; D.D. Coats, Second Lieutenant; W.M. Johnson, Ensign.

Flat Rock Minutemen — Forty men signed up. Colonel D.D. Kirkland, Captain; Dr. J.I. Trantham, First Lieutenant; Captain G.R. Miller, Ensign.

Lysenby's Minutemen — Forty-five men signed up. T.B. Cantey, Captain; Finley McCaskill, First Lieutenant; Andrew Raley, Second Lieutenant; Moses Hough, Ensign.

In November, the Mounted Minutemen, known as M.M.M., was formed out of the Camden Minutemen Association. They have embraced some of the finest flowers of its youth. An Artillery corpse has also been determined, and we soon shall have the finest little army in the land in Kershaw District. How they will perform when the "tug of war" comes, we can only judge by what our boys have done in the past. The bones of our gallant dead, upon Mexican soil, and those which have found a resting place upon the bosom of their mother earth, attest the truth that Kershaw District has never failed to have a prominent place in the picture.[7]

November came, and the presidential election took place. On April 23, 1860, in Charleston, South Carolina, the democrats held their convention.[8] Turmoil occurred between northern senators and southern senators with views for and against strongly spoken. Senators William Lowndes Yancey of Virginia alongside Edmund Ruffin exchanged words with Senator James Buchanan of Pennsylvania.[9] Talk from the South focused on the actions of John Brown and his acts in blowing up Harper's Ferry in 1859.[10] Other arguments that transpired were about the factions for slavery and those opposed, the undue influence of the North upon the Southern states, and failure to reach a compromise because of all these strong feelings for and against.[11] However, the election proved misery for all as the North and the South despised Abraham Lincoln. The southern states, especially South Carolina, had few or no electoral votes. South Carolina and the South went for John C. Breckenridge, three states went for John C. Bell, Stephen Douglass fell in second place, and Abraham Lincoln carried the West and Midwest to carry the rest of the votes and win the electoral vote by sixty-nine percent.[12] The actual electoral votes went as follows: Abraham Lincoln had 69 percent, Stephen Douglass took 4 percent, John Bell had 13 percent, and John Breckenridge had 24 percent. The results caused quite a stir in South Carolina.

In Camden, at the Peck Academy, a group of students were busy at work on a flag. No one in leadership gave them the authority to work on such a flag. Thursday after the election, these brave, opinionated, and service for the cause-minded students displayed what could be considered the first succession flag in Camden and in

---

[7] The Lancaster Ledger, November 7, 1860
[8] McClure, J. M. United States Presidential Election of 1860. (2011, April 5). In *Encyclopedia Virginia*. Retrieved from http://www.EncyclopediaVirginia.org/United_States_Presidential_Election_of_1860.
[9] Ibid.
[10] Ibid.
[11] Ibid.
[12] Ibid.

the state of South Carolina, on the flagpole at the academy with Colonel Peck's approval to fly with honor for the causes. The only thing mentioned about the flag was that it had a palmetto on it with the words "South Carolina" underneath. [13]

Talk of succession became the talk of the day in Camden and in small and big towns across this state. Then, a succession convention was called, and many representatives came to voice their opinion. Kershaw District sent Judge Withers, Joseph B. Kershaw, and the eloquent and masterful senator, James Chesnut, Jr. When the votes came at the end of December, succession began for the state of South Carolina. With it, celebrations occurred across the state. In Camden, the people shouted, fired guns in the air, and on every porch, a candle was lit in jack o' lanterns, which could be seen for miles. Some people in the celebration may have gotten killed, as some reports suggested. This happened despite a small-pox epidemic in Camden and in areas like Columbia, South Carolina. [14] The original meeting place was in Columbia, and then the meeting place was moved to Charleston to prevent the spreading of measles throughout the state. While in Columbia, several ballots were done for a permanent president. On the third ballot, Chesnut had seventeen votes, Orr had thirty-two votes, and Jamison had sixty-four votes. On the fourth ballot, Jamison won, with Orr receiving thirty, and three to others. [9]

Just as the succession convention ended, the Charleston mayor approached Camden's Gamewell to design the telegraph system for Charleston and eventually the state.

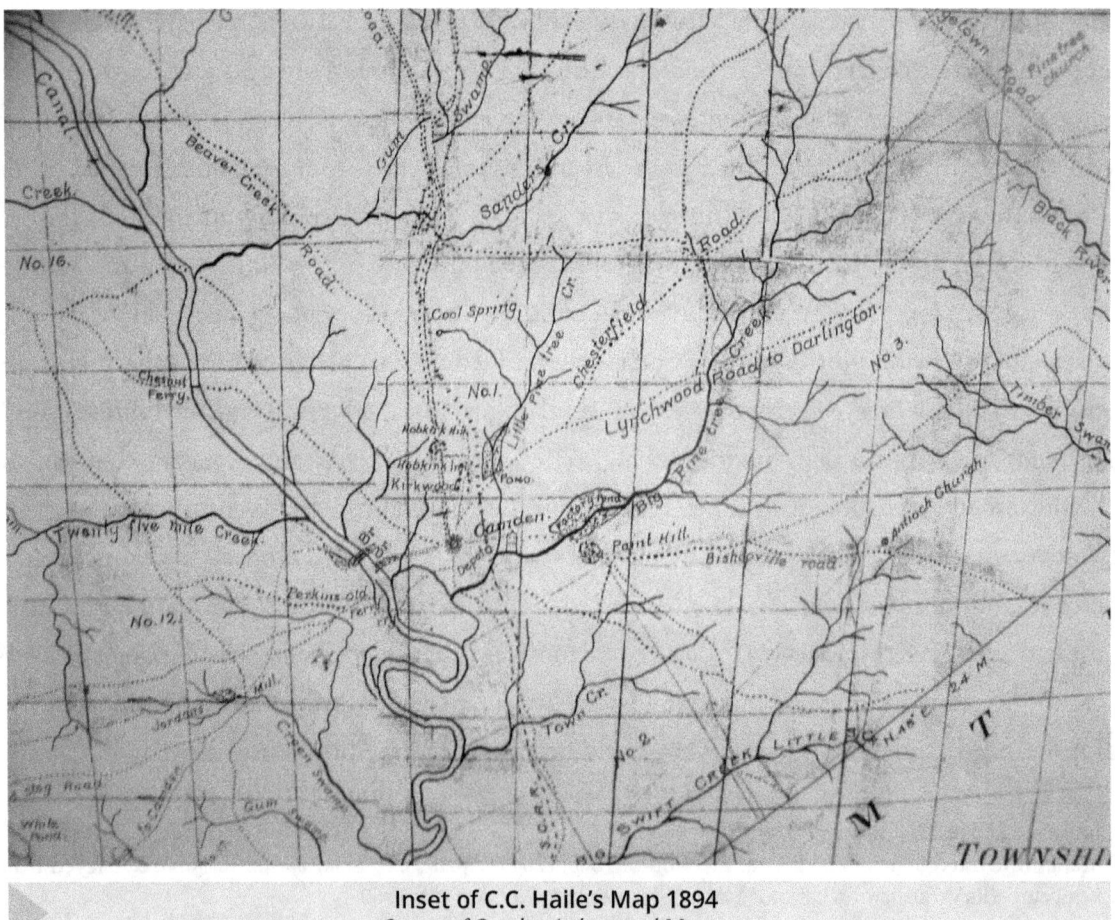

Inset of C.C. Haile's Map 1894
Coutesy of Camden Archives and Museum

---

13   The Lancaster Ledger, Lancaster, South Carolina, November 1860.
14   The Daily Dispatch Newspaper, Richmond, Virginia, December 17, 1860

1861: The Beginning of the War

IN 1861, PLANS WERE BEING made as to what to do next. The local militia was activated. A military defense was being planned and regiments activated. One of those nominated was Joseph Brevard Kershaw of Camden. He was to command and be a part of a large state military organization.

Correspondents were coming to Camden to see what was going on in the area. They wrote of "the Hill" as the Kirkwood suburb was so eloquently called by the locals.[15] The area of Camden near the railroad area was described as like a selvage. It gave a neutral ground to the rest of the area. The Kirkwoodians did their shopping by equipping themselves with fast horses, fast paces, and a fast, hurried travel up the streets.[16] Men shopped occasionally, going into grocery stores and making their way in the back dirty room to sip on Mumm's quarts, and intake their favorite sardines and crackers.[17] The feeling was that the Union would not be bad but they feared that something else would be worse and that was not in their interest.[13] The fear remained that actual business would slow to a crawl, selling cotton would become hard, getting any money difficult, thus forcing them to do without the comforts and luxuries that the North had. Upon hearing this, people acted with a naughty-boy, poutiness attitude.[18] These people treasured their leisure time. They disliked being forced to run fast to get things done.[19]

In a letter (dated February 24, 1861) from Henry C. Roberts to his nephew Henry C. Burns, the following was said: The companies were encamped for a week after you left and had a drill every Saturday since your departure. The company will soon be callled out under Colonel Kershaw's Brigade, and that Fort Sumter will be taken by the fourth, had the greatest display of jubilation upon hearing the news of the Confederation Ordinance, as the town was illuminated, fences, trees, and all sorts of contrivances and representations, Old Abe was manufactured out of large pumpkins and illuminated inside and labeled Old Abe, the Minutemen are to guard duty and Negroes prevented from going after the bell ring, Old Colonel Chesnut is finishing off his new house nearby, as he intends to move here and give his Mulberry to his son at once (he is eighty-eight and his wife is eighty-seven, his daughter is near fifty but could pass for a thirty-year-old, a Negro driver of Captain

---

[15] The Philadelphia Inquirer, Philadelphia, Pennsylvania, January 21, 1861.
[16] Ibid.
[17] Ibid.
[18] Ibid.
[19] Ibid.

Mungo killed a Negro boy some days ago and was sent off to Alabama and sold before he could be arrested, the Volunteers look good; however one was expelled for _____ and fighting, and he and another got to fighting after a parade. During all of this, rain was coming down to the ankles and Clyburn stood over them with a revolver and kept them from separating until they reached the point of nearly drowning.[20]

A chaplain was selected for the 2nd Regiment. That individual was Reverend E.J. Meynardie, pastor of the Methodist church.[21] Reverend Meynardie was asked by Colonel Kershaw, and he accepted the appointment. That Saturday, he left for the war, and with it, his patriotism, his unselfishness, his devotion to duty, and prayers from the community for his safety and safe return."[22]

Mail that needed to get to Captain Kennedy's group could be sent to the name of the person, Captain Kennedy's Company, 2nd Regiment, S.C.V., Morris Island, South Carolina.[23] Captain Kennedy received orders to go to Charleston, South Carolina. He left in the afternoon because many were scattered through the district, with couriers dispatched in every direction to alert the soldiers that their time had come to go to war.[24]

On a Tuesday afternoon, an escort was provided by Peck's Academy, and it was Peck's cadets that led the way to the train depot, where many citizens were there to send them on their way.[25] While at the train depot, Thomas J. Warren addressed the soldiers. Then Captain Kennedy spoke a few words, then Chaplain Meynardie said a prayer, and at five o'clock in the afternoon, the train with all the soldiers from Camden left to go to Charleston.[26] The group stopped in Kingsville and waited for others as more from Camden would be coming in the next day. That Wednesday, a detachment under Lieutenant William L. DePass arrived, with another group under Corporal Henry G. McKagen arriving that same day.[27] On Friday, the arrivals stopped, and with it the detachment under Lieutenant E.E. Sills, making the total number of soldiers on duty ninety- two soldiers.[28] The question on the minds of the people reflected not who was leaving for the war, but who was staying home to protect those here.

Ironically, the arrival of Captain Kennedy's troop found them watching the bombardment of Fort Sumter from their quarters at Morris Island.[29] During this bombardment, Colonel Kershaw had telegraphed Adjutant Goodwin for the commissary captain, James T. Villepigue, and special aid, James A. Doby, and the regimental surgeon, Dr. Thomas W. Salmond.[30]

The Camden area had a special group that came into town last week. This group was the Lancaster Greys, and they were traveling from nearby Lancaster, in route to do their service for the cause. As this company came close to the city line, the Lancaster Greys were met at the Kirkwood Boundary by the Kershaw Cadets, which

---

20 Letter from Henry Cassel Roberts to Henry C. Burns, February 24, 1861; Camden Archives and Museum, Camden, S.C. (Burns Family Collection)
21 The Camden Weekly Journal, Camden, S.C., April 16, 1861.
22 Ibid.
23 Ibid.
24 Ibid.
25 Ibid.
26 Ibid.
27 Ibid.
28 Ibid.
29 Ibid.
30 Ibid. (note: Goodwyn left on Saturday; James Villipigue left on Tuesday with Doby, and Dr. T. W. Salmond,)

were being led by Captain James Doby, who escorted these fine soldiers, who were under the command of Captain John D. Wylie, to the Laurens Square. When this group arrived, they were met with three excitable cheers that could be heard all over the area for miles and miles around. There was so much excitement and exuberance for a cause that had brought all the communities together. A cannon was shot. Now, Thomas Warren, the editor of the *Camden Weekly Journal* and the selected representative of Camden, gave a short but appropriate welcome speech. He went on to invite these men to their town's hospitality. And with his usual grace and eloquence, Captain Wylie gave a gentle, warm speech, only reminiscent of patriots and soldiers of old to the solders now in service. Then, citizens led a procession, followed by the cadets, forming an escort to be led to the town hall, and under flags flying from the buildings of the Mansion and DeKalb house, there they would stay for the night. The Lancaster Greys totaled one hundred men, and their officers were John D. Wylie, captain; John N. Crockett, first lieutenant; J.R. Wade, second lieutenant; and W.G. Stewart, third lieutenant. The correspondent of the *Lancaster Ledger* wrote of Camden, the heritage that this area has seen. From the baptism of blood in the Revolution War, to the War of 1812, the Florida Indian battles, the Mexican War of 1847-48, to now. Camden had always been the leader in the state in the struggle for independence. Camden was well deserved as being known then as "Cockade Town." She has earned it so well because of her patriotic leadership and men to fight for such a cause. [31]

The following is the roster of the Camden Volunteers, 2nd Regiment:[32]

J. D. Kennedy, Captain
W. Z. Leitner, First Lieutenant
E.E. Sill, Second Lieutenant
W.L. DePass, Third Lieutenant
E. Niles, First Sergeant
J. J. McKain, Second Sergeant
J.D. Dunlap, Third Sergeant
J. L. Haile, Fourth Sergeant
J. J. Drakeford, Fifth Sergeant
A. Niles, First Corporal
H. G, McKagen, Second Corporal
B. Hornet, Third Corporal
W. C. Dutton, Fourth Corporal
J. P. Boswell, Fifth Corporal
J. A. Perry, Sixth Corporal

Privates

W. R. Allen	J. T. Graham	C.J. Pegues
J. H. Arrants	J. E. Hinson	J. R. Pickett

---

[31] The Camden Weekly Journal, Camden, S.C., April 30, 1861.
[32] Charleston Mercury, Charleston, S.C., April 24, 1861.

B.M. Baer	E. H. Jenks	T. W. Pope
J. R. Beaver	A. Johnson	R. W. Procter
Y. F. Brasington	W.E. Johnson	J. H. Riddle
J. S. Brown	George King	R.F. Small
W. Bowen	Robert Kirkley	John Smith
T. F. Boykin	R. R. Kirkland	W. W. Stokes
W. M. Bullock	J. M. LeGrand	R. R. Strawbridge
A. Campbell	M. L. Lemmond	James Stuart
T. M. Crump	James McIntosh	John Team
Patrick Cussick	Joel McMillian	W. M. Turner
J. T. Davis	C. J. McDowell	L. M. Vaughan
F. J. Devine	J. W. P. McKagen	W. W. Watts
George Evans	S. B. Meanes	J. O. Warren
J. R. Ferrel	J. P. MIckle	L. A. Wethersby
J. H. Francis	D. J. Middleton	R. R. Wilson
L. T. Gardner	C. R. Miles	J. R. Winder
R. L. Gerald	M. W. Morrison	J. H. Witherspoon
H. R. Gibson	George Nelson	P. C. Woods
John A. Green	Hiram Nettles	Jessie Nettles
W. H. Wright		

During this time, the following troops were activated to go to Richmond to join Colonel Kershaw and build the soldier count from South Carolina. Those troops joining are Captain McManus from Lancaster, South Carolina, Captain Boykin's Troop from Camden, which will join up with Colonel Gregg's regiment, Captain Cantey's Mounted Rangers, Butler Guards from Greenville, Captain Richardson's Company, and Captain Perryman's company from Abbeville.[33] When these companies arrived in Richmond, Colonel Kershaw's force would be between sixteen and seventeen hundred strong.[34]

In Camden, news spread that John Brown's steam mill, located near Camden, South Carolina was burned on May 28, 1861, with a valued loss of over ten thousand dollars.[35]

In Charleston, South Carolina, a big celebration took place at the hotel in Charleston on April 12, 1861.[36] The arrival of the Honorable Roger A. Pryor, of Virginia, at the Charleston Hotel, last night, took his friends by surprise. Notwithstanding the absence from the city of so large a proportion of our citizens, now on duty at the harbor batteries, quite a large concourse assembled with a brass band in front of the portico of the Charleston Hotel, and stirring strains of "Dixie" and the Marseillaise, succeeded by hearty calls, Mr. Pryor came in sight. At that very time, the lines from Clarendon and Kershaw appeared just arriving in town. They, however, were hurrying toward the boat, and could not wait to hear Mr. Pryor's speech. As the sound of their drums died away in the distance, Mr. Pryor rose, and after the cheering, which had greeted him had subsided,

---
[33] Ibid.
[34] Ibid.
[35] The Daily Dispatch, Richmond, Virginia, April 10, 1861
[36] The Daily Dispatch, Richmond, Virginia, April 13, 1861

addressed the assemblage. From his speech: "For this demonstration of your regard, I beg to return my grateful acknowledgments. I am here in Charleston in pursuance of a pledge, voluntarily given, that so soon as I might be able to release myself from certain very imperative engagements in Virginia, that I would come hither, and, upon the soil of South Carolina, offer in person the tribute of my infinite admiration." As sure as to-morrow's sun will rise upon us, just so sure will Old Virginia be a member of this Southern Confederation. [Applause.] And I will tell you, gentlemen, what will put her in the Southern Confederation in less than an hour, by Shrewsberry clock. Strike a blow! [Tremendous applause.] I do

The Charleston Hotel, 1861
Courtesy of Library of Congress

not mean to say anything for effect upon military civilian, who never sent a squadron in the field …"[37] Later that night, Colonel J.B. Kershaw's troops left for Richmond by train. Another side to this story is that the regiment formed in front of the American Hotel and marched to the Charleston Hotel.[38] As the regiment and the people gathered at nine o'clock, Governor Manning had been chosen to present a flag on behalf of the Ladies of Sumter for the Second Regimental Volunteers. The flag was at the Mr. Louis D. DeSaussure's house on Number 1, East Bay Street.[39] Governor Manning, in his speech, addressed Colonel Kershaw and said: "I am deputed by fair ladies whose fathers, husbands, brothers, sons, and lovers are about, after fighting the battle of their own country and their own state, to march forward to the assistance of those who are struggling for our great constitutional rights in another and a distant state, to deliver to you this standard; this standard, which embodies the idea of unity, which is obedience, this standard which embodies the idea of patriotism; and more than that, this standard which embodies in itself all the ideas of sacred home, of your thoughts, your hearthstones, and all the tender joys which , as men, you have ever known in this world. Tremblingly their hands have worked its device, tearfully their eyes have poured over their labor, and prayerfully they bid you Godspeed in the noble march of the future. The march was as noble a march as ever for soldiers to put forward a step. It is to battle for the rights of your wives and your children; it is to battle for the glorious heritage left to you by your ancestors; it is to leave a noble inheritance to your posterity." Applause has set in. "In the olden time Virginia, almost the mother of the republic, gave out land here surges, her statesmen, and her warriors, and it is to Virginia that you are now to march, and the battle is again to be fought on that soil, which established first the independence of America. And although there has been somewhat of a cavalry in settlement between you as to who has been the most patriotic to maintain our rights and liberties, and to establish our past glories,

---

[37] The Daily Dispatch, Richmond, Virginia, April 13, 1861.
[38] The Charleston Mercury, Charleston, S.C., April 26, 1861.
[39] Ibid.

that rivalry has now ceased, and you are to march forward tonight and take your place alongside of her, and to unite in a new and fresh struggle for your liberties, and upon the strength of your arm, upon the establishment of your supremacy as trained and disciplined soldiers, is to rest the inheritance of your children. The beast that will exist in future life, will be that Virginia and South Carolina, the first and the last to strike, are about to be united upon a new field. And then you may state as has been stated before — as on this glorious and well-fought field, they kept together in their chivalry."[40] Colonel Kershaw then got up and told the soldiers: "I misconceive the manly hearts which beat in your stalwart forms, if a word of mine could add ought to the reverence with which you regard this sacred emblem of the confidence of the Ladies of Sumter. Upon you it devolves to justify the distinction expressed in this gift upon the battlefield. You may die beneath it, but you can never dishonor it." Cries of "never" and applause erupted.[41] With that, Colonel Kershaw and his regiment went to the eleven o'clock train of the Northwestern Railroad and left for the Old Dominion.[42]

The spokesman for the Ladies Society from Sumter was Mrs. Elizabeth Garden.[43] The flag was described as being from the best Parisian silk, and doubled, and of regimental proportions at six feet long and four feet wide, had a blue silk Union and a palmetto tree worked with white floss silk, with a crescent on the right-hand corner.[44] Golden fringe with golden tassels formed the trimming on the flag, with an inscription on one side that read Second Regiment South Carolina Volunteers, 1861, encircled by a wreath of honeysuckles with roses in full bloom.[45]

One important bill was enacted and confirmed on April 21, 1862, by the Congress of the Confederate States of America. In this bill, the enrollment of cooks was explained. Briefly, the captain or commanding officer oversaw the hiring, four cooks would be retained and would take responsibility of supplies, utensils, and other things. These cooks would be white, free black, or slave, if slave had the written consent of the owner, be put on the muster roll at time of enlistment, be paid twenty dollars if head chef, fifteen if assistant to each of the assistants, and have the same clothing allowance as the others.[46] Two such individuals may very well be Washington Drakeford, who in his Confederate pension, is mentioned to have been a cook, and a slave belonging to William Drakeford, and Ellison Haile, a slave belonging to Captain C.C. Haile. On one of C.C. Haile's actual Confederate service records, he was listed as having been in the hospital.

On April 25, 1861, Captain Boykin left Camden, for Richmond, to arrive ahead of Kershaw, and with Boykin was more of the regiment of the 2nd South Carolina Volunteers.[47] On April 28, 1861, Colonel Kershaw and his troops finally arrived in Richmond by way of the Petersburg Railroad, and went to Jarret's Hotel for breakfast.[48] When finished, the companies were escorted to the Richmond Depot by the local home guard.

---

40 Ibid.
41 Ibid.
42 Ibid.
43 Ibid.
44 Ibid.
45 Ibid.
46 War of the Rebellion Official Records of the Union and Confederate Armies, Series IV, Volume 1, Confederate Correspondence, pages 1079, 1080.
47 The Daily Dispatch, Richmond, Virginia, April 26, 1861.
48 The Daily Dispatch, Richmond, Virginia, April 29, 1861.

Passing through several streets, flags could be seen everywhere with every type of description and on many devices. When the company arrived at the corner of Bank and Sycamore streets, the group was halted. As the group was marching down the street, windows and openings were filled with people waving their handkerchiefs in support of the arriving troops. Shouts of jubilation and support could be heard for the mighty volunteers from Camden, South Carolina. Among them, a palmetto flag hung across the street, highlighting their arrival to help with defending the southern cause. One can only imagine, the ladies showed their lips and shouted sweetly with admiration for their troops from the South. Judge T. S. Gholson met the soldiers at the depot. There he talked of the willing, brave hearts and difficulties that this noble state was in with such support and confidence being shown. Captain Carson filled in with the absence of Colonel Joseph Kershaw and gave a response that was not only appropriate but very patriotic under these circumstances.[49]

2nd Regimental Volunteers South Carolina
From Kershaw County Roster

J. W. Allen	D. Graham	William Parker
W. R. Allen	J. T. Graham	C. J. Pegues
R. B. Arrants	B. F. Harrison	R. H. Pegues
J. H. Arrants	J. E. Hinson	J. R. Pickett
B, M. Baer	E. H. Jinks	T. W. Pope
J. R. Beaver	A. Johnson	R. W. Procter
Y. F. Brasington	W.E. Johnson	J. H. Riddle
J. S. Brown	George King	R. F. Small
W. Bowen	Robert Kirkley	John Smith
T. F. Boykin	R.R. Kirkland	W.W. Stokes
W. M. Bullock	J. M. LeGrand	R. R. Strawbridge
A. Campbell	M. L. Lemmond	James Stuart
T. M. Crump	James McIntosh	John Team
Patrick Cusick	Joel McMillian	W. M. Turner
J. T. Davis	C. J. McDowall	L. M. Vaughan
F. J. Devine	J. W. P. McKagen	W.W. Watts
George Evans	S. B. Meanes	J. O. Warren
J. R. Ferrel	J. P. Mickle	J. A. Wethersby
J. H. Francis	D. J. Middleton	R. R. Wilson
L. T. Gardner	C. R. Miles	J. R. Winder
R. L. Gerald	M. W. Morrison	J. H. Witherspoon
H. R. Gibson	George Nelson	P. C. Woods
John A. Glenn	Hiram Nettles	W. H. Wright
	Jesse Nettles	

---

[49] Ibid.

All was presented to Kershaw in Charleston, South Carolina, by the ladies of Charleston. The call from Virginia was accepted by South Carolina to come and help defend the state of Virginia.

In return, there was a gallant approval and noble consideration by this these specific soldiers.[50] One extraordinary event was the number of Negroes that had come to Norfolk. They came to help and support and be present at this celebration and numbered around one hundred. The Negroes came willingly and were not forced, with more outside the city offering their special talents to do what they could. One even gave one hundred dollars to help the cause.[51]

May first found an attachment of 2nd Regimental South Carolina Volunteers arriving in Richmond at half-past five the day before via the Petersburg Railroad.[52] Two hundred eighty-three soldiers comprised Captains McManus, Hale (Haile), and Richards, with their destination being to encamp at the Central Fairgrounds.[53] Again, the volunteers went to Jarrett's Hotel and were spoken to by Reverend Theodore Prier. Colonel J.B. Kershaw, in a strained but eloquent voice, gave his usual response at such an occasion. One prayer that stood out was that of the chaplain, Lieutenant Maynardie, whose patriotic words were most inspiring and crowd pleasing for the cause.[54] One side note is that one of the Lancaster Invincibles fell and became quite ill.

Word came that one of the prominent and well-respected citizens of Camden, South Carolina, had died. That gentleman was C. Matheson, Esquire. He had passed in Gainesville, Florida.[55]

The camp of Colonel Joseph Kershaw's troop moved from the northeast part of the city to a camp near Trotting Park, in Henrico County.[28] Word had surfaced that one soldier had died, but no verification on that had been made, yet.

Word on the streets in Camden began. Talk was about a certain individual sending and receiving letters from the North, and an investigation was in place.

On May 13, 1861, a flag was presented by Colonel J.B. Kershaw to the Camden Light Infantry under the command of Captain Kennedy. The flag was a gift from the ladies of Camden and made of silk.[56]

On May 26, 1861, a railroad collision took place at the Central Depot in Richmond. Three trains occupied by the troops of Colonel J.B. Kershaw and the 2nd Regiment were involved. Information sent from the Orange Courthouse by the conductor explained that a mail truck coming in came in too fast and hit the train.

Word of some deaths and many wounded was sent out by telegraph.[57] One story told of an amputation of one soldier below the knee, and some of the injured were now dead in Gordonsville.[58]

Camden was quite honored to have two people selected as new members of the Confederate Congress around the first of June. They were James Chesnut and Judge T.J. Withers.[59]

---

[50] Ibid.
[51] Ibid.
[52] The Daily Dispatch, Richmond, Virginia, May 1st, 1861.
[53] Ibid.
[54] Ibid.
[55] The Daily Dispatch, Richmond, Virginia, May 3rd, 1861 [28] The Daily Dispatch, Richmond, Virginia, May 4, 1861.
[56] The Daily Dispatch, Richmond, Virginia, May 14, 1861.
[57] The Daily Dispatch, Richmond, Virginia, May 27, 1861.
[58] Ibid.
[59] The Daily Dispatch, Richmond, Virginia, June 4, 1861.

During this time, in Camden, talk of a traitor surfaced, and now that person had a name. He was a music teacher at Peck's Academy and from the North. People got angry and wanted justice. They wanted to hang him, but James Chesnut stepped in and cooler heads prevailed. The person was Frank Devine, and he wanted to serve with the 2nd Volunteers under Kennedy, but because of his birth being up North, he was sent to Charleston to work in an office. Further details on this case state that Judge Withers declared that this offense was treasonous.[60] Many letters had been sent to the North. The last one said that Camden was vulnerable to attack, on the verge of starvation and discord, and that Camden would be easy to overtake, especially with the men in Virginia.[61] Even in the Diary of Mary Boykin Chesnut, she wrote that the women were yelling for him to be hanged, but Mr. James Chesnut spoke for him and concluded that no real treasonous crime had been committed so he sent DeVine to Fort Sumter to save this poor Frenchman. Chesnut's arguments were very compelling and convincing to the group at the Bank of Camden meeting room.[62]

Colonel Joseph B. Kershaw on June 26, 1861, sent the following letter about where to send and how to send letters to his regiment:

"All letters intended for the members of the 2nd Palmetto Regiment South Carolina Volunteers will be directed here until further notice: Mr. _____, Captain's _____ Company, 2nd Palmetto Regiment Volunteers, Fairfax Courthouse, Virginia.[63]

On July 20, 1861, a report from Manassas told of Joseph Kershaw's men killing an officer, his horse, and found seven hundred dollars in gold on this person.[64]

On Saturday evening, July 21, 1861, Captain E.B. Cantey arrived with his Kershaw Troop by way of the Petersburg Railroad with over one thousand solders.[65]

News came in with causalities in Colonel Kershaw's Brigade. Two local companies with casualties were:

Captain Haile's Company — Reuben Patterson, slightly wounded; Private M.C. Love, missing; J.C. Cook, missing; S. Sowell, missing; W.J. Lyles, missing; R. Lowry, missing; W. Lowry, missing; W. Wright, missing.

Captain Kennedy's Company — Lieutenant DePass, severely wounded; Corporal Pegues, slightly wounded; Privates: Barrett, killed; Jesse Nettles, mortally wounded; J.H. Francis, slightly wounded; A.W. Farin, slightly wounded; L.W. Scarborough, slightly wounded.

---

[60] The Charleston Mercury, Charleston, S.C., June 21, 1861.
[61] The Charleston Mercury, Charleston, S.C., June 6, 1861.
[62] The Charleston Mercury, Charleston, S.C., June 21, 1861.
[63] The Daily Dispatch, Richmond, Virginia, June 26, 1861.
[64] The Daily Dispatch, Richmond, Virginia, July 20, 1861.
[65] The Daily Dispatch, Richmond, Virginia, July 22, 1861.

From Bull Run, July 19, the following was sent in: "These are observations from a special correspondent. The battle occurred on July 18. The two parties involved was the Army of the Potomac under General Beauregard and the Grand Army of the North under General McDowell. Many felt that no action was going to take place over the days of Monday and Tuesday, but then on Wednesday, everything began to change. Booming of cannons took place, followed by the rattling of small arms, and the rapid departures of hastening couriers seen in the midst. The Yankees were advancing on Fairfax Courthouse, where the Bonham Brigade of South Carolina held the advance post of the Confederate Army. They were firing upon one of our pickets. Captain Haile, with all his company and half of Brook's Guards, was on picket from two to four miles from camp, the enemy was advancing across their line of retreat at about one mile. From Colonel Kershaw's camp, the most advanced, the glitter of the enemy's guns in the morning sun illumined hill after hill. However, no time for observation. The long roll beat and each company fell promptly into line. Colonel Kershaw gallops in, and to the interrogatory, 'How is the picket?' The reply came back alright. Captain Rhett was ordered to take the other half of his company and hold a house, at the intersection of the two roads, until the picket reached that point. Brooks, elated at the prospect of a fight and anxious for the fate of their exposed comrades, set off at a brisk pace, and soon reaching their place of destination, were preparing to keep the Yankees at bay until the safe passage of their friends."

News came from Camden that a well-known citizen had died. That person was Captain Benjamin McCoy of the Camden District, South Carolina, passing away on the fourteenth. During the War of 1812, he was a member of Captain Levy's Corp stationed at Haddrell's Point.[66]

On August 2, talk of a formation of a Ladies Aid Society in Camden was being discussed from the offices in Charleston, South Carolina.[67]

The impact of women should be noted by the following:

> "One and all feel that the utmost that can be done by the women, in this, our great trial, seems so little when compared with what our brother soldiers are daily sacrificing for the protection of our rights and homes, that the proceedings of our district newspaper, now discontinued, as its brave and patriotic editor has thrown aside the scissors and pen to take up the sword. We have nevertheless worked diligently; and as the result of our labors, have sent five large boxes to Mrs. Randolph, President of the Society in Richmond, and three to the Reverend Mr. Barnwell; besides shirts and drawers to the companies of Captain Kennedy, Second Regiment, and Captain Cantey, Ninth Regiment, South Carolina Volunteers. We now have on hand between two and three hundred flannel shirts and drawers, by which we hope to add to the comfort of the volunteers from Kershaw District during this coming winter."

---

[66] The Daily Dispatch, Richmond, Virginia, July 29, 1861.
[67] The Charleston Mercury, Charleston, South Carolina, August 2, 1861. [38] Ibid.

By this you will see that the women of Kershaw are awake, as well as the men, of whom we shall soon have six companies in active service; and we doubt not that they proved as well drilled and appointed, and as thorough in the performance of every duty, as any that have been sent from this state.[66]

On August 3, reports came in on the death of Lieutenant William H. Hardy, aid-de-camp to Colonel Kershaw. Only eighteen years old, he died gallantly leading a Virginia Regiment in the Battle of Manassas on the twenty-first. Hardy distinguished himself, not only on the field of battle, but in the army for Jesus Christ.[68] His body was found a day later by a member of the regiment. A notice was sent out trying to find where Hardy was buried. His body was picked up and taken for burial by two men who knew of Colonel Kershaw and told his grave would be marked and that all information on Hardy's burial would be sent to Colonel J.B. Kershaw or Lieutenant Alfred Doby, 2nd Regiment South Carolina Volunteers. [69]

News came to Virginia that one of the old residents of Camden had passed away. Captain Burrell Boykin had died recently in the Kershaw District.[70]

Coming out is a list of wounded at the General Hospital in Charlottesville, Virginia. On the list from the Camden area were: Atkinson, S.C. Hampton's Legion in head; J.H. Francis, 2nd Company H in buttocks; Samuel McPherson, 2nd Company A, jaw bones joint broken; W.J. Falconbery (Faulkenbery), 2nd Regiment Flat Rock Guards on July 28. In the August 26 paper, W.I. Falkenbery of the Flat Rock Guards was injured.

The Old Camden District would soon come out with another fine and noteworthy company. This company would be led by Captain William M. Shannon and would be in the field in three weeks.[71] This cavalry would be the composite of a horse, composed of picked men; specifically, this makeup included those of the minuteman that came into the picture in the fall of last year to show independence in the area and for the state.[72] These soldiers would have a blue cockade on their hats and a purpose in their minds and in their hearts. Soon they would leave for Virginia.[73] On September 9, this unit met at the Hawthorne Course in Camden, and began training.[74] Recruits would come mounted and equipped to begin.[75]

In the August 27 edition, an unusual presentation occurred. This presentation was in honor of Colonel Kershaw's men for their bravery and appreciation for what they were doing in the war effort, especially in the Battle of Manassas. The ladies of Columbia made palmetto stars, made from genuine palmetto leaves, finely designed and braided.[76] The ladies are now in the summer residence in Pendleton. Given to Colonel Kershaw was a palmetto tree, wonderfully designed and made in a badge so beautiful by those who saw it, as well as the

---

68 The Daily Dispatch, Richmond, Virginia, August 3, 1861.
69 Ibid.
70 The Daily Dispatch, Richmond, Virginia, August 5, 1861.
71 The Charleston Mercury, Charleston, South Carolina, August 17, 1861.
72 Ibid.
73 Ibid.
74 The Charleston Mercury, Charleston, South Carolina, August 30, 1861.
75 Ibid.
76 The Daily Dispatch, Richmond, Virginia, August 27, 1861.

other objects made.[77] Next came many pouches and needles for the soldiers, which contained needles, pins, buttons, with a pretty piece of poetry and verse done in a manuscript style.[78]

September 9 came and news originating out of Fairfax, Virginia, from September 5 brought word of an event that happened halfway between Falls Church and Fairfax Courthouse.[79] What remained was half of what the regiments started with, which was 900 men. Those companies were Kershaw, Cash, Bacon, and Wilson.[80]

On September 19, a deposit was made in the Farmer's Bank for the wounded, sick, and disabled from the state of South Carolina for the troops in Virginia.[81] Joseph Kershaw did this under the instructions of Governor Pickens and was subject to under the guidance of Colonel Joseph Kershaw since he was the senior colonel out.[48]

In the *Charleston Mercury* of October 8, 1861, following the Battle of Manassas, Colonel J.B. Kershaw sent in a report of Sunday July 21 of those in the area. The most devastating injury was that of Lieutenant DePass, as he was struck in the head. Captain Kennedy was struck in the side by a ball and bruised. Captain Haile was one of three commanding officers singled out for his encouragement to lead and keep his company going in the heat of the battle, and Lieutenant Colonel Jones fulfilled his duty during this trying time by showing tremendous courage. Captain Sill, adjutant, and Sergeant-Major Haile were very active and quite efficient in this time, and in their service, the use of the pistol by Sill and the use of the musket by Haile in battle. Dr. Salmond, surgeon, tended to the wounded on the field, and Reverend E.J. Meynardie gave his time as chaplain to the unfortunate comrades. The flag of Captain Kennedy was struck once during the exchange in battle.

Camp life in the Kershaw camp was described as the following: An extract of a letter from Munson's Hill, Advance Piguet, Army of Potomac, September 21, 1861: Breakfast consisted of coffee, beefsteak, or fried bacon, nice raised bread, with potatoes sometimes, and our dinner yesterday consisted of roast beef, Irish potatoes, cabbage, bacon, tomatoes and rice boiled together.[82] Overseeing nine, the bill from July 23 comes to four dollars and a half and that was for extras. I know that I will be good in making raised bread and as cook can't satisfy all.[83]

The local paper in Camden was the *Camden Confederate*. Brief goings-on were highlighted as to the town, county, state, and the war efforts.

November 1, 1861 had the following highlights: Our Volunteers in Virginia, a congressional election the following Wednesday; Adjutant Sill has returned from the 2nd Regiment SCV, from being sick two weeks ago; George A. Young and Chesnut Whitaker had come home sick from the Boykin Rangers. Lieutenant Niles has returned home to the front after being home with sickness since the last of August. Captain Thomas J. Warren paid a visit last week and said his company was in good health. Colonel DeSaussure's right wing will start this week for Summerville. Uniforms had not gotten to Captain Cantey's company, and the hope was that the ladies would send them soon. Despite material goods acquisition problems, the Boykin Rangers under Captain

---

77 Ibid.
78 Ibid.
79 The Daily Dispatch, Richmond, Virginia, September 9, 1861.
80 Ibid.
81 Richmond Enquirer, Richmond, Virginia, September 19, 1861. 48 Ibid.
82 The Daily Dispatch, Richmond, Virginia, October 12, 1861.
83 Ibid.

H.H. Boykin had received many articles that were shipped for their comfort and use. The Kirkwood Rangers, under Captain Shannon, were doing well despite a three-week march from Camden, South Carolina, arriving on the sixteenth, and received much attention during the route to Old Dominion, and the Flat Rock Guards, under Captain Haile were doing well with all the friends of the company and area sending them articles for the coming winter, and Mr. D.D. Perry was elected to fill the vacancy left by Captain Shannon due to the war for being a representative in our state legislature. One the most important things were the military elections, occurring on the previous October 19. The officers that were elected for Beat 2, 22nd Regiment at Camden were: A.M. Kennedy, captain; W.E. Hugheson, first lieutenant; J.J. Workman, second lieutenant; C. Shiver, third lieutenant. At the Cureton's Mills Beat 1, the following was elected: E. Parker, captain; J.J. Nelson, first lieutenant; D.G. Robertson, second lieutenant; and J.J. Hogan, third lieutenant.[84]

Captain Thomas Warren sent a letter thanking the people of the community for the articles sent to his company. The letter said:

> "To the citizens of Camden and vicinity, and especially to the ladies, I desire in behalf of the company we have the honor to command to a return sincere thanks and grateful acknowledgement for the kind sympathies and valuable liberal and opportunity extended it on to liberal donations in money, we have a good supply of clothing furnished for the comfort of the soldiers, besides many types of kind appreciation, which is by means in the regard of every honest man status to do his duty to the country in this emergency.

We trust the future course will prove the sincerity of profession, and the measure of gratitude which animates us in the charge of defense.

Thos. J. Warren
Captain, 15th Regiment S.C.V.[50]
The rolls of the 15th Regimental unit were also given: [85]
Kershaw Guards, Company D, 15th Regiment, S.C.V.

Thomas J. Warren, Captain
Joel A. Shrock, 1st Lieutenant
C. B. Bell, 2nd Lieutenant
Charles A. Fisher, 3rd Lieutenant
A. Sommers, 1st Sergeant
J. J. Huckabee, 2nd Sergeant
John J. Davis, 3rd Sergeant
R. Springer, 4th Sergeant

---

84   The Camden Confederate, Camden, South Carolina, November 1, 1861. 50 Ibid.
85   Ibid.

P. A. Man, 1st Corporal
Eugene Wolfe, 2nd Corporal
Johnson, B. F., 3rd Corporal
George Buff, 4th Corporal

Privates

H. Ammons	William A. Ammons	John Brannon
Robert Brannon	J. P. Capell	J. Corbett
W. Capell	F. E. Creighton	Daniel Cromer
John J. Davis	James Fulghum	John Faulkenberry
D. G. Fletcher	E. J. Ford	Lewis Gardner
William Graham	Stephen Griffin	James Hall
Joseph Hayes	Emanuel Hayes	James Harrel
John Harrel	Samuel Hornsby	Hollis Hough
B. F. Hinson	W. B. Hinson	Douglass Jackson
W. Jordan	Daniel Kirkley	Warren Kemp
Tia Kemp	A. Kirby	J. W. Kirby
A. J. Munn	N. H. McInnis	Samuel Mattox
Isaac Mattox	James Mattox	N. A. McLeod
John Mooneyham	James Marsh	Gates Marsh
John Morris	John E. Outlaw	William E. Parker
Redding Parker	J. J. Richbourgh	Manning Scott
Hasting Scott	Jesse P. Shield	Jesse W. Smith
W. J. Spradley	James Ray	John W. Turner
A. Von Hasselin	Joel Wilson	Paul H. Wilson
Henry Wilson	B. F. Williams	W. W. Watson
William Warren	A. W. Williams	John Watts
Columbus Watts	Samuel Yates	Willis Yates

First Lieutenant J.M. Davis appointed adjutant; Reverend B. McCallum, chaplain; Second Lieutenant J.V. Lyles, resigned; Privates S.B. Capell, H.F. Corbett, and K. Kemp, died.

Reported dead in obituaries:

H. Corbett, son of H.H. Corbett, Esquire of Sumter. Died at the residence of John Beard after being moved from the fairgrounds of disease. Sidney B. Capell died at the fairgrounds Sunday morning, October 13, 1861. Enlisted the twenty-sixth of September, on duty at Camp Lightwood Knot Springs for instruction, and died of measles due to an outbreak in the camp. Tira Kemp died October 19, 1861, of measles at the fairgrounds. John Team died in September in Lynchburg, Virginia, age eighteen, of typhoid fever, as well as W.W. Turner, age eighteen, and Lewis M. Vaughan, age twenty-one, also died of typhoid fever in Lynchburg, Virginia.

Tragedy strikes in war and at home. Those dying are H. Corbett, son of H.H. Corbett, private in Captain Warren's company, at the home of John Beard in Columbia, South Carolina by disease; Sidney B. Capell, died Sunday morning at the Columbia Fairgrounds, October 13, enlisting the twenty-sixth of September, dying of measles; Tira Kemp, dying the nineteenth at the Columbia Fairgrounds of measles; John Team, dying in September at Lynchburg, Virginia, of typhoid at eighteen years old; W.W. Turner, eighteen years old and Lewis M. Vaughan twenty-one years old, both dying of disease at Lynchburg; and Carolina H. Kennedy Whitaker, whose father was Captain Wm. Kennedy and whose husband was John Whitaker, Jr., died at her father's home at just twenty-two years, two months, and eleven days Saturday last.[86]

Finally, the following needs to be mentioned:

A Prayer for Our Soldiers

"While our people are mindful of the temporary comforts of our gallant defenders, it will revive the heart of many in camp to know that on every Friday afternoon the people of God meet and pray specially for the protection and blessing of God upon our soldiers, and the cause in which they are engaged, and that discretion and guidance may be given to all our civil authorities in these troubled times."[87]

In the next issue, November 15, the following was told: A message from Captain Thomas Warren, which said: "Say to our friends, that although we were in the Battle of Hilton Head on the seventh, and was shelled to our heart's content, all the Kershaw Guards are safe and well."[88]

J.J. McKain was in Virginia on service, and Mr. Hudson handled all the drugstore needs. The following merchant stores were closed under the time that military drills were occurring in Camden —The merchants being A.M. and R. Kennedy, E. W. Bonney. George Alden, James Dunlap, F. McLarnon, Koopman and Summers, John Workman and Company, C. Shiver, Thomas Harris, Matheson and Company, A.T. Latta, C.A. McDowell, and T.S. Myers. Reverend Manning Brown began the organizing of a company for Colonel James Chesnut by putting out a call and request for volunteers' due to Chestnut's overwhelming influence and leadership in the town, county, and state.[89]

The Lucas Guards under Captain Blair were camped at the old Cornwallis quarters for instruction and drill.[90] The volunteers were ready to be mustered in and ready for service in the war and were fine examples of the qualities of men found in the area. This would be the seventh company formed in Kershaw District.[91] The officers were L.W.R. Blair, captain; Benjamin Simon Lucas, first lieutenant; Dove Segars, second lieutenant; Finley McCaskill, third lieutenant; A.W. Raley, first sergeant; and Wm. McSween, second sergeant.[57] In the next

---

86 Ibid.
87 Ibid.
88 The Camden Confederate, Camden, South Carolina, November 15, 1861.
89 Ibid.
90 Ibid.
91 Ibid. [57] Ibid.

few days, this company would leave for service.[92] Lieutenant Alfred Brevard from Captain Cantey's company paid a short visit the week before.[93]

Major John L. Jones would seek to organize a troop in the area. Beat number 2 would have Captain A.M. Kennedy to take over since William Clyburn went into service in Virginia.[94] A fellow named W.T. Sherman sent correspondence over the state from Port Royal demanding that the people of South Carolina needed to rethink their actions.[95] Sherman further stated that upon his return he planned to steal our property, burn our cities and towns, ravish our women, and lay waste this fair heritage. As there is a righteous God who rules in heaven and earth, to aid and strengthen those relying on Him. He will be taught[96] a lesson he will never forgot — that a free and brave people can never be cajoled by honied phrases, and that the people of South Carolina, who asserted their independence on the twentieth of December last meant what they said and treat with that contempt and loathing any utterances emanating from such a source. J.V. Lyles was selected to be receiving agent for the Camden District.[97]

William L. DePass is ready to start the process of organizing a company in this area.[98] Other items of interest was the fire on the roof of Dr. Thomas W. Salmond in the Kirkwood section, a meeting of the newly organized company under Major John Jones, and a listing of articles and contributions by the Ladies Aid Society.[99] Beat Number 2 had a parade from ten to twelve in the morning under Captain A.M. Kennedy called "The Day We Celebrate."[100] A meeting at town hall takes place, and a list of Kershaw Guards by Lieutenant J.A. Shrock is announced.[101] Cornwallis Quarters is being filled by the Kershaw Guards under Major John L. Jones, while W.L. DePass is meeting with his newly formed company at the town hall.[102] A concert was held by Professor Henry E. Eckel, assisted by Mr. Henry Bard of Camden.[69]

Returning from Camp Gist were Lieutenant J.J. McKain and James Riddle from the Kershaw Guards under Captain Warren's Company. Private Yates from Camp Gist and a member of Captain Warren's company brought home the body of John L. Richards.[103]

December 16, 1861 ended with a public meeting at town hall in Camden, South Carolina. In an article in the *Charleston Courier* on December 20, 1861, the following highlights were told: The intendant of the town, Mr. James Dunlap (another name is the mayor of today), called a meeting. In this meeting, the citizens were asked to adopt measures to help relieve the sufferers of the fire in Charleston, South Carolina. Mr. J.S. DePass made a motion that Mr. James Dunlap act as the chair, and acting secretary would be John J. Workman. As with many meeting during this time, prayer was opened by Reverend S.H. Hay. During this meeting, five

---

[92] The Camden Confederate, Camden, South Carolina, November 22, 1861.
[93] Ibid.
[94] The Camden Confederate, Camden, South Carolina, November 29, 1861.
[95] Ibid.
[96] Ibid.
[97] Ibid.
[98] The Camden Confederate, Camden, South Carolina, December 6, 1861.
[99] The Camden Confederate, Camden, South Carolina, December 13, 1861.
[100] The Camden Confederate, Camden, South Carolina, December 20, 1861.
[101] Ibid.
[102] The Camden Confederate, Camden, South Carolina, December 27, 1861. [69] Ibid.
[103] Ibid.

were selected based upon being retired and willing to serve when asked by the chair. Those chosen were A.M. Kennedy, C.J. Shannon, E.W. Bonney, Dr. J.J. Hankell, and Reverend S.H. Hay. The following resolution was said: The citizens of Camden are convened today to give expression to their feeling of sympathy with their neighbors and friends of the City of Charleston, in the great calamity that has befallen them in the terrible conflagration of the past week, by which so vast an amount of property has been destroyed and so many of her citizens have been deprived of their homes and reduced from comfort to want.

In public buildings destroyed, the Hall, where the Ordinance of Succession was signed with our views to repel the attacks of northern tyranny by the government, was crushed. Mr. Bews gave a concert in connection with Professor Eccol, of Harmony College, with the proceeds going to the same.

The Southern Cross

In the name of God, men
Stand for our Southern rights,
Over ye Southern men
The God of Battles fights!
Fling the invaders far,
Hurl back their work of woe—
The voice is the voice of a brother,
But in the hands are the hands of a foe.
They come with a trampling army,
Invading our native sod—
Stand, Southerners, fight and conquer,
In the name of almighty God!

They are singing our song of triumph,
Which was made to make us free,
While they're breaking away the heart-strings
Of our Nation's harmony —
Sadly, it floateth from us,
Sighing o'er land and wave,
Till mute on the lips of the poet,
It sleeps in his Southern grave.
Spirit and song departed!
Minstrel and minstrelsy!
We mourn thee heavy hearted—
But we will, we shall be free.

They are waving our flag above us,
With a despot's tyrant will,

With our blood they have stained its colors,
And call it holy still.
With tearful eyes, but steady hand,
We'll tear its stripes apart,
And fling them like broken fetters,
That will not bind the heart.
But we'll save our stars of glory,
In the might of the Sacred Sign
Of him! Who had fixed forever
Our Southern Cross to shine.

Stand, Southerners! Fight and conquer.
Solemn and strong and sure —
The strife shall not be longer
Than God shall bid endure,
By the life which only yesterday,
Come with the Infant's breath!
By the feet, which ere the morn may
Tread to the soldier's death!
By the blood which cries to heaven!
Crimson upon our sod,
Stand, Southerners! Stand and conquer!
In the name of the mighty God!

The Camden Confederate — October 10, 1862.

1862

EIGHTEEN SIXTY-TWO STARTED OUT WITH several things: Correspondence from Camp Gist about the Camden soldiers, an unsigned letter from a Camdenite fighting in Louisiana, Beat Number 2 visited the homes of Colonel J.B. Kershaw and Captain Kennedy, the concert by Eckel was held at the town hall, Captain DePass's Wateree Guards had encamped at the Cornwallis Headquarters, Captain Jones's Kershaw Greys began their march to Camp Wade Hampton near Columbia, and the following names for public offices were posted for colonel, R.M. Kennedy; lieutenant colonel, William Dixon; and for mayor, Emanuel Parker.[104] Field officers for the upcoming election for the 22D South Carolina Militia for Camden were Colonel Burrell Jones, Lieutenant Dr. J. I. Tratham, and Major Stephen Clyburn, those of the general town offices.[105]

There was another death from the war. This time from the Battle of Manassas. His name was Jesse S. Nettles who fell mortally wounded on the field.[106] He was brought home by his brother Hiram Nettles, and both was escorted to the Baptist church to lay at rest. Both were of the same company and even Beat Number 2 soldiers turned out to pay tribute to their fallen comrade.[107] Also, W. Turner's remains were brought home by J.W.P McKagen, who died of disease and was slated for burial at the Baptist church at eleven o'clock the next day.[108]

The following is a list of public officers, appointed by the legislature recently:

Magistrate — John K. Witherspoon; Commissioners of Free Schools — Jesse Truesdel and W. McClure; Commissioners of Fish Sluices (opening around a dam or other obstacles to allow fish to travel) from Graves' Shoals to Fishing Creek on the Wateree River — James L. Reed II, J. Jayden, W.E. Johnson Jr., William C. Brown, John Perry, John Nelson, John Mickle, Robert Scuyler, Daniel McCulloch; Soldiers of the Board of Relief — James Dunlap, L.H. Deas, John Milling, Edward Barnes, James Team; Managers of Camden Elections — John S. Merony, C.A. McDonald, W.D. Anderson; Cureton's Mill — Frederick Bowen, James Team, Eli Parker; Flat Rock — J. Fletcher, J.B. Hughes, Jesse Truesdel; Lyzinby — Lauchlin McKinnon,

---

[104] The Camden Confederate, Camden, South Carolina, January 3, 1862.
[105] Ibid.
[106] Ibid.
[107] Ibid.
[108] Ibid.

Wilson Yarborough; Buffalo — William Mungo, Gilliam Sowell, William Cato; Schrock's Mill — B.T. McCoy, Henry Ratcliffe, Alexander McLeod; Goodwin's Store — A.J. McDowell, Benjamin Cook, R.C. Drakeford, and Liberty Hill — A.D. Jones, R.C. Patterson, Robert B. Cunningham.[109]

The military election was set for 10 a.m. with polling to take place at the town hall on January 15, 1862.[110] In the final tally, Burrell Jones was elected colonel, William Dixon was elected lieutenant, and W.A. Antrum was elected mayor.[111] For Beat 2, W.E. Hugheson was elected captain, J.M. McLernon was elected first lieutenant, William Billings was elected second lieutenant, and L. Sommers was elected third lieutenant.[112]

From Virginia, a letter from Captain C.C. Haile stated his troops was near Centreville at Camp Camden and wanted to thank the Ladies Aid Society of Flat Rock and Liberty Hill for their donations sent from time to time to the Flat Rock Guard, and Captain DePass who had left Camden with his Wateree Guards for Camp Hampton.[113]

During this time, the Ladies Aid Society of Camden began to meet at the town hall at eleven o'clock to discuss what more they could do or needed to do for the soldiers.[114]

The Kershaw Masonic Lodge Number 29, A.F.M. elected the following for the upcoming years: Brother J. Stakeley, Worshipful Master, Brother T.W. Smith, Senior Warden, Brother D.D. Hocott, Junior Warden, Brother H. F. Hodson, Treasurer, Brother J. Jones, Secretary, Brother W. H. Hocott, Senior Deacon, Brother R. Latta, Junior Deacon, and Brothers W.D. Anderson, S. H. Blodget, Stewards, and Brother F. J. Oakes, Tyler.[115]

A war tax collector was chosen in Captain A.M. Kennedy.[116] He will oversee collecting taxes in accordance with the wishes of the Confederate Congress, which will include collecting taxes for property owners to make returns to the assessors before the first day of February next disclosing property ownership or by October first, lose their property.[117]

In the next issue of the paper, the Ladies Aid Society of Camden had elected the following to serve: President, Miss Sally Chesnut; Vice-President, Mrs. H.M. Howard; Treasurer, Miss Louisa Salmond, and Secretary, Miss Emma Reynolds. In this issue, Captain J.L. Jones sent a thank you note to the ladies for socks sent to his soldiers.

Camden was now a military organized town to deal with the needs of soldiers and the needs of those in the town and vicinity.

In the January 31 paper, the following soldiers had returned to camp Monday last: Colonel J.B. Kershaw, Colonel T.J. Ancrum, Lieutenant J.J. McKain, A. Doby, and Sergeant Barnes for camps in Virginia. Captain DePass sent a thank you note from the Wateree Guards to the Camden Ladies Aid Society for their package of

---

[109] Ibid.
[110] The Camden Confederate, Camden, South Carolina, January 10, 1862.
[111] The Camden Confederate, Camden, South Carolina, January 17, 1862.
[112] Ibid.
[113] Ibid.
[114] The Camden Confederate, Camden, South Carolina, January 10, 1862.
[115] Ibid.
[116] The Camden Confederate, Camden, South Carolina, January 17, 1862.
[117] Ibid.

thirty-six shirts, twenty-four pairs of drawers, and eight pairs of socks from Mrs. James Chesnut. The ladies even sent to the Blackville Hospital in need of supplies.[118]

Captain John L. Jones of the Kershaw Greys sent a notice telling the community that his unit was near Magnolia Gardens, Charleston, and letters could be sent to in care of Captain John L. Jones, Kershaw Greys, Charleston, South Carolina.[119] In the next paper, a thank you note sent to Miss Sally Chesnut had been received for supplies sent to Rickerville Hospital by Samuel Logan. That list includes nine mattresses, eighty-one pillows, thirteen comforters, five blankets, one piece of carpet, thirty-four shirts, four dressing gowns, eight-night caps, twenty-five pairs slippers, twelve pairs of socks, seventy-seven pillow cases, one coat, sixty-eight towels, twenty-four bottles of wine, one bottle of honey, one bag of hominy, etc.[120]

Mr. Duncan Sheorn was elected sheriff as E.E. Sill went off to serve in the war. News got to Camden that Colonel J.B. Villipeque was wounded in the arm in Pensacola, Florida.[121] His father, Paul F. Villepigue, died on January 31 in Camden at the age of sixty-eight. He'd come to this country from the West Indies early in his life and had settled in Charleston first before coming to Camden in 1825.[122]

The town got an unusual request that must be told. Letters came in wanting books and pamphlets to be sent to the soldiers of the Camden Volunteers. There was a need for the soldiers to read doing their breaks and to relax doing the winter months of the war.[123] These items could be dropped off at either J.J. McKain's store or at R.M. Kennedy's store.[124]

News from Virginia brought news that Joseph B. Kershaw had been promoted to brigadier general.[125] One can only imagine the town was pleased over one of their own receiving such an honor. Two different soldiers were in town to sign up more volunteers. Captain E.B. Cantey would be at the M. Baum and Brothers store, and Lieutenant Leitner would be at the James Dunlap store.[126] Those wanting to sign up and join the war efforts needed to go to those stores. Captain Warren would be returning next week and advised those wishing to send letters to drop them off at this house on DeKalb Street.[127] He went on to state that small packages could also be sent but the distance from the railroad to the camp made it inconvenient to carry big boxes and bundles.[128]

Captain J.D. Kennedy paid a visit to Camden, returning to Manassas.[129] On his visit, Captain Kennedy is on a recruiting trip and can be found at McKain's Drug Store from ten to five of a day.[130] The Ladies strongly

---

[118] The Camden Confederate, Camden, South Carolina, February 7, 1862.
[119] The Camden Confederate, Camden, South Carolina, January 31, 1862.
[120] The Camden Confederate, Camden, South Carolina, February 14, 1862.
[121] Ibid.
[122] The Camden Confederate, Camden, South Carolina, February 7. 1862.
[123] The Camden Confederate, Camden, South Carolina, February 14, 1862.
[124] Ibid.
[125] The Camden Confederate, Camden, South Carolina, February 21, 1862.
[126] Ibid.
[127] The Camden Confederate, Camden, South Carolina, February 28, 1862.
[128] Ibid.
[129] The Camden Confederate, Camden, South Carolina, March 1, 1862.
[130] Ibid.

considered the possibility of a soldier's rest in Camden.[131] There was further news that Camden was a possible choice to begin five more regiments in the area.[132]

Camden was in the process of evaluating a Confederate tax in the district.[133] **Results show the following:**[134]

Real Estate	$1,636,336
9,371 Slaves	4,552,110
Merchandise	129,425
Bank Stock	450,000
Bridge Stock	10,000
Money at Interest	1,576,110
Cash on hand	32,147
259 Gold Watches	21,147
Horses	585
Gold and Silver Plates	27,205
91 Pianos	17,465
322 Carriages	34,558
Cooperation Stock	6,670
Total amount	**$8,482,255**
Percentage	**$42,412.77**

Death in the community came with the news that the wife of Major Joseph Mickle, major from the War of 1812, Martha Belton, had died on the sixteenth of February in her eighty-fifth year of age, leaving six children, Mrs. Rice Dulin, Mrs. James V. Lyles, Captain Joseph Mickle of Columbia, Mrs. J.J. Nelson, Mr. Robert Mickle, and Captain John Belton Mickle.

More talk highlighted the next issue, which concerned recruiting more volunteers. Five more regiments were planned without having to have a draft, including a new formation of a beat company, where recruits needed to be between the ages of sixteen and sixty.[135]

More information on the Soldier's Wayside Resting Place in Camden was announced. The place would be next door to the Dekalb Hotel, and would be looked after by the Mr. Rodgers of the hotel.[136] Many soldiers passed through Camden with little or no money, so this place would serve them, allowing them to eat and rest before going on to their destination, whether it be home or back to the war.[137] Any donations could

---

[131] Ibid.
[132] Ibid.
[133] Ibid.
[134] The Camden Confederate, Camden, South Carolina, March 14, 1862.
[135] The Camden Confederate, Camden, South Carolina, March 21, 1862.
[136] Ibid.
[137] Ibid,

be sent to Mr. Rodgers at the Dekalb **Hotel**.[138] A new formation of a beat company was announced by Captain Hugheson, with all interested persons needing to report at the Market Saturday for reserve duty, if between the ages of sixteen and sixty.[139]

Those wishing to become recruits needed to report to Captain Kennedy, Lieutenant J. A. Shrock, or Sergeant Baum, as they would leave Monday night for Virginia or the coast.[140] *The following details were* given: Those with Captain Kennedy would meet and leave March 31. Lieutenant Shrock recruits would meet at the Post Office on Monday, March 31, and leave at half-past nine, and Captain E.B. Cantey's recruits would meet and report to Sergeant Baum to leave Saturday morning at nine o'clock.[141] A fifty-dollar bounty would be paid.

DeKalb Hotel- 1890's

In total, Kershaw County had a wonderful citizens' turnout for the war effort. The companies now in Virginia were Captains Kennedy, Cantey, and Shannon. Along the coast were Captains Warren, Blair, and Jones. Those who enlisted with Lieutenant W.L. Depass for the Captain Johnson's Artillery Company were stationed on James Island. The amount now is 150 with the total taken over 850 from a county with a voting population of over one thousand.[142]

During this time, exemption from the war took place. The board consisted of Dr. J.L. Trantham, Colonel Burrell Jones, Lieutenant-Colonel William Dixon, and Major W.A. Ancrum. Usually about a one-fourth would be deemed exempted from serving. The following was the list at that time:

List of Exemptions

R. R. Williams	James L. Downs	John S. Fletcher	James L. Stover
L. B. Stephenson	S. J. Truesdale	James R. Sowell	Isaac S. Huff
Laurence C. Jones	Joseph A. West	Issac Shirah	J. L. Hogan
W. D. Hogan	John McCaskill	James Motley	Allen Young
J. L. Gattis	W. L. Cook	James Kelly	A. Rabon
Mason D. Wood	W. J. Ross	Isaac Owens	J. T. Truesdale
A. A. McDowell	W. W. Gardner	A. L. Haile	L. McKinnan
J. B. Gaskin	John Barefield	Burwell Outlaw	John Brennon
J. A. Elliott	M. Ingraham	M. McGougan	M. Yarborough

---

138 Ibid.
139 Ibid.
140 The Camden Confederate, Camden, South Carolina, March 28, 1862.
141 Ibid.
142 Ibid.

Samuel Cato	Nathan Umfrees	Wiley Watkins	Bently Outlaw
H. F. Hodson	Joseph W. Doby	C. Gooding	J. A. Boswell
L. McCandless	C. H. Peak	Rev. J. S. Hankel	Rev. S. H. Hay
Joseph Sommers	F. L. Zemp	Dr. D. L. Desaussure	J. T. Hershman
J. L. Witherspoon	H. Pate	Joel Gardner	Duncan Sheorn
William R. Taylor	W. Croswell	William Ostin	J. B. Hammond
Adam Team	George Taylor		

[143]

In the April 4th edition of the paper, two companies were mentioned. Major W.Z. Leitner was to organize a Cavalry company, and Captain Johnson's Artillery Company was to form in the town of Camden and Kershaw District.[144] Captain J.D. Johnson would command, with W. L. DePass Sr. to be first lieutenant, Alexander Y. Lee Jr. would be second lieutenant, and D.M. Rodgers Sr. would also be second lieutenant.[145] They would be encamped on James Island, but they had no equipment at that time.

During the municipal election, James Dunlap was elected intendant or the equivalent of mayor today. L.M. Boswell, N.D. Baxley, R.M. Kennedy, and D.D. Hocott were elected wardens or the equivalent of our city council of today.[146] Also, of great importance that people were compiling a list of soldiers from Kershaw County but in researching further, no list was found.

During this time, the Kershaw District was being divided in beats. One beat was Beat Number eight, where J.L. Hogan, W.D. Hogan, and D.M. Cloud was elected to head.[147] The Kershaw Aid Society received a thank you note from Captain W.L. DePass for the receipt of forty pairs of socks for the soldiers.[148] Sad news came as the town and area was told of the death of Lieutenant John J. McKain, the druggist who went to serve for such a worthy cause.[149] His loss will be felt as a druggist and his knowledge of medicine and above all as a soldier who gave his life. More sad news came in from the war when it was learned that Camden's beloved Brigadier General John Bordenave Villipique had died.[150] More news came that the church bells of four different churches would be used to make cannons for the war effort, enough to make two twelve pounders.[151] However, the bells were not used and came back later to ring out for the people of Camden.

W.L. DePass wrote a letter to the subscribers of the Fund for Camden Volunteers. In this this letter, DePass wrote: "Gentleman: Having served my connection with the Camden Volunteers, by the tender of my resignation of my position I held in the Company, on the 13th day of December, 1861, and accepted on the 13th of January, 1862, on account of my inability again to enter the service of the Confederacy, from the effects

---

143 Ibid.
144 The Camden Confederate, Camden, South Carolina, April 4, 1862.
145 Ibid.
146 Ibid.
147 The Camden Confederate, Camden, South Carolina, April 25, 1862.
148 Ibid.
149 Ibid.
150 The Camden Confederate, Camden, South Carolina, May 30, 1862.
151 Ibid.

of my wound received in the battle of Manassas, it is due to you as well as to myself, to produce some evidence that my financial connection with the said company has also ended, which appears by an enclosed receipt given with this letter and referenced. Some of you are aware that the fund so liberally subscribed by you, for the uses and necessities of the company to which I have collected, was managed and disposed of by a Board of Finance, consisting of the commissioned officers — Captain J.D. Kennedy, as chairman, myself as treasurer, and the Orderly Sergeant as secretary, or with authority to countersign all orders for payment of money, which this rule was strictly adhered to. To this board, I submitted a report and an account of my receipts and expenditures as treasurer, (before the acceptance of my letter of resignation by the War Department at Richmond) which authorized its chairman to settle the same with me, which was done by him during his visit home."[152]

Exemptions came in for the 22nd Regiment South Carolina Militia of the Camden Area. Those were included in beat sections of the county and numbered 112.

Beat Number 1
Liberty Hill Section

P. B. Hammond, A. D. Jones, Jr., W. C. Cunningham, Joseph Simpson, J. G. Richards, D. Harrison, R. C. Patterson, J. D. Stanley, Thomas McDow, John McCaa, and J. Vinson- eleven people.

Beat Number 2
Flat Rock Area

J. W. Ford, J. L. Downs, E. Gaskin, William H. Martin, John S. Fletcher, G. R. Miller, J. L. Stover, L. B. Stevenson, D. G. Lanier, and S. J. Truesdel – ten people.

Beat Number 3
Buffalo Area

J. R. Sowell, J. S. Hough, L. C. Jones, J. A. West, and C. West- five people.

Beat Number 4
Westville Area

J. A. Kirkland, A. J. McDowell, Richard Hocott, Isaac Owens, James T. Truesdel, A.A. McDowell, W. W. Gardner, A. J. Haile, J. Shailor (Shaylor), and J. B. Gaskin—ten people.

Beat Number 5
Camden Area

W. C. Gerald, James W. Team, H. F. Hodson, J. W. Doby, Charles Gooding, G. M. Turner, J. A. Boswell, L. McCandless, C. H. Peck, Rev. J. S. Hankle, Rev. S. H. Hay, Joseph Sommers, F. L. Zemp, Dr. D. L. Desaussure, J. K. Witherspoon, Duncan Sheorn, William R. Taylor, Monroe Crowell, William Osteen, J. B.

---

[152] The Camden Confederate, Camden, South Carolina, April 30, 1862.

Hammond, Adam Team, George Taylor, Thomas Davis, Jr., W. Koopman, John Nettles, Robert Robertson, J. J. Thompson, J. M. Gayle, J. A. Perry, J. M. Rogers, N. Froleich, and T. L. Shiver—thirty-two people.

Beat Number 6
Bethune Area

L. McKinnon, Peter Stewart, John Barefield, Burwell Outlaw, John Brannum (Brannon), J. A. Elliott, Moody Ingraham, M. McGougan, M. K. Yardborough, Samuel Cato, Wiley Watkins, Bently Outlaw, and C. P. Mungo- thirteen people.

Beat Number 7
Tiller's Ferry Area

John Kelly, Nathan Umfrees (Humphries), J. J. Tiller, W. Blackwell, William M. Kelly, J. Kirby, A. J. Melton, J. A. W. Berry, and Thomas Holland- nine people.

Beat Number 8
West Wateree Area

Isaac Shirah, J. Morgan, W. D. Morgan, D. McCloud, John McCaskill, Samuel Brannum (Brannon), James Motley, Allen Young, A. L. Gattis, W. L. Cook, James Kelly, David Robertson, A. Rabun, Joel Gardner, J. D. Isbell, Mason D. Wood, William J. Ross, William Christmas, William R. Jenkins, A.A. Huckabee, and J. J. Nelson- twenty-one people

J.B. Alexander brought in a saucer of strawberries to the paper, and the people at the paper thought the strawberries may very well have been the first of the season.[153]

Cows were dying in Camden, and the culprit seemed to be the leaves and trimmings of the mock orange trees which were poisonous. The leaves and trimmings were placed in the streets and the cows ate them and died.[154]

Sad news came from the war as John J. McKain's death reached the community on Thursday. He was a valuable citizen, a warm-hearted friend, an ardent patriot, and he died as a fallen martyr to his beloved country and for her deepest rights, which this country deserved and respected. He was a lieutenant and was the first to volunteer in the area and join the Camden Volunteers. The places he had been in the war were Morris Island when Fort Sumter surrendered, Virginia, Lewisville, and in the retreat with the 2nd Regiment from Fairfax to Bull Run under fire until July 18, when the enemy was repelled. He was involved in the victory at Manassas. On the morning of the fifteenth, he was hit with a Minnie ball, and even though his friend and doctor, Dr. Thomas W. Salmond, did all he could, his life came to an end. Through the ordeal, he lost his right leg to amputation. On the seventeenth, his life and his spirit went, and with it, his last breath of life. Mr. J.W.P. McKagen and P.E.

---

[153] The Camden Confederate, Camden, South Carolina, April 25, 1862.
[154] Ibid.

Woods brought his body to the depot in Camden on a Sunday afternoon. Many people came to mourn his life and see him put in his final resting place. Reverend Hay of the Presbyterian Church performed the service. He was only twenty-six years of age, and he left a widow and two children. He grew up as orphan young in life, but the difference he made was the impact people will miss.[155] A tribute of respect was sent from the company by E. Niles, secretary, in the next paper for his service and loss to those who knew him.

Thanks came from Captain W.L. DePass for forty pairs of socks sent to the company from the Kershaw Aid Society.[156] The wheat crop is looking good and bountiful in the upper part of the county and in Lancaster County, and should provide some help for the families.

Mr. A.M. Kennedy, James Dunlap, and J.H. McLeod were selected commissioners to open the books for cotton in the area.[157] Also, there was the news that the Hunt Hotel was now in the hands of Mr. T.S. Nickerson; he was also the owner of the Mill's house.[158]

Death came to the community, when they learned of the death of John Mickle, who had passed on April 29, 1862. He had a commission in the War of 1812, and one who suffered with others on Sullivan's Island during the war and was a member of the Baptist church. He had had nine children (six still living) and a wife.[159]

On Friday, like most Fridays, people had prayer meetings, and were lifted by God to ask that every soldier be delivered from the enemy, safe and back in the community.[160]

A fire occurred at the Terebene Distillery of Hocott and Sutherland. The loss to the building was between $400.00 and $500.00, but the barrels of terebene were saved. Terebene was a form that some people burned.[161]

The second regiment had now been reorganized. The field officers were: Captain J.D. Kennedy for colonel, Major A.D. Goodwin for lieutenant colonel, and Franklin Gaillard for major. The captain would be W.Z. Leitner; first lieutenant would be E. Niles; second lieutenant would be J.D. Dunlap, and third lieutenant would be J.J. Drakeford. Lieutenant Niles had also been appointed quartermaster of the regiment.[162]

The Flat Rock Guard now had J.P. Cunningham as captain, Jesse Truesdale as first lieutenant, Samuel Benton as second lieutenant, and William Patterson as third lieutenant.[163]

Mr. J.W. Rodgers, of the Dekalb house, gave out baskets of blackberries last week, and the paper was given a basket to enjoy.[164] It was good to have blackberries this early in the season that looked and tasted so good. The bells of the Presbyterian, Episcopal, Methodist, and Baptist churches were taken down to possibly be used to make a cannon.[165]

---

[155] Ibid.
[156] The Camden Confederate, Camden, South Carolina, May 2, 1862.
[157] The Camden Confederate, Camden, South Carolina, May 16, 1862.
[158] Ibid.
[159] Ibid.
[160] The Camden Confederate, Camden, South Carolina, May 23, 1862.
[161] Ibid.
[162] Ibid.
[163] Ibid.
[164] The Camden Confederate, Camden, South Carolina, May 30, 1862.
[165] Ibid.

News came that General John B. Villipique had been promoted officially and was commander of Fort Pillow.[166] He is remembered for his refusal to obey an order from General Hallock to receive men who had the small pox, in exchange for Yankee prisoners, so as not to allow the disease to come into camp.[167]

The official list of the Second Regiment is as follows (Formerly Kershaw's):

J. D. Kennedy- Colonel
A. D. Goodwin- Lieutenant-Colonel
F. Gaillard- Major

Company A	Company F
S. L. Leaphart- Captain	W. W. Perryman- Captain
P. H. B. Shuler- First Lieutenant	J. C. Maxwell- First Lieutenant
R. Brown- Second Lieutenant	George McDowell- Second Lieutenant
W. M. Myers- Third Lieutenant	W. L. Appleton- Third Lieutenant
Company B	**Company G**
R. C. Pulliam- Captain	J. P. Cunningham- Captain
W. R. Powell- First Lieutenant	J. E. Truesdale- First Lieutenant
A. Isaacs- Second Lieutenant	S. J. Benton- Second Lieutenant
J. W. Coates- Third Lieutenant	W. W. Patterson- Third Lieutenant
Company C	**Company H**
W. Wallace- Captain	B. R. Clyburn- Captain
S. Lobick- First Lieutenant	A. M. Perry- First Lieutenant
C. M. Goodwyn- Second Lieutenant	J. F. Perry- Second Lieutenant
E. Wallace- Third Lieutenant	G. C. Brasenden- Third Lieutenant
Company D	**Company I**
L. W. Barlett- Captain	G. B. Cutchbert- Captain
J. D. Graham- First Lieutenant	T. D. Brownfield- First Lieutenant
W. W. Wilder- Second Lieutenant	R. E. Elliot- Second Lieutenant
J. Jacobs- Third Lieutenant	Samuel Robinson- Third Lieutenant
Company E	**Company K**
W. Z. Leitner	J. F. Mooner- Captain
E. Niles- First Lieutenant	W. M. Dwight- First Lieutenant
J. D. Dunlap- Second Lieutenant	DeSaussure- Second Lieutenant
J. J. Drakeford- Third Lieutenant	T. W. Bradley- Third Lieutenant

[168]

---

166 Ibid.
167 Ibid.
168 The Camden Confederate, Camden, South Carolina, June 13, 1862.

A large potato grown by Captain A. M. Kennedy in his garden was brought in to the paper to be looked at.[169] The potato measured over ten inches in circumference and could have grown larger if not had been pulled up. This was grown from last year's seed.[170]

Sally Chesnut, President of the Ladies Aid Society, gave a list of things given to the soldiers in Virginia.[171] Those things being 298 dollars cash, 7 pairs sheets, 5 pairs of pillows, 12 pairs of pillow cases, 5 counterpanes, 58 towels, 22 shirts, 27 pairs drawers, 7 handkerchiefs, 3 pair socks, 5 arm pillows, bandages, compresses, linen rags, lint, dried beef, honey, dried fruit, 45 bottles wine, 2 gallons wine, 2 jars preserves, 1 jar pickles, arrow root, corn starch, sage, jelletine, spices, flax seed, 3 pounds sugar from Little Willie Shaw, 3 pounds of sugar from another little boy, and 25 cents from another little boy.[172]

The crops and water were rough on the growing season. Rust had come in on the wheat and needed to replant in the fall, cotton had hail beat it down and ruin, corn had to be planted in place of wheat if time would allow, and peas and corn looked good in the upper section, but in the lower sections were bad.[173] Times were beginning to look bad.

The Battle of Seven Pines took place and only one of our troops took part. Company C, 6th Regiment SCV under Captain E.B. Cantey. Sergeant Baum sent the following list of casualties: Sergeant J.A. McLeod, slightly wounded in the side; Sergeant Marcus Baum, in the arm; Corporal J.B. Arrants, in the shoulder; J.J. Brown, in the foot; J. Beeton, in the foot; Jacob Cotton, severely; J. Jackson, severely in the leg; W. Marthias, slightly in the side; J. Mosely, slightly in the foot; Z. Shiver, slightly in the arm; J.W. Hough, B. Hough, missing; --- Moye, missing; L. Watts, missing; W. Stewart, missing.[174]

On James Island, another group was in action on the twenty-fourth. This group was Captain W.L. DePass of Light Artillery, Company G, in Major B. White's Battalion.[175] DePass's officers included Dr. D.M. Rodgers of Camden, as first lieutenant; A.A. Gilbert Jr., first Lieutenant and editor of the *Sumter Watchman*; Samuel W. Richardson, Sr. second lieutenant, and J. Randolph Mordecai, Jr. second lieutenant.[176] Major White expressed admiration for Captain DePass for this gallantry on the bloody field and to the wound he received in battle and to the scar which he bore on his forehead. It was quite a memento of his service. He performed highly in battle and with much modesty doing his service as a soldier and patriot, along with his graceful and eloquent oratorical skills during battle.[177]

---

[169] Ibid.
[170] Ibid.
[171] Ibid.
[172] Ibid.
[173] Ibid.
[174] Ibid,
[175] Ibid.
[176] Ibid.
[177] Ibid.

Dr. E.M. Boykin announced in June 27 edition that all persons assigned to the first corps of reserves to come and sign up in his Cavalry unit.[178] I.B. Alexander brought in a peach from his orchard. Peaches at the Camden market were now eight dollars a bushel.[179]

Captain William M. Shannon had now been appointed as chief enrolling officer for the Kershaw District. His duties included receiving all applicants, exemption applicants, and conscription applicants.[180] The grain and flour mill of James H. Vaughn had just been readied for use.[181] If one was traveling out of state, then one would need to see J.M. DeSaussure to get a passport, as he was the government official who gave these passports out.[182]

The Kirkwood Cavalry had just released the new reorganization in the unit. The unit now had James Doby as captain; U.P. Bonney, first lieutenant; James Jones, second lieutenant; James D. Matheson, third lieutenant; George Barnes, first sergeant; Jesse Burch, second sergeant; James L. Haile, third sergeant; John B. Lee, fourth sergeant; Harvey McRae, fifth sergeant, A.W. Thames, first corporal; William Whitaker, second corporal; James Cureton, third corporal, and Daniel Kirkland, fourth corporal.[183]

The figures from South Carolina were 85 killed, 614 wounded, 45 missing for a total of 744.[184]

Another death had reached Camden. This time, Henry M. DeSaussure was killed in an engagement near Richmond.[185]

The Ladies Aid Society in Camden had a contribution of goods to McPherson Hospital.[186]

Causalities in Captain E.B. Cantey's Company.

Battle of Wilderness

Killed — none

Wounded —

Corporal A. Wittowsky, dangerously in the leg

Privates:

J. Robert Seay - slightly in the arm.

J. Henson - slightly in the thigh

W.J.C. Bass - missing in action

Battle of Seven Pines

Killed — none

Wounded —

---

[178] The Camden Confederate, Camden, South Carolina, June 27, 1862.
[179] Ibid.
[180] The Camden Confederate, Camden, South Carolina, July 4, 1862.
[181] Ibid.
[182] Ibid.
[183] Ibid.
[184] Ibid.
[185] Ibid.
[186] Ibid.

Sergeant J.A. McLeod - slightly in the side
Corporal J.B. Arrants - severely in shoulder

Privates:
J.J. Motley - dangerously in foot
J. Bedon - severely in foot
M. Baum - severely in arm
J.J. Brown - severely in arm
B. Hough - severely in leg
J. Jackson - severely in thigh
J. Cotton - severely in hip
C.C. Stuckey - slightly in arm
Z. Shiver - slightly in arm
W. Marthers - slightly in side
L. Watts - slightly in thigh
W.L. Moye - slightly in leg
William Stewart - missing in action

Battles of the twenty-eighth and thirtieth of June
Killed - Lieutenant H. W. DeSaussaure - commanding the company at that time

Wounded -
Lieutenant A. Brevard - in the hand and breast
Private R. Oxindine - mortally

Privates wounded:
W. Hough - mortally in leg and thigh
J. Robert Seay - severely in chest and arm
J.P. Wesberry - severely in head
L.C. Gerald - severely in thigh
W.R. Watts - slightly in arm
F.M. Stokes - slightly in hip
C. Stewart - slightly in leg
H.A. Barnes - slightly in hand

In August, Alexander L. McDowell was announced as a candidate for tax collector.[187]

---
[187] The Camden Confederate, Camden, South Carolina, August 15, 1862.

Mr. C.H. Peck, who ran the boy's military academy, brought in an Irish potatoe, which is the best seen grown either in the South or North. The variety was Prince Albert. Grown in his garden, this variety of potatoe's yield is incredible. The potatoes grown and brought to us came from a single hill and amounted to near a peck.

The Ladies Aid Society received ten dollars from the Ladies of Flat Rock Aid Society and their president, Miss Emily E. Perry.[188]

Again, death reached Camden when news came of the loss of Mr. James Shropshire.[189]

A military election took place for the Wateree Mounted Rifles. E.M. Boykin was elected captain; T.J. Ancrum was elected first lieutenant, John Cantey, second lieutenant, and Duncan Whitaker, third lieutenant.[190]

The Kershaw County Bible Society met for their forty-second annual meeting.[191]

The news of two more soldiers' deaths reached the area. They were John K. Witherspoon and John McLeod.[192]

The Flat Rock Guards sent a thank you note to the Ladies Society of Flat Rock for their boxes of wine, cordials, and bandages forwarded to the South Carolina Hospital at Manchester, Virginia, for the sick and wounded of the company.[193]

Dr. H.H. Clark of Longtown received news from the Battle of Maryland that his son, Caleb, died during this battle.[194]

Edward B. Lang died in Arkansas, of disease in camp on July 31, 1862.[195]

Colonel Warren dismissed that he was a candidate for legislature as he was in service.[196]

A former Camdenite, Lieutenant F.L. Villipigue, brother of Brigadier General John B. Villipique, was doing well in Florida.[197]

The following were casualties from the Sharpsburg and Boonsboro Gap: Company C with Captain E.B. Cantey: Private Barwick killed, wounded; C. Stuckey, mortally; Captain E.B. Cantey, severely; Sergeant Robert Seay, slightly; Sergeant McLeod, slightly, and Private R. McGinnis, slightly. At Boonsboro Gap, Edward B. Lang, who had a lot of relatives here in Kershaw County, died in Arkansas, July 31, in camp in of disease. He was in Captain McCray's Company, "The Hough Rangers," of General Hindman's army. He left behind a wife and a child in Texas.[198]

---

[188] The Camden Confederate, Camden, South Carolina, August 22, 1862.
[189] Ibid.
[190] The Camden Confederate, Camden, South Carolina, August 29, 1862.
[191] Ibid.
[192] Ibid.
[193] The Camden Confederate, Camden, South Carolina, September 5, 1862.
[194] The Camden Confederate, Camden, South Carolina, September 26, 1862.
[195] Ibid.
[196] Ibid.
[197] Ibid.
[198] Ibid.

Also, dead was William H. Albert, of Kershaw District. He was born on October 19, 1830, and died in his home in Gadsen County, Florida, on August 29, 1862. At Adam's Run Hospital, below Charleston, Mr. John Campbell, third son of Benjamin J. Campbell, died at twenty-five years old of the fever.[199]

Lieutenant J.A. Schrock had sent a list of casualties in Company D, 15th Regiment SCV in battles fought since August 29.

August 30	—	Lieutenant C.A. Fisher, wounded slightly in leg; Sergeant J.W. Young, knee; Private W.D. Warren, foot; Private Samuel Yates, leg; Private James L. Gardner, foot slightly
September 14	—	William Brown, neck slightly; D. Jordan, shoulder; W.H. Capell, dangerously in head; M. Scott, neck slightly; E. Watts, hip severely.
September 17	—	Lieutenant C.A. Fisher, seriously, leg amputated; Private John Ervin, shoulder; Private Samuel Hornsby, both arms and legs, severely; Private B.F. Johnson, shoulder; Private James Mattox, both ankles; Private W. Brannon Jr., foot; Private Lewis Gardner, hip; Private Frank Watts, hip slightly.
Missing	—	W.J. Spradley, D.G. Fletcher, J.B. Capell, and W.W. Watson. Sick and in the hospital was Captain Warren, and Lieutenants Shrock and Burns, expected to get well soon.201

In the Battles of Blue Ridge and Sharpsburg, Kershaw District Casualties occurred. The following was a report of those soldiers:

Colonel J.D. Kennedy's instep of his foot was slightly bruised and tendon of his heel wounded; Adjutant Sill had a piece of his head cut out by a piece of shell. The 2nd regiment had eleven killed and between eighty and ninety wounded.

Adjutant J.M. Davis of the 15th Regiment was slightly wounded. Captain E.B. Cantey was severely wounded in both thighs, but a good recovery was expected.

Sergeant William C. Dutton fell mortally but feels he was wounded and left alive at last accounts and was sent back by the enemy to our side of the line. He was in Captain Leitner's Company and in Winchester, not expected to live.

Hiram Nettles was slightly wounded in the leg; J. Arrants and James Cooper were killed on the field of battle; J. Freeman, Sergeant D. Ryan, and C.R. Pearson were slightly wounded; R.T. Gardner was left to take care of himself, wounded and left in the hands of the enemy.[200]

---
199 Ibid.
200 Ibid.

An election in Kershaw District was to take place and people to man the polls the second October next, was listed as the following:

Camden — John S. Meroney, Charles A. McDonald, W.D. Anderson
Cureton's Mills — Frederick Bowen, James Team, Eli Parker
Flat Rock — James Fletcher, J.B. Hughes, Jessie Truesdel
Buffalo — William Mungo, Gilliam Sowell, William Cato
Lizenby's — Lauchlan McKinnon, Wilson Yarborough, Jonathan Newman
Schrock's Mills — B.T. McCoy, Henry Ratcliffe, Alexander McLeod
Goodwyn's Store — A.J. McDonald, R. D. Drakeford. Benjamon Cook
Liberty Hill — A.D. Jones, R.C. Patterson, Robert J. Cunningham

Also, two more representatives needed to be elected. The polls would be open for one day only. Managers would count the votes at the close of the day, make out a certificate of the results, and take it to the courthouse to declare the results of that precinct.

Signed by John S. Meroney, Charles A. McDonald, and W.D. Anderson [201]

More results of casualties in the Flat Rock Guards were reported by Captain J.P. Cunningham. These occurred in the battle on September 17 and were as followed:

Lieutenant W.W. Patterson, in the leg slightly
James J. Truesdel, killed
Corporal D.M. Kirkley, right arm broken near the shoulder, and since amputated
J.A. Sowell, severely in left breast
W.J. Fletcher, shoulder
J.B. Hall, sides
John Williams, slightly in leg
Sowell, Kirkley, and J.B. Hall were left in the hands of the enemy.[202]

The ladies aid society appealed for blankets and woolen garments for the upcoming winter for the soldiers in service, asking each family to give one blanket dyed and cut up into coats.[203]

The election was held and the following results tabulated. House of Representatives had no opposition: John M. DeSaussure and D.D. Perry were elected. Also, without opposition were the votes for ordinary where William M. Bullock won.

For tax collector, McKain won with 439 votes; second was Pate with 329 votes; third was McDonald with twelve votes, and fourth was Arrants with four votes.

---

[201] Ibid.
[202] The Camden Confederate, Camden, SC., October 10, 1862.
[203] Ibid.

No opposition for the Commissioners of the Poor as E. Barnes, A.A. McDowell, J.O. Higgins, J.S. DePass, and R.M. Kennedy were elected. [204]

The DeSaussure Light Artillery Unit. The last company organized in the Palmetto Battalion, or Light Infantry, will be called the DaSaussure Light Artillery, and well equipped.

The following correspondence refers to this Corps and its designation:

Camp Gilbert, September 29, 1862

Major John M. DeSausure:

Major: - I have the honor to inform you that at the meeting of my Company it was unanimously resolved, that in appreciation of that manly and upright course of integrity, which has ever marked both your public and private life, to designate the organization as the "DeSaussure Light Artillery." Be assured that this mark of affection and respect proceeds not from honored name you bear, alike distinguished at the Bar and in the public council of the country, but for that veneration we entertain for your own individual character, so signally displayed in those acts of patriotism which have been exhibited in this present contest for our liberty and independence. And more particularly, in the active sympathy and ready assistance which you have extended to the soldier and to his family in their need. I enclose your Roll of Officers and Privates of the Company.

I am, Major, yours, more respectively,
W. L. DePass
Captain DeSaussure Light Artillery[205]

Roll of the Officers and Privates of the DeSaussure Light Artillery

W. L. DePass, Captain
D. M. Rogers, Senior First Lieutenant
A.A. Gilbert, Junior Second Lieutenant
S. M. Richardson, Senior Second Lieutenant
J. R. Mordecai, Junior Second Lieutenant
J. N. Corbett, Quartermaster and Ordinance Sergeant
John Magnet, Orderly Sergeant
Isaac Holland, First Chief of Piece
Joseph F. Rhame, Second Chief of Piece
Wiley Bradley, Third Chief of Piece
G. W. Reardon, Fourth Chief of Piece
J. M. Hill, Fifth Sergeant
E. G. Robinson, Sixth Sergeant
William M. Campbell, First Corporal

---

204   The Camden Confederate, Camden, SC., October 17, 1862.
205   The Camden Confederate, Camden, SC., October 24, 1862.

S. P. Durant, Second Corporal
J. W. DePass, Third Corporal
G. W. Stoudemire, Fourth Corporal
B. H. Cross, Fifth Corporal
B. J. Humphries, Sixth Corporal
John Goff, Seventh Corporal
Julius J. Cooper, Eighth Corporal
James T. Flowers, Ninth Corporal
A. M. Dunn, Tenth Corporal

Privates

W. R. Atkinson	T. W. Atkinson	Thomas Adkinson
Ezekial Adkinson	A. L. Barnes	P. Baxley
John Bordenave	P. Bowen	C. P. Bowen
James Bradley	George Brown	Samuel J. Brown
Richard Brown	Daniel Brunson	J. P. Boswell
J. W. Bessinger	J. W. Baker	T. M. Cassels
Charles Clark	John A. Counts	John A. Capell
John Campbell	C. W. Davis	W. E. Deloache
J. E. DePass	T. Dickert	B.E. Evans
E. L. Galloway	L. B. Gay	R. T. Gee
S. Griffin	B. F. Gordon	John Gillis
Charles Hayden	M. Henderson	John Holland
George Holley	J. Dargan Jones	S. I. Jones
E. C. Jones	Jessie A. Jones	G. W. Johnson
James Langley	J. L. Lyles	Alfred Marsh
T. J. McCants	T. B. Miller	John McGowan
T. A. Merony	E. Owens	D. Owens
V. Parsons (Farrier)	E. Parsons	John Parker
Richard Potee	I. P. Sharp	John W. Smith
James Smith	J. T. Setzler	Frank Stevens
James Tisdale	Davis Thomas	R. H. Vaughn
Samuel T. Wilson	Robert Wilson	Judge Wilson
H. C. Wilson	John Wooten	J. M. Wilson
Jessie Yates		

---

[206] Ibid.

The following letter was in the Camden Confederate, October 24, 1862

Camden, October 4, 1862

Captain W. L. DePass, Commanding DeSaussure Light Artillery

Captain: I am honored with your favor of the 29th ult., informing me that your command had been pleased to designate their corps by my name.

I feel honored by this resolution of the Company as well for the distinction itself as coming from the men who have been pleased to bestow the honor- many of whom I know, and knowing them, have a perfect conviction that they sustain the honor of their flag to the last extremity.

Men who abandon home and all its charms and enjoyments to meet the common foe of the country and expose their lives for that country are earned men, and truly an honor bestowed by them must be highly appreciated by everyone. I feel sure that in that fierce trial which the times foreshadow will probably come upon you this fall or winter, every man of your command will march to the cannon's mouth without flinching and force victory to perch on their banner. In you, sir, they will find a leader who has felt the power of the foeman's lead in the first battle of Manassas, and gallantly performed his part there. A son of Kershaw never surrenders. Be pleased to tender to the company my warmest thanks for this, their mark of honor to me, and assure them that I shall watch their movements with great solicitude and shall do all for them and their families in my power.

With great respect, yours, most truly,
John M. DeSaussure[207]

Captain E.M. Boykin's Wateree Mounted Rifleman were now in camp at the race course for drilling, instructions on camp life, and would remain for a few weeks before their duty on the coast.[208]

Due to the death of Major W.A. Ancrum, an election for major of the Lower Battalion South Carolina Militia for Kershaw District would take place on November 7 by General Order of Colonel Witherspoon.[209] Captain A.M. Kennedy won the election as major.[210]

An obituary was in the paper in honor of James D. Cooper, who died on September 17 in the Battle of Sharpsburg. He was sixteen and four months old, and a native of Kershaw District. Only a few short months, did he enlist with Captain Leitner's Company, the Camden Volunteers, attached to Colonel Kennedy's 2nd South Carolina Regiment. His officers gave testimony on that gallantry he performed on the day he died. It was a bloody battle scene which terminated his life and took his final breath, and with enemy just a few feet from their guns, he fell and gave his life for the cause, his country, and his comrades.[211]

Mr. C.A. McDonald had brought to us a yam potato, which grown in his garden weighed eight pounds, twenty-four inches in length, and sixteen inches in circumference.[212]

---

[207] Ibid.
[208] Ibid.
[209] Ibid.
[210] The Camden Confederate, Camden, SC., November 14, 1862.
[211] The Camden Confederate, Camden, SC., October 24, 1862.
[212] The Camden Confederate, Camden, SC., October 31, 1862.

The Ladies society would like to thank Mrs. Lemuel Boykin for her donation of fifty yards of hair cloth for the soldiers.[213]

Word has come down that Captain E.M. Boykin's company, who had been training at the race course, would be leave for the coast next week.[214]

In our newspaper office (Camden Confederate), a gentleman claimed to have a fine, wooden, soled shoe for the negroes made on the J.R. Dye Plantation at Red Hill and is of fine quality. The shoe is neat, finish, and substantially made. The shoe is light, durable, and made of leather. The wood used is walnut and secured to the upper leather being fastened by screws. At this time, no intention is being given toward manufacture of this shoe on a wide scale. It is our belief at this newspaper, its need for production is greatly needed. [215]

On the plantation of our fine, gallant Colonel J. D. Kennedy, a bottle of extra fine Chinese Sugar Cane Syrup was brought in. Made on his plantation, Major A. M. Kennedy told us that "with good cultivation" that fifty gallons could be made per acre. [216]

Captain B.S. Lucas has sent us the casualty report from the Battle of Pocataligo on November 22, under the Colonel P.H. Nelson, commanding the 7th South Carolina Battalion Infantry. [217] **This letter was dated November 7, and from Adams Run, Camp Cantey.**

Company A	—	Lucas Guards - Under Captain B.S. Lucas, Jr. - Killed – none; Wounded - James Sinclair, severely in thigh.
Company D	—	Kershaw Greys - Commanded by Lieutenant Young - Killed and Wounded none.
Company F	—	Lucas Rifles - Commanded by Captain Dove Segars – Killed - Corporal S.T. Folsom and Private James Hall; --- John McGougan; Mortally (since dead); R. J. Turner and James Bruce—supposed mortally; R. D. Turner, James Hopkins, and J. W. Horton, slightly.
Company G	—	Moffatt Rifles- Captain William Clyburn, commanding, Killed- none. Wounded—Martin Gilbran- severely in both thighs; J. A. Smith- flesh wound in the right fore arm; William Justice- slightly in chest; A. F. A. Hughes- flesh wound in thigh; H. A. Tiller and D. R. Smith, slightly.

End of List received.

Near Georgetown, South Carolina, near the coast, Captain E.M. Boykin sent us a roll of the Wateree Mounted Riflemen:

---

[213] Ibid.
[214] The Camden Confederate, Camden, SC., November 7. 1862.
[215] The Camden Confederate, Camden, SC., November 14, 1862.
[216] Ibid.
[217] Ibid.

Officers:

E. M. Boykin, Captain
Thomas A. Ancrum, 1st Lieutenant
John Cantey, 2nd Lieutenant
Duncan Whitaker, 3rd Lieutenant
S. Sumter, 1st Sergeant
D. P. Dubose, 2nd Sergeant
J. P. Kirkland, 3rd Sergeant
C. L. McCoy, 4th Sergeant
John M. Cantey, 1st Corporal
James Truesdale, 2nd Corporal

Privates

H Arrants	Joseph Arrants	T. S. Boykin
W. T. Boykin	M. N. Brown	Samuel Barfield
H. Baruch	B. J. Baker	R. Collins
B. J. Campbell	James Clyburn	D. J. Cook
William Christmas	R. H. Douglas	L. H. Deas, Jr.
Allen Deas	E. W. Davis	W. G. Duncan
J. R. Davis	J. M. DeSaussure	G. A. DeBruhl
Ben DeBruhl	J. W. Doby, Jr.	M. Evans
Thomas Elliott	D. J. George	W. J. Gerald, Jr.
-----Garner	M. G. Huckabee	James R. Kirkland
M. W. King	S. R. Kirkland	R. L. Logan
B. H. Matheson	A.L. McMullen	Washington Myers
W. D. McDowell, Jr.	J. P. Mickle	Thomas Nelson
B. Nunnery	Jonathan Newman	R. R. Player
J. R. Pickett	J. R. Pace	J. J. Ross
B. J. Ratcliff	W. H. Ratcliff	W. T. Russell
W. J. Reynolds	W. W. Stokes	P. E. Woods
O. W. Watts	John Williams	H. K. Witherspoon
G. G. Young	J. N. Young	Wilson Yarborough

218

Camden was again touched by death, and with this death, the remains of Lieutenant H.M. DeSaussure arrived in Camden. He fell on the battlefield near Richmond, leading a command. His body would be in a vault in the city cemetery (Now referred to as the Quaker Cemetery). The men of his company, his friends, and family would miss the gallant officer.

Also, news came of the death of Lieutenant Edward Niles, who fell to the wounds of war fighting for a cause he believed in. He would forever remain in the hearts of those who knew his fight and would miss the efforts of yet another gallant soldier.[218]

The paper got a letter of thanks for the kind accommodations given to the staff of General Villipigue during their stay to honor their fallen leader.[219]

Captain E. M. Boykin announced that anyone wishing to send a letter or package could send it to Captain E.M. Boykin, W.M.R. Conwayboro, Horry District, South Carolina for the Wateree Mounted Riflemen.[220]

The Camden Ladies Aid Society received a thank you note for the twenty suits of underclothing for the DeSausure Light Artillery by Captain W.L. DePass.[221]

The Camden Ladies Aid Society received the following:

From Dr. LaBorde, of nearby Columbia, for the four companies presently in Virginia - Captains Doby, Chesnut, Leitner, and Warren; forty blankets, forty shirts, forty pairs of drawers, twelve carpets, twelve comforters, eight pairs of hair pantaloons.

To Captain DePass, twenty shirts, twenty pairs drawers, twenty pairs of socks, two blankets, and two carpets.

Other collections from other sources from Camden and the vicinity included: shoes for the soldiers at $726. 50; $6 from James Young, $16 from raffled rocking horse won by Master Blanding DeSausure, and sent to Captain Cantey's Company: twelve pairs of drawers, twelve shirts, twelve blankets, twelve pairs socks, three carpet blankets, one coat, two pairs pantaloons, two scarves, and one pair gloves.[222]

Death had surfaced once again in the community with the word that Lieutenant C.A. Fisher had been killed. Though being from nearby Sumter District, his childhood was spent in Camden growing up. He graduated from South Carolina College with high honors, and those who knew him best said of him that was a brave, gallant soldier, an efficient officer, genial and warm person, who would be missed by those duties he loved so much. He was wounded in the battle of Manassas, but persevered on with his company, before falling in the mighty battle of Sharpsburg, leading the heroic charge against the enemy with his company.[223]

The ladies of Liberty Hill Society Aid Association received the following donations: Mr. Kilgore, one felt cloak, $25; Mrs. William Dixon, two blankets, one comfort, and five pairs of drawers; Mr. R.B. Cunningham, $25; Mrs. R.B. Cunningham, six pillows, two carpet blankets; Miss M. Cunningham, one pair of socks; Miss S. Cunningham, one pair of socks; Miss Maggie Cunningham, one pair socks; Mrs. J.L. Jones, three carpet blankets, two pairs drawers; Mr. J. Brown, $25; Mrs. J. Brown, one carpet blanket, one blanket; Mrs. L.W. Wardlaw, seven carpet blankets; Mr. D.D. Perry, $25; Miss N. Perry, two blankets, one pair of socks; Miss H. Perry, one pair of socks; ;Mr. A.D. Jones, $20; Mrs. A.D. Jones, two blankets; Dr. T. McDow, $10; Mrs. McDow, one blanket, one pair of drawers; Mrs. Montgomery, two pairs of socks; Mrs. W.E. Johnson, one blanket; Mr. William Cunningham, $40; Miss Mary Cunningham, one pair of socks; Miss Lizzie Cunningham,

---
218 Ibid.
219 Ibid.
220 The Camden Confederate, Camden, South Carolina, November 28, 1862.
221 Ibid.
222 Ibid.
223 Ibid.

one pair of socks; Master Joe Cunningham, one woolen shirt, which he insisted be made of cloth and not from his own jacket; Miss S. George, four blankets; Mr. J.S. Thompson, $25; Mrs. J.S. Thompson, four blankets; Mrs. A.B. Wardlaw, nine carpet blankets; Mrs. W. Patterson, one blanket; Mr. L.J. Patterson, $50; Mrs. L.J. Patterson, four carpet blankets; Mr. Wiley Patterson, $25; Mr. John Perry, Jr., $5; Mr. A.D. Hillard, $5; Mr. William Brown, $20; Mr. H.R. Brown, $10; Mr. J.R. Gilbert, $5; Mr. R.C. Patterson, $5; Mr. D. Harrison, $5; Mr. John Montgomery, $25. This list was sent in by Mrs. L.J. Patterson, president of the Ladies Aid Society in Liberty Hill. She also noted that during the past week, the following items were sent to soldiers in Virginia: twenty-eight carpet blankets, eighteen blankets, twenty pairs of pants, four vests, fifty-nine shirts, forty-eight pairs of drawers, and eighty-seven pairs of socks. [224]

The Soldier's Rest released the following contributions: Mr. W.C. Cauthan, seventy-one dollars; J.M. Ingram, two dollars; J.B. Mobley, ten dollars; Osborn Floyd, five dollars; Thomas Cauthan, ten dollars; Miss Susan Cauthan, five dollars; Mrs. Dr. Cauthen, five dollars; L.M. Cauthan, five dollars; Dr. B.L. Beckham, four dollars, and J.T. Cauthan. [225]

The Masonic Lodge, Number 29, held elections. Those to serve for the upcoming year would be:

>Brother J. Steckley, W.M.
>Brother T.W. Smith, S.W.
>Brother D.D. Hocott, J.W.
>Brother C.A. McDonald, Treasurer.
>Brother J. Jones, Secretary.
>Brother D. L. DeSaussure, S.D.
>Brother R. Hocott, J.D.
>Brother W.E. Hughson, Chaplain.
>Brother W.D. Anderson, Steward
>Brother S.H. Blodget, Steward
>Brother F.J. Oakes. [226]

Camden learned of casualties in the Camden Volunteers under the command of Captain Leitner. No real details were given but the initial information had James Witherspoon, severely in thigh; James R. Brown, severely in thigh; Henry McKagan, severely; R.W. Proctor, with __Crenshaw, __Laurence, C.J. Pegues, R.W. Allen, Alexander Monroe being slightly wounded; George Monroe, leg amputated, and three others unnamed.[227] Also, in the 2nd Regiment, three were killed, and seventy-five wounded. Among them was Major Gaillard, slightly wounded; Lieutenant Elliot, severely in the groin, W. Adams, mortally; and Captain Doby, slightly.[228]

---

[224] The Camden Confederate, Camden, South Carolina; December 5, 1862.
[225] The Camden Confederate, Camden, South Carolina, December 12, 1862.
[226] The Camden Confederate, Camden, South Carolina, December 19, 1862.
[227] The Camden Confederate, Camden, South Carolina, December 26, 1862.
[228] Ibid.

The obituary was made known to the Camden area of Benjamin F. Leitner, who died at Savage Station, June 29, 1862. Though born in South Carolina, he was raised a portion of his life in Florida. He went to the University of Virginia, left the university, and enlisted in the Camden Volunteers in August 1861, as a private. He fought at Manassas in the snows, fatigue campaigns of the Peninsula; he was acting color bearer the day he died, when General McGrugor's Corp attacked General Sumner's at Savage Station. Wounded, he was carried to Richmond, and perished on July 13. Others who died were Ellen Whitaker Chesnut, age twenty-three, in Florida on the twelfth, and Mrs. C. Collins, ninety-nine years old, on November 25 in Kershaw District.[229]

The Camden Ladies Aid Society released the name of Mrs. A.E. Peay, who gave fifteen dollars, along with two bundles hospital stores.[230] Other donations were fourteen dollars and seventy-five cents from the proceeds of an embroidered cushion from Ann Salmond, one dozen cups given, one bunch yarn from Mrs. Humphreys, one pair socks from Miss Dabney, and a large quantity of scraps for making caps.[231]

---

[229] Ibid.
[230] Ibid.
[231] Ibid.

1863

Casualties began to come in more readily. The mood of Camden, though trying to be upbeat, grieved for those families with dead, sons, husbands, and other love ones now gone. The 2nd Regiment had casualties, but the Flat Rock Guards under Captain J.J. Cunningham had J. Herby, severely in neck; E.D. Williams, severely in arm; and J.Q. Cranton, slightly in head. Captain T.J. Warren's company in the battle of Fredericksburg had W.J. Spradley, H. Scott, and John Bradley, slightly wounded.[232] The war was taking its toll on those from Kershaw District units. Sickness and disease, not to mention, battle wounded and dying on the field of battle were taking our beloved fathers, sons, brothers, and friends for the cause.

And of all things, a court martial was instituted for the 22nd Regiment with Lieutenant Colonel William Dixon, President; Captains W.E. Hugheson, John. B. Mickle, John Thompson, L.J. Patterson, J.J. Nelson, and Judge Advocate J.M. Gayle.[233] The Supernaires were Lieutenants Gilliam Sowell and Tobias Folsom.[234] No details known.

Another death occurred in December on the eighteenth, 1862, when Washington Myers, forty-seven years old, died of disease.[235] Edward P. Niles, also, died.[236] William K. Arrants died. His parents were Nathan and Mary Arrants. He had joined the command of General Benjamin McCullough in Arkansas, before transferring to the company of General Price, serving until November 14, when, on detached service in the Cumberland Gap, Tennessee, he fell. He was born on February 4, 1839, and united with the Camden Baptist Church in April 1856.[237]

More casualties came from Captain T.J. Warren's Company D, 15th Regiment.[238]

(paper blackened and hard to read)
Unknown (unreadable), present for duty.
Lieutenant J. A. Shrock, present for duty.

---

[232] The Camden Confederate, Camden, South Carolina, January 2, 1863.
[233] Ibid.
[234] Ibid.
[235] The Camden Confederate, Camden, South Carolina, January 9, 1863.
[236] The Camden Confederate, Camden, South Carolina, January 16, 1863.
[237] The Camden Confederate, Camden, South Carolina, January 23, 1863.
[238] Ibid.

C. B. Burns, present for duty.

Geo. Crosby, absent sick at hospital.

J. L. (letter not clear) Huckabee, absent sick at home.

J. J. Davis, present for duty.

Sergeant R. Springer, absent sick, at Macon, Georgia.

Sergeant E. Wolff, absent sick, at hospital in Lynchburg.

Sergeant J. W. Young, present for duty.

Corporal N. A. McLeod, absent sick, at hospital in Richmond. (pneumonia)

Corporal A. J. Munn, present for duty.

Corporal D. C. Kirkley, absent sick, at hospital at Richmond, (pneumonia)

Corporal A. W. Williams, present for duty.

H. Ammons, present for duty.

John Brannum, present for duty.

D. Brannum, present for duty.

R. Brannum, present sick.

W. Brannum, present for duty.

W. Brannum, absent at hospital at Richmond, (wounded)

W. Brown, present for duty.

John Bradley, present for duty.

J. C. Corbett, absent sick at home.

W. H. Capell, absent sick at home.

H. L. Creighton, present for duty,

F. E. Creighton, absent sick at home.

F. J. Collier, present for duty.

Samuel Ervin, absent sick at home.

John Ervin, absent at home, (wounded)

E. J. Ford, **deserted.**

D. G. Fletcher, missing since the battle of Boonsboro.

J. L. Gardner, absent at home, (wounded)

Lewis Gardner, absent at home, (wounded)

Stephen Griffin, absent sick, at hospital at Richmond, (pneumonia)

Joseph Hays, absent sick at home.

E. Hays, present for duty.

James Hase, present for duty.

James Harrall, died at Richmond, (date unknown)

Samuel Hornsby, died from wound at Shepardstown, (date unknown)

Joseph Hornsby, present for duty.

S. W. Hornsby, absent sick, at hospital at Richmond.

Hollis Hough, absent sick, at hospital at Lynchburg.

John Hinson, absent sick at home.

A.A. Hunter, missing since the latter part of August, (deranged)

R. J. Hall, present for duty.

B. F. Johnson, absent at home, (wounded)

W. B. Johnson, absent at home, (wounded)

W. H. Jourdan, present for duty.

D. Jackson, present for duty.

Warren Kemp, absent sick at home.

A. Kirby, present for duty.

J. W. Kirby, present for duty.

B. P. Kelly, present for duty.

Jno. Mooneyham, present for duty.

Jas. Mattox, present for duty.

George Mattox, absent sick at home.

Isaac S. Mattox, present on duty.

John Morris, absent, (disabled by wound)

J. B. Minton, present for duty.

Columbus Minton, present for duty.

Henry McGuire, missing from about September 1st.

J. E. Outlaw, absent at hospital at Richmond, (pneumonia)

W. E. Parker, absent sick at hospital at Richmond.

R. Parker, present for duty.

B. B. Parker, present for duty.

H. Scott, absent sick at hospital at Richmond, (pneumonia)

M. Scott, absent sick at hospital at Richmond.

Joseph Shira, present for duty.

J. P. Shedd, absent sick at hospital at Richmond.

John Spradley, present sick.

W. J. Spradley, present for duty.

T. S. Shaylor, absent sick since October 1st, (whereabouts unknown)

C. H. Shaylor, present for duty.

J. F. Turner, present for duty.

Joel Wilson, present for duty.

P. H. Wilson, absent sick at home.

Henry Wilson, absent sick at home.

W. W. Watson, missing since the battle of Boonsboro.

W. D. Warren, missing since 8th September- last seen at Warrenton.

N. T. Waddill, absent sick, (whereabouts unknown)

John Watts, absent sick at home.

F. Watts, present for duty.

Columbus Watts, wounded at Boonsboro and missing since then.

John Ward, *deserted.*

Willie Yates, present for duty.

Samuel Yates, absent sick at home.

Sent in by J. A. Shrock, 1st Lieutenant Commanding
Company "D", 15th Regiment S.C.V.

Mr. George Douglass had a fire at his cotton house, where the house burnt down, taking with it three hundred seventeen bales of cotton, two hundred seventy-six covered by insurance, forty bales of cotton, and ten having no insurance. Douglass owned the building but had no insurance on the building itself.[239]

More deaths came in. Captain John McCaa, Henry G. McKagan, and James M. Witherspoon.[240]

A bright spot had been seen in the form of Spanish yams grown on the plantation of Mrs. A.F. Cougar of nearby Bishopville.[241]

General James Cantey was promoted to Brigadier General and with this honor, a command of forces at Poland, Alabama.[242] Enrolling notices in Camden occurred. One such was Captain James Doby recruiting for the Kirkwood Rangers.[243] The Upper Battalion of the District of the 22nd regiment was named. John Thompson was captain, Thomas J. Cauthen as first lieutenant, Joseph G. Brun as second lieutenant, and Richard C. Drakeford as third lieutenant. The Lower Battalion of 22nd would have A.M. Kennedy as captain, B.T. McCoy as first lieutenant, Jessie Arthur as second lieutenant, and A.H. Boykin, Jr. as third lieutenant.

Election came around again in March. James V. Lyles was elected intendant, with Robert M. Kennedy, Joseph W. Doby, Joseph W. Gayle, and C.A. McDonald elected wardens.[244]

The Liberty Hill Aid Society received the following donations: Mr. W.E. Johnson, twenty-five dollars; Mrs. J.S. Thompson, the weaving of thirty yards of woolen cloth; Miss Cornelia Cunningham, one woolen cap; Miss Sallie Cunningham, one pair of woolen socks: Mrs. Robert McDow, six pairs of woolen socks, and the yarn for knitting six more pairs; Mrs. S. Watt Wardlaw, three flannel shirts; Mrs. John Brown, two pairs of socks. Sent earlier to Virginia were thirty-four pairs of pants, sixty-two pairs of drawers, three flannel shirts, one cotton shirt, one cap, fifty pairs of socks, eight vests, and six pillows.[245]

---

[239] The Camden Confederate, Camden, South Carolina, January 30, 1863.
[240] Ibid.
[241] The Camden Confederate, Camden, South Carolina, February 4, 1863.
[242] The Camden Confederate, Camden, South Carolina, February 20, 1863.
[243] Ibid.
[244] The Camden Confederate, Camden, South Carolina, March 13, 1863.
[245] Ibid.

A Letter of thanks came in for the Ladies Aid Association of Camden which read:

Camp White, Sea Shore
February 22, 1863
Miss Chesnut, Pres't Ladies Aid Association:

Your kind and considerate present of clothing and caps has been received, and would not have been sooner acknowledged, had I not been necessarily out of the way when they arrived. Permit me in my own behalf, and that of the Wateree Mounted Rifles, to thank you for them. It is but another of the many kindness done towards the soldier by the women of our country — acts not done in vain, for they show to him that kindly eyes are watching him, and kindly hands are caring for his comfort, and he would not be the man he is, did he not strive in some measure to return their great kindness.

Accept for yourself, and the Ladies of the Society, our highest regard, and believe me most
Truly yours,
Edward M. Boykin
Captain Wateree Mounted Riflemen[246]

The Ladies Aid Society of Camden gave the following list and requests to those who give: Mrs. John McRae, nine pairs of socks, Mrs. John Whitaker, twenty-eight pairs of socks, Mrs. A.D. Jones, nine pairs of socks, five dollars cash, and to Master Willie McCreight for neatly packaging fifty-nine pairs of shoes for the soldiers.

This morning, three packages left for Virginia, to Captains Cantey, Leitner, and Warren. Included are thirty-five pairs of socks, twenty pairs of drawers, twenty shirts, twelve pairs shoes, ten caps, one knit shirt, two pairs of gloves, one woolen jacket, and one scarf. Those who are making socks should make sure the socks have the following dimensions: twenty-four stiches on each needle, length of the leg to the heel, nine-inches length of the heel, four inches; length of the foot from back of heel, nine inches.[247]

One interested side note is that an ordinance was passed to prevent sheep from roaming in the Town of Camden.[248] Sheep were used for weaving purposes and for food when necessary.

Brothers were found dead in the woods.[249] Coroner Maroney on March eleventh held an inquest into the deaths of Edmond and William Wages, found dead in the woods, but because their residence was in Richland County, the inquest was dismissed. It was said that William Wages was a deserter from Captain Waites's Artillery Company, and his brother eluded the proper authorities to keep them from finding them. On a Tuesday night, both were shot to death, with no evidence as to who did the deed.[250]

Captain William Clyburn of the Moffat Rifles gave thanks to Miss Francis Hay for the knit socks she sent the company.[251]

---

[246] Ibid.
[247] Ibid.
[248] Ibid.
[249] The Camden Confederate, Camden, South Carolina, March 20, 1863.
[250] Ibid.
[251] Ibid.

Another election for the Town of Camden had taken place. Elected intendant was James Dunlap, Robert M. Kennedy, Joseph W. Doby, Joseph M. Gayle, and C.A. McDowell were elected wardens.[252] N.D. Baxley remained the tax collector.[253]

News arrived that W.C. Dutton was dead from the war.[254] He died near Sharpsburg, Maryland, on the nineteenth of September, dying from wounds received on the seventeenth. He was born and raised in Camden, and in service, he rose from private to corporal to orderly sergeant of his company.[255]

B.P. Parker, son of Mr. Vincent Parker of Kershaw District, died in camp, and was buried here. Also, W. H Jordan died at hospital in Lynchburg during the past month.[256]

Orders came down from General Longstreet through G.M. Sorrel, A. A. General for U.P. Bonney, Lieutenant Commander of Kirkwood Cavalry. These orders said that the services of Captain James Doby's troop of South Carolina Cavalry would no longer be needed in escorting services from headquarters. Instead, they could be assigned to another duty and thanks was expressed for their courage.[257]

A new chief enrolling officer for the town of Camden and Kershaw District was selected in E.B. Cantey.[258]

Camden saw the observance of Christian duty on Friday. This was set apart by the president of the Confederacy as a day of fasting, humiliation, and prayer from people that truly believed in the Christian duty.[259]

Fire struck again on the plantation of Mr. S.H. Young at his cotton house twelve miles from Camden.[260] Lost and insured for cost only were forty bales of cotton belonging to Messengers Koopman and Sommers.[261] Also, not insured and lost was five bales of cotton belonging to Washington Bracey, thirty-three hundred pounds of guano, five hundred bushels of cotton seed, and seventy bushels of peas.[262]

James Dunlap was elected intendant, along with R.M. Kennedy, N.D. Baxley, L.M. Boswell, and D.D. Hocott.[263]

Major L.W.R. Blair resigned and returned to Camden.[264]

Again, more donations for the Camden Ladies Society: Reverend Manning Brown, fifteen dollars; Mr. George Alden, twenty dollars; twelve dollars came from the proceeds of a work basket by Mrs. H.W. Conner, Jr.; scissors by Dr. James Young; Mrs. A.D. Goodwyn, one pair of socks; Miss H.M. Whitaker, two pairs of socks; Mrs. William Kennedy, one pair of socks and twelve hanks of yarn; given to Captain William Clyburn's company, twelve pairs shoes, twenty-five pairs of drawers, fifteen shirts, twenty-five pairs of drawers; sent

---

252 Ibid.
253 Ibid.
254 Ibid.
255 Ibid.
256 Ibid.
257 The Camden Confederate, Camden, South Carolina, March 27, 1863.
258 The Camden Confederate. Camden, South Carolina, April 3, 1863.
259 Ibid.
260 The Camden Confederate, Camden, South Carolina, April 10, 1863.
261 Ibid.
262 Ibid.
263 Ibid.
264 Ibid, Captain J. L. Jones was chair. Lieutenant W. J. Taylor, secretary. The meeting was held at Camp Cantey near Adams Run. Unit is the 7th Battalion S. C. Volunteers.

through Dr. Laborde to Captains Chesnut and Doby in Virginia, twelve pairs of shoes, twenty-five pairs of drawers, thirty-five pairs of socks, twenty-five shirts, twenty caps; Miss Milling, one pair of gloves and two pairs of socks; Mrs. Dehone, ten dollars; Mrs. Thornton, one pair of socks; six dollars and twenty-five from proceeds of a hat made by Miss Carrie Mickle of Florida and given to the association.[265]

In April, an ordinary election took place with A.L. McDonald being elected.[266]

In May, a public meeting took place in the Camden District at the town hall for the sole purpose of fixing the price of corn that would be furnished to the army by the citizens of Kershaw, appointing Beat committees, which would aid the quartermaster, Captain Cole, in the procurement of the surplus corn. Those in charge of the meeting were A.H. Boykin, D.D. Perry, and J.M. DeSaussure.[267] The public meeting took place on the sixth. Upon a motion of Major John M. DeSaussure, W.E. Johnson, Esquire was the chairman, and A.M. Kennedy, the secretary. The purpose of the meeting was explained to assist the government in getting supplies. A committee was chosen to coordinate the beats. Those on this committee was D.D. Perry, James Team, E. Barnes, J.B. Mickle, and James Dunlap. Those heads in the beats would be:

Cureton's Mill: E. Parker, J.J. Nelson, W.B. Huckabee, L.L. Whitaker, and R.L. Whitaker
Goodwins: J.B. Mickle, Dr. J. Milling, Jessie Kilgore, Dr. J.I. Trantham, and J.L. McDowell.
Liberty Hill: William Dixon, D.D. Perry, J.R. Dye, L.J. Patterson, and R.B. Cunningham.
Flat Rock: L.B. Stephenson, John Thompson, R.G. Miller, Jessie Truesdell, and Thomas J. Cauthen.
Buffalo: Seaborn Jones, Craddock Mosely, S.F. Clyburn, Colonel Burrell Jones, and Captain C.C. Haile.
Lizenby's: William Mungo, Gilliam Sowell, C. Raley, Angus McCaskill, and D. Bethune.
Shrock's Mill: Dr. B.S. Lucas, Captain Wiley Kelly, J.R. Shaw, B.T. McCoy, and E. Barnes.
Camden: E.W. Bonney, A.M. Kennedy, B. Perkins, John Whitaker, and John Boykin.[268]

A new ordinance was enacted for the town of Camden. The tax was imposed on country produce and poultry, etc. The following is the list of goods:

Flour per bag of 98 pounds	5.00
Corn per bushel	.50
Peas per bushel	.35
Oats per bushel	.25
Turkeys each	.75
Geese each	.60
Ducks each	.60
Chickens each	.50

---

265 The Camden Confederate, Camden, SC; April 17, 1863.
266 The Camden Confederate, Camden, SC; April 24, 1863.
267 The Camden Confederate, Camden, SC; May 1, 1863.
268 The Camden Confederate, Camden, SC; May 8, 1863.

Eggs per dozen	.25
Bacon per pound	.30
Beef per pound	.20
Mutton per pound	.20
Pork per pound	.25

The fine for violating this was, at least, five dollars and no more than twenty dollars. Free Negroes shipping any of these articles would be charged double.[269]

In Kershaw County, the following is those with a statement of conscripts enrolled:

Total Number Enrolled	163
Exempt by Law	82
Accepted by Surgeon	33
Rejected by Surgeon	48

These were reported by the enrolling officer, Captain E. B. Cantey, and the surgeon was Dannelly.[270]

Donations were sent for Charleston hospitals by the aid society. Collected and sent was wine, brandy, sugar, rice meal, corn starch, coffee, hominy, $321.10 in cash, and a doll, raffled for $26.50. The doll was made by Mrs. Conner and won by Mr. John Witherspoon.[271] More donations came in for the Camden Ladies Aid Society. Those donations consisted of two pairs of socks made by Miss Helen Whitaker; an amethyst breast-pin from Mr. J. McEwen, which was raffled and brought in $21.50, and was won by Miss Lottie Ancrum.[272]

More casualty reports came to the Camden Area. There were losses in Captain Leitner's Company. Those being Sergeant David H. Ryan and Private D.E. Kelly, who were hurt slightly. Captain J.P. Cunningham had one. Lieutenant William Patterson, hurt slightly. Colonel J.D. Kennedy's 2nd Regiment passed through the thickest and bloodiest part of the battle and came out without a loss.[273] However, the obituary arrived for Corporal N. A. McLeod. He died January 18, 1863, of typhoid pneumonia. He was born April 6, 1839, and his parents were Alexander and Harriet McLeod, and he was the eldest son. He volunteered and helped form the company at Camden, commanded by Captain T.J. Warren, Company D, 15th Regiment, SCV on August 1861. He went into Lightwood Knot Springs, Columbia, for camp. Cold on his lungs developed, and he came home to recuperate, and soon he returned to his comrades at Beaufort, South Carolina and went along the coast and Charleston till July 1862, when his company left for Richmond, Virginia. He went from Richmond

---

269 The Camden Confederate, Camden, SC; May 1, 1863.
270 Ibid
271 Ibid.
272 The Camden Confederate, Camden, SC; May 8, 1863
273 The Camden Confederate, Camden, SC., May 15, 1863.

to Maryland to participate in the September 17 battle at Sharpsburg. Hurt slightly on side of his face, his next battle was in Fredericksburg on February 14. On December 14, he left the bloody battle, unhurt. Soon thereafter he came down with pneumonia and was sent to a hospital in Richmond. His father, hearing of the illness of his son, left and went to Richmond. Upon arriving, he was too late. His son had died and had been buried, and as his captain remarked, a fine soldier had passed. His father had his remains returned home on April 14, 1863. A large gathering took place on April 16, at Antioch Baptist Church, where Reverend J.E. Rogers preached the service for this fallen warrior.[274]

Lieutenant Commander R.M. Cantey sent a thank you note for the continued support given of clothing, and the constant comfort shown to the soldiers of the 6th Regiment. This kindness showed the patriotism of the women and their horrific struggle to help in this way during this war, especially those back home.[275]

On May 9th, in Fredericksburg, the officers of the 15th SVC Regiment presented Colonel W.D. DeSaussure with a horse and equipment. The letter from that day said:

> **Colonel:** It gives me great pleasure, as the organ of the officers of your command, to present you with a horse and trappings, in token of their esteem and appreciation of your ability and efficiency as an officer, and of the personal regard for you as a gentleman. We have the proud satisfaction of knowing that you have never shrunk from the prompt and manly discharge of duty on any occasion, and during danger, most imminent, your coolness, self-procession, and courage has cheered our hearts and elicited our highest admiration.
>
> The horse is the gift of the commissioned officers, and the trappings of the Sergeants of the Regiment, who desired to join in the testimonial.
>
> Accept them, sir, as an earnest of our well wishes, that a kind Providence which has often 'shielded your head in the day of battle' may continue, and that your life may be spared, now so necessary to your bleeding country and its sacred cause.
>
> I am, sir, very truly,
> Thomas J. Warren
> Captain Company D, 15th Regiment S.C.V.,
> For the committee.[276]

The Ladies Aid Association received twenty dollars from the proceeds of a palmetto hat presented by Mrs. Hammerslough, and twenty-five dollars from Mr. James Jones.[277]

Once again, news of death reached Camden. James Lawrence Haile, age twenty-nine, seven months, and seven days died on Sunday, May 17, 1863, of typhoid fever, in Shelbyville, Tennessee. Also, Henry Green McKagen, born March 20, 1838, joined the Methodist Episcopal Church, Camden, South Carolina in 1854.

---

[274] Ibid.
[275] The Camden Confederate, Camden, S.C., May 29, 1863.
[276] Ibid.
[277] The Camden Confederate, Camden, S.C., June 5, 1863.

On December 13, 1862, on a battlefield in Virginia, he received a mortal wound, and died on January 1, 1863. In a letter written the day before the battle, he wrote, "All is ready, now waiting for the signal to be given. I have no fears as to the result. The God of battle is with us, and I know all will be well. Into his hands, I commit myself."[278]

Clark's Diary from the beginning of the war to the first of 1863 had these figures:

Nationals (Union) – Killed 43,373; wounded 97,029; Died of Disease 120,000; and prisoners 69,218.
Confederates - Killed 20,898; wounded 59,015; Died of Disease 120,000; and prisoners 22,169.[279]

Miss Chesnut of the Ladies Aid Society acknowledged the donations of Mrs. Benjamin Perkins, ten dollars; Mrs. R.G. Perkins, ten dollars; five dollars from M.H.; a pair of socks from M.H.; Mrs. Hay sent one pair of socks; and Mrs. Ann Salmond gave ten dollars.

She also received this letter:

Dear Miss Chesnut;

I write from my sick bed, where I have been for some time, to acknowledge and thank the Aid Association for the acceptable $150. We are in want of funds now.

Your respectfully,

R. W. Barnwell, Jr.[280]

The Confederate War Tax appointments for Kershaw County were made by J.D. Pope, Esq., Major A.M. Kennedy, Collector, and Mr. William McKain, Assessor.[281]

Though not of this county but of the Sumter District, John Holland died of typhoid dysentery, on May 12 at the Ladies Hospital in Columbia, South Carolina. He had been a member of Captain DePass's Company for the last twelve months and had been stationed on James Island. Born in 1836, his father died when he was nine, and he assumed the care of his mother. He was baptized in October of 1860 at Antioch Baptist Church, alongside with his wife, who he married in 1857. He, also, left two children.[282]

A hail storm on June 21 hit several plantations, whose owners were W.A. Ancrum, Colonel T.J. Ancrum, Major Alexander H. Boykin, and Colonel J.D. Kennedy.[283]

C.H. Peck, Esq. passed away in Camden. He oversaw the boys' military academy. He had been feeble for some time. Those who knew him knew he was a faithful teacher, devoted to the rigors of military training. The

---

[278] Ibid.
[279] The Camden Confederate, Camden, South Carolina, June 12, 1863.
[280] Ibid.
[281] The Camden Confederate, Camden, South Carolina, June 19, 1863.
[282] Ibid.
[283] The Camden Confederate, Camden, South Carolina, June 26, 1863.

next day, on a Saturday, he was placed by his faithful students and alongside those scholars he had known and taught. He was a Masonic member.[284]

Entertainment came to Camden as Mr. Sloman and his daughters gave a performance at the town hall for the people of Camden. They are well-known all over the state and in this community.[285] The concert was a musical treat with songs like "Tubal Cain" (repeated by request), and the acting and singing of "Seven Ages," and "London Newspapers."[286]

Miss Chesnut from the Ladies Aid Society received one pair of socks from Mrs. W.E. Johnson, one pair of socks from Mrs. William Anderson, five dollars from Mrs. McCandless, and five dollars and thirty-five cents, proceeds of the raffle of a caster cover was presented by Mrs. Gatewood.[287] W.L. DePass, for Captain DeSaussure, sent a letter thanking the Ladies Aid Society for the package of clothes and shoes for the company. He further stated that the delay in acknowledgement was due to movement of the company to different places along the coast for the last six weeks. He went on to say, "To say that we are thankful to you for your kind remembrance would barely express the sentiment that exists in the heart of every brave and patriotic soldier, who sacrifices all for the common defense of his country, but that his highest reward is to feel that those to whom his best and purest affections are ever given, appreciates the sacred offering — appreciates it by the ministrations to his wants and necessities in the hospital and on the tented field — appreciates it by the thousand prayers which ascend daily to the throne of the Most High for his protection from the dangers, diseases, and hardships of a cruel and relentless war. Then feel assured that so long as you sustain the wearied routine of the day — that stands at the door of every half-fed, half-clothed soldier, away from his home and all that his clings to in the distant camp — by your generous deed, our cause, though a deluge of flame and blood, will yet come forth honored and regenerated for all time to come. And upon no more than yourselves will reflect the brightest luster and undying honor."[288]

A notice came out in the newspaper to the importance of organizing and guarding against any raids that the enemy might have brought. Companies, such as mounted infantry and artillery, would be formed for citizens to sign up. Lists were found at J. Dunlap's store for the Camden area, and for the Flat Rock area, the list was found at the L.B. Stephenson's store. When thirty names were written down, a meeting was called.[289]

Colonel Jones assembled the 22nd Regiment South Carolina Militia last week. He was seeking 105 members for home service between the ages of forty-five and fifty years old. He only needed ninety-seven as eighteen was credited to this company. An election was held and C.C. Haile was elected captain, T.J. Ancrum, first lieutenant; John Thompson, second lieutenant, and T.J. Cauthen, third lieutenant.[290]

The Fourth of July was celebrated with the quietness that one may feel on the Sabbath. Stores were closed. Streets were deserted. The usual pomp and circumstance, like noisy and boisterous fireworks, were missing. But

---

284 Ibid.
285 The Camden Confederate, Camden, South Carolina, July 3, 1863.
286 The Camden Confederate, Camden, South Carolina, July 10, 1863.
287 The Camden Confederate, Camden, South Carolina, July 3, 1863.
288 Ibid.
289 The Camden Confederate, Camden, South Carolina, July 10, 1863.
290 Ibid.

as citizens, we must never forget the independence won in 1776, the struggles fought and won, the times that each us have come through, and, of course, the battle that we are in now.

News came of two deaths — Captain Thomas J. Warren and Captain J.P. Cunningham.

Captain Joseph P. Cunningham, Company, 15th Regiment SCV, was killed near Gettysburg in one of the many battles. He was a native of Liberty Hill and a fine young man of great talents and a disposition to match.[291]

Captain Thomas J. Warren was killed at Gettysburg. He was a native of Camden, editor of *The Camden Journal* since 1845, filled several public offices when the need arose, attended the Methodist Episcopal church, and, in two years, raised a company and fought from Port Royal to Gettysburg.[292] Word came that Captain W.Z. Leitner had his leg amputated due to him being severely injured.[293]

Casualties in the Seventh Battalion under Major Rion included:

Company A: Captain Lucas commanding (Lucas Guards) Killed - none. Wounded - Sergeant Outlaw, Corporal Daniel McLaurin, Isaac Mosely, and John Pitts.

Company B: Maurice Cohe, orderly. In the hands of the enemy as prisoner.

Company C: Lieutenant Pearson commanding. Killed – none. Wounded – P. Hawkins, severely and prisoner; D. Outen, slightly; Missing: Sergeant W. R. Myrant, Hugh Price.

Company D: Captain Jones commanding. Killed - H. Capell, R. Gaskins. Missing and wounded - C.T. Billings, J.W. Allen.

Company E: Lieutenant Gaillard commanding. Killed - Private J.M. Ives. Wounded - Privates J.P. Allen and W.H. Cater.

Company F: Captain Segars commanding. Killed – None. Wounded - B.W. Newman, A. McGougan.

Company G: Captain Clyburn commanding. Killed - Stephen Meggs. Wounded - Corporal Daniels.

Missing - Captain Clyburn, Sergeant Murray, George Dean.

Company H: Captain Brooks commanding. Killed: J.S. Holloway. Wounded - Jep. Thomas, John Collen, R. Dunning. Dr. Hannahan in the hands of the enemy.

Sent in by S. Warren Nelson, Adjutant Seventh S.C. Battalion.

Total killed, wounded, and missing- 183.[294]

---

[291] The Camden Confederate, Camden, South Carolina, July 17, 1863.
[292] Ibid.
[293] Ibid.
[294] Ibid.

The updated list will include information to clear up reports of exaggeration. This report sent by B.S. Lucas, Captain, Company A, 7th S.C. Battalion. These include the engagements at Morris Island up to the evening of the fourteenth.

Kershaw Greys - Captain J.L. Jones, commanding. Killed - Privates Ransom, Gaskins, and Hartwell Capell.
Wounded - J.W. Allen (since dead); W.J. Bryant, slightly in the head; C.J. Billings, severely in the leg, and in the hands of the enemy.

Lucas Rifles - Captain Dove Segars, commanding. Killed - none. Wounded - B.W. Newman, in the head; Angus McGoughan, severely. Missing - none.

Moffat Rifles - Captain William Clyburn, commanding. Killed - Stephen Meggs. Wounded - R.H. Fields, John Wilson, J.Y. McNeil, and W.L. Smith. Missing - Captain William Clyburn, Sergeant Murray, and Private George Dean.

Lucas Guards - Captain B.S. Lucas Jr., commanding. Killed - none. Wounded - Corporal Daniel McLaurin, Isaac Moseley, and John Pitts, slightly. Missing - none.[295]

Results of the Battle at Gettysburg brought bad news of more casualties.[296]
Second South Carolina Regiment:

Colonel J.D. Kennedy, wounded severely in the head and slightly in the hip; Captain William Wallace (acting major), severely in arm; Adjutant E.E. Sill, in foot severely.

Company E - Captain W.Z. Leitner, commanding. Killed - D.R. Ryan, Privates W.R. Riley and J. W. Polk.
Severely wounded - W.Z. Leitner, leg amputation; T.E. Gardner, in abdomen, and Private G. Smith, in head. Slightly wounded - Private B.R. Arrants, in leg, and D. Tidwell, in shoulder. Killed 3, Wounded 5.

Company G - Captain J.P. Cunningham, Commanding. Killed - Captain Joseph P. Cunningham, Privates R.M. Love, John Gaskin, and W.W. Johnson. Seriously Wounded - S. Coonin, leg and breast; John Falkenberry, knee; B. Parker, leg amputated; W. West, leg and thigh; and J.O. Croston, knee. Severely wounded - Lieutenant J.E. Truesdell, neck; Corporal J.A. Sowell, thigh and hand; Privates W. Bird, hand and breast; John Boon, head and arm; William Huff, breast and leg and John Roe, arm. Slightly wounded - Lieutenant S.J. Benton, arm; Sergeant R.B. Patterson, hand; Corporal T.G. West, head; Privates D. Davis, breast and foot; W.J. Dunn, foot; J. Polley, thigh; William Mahaffey, head; W.C. Huff, head;

---
[295] Ibid.
[296] The Camden Confederate, Camden, South Carolina, July 24, 1863.

W.T. Phillips, breast; B. Raley, leg and arm; E.H. Robinson, shoulder, and L.D. Robinson, thigh. Killed 4, Wounded 24.

Colonel Kennedy's Regiment sustained a loss of 27 killed, 125 wounded, and 2 missing. Total 154.

Fifteenth South Carolina Regiment Field and Staff:

Killed - Colonel William D. DeSaussure, Acting Major Thomas J. Warren
Wounded- Adjutant James W. Davis
Company D - First Lieutenant C.B. Burns, commanding. Killed - Privates J.C. Corbett, C. Minton, and F.W. Watts. Wounded - Lieutenant George Crosby, leg; Corporals P.H. Wilson, arm flesh; J.B. Shedd, foot severely; Privates - William Brannon, loin, slight; S. Griffin, contusion of thigh; S.W. Hornsby, flesh, leg; A. Kirby, groin, severely, and C.H. Shingler, chest, slight. Missing- D. Brannon, John Spradley, and J.W. Kirby.[297]

The following is the roll of officers and men between the ages of forty and fifty who signed up for duty in Kershaw District under a late call from Jefferson Davis.

C. C. Haile, Captain
T. J. Ancrum, 1st Lieutenant
John Thompson, 2nd Lieutenant
T. J. Cauthen, 3rd Lieutenant
R. B. Cunningham, 1st Sergeant
R. C. Drakeford, 2nd Sergeant
J. G. Bruce, 3rd Sergeant
A. Owens, 4th Sergeant
R. McKee, 1st Corporal
A. J. Faukenberry, 2nd Corporal
William Cato, 3rd Corporal
Angus McLeod, 4th Corporal

Privates

W. C. Cunningham	Thomas E. Shannon	J. S. Thompson
Ey	W. W. Newman	Daniel Baker

---

[297] Ibid.

H. F. Warren	Thomas Dawson	John Holley
Daniel McCaskill	A. Rabon	Henry Thorn
Wiley Outlaw	Thomas Mickle	Wiley Brannon
A. McClester	Joel Hough	George Pettigrew
Joel H. Brown	John Young	J. T. Bowers
Lewis Phillips	W. C. Denton	David Barefield
H. C. West	J. E. King	Levi Kennington
William Johnson	S. A. B. Shannon	John J. Stokes
L. B. Boswell	Thomas Birkett	W. M. Billings
Nathan Humphries	William K. Robertson	Nathaniel Humphries
J. J. Stokes	George Norris	Alfred Davis
H. Norris	E. Deas	J. A. W. Berry
W. Bass	M. Watson	E. Harrell
William Price	W. Bradley	Wilson Steen
R. Hocott	W. J. Hall	George Outlaw
James Holland	J. T. Barker	Thomas English
Robert Mann	William English	Isaac Shiver
John Spradley	R. J. Dowie	Wiley Watkins
J. J. Roach	Thomas Watkins	Robert Brannon
Calvin Jones	Warren Brannon	E. Atkinson
M. D. Wood	James Wilson	R. J. McCreight
William Goff	F. J. Oakes	J. J. Ross
William Branham	William Ross	R. Hinson
Calvin Ross	Thomas Holland	John Rush
B. T. McCoy	Thomas Sessions	Jonathon Page
Thomas Peak	John N. Gamewell	William Christmas

[298]

Despite the need for more recruits by Captain James Doby, another casualty came in the form of the news of the death of Captain Joseph P. Cunningham.[299]

The President of the Soldier's Rest announced that the following donations were given: Mrs. Oppenheim, a bundle of rags; Mrs. Lang, fourteen eggs; and Miss Grant, one ham, rice, and tea.[300] The Camden Ladies Aid Association received the following, according to Miss Chesnut: One hundred fifty dollars from the Young Ladies Tableaux; eighteen eighty, proceeds of a basket presented by Mrs. Bonney, raffled and won by Mr. Willie McDowell; five dollars from a regular contributor; two dollars from Mrs. T.J. Ancrum; seven dollars from Alfred Doby; thirty dollars, proceeds of a collar presented by Mrs. Bonney, and raffled off and won by Mrs. J.T. Hershman; fifty-five cents from Joe Bonney; six dollars and ten cents, from Lizzie Haile, proceeds of a seen

---

[298] Ibid.
[299] The Camden Confederate, Camden, South Carolina, August 7, 1863.
[300] Ibid.

basket. Won by Mrs. Oppenheim; three dollars from Miss Habbersham; ten dollars from Mrs. Rodgers; one pair of socks from Mrs. DeHone; two pairs of socks from Mrs. J. Whitaker; and three pairs of socks from Mrs. McRae.[301] Captain James E. Doby, captain of Company E, Holcombe Legion, wrote a thank you letter on behalf of the Kirkwood Cavalry to the ladies of the association for their fine and liberal donations of clothing, which were so appreciative and the impact to the moral of the men to continue their efforts.[302]

Mr. Ellerbe's Flour and Grist Mill was working well these days and was in good condition.[303]

To prepare for anything that might happen, the Aid Association made an appeal for hospital supplies. The appeal was made by the Ladies of Charleston. The appeal included vegetables, fruits, and any provision in kind for soldiers and hospitals within the city of Charleston. Collection would be mid-Thursday. The train that came every Thursday would pick up donations and collections.[304]

On a side note, the Miss Chesnut of the Aid Society had received three bushels of meal from A.M. Kennedy; two boxes and one basket of vegetables sent to Miss Fannie DeSaussure on the sixth, and eight bushels of meal to Dr. J. Bachman for the use of the soldiers.[305]

Colonel William M. Shannon had been asked to raise a cavalry squadron that would be attached to Hampton's Legion. His past record in doing this was impeccable and one that the state would have the honor of having represent this state in battle.[306]

The chief medical examiner, Dr. F. Olin Danally would be coming to Camden to examine all those recruits liable to conscription for their claim of exemption for the war on Monday, August 31.[307] He would also be in September 29 or 30 to do the same tasks.

Many announcements came in during the month of September. On the fourteenth, the farmers and planners had a meeting to determine the amount of wheat, flour, meal, bacon, and beef cattle that would be given to the army, at the town hall at noon.[308]

Good news came in as Captain E.M. Boykin's Company was expected to arrive today. They would rest for a couple of days, and then move on over to Columbia, and then to some mountainous region.[309] The 4th Regiment, under Colonel Witherspoon, left for Georgetown by way of Kingstree yesterday.[310]

The DeKalb House, a local motel, was sold to Mr. J.H. Jungbluth for $21,000 dollars.[311]

Aid and donations continued to come in as the Camden Ladies Aid Association received the following: From Mrs. Seibring, $25; Miss D, $5; Miss M, $2; a friend, $10 and a pair of socks; Mrs. C, for hospital, $5; B.M. Lee, $2; Mrs. William E. Johnson, $25 (proceeds of fans presented to the association); Fannie McCandless, $4.20

---

301 Ibid.
302 Ibid.
303 Ibid.
304 The Camden Confederate, Camden, South Carolina, August 14, 1863.
305 Ibid.
306 The Camden Confederate, Camden, South Carolina, August 28, 1863.
307 The Camden Confederate, Camden, South Carolina, August 21, 1863.
308 The Camden Confederate, Camden, South Carolina, September 4, 1863.
309 Ibid.
310 Ibid.
311 Ibid.

(proceeds from a box raffled and won by Miss M. Wilson; Mrs. Adamson, $5 for vegetables; $32.50, proceeds of a box presented by Mr. Alden, and won by Miss Dunlap. A box was sent to the 27th to Miss DeSaussure and Dr. Backman for the soldiers in Charleston. One bale of goods was sent to Captain John Chesnut in Virginia, containing 25 shirts, 25 pairs of drawers, 25 pairs of socks, and 6 pairs of shoes. To Captain Cantey's Company, 25 shirts, 25 drawers, 25 pair socks, and 6 pairs shoes were sent.

At a meeting of the aid association, the ladies adopted a plan to make every effort to secure shoes for the soldiers. Any money, donations, or leather, etc., would be used for that purpose.[312] On August 4, Miss Fannie Augier died at sixty-six years of age. She was a member of the Camden Baptist Church for over forty years.[313]

Celebrations were in order as the Kershaw District Bible Society held its forty-third anniversary at the Presbyterian Church in the morning, and one celebration at the Methodist Church in the afternoon. The president was C.J. Shannon, with W.H.R. Workman, secretary.[314]

An unknown friend, who wished to be express thanks for what the ladies aid society was doing gave two hundred dollars, while Mr. George Trenholm gave five hundred dollars.[315] The Flat Rock Aid Association gave fifteen dollars to the Soldier's Rest in Camden by Miss E.E. Perry.[316]

Mr. Crammond, a well-known landscape gardner, had arrived in town to lay out the cemetery. This was the city cemetery, which led to being called Quaker Cemetery in future years.[317]

The Camden Ladies Aid Society acknowledged the donations of September. A painting presented by Miss Hymes could be seen at Dr. Young's store, a vase of flowers by Miss Chesnut, some knit counterpanes by Miss Neile, a fly brush from Charleston, raffled and won by Mr. Youngbluth, three pairs of socks from Miss M; two pairs of socks and six pairs knitting hanks from Miss C.; ten hanks of cotton from Miss Cantey; one pair socks from Miss H, and ten dollars from Mrs. T.J. Ancrum.[318]

The newspaper announced the death of Sergeant R.R. Kirkland, who fell in the Battle of Chickamauga at twenty-three years of age. He participated in every battle in Virginia that the Kershaw Brigade was involved in, every battle from Bull's Run to this latest battle in Chickamauga.[319]

One of the most interesting things that I found was the Camden and Kershaw County Bible Society. A celebration took place on October 13 at the Presbyterian church. The service was led by Reverend Allison, who read Palms 119 and 120, focusing on "The Entrance of thy Words Giveth Light." This also marked the forty-third anniversary of this society. On October 20, the society met in the United Methodist Church, where Reverend S.H. Hay gave the sermon. During this session, a letter was read by General D.H. Hill, a life director

---

[312] Ibid.
[313] Ibid.
[314] The Camden Confederate, Camden, SC, September 11, 1863.
[315] Ibid.
[316] The Camden Confederate, Camden, SC, September 18, 1863.
[317] The Camden Confederate, Camden, SC, September 25, 1863.
[318] The Camden Confederate, Camden, SC, October 9, 1863.
[319] The Camden Confederate, Camden, SC, October 16, 1863.

of this society in the Confederate States Bible Society.[320] During this meeting a tribute was given to Captain T.J. Warren, who fell in Gettysburg, and General J.B. Kershaw was voted a life director of the Bible Society.[321]

Even during war, some bright hope existed. A marriage took place on October 15, between Mr. William McKain, and Miss L.A. Kilgore, daughter of the late James L. Kilgore at the residence of her grandfather by Reverend W.E. Hughson Jr.[322]

Two years ago, before the war began, Robert F. Small relocated to Camden from Mecklenburg, North Carolina on July 3, 1863. He was mortally wounded. He had fallen on the bloody field at Gettysburg, expiring on July 7. He volunteered with the Camden Volunteers, the first to leave the district to be present at Fort Sumter, re-volunteered in his company in Virginia, and participated in the battles of Bull Run. He was the flag bearer of his company. Then, he joined the Garden's Battery of Light Artillery upon the reorganization period, being in second Manassas to Gettysburg.[323]

From Charleston Wayside Hospital on September 17, 1863, Corporal Charlie Campbell died of congestive fever. He was a member of Captain Lucas's Company 7th South Carolina Battalion. At the first sign of this conflict, he was quick to enlist and respond to the call of his country, and, soon thereafter, became a member of the Captain Thomas Boykin's Company of the 1st South Carolina Regiment under Gregg. His service ended then with the skirmish at Vienna, and his unit disbanded, and he returned home to Kershaw District. He then enlisted with this company. His battles included Pocataglio, Morris Island, the assault on Battery Wagner on July 11, and an occupant of the battery six days during its bombardment. Passing through all this unhurt, disease set in on this fine soldier. When his death was announced at camp, a gloom fell over his comrades. He was described as an amiable young man, who displayed courage on the battlefield. He was a brave and true soldier. Battery Marshall, October 10th, 1863.[324]

The new growth of a pear tree had emerged. Mr. L.B. Alexander brought in six pears that were the size of a turkey egg. The species was Burgamot. [325]

Around this time, the State War Tax office under Joseph Daniel Pope, South Carolina State Collector, issued a new statement concerning animals for personal and animals for agriculture. "In taxing horses, lay the tax on everything not used in agriculture. All carriages, buggies, and saddle horses are accessed and taxed; they are not used in agriculture. Nor is an overseer's horse exempt. The Act contemplates only such as actually used in tilling the soil. Mules, oxen, wagon, and cart horses, and those used in the plough, etc., and none others, are exempt. You cannot inspect and value every horse. You must, therefore, arrive at a fair average of this class of property. Horses include all mares and colts. Those processing peculiar value — such as a race horse or blood horse — must be assessed according to their intrinsic value. So too with the tax on meat cattle. This includes all cows, yearlings, and calves; all milk cows included of course. The Act makes no exception. The value of all beeves sold prior to the first of November, from the passing of this Act (24 of April 1863), shall be taken

---

[320] Ibid.
[321] Ibid.
[322] The Camden Confederate, Camden, SC, October 23, 1863.
[323] Ibid.
[324] The Camden Confederate, Camden, SC, October 30, 1863.
[325] Ibid.

according to the gross proceeds of such sales — making such deduction as to the Act specifics, and such sales shall be added to income. About potatoes and all other crops, the act lays a tithe upon all planted, as well as gathered. If an estimate can be formed of the ingathered crop, the tithe to the Government can be collected from that which is gathered."[326]

Mr. W.D. McDowell had received the wool cards for the Kershaw District, which was slated for wives of poor soldiers, and those whose means were too limited to purchase at the present expense.[327]

During this time, another death had been heard about — Mr. Michael Parker, father of Redin Parker, was sent this note:

"Your son, Redin Parker, died at hospital, in Gordinsville, Virginia, on the 29th of July last. There is one thing that I can say in truth, for the gratification of the loved ones at home — the Confederacy had no better soldier under arms than was Redin. In everything respecting his duty as a soldier under arms as a soldier, he was willing and obedient — enduring all fatigue, hardships, and exposure without murmuring. In time of battle, he was always at his post, and never was known to shrink from any portion of danger. In fact, he was everything that could be desired, in these times, when we need good and true men. Thus, has passed one that all loved for his many good qualities, and at the same time, let me assure you, that we, as a company, deeply sympathize with you in your time of trouble, and hope your loss may be his gain."

Lieutenant C.B. Burns

Commanding Company D, 15th Regiment[328]

On October, Thursday 22, the ladies at the request of Colonel J.D. Kennedy met to form another society at the Temperance Hall. This society will be known as the Ladies Benevolent Society of Camden. The president would be Mrs. Joseph Lee, Vice Presidents would be Mrs. Bronson, Mrs. Capers, Miss Lou Kennedy; secretaries would be Mrs. H. Conner Jr., Mrs. Zack Leitner; treasurer would be Mr. R.M. Kennedy, and a finance committee consisting of Mrs. A.D. Goodwyn, Mrs. A.E. Doby, Miss C. Boykin, Miss Ella Reynolds, and Miss Eliza B. Lee. For a dollar membership due, the following joined:

Mrs. A. M. Kennedy	Mrs. Alexander
W. Kennedy	A. M. Lee
W. E. J. Hinson	R. Blair
Robert Johnson	Miss Chesnut
J. Oppenheim	Trapier
----- Oppenheim	Mrs. L. DeSaussure

---

326 The Camden Confederate, Camden, SC, November 13, 1863.
327 The Camden Confederate, Camden, SC, November 21, 1863.
328 Ibid.

Robert Young	M. McDowell
Charles Shannon	H. Shannon
B. M. Lee	C. Boykin
J. M. DeSaussure	Godfrey
Tom Salmond	L. Salmond
E. W. Bonney	Sue Bonney
G. -------	Emma Reynolds
W. ------	Sallie Reynolds
J. Whitaker	Essie Reynolds
James Cureton	Eliza R. Lee
J. Sutherfield	Ella Reynolds
B.-----	Meta Deas
L.-----	Fattle Dunlap
James Dunlap	M. Ancrum
G. Reynolds	M. Lee
James Davis	Kennedy
L. DeSaussure	M. Ancrum
Zemp	

The following donations have been received:

Colonel J. D. Kennedy ------ $200	J. S. DePass------$5
Mr. Alden------$200	A. D. Goodwyn----$50
Mrs. James Chesnut---$50	Koopman and Sommers----$50
E. A. Salmond—Fifty Bushels of Corn	C. J. Shannon-- $50
J. Whitaker—Two Bushels Potatoes, One Bushel Meal	Morris Meyer-- $20
Mrs. D. L. DeSaussure-- $5	Reverend Thomas F. Davis--$10
James E. Doby--$20	J. B. Cureton--$50
A. E. Peay-- $5	Mrs. Joseph Kershaw-- $10
J. E. Peay—11 pounds Cotton	Hay-- $5
J. M. DeSaussure- $5	Mr. D. D. Hocott- $200
L. DeSaussure- $12	James Dunlap- $100
Hughson -$5	J. W. Young- $50
Lege- $5	J. T. H.- $10
Peach- $30	J. K. Witherspoon- two four horse loads wood
H. W. Conner- $25	Henry Conner- $25
W. C. Gerald & Company- $10	Oppenheim-$10
N. D. Baxley- Three one horse top of wood	Julius Oppenheim- $5
W. M. Shannon- $5	W. E. Johnson- $25
Robert Johnson- $15	Cash- $100
A. E. Doby- $10	W. L. DePass- $50
Trapier- $6	A. D. Goodwyn- $5

J. F. Sutherland- $50	J. N. Gamewell- $5
W. Z. Leitner- $25	A. M. Kennedy- $5
W. E. Hughes- $25	J. Lee- $5
J. L. Sheorn- $20	R. Blair- $2
Dr. John McCaa- $10	J. V. Lyles- $2
C. J. Shannon- $10	A. M. Lee- $50
Mr. J. B. Clark- $50	A. Latta- $1
W. McKain- $25	Miss Emma Reynolds- $5
Dr. L. H. Deas- $10	Ella Reynolds- $5
F. L. Zemp- $20	Cash- $5
Mr. William M. Shannon- $50	H. Shannon- $10
W. D. Anderson -$ 5	Matheson and Company- $25
Thomas E. Shannon- $50	Mr. W. L. McCaa- $10
Duncan Whitaker- $5	S. C. DePass- $5
T. W. Bracey- $50	A. T. Latta- $5
Charles Hoffendine- $10	Cash - $10
W. H. R. Workman- $5	J. Young- 50 cent piece
L. M. Boswell- $10	R. Sotaers- $10
J. A. Boswell- $ 10	J. A. Berry- $5
Wiliam Kennedy, Jr.- $20	Joseph M. Gayle- $5
J. M. Cantey - $25	T. M. Cantey- $5
S. W. Nelson- $5	J. H. Oppenheim- $5
C. A. McDonald- $5	C. M. Weinges- $5
Cash- $5	M. Drucker- $10
J. M. Baum and Company- $50	S. Hammerslough- $10
A. M. Kennedy- $50	A. Witkowski- $5

Any other donations or provisions can be left at Mr. Robert M. Kennedy's or Messrs. Gerald. Mrs. J. Lee, President Benevolent Society, November 16[329]

More news came in on the life of Captain Thomas J. Warren. E.J. Meynardie wrote the following about him: He was late editor of *The Camden Journal,* and taken down in Gettysburg being shot through the head leading his men in a charge against the enemy in the thickest of battle, July 2, 1863. When he was sixteen, he joined the M.E. Church and made his profession to Christian service. While in the church, he had such positions as steward, class-leader, and Sunday school superintendent in the Church of Camden. He volunteered at the beginning of the war, and he bravely led and fought in many battles under the age of thirty-eight, when his fighting spirit came to an end on the battlefield.[330] He was laid beneath the soil as a reminder to those who come and remember.

---
[329] Ibid.
[330] The Camden Confederate, Camden, SC. December 4, 1863.

Kershaw District had several appointments to the South Carolina Military Academy for the year 1864. Those were P. Bracy Villipique, W.R. Withers, John Kershaw, William E. Johnson, and Benjamin H. Shannon.[331]

More excitement occurred in the community as two marriages took place. On the twenty-fifth of November, Rev. J.L. Shuford married Mr. J.J. Thompson to Miss E. Prescott, and Mr. L.R. Isbell was wed to Miss Kittie Team by the same reverend at the bride's father's house on the twenty-fourth.[332]

The Wateree Mounted Riflemen had now been in Tennessee. Once they were there, Colonel E.M. Boykin's troop joined forces with General Vance and his North Carolina State Troops. General Vance said of the Rifleman that they were gallant, brave, and fought well under the circumstances and proved themselves well in battle and could now return to the normal duties. They fought against immense odds and numbers.[333]

This past Sunday, bells could be heard from the Episcopal church. This sound was quieted as the bells of the town were sent to make a cannon. All bells would be returned later to Camden and heard joyfully on Sunday mornings.[334]

---

[331] Ibid.
[332] Ibid.
[333] The Camden Confederate, Camden, SC., December 11, 1863.
[334] Ibid.

1864

THE START OF THE YEAR brought the inauguration of another newspaper, or rather the restart of *The Camden Journal*. D.D. Hocott, who was the owner, took over the paper, which was formerly owned by Thomas J. Warren, who died in the Battle of Gettysburg.[335]

Two deaths were reported to have left the community. Those being J.W. Doby on December 22, and James V. Lyles, Esq. Doby was forty-five years old, had a large family and relatives, worked as a cashier at the Bank of Camden before taking over as president, when C.J. Shannon went to war, but died three years later. The tribute by the bank appeared in the next issue of *The Camden Journal*, January 8, 1864. Lyles had been in Camden for only a few years, but he was well liked.[336] In the January 8th issue, it was discovered that he was from Newberry District, being born August 2, 1810. He was a Christian and attended the Baptist church and felt very strong in his values and with serving the Lord. He had the following positions in his life: First President of the Exchange Bank in Columbia, South Carolina, Warden and Intendant of Columbia, South Carolina. He had said to many people who knew him that the North and South was destined for separation, and when it occurred, he would do all in his power to make sure that this state and the South accomplished the great call for Southern Independence and win. He'd moved to Camden six years ago.

A.M. Kennedy, the Kershaw County tax collector, released information of taxes collected.

Naval Stores	$27,882
Wines	5,673
Cotton, Bales	10,319
Cotton, unpacked 1,402	1,875,477
Sea Island, unpacked	569
Tobacco	1,200
Flour	500
Rice	2,200
Other agricultural products	66,240
	$1,979,172- SC $15,833,376

---

[335] The Camden Journal, Camden, S.C., January 1, 1864.
[336] Ibid.

Gold Coin, $1,766; value	$14, 128
Silver Coin, $1,625; value	11, 376
Cash in hand and deposits	409,542
Credits	1,272,988
	$1,765,833 — SC 1,705,833
	$60,000[337]

The Masonic Kershaw Lodge No. 29 election took place Tuesday evening last, and the following were elected:

Jacob Stakely, Worshipful Master
T.H. Smith, Senior Warden
D.D. Hocott, Junior Warden
C.A. McDonald, Treasurer
Thomas I. Jones, Secretary
F.J. Oakes, Tyler
D.S. DeSaussure, Senior Deacon
Richard Hocott, Junior Deacon
W.D. Anderson, Steward
S. Blodgett, Steward
W.E. Hughson, Chaplain [338]

The state legislature recently released their appointments for Kershaw County:

Managers of Election

Camden: John S. Maroney, C. A. McDonald, William McKain
Cureton's Mill: Frederick Bowen, James Team, Emanuel Parker
Flat Rock: Jessie Truesdel, James Fletcher, George R. Miller
Buffalo: William Mungo, Gilliam Sowell, William Cato
Lizenby's: John McGougan, Daniel McCaskill, Donald McDonald
Schrock's Mill: B.T. McCoy, Alexander McLeod, Henry Ratcliffe
Goodwin's Store: Benjamin Cook, John B. Mickle, James H. Vaughn
Liberty Hill: A.D. Jones Jr., R.C. Patterson, R.B. Cunningham

---

[337] Ibid.
[338] Ibid.

Commissioners of Free Schools:
W.H.R. Workman, Wiley Kelly, William Dixon, James Team, C.C. Haile, Jessie Truesdel, Daniel Bethune, A.L. McDowell

Commissioners to Approve Public Securities:
John Workman, R.M. Kennedy, R.B. Johnson, F.L. Zemp, L.W.R. Blair, James B. Cureton, William D. McDowell

Magistrates:
J.K. Witherspoon, William D. Hogan, W.R. Taylor, Cradock Mosely, Henry Brace, John R. Shaw, Richard Whitaker, ---- Barker.

Commissioners of Roads:
L.L. Whitaker, B.T. McCoy, William E. Hughes, Daniel D. Kirkland, James L. McDowell, Lewis J. Patterson, J. English Doby, David G. Robertson, Lynch H. Deas, Gilliam Sowell, Richmond R. Terrell, and John Cantey.

In accordance with the sixth section, "Act to establish certain roads, bridges, and ferries," passed December 17, which stated that each commissioner in office, new, shall serve, whether new in office, or appointed, until a new successor was appointed, and accepted during this time of war.[339] On December 27, the Ruling Elders of the Presbyterian Church, Reverend S.H. Hay, Pastor, John Workman, W.H.R. Workman, R.J. McCreight, and A.M. Kennedy, met and issued the following resolution concerning Charles J. Shannon. The Ruling Elders of the Church wished to honor Charles J. Shannon, who had been a Ruling Elder since October 28, 1832, when he was ordained, joining the church the May before under Reverend S.S. Davis. He was a loved and beloved member that would be missed.[340]

Another obituary mentioned was the death of Emma W. Stockton, occurring on December 15 at age twenty-five. Her husband was Lieutenant Edward C. Stockton, USN. She was of the Catholic faith.[341]

A soldier's obituary was now listed. A memorial was placed for R.L. Gerald, who on September 21st, on the battlefield in Chickamauga, fell on the bloody field of battle. He enlisted April 8, 1862, as a private, and now had risen to the rank of sergeant by May 15, 1862. He was in the battles at Manassas Plains, around Richmond, Maryland Heights, Sharpsburg, Gettysburg, and Chickamauga, where he took his final breath. He was in Company F, 2nd South Carolina regiment.[342]

On Tuesday, the twenty-second, Camden played host to a long, well-travelled friend. General Joseph Kershaw arrived home for just the third time since the beginning of the war. It must have been a miracle that he

---
[339] Ibid.
[340] Ibid.
[341] Ibid.
[342] Ibid.

was still living going through all those battles, and one can only imagine what his immediate family and friends must have thought. History would remember what the glorious Kershaw Brigade did during this conflict when this war was over. No one person could be ashamed of anyone's name that was emblazoned across this brigade and what it stood for, leaving no doubt of casting dishonor upon the Palmetto State. Their banners had been and held high throughout the war in each battle starting with Manassas, in battles around Richmond, second Manassas, Heights of Maryland, Sharpsburg, Fredericksburg, Chancellorsville, Gettysburg, Chattanooga, and the recent conflict in Knoxville, not to mention the many skirmishes his brigade must have been involved in. The people of Camden had high admiration and would put the name of Kershaw on a higher plateau of admiration, bravery, gallantry, and leadership of patriotic and giving soldiers. With that, the people would give a hearty welcome to Kershaw, and the people knew that the Almighty had a hand in his safety up to now. When the conflict came to an end, one would be able to look back and thank Kershaw for his leadership on the field, his courage, and the skills to cope with the rigors of war, even though Kershaw's future was unseen as what would really happen.[343]

One observation of the citizens of Camden and their attitude was that these people were willing to do what they had to for the Confederacy. The citizens in Camden would do what they needed to advance the cause for those who were dying and bleeding for her defense. This faith was as strong as Noah and his family as Noah faced uncertainty in taking his family on the ark, with only the faith that God would protect those who did his will. Hope, courage, and triumph would blaze a glorious victory. While also, we have some like Cain, acting cowardly, skulking, and feeling guilty for not lifting, or lending a helping hand in their country's time of need, dodging from service, and the responsibility and struggle their fellow friends were enduring. We must look at the reality of what may happen should they fail. Our fate will be grim and miserable, and likened to the nations and kingdoms of all the earth overthrowing another people and making havoc on their lives, as mentioned in the Bible.[344]

A newspaper writer wrote the following: "History has taught us that the more ignorant, the more depraved one feels on power and authority, the more tyrannical and abusive one may be toward the governed. So, it will be like that with us. We know that our enemy is seen as stupid, proud, boastful, and an arrogant race on earth. What else can one think as this enemy will reduce our soul to the lowest degree on Earth? Look at Ireland and Poland and their fate. Under rule of a generous and giving ruling government. In contrast, the Yankees know nothing of this attitude and will be worse. We will lose our dignity, our property, our means to defend ourselves, our arms taken away from us, and under military rule watching our thoughts, our doors, and controlling our southern ways. Yankee spies will soon if not already in our midst. Soon, Yankee judges, generals, legislatures, constables, magistrates, sheriffs, clerks, and anything the Yankees can get in and will.[345]

Our south with all its beauty and customs, home of the brave, the free, will become a den of thieves, through the use of midnight assassinations, wholesale murder, foul plots, arson, rape, butchery of men, women,

---

[343] The Camden Journal, Camden, S.C., January 22, 1864.
[344] Ibid.
[345] Ibid.

and children will become common in our walk during our daily routine. Arouse all of you, our sons, strike for our freedom, for our price of heritage is on the line. To lose will mean our South is over."[346]

A tribute of respect came in from the Kershaw Lodge, No. 29, A.F.M., January 12, A.L. 5864. This was in response to the lives lost with fellow brothers, John N. McLeod, Charles H. Peck, and Z.J. DeHay. A page would be left blank in their honor.[347]

Several obituaries came in. One was concerning Joseph William Doby. He was born in Waxhaw, above Camden, July 22, 1818. He received his education in schools in Camden, before going to South Carolina College in the fall of 1835, with the likes of Ed Salmond, Thomas Anderson, Edward Boykin (now captain), and James Cantey (now General Cantey in Alabama). After the first session, he left school and pursued agricultural and mercantile business interests, until elected to the position of cashier at the Bank of Camden. There he remained until he became sick, acting as both the cashier and president of the bank. He was a husband, father, and had strong Christian values. He was liked by many citizens in Camden and surrounding areas. He would be missed. On December 22, 1863, at his residence, Joseph William Doby's life came to an end after an illness of pneumonia, at forty-five years of age.[348]

Word came to Camden to announce the death of thirty-year-old William Lowndes McCaa on December 29, 1863, in Carlowville, Alabama. He was born in Camden, and after a week of illness, he passed away.[349]

Notice came from the C.S. engineer's office on January 13 that the area and surrounding areas would provide Negroes who would be put on the nearest depot on the second of February and sent to Charleston. All that was needed was a total of two thousand Negroes, but Kershaw District's share would be two hundred sixty-five.[350]

Dr. John Bachman, servant of the Lord and of this state, paid a visit earlier in the week to ask for comforts that the soldiers, who were fighting and giving their all, needed in the hospitals all over the state. These needs were flour, meal, hominy, bacon, lard, butter, eggs, chickens, sweet potatoes, red pepper, or anything they could send. They could be dropped off at store of Mr. W.F. McDowell. Everyone was urged to "get involved and do it yourself. Don't depend on your neighbor to do it. Doing this will give you a blessing."[351]

A memorial for the passing of Zachariah J. DeHay on December 26, 1863, was held at his residence in the town of Camden. He was born in Charleston, South Carolina, November 14, 1819. He spent his youth in Charleston, then he moved to Columbia to learn the apothecary business. On January 1, 1848, he moved to Camden to begin the duties of his calling. He was a member of the Great Temperance Reform in Camden. He was the recording scribe of the Wateree Division, and for several years, the recording scribe of the Grand Division, Sons of Temperance, and the State of South Carolina. He was a member of the Odd Fellows and the Masons.[352]

---

[346] Ibid.
[347] Ibid.
[348] Ibid.
[349] Ibid.
[350] Ibid.
[351] Ibid.
[352] The Camden Journal, Camden, S.C., January 29, 1864.

On December 17, 1863, the legislature passed an act to make provisions for the families of soldiers of this state when Kershaw District was divided into twelve sections with a separate board member over each section.[353]

Section number one would be from the Sumter line to Swift Creek, then over to Hughes' Mill, to McKinnon's Old Stand, to Sander's Creek, and over to the river and down the east side of the Wateree River to Sumter. Section number two would be from the mouth of White Oak Creek to Beaver Creek Road, to Liberty Hill Beat Line, to Lancaster line, and over to the river.[354] These two sections would carry the large surplus of grain derived from the two percent tax in kind. These sections would carry the burden to supply the other portions of the district, as there would be a major shortfall in other parts of the district, specifically the eastern part of the district.[355]

From current data projection, there would be a two-thousand bushel deficient in the district to supply those under the act guidelines, which each person was entitled to ten bushels per person.[356]

Each board member would oversee the process by directing the person within that district section to a producer in that a specific section. It would have been very troublesome for a person to go to section number 1, where a lot of river planters existed unless that person had a way to transport it or haul their share. One of the problems would be that females might not be able to do this, especially with small children that may be present, and may have to go without and suffer going without. The class of persons would be individuals and necessities to consist of no slaves, and rarely use of a horse. These women were seen walking the roads, with their allowance of meal on their heads, carrying for miles. Their male relatives were in the army during military duty and putting their lives in service, protecting the property and their lives at home. To help with this, those who paid the two percent tax in kind of grain, those in section one would haul and deliver in Camden, and those in section two would deliver their grain to Mr. John Gaskin's mill. Paying for the grain to be hailed to the mill was expensive. J.M. Gayle would have the Soldier Families Depot at his store and would be the agent in Camden. This act was being overseen by the Board of the Soldiers Relief and the board under Chairman John M. DeSaussure.[357]

Mrs. J. Lee, president of the Camden Ladies Society, announced the following donations to the Ladies Aid Society. Mrs. J. Whitaker gave two bushels of meal, Mrs. B. Boykin gave a half bushel of meal, Mrs. J. DeSaussure gave ten dollars, Mrs. J. Lee gave one bushel of peas, Miss Mary L. Boykin gave nice things for a wounded soldier, Mrs. L.L. Whitaker, for Soldier's Rest, one bushel of potatoes and meat, Mrs. Cureton gave five dollars, and from a friend, one ham and one bushel of peas.[358]

On January 5, 1864, forty-year-old John Myers, died in Hardeeville, South Carolina. He was born and raised in Kershaw County, and was in Captain W.L. DePass' Company, the Light Artillery Palmetto Battalion. He was living in that county at the time of his death. He first married the daughter of James Corbett in Sumter County, which lasted a few years till her death. When he married the second time, he married the daughter of

---

[353] Ibid.
[354] Ibid.
[355] Ibid.
[356] Ibid.
[357] Ibid.
[358] The Camden Journal, Camden, S.C., February 12, 1864.

Sheriff Barnes; however, a short time later, she died. The third marriage was to the daughter of John Boykin of Sumter County. The churches he joined were the Spring Hill Methodist Church, in the Spring Hill Area, and then the Antioch Baptist Church in the Antioch area. He was a faithful member of the church and was loved by these friends and the congregation at the church. He was affected health wise in his latter life, but because of his wanting to serve, found camp life hard to take. Because of his being a good soldier and a good, devoted worker, he could work and live at home. On his last time at home, he felt ill but went back to battle for the cause of the war and to do his part. He was not allowed to stay at home that last time. Another brave son had now departed the Palmetto state. He left one child from the first wife, one by the second wife, and three by the third wife. He would be missed by relatives and friends. He was a farmer by occupation, and would be remembered as a tender parent, affectionate husband, and a humble and sincere Christian soldier of the cross. His remains were brought back to Antioch, where Reverend J.E. Rogers preached his funeral, and he was buried in Antioch Cemetery.[359]

A call for Bibles had taken place, so the soldiers could have comfort during the war. In Camden, contributions were sent to A.M. Kennedy, Esq. and the Bank of Camden. This request came from the Bible Society in Augusta, Georgia, by Reverend E.A. Bolles. This request was asked for by chaplains and missionaries in the units needing to distribute the word to the soldiers.[360]

In Columbia, a big reception took place. In attendance were many high-ranking military and public figures. One was Colonel John D. Kennedy, who gave an eloquent and moving speech. No record of his speech was located. However, the following is the copy of General Joseph Kershaw's Speech: General Kershaw was introduced by Columbian Major Goodwyn at the Jenny's Hotel.

"My Fellow Citizens: A demonstration of this character was more than I expected on casual visit to your city, and I am overwhelmed with emotions to which I am entirely unaccustomed. At the commencement of this revolution, I had the honor to be elevated to the command of the Second Regiment. Three years have rolled away - three years pregnant with the grandest events that ever occupied the attention of the universe - three years prolific with the destinies of the human race - three years whose influences will either forever establish or destroy the grand problem of human liberty. During this time, I have been a stranger to South Carolina, and a soldier - citizen of our sister state Virginia. I thank God in my heart of hearts that, except as an invader, I have never rested my foot on the dust of a free-soil State. (Cheers) Three times only during that three years have I returned to the land of my nativity to enjoy those associations which are dearest to the human heart, but while I stand here, I have the consolation of knowing that my brigade — your sons, and husbands, and brothers, whom it is my proud privilege to command — still occupy their places in the front; a wall of patriotic hearts between the invader and your homes. (Cheers)

"Since I came among the people of South Carolina, I have learned, for the first time, that there were some here who was desponding, tremulous, and doubtful as to the result of our struggle. I thought I was acquainted with the history of our country during the last twelve months. I had a part of it and become familiar with the sentiment of the army, but I must confess my surprise, nay, mortification, that here, in

---
[359] Ibid.
[360] The Camden Journal, Camden, S.C., February 19, 1864.

South Carolina, in Columbia, the hot-bed of secession, the spirit of the people has sunk so far below that of your brave defenders in the field, as to make it almost doubtful whether you are kin to that glorious community who, at the beginning of this war, initiated this gigantic struggle. (Profound silence in the crowd, and murmurs from the soldiers, that's right) Proud I am to come from South Carolina, but God forbid that I should ever stand the representative of such demoralizing sentiments as those to which I allude. Where exist the cause of despondency? Twelve months ago, you were full of courage and confidence. Why doubt now? We have lost Vicksburg, but what was Vicksburg? One of two outposts on the Mississippi River, whose object was, first impede navigation on the river, and secondly, to prevent the enemy, who had obtained possession of New Orleans, from holding intercourse with the people of the North by the river routes; in brief; to make the Crescent City the barren fruit of victory. Port Hudson and Vicksburg have fallen, but is the country lost because a few gunboats continue to ascend and descend as they have been in the habit of doing? Is not commerce restricted? Do vessels pass at will from St. Louis to New Orleans? Does not every newspaper bring tidings to your ears of brave men operating along the banks, as effectually baring the navigation as if a score at Vicksburg existed still? What then have we lost there? Nothing. If you think of the Trans-Mississippi department separated from us, remember that that department has done ten-fold better than before its isolation. What else to pronounce despondency? Why, the people have said we lost Tennessee. Let us see how we stand there, at the beginning of fall, we had a glorious victory, and the advancing enemy were rolled back to the point from whence they started. The whole of East Tennessee was occupied by federal troops, and what was the result there? They succeeded as they always do, in making of traitorous Union men bad Southerners. Soon afterwards, Longstreet went in that section with the purpose of driving out the Yankee Burnside. Meanwhile, our army in front of Chattanooga was driven back into Northern Georgia, and yet, in the face of this apparent misfortune, our Western Army, today."

From Camp Kizey, the following letter was sent to the newspaper to and printed March 4, 1864: Camp Kizey, Bottom Falls, Virginia, February 8, 1864:

"At a recent meeting of the Kirkwood Rangers, the following was unamaniously adopted:

We, the officers and members of the Kirkwood Rangers, Company E. Holcombe Legion Cavalry, S.C.V., appreciating the fully the great principles involved in this present war, and witness, to a great extent, of the cruelty and ferocity, practiced upon those of our countrymen, whom they have overrun, and the devastation and misery they have inflicted upon our fair country, do unamaniously. Resolved, that we, to a man, re-enlist for the war, and never lay down our arms until the last vandal is driven from the land, and enjoy the peace and liberty, which by nature is ours.
Corporal W. F. Jones, Chairman
R. K. Challes, secretary"[361]

---

[361] The Camden Journal, Camden, S.C., March 4, 1864.

In a camp near New Market, East Tennessee, two notes of thanks came in to the Camden Ladies Aid Society. One was from J.J. Drakeford, Lieutenant, Commanding Company K, 2nd Regiment. S.C.V. for twenty-four pairs of socks, two pairs of drawers, and one pair of gloves. All came in good and appreciated. The other was from J.E. Truesdel, Captain, Company G, 2nd Regiment, S.C.V., for thirty-five pairs of socks, and two pairs of drawers.[362]

W.E. Johnson was recently named in charge of the Confederate State Depository in Camden. This depositary funds treasury notes and exchange (after April 1st) the present currency for the new currency issues. The rate will be three of the old currency for two of new issues coming out.[363]

Robert M. Kennedy reminded the citizens of Camden of the condition of the cemetery, a process started but needs help to finish completion by Mr. Crammond. "Enclosures are nearly finished, wagons are needed, help needed for a couple of days, trees, turf and gravel needs to be hauled, and these needs require the work be done quickly, and not a month from now. When this process is completed, then the grounds can be leveled, cleared of rubbish, and ploughed in. Then, the place will look clear and without trees, looks like a clearing filled with ornate enclosures, and the grounds wonderful to vison. The Society will give money, but what is needed is helping to do the work. This is the cemetery for the people of Camden and looking appropriate is needed. Labor is scare but if we give servants a day to two to give help, each of us give time, then the task at hand can be completed and done."[364]

Captain C.B. Burns, Company D, 15th S.C. Regiment sent a note of thanks to the president of the Ladies Aid Society, Miss Sally Chesnut, for thirty-four pairs of socks, two pairs drawers, and one pair gloves.[365]

Death in the community occurred when Dr. John Milling died at his residence in Camden at seventy-four years of age.[366] Another death occurred with Mrs. Mary A. Hughson, wife of Reverend W.L. Hughson. She was born February 2, 1816, in the City of Charleston, and died March 4, 1864. The Ladies Benevolent Society President, Mrs. J. Lee, put a notice of tribute to Mrs. Mary Hughson for her work as vice-president in that organization.[367]

Another election took place in Camden in late March. Reelected recently was James Dunlap for intendant, and Robert M. Kennedy, D. D. Hocott, L. M. Boswell, and N. D. Baxley for wardens.[368]

Six-year-old Margaret Love, gave yarn, spun and prepared for knitting two pairs of socks. These were given to the Ladies Aid Society, as well as twenty-five pairs of socks from Mrs. John Whitaker.[369]

A report came in from the assessors of Kershaw District, Cantey and Kennedy, from the office of the Chief Commissary of Kershaw District, Mr. Devereaux. In this report, the following was given on the return of crops figures from 1863: Wheat gross crop, 9,082 bushels; corn gross crop, 325,444 bushels; Rice corn gross, 2,175 bushels; peas gross crops, 23,230 bushels, and bacon not closed at 60,000 pounds, with 45,000 already

---

[362] The Camden Journal, Camden, S.C., March 4, 1864.
[363] The Camden Journal, Camden, S.C., March 11, 1864.
[364] Ibid.
[365] Ibid.
[366] Ibid.
[367] The Camden Journal, Camden, S.C., March 18, 1864.
[368] The Camden Confederate, Camden, SC, April 6, 1864, The Camden Journal, Camden, April 8, 1864.
[369] The Camden Journal, Camden, S.C., April 8, 1864.

delivered.[370] Not yet given was the government share of the crops: 200 bushels of wheat, 1150 bushels of peas, 180 bushels of rice, and 10000 bushels of corn.[371] Three hundred fifty head of beef cattle had been sent from the district for the soldiers along the coast, for soldiers drafted for the war, for people in the Kershaw County area, and for those who had snuck over from Columbia and take with undesirable means a share of beef.[372]

W.Z. Leitner, the chief enrolling officer of Kershaw District, put a notice about conscription draftees. All people between the ages of 17 and 18 and 45 and 50 needed to come down to the office on or before April 16 to enroll, or face conscription orders from this office.[373] Also, all free Negroes and free persons of color between the ages of eighteen and fifty needed to report to work on fortifications for military defenses, working in productions of production or materials for war, and military hospitals.[374]

N.D. Baxley and W.D. McDowell were elected cashiers of the Bank of Camden. Baxley was the former teller of the bank, and McDonald replaced W.H R. Workman, who resigned.[375]

On April 16, a military election occurred for the overseeing of reserves in the Kershaw District. Those elected were Captain John Thompson, First Lieutenant Thomas J. Cauthen, Second Lieutenant John Kirkland, and 3rd Lieutenant Chapman L. McCoy.[376]

The Examining Board would be in Camden, April 28 and 29, to examine those with current disability papers for dismissal and those liable to be reexamined as ordered by headquarters.[377]

Two deaths occurred in the Camden Community, and these losses would be felt by the citizens. Those were Mr. L. Lawrence Whitaker, former bank director of SC State Bank in Camden, dying April 2, 1864, and Mrs. Eliza H. DeSaussure, wife of Major J.M. DeSaussure, dying March 11, 1864.[378]

The District released the amount collected under the act to impose a tax for the soldier's families. Those are as follow:

	From Producers	
Corn	2613	bushels
Wheat	171	bushels
Rice	29	bushels
	From Toll Mills	
Corn	137 ½	bushels
Wheat	29	bushels
Total Grains	4767 ½	bushels

---

[370] The Camden Confederate, Camden, SC, April 13, 1864.
[371] Ibid.
[372] Ibid.
[373] Ibid.
[374] Ibid.
[375] The Camden Journal, Camden, S.C., April 15, 1864.
[376] The Camden Journal, Camden, S.C., April 22, 1864.
[377] Ibid.
[378] Ibid.

Tan yards	
Leather	257 pounds

Commutations	
Leather made and sold before the Law	37
Shoes made and sold before the Law	90
Turpentine, Rosin, Terbium	1194
Copper Ware	1.75
Lumber	329
Money received	$1581.75
Total Number of receipts	1064 [379]

W. McKain and D.D. Hocott oversaw commissary of liquor and medicine. And could be found at the post office.[380]

Leitner put a notice out in the local newspaper on the enrollment of free Negroes in the area.

Captain J.H. Tucker and his two companies of cavalry camped in the suburbs of Camden for a few days before continuing their journey to meet up with the Holcombe Legion shortly.[381] Their appearance was welcomed and very appreciated by the community.

Word got out by R.J. McCreight, Orderly of Beat No. 5: All members of the company needed to meet Friday next for guard duty during an execution of a boy called Bob.[382]

A strawberry basket was brought in by Mrs. L.B. Alexander, and they were good and early for the season, which brought hope for a good harvest this year.[383] The Soldier's Rest received a gift of $202 toward the purchase of sheeting and bedding from Mr. M. Drucker.[384]

Those wishing to distribute and sell liquor needed to send their application to the district's representative, D.D. Hocott, at the Camden Post Office.[385] W. McKain was the agent selected for Kershaw District to receive prospective agents wanting to be agents for the district.[386] McKain will be located at the post office.

Captain Owen had sent out a plea that the corn had been depleted and more was needed. It was stated to "Please contact him if you have more to spare as shortages will now occur in Kershaw District and other area."[387]

News had arrived about the enemy holding the Petersburg and Danville Railroad. In the news, Colonel J.D. Kennedy was wounded in the right shoulder in the battle near Rappahannock, and was now home recuperating, while tragedy occurred in the death of a member Kershaw's staff, Alfred E. Doby, and another member in high

---

[379] The Camden Journal, Camden, S.C., May 13, 1864.
[380] Ibid.
[381] The Camden Confederate, Camden, SC., April 27, 1864.
[382] Ibid.
[383] The Camden Confederate, Camden, SC., May 4, 1864.
[384] Ibid.
[385] The Camden Confederate, Camden, SC., May 11, 1864.
[386] Ibid.
[387] Ibid.

position, Marcus Baum. Alfred English Doby was twenty-four years old.[388] In the May 19, 1864 issue of the ***Charleston Mercury***, the deaths were written about: "We regret to announce that Captain Alfred Doby and Marcus Baum, of Kershaw's Staff, (from Camden), were killed by the same fire which brought down Generals Longstreet, Jenkins, and Major Latrone.

"At twenty-four, W.H. Lewis died in Camden of disease. He was a member of the 7th Battalion, S.C.V., and had escaped harm in numerous fights on Morris Island. He entered the war three years ago at the start before the enemy's bullet sent him to be with the Lord. He leaves a wife and two children, and numerous relatives and friends."

From May 16, word came from Drury's Bluff of soldiers that had been killed and wounded. The Camden area was again saddened by the loss of life and those wounded in action. The following list was sent from the Nelson's 7th SC Battalion under Lieutenant Colonel P.H. Nelson:

Field and Staff: Major Rion, slightly but still on duty

Company A Commanded by Captain B.S. Lucas:
  Killed - Corporal W.H. Atkinson, Jesse D. Bush
  Mortally wounded - J.D. Rodgers, J.W. Barr, M.T. Blackwell, and W.J. Stokes, J.S. Mixon
  Seriously wounded - Sergeant M.J. Outlaw, J.M. Tiller, Samuel Webb, J.D. McCaskill, J.R. Clyburn, L.C. Rodgers, James Watson
  Slightly wounded – M. Hough

Company B commanded by Captain J.D. Kennedy
  Killed - J.A. Potut, James S. Lee, A.S. Jimie, John S. Harrison, J.A. Rose, Alan Trap, E.J. Blizzard
  Mortally wounded - Daniel Reid, T.H. Christmas
  Severely wounded - S.G. Perry, Allan Perry, W. Brown, E.J Haynes, R.L. Phillips
  Slightly wounded – G.O. Williamson, H. Dawkins
  Missing - Lawrence Powers

Company C commanded by Captain P.P. Gillard
  Killed - J.W. Benton
  Severely wounded - Sergeant C.M. Atkinson, R.C. Brown, J.B. Haley
  Slightly wounded - A. Scott, James Catoe

Company D commanded by Captain Dove Segars
  Killed – R.E. West, Joseph Hall

---

[388] The Camden Confederate, Camden, SC., May 18, 1864. Also, The Camden Journal, Camden, S.C., May 20, 1864.

Mortally wounded - George King, James Herron

Severely wounded - Lieutenant William McSween, Sergeant G.B. King, C.W. McCaskill, W.C. Radcliffe, J. Wiley Sowell, E.N. Yarborough

Slightly wounded – L.C. Hough, C.J. Phillips, C. Pate, D. Raley, J.M. Hazzard, N.W. Jones, Jesse E. Watkins, G. Robertson

Company G commanded by Lieutenant L.L. Clyburn

Killed - John C. Holland, C.L. Gardner, John J. Perry, John Kirby, T.G. Sutton, Henry McNeil, G.W. Gaskins, J.N. Clyburn, Bently Outlaw, W.L. Bagley, Joseph West

Mortally wounded - Sergeant J.G. Mayrant, W.M. Wilson, T. Kirby, J.N. Williams, S.W. Augustine, D. Hornsby

Severely wounded - Sergeant S.C. Clyburn, T.J. Smyrl, William Gaskins, James Corder, D.T. Bradley, C.B. Gay, W.R. Gardner, J. Hill, William Peach, G. Sutton, Corporal R.T. Spears, J.A. Smith, J.B. Williams

Slightly wounded – L.O. Jones

Slightly wounded and in the hands of the enemy - Corporal W.J. Cooper, H. Gardner, P. Martin, E.T. Brown, J.T. Villipigue, Richard Outlaw

Company H commanded by J.H. Brooks

Killed - Sergeant R.L. Motley, Sergeant J.H. Outz (Color Bearer), Corporal J.B. Robertson (Color Corporal), Corporal J. Hunsucker, Joseph Addison, John Bailey, Alford Cheatham, Ely Douglass, George Dust, Fletcher Elkins, Robert Harris, John Harris, William Holloway, Allen Kennedy, William A. Rush, Jasper Rodgers, William Taylor, John Walton, J.M. Young

Mortally wounded - Corporal John Gregory, M. Ellenburg, J. Hawley, John Cotton, Rush McLaughlin

Severely wounded - Captain J.H. Brooks, Lieutenant B.J. Randell, Sergeant A.P. Irby, Sergeant E.P. Walker, Corporal Rush, Corporal Bradby, H T Addison, Randell Johnston, James W. Johnson, George McCants, R. Minor, R. Strut

Slightly wounded - Lieutenant William Weston, J.S. Brooks, R.M. Cogburn, W.N. Franklin, J.C. Gillabou, J.C. Henderson, R. Langley, James Millar, James Minor, D. Roberts, Samuel Shirley, S. Strickland, W.S. Tolbert, W. Tyson, J.B. Vandiver, B.B. Wright

Missing – W.H. Bell, Asa Hammond, William Jones, Daniel Jones, S. Milers, William Roberts, B. Stalnacker, Richard Stalnacker, Thomas Sturgeon, L.D. Tinkler, J.T. Walton, E.B. Wright, L. Wyrick

List of Casualties of Companies D and E, 7th SC Battalion,

Commanded by Lieutenant Colonel S. Warren Nelson

Skirmish in front of works near Drury's Bluff, May 15, 1864

Company D Commanded by Captain J.L. Jones

Slightly wounded - Lieutenant R.W. Young

Company F Commanded by Captain D. Segars

Severely wounded – C.A. Jamison

Slightly wounded - Tim Scott, S.L. Gardner, R.J. Bell, G. Cannington

Casualties in 15th Company Commanded by Captain Burns

Company D Commanded by Captain Steen

Killed – John Spradley, S.W. Hornsby

Wounded - Sergeant J.W. Huckabee, severe shoulder, A. Kirby, contusion arm slight, J.C Outlaw, arm flesh severe[389]

Recapulation of the Drury Bluff Encounter on This Confederate Side

Killed	42
Mortally Wounded	20
Severely Wounded	47
Slightly Wounded	39
Missing	21
Total	169[390]

From a private dispatch received during the last day before going to print, the following information was contained that concerns the Camden area and vicinity:

"The following casualties from Shingler's Regiment, a part of the Holcombe Legion: J.B. Cureton, Jr. - Killed; John Lee, slightly wounded in the hand; William Whitaker, slightly in the head; Henry C. Salmond, slightly in the hand; J.M. DeSaussure, slightly in the foot, and T.H. Clarke, in thigh. Many officers took the brute of the battle and didn't fare well, but Camden's officers came out well.[391]

Chancellorsville and Spotsylvania Courthouse Virginia sent news of those conflicts and with more news of soldiers from the vicinity in the 2nd Regiment, S.C.V.

Company A – Wounded - Corporal George Bruns, leg amputated; P.H. Joyner, slight

Company B – Wounded – N.P. Henning, R.H. Bramlet, slight; Thomas Johnson, severe; G.W. Williams, at first mortally, then eventually he died.

---

[389] The Camden Confederate, Camden, South Carolina, June 1, 1864,
[390] Ibid.
[391] Ibid.

Company E – Wounded – J.E. Nettles, leg amputated

Company F – Killed - John Robinson; Wounded - Captain W.C. Vance, William Chipley, J.S. Chaney, slight; Lieutenant Alex McNeill, P.M. Fuller, severe

Company G – Killed - Sergeant J.J. Murchison; Wounded – B.J. Blackman, J.W. Bone, Slight; W.W. Blackman, A.J. Small, severe; E.B. Robinson, dangerous condition.

Company H – Killed – S.A. Douglass, A.M. Williams; Wounded – S.C. Gardner, J.B. Kennington, B. Sutton, severe; W.C. Adkins, leg amputated; J.B. Harris, slight

Company I – Killed – E. Kerrison, W.D.S. Frieks; Wounded - Sergeant R.H. Scriven, J. Brown, slight

Company K – Killed - Captain John Webb, Sergeant J.R. Simmons, and J. Bull; Wounded - Sergeant F.C. Ferrura, J. Baily, W.P. Bell, slight; J.M. Benson, hand amputated. [392]

At a crossroads near the Old Church, May 30, 1864, a cavalry conflict took place that involved two units from the Camden area. Commanded by Lieutenant A.C. Haskell, and with units captained by James L. Doby and D. Dubose (this unit late E.M. Boykin). Field Officers – Wounded: Lieutenant Colonel E.C. Haskell, severely, not dangerous; Major E.M. Boykin, severely in thigh; Captain James Doby's Company: Killed - Corporal J.B. Cureton; Wounded - Sergeants John B. Lee, in wrist severely; W. Whitaker, slightly in head; Corporal H.C. Salmond, Privates John Turnball, John Mulholland, John Player, E.W. Parker, all slightly in hand; T.H. Clarke, in thigh; Missing - Lieutenant U.B. Bonney, Privates D. McRace, S.B. Edwards, J.A. Davis, A. Massey; Captain D. Dubose's Company: Wounded - Captain Dubose, leg painful; Lieutenant J.W. Arrants, leg slightly; Privates A. Neuffer, mortally and missing; S. Kirkland, leg and hand severely; S. Beckham, shoulder severely; J. Dusenbury, face severely; J.M. DeSausure, foot slightly; E.D. Cole, face; G.G. Young, arm severely; Missing- Lieutenant W.E. Johnson, Sergeant T.L. Boykin, Privates L.H. Deas, T.A. Huggins, D.B. Strother — Sent by S. Watt Wardlaw, Adjutant [393]

Special Order number 8 was sent by the secretary of South Carolina.

The following is a list of war-taxable items that those with any of these items were responsible for paying taxes:

1. Number of acres of land.
2. Number of slaves.
3. Number of horses, mules, asses, and jennets.
4. Number of cattle.
5. Number of sheep, goats, and hogs.
6. Number of pounds of tobacco.

---

[392] The Camden Confederate, Camden, South Carolina, June 8, 1864.
[393] Ibid.

7. Number of pounds of cotton and wool.
8. Number of bushels of wheat, corn, oats, rye, buckwheat, rice.
9. Number of bushels of potatoes of all kinds, peas and ground peas.
10. Flour, meal, sugar, molasses, bacon, lard, and all other groceries, goods, wares, or merchandise, spirituous liquors, wine cider, and vinegar.
11. Value of all household and kitchen furniture, agricultural tools, implement of mechanics, musical instruments, and all other articles of household use.
12. And every species of vehicles on wheel.
13. All gold and silver wares, and plate, jewels, jewelry, and watches.
14. Books, maps, pictures, paintings, statuaries, and other works of art.
15. Number of shares in any bank, railroad, and other joint stock companies.
16. Gold or silver coins, bullion.
17. Value of all other property not enumerated in the foregoing.

All kinds of property owned by February 11 would be taxable and came under this act.[394]

A list of casualties was sent in for the 7th SC Battalion, commanded by Lieutenant Colonel P.H. Nelson covering May 17 to June 6.

Company A – Commanded by Captain B.S. Lucas: June 2: Wounded severely - Corporal J.C. Pitts; June 8: Killed - Angus McClarin, J.J. Hall; wounded severely - Captain B.S. Lucas, Corporal D. McClarin, Thomas Randall, J. Sinclair; Slightly wounded - Sergeant B.F. Outlaw, S. Stokes, E. Brannon, W.H. Allen, and C.W. Hyott.

Company D – Commanded by Captain J.J. Jones: May 24: Severely wounded - Sergeant W.J. Jones; June 1: Slightly wounded – J.J. Bell, W.C. Denton, R.J. White: June 2: Severely wounded – J.F. Ballard: June 3: Severely wounded - Josiah Vincent, S. Self, Corporal J.R. Sheorn: Slightly wounded - Corporal R.T. Lewis, L.C. Bell, Z. Boon

Company F – Commanded by Captain D. Segars: May 18: Slightly wounded – J.J. Folsom, R. Barns, Dan Clanton, J. Hough, severely: May 20: Severely wounded - E McClendon: May 29: Severely wounded – C. Stokes: Slightly wounded - William Raley, J.R. Hall, John E. Watkins, J.J. Watkins, James Sullivan, Jeff Gardner: June 4: Severely wounded – B.W. Newman, Curtis Outlaw.

Company G – Commanded by William Clyburn: June 3: Severely wounded - Joseph Mickle.[395]

---
[394] The Camden Confederate, Camden, SC, June 15, 1864.
[395] The Camden Confederate, Camden, SC, June 28, 1864.

E.R. Lee, treasurer of Soldier's Rest, announced a gift from the president of the Flat Rock Ladies Society, Miss Emily Perry, for $5.80. Also, worthy of note was that the Soldier's Rest was getting anywhere from three to a dozen or more nightly traveling through for rest, sickness, wounds, and disease.[396]

A new newspaper had come to print in Camden last Friday. The name was *Camden Daily Journal*.[397]

The Soldier's Rest reported that donations from all over the county would be acceptable as the rest were having as many as three to a dozen every night. Each soldier passing through was headed to their homes in different districts, and at times, some needed to stay longer to recover from their wounds and diseases. This report was from the treasurer of Soldier's Rest, E.R. Lee.[398]

Mrs. James Jones of Camden brought to the Soldiers' Rest, the following articles from the Flat Rock Ladies Society from Mrs. Perry and Miss Lizzie Brown— two hams, one peck of rice, twenty-one eggs, one-gallon syrup, one peck of wheat, coffee, and cornmeal.[399]

During the last week, letters came in from local soldiers in prisons in Delaware and Washington. Those soldiers were E.B. Cureton and Samuel H. Boykin. They were in prison at Fort Delaware and would be in prison for over twelve months, and Lieutenants W.E. Johnson and U.P. Bonney, with T.L. Boykin and Lynch H. Deas, were still recovering from a severe thigh injury, after being in prison in Washington.[400]

On the evening of Saturday July 23, the following soldiers arrived at the Soldier's Rest. Those soldiers were J. Moneyham, 20th S.C.R., wounded from Sumter; W.W. Folsom, 7th S.C. Battalion, sick from Kershaw; Martin from Lancaster; and C.H. Horton, from Kershaw, both sick - regiment to which they belonged unknown.[401] On the evening of July 25, the following soldiers arrived at the Soldier's Rest. Those being N. Hough, Company G, 2nd S.C. Regiment, sick from Kershaw; C.R. Hatfield, Company G. 2nd S.C. Regiment, sick from Sumter; J.H. Clyburn, Company A, 7th S.C. Battalion, sick from Kershaw; and G.P. Copeland, Company D, 7th S.C. Battalion, sick from Kershaw.[402] Arrivals on the evening of July 28 includes G.R. Bowers, Company A, 1st S.C. Infantry, sick from Lancaster; J.N. Jowers, Company A, 4thRegiment S.C.V., sick from Chesterfield; William Shannon, 6th Regiment S.C.V., sick from Kershaw; and J.A. Falkenberry, Company D, 7th S.C. Battalion, sick from Kershaw.[403] Arrivals on the evening of July 10 included John Laney, Waites Battery of S.C., wounded from Lancaster; Joseph Adams, Company A, 1st S.C. Infantry, sick from Lancaster; and Uriah J. Stephenson, Company K, 5th Texas, from Clumbers County, Texas.[404] On the evening of August 2nd, J.J. Jeffords, Company G, 20th Regiment, wounded from Sumter, arrived.[405] Arriving on the evening of August 6 included W.B. Johnson, Company D, 15th Regiment S.C.V., sick from Kershaw; W.M. Frail, Company J,

---

[396] The Camden Confederate, Camden, SC., July 6, 1864.
[397] Ibid.
[398] The Camden Daily Journal, Camden, S.C., July 7, 1864.
[399] The Camden Confederate, Camden, SC., July 13, 1864.
[400] The Camden Confederate, Camden, SC., August 3, 1864.
[401] The Camden Daily Journal, Camden, S.C., July 25, 1864.
[402] The Camden Daily Journal, Camden, S.C., July 27, 1864.
[403] The Camden Daily Journal, Camden, S.C., July 29, 1864.
[404] The Camden Daily Journal, Camden, S.C., July 30, 1864.
[405] The Camden Daily Journal, Camden, S.C., August 3, 1864.

17th S.C.V., sick from Lancaster; T.O. Wilkinson, Company D, 4th Regiment S.C.V., sick from Lancaster; J.B. Hilton, Company D, 1st Regiment S.C.V., sick from Lancaster; and John F. Hammond, Company H, 4thRegiment, S.C. Cavalry, Butler's Brigade, sick from Lancaster.[406] On the evening of August 8, the following arrived at the Soldier's Rest: J.E. Atkinson, Company J, 20th Regiment S.C.V, sick and from Kershaw; W.A. Funderburk, Company J, 1st Regiment S.C. Infantry, from Lancaster; Joel Hough, Company G, 2nd S.C. Regiment, sick from Kershaw; George DeBruhl, Company F, 7th S.C. Cavalry, sick from Kershaw; and George Self, Company G, 7th S.C. Battalion, sick from Kershaw.[407] On evening nights of the eleventh through the thirteenth of August, the following arrivals came: John W. Wilson, Company C, 12th S.C. Regiment, on furlough from Kershaw; H. Bass, Company C, 12th S.C. Regiment, on furlough from Kershaw; J. Williams, Company K, 7th S.C. Battalion, sick and from Kershaw; Wesley Allen, unknown regiment, from Kershaw; Samuel Mackey, Company B, S.C., Siege Train, sick and from Charleston; M.S. Veney, Company D, 2nd S.C. Regiment, sick and from Virginia; J.A. Gregory, Company E, 43rd Alabama, wounded and from Alabama; J.J. Funderburk, Company E, 22d S.C. Regiment, wounded from Lancaster; and Chapman Estridge, Company E, 22nd S.C. Regiment, wounded from Lancaster.[408]

More tragedy came in the form of a letter announcing to the citizens of Camden the recently killed, wounded, and those soldiers taken as prisoners. This letter is a personal letter from Captain William Clyburn after a fight near Petersburg, and the hardest hit were thirteen captains and lieutenants. Those soldiers are from Company A - Lieutenant Finley McCaskill; missing Lieutenant James Gardner; Company B - Lieutenant Douglass, wounded in the thigh severely; Lieutenant Isbell, wounded severely and in the hands of the enemy; Lieutenant Kennedy, wounded severely and in the hands of the enemy; Company D - Captain J.L. Jones became a prisoner, as wells as Lieutenant E.A. Young, who was taken as a prisoner; Company F - Captain Dove Segars, wounded slightly in the side; Lieutenant H.D. Tiller, wounded severely in the shoulder; Lieutenant King, wounded slightly in the side; Company G - Lieutenant L.L. Clyburn, wounded in the leg; Lieutenant T.W. Sligh was missing; and Company H – W. Weston, wounded through the thigh severely.[409]

An appeal came in from the president of the Soldiers' Rest. This appeal was for ladies to come and redo the mattresses and pillows at the rest as the soldiers were finding them very uncomfortable and needed to be taken care of. "We are asking that each lady takes one matrass or four pillows and wash the ticks and adding some wheat straw and or shucks to the cotton."[410]

---

[406] The Camden Daily Journal, Camden, S.C., August 8, 1864.
[407] The Camden Daily Journal, Camden, S.C., August 9, 1864.
[408] The Camden Daily Journal, Camden, S.C., August 15, 1864.
[409] The Camden Confederate, Camden, SC., August 31, 1864.
[410] Ibid.

During this time, a list of the District Directory was put into the *Camden Daily Journal* about July 2, 1864:

District Officers

Legislatures
A.H. Boykin — Senator
John M. DeSaussure, D.D. Perry — Representatives

Magistrates
John K. Witherspoon, Wm. D. Hogan, W.R. Taylor, Henry Brace,
John R. Shaw, Richard L. Whitaker, J.T. Barker

Commissioners of Roads
J. M. DeSaussure, Chairman; B.T. McCoy, W.E. Hughes, Daniel D. Kirkland,
James L. McDowell, Lewis J. Patterson, J. English Doby, Fred Bowen, John L. Mickle,
Gilliam Sowell, Richmond R. Terrell, Emanual Parker.

The sixth section of the "Act to establish certain Roads, Bridges and Ferries," passed on December 17 and is as follows:

"That each commissioner of Roads now in office, or hereafter, appointed, shall serve until a successor is appointed, and has accepted. This section is to be in force during the war."

Commissioners of Free Schools
Willey Kelly, William Dixon, James Team, C.C. Haile, Jessie Truesdale, Daniel Bethune, A.L. McDowell

Commissioners of Public Buildings
John Workman, R.M. Kennedy, B.B. Johnson, F.L. Zemp, L.W.R. Blair, James B. Cureton, William D. McDowell, Chairman; C.P.B., Collin Macrea, Treasurer

Commissioners to Approve Public Securities
John M. DeSaussure, James Dunlap, William E. Johnson Sr., A.M. Kennedy, Thomas E. Shannon

Commissioners of the Poor
E. Barnes, A.A. McDowell, John O. Higgins, R.M.W.E. Hughson, Secretary and Treasurer

---

President and Director of Camden Bridge Company
President - John M. DeSaussure

Directors - Joel Macrae, B. Perkins, James Team, Collin Macrae (secretary and treasurer)

Soldier's Board of Relief
John M. DeSaussure, E. Barnes, James Dunlap, J. Ross Dye, C. Mosely, James Team, Jesse Truesdel, John B. Mickle, Charles Raley, John Gaskin, Daniel Gardner

Coroner
John S. Meroney
Manager of Elections
Camden - John S. Meroney, C.A. McDonald, William McKain
Cureton's Mill - Frederick Bowen, James Team, Emanuel Parker
Flat Rock - Jesse Truesdel, James Fletcher, George R. Miller
Buffalo - William Mungo, Gilliam Sowell, William Cato
Lizenby's - John McGougan, Daniel McCaskill, Donald McDonald
Schrock's Mill - B.T. McCoy, Alexander McLeod, Henry Radcliffe
Goodwin's Store - Benjamin Cook, John B. Mickle, James M. Vaughn
Liberty Hill - A.D. Jones Jr., R.C. Patterson, R.B. Cunningham

---

Officers of Court
Joseph D. Dunlap - Commissioner in Equity
W. Clyburn - Clerk
A.L. McDonald - Ordinary
Duncan Sheorn- Sheriff

Tax Collector
William McKain

Confederate Enrolling Officer
W.Z. Leitner

Confederate War Tax Collector
A.M. Kennedy

Assessors
John Cantey, R.M. Kennedy

Collector of Tax in Kind
James Jones

Chief Commissary Agent
J. H. Devereaux

Confederate Quartermaster's Agent
James Sowers

State Quartermaster's Agent
A. Markley Lee

Receiving and Delivering Agent
J.M. Gayle

Officers of the Town of Camden
Intendant
James Dunlap

Wardens
N.D. Baxley, D.D. Hocott, L.M. Boswell, R.M. Kennedy

Recorder
R.M. Kennedy

Marshal and Market Clerk
William Johnson

Professional:
Physicians now Practicing
L.H. Deas, D.L. DeSaussure, T. Reenatjerna, W.R. Sikes, Benjamin H. Matherson, J. McCaa, J.L. Trantham, W.L. Pickett, B.S. Lucas, T.F. McDow, Lewis DeSaussure, Thomas W. Salmond, F.L. Zemp

Lawyers
William M. Shannon, W.Z. Leitner, W.M. Kennedy, W.R. Taylor, Joseph D. Dunlap

Dentist
M. Bissell

Surveyors
Colin Macrae, Daniel Bethune, C.C. Haile

Scholastic, Mercantile, and Mechanical
Academies and Primary Schools in Camden

L. McCandless, Male Academy; F. Staudemyer, Male Academy; G. Bailey, Professor of Foreign Languages; Mrs. McCandless's Academy for Young Ladies; Mrs. McCreight, Miss Dawson, Mrs. Peck, Miss Maggie DeNoon

Dealers in Dry Goods, Groceries, Hardware
E.W. Bonney, James Dunlap, George Alden, Mrs. M.T. Campbell, R. M. Kennedy, Mrs. McLeish, Mendal Smith, Mrs. Conner, Mrs. Crosby, Benjamin Matheson and Company, A.T. Latta, W.D. McDowell, S. Oppenheim, M. Baum and Brothers, Meroney, Bowell, and Brothers, J.M. Gayle, Joseph Sommers, T.S. Myers, James McEwen, W.C. Gerald and Company, George Douglas, J.H. Oppenheim and Brothers, William Johnson, D.D. Hocott, B. Sikes.

Druggists
William McKain, F.L. Zemp

Book Seller and Stationer
James A. Young

Watches and Jewelry
James A. Young, I.B. Alexander, A.W. Wehrhan

Blacksmiths, Wagons, and Carriage Makers
Samuel Shiver, Robert Man, Nathan B. Arrants, Thomas Shiver, R.R., Blacksmith

Cabinet Water rooms and Undertakers
C.L. Chatten, William Tarver, J.F. Sutherland

Builders
J.F. Sutherland, C.L. Chatten, H.C. Roberts

Merchant Tailor
Charles A. McDonald

Saddlery and Harness
F.J. Oakes

Wheelright and Ginmaker
R.J. McCreight

Bakers
Mrs. A.M. Kennedy, F. Shoemaker, William Daasch

Tan-Yards
L.B. Stephenson, F.L. Zemp, John S. Bradley, Alexander McLeod,
Lewis J. Patterson, John Brown

Hotels
Mansion House by E.G. Robinson
DeKalb House by J.H. Jungbluth

Private Boarding
J.W. Rodgers

Milinary and Dressmaking
Miss D.H. McEwen, Mrs. Hammerslough

Churches
Methodist - J.T. Wightman, Pastor
Presbyterian - S.H. Hay, Pastor
Episcopal - T.F. Davis Jr., Pastor
Baptist - W.E. Hughson, Pastor

Grain and Lumber Mills
F.L. Zemp, flour and grist
James H. Vaughan, flour and grist
James A. Kirkland, grist
J.F. Sutherland, lumber and grist
W.E. Hughes, lumber and grist
Charles Perkins, lumber
Colonel James C. Haile, lumber and grist
A.H. Boykin, flour, grist, and lumber

L.W.R. Blair, *flour and grist*
Charles Raley, *flour and grist*
J.R. Sowell, *grist*
John W. Gaskins, *flour, grist, and lumber*
John A. Young, *grist and lumber*
T.J. Cauthen, *lumber*
Robert Kirkley, *grist*
Estate of William Shields, *grist and lumber*
George R. Miller, *flour and grist*
L.J. Patterson, *flour and grist,*
John S. Miller, *flour and grist*
Estate of T. Lang, *grist and lumber*
W.M. Kelly, *grist*
John Chesnut, *grist and lumber*
James Chesnut, *grist and lumber*
John McRae, *grist and lumber*
John Brown, *grist*
Estate of Burwell Boykin, *grist and lumber*
Estate of Lemuel Boykin, *grist and lumber*
Mrs. Jane J. Knox, *grist*
Richard Hyatt, *flour and grist*
Lewis Peoples, *flour, grist, and lumber*

Bank Officers and Directors
Branch Bank of the State of South Carolina
President - William M. Shannon
Cashier - N.D. Baxley
Bookkeeper - J.E. Nettles
Assistant Bookkeeper - W.D. Anderson
Directors - J. Ross Dye, L.H. Deas, John Cantey,
E.W. Bonney, A.D. James Sr.
Bank of Camden
President - W.E. Johnson Sr.
Cashier - W.D. McDowall
Directors - H.B. Johnson, William M. Shannon, Benjamin Perkins,
W.D. McDowall, John Workman

Post Office, Camden, S.C.
Mail Arrangements

Richmond, Charleston, Columbia, Western, and Way Mails
Due daily by 7:30 P.M.
Close Daily by 6:00 P.M.

Lancaster, Flat Rock, and C.
Due - Monday, Wednesday, Friday by 12:00 M.
Close - Same days at 11:00 A.M.

Red Hill, Russell Place and C.
Due - Thursday by 12:00 M.
Closes - Same day at 11:00 A.M.

Tiller's Ferry, Jefferson, and C.
Due - Monday by 12:00 M
Closes - Friday at 10:00 A.M.

Office Hours
From 8:00 A.M. to 2:00 P.M., and for a short time after opening the mail at night.
T.W. Pegues, P.M.
[411]

The president of the Soldiers' Rest released a report of subscriptions and donations for the month of August. The following was a list and by whom:

Cash Monthly - Five dollars from Mrs. Leslie McCandless, Mrs. W.M. Shannon, and those omitted from last month, Mrs. Sebring, ten dollars; Mrs. B.M. Lee, five dollars; Mrs. Courtney, five dollars; Mrs. McCreight, two dollars.

Provisions Monthly - Mrs. W.E. Johnson gave a half bushel each of hominy and meal; Mrs. J. McRae gave one bushel of meal, one gallon of syrup, one bucket of lard, and four candles; Mrs. Gamewell gave one peck of hominy; Mrs. B. Boykin gave four chickens, one and a half pecks of hominy; Mr. J. Boykin gave one bushel of meal, one quart of rice, and vegetables; Mrs. L.L. Whitaker gave one and a half pecks of flour, two watermelons,

---

[411] The Camden Daily Journal, July 2, 1864; Camden, S.C.

and Irish potatoes; Mrs. E.A. Salmond gave one and a half pecks of rice; Mr. Owens gave one basket of greens; Mrs. J. Whitaker gave one shoulder of meat and vegetables.

Donations - Mrs. Lyles, five dollars; Mrs. Thornton, five dollars, Little Miss Bessie Courtney, ten dollars proceeds from a hat she made; Little Miss Fannie B. Lee, ten dollars proceeds from a hat she made; Mrs. Arthur gave three gallons milk and a pitcher of soup; Mr. Marshall, Lynches Creek, gave one peck of apples; Mrs. Boswell gave one pint syrup; Miss Bonney gave one bowl of prepared tomatoes; Mr. James Team gave one half bushel each of meal and hominy; Mrs. West gave four pounds of beef; Mrs. Chatten gave one plate of biscuits and one bucket of milk; Mrs. Dunlap , Mrs. Sebring, and Mrs. A.F. Doby, renewing four pillows each for "Rest"; Mrs. B. Haile, Mrs. John Cantey, and Miss Ancrum each renewed one mattress each; Mr. Deasch gave loaves of bread; Miss McEwen gave supper for the soldiers on the seventeenth; Mrs. Sebring gave one peck of rice, one dozen hymn books, and six tracts; Mr. R. Mickle gave seven pounds of beef; Mr. Newman and Mr. James Boykin gave three pounds of beef; and Mr. E.P. Baker gave three pounds of mutton.

Providing Meals per Day on Specific Days of the Month

1st - Mrs. I.B. Alexander	17th - Mrs. Rogers
2nd - Mrs. Hyams	18th - Mrs. James Davis
3rd - Mrs. J.H. Anker	19th - Mrs. McDonald
4th - Mrs. James Dunlap	20th - Mrs. H. DeSaussure
5th - Mrs. A.M. Kennedy	21st - Mrs. G.S. Douglass
6th - Mrs. C.L. Chatten	22nd - Mrs. Stakely
7th - Mrs. Joseph Kershaw	23rd - Mrs. J. Lee
8th - Mrs. R.M. Kennedy	24th - Mrs. J.M. Gayle
9th - Mrs. D.D. Hocott	25th - Miss McDowell
10th - Mrs. Joseph Oppenheim	26th - Mrs. Sutherland
11th - Mrs. E.W. Bonney	27th - Mrs. Deas
12th - Miss Chesnut	28th - Mrs. Anker
13th - Miss Salmond	29th - Mrs. Reynolds
14th - Mrs. T.F. Davis, Sr.	30th - Mrs. Edward Boykin
15th - Mrs. T.F. Davis, Jr.	31st - Mrs. James Jones
16th - Mrs. R. Young	

"The Medical Purveyor of Columbia, Mr. Chisolm, has responded with medicines upon hearing of our appeal. Thanks to our own Dr. Lewis DeSaussure, who has allowed attention to the wounded and sick at this home. Our thanks to Mr. Witherspoon and Colonel Kennedy to relieve the foot worn soldier." [412]

---

[412] The Camden Confederate, Camden, SC., September 7, 1864.

The Fifth Brigade composed of the 20th, 21st, 22nd, 23rd, and 44th Regiments at Camden was under the command of Lieutenant Colonel A.H. Boykin, A.D.C.[413]

Three escaped prisoners were recaptured on August 11, 1864. Those being Mr. Joseph Barber, Dr. William R. Sikes, and Mr. William Christmas. They were in the Wateree Swamp about five miles below Camden. The two Yankees were probably escaped prisoners making their way to the coast. On being searched at Captain Leitner's office, there was found upon them, among other things, two well-executed maps — one of the Georgia Railroad, and the other of the country from Columbia to Beaufort, North Carolina. The prisoners were lodged provisionally in the jail, and forwarded this morning, under guard, to Columbia.[414]

In an ad on September 4, 1864, the Fifth Brigade was organized in Camden, South Carolina. This unit was composed of the 20th, 21st, 22d, 23d, and 44th Regiments, and under the command of Lieutenant Colonel A.H. Boykin, ADC. On note, another Camdenite, Lieutenant Colonel Wilmont G. DeSaussure oversaw a unit consisting of the 16th, 17th, 18th, and 19th Regiments in Charleston, South Carolina.[415]

The following prisoners of war from this district were unhurt: Captain J.L. Jones, Lieutenant E.A. Young, Privates L.M. Cauthen, S. Bell, G.L. Dixon, David Peach, S. Herbert, G.B.P. Copeland, W.J.C. Stokes. Thomas Fitzpatrick, and J.H. Coward, all belonging to Nelson's Battalion.[416]

Captain William Clyburn gave a donation of twenty dollars for the support of the Soldier's Rest.[417] Coming from the services of battle, Captain Clyburn was doing his part for the soldiers coming through from doing their part on the battlefield.

In late October 1864, an accident occurred at a nearby mill. The mill was twelve miles from Camden, relating to a sugar mill. Miss Sill, the sister of E.E. Sill, was caught in the cylinders of one of those mills, and both arms were crushed to cause immediate amputation. One was taken off at the shoulder joint, the other above the elbow. She was making sorghum as many farmers were trying to do.[418]

---

413 Ibid.
414 The Camden Daily Journal, Camden, S.C., August 12, 1864.
415 The Camden Daily Journal, Camden, S.C., September 8, 1864.
416 The Camden Daily Journal, Camden, S.C., September 20, 1864.
417 The Camden Confederate, Camden, SC., September 22, 1864.
418 The Camden Daily Journal, Camden, S.C., November 1, 1864.

1865

The Ladies Aid Association received the following donations: Mrs. John Whitaker, eighteen pairs of socks; Mrs. James Chesnut, twelve pairs of socks; Mrs. W.E. Johnson, five pairs of socks, three bundles of yarn; Mrs. David Robinson gave three pairs of socks and five dollars cash. Also, the aid association announced that "the meeting will be held from now on at the Temperance Hall every Tuesday at eleven o'clock." [419]

Here is a look at what Sherman said about the southern soldier. This was taken from a letter a lady in Atlanta wrote just before leaving Atlanta and having a conversation with Sherman. This letter was sent to Reverend George G.N. McDonald. In that letter, Sherman said that the southern soldier was "the bravest in the world but in a fair fight, they would lose two to one." He further stated to the lady that "your southern soldier can beat us in fighting, but where the South falls short is that that we (Yankees) can outmaneuver you. Your officers work half the time as ours, who work day and night to spare no labor or pain to carry out the plan."[420]

The President and Committee of the Soldier's Rest acknowledged the following for the month's donations:

Donations monthly - Mrs. McRea for one peck of meal, one gallon of syrup, one mess of potatoes, and two heads of greens; Mrs. H. Whitaker, one middling of bacon, and two packages of rags; Mr. Deach, sixty loaves of bread, six pounds of salt, six pounds of rye and flour; and Mrs. W.E. Johnson, half a bushel of meal, and a half bushel of hominy.

Donations - Mrs. Charles Perkins, one fore-quarter of beef; Mrs. Sommers, piece of beef; Mrs. Hamilton Boykin, lard, flour, spareribs, and backbones; Mrs. McCreight, one peck of meal, one loaf of bread; Mrs. Dunlap, one-peck meal; Miss M.A. Brown, Liberty Hill, one-gallon syrup, one half-bushel rice; Mrs. Isabella Peay, one bag of sage, one bag of mustard seed and pepper; Mrs. E.K. Doby, ten dollars; Mr. Sutherland, one load of pine wood; and Mr. Hughes, one load of oak wood; and Colonel R.B. Johnson, one load of pine wood.

Cash monthly donations - Mrs. Sebring, ten dollars; Mrs. McCandless, five dollars, Mr. B.A.S., ten dollars; Mrs. Louisa Haile, ten dollars; Miss Sue Bonney, Miss E.K. Lee, each gave fifty cents, and Mrs. McCreight, two dollars.

---

[419] The Camden Confederate, Camden, SC; January 2, 1865.
[420] Ibid.

Providing Monthly Meals on Specific Days of the Month

1st - Mrs. I.B. Alexander	17th - Mrs. Rogers
2nd - Mrs. Hyams	18th - Mrs. James Davis
3rd - Mrs. J.H. Anker	19th - Mrs. McDonald
4th - Mrs. James Dunlap	20th - Mrs. H. DeSaussure
5th - Mrs. A.M. Kennedy	21st - Mrs. G.S. Douglass
6th - Mrs. C.L. Chatten	22nd - Mrs. Stakely
7th - Mrs. Joseph Kershaw	23rd - Mrs. J. Lee
8th - Mrs. R.M. Kennedy	24th - Mrs. J.M. Gayle
9th - Mrs. D.D. Hocott	25th - Miss McDowell
10th - Mrs. Joseph Oppenheim	26th - Mrs. Sutherland
11th - Mrs. E.W. Bonney	27th - Mrs. Deas
12th - Miss Chesnut	28th - Mrs. Anker
13th - Miss Salmond	29th - Mrs. Reynolds
14th - Mrs. T.F. Davis, Sr.	30th - Mrs. Edward Boykin
15th - Mrs. T.F. Davis, Jr.	31st - Mrs. James Jones
16th - Mrs. R. Young	

[421]

A tribute of respect was given to Lieutenant William McSween. The following was said of him: "Kershaw District has lost many noble and gallant sons in the war. Their names and memory should ever be cherished while liberty, right, and justice have a place among us. Prominently among her worth deeds, should ever stand the name and memory of Lieutenant William McSween. He was truly patriotic and had not aspiration for office. The earnest of his heart, was faithful performance of his duty, and he did his duty, his simple duty, and laid down his life on the altar of his suffering country. He was a good officer. While he showed zeal and devotion in our righteous cause, he never failed in acting with kindness and generosity to the humblest of privates. This day Billie's grave will have soldier's tears to remind us what we have lost in his generosity and the soldier he was. The wound he received, which caused his death, occurred when he was leading his men forward in the successful repulses of the enemy at Petersburg in last March. He died in the hospital, not long after he received his wound. I understand the sadness felt upon your parents and sisters, and their wish to be with him again. His wish was to have his body near his Carolina home during this time of his life. Recently, his remains were [sic] unearthed on the banks of the majestic Roanoke and placed where he wanted to have as his place of rest. The many sorrowing friends around his grave testified the effection and high esteem felt for him. His death was a loss to this community, which he lived, and especially to his relatives. The war may pass away, but the tears and sorrows it has made will remain with us, for many days and years to come." [422]

---

421 The Tri-Weekly Journal, Camden, South Carolina, January 6, 1865.
422 The Tri-Weekly Journal, Camden, South Carolina, January 18, 1865.

"Forty-eight hours in a tree top occurred near the Chesnut plantation, near Camden. The plantation was three miles from Camden on the Wateree. Intelligence had reached me, D.D. Hocott, on Wednesday last that the river was rapidly rising. I took a lantern, in company with a strong manservant, and pushed off to rescue any stock that may be trapped in the river. While engaged in capturing three fine hogs, the head dam broke on the plantation and let loose a flood that swept everything way before it. This burst spread to two miles wide from bank to bank. In attempting to get out of the bateau (a flat-bottomed boat), got washed away by the current against a tree, capsized, and with the pigs that drowned. The boat was caught by the tree in midship, and we managed to get on the bottom, where we stood three feet in water. Our boat anchor began to give way, but there was another tree ten feet away distantly beyond the reach from the boat, and crawling as far as we could, and then placing the end of the boat pole in a fork of the tree, holding the other end. My companion, in distress, made his escape, and held the pole for me. It was in a cotton tree, seventy inches at the root, and about forty feet high. We had scarcely perched ourselves in its boughs before the tree, and the boat was swept away. Here we were up this slender tree, with angry torrent twenty-five deep sweeping five feet below us, and the river more than a mile on either side. From this time, Wednesday twelve o'clock, until Friday two o'clock, we clung for life to these frails but faithful limbs. The river reached its best on Wednesday evening at five o'clock, and its roar and width prevented our cries from being heard until the next day. All the first day and night, and all the second day and night, we shouted for help, and we began to give up hope. In my exertion to save the boat, I had thrown off my coat, and lost it, and the only way we kept ourselves from freezing to death was by violently and constantly kicking each other, kicking the tree. Thursday night the boy slept soundly, and it was with difficulty I supported him, and cheered him from giving up entirely. We ate no food and drank no water and felt like doing either. However, we did moisten our lips to keep see who could yell the loudest. The waves surged about us, but we were fearful the tree would wash away. The waves seemed to grow in the track toward us. Though almost my entire stock of mules, beef cattle, hogs, fodder, etc. was swept away, I scarcely thought of them in my peril. Several gentlemen made attempts to rescue us, but to no success due to the swift current and heavy for a boat to survive. A bateau with two Negroes came within a hundred yards of the tree, when it was swamped, they barely escaped clinging for their lives. About two o'clock on Friday, Mr. Rush (John Jason Rush), the overseer on Colonel Chesnut's plantation, with two colored men, reached the tree in a boat. He, with one of them, took our places on the tree, and we safely reached the shore, stiff, and bruised from the fearful exposure. The boat returned and brought the other parties to shore. My colored boy is confined to a bed, but he is doing well. I am sore in the limbs and hoarse but suffered in no other way. I am nothing but gratitude for the Providence for rescuing us from a watery grave. I will always remember January 11, 1865. The plantation is badly washed, in some places, heavily deposited with sand. Every dam was carried away. The river rose two to three feet higher than any mark within the memory of the oldest citizens, I hereby give thanks to those who nobly periled their lives to save ours, and especially to Mr. Rush. My loss contained eleven head of horses and mules, two jennets, about twenty head of cattle, seventy-five head of hogs, forty-five sheep, a large amount of fodder, peas, etc." [423]

---

[423] The Tri-Weekly Journal, Camden, South Carolina, Wednesday, January 18, 1865. Note: two papers with the same date, make sure you get Wednesday and not Friday.

During this time the commissioner of roads, R. B. Johnson, came with guidelines for the Enrolling Officers for each incorporated city, town, and village. Their responsibility would be to furnish the sheriff within thirty days the names of the slaves to be used for road work in the area or where road work may be needed. The slaves must be between the ages of eighteen and fifty years old. The assessment of slaves would be as follows:

The Owner of 2 Road Hands will furnish 1 for two months.
The Owner of 3 Road Hands will furnish 1 for two months.
The Owner of 4 Road Hands will furnish 1 for four months.
The Owner of 5 Road Hands will furnish 1 for four months.
The Owner of 6 Road Hands will furnish 1 for six months.
The Owner of 7 Road Hands will furnish 1 for six months.
The Owner of 8 Road Hands will furnish 1 for eight months.
The Owner of 9 Road Hands will furnish 1 for eight months
The Owner of 10 Road Hands will furnish 1 for twelve months.

In like manner with fractions above ten. If it is desired, several owners having fractions above or below ten, may unite and furnish one slave for twelve months. Delivery will begin on February 8 at points named by the district. If the slave does not show up, the sheriff will come for that slave. It is to the owner's interest to comply with this act, and make sure the slave doing the labor can do the actual job asked of the slave, if not the slave will be returned and another gotten.[424]

On February 3rd, the Bank of Camden honored the late Jessie S. Nettles. The following was said:

> "Jessie S. Nettles, late discount clerk of this bank, has been in office for nearly thirty years, doing all of this time, not only have his duties been fully accurately and satisfactory discharged, but in all his intercourse with the members of this Board, he has ever impressed them deeply by the sterling worth of his character, as well as by his general and amiable disposition. Time had silvered his hair and bowed his form but had failed to impair his faculties or break his spirits. He died, as he had lived, cheerfully, and bowed to the decree which called him hence with a beautiful and touching faith. A page in the minutes of this bank will be blank in honor of him."
> This was given by the president of the bank, William M. Shannon.[425]

The 7th Battalion, per a letter received by a neighbor of Captain William Clyburn, reported that the letter came from Fort Anderson. In this letter, the 7th is safe and is about to go near Fort Fisher, until orders came for the unit not to go. The grounds for such a remark came as Hagood's Brigade arrived at Fort Fisher, prior to the capture of that stronghold. Providence came to the battalion as Fort Anderson was only three miles from Fort Fisher. The portion of the brigade at Fort Fisher were taken as prisoners, but his battalion was not involved. Captain Clyburn stated, "They are far from being safe, the enemy's boats are moving up the river, and the point

---
[424] Ibid.
[425] The Tri-Weekly Journal, Camden, South Carolina, February 3, 1865.

where they are stationed is weak at best. The Confederacy can boast of no truer, nobler, chivalric sons, than those that compose the 7th South Carolina Battalion. Kershaw District can be proud of the four companies which hail from their district, and each being led by officers having the interest of this country at heart. They know no fear where the cause of independence is at stake."[426]

On February 3, the Camden paper told of General Hood arriving at noon the day before. He was met with a large assemblage of people, and made a speech that was patriotic in nature. The speech was eloquent and impressive, combining the cannon shot and sabre stroke, and elicited the hearty applause of the crowd. The battle-scarred hero was hopeful and confident.[427]

The Bank of Camden paid homage to Jessie S. Nettles, who being a late discount clerk of this bank, who had been in this office for thirty years, and who had died in the war. His dedication to his duties and his faithfulness the board will always be remembered.[428]

Inset from C. C. Haile Map of 1894

Toward the end of February, Sherman and his troops, came into the upper part of Kershaw District. Sherman's forces left Columbia toward this direction about February 20. The left wing and cavalry moved toward Winnsborough, which General Slocam reached on the twenty-first. General Slocam's damage included the railroad to be destroyed, Black Stocks Depot, and then went to Rocky Mount on the twenty-second on the Catawba River. The twentieth corps reached Rocky Mount on the twenty-second and began to lay a pontoon

---

[426] The Tri-Weekly Journal, Camden, South Carolina, January 20, 1865.
[427] The Tri-Weekly Journal, Camden, South Carolina, February 3, 1865.
[428] Ibid.

bridge and crossed on the twenty-third. Kilpatrick's Cavalry crossed over on the twenty-third in a terrible rainstorm during the night and made way to Lancaster and onward in the direction of Charlotte, North Carolina. The heavy rains made the roads hard to maneuver and passable, and the river swelled to a flooding state. Finally, about the twenty-sixth, the Twentieth Corps reached Hanging Rock, and waited there until the Fourteen Corps to arrive. Due to the heavy rains swelling the river, the pontoon bridge broke. General Davis finally got the bridge repaired to get his command across. He succeeded, and the left wing went on toward Cheraw direction.

The Right Wing broke up the railroad to Winnsborough and turned their sights in the direction of Peay's Ferry. They crossed before the rains set in. The Seventh Corps moved straight on Cheraw Crossing at Young's Bridge. The Fifteenth Corps went by Tiller's bridge and the Kelly Bridge. The latter group sent attachments into Camden to burn the bridge over the Wateree, along with the railroad depot, stores, etc. A bad road was encountered at Lynches Creek, which delayed the Right Wing about the same amount of time as the Left Wing because of the delayed crossing the Catawba.

The following is a timeline: Second Division

February 20 - Marched on Camden Road eleven miles, then took road to Muddy Springs, camping for the night.

February 21 - Marched twenty-two miles and camped on Dutchman's Creek.

February 22 - Crossed the Wateree River on pontoons, marched two miles, and camped at Singleton's Creek.

February 23 - Marched at one p.m., passing through Liberty Hill, marched on the Camden Road six miles, marched on a settlement road across to Lancaster and Camden Road, camped at Red Hill Post Office, near Flat Rock.

February 24 - Marched in the direction of Camden, passing the town of Camden on the right, and camped at Marengo Mills, six miles from Camden.

February 25 - Marched to Sandy Grove Church and camped.

February 26 - Marched on Darlington Road, reaching Kelly's Bridge about eleven a.m. Found water so high the men had to cross waist deep. Trains could not cross, too high.

February 27 and 28 - Still at Kelly's Bridge. Water dropping slowly.

March 1 - Division moved to Kellytown, Darlington County. Distance six miles.

First Brigade, Second Division Timeline:

February 20 – March 1 - Crossed Lynches Creek on March 1. Went toward Fayetteville, North Carolina.

Third Brigade, Second Division Timeline:

February 22 - Marched eleven miles and crossed Wateree River.

February 23 - Marched ten miles.

February 24 - Marched seventeen miles.

February 25 - Marched eight miles.

February 26 - Marched ten miles.

February 27 - Crossed Lynches Creek.

February 28 – Camped.

March 1 - Moved at 5:30 p.m.; marched six miles and camped at Kellytown.

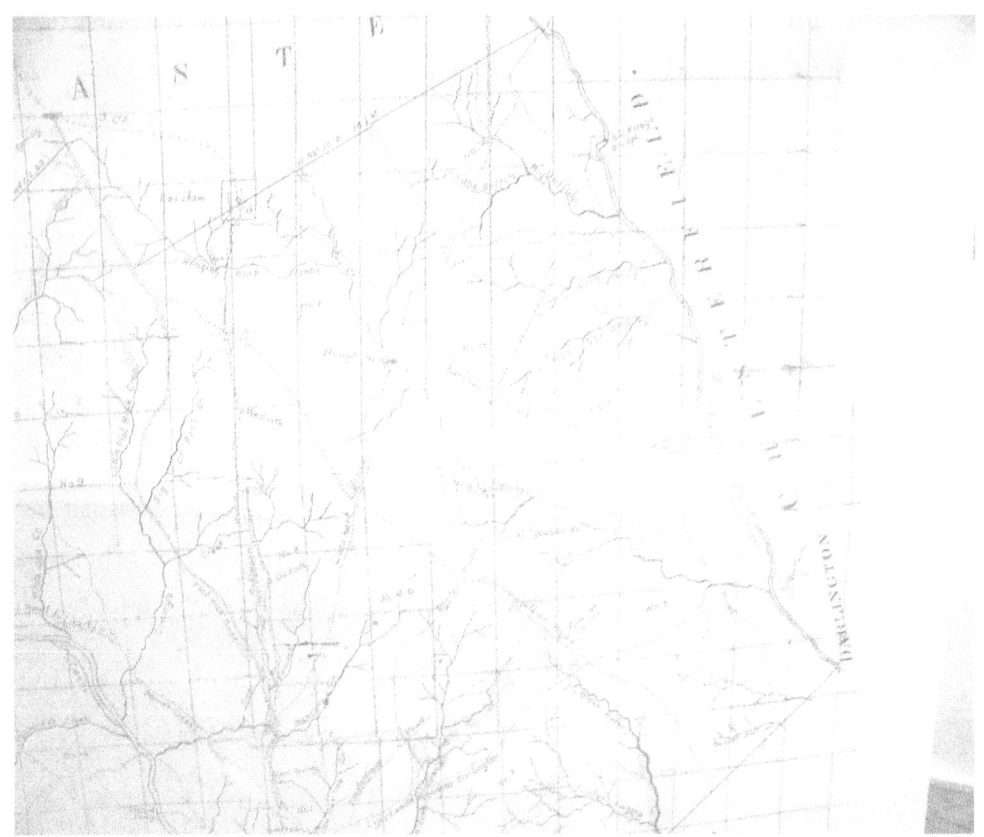

Inset of C.C. Haile Map of 1894

Third Division Timeline:

February 22 - Crossed Wateree River and camped near the same.

February 23 - Marched toward and near Flat Rock.

February 24 - Marched to West's crossroads.

February 25 - Command attacked by Butler, who lost severely.

February 26 - Marched to Kelly's Bridge on Lynches Creek.

February 27 – 28 - Waited for bridge to be built across Lynches Creek.

March 1 - Waited for bridge to be completed at Kelly's Bridge across Lynches Creek.

March 2 - Crossed Lynches Creek over bridge 580 yards long, built by pioneer corps, and marched to Kellytown.

First Brigade, Third Division Timeline:

February 20 - Left Columbia and marched near Poplar Grove Post Office, Peay's Ferry, on Wateree River, and Flat Rock Post Office to within one mile of Kelly's Ferry on Lynches Creek, arriving there February 26.

February 27 and 28 - In Camp.

March 1 - Camp at Kelly's Ferry.

March 2 - Crossed Lynches Creek at Kelly Ferry Bridge in the direction of Big Black Creek.

Second Brigade, Third Division Timeline:

February 20 - Left Columbia, coming toward this direction and crossing Lynches Creek on March 2.

Fourth Division Timeline:

February 20 - Moved to Muddy Creek and there over parts of Camden and Rocky Mount Roads, crossing Dutchman's Creek by way of Poplar Springs, to Peay's Ferry, on the Wateree River.

February 23 - The march continued the Camden Road, by way of Liberty Hill, crossing White Oak Creek and Saunder's (Sander's) Creek, passing to the left of Camden. A portion of the division passed through Camden, traveling upon the Camden and Cheraw Road, by way of the Pine Tree Meeting House, to Tiller's Bridge, on Lynches Creek, now on February 28. This division had skirmishes at Camden and Lynches Creek, and place twenty miles of corduroy.

March 1– Marched from Lynches Creek (Tiller's Ferry) to Goldsboro, North Carolina.

Inset of C.C. Haile Map of 1894

Second Brigade, Fourth Division Timeline:

February 20 - March taken up toward Camden direction.

February 24 - Colonel Adams received orders to take a detachment of his command and proceed to Camden, South Carolina. Camden was entered after a slight skirmish with the enemy without loss. Fourteen Union soldiers were released and the six rebels guarding them captured. Two Depot buildings, an engine house, and a building containing a large amount of commissary stores were destroyed. About 2,000 bales of cotton and a flouring mill, containing a large quantity of grain also destroyed. Upon entering the town, a skirmish happened with one of the enemy killed and eight captured. This detachment rejoined the division six miles northeast of Camden.

February 26 - The brigade reached Lynches Creek. The command was camped on the north bank of the stream.

March 1 - Brigade left Lynches Creek and moved toward Black Creek, South Carolina.

The Right Wing of the Union Army consisted of the following:

	Infantry		Cavalry		Artillery	
	Officers	Men	Officers	Men	Officers	Men
Fifteenth Army Corps -	733	14,076	2	12	14	348
Seventeenth Army Corps -	441	10,675	4	42	5	266
Total	1174	24,751	6	54	19	614

The Left Wing of the Union Army (Army of Georgia) consisted of the following:

	Infantry		Cavalry		Artillery	
	Officers	Men	Officers	Men	Officers	Men
Fourteenth Army Corps	571	12,192	----	----	7 438	348
Twentieth Army Corps	610	12,300	----	----	23 481	266
Total	1181	24,492	----	----	30 919	614
Kilpatrick's Cavalry	----	----	173	4,168	4	91
Aggregate	2355	49,243	179	4,222	53	1624[429]

The headquarters guard provided by the 7th Ohio Sharpshooters under Lieutenant James Cox.

The engineers and mechanics were the 1st Michigan, under Colonel John B. Yates and the 1st Missouri (five companies), under Lieutenant Colonel William Tweeddale.

Artillery was under Brevet Major General William F. Barry

The Right Wing was under Major General Oliver O. Howard (Army of the Tennessee).

---

[429] The War of the Rebellion: A Compilation of the Official Records of the Union and Confederate Armies, Series 1- Volume XLVII- In Three Parts, Part 1- Reports; Washington: Government Printing Office, 1895, page 43.

Escorted by the 15th Illinois Cavalry, Company K, under Captain William Duncan, and the 4th Company Ohio Cavalry, under Captain John L. King.

The Pontoon Train Guard was under the 14th Wisconsin Company E, under Captain William I. Henry.[430]

The Fifteenth Army Corps was under Major General John A. Logan.

The first division was under Brevet Major General Charles A. Woods.

The first brigade in this division was under the leadership of Colonel Milo Smith, and Brevet Brigadier General William B. Woods. The following units were under this brigade: 12th Indiana under Colonel Reuben Williams; 26th Iowa under Major John Lubbers; 27th Missouri under Colonel Thomas Curly; 31st and 32nd Missouri (six companies) under Colonel Abraham J. Seay; and the 76th Ohio under Lieutenant Colonel Edward Briggs.

The Second Brigade in this division had Brigadier General Charles C. Walcutt leading, and Colonel Robert F. Catterson. The following units under this brigade: 26th Illinois, under Lieutenant Colonel Ira J. Bloomfield, 40th Illinois, under Lieutenant Colonel Hiram W. Wall; 103rd Illinois, under Lieutenant Colonel George W. Wright; 97th Indiana, under Captain George Elliott and Lieutenant Colonel Aden G. Cavins; 100th Indiana, under Major Ruel M. Johnson and Captain John W. Headington; 6th Iowa, under Lieutenant Colonel William H. Clune; and the 46th Ohio, under Lieutenant Edward N. Upton.[431]

Timeline of the following Companies of the Union:

Fifteenth Army Corp – February - Captured from enemy six commissioned officers and 139 enlisted men.

March - Marched from Big Lynches Creek to Cheraw, etc.[432]

First Brigade, First Division –

February 20 - Moving toward and reached Lynches Creek on the twenty-sixth. Encamped till February 26 at Lynches Creek. Distance marched during February was 225 miles. Lost eight enlisted men, who were supposed to be captured.

March 1 - left Lynches Creek toward New Market.[433]

Second Division –

February 20 - Marched on Camden road eleven miles, took road to Muddy Springs, where they camped for the night.

February 21 - Marched twenty-two miles and camped on Dutchman's Creek.

February 22 - Crossed the Wateree at Peay's Ferry on pontoons; made two miles and camped on Singleton's Creek.

---

[430] Ibid, p. 46
[431] Ibid, p. 46.
[432] Ibid, p. 77.
[433] Ibid, p. 77

February 23 - Marched at one p.m., passing Liberty Hill and marched on Camden Road six miles; then on settlement road across to Lancaster and Camden; camped at Red Hill Post Office, near Flat Rock.

February 24 - Marched in the direction of Camden; passed by, leaving the town on the right, and camped at Marengo Mills, six miles from Camden.

February 25 - Marched to Sandy Grove Church and camped.

February 26 - Marched on Darlington Road, reaching Kelly's Bridge at eleven a.m. The water was high and rising, extending a mile in width. Two brigades crossed by wading waist deep. It was impossible for the train to cross. February 27-28 - Division still at Kelly's Bridge; water falling slowly.

March 1 - Division marched from Kelly's Bridge to Kellytown, six miles, and onward to Cheraw on March 4.[434]

First Brigade, Second Division -

March 1 - Marched with the division, crossing Lynches Creek and continued up to Fayetteville, North Carolina.

Third Brigade –

February 22 - Crossed Wateree River after marching eleven miles.

February 23 - Marched ten miles.

February 24 - Marched seventeen miles.

February 25 - Marched eight miles. Command was attacked by Butler's Cavalry Command. The enemy was driven off having list severely.

February 26 - Marched ten miles.

February 27 - Crossed Lynches Creek.

February 28 - Remained in camp.

March 1 - Left at 5:30 p.m. and marched six miles to Kellytown.[435]

Third Division –

February 22 - Crossed Wateree River and Camped.

February 23 - Marched near Flat Rock.

February 24 - Marched to West Crossroads.

February 26 - Marched to Kelly's Bridge on Lynches Creek.

February 27-28 - In camp, waiting for the bridge to be constructed over Lynches Creek, water too high.

---

[434] Ibid, p. 79.
[435] Ibid, p. 82.

March 1 - In camp at Kelly's Ferry, waiting for bridge to be built across Lynches Creek.

March 2 - Crossed Lynches Creek on bridge across Lynches Creek 580 feet long, which was constructed by the pioneer corps, and marched to Kellytown.[436]

First Brigade, Third Division –

February 20 - Left Columbia, and marched to, by way of Poplar Grove Post Office, Peay's Ferry, on Wateree River, and Flat Rock Post Office, to within one mile of Kelly's Ferry, on Big Lynches Creek on February 26.

February 27-28 - In camp. Marched during the month, 230 miles.

March 1 - In camp at Kelly's Ferry, South Carolina.

March 2 - Crossed Lynches Creek at Kelly's Ferry Bridge (went onward toward Cheraw).[437]

Second Brigade, Third Division –

February 20 - Left Columbia and headed this way. By March 2 was crossing Lynches Creek.[438]

Fourth Division –

February 20 - Moved to Muddy Springs, and over portions of Camden and Rocky Mount Roads, crossing Dutchman's Creek, by way of Poplar Springs, to Peay's Ferry on the Wateree River.

February 23 - Marched from this point on Camden Road, by way of Liberty Hill, across White Oak and Saunder's (Sander's) Creeks, to the left of Camden, a portion of the division passing through Camden; then upon Camden and Cheraw Roads, by way of Pine Tree Meeting House, to Tiller's Bridge, on Lynches Creek, where the command was now (February 28) in position and on bivouac. The division had slight skirmishing at Camden and Lynches Creek, and placed twenty miles of corduroy.

March 1- This division marched from Lynches Creek to Goldsborough, North Carolina.[439]

Second Brigade, Fourth Division –

February 20 - March taken up from Columbia, South Carolina.

February 24 - Colonel Adams ordered to take a detachment of his command and proceed to Camden, South Carolina. The place was entered after a light skirmish with the enemy without loss. Fourteen soldiers, who were prisoners, were released, and six rebels, who were guarding them captured: Two Depot buildings, an engine house, and a building containing a large amount of commissary stores were destroyed. About 2,000 bales of cotton and a flouring mill containing a large amount of grain were destroyed. In the skirmish on entering the town, one of the enemy was killed, and eight captured. This detachment rejoined this command six miles northeast of the town.

February 26 - The brigade reached Lynches Creek, and in camp on the north bank of the stream.

---

[436] Ibid, p. 84
[437] Ibid, p. 85.
[438] Ibid, p. 86.
[439] Ibid, p. 87.

March 1 - The brigade broke camp and left Lynches Creek. Heading toward Cheraw and entering on March 4.[440]

First Division –

February 20 - Moved at seven a.m. on Winnsborough Road and camped.

February 21 - Moved in and camped near the town of Winnsborough.

February 22 - Destroyed two miles of railroad tracks; passed through the town and camped at Poplar Springs, a distance of fifteen miles.

February 23 - Moved at eight a.m. on Peay's Ferry road; crossed Wateree River, and camped at Liberty Hill, a distance of fifteen miles.

February 24 - Moved at six a.m. on Camden Road; passed through Liberty Hill and camped on Patterson's Plantation, a distance of sixteen miles.

February 25 - Moved at seven a.m. on Georgetown and Camden Road and camped a distance of fifteen miles. February 26 - Moved at seven a.m.; crossed Little Lynches Creek and camped on Big Lynches Creek a distance of twelve miles.

February 27 - Moved at seven a.m. on Cheraw Road; crossed Big Lynches Creek and camped on the other side a distance of two miles. Went toward Cheraw the next day.[441]

Second Brigade, First Division –

February 22 - Marched fifteen miles passing through Winnsborough to Poplar Springs.

February 23 - Marched eight miles.

February 24 - Marched fifteen miles, passing through Liberty Hill.

February 25 - Marched fourteen miles to Little Lynches Creek, Hough's Ferry.

February 26 - Marched to Big Lynches Creek, ten miles and a half away.

February 27 - Moved across creek two miles, camped and waiting for trains.

February 28 – March 3 - Moved twenty-nine miles and camped at Cheraw.[442]

Third Division –

February 20 - Marched near Winnsborough.

February 21 - Marched to Simpson's Station, fifteen miles.

February 22 - Marched to Poplar Springs, fifteen miles.

February 23 - Marched to and crossed Wateree, seven miles.

February 24 - Marched to Russell's Place, twelve miles.

February 25 - Marched to Copeland, twelve miles.

February 26 - Marched to Little Lynches Creek, eight miles.

---

[440] Ibid, p. 87-88.
[441] Ibid, p. 92.
[442] Ibid, p. 96.

February 27 - Marched to Big Lynches Creek, thirteen miles.

February 28 - Marched in direction of Cheraw, eighteen miles; total 268 and 1/2 miles. Twenty-one railroads destroyed, 14,485 yards of corduroyed built, 263 bridges built, 54,560 yards of side roads built, and 650 yards clearing roads obstructed by enemy.[443]

Second Brigade, Third Division –

February 21 - Marched toward Winnsborough, destroying two miles of railroad.

February 22 - Marched to Poplar Springs, sixteen miles; destroyed two miles of railroad.

February 23 - Marched six miles; crossed Wateree River.

February 24 - Marched twelve miles, Liberty Hill Post Office.

February 25 - Marched eleven miles.

February 26 - Marched eight miles; bridged Little Lynches Creek.

February 27 - Marched twelve miles to Big Lynches Creek.

February 28 - Marched sixteen miles on Cheraw Road; crossed Big Lynch's and Black's Creek; built fortifications within thirteen miles of Cheraw.[444]

Third Brigade, Fourth Division –

February 18 - Moved toward Winnsborough, destroying the Charlotte Railroad for two miles.

February 20-28 - On March, by way of Simpson's Station, Winnsborough, Poplar Springs Post Office, Liberty Hill, Patterson's Crossroads; three miles of railroad on the way. Distance marched 261 miles, destroying ten miles of railroad.

March 1 - Thirteen miles from Cheraw.[445]

First Brigade, First Division –

February 20-21 - Marched on Winnsborough Road and passed the town of Winnsborough on the twenty-first.

February 23 - Got within three miles of Catawba River. The rest of the day was spent reaching the opposite bank of the river.

February 28 – Marching forward toward Hanging Rock today from leaving the banks of the river on the twenty-third.

March 1 - Brigade left Catawba river, moved fifteen miles, mostly over corduroy, with the division and corps. March 2 - Passed Hanging Rock; had pontoon train in charge; roads and weather bad.

March 3 - Moved at six a.m.; Lynches Creek was crossed at four p.m.; enemy's cavalry made an unsuccessful attempt to capture pontoon train; camped at twelve p.m.; marched twenty miles.[446]

---

[443] Ibid, pgs. 97-98.
[444] Ibid, pgs. 100-101.
[445] Ibid, p. 104
[446] Ibid, p. 109.

Second Division –

March 1 - Division left camp from Clyburn's House in Lancaster District.[447]

Third Division –

February 23 - Passed through Gladden's Post Office and went into camp near the Wateree. Marched twelve miles.

February 24 – 26 - Division remained in camp on the south side of the Wateree, the rise of the river caused by the late heavy rains having broken the bridge. Many delays and difficulty in repairing the bridge, the division crossed at eleven p.m. at Kingsbury Ferry (Lancaster County) on the twenty-seventh.

February 28 - Camped on the north bank of the river.

March 1 - Marched from the camp at Catawba River twelve miles, camped at Ingraham's Mills near Hanging Rock. Found the roads unfathomable in depth.

March 2 - Crossed Little Lynches Creek, Lick Creek, and Flat Creek. Marched fifteen miles.

March 3 - Passed Lynch's Creek and Mill Creek, marching sixteen miles. Camped at Edgeworth's Mills (Chesterfield County). Lost many men to rebel cavalry during the day. First sign of the enemy since leaving Catawba River.[448]

First Brigade, First Division –

March 1 - Marched from point three miles east of Catawba River, eight a.m., and camped on the Hanging Rock Battleground.

March 2 - Marched at ten a.m. arriving at Lynches Creek to camp for the night. Went on toward the Peedee River.[449]

Twentieth Army Corps –

February 21 - Marched through Winnsborough and camped on Beaver Dam Creek.

February 22 - First and Third Divisions marched to Catawba River at Rocky Mount Post Office; Second Division stayed near Winnsborough and destroyed the railroad.

February 23 - First and Third Divisions crossed Saluda River, camping five miles north from Colonel Ballard's farm; Second Division rejoined the corps.

February 24 - Marched four miles and camped on the Hillard Farm.

February 25 - Stayed in camp.

February 26 - Marched to Hanging Rock Post Office.

February 27 - Crossed Hanging Rock Creek.

February 28 - Marched to Horton's Store.

---
[447] Ibid, p. 112.
[448] Ibid, pgs. 115-116.
[449] Ibid, p. 119.

March 1 - Marched from Clyburn's Store to Brewer's farm a distance of fourteen miles. Roads were miry, weather cloudy, with little rain.

March 2 - Went to Chesterfield Court House.[450]

First Division –

February 23 - Crossed Catawba River at Rocky Mount.

February 27 - Crossed Hanging Rock Creek near Hanging Rock. In the early part of the month, only one-half rations of coffee, sugar, and hard bread were issued to the troops. On the eleventh, the rations were cut to one-quarter. Rainy weather occurred most of the month and the roads were bad.

March 1 - Crossed Lynches Creek and, by March 2, had reached Chesterfield.[451]

First Brigade, First Division –

February 23 - Crossed the Wateree. This command existed on the country, foraging parties of one commissioned officer and fifty men being sent out daily by commanders.

March 1 - Reached a point near Hanging Rock.

March 2 - Reached Chesterfield Court House.[452]

Second Brigade, First Division –

February 23 - Crossed the Catawba.

February 27 - Crossed Hanging Rock Creek.

February 28 - Crossed Little Lynches Creek, near Hickory Head (Lancaster County).

March 1 - Left Hickory Head; marched fifteen miles, crossing Big Lynches Creek.

March 2 - Entered Chesterfield.[453]

Third Brigade, First Division –

February 21 - Troops on rations and camped near Winnsborough, three miles above the town.

February 22 - Marched at ten a.m.; crossed the Wateree Creek and camped at Rocky Mount Post Office around midnight.

February 23 - Marched at seven a.m.; crossing the Wateree River at ten a.m.; camped four miles beyond and had gone five miles.

February 24 - Marched at 7:30 a.m., wet weather and roads heavy. Only traveled three miles and camped at Patterson's plantation.

February 25 - Remained in camp at Patterson's plantation. Still wet weather.

---

[450] Ibid, p. 122.
[451] Ibid, p. 124.
[452] Ibid, p. 126.
[453] Ibid, p. 127.

February 26 - Marched at two p.m. and camped two miles from Hanging Rock Post Office at night fall only marching six miles.

February 27 - Marched at 6:15 a.m., passing the Hanging Rock Post Office and crossing the Hanging Rock Creek before camping on Mobley's plantation at nine p.m. Only went three miles.

February 28 - Remained on Mobley's plantation.

March 1-2 - Brigade marched from Little Lynches Creek, a distance of four to twelve miles beyond Big Lynches Creek. The next day, March 2, reaching the Chesterfield Courthouse.[454]

Second Division –

February 23 - Crossed Catawba at Rocky Mount.

February 24 - Marched four miles.

February 26 - Marched five miles to Hanging Rock Post Office.

February 27 - Marched three miles, crossing Hanging Rock Creek.

February 28 - Marched eight miles, crossing Little Lynches Creek. Camped at Clyburn's Store.

March 1 - Marched from Clyburn's Store beyond Big Lynches Creek, twelve miles. By March 3, had reached the Chesterfield Court House.[455]

First Brigade, Second Division –

February 21 - Ordered to act as provost guard for the town of Winnsborough, until the army went through. On the twenty-second, marched from 3:30 to the Wateree Church to rejoin the division.

February 23 - Marched to the Catawba River and crossed at Rocky Mount Post Office and went into camp. February 24 - Hillard's farms staying until the twenty-sixth.

February 26 - Marched to Hanging Rock Post Office.

February 27 - Crossed the Hanging Rock Creek and camped two miles east.

February 28 - Marched to Clyburn's Store.

March 1 - Moved at twelve p.m. This brigade had 114 wagons to guard, and to render assistance to help it along the way should the need arises. Crossed Lynches Creek at Ferley's Bridge for the night. A distance of a mile and a half east.[456]

---

[454] Ibid, p. 130.
[455] Ibid, p. 133.
[456] Ibid, p. 136.

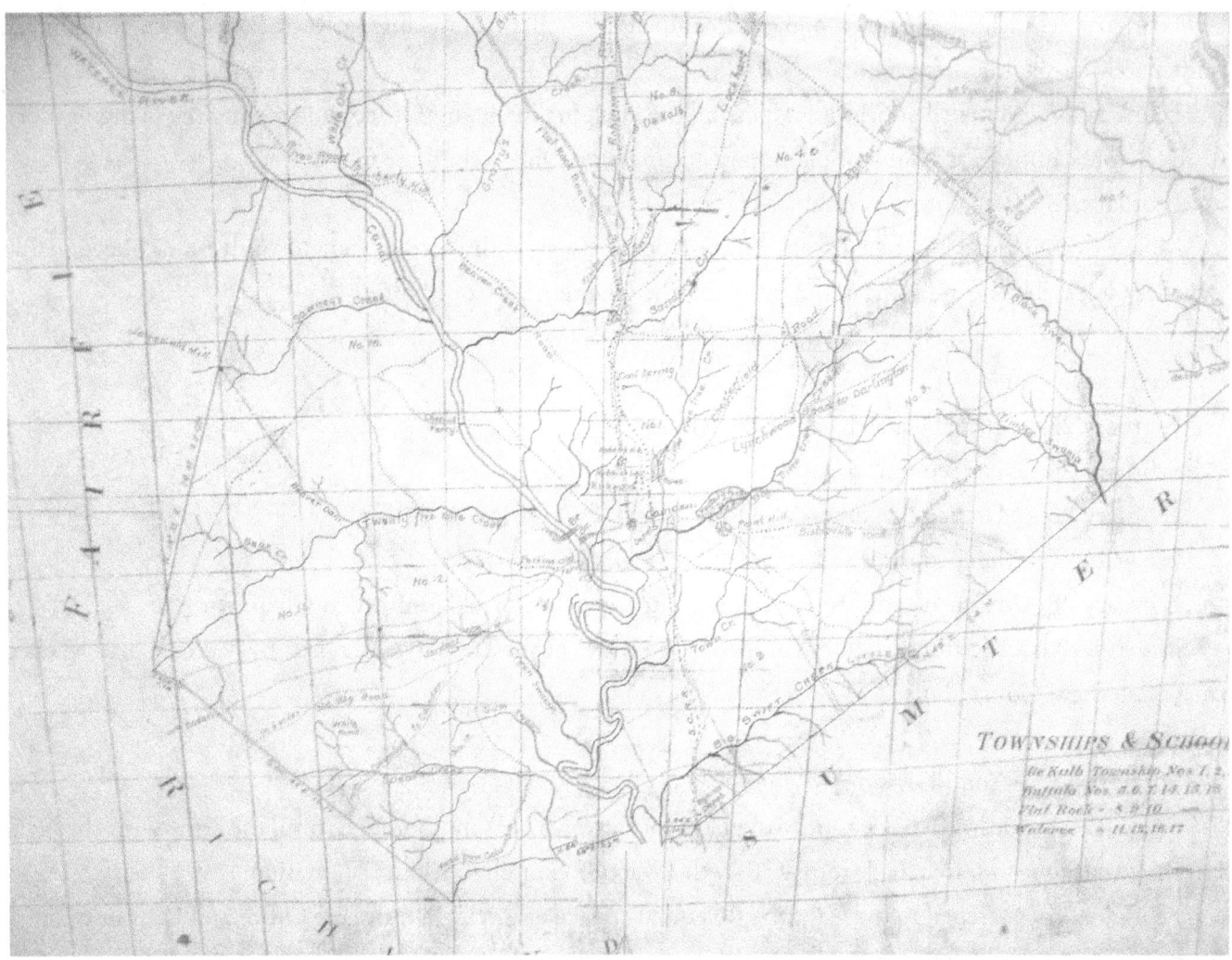

Inset of C.C. Haile Map of 1894

Third Brigade, Third Division –

February 21 - Marched through Winnsborough.

February 23 - Crossed the Wateree River.

February 25 - The division did not move. This brigade corduroyed the road from camp to Russell's Crossroads, a distance of three miles and a half.

February 26 - Marched from Russell's Crossroads to Hanging Rock.

February 27 - Marched on the Chesterfield road northeast.[457]

Third Cavalry Division –

March 1 - Camped seven miles east of Lancaster.

March 2 - Moved across Lynches Creek to Blakeney's Crossroads. Traveled within ten miles of Wadesborough, North Carolina.[458]

---

[457] Ibid, p. 143.
[458] Ibid, p. 146.

First Brigade, Third Cavalry –
February 25 - Reached Lancaster, South Carolina, and stayed the rest of the month.
March 1 - Camped at Taylor's Crossroads in Lancaster District.
March 2 - Went on to Chesterfield. [459]

In the report of Brevet Brigadier General Orlando Poe, Corps of Engineers, U.S. Army, Chief Engineer, the following was told:

> "At Winnsborough, the whole army was concentrated, and the Left Wing assisted in the destruction of the railroad northward. From Winnsborough and White Oak, the Left Wing and the cavalry moved to Rocky Mount, and the Right Wing to Peay's Ferry. A pontoon bridge was thrown over the Catawba River (Wateree River) at each of these points, and with a great deal of trouble, due to the rising water, swift currents, and muddy roads, the army went from over one side to the other side. This crossing begun on February 23 and finished on February 27, after one bridge at Rocky Mount had be carried away. It was 700 feet in length, with about 200 feet of it lost. The balance of the bridge was recovered and rebuilt. By this time, the cavalry had passed through Lancaster, the Twentieth Corps was at Hanging Rock, and the Right Wing was at Tillersville, in the vicinity that crossed Lynches Creek, after almost incredible labor in building bridges and corduroying roads. The remainder of the army crossed at Fenilly's and McManus's Bridges, going to Cheraw."[460]

In the report of Surgeon John Moore, U.S. Army, Medical Director, he described the Wateree area as being high and rolling, with occasional outcroppings of granite formations, a more fertile region and better cultivated than any passed in South Carolina.[461]

In the report by Major General O.O. Howard, the following was stated about his movements in this area: "Monday, February 20, the command commenced northward, General Logan's column made a detour, by way of Robert's Crossroads and Muddy Springs, his head of his column readying Rice Creek. General Blair followed the railroad, destroying it as he went marching fifteen and sixteen miles. The next day, General Blair continued the same work to within five or six miles of Winnsborough, and the Fifteenth Corps camped with two columns, one at Harrison's Crossroads, and the other at Longtown. My headquarters were at Harrison's Crossroads. The next day the Fifteenth Corps moved in two columns to the area known as Peay's Ferry. General Blair continued the destruction of the railroad to Winnsborough, where he joined the work of the Twentieth Corps, and went up to closing the distance to the Poplar Springs Post Office. The work of laying the bridge across the Wateree River commenced at one p.m. Our crossing at that point did not seem to be anticipated. Here we found the country high and rolling and the banks of the river steep. General Logan crossed two of the divisions after the

---
[459] Ibid, p. 147.
[460] Ibid, p. 171.
[461] Ibid, p. 188.

completion of the bridge. Thursday, February 23, the Fifteenth Corps reached Flat Rock with the head of its column. The Seventeenth Corps crossed the river and camped near Liberty Hill with its mounted infantry at Russell Place. My headquarters, with one brigade for guard, took an intermediate position near Patterson's Crossroads. Before General Blair completed his crossing of the Wateree, a heavy rain commenced and continued all the following night and the next day. The soil, which was hard during fair weather, became slippery and muddy, causing great difficulty in climbing the steep hills. The 24th under General Blair continued his march, by way of Russell Place, and upon finding a straight road from Russell Place to Flat Rock, he took that route. However, he came upon quicksand and had to turn back to move further South. His head of his columns were at Flat Rock. General Logan had moved the Fifteenth Corps in three columns, one, by way of McDowell's Mill, to a point between Williams's and West's Crossroads, and the left column, consisting of two divisions, to a point on Saunder's Creek (Sander's Creek). The rain and bad roads had prevented the completion of each order of the march to the point that the troops became scattered. The country, after passing Flat Rock, was, for the most part, sandy, with pine forests, filled with numerous roads and crossroads. The rebel cavalry annoyed us a good bit, capturing our foragers and a few wagons from General John E. Smith's Division. On February 25, the Fifteenth Corps closed near twelve or fifteen miles from Tiller's Bridge. Two regiments of General Corse's division had entered Camden and had destroyed a quantity of cotton and public stores. Afterward, a party of mounted men, under charge of Captain Duncan, by my direction, destroyed the Camden bridge and the depot and a quantity of cotton. The Seventeenth Corps reached Hough's Bridge over the Little Lynch's. The pontoon train, with its guard, closed at the Williams Crossroads. During the day, General Logan had sent forward his mounted infantry with instructions to secure Tiller's Bridge. Upon arrival, they surprised and captured a camp of rebel militia numbering one hundred people. At Tiller's Bridge, General Corse had two brigades wade the creek immediately upon his arrival, and a few wagons succeeded in crossing to the other side. At Kelly's Bridge, General Hazen did much the same thing, sending over a part of his infantry and a few wagons. General Corse had hardly reached the mainland when the foragers and skirmishers were assaulted by the rebel cavalry. The assault was met and pushed back. The rebels suffered a loss of both killed and wounded. Many horses of the enemy were also killed.

"During the night, the water rose two feet. The passing over the bridge became impassable, with only bridging helping any success. I dispatched the same day Captain Duncan, with all available mounted men at my headquarters. When assembled, the instructions to the sixty in the audience were to penetrate as far as Charleston and Florence Railroad, and break the road by burning some of the bridges west of Florence. At Peay's Ferry, news arrived that Charleston had been evacuated. The news was collaborated by prisoners taken at Tillers Bridge. Lieutenant McQueen, the chief of scouts, accompanied Captain Duncan with a cipher message to send to Charleston. Captain Duncan crossed below Kelly's Bridge reaching Mount Elon Post Office. There he was followed by many rebel cavalry, which outnumbered his own forces. Upon the approach of this force, he held his command well and fought them desperately. The commander, Colonel or Brigadier General Aiken, with some of his six or seven of his men, were killed, with fifty or sixty reported wounded. Captain Duncan had two killed, with three or four wounded. One who was wounded severely was Lieutenant McQueen.

"Duncan drove the enemy from the field, but because of the opposition met, turned back and went to headquarters. February 27 saw rain all day. General Blair put his entire corps to work and succeeded in bridging the approaches to the main stream. Some crossed at evening. General Logan had a footbridge constructed from mainland to mainland. The pontoon was put down on the west side. The bad places were filled in with brick, while other points corduroyed under water. The corduroy being pinned down. However, some difficulties remained. No wagons could cross. Thankfully, the water was finally going down. On February 28, the bridging at Tillersville continued. A few wagons crossed and animals with great difficulty. General Hazen had completed a plank bridge and promised to have a good one completed early the next day. On March 1, the water had subsided, and a roadway completed by noon at Tiller's Bridge. At Kelly's Bridge, General Hazen completed his plank bridge at 3:30 p.m., of nearly a half mile. One complication was the quicksand that the trestle settles upon in the building of the bridge. Reconstruction had to take place and be finished so wagons, loaded down with weight making them heavy, could travel. I accompanied two of General Hazen's brigades as far as Kellytown."[462]

The following is a report of Major General John A. Logan. U.S. Army, commander of the Fifteenth Army Corps: "On February 21, the country was found to be barren and hilly, with little forage for man or animal, as we approached Dutchman's Creek with our three divisions. Also, General Woods's division was at Longtown, on the Camden and Winnsborough Road. The next day, we corps moved to the Wateree, the left column, by way of Poplar Springs, to Peay's Ferry, at which place was directed to the river. General Woods was directed to move along the road to Nichol's Ferry, cross, and meet at the most direct route at Peay's Ferry. No signs of the enemy were seen. The pontoon was laid down. General Hazen crossed his command, taking up position on the opposite side. The rest of the corps camped ready to cross in the morning. On February 23, the corps continued to cross the Wateree. Upon reaching Liberty Hill, we broke into two columns. The left wing, consisting of the First and Third Division, moving to Flat Rock Church; the right wing, composed of the Second and Fourth Divisions, to the neighborhood of Red Hill Post Office. The object of the movement was to strike the system of roads leading from Camden to Cheraw, across Lynches Creek, by Tiller's and Kelly's Bridges, and to attain this object the left column was moved on the morning of February 24 to West's Crossroads, the right column making Big Pine Tree Church on the Camden and Cheraw Roads. Detachments from the Second and Fourth Division entered Camden, destroying all public buildings to be found in that place. No enemy was encountered on this detour.

> "The following morning this column moved up with the other divisions into position near Pine Tree Church, with one brigade at McCaskill's Crossroads, making communication complete. While our troops remained at West's Crossroads, the enemy maneuvered on our flanks, and succeeded in picking up a few of our foragers and stragglers, but no serious inconvenience was experienced from their presence. On February 26, the corps marched to Lynches Creek, the Fourth and First Divisions to Tiller's Bridge, and the Second and Third to Kelly's Bridge for preparations to cross. The rains of the previous week had swollen the stream so much, but the

---

462   Ibid, pgs. 200-201.

bridge remained on either side deep enough for a horse to swim and presented an obstacle for our trains to cross. Upon reaching the creek, General Corse pushed his division across, his men wading up to their armpits, holding above their heads their muskets and cartridge boxes. Upon reaching the other side, he skirmished with and drove Butler's division of rebel cavalry. There this division stood to hold and protect the crossing. The same character of stream was found at Kelly's Bridge, as at Tiller's Bridge, having the same obstacles to crossing. On February 27 and 28, the time was consumed in building footbridges. The bottoms were irregular and hard to deal with. Several deep holes were bridged and sunken corduroy put in wherever the water subsided enough to permit work on the bottom. The water had fallen enough to attempt crossing our trains on March 1. In crossing, the hard bread and ammunition was raised five to six inches in the beds of the wagons. The Fourth Division train and a portion of the First Division passed over with little or no damage. Before General Woods found the train inadequate to use for the rest of the wagons could pass, another bridge of great length would have to be built to last until March 2, to cross the rest of the wagons. General Hazen met with even more obstacles at Kelly's Bridge. As the wagons were crossing, the bridge gave way. Rebuilding began again. By the evening, General Woods and all the men had come and lent a hand in getting across."[463]

The following is report from General W. B. Hazen, Major General: "Reached Peay's Ferry on February 22, moved through Liberty Hill on the twenty-third, moved on the twenty-fourth to Marengo Mills, passing the suburbs of Camden, one regiment passing through today. Met with some skirmishing today with one rebel killed and several wounded. On February 25 and 26, moved to Kelly's Bridge over Lynches Creek. Remained till the 28, while the water subsided. Construction of a trestle bridge took place. This bridge contained over ninety trestles and was completed in twenty hours. We then moved on to Black Creek."[464]

Captain C. A. Earnest of the Thirteenth Ohio Volunteer Infantry, reported that on February 23: "Marched at the rear of Third and First Divisions, passing Liberty Hill, and marching on the Camden road six miles, then on a settlement road across to Lancaster and Camden Road on White Oak Creek, five miles from Flat Rock, one mile south of Red Hill Post Office, camping for the night at five p.m., having traveled for twelve miles this day. On February 24, marched at nine a.m., in rear of the Fourth Division on the Camden Road. Passed Saunder's Creek (Sander's Creek), six miles from Camden, turned to the left, crossing the Camden and Lancaster Roads at Cool Springs, leaving Kirkwood on the right, striking the Cheraw and Camden Roads two miles from Camden. We camped at Marengo Mills, six miles from the northeast of Camden at nine p.m. The day was rainy and the roads heavy to travel. Foragers killed one rebel in a skirmish at Cool Springs. On February 25, marched at eight a.m. in advance on the Cheraw Road. Roads good; timber, pine. Camped at Sandy Grove Church at one p.m., having traveled eight miles. The First Brigade went forward to Tiller's and Kelly's Bridges, on Lynches Creek. They secured both points. On February 26, marched to Darlington road at eight a.m., reaching Kelly's Bridge

---

[463] Ibid, pgs. 228-230.
[464] Ibid, p. 273.

at eleven a.m.; eight miles with roads good. The water was found high, appearing a mile in width, and crossing of trains impracticable. The Second and Third Brigades and the battery were pushed across with so much difficulty, a halt became obvious and the idea abandoned. The Second and Third Brigades, under the command of General Oliver, took up a defensive position one mile from the bridge. On February 28, held the position, and water began to recede. Building of a bridge continued. General Oliver pushed on toward Darlington."[465]

The Thirtieth Ohio Infantry under Colonel Theodore Jones followed the same path as the previous one in coming through the county.[466]

Captain William S. Bunn, Acting Inspector General, 1st Brigade, 2nd Division, Army Corps, told that the camp was near Big Pine Tree Creek, and the camp was located on King's Plantation on the Tiller's Ferry Road.[467]

Lieutenant Colonel Louis von Blessingh, Thirty-Seventh Ohio Infantry, told of his people wading with the Fifty-Fourth Ohio Volunteer Infantry on February 26.[468]

Brevet Major General John Smith reported:

"On February 22nd, near Peay's Ferry, all surplus animals were handed over to the chief quartermaster, Colonel G.L. Fort. On February 23, camp was on J.R. Dye's Plantation, near Flat Rock. Near West's Crossroads on February 24, the left flank saw Butler's Cavalry. On February 25, Young, command of Butler's Cavalry of about 600–700 cavalry strong, captured seven wagons, seven enlisted men, and four contrabands, while after corn at plantation two miles in the rear of camp. Some of the enemy came within fifty yards of the picket line, when one of their horses were shot. Upon hearing of this, I ordered on regiment to drive them off and hopefully recover one of our wagons. The Forty-Eight Regiment Indiana Volunteers was selected, along with deployed skirmishers moved out. They drove the enemy back off the Camden Road, and our wagons were driven across the Little Lynches Creek never to be seen again. In this skirmish, two enlisted men [were] killed and one wounded. Two of our men were brutally murdered with our skirmishers looking having surrendered. In retaliation, two of their men in uniform were shot on the spot. On February 28, trains were inspected, and about 3,000 pounds of tobacco and sundries were made at West Crossroads."[469]

Another unit that went through was the Twenty-First Wisconsin Infantry under Brevet Brigadier General Harrison C. Hobart. His company went through on February 28 to March 1, going through and passing Russell Place, Hanging Rock, Clyburn's Store, and crossing Lynches Creek. During this time, Butler's Cavalry was seen scouting their camp. Butler even captured a few of the foragers following the unit. On February 28 about twelve p.m., attacked our picket lines "but I withdrew my troops and they left," he reported.[470]

---
[465] Ibid, p. 281.
[466] Ibid, p. 287.
[467] Ibid, p. 292.
[468] Ibid, p. 307.
[469] Ibid, pgs. 318- 319.
[470] Ibid, p. 452.

Major John H. Widmer, 104th Illinois Infantry, came through the area. He reported: "This infantry unit, on February 23, marched to Rocky Mount Post Office, and camped the twenty-fourth and twenty-fifth. I then ordered Captain William C. Ross, Company B, to carry with him a group of foragers from this unit to join the unit from the 88th and 42nd Indiana Regiments to gather subsistence from the surrounding country. Captain Ross's detail crossed Rocky Mount Creek and passed the Cloud House, moving in the direction of the Stroud Mill. When Captain Ross's detail got close to the mill, the enemy attacked his group, capturing Captain Ross, Privates William Buckley, Company A; John Mellon, Company B; C.G. Phillips, Company D; C. Brook, Company F; James C. Carns and John H. Misner, Company G; William Lakin, Company H; and M.B. Bushnell, Company K. The next day, February 27, I was ordered by General Hobart to take a detail to Stroud's Mill to forage the area. This detail sent out was under Captain White, with orders to be back by four p.m. At the point, the one hundred members of my troop, got close to crossing the Rocky Mount Creek bridge and moving up near the Cloud's, at the junction of the road to Stroud's Mill and the Lancaster road, a skirmish occurred. Then we moved to the mill and then to the creek, but found the creek swollen and impassable. We went back to camp at five p.m. On March 1, camped at Hanging Rock, and crossed Little Lynches Creek on March 2, camping at Wharton's Tavern.[471] Ninety-Fourth Ohio Infantry, under Major William H. Snider, also came through. This group encounter one skirmish with the rebel cavalry during February late.[472] The Seventy-Ninth Pennsylvania Infantry also skirmished with Rebels near Rocky Mount coming through this period."[473]

The journal of the Second Division Fourteenth Army Corps was as follows:

February 23 - Division moved at six a.m. First Brigade in charge of corps trains at railroad near White Oak Station. Camped at Rocky Mount after traveling ten miles. Trains came into the camp at two a.m. Captain Wilde and Lieutenant Floyd captured. The order of march was Third Brigade, battery, First Brigade, and Second Brigade.

February 24 - Division moved at 10:30 a.m. in the rear of the Twentieth Corps Train. Roads were muddy due to the constant rain. Crossed the Catawba River with Wilde and Lieutenant Floyd. February 27 saw six regiments of our division alongside that of the thirteenth Michigan make up a road to an old one in the afternoon.

March 1 - Camped two miles east of Little Lynches Creek, passing Hanging Rock Creek near Ingraham's Plantation.[474]

During this time of the Yankees in the Flat Rock area, Sherman spent three nights and three days in the home of my great-grandfather Kirkland (Richard Kirkland's father and the land he grew up on) on his famous march to the sea. At that time, my grandfather, James Allen Kirkland, hid in the woods, and was supplied food

---

[471] Ibid, pgs. 455-456.
[472] Ibid, p. 462.
[473] Ibid, p. 480.
[474] Ibid, p. 491.

by the slaves who could be trusted, the rest went off with the Union Army. James Allen Kirkland did not go to war.[475]

In a letter in Confederate dispatches from a Headquarters of the Cavalry Division, on a road from White Oak to Rocky Mount, February 26, 1865, at six a.m., the following was sent:

"We wrote you yesterday by a scouting party from the Eighth Confederate that the enemy had all crossed Peay's Ferry and Camden and tried to cross and sent our scouts night before last to ascertain the condition of things, then they found every boat destroyed, and no means of crossing the river. Wateree Creek was past fording, and we moved up it and got upon this road, and are moving this morning to Landsford, and will cross the Catawba first chance. Our men ran out of rations yesterday, and every mill on this side has been burned by the enemy; consequently, we move as rapidly as possible until we get rations and will overtake you as soon as possible. If we had been done a day sooner, could have gotten one hundred stragglers. It would be of great service to people to have a force in the rear, all the while to prevent these stragglers committing so many depredations. If we can cross at Langsford will do so, aim to reach that vicinity tonight, and would be glad to receive orders as to what to do there. Unless ordered, shall move up the command, unless I can see an opportunity of accomplishing something in the rear.

"The enemy have large droves of cattle and very large wagon trains, all guarded by infantry. Sometimes large guards and at others small. Negroes report they hung eighteen Confederates soldiers in retaliation for killing theirs, but I can't find out certainty. They say it was done between the Wateree Meeting house and Rocky Mount. I have sent a scout down this side of the creek to learn certainty. They burned a great many houses through the country, robbed everyone, have caused Negroes to take everything they wanted out of the houses, and defied the owners to molest them. We yesterday saw a Mrs. Mobley (whom was living in a Negro cabin, and her Negroes in possession of her band, her husband is in the Second South Carolina Cavalry), an intelligent lady, clothing, bedding, bacon, etc. I sent a detail and had it all gathered up and returned and her moved to another house. Such is the case wherever they go. A small party could accomplish much for the citizens in regulating the Negroes. I am more than willing to bring up the rear if I can co-arrange it as to feed the men and hope not to be bothered by high water again. It has rained incessantly, and every creek is overflowed. The Yankees cleaned out every horse, mule, and cow in their line. Their infantry treated citizens much worse than cavalry. All express the greatest horror at the idea of falling into the hands of Wheeler's cavalry. Very respectfully,
G. G. Dibrell, "Colonel"
From the Headquarters of Butler's Cavalry Division, February 27, 1865, 12:30 a.m.

---

[475] Descendants of Richard Kirkland's Brother, James Allen Kirkland, by Mrs. Paul Sanders, found in the Kirkland family folder, Camden Archives and Museum, Camden, S.C.

The following dispatch was sent:

"Lieutenant General Hardee: I encountered the Fifteenth Army Corps, General Logan commanding, at Tiller's Bridge this morning, engaged them, and captured some prisoners. Their foragers have extended from the river as far as Kellytown, where I am now encamped. On the twenty-fourth, the Fifteenth Corps, leading the enemy's advance, moved from Flat Rock, in the Kershaw District, and encamped near Porter's Bridge, on Little Lynches Creek. The Seventeenth Corp was then moving from the Catawba River about Liberty Hill toward Flat Rock. The Fourteenth and Twentieth Corps at that date were in the rear of the other two corps. The general movement of Sherman's forces at that time were understood to be upon Camden, which, I presume, was occupied on the twenty-third and twenty-fourth. The Fifteenth Corps, which has been encamped on the south side of Lynches Creek for two days, seems to have been halted to await the arrival of the other three corps. Their next movement will probably be developed tomorrow, whether on Cheraw, or toward Florence, I have not been able to form any definite conclusion. I think that if our troops were concentrated now, and thrown rapidly upon the Fifteenth Corps, very serious damage may be inflicted. If the enemy turn down Lynches Creek, I will endeavor to cross over into Sumter District, and get in front of them. I should be glad to have all the available mounted men sent to hold the bridges on Lynches Creek, and the country between that stream and the Peedee River, so that I may be able to effect the withdrawal of my command from Sumter or Williamsburg District. I have not been in communication with General Hampton or General Beauregard since the twenty-first. After leaving Winnsborough, I was ordered to attempt to reach the rear of the enemy, who was then moving on to Chester, the Fifteenth and Seventeenth Corps on the east side of the railroad constituting this right wing, and the Fourteenth and Twentieth, his left wing, on the west side. The enemy changed direction on the twenty-first toward the Catawba River and Camden. I have been on his left flank ever since. Prisoners taken on the twenty-third report Sherman's army to have only five days' ration, and were moving toward Wilmington or Georgetown. He has been foraging very extensively along his line of march, no house within reach of his main column has been passed by, and all supplies have been taken from the inhabitants, by foraging parties of infantry mounted on captured horses."
Respectively,
M. C. Butler,
Major- General.

On March 10, 1865, the issue of the newspaper, *The Journal and Confederate,* in Camden, began to publish. On the front page, the following was written in bold letters: **The Occupation of the Enemy in Camden.** In that article, the following was said: "The storm has at length burst upon us; the anticipated blow has fallen, and Camden has been made to undergo, in her turn, all the horrors of a Yankee invasion. The raid, though expected, was so sudden, and its duration so brief that we feel stumped, as it were, and hardly able to realize that a Yankee force has been in our midst, plundering and destroying, as is their want, although the blackened and smothering ruins around us painfully attest the fact. God grant that it may be long with such scenes of horror are again reenacted in our peaceful town.

"Most of our neighbors having sought refuge in the neighboring swamps, from which they are only now venturing to return, and small bodies of Yankees still reported hovering at no great distance from the town, render it somewhat unsafe to stir abroad, as we have not been able to, up to this date of this writing, gather full particulars of this invasion and capture of Camden.

"The enemy made their first appearance in our midst on Thursday evening the nineteenth, having crossed the Wateree at Peay's Ferry and Jones Ferry, about twenty miles above Camden. They were in small number, some thirteen, and a formed a line. Major John Whitaker's residents, where the militia, under the command of Colonel Jones, confronted them, but after a few shots were exchanged, the enemy withdrew, wounding, and capturing Mr. R.C. Drakeford of Flat Rock. They returned on the following day (Friday) and reached Camden at two p.m., entering the town from the north, with a force of two detachments of cavalry and infantry, numbering in all, two hundred and fifty men. A portion of the cavalry and the bulk of the infantry proceeded directly down main street, into the heart of the town. The remainder stopped to plunder along the way. All the houses on the road were entered and pillaged, according to the caprice of the robbers. Soon after the main body reached Jungbluth's hotel, the orders from headquarters began by destroying the government stores and public stores. The first building fired was the passenger depot, next the freight depot at the railroad; then the Cornwallis house; and the building occupied as a commissary store house and office, located on the corner of DeKalb and main streets, were next fired. From the fire on the commissary house, the flames went to the other adjoining buildings, and all the houses fronting main street on that square were destroyed. They burnt Mr. George Douglas's store, the cotton sheds in the rear of Mr. Gerald's and Mr. Bell's stores, and the bridge over the Wateree. The Masonic Hall, the three-story brick dwelling, adjoining, occupied the enrolling office, of Captain Colclough and the residence of Mrs. S. Oppenheim, McKain's drug store, and the three wooden buildings to the south, were also burned, but some feel that the Yankees was not the culprit in that burning. All the stores were opened and pillaged. The Yankees took what they wanted and threw the balance of the goods in the street. Witnesses say the Negroes took these goods off, being encouraged by the Yankees. The destruction of property was very heavy, with years of labor required to rebuild. The devastation is so complete and heart rendering to contemplate that such an act would be done to their town. After the cotton, government stores, etc. had been burned, most of the Yankees dispersed in small squads on the town to rob private accounts. Nearly every house in Camden and Kirkwood was visited. In fact, we have heard but two that escaped, besides those in the immediate vicinity of Bishop Davis's residence, before which a guard was placed. The conduct of the invaders varied in different locations, according to the dominant instincts of the individuals who composed the different squads. In some rare case, some soldiers behaved well and with courtesy and gentleness, neither plundering nor insulting the inmates, and limiting their demands to a dinner, or a bed. The others and majority of the Yankees ran through the gamet, from disrespect to gross outrage, and from simple petty pilfering to wholesale spoilage and robbery. Many families have been stripped from everything they had in the world, and for them especially we should speak the sympathy, and aid of those who suffered less. In one neighborhood, several barrels of liquor had been buried by the owners and dug up by the Yankees. Drunkenness led to stimulate outrage and intensified the scene with horrors. They seemed to delight in frightening women and children and setting fires to private dwellings. All of this done under the most heartless and cruel circumstances. The loss of property and the pollution from their presence is all we can endure. The quiet now will satisfy us for a while and a long time to come.

"True to their instincts, they sought affiliation with the slaves, and devoted a portion of their time to persuade them to leave their owners. All in the name of being blessed by Yankee freedom. About two hundred and fifty from the town and plantations in the vicinity have been deluded in going off, but the large majority of slaves have remained faithful to their masters. Great praises are due those who stayed, especially those house servants, who stuck by their mistresses, and by their earnest and active efforts, aiding greatly in preventing outrage and saving property.

"Although the force which entered Camden was small, there were large bodies of Yankees in the vicinity. The whole of Sherman's army passed within twenty miles of us. The party who came in on Friday left on Saturday night, but stragglers can still be seen in the vicinity and more in the distance. Whether Sherman is going, we have no means of knowing with any accuracy. Being cut off from the outside world, we feel isolated as to what is going on in the area and out of the area. It's very possible that the Yankees are in Cheraw, but we have no way of knowing that fact and realizing our unwelcomed visitors are truly gone for the present. We have a lot to be thankful for. We have lost much and we have suffered much, but we might have lost and suffered more heavily; and in so glorious a cause who could not suffer gloriously! Let us keep a stout heart, trusting that he who endures all things wisely, will know how to bring the good out of evil, and bestow on us in a glorious future an overflowing compensation for the sad present.

"During this dark cloud, a silver lining has come through. Requiting their exertions to heal the sick, minister to the wounded, and clothe the naked, the woman of Camden has cheered the battle worn soldier, and approached with a gentle but powerful voice. They have such a fixed belief in using a well-regulated mind that a cause so just in itself as ours is just with such potent influences brought to bear in support, cannot, will not, under the rulings of such a Providence, be allowed to fail.

"During the recent occupation in Camden, the ladies proved no exception to the heroic conduct of their sisters in other parts of the Confederacy under like distressing circumstances. Calm, dignified, unawed, they received the intrusion of the dasterling thieves and plunderers, with true women bearing — overpowered, but unconquered; oppressed, but still patriotic, they have seen our barbarous foe depart, without the comfort of one word of sympathy, of aid, or hope for their cause, breathed by a woman's voice.

"Were the men of the Confederacy being as true and devoted to the cause of our country as the women, where would be the absentees without leave, the occupiers of impenetrable bomb proofs? We hope and believe that even considering the universal private sufferings inflicted, that the late invasion will be productive of good; that like the tropical tornado, it will purify the atmosphere that has recently be made unpure. Hopefully, no private injury has been made to the spirit of patriotism but will be a means of working out the great cause of Southern Independence.

"During this invasion, much was taken. The people were asked to return that which were stolen doing the recent thefts. These goods can be returned to the storehouses of Bell and Matheson. Much has been returned and under the watchful eye of Mr. Bell, who will take charge of receiving and delivering the goods. Captain Colclough should be commended for returning stolen property and goods to the rightful owner. Him being the enrolling officer and very intelligent and gentlemanly in his manners. Dr. Young has told that a lot of his books have been returned, except those of great value that fell in the hands of the servants. One of the most interesting aspects is that a pair of scissors was taken. The individual who had these scissors taken had a few choice words. He called the culprit a 'piffering scamp,' and said, if he would return the scissors in person, no questions would be asked, but he would be handsomely done for.

"Mr. Witherspoon has finally got the telegraph lines working as of the printing of March 10. Mr. W.E. Hughes suffered a great loss during the invasion. He lost his grist mill, the Yankees carried off his Negroes, burnt his corn crib, took all his meat, and even his horse and mule so he could not grow anything."[476]

"One interesting occurrence came when the Yankees, moving from Columbia toward Camden, began the seizing of trains cars. On one of these excursions, a group of Yankees came across two officers that were going to be in a duel. One was to be a principal and the other, his second. Those officers were Captain W.D. DePass and Captain W. Courtney, a fighting quartermaster. The Yankees did everything they could to allow these two to finish their affair.[477]

"As the Yankees coming into Camden, under the command of Major Hazen foragers, they skirmished with cavalry just outside of Camden. They eventually pushed them into the Camden. These foragers were supported by the 112 Illinois, under Colonel Adams, of the Corse's Division. While there, they found fifty thousand rations of corn meal, and four thousand bales of cotton, which were destroyed. Captain John H. Devereaux, of Charleston, Post Commissary of Camden, was captured as he was retreating by horse and rode into the Yankee troops. The mayor and city council of the town had an elaborate speech planned for surrender but, because of the swiftness of the enemy, such a speech didn't happen as planned for General Sherman. However, the presence of the foragers made the situation rough. At Lynches Creek, delays occurred because of the swelling creeks, and corduroys would have to be made under General Hazen. One was over three hundred feet. One group crossed at Tiller's Creek, and another at Black Creek had to build a corduroy, as the water was over one hundred yards beyond the bridge. The Seventeenth Army crossed at Young's Bridge. There, two regiments wading through the creeks, and corduroyed the brigade and all for a quarter of mile. Captain Duncan of the Fifteenth Illinois, Fourth Ohio Independent, and fifteen of the Signal Corps had a confrontation with the Seventh Cavalry, near McEnlow. In that skirmish, the Yankees lost the chief scout of General Howser, Lieutenant Quint, and three men. The Confederates lost Acting Brigadier General Aiken and five killed.[478]

"Fires begun March 13 in the early morning hours. Mrs. Lee had a fire at her dwelling about four in the morning. The fire was set by someone in the town and set afire a shed that was attached to the dwelling. That

---

[476] The Journal and Confederate, Camden, South Carolina, March 10, 1865.
[477] Sherman's Grand March: The Campaign in the Carolinas: Interesting Details of the Grand March from Savannah to Fayetteville, Albany Evening Journal, Albany, New York.
[478] Ibid.

dwelling had no real damage, and that structure is known today as the Green Leaf Villa. Down the street at the other end of town, a warehouse owned by Mr. Bonney was set fire, just as the fire at Mrs. Lee was under control. The adjoining building of Russell and Jones caught fire next door of the Bonney warehouse. The contents of books were saved as were the building. However, the contents of Bonney's warehouse, cotton, furniture, and other goods were destroyed. The next door above, being a commissary store, caught fire, but the only damage was the damage to the goods being saved getting out of the building. Mrs. Joy's residence was torched when someone put fire underneath the piazza a few days ago. Yesterday in the morning, Mrs. Arthur's stable had a fire, killing two valuable horses. It's bad enough that these folks had weathered the invasion, but now have got to cope with the forces of their scrupulous people that could be their neighbor doing these horrible acts." [479]

More details were given in Charlotte about Camden. The enemy burned McKain's drug store down to the Branch Bank, and on either side of main street, from Drucker's corner to the new brick hotel. They burned Zemp's Mill, the Cornwallis house, George Douglas' store, and Mrs. Lang's house. The Yankees got intoxicated as they did in Columbia and caused havoc. This influence caused the soldiers to do many acts that maybe normally they would not due. Estimates was that about 4,500 Yankees had come into town. They went down Boykin way. They didn't bother Messengers Boykin or John DeSaussure's place, nor the inhabitants that way, but they did bother General Chesnut's plantation. General Chesnut lost horses, mules, provisions, but his dwellings were saved by one of the Negroes. Among the horses captured on the Chesnut plantation was the superb stallion presented to President Davis by the Viceroy of Egypt. One of the Yankees, after riding the stallion down the streets in Camden, took off the saddle, patted him on the rump, and said that the horse was too fine to ride in these parts, so he would give him to Old Abe. In fact, he (the Chesnut Negro) stood up against the Yankees and told them, "Massa, come dar 'bout once in two year and dey allers give him something to eat, but dat was all; and if ye bun de place, dey jis tun poor nigger out in de cole." It looked as if they had adopted the Ethiopian philosophy to save the old and valuable property.

One of the ladies acted with great courage. The Federals entered her house and demanded all the silver. She told them that she hid it, so they would never get it. The Yankees threatened they would burn her house. She told them to burn it 'cause they won't find it. One of the Yankees dropped a match on the bed and started a fire. Soon however, they distinguished the fire and left the premises. In another incident, an informant told us he was on his way from Columbia. On the way, he passed a lot of Negroes, who had gone with the enemy, going back to the plantations in disgust. One of them told him, "Well, Boss, did ye ebber see such a people." All looked as if they had seen hard times. [480]

In the April 24, 1884, edition of the *Kershaw Gazette*, Colonel Zimmerman Davis wrote of incidents during the Sherman's Invasion of 1865 in the Camden area: "Among many brilliant exploits of our major-general, M.C. Butler, was a morning attack upon one of Sherman's wagon trains on the west side of the Little Lynches Creek, in Kershaw County, on February 22 or 23. The night before was cold, dark, and rainy, when he boldly marched his command into the very midst of Sherman's army, and about eleven o'clock went into camp insight

---

[479] The Journal and Confederate, Camden, South Carolina, March 17, 1865.
[480] The Western Democrat, Charlotte, North Carolina, March 21, 1865.

of and between the camp fires of two army corps. His men were in the saddle again before dawn, and by sunrise were drawn up in column of fours in close proximity to an encampment of wagon trails, anxiously awaiting the opportune moment to charge. Just as the wagons were hitched up and had been driven into the road for the purpose of beginning the day's march, their escort in front, the shrill blasts of our bugles sounding the charge awoke the echoes the in the forests around, and away we went shouting, shooting, and hewing with sabers. It was but the work of a few minutes, and in an incredibility short space of time about two hundred prisoners and nineteen splendid army wagons, each laden to the very top with corn or bacon, and drawn by six flue mules, clad with harness as our Confederate teamsters had not seen for many a day, were put across the stream into the peninsular formed by the Little and Big Lynches Creeks, where they were safe from rescue. After the charge, while waiting in the road in column of fours, prepared to resist a counter charge from the enemy's main body, should one be attempted while the captured train was crossing the creek, I observed a horse running through the woods without a rider, and dispatched Private McElroy, of my old company, the South Carolina Rangers, to capture and bring him to me. He did so, and as the horse was equipped with a perfectly new English bridle and martingales of soft yellow leather, I lost no time in transferring them to my own horse. I swapped saddle pouches, too, as the captured one was also new. One side of the pouch was empty, the other side contained nothing but a book, which upon examination proved to be the 'Diary of Lieutenant John A. McQueen, 'of the Fifteenth Illinois Mounted Infantry, from the time he left Chattanooga with Sherman's army down to two days before it came into my possession; the last entry, I think, describing his destruction of the depot buildings at Kingsville by order of his commanding general. This diary showed its writer to be, what you found him to be — a Christian gentleman. Of course, at this distance of time, I remember very little of its contents, though it was frequently referred to and discussed by General Butler, Colonel Aiken, and myself, during the next day or two as we had the opportunity to do so on the march. I believe I quote his very words recorded of Columbia: 'It was heart-rending to see the wanton destruction of property and the insults visited upon the defenseless women and children of Columbia by our Union soldiers. I did all I could to prevent it but was powerless.' And this tone seemed to pervade the entire book, which appeared to be written for the perusal of some loved one at home; at least such is my remembrance of the impression created in our minds as we read it, and we determined to be as kind as we could to such an enemy should the fortunes of war place him in our power. I kept this diary until the morning of the twenty-fifth, when my impression is that it was left upon a table at some farm house on the road to Cheraw, where I procured a hasty breakfast. How little did I then suppose that only the night before I had strangely interfered with the future plans of the writer."[481]

Matthew C. West said in an article of the War Between the States that he remembered the war very well. "His father died during the war. He still remembered how he looked, and he believes that someday he will know him when he sees him again. His mother was left to raise the children. She nor any of the children ever wore a piece of cloth of any kind unless she had made it. She spun the thread and wove the cloth. The Yankees camped two and half miles from their place near Providence Church. One day five of them came to our place and began to catch our chickens. We had virtually been living off these chickens. After they had caught them,

---

[481] "Incidents of '65", The Kershaw Gazette, April 24, 1884.

one of the Yankees turned to my mother and said, 'Give me a string to tie these chickens with.' My mother had a belt around her waist which she had woven herself. She took it off and gave it to him. The Yankee looked her in the face real hard and turning to the men [and] said, 'Turn those chickens loose.' Biscuits were a rarity in those days. Most of the time, we ate cornbread or rye bread."[482]

Peay's Ferry was a special project of General Sherman. Sherman made a special trip through Fairfield County to burn the Colonel's (Nicholas Peay) mansion-in-progress. The mansion in question was Melrose and only ruins remain. Two on the columns are the entrance to the Longtown Presbyterian Church Cemetery. Before the mansion was burned, two union soldiers made a mistake and sampled the wine cellar. Problem was they got so drunk that when the fire started, they couldn't get out. After burning the mansion and freeing the slaves, Sherman's army crossed the Wateree at Peay's Ferry- the same one the family that used to take slaves up the Wateree from Charleston- to continue on to Camden and beyond. All 2000 slaves were now free. These slaves couldn't read, couldn't write, and had no money. Around 750 of them went to Lancaster County, and built Camp Welfare, an encampment of "bush harbor" houses, built of branches with dirt floors. Those are gone from yesterday, but cabins are there for revivals held every year.[483]

April 3rd brought news of the death of Mr. Allie Shannon the oldest son of Mr. T. E Shannon. He died while guarding the bridge on the Neuse River. Also, killed at the same place and time was Mr. Allen Young. Mr. George Young, who was also there, got captured. Both were members of Captain John Chesnut's Cavalry from the area. The news came from servant of Captain Chesnut's command.[484]

In April, another election took place in the city. James Dunlap would be the intendant, along with wardens Robert M. Kennedy, D.D. Hocott, L.M. Boswell, and N.D. Baxley.[485] Fires are still erupting by villains. At one o'clock Tuesday morning, yesterday, the kitchen of Mrs. Martha Dutton was set ablaze, and before anyone could save it, the building was consumed and lost. At four o'clock, the barn containing carriage horses of Miss Martha Shannon was set on fire and lost. At quarter by four in the morning still, the barn and stable of Major L.W.R. Blair was set on fire, and firemen saved his residence. His residence was on Monument Square, the first house on the extreme right facing the square.[486] The house is known today as Alberdeen.

April 11 brought word that another Yankee invasion was heading toward Camden. Brigadier General Edward E. Potter was bringing groups of the 157 New York, a detachment of 56 New York, coming up on the enemy's rear through the swamp. This was at Dingle's Mill. The purpose of this expedition will be to destroy all rolling railroad stock between Camden and Florence. At Summerville, Potter destroyed all railway buildings and machine shops, four locomotives, and twenty cars. Trestle work was burned for six miles either side and track torn up. At Manchester, eight locomotives were destroyed and forty-five cars. We burned the Wateree Trestle, and track toward Camden and back toward Sumterville. Major General Young of the Butler's Cavalry came into the scene and digging in at Boykin's Mill, eight miles from Camden. Young was waiting for a showdown

---

[482] "County's Oldest Citizen Talks of the Remarkable Growth of Camden," The Camden Chronicle, undated, found in the West folder at The Camden Archives and Museum.
[483] "A House United: Descendants of Slaves, Their Owners Gather," The State newspaper, July 7, 1990.
[484] The Journal and Confederate, Camden, South Carolina, April 3, 1865.
[485] The Camden Confederate, Camden, South Carolina; April 5, 1865.
[486] Ibid.

with Potter. On April 15, Potter moved in the direction of Statesburg. Potter drove the enemy back toward the Camden direction. Potter used night marches to gain speed in getting the Camden direction. Opposition and skirmishes existed until we reached Camden, where there was no opposition, and we could occupy Camden. We found the railroad trains had been moved below Boykin's Mill on Swift Creek. This expedition ended with Potter capturing three guns, one battle flag, fifty prisoners, three hundred horses and mules, destroying thirty-two locomotives, two hundred-fifty cars, many government stores, railway stations, freight houses, machine shops between Camden and Mayesville, large portions of railway at these points, and twenty-five hundred bales of cotton. Nearly five thousand Negroes followed us behind our column. [487]

In the ***Journal and Confederate***, published in Camden, South Carolina, the following was said about the confederates and what they were doing: "We entered camp at Pine Tree, on Tuesday evening, the eleventh, about sunset, with Colonel Brown's battalion of reserves, and was placed on the picket line at Chesnut's Crossings. We were relieved at nine a.m. the next morning, to return and report to Captain Kennedy. Kennedy had informed us that we had a military function at ten a.m., and we must be there. We had to be armed and equipped for this emergency was a pressing one. We then refreshed ourselves with our thimbles of XX. We were placed in charge of function No. 2; however, we were chosen to be placed in charge of function No. 3. As we marched to the Depot, we saw the telegraph lines being repaired. We were ordered to guard the magnetic operator. When fixed, we could send telegrams as far as Danville. Upon arrival at Camp Boykin, we were stopped by Captain Team, who informed us the enemy was occupying Statesburg. We then made a dash to return to Camden. We reported to Captain Kennedy, who told us to guard function No. 2, with orders to report to the guard house at eight p.m. As reported, we were on duty at the guard house when at eleven p.m., we were supplied with cartridges near function No. 4, and told to go to the line at function No. 5. We marched to the railroad and we entered the cars, and then we were off to Camp Boykin. We arrived about one p.m. We were exhausted and fatigued by all these orders and the drills at all those different function points. We laid down on the ground and fell asleep. On Thursday morning, the next day, we were awakened at sunrise. However, our awakening was not by soft music, but rather a sergeant ordering us to fall in, turn right face, and march. We then enjoyed our one third of hard tack and then proceeded to the slaughter pits, which were strongly made with the joint superintendent of Captains Colclough and Team. While waiting, the pits were visited by some ten to twelve men, some of whom were fat and some that were lean but showed remorse in their chubby faces. The horrors of war have left scars that could be seen. Those scars being wrinkled faces, their eyes dilated, their nose elongated, their mouths showing exclamation, but the chin, the description can't go on. Their looks were that devastating. It was as if they were saying, 'He who is in battle again will never live to fight again.'

"Two hours later, joy began to set in. The arrival of the Lewis's Kentucky Brigade and their five hundred men brought hope to their cause and sighs of relief.

"On Friday morning, they pressed toward the enemy's line, remaining quiet but vigilant till Saturday. Our little unit under Captain Conner, proceeded during this time toward Claremont. As we got an hour in

---

[487] The War of the Rebellion: A Compilation of the Official Records of the Union and Confederate Armies, Series 1- Volume XLVII- In Three Parts, Part 1- Reports; Washington: Government Printing Office, 1895, p. 1026-1027.

our march, the enemy attacked General Lewis's Brigade, four miles from Statesburg, who repulsed then with slaughter. Put loss was one killed and two wounded. That afternoon, the enemy assaulted our lines with even a greater force. Their numbers being so great, we had to admit to the flanking process, and our men began their way back in the direction of Camden, and left Statesburg to the Yankees. We were silent even being five miles away. We went back to Camp Boykin and stayed till Monday. Then, we discovered the Yankees had crossed Swift Creek, and closing in on Camden.

Sadness fell on the men at Boykin's Mill, especially the men of Captain Colclough, that Camden would be sacrificed and given to the enemy without a fight. Captain Colclough's men was waiting at McLeod's crossing for the enemy, while others were contemplating getting the railroad cars in Camden and hiding to have some defense of Camden. General Elliot, wounded, commanded the distribution of forces on the north of the creek. Then, moved his men to the south of the mill and creek. With Elliot, was the forces of Colonel Brown and Colonel Shannon. With those forces in place, a stronger line was created. Rifle pits were thrown up along the railroad, and some but a few to the rear and west of the road. On an elevation, rifle pits were put up along the whole way to the main road by the mill. Doing this, command of the whole swamp between the railroad and the mill and on the extreme right our position had control by the main road. We felt that we were as tight and strong as a cotton press, the grist mill, saw mill, and the right line of rifle pits offered complete shelter. The flanking position was made even stronger under the direction of Colonel Bull. Bull used timbers to double the strength from the saw mill up to the right of the line. Ten o'clock came, Tuesday the eighteenth, word came the enemy was approaching. Soon black smoke could be seen caused by their burning of gin houses of Colonel T.J. Ancrum, Dr. C.J. Shannon, and Benjamin Prescott. Colonel Brown's Fifth Battalion Reserves were put in the rifle pits on the extreme left, and twenty men from Conner's company joined at the railroad crossing. The central line contained soldiers of Captain Conner. His company formed the right wing of the battalion and was under the command of Colonel William M. Shannon. The right of the line was occupied by the Lewis Brigade sharpshooters. One of the cannons was placed to command the railroad and the other the main road. Waiting was short as the hearing of the sharpshooters commenced. Then, a skirmish broke out. As expected, the fighting was strongest on the railroad. Colonel Conner's detachment and Colonel Brown's men were full with their work, and the Yankees would not show themselves before they got evidence of us. The firing was rapid and destructive. After a few efforts, the skirmish lines drew back and the cannon, paid its respects shooting but only dusting a few of the men. The enemy tried to approach from the main road but the Kentuckians thwarted their attempt from the saw mill. Few tried but passing in front became impractical for the enemy and was driven toward the front of Captain Conner's company, and left of the Kentuckians. The enemy got tired of their futile efforts. Then, they decided to build a crossing directly toward the center works. However, the rifles discouraged their movements. The enemy tried below. Soon, we heard the shelling and the charging on the extreme left and knew the enemy had flanked us. General Elliot ordered Colonel Brown and Major Shannon to withdraw their men from the pits. So beautiful was this action executed, with the militia falling back to the skirmish line. Now, we are ready for renewing this fight. A battalion composed of Colonel Brown's battalion and Captain Conners was placed on a hill beyond the mill, toward Captain John Boykin. General Elliot directed the movements and lead toward the Providence road. At about three thirty, and very hot, we had to cross an open field. Feeling that

that the enemy might have opened up the path, the gallant general knows how to fight his troops, and to take care of them. Quickly, the general got us to a pine grove beyond the field. Taking up the march, and just getting after dark, we turned flanked the enemy in front of Dinkin's Mill. We were in a rapid march, though rain set in, but soon the fires dried us off. As soon as we fell off to asleep, another rain came in. Now, we had little sleep that night, except by veterans, whom water did not disturb, as long as symptoms of drowning was exhibited. Early on Wednesday, we marched to the railroads crossing on Rafting Creek. We immediately threw up defenses to prepare for the enemy. As soon as that was done, orders came for us to return to Dinky's Mill. The enemy was making a movement there. Though we hurried back, we did not participate in the fight. We merely rested on our four guns, two parrots, discoursed sweet music, and dealt heavy blows upon the columns of the enemy. The biggest portion of General Young's command consisted of Lewis and Hannon brigades. We fought the enemy back to Statesburg. A portion of the cavalry and reserves stayed at Providence. On Thursday morning, the determination was given that the infantry could not keep up with the movements of the cavalry, and the reserves, and the militia, including Colonel Colclough's mounted men, were ordered home. The enemy having passed beyond the region of the homes they wanted to defend, undertook a march of twenty miles between ten o'clock and dark. The long, hard week they have done, and all arrived safe, covered in dirt and with glory."[488]

"Leaving there, we encamped at Singleton's plantation, and sent two thousand contrabands to Georgetown in charge of the 32 U.S.C.T. When they returned, we started upon our mission - and from that time, the fourteenth, we fought every day with the rebels, and drove them before us. But at length they made a stand at Swiss Creek and fought desperately. We captured nine prisoners. On the fifteenth, we left for taking Camden, which we did capturing all the rebel sick and wounded there, numbering, a least, from three to four hundred men."

The following came out of the diary of W.N. Collins, Orderly Sergeant of Company H, 54th Massachusetts Infantry: "On the sixteenth, we left Camden, and from that we fought until we got to Swiss Creek, where the rebels again made a stand. Cos. F and H were on the skirmish line, the battalion on the reserve, that 102d U.S.C.T. in the center, and the 3rd U.S.C.T. on the left wing. We drove them to their den, when they fought quite desperately for a time. For if they flee from the horsemen, how can they contend with the footmen? The rebels had a dam constructed all around them, and there was no way of getting at them but to pass over it in single file. The left wing went to the extreme right for flanking Johnny and there it was that we lost our noble Lieutenant [Edward L. Stevens]. Who will help us mourn his loss — for he fell in defense of the dear old flag?

"[Corporal James P.] Johnson and Corporal [Andrew] Miller of Co. He had six privates wounded. But the 54th stormed the hill and carried it at the point of the bayonet, making themselves masters of the field, as they always do. Just like them! Brave boys they are! Who will say, Three cheers for the 54th Mass. Vols., 32nd and 102nd U.S.C.T., and for the 25th Ohio Vols., the 107th Ohio Vols., 15th and 56th N.Y. vols., and the 4th Mass., and the 3rd New York Artillery, and for General [Edward E.] Potter's brave troops? For we are the ones that destroyed and drove the rebels from the field, totally demoralizing them."[489]

---

488 The Journal and Confederate, Camden, S.C., April 24, 1865.
489 A Brief Historical Background of Potter's Raid," by W.N. Collins, Orderly Sergeant, Company H, 54th Massachusetts, vcwsg.com/PDF%20Files/A%20BRIEF%20HISTORICAL%20 on the Web.

On 11 April 1865, near Camden, South Carolina, 1st Lieutenant Stephen Atkin Sails, 54th Massachusetts, was wounded for a second time. While the 54th was on reconnaissance near a railroad junction, several locomotives, one with the steam up, were observed after dark. A detachment led by Lieutenant Swails rushed the trains and captured them. As Lieutenant Swails entered the cab of one locomotive, he waved his hat in triumph. However, sharpshooters deployed to shoot the trainmen if they tried to escape, mistook him for an engineer, fired and wounded him.[490]

Ironically, the plantations of Boykins and John DeSaussure was visited. Some evidence may "lead us to a deal made with the Yankees to save their places."[491]

Mary Boykin (Miller) Chesnut wrote in her Journal, *"A Diary of Dixie"*: (We drove) "to our house at Mulberry. On one side of the house, every window was broken, every bell torn down, every piece of furniture destroyed, every door smashed in. The other side was intact. A servant explained, 'They were working like regular carpenters, destroying everything, then the General came in. He said it was a shame to destroy such a fine old house like this, whose owner was over ninety years old. He would not condone it done for the world. It was wanton mischief.' They carried off sacks of our books and our papers, our letters were strewed as far away as Vance's Ferry. This was Potter's raid. Sherman only took our horses. Potter's raid, which was after Johnston's surrender, ruined us. He burned our mills and gins, and a hundred bales of cotton. Indeed, nothing was left now but bare land, and debts incurred for the support of these hundreds of Negroes during the war."

The household staff, led by a servant named Claiborne, extinguished the fire set by an earlier contingent of Union soldiers after they had left stacks of brush ablaze along the sides of the house.[492]

In May, Mr. James Jones, of the Railroad Depot, had put in a new grist mill for grinding meal and hominy at the Depot. His mill "will be operating at all hours of the day. Please come use the mill to grind your wheat and corn."[493]

On Saturday night, April 9, 1865, John S. Capers, Adjutant of the 7th Cavalry, was killed near the Appomattox Court House. At the onset of war, he enlisted in the Kirkwood Rangers under Captain Wm M. Shannon. In the campaigns of 1862 and 1863, he served as a private. In 1863, his company was taken into the Holcombe Legion.

In June, occupation forces of two companies of the 25th Regiment Ohio Volunteers came into Camden. They were under the command of Captain C.W. Ferguson. Ferguson had "assured us as long as the citizens remain law-abiding, no harm will come to them." In doing this, Captain Ferguson issued the following orders: General Order Number 1: any citizen having in their property that rightfully belongs to the United States Government will report to the headquarters as the terms of the surrender was agreed upon. Persons having mules, horses, and wagon will be allowed to keep them for the moment, and for their work. Any persons failing to comply will be deprived of such property and subject themselves to military authority.

---

[490] Stephen Atkin Swails. Wikipedia, Inc.
[491] Cook, Harvey T.; Sherman's March Through South Carolina in 1865, July 1938, Greenville, S.C., p. 13.
[492] Mulberry Plantation: An Old Camden Landmark in a Changing World, Daniels, Martha Williams, October 8, 1970. Was done for an article sent to Mr. Gregg Smith, Camden Chronicle, October 8.
[493] The Journal and Confederate, Camden, S.C., May 12, 1865

Special Order Number 2: To prevent any disturbances, the improper use of liquors, no selling of liquor will be sold or given away to any citizen or soldier, unless permitted is granted from these headquarters. Anyone found guilty of these violation, their goods will be confiscated and subject to punishment of military law.

Special Order Number 3: Information has been received that a "band of marauders are infesting the country and committing depredations on the peaceful citizens. It is ordered that all persons comprising such will be considered outlaws, and if caught will receive the severest penalty of military law. It is the desire of the United States Government to protest all peaceful and law-abiding citizens, and they will confer favor on these headquarters, and do justice to themselves, by giving any information they may have in their procession concerning the names and movements of such bands and aiding in their capture."[494]

---

[494] The Tri-Weekly Journal, Camden, South Carolina, June 16, 1865.

Horse and Jefferson Davis
Permission to use by Norton Rare and Antiquarian Research Library, New Orleans, Louisiana

The White Arabian: Jefferson Davis's Horse

To tell this story, one must tell of the swashbuckling adventurers known as blockade runners. One must relive the tales of being shot at by the Yankees, and one must learn how to play chess to slide by the enemy without being caught and possibly hanged. One blockade runner was Thomas Taylor, a young Englishman, who was working as an assistant for a Liverpudlian firm merchant.[495] In 1862, the firm that he was working for bought shares in a blockade-runner, and Taylor was asked if he would like to accompany the ship as a per cargo (owner's representative).[496] Taylor made seven trips from Bermuda or Nassau.[497]

However, this story begins in a faraway land in the Middle East. A friendship had developed between Edwin DeLeon, a consul-general in Cairo, Egypt, from the United States, with the Khedive, and the story was told by the son of the infamous Mehement Ali, and the uncle of Abbas Pasha, who was strangled by two of his slaves.[498] Abbas Pasha and his kinswomen, Nexie Khanoun, played leading parts in that romance, which Lew Wallace undoubtedly drew upon to form the ground plan of *Ben Hur*. Pasha was having troubles of his own in a weak attempt to suppress the slave trade, and DeLeon, fresh from a country where slavery was a burning issue, could well sympathize. Pasha became fond of him, and as a mark of his regard presented him with a pure Arabian Stallion, a noble breed, white in color, and with all the fine points of his breed.[499] At one point, the thinking by DeLeon was to send the horse to be stabled at Mulberry Plantation in Camden, South Carolina, as DeLeon knew General Chesnut's love of horseflesh.[500]

In 1903, the following was written about the Arabian Horse: "The Viceroy of Egypt, Abbas Pasha, who about twenty-five to thirty years ago, undertook to breed Arabs, thinking Egypt could supply the great and constantly increasing demand from the nations of the old world, expended much money in purchasing Arab horses and mares through agents, then entrusted the handling, care, and breeding to servants; with the results being such great uncertainties in sizes, colors, and characters, that he gave it up, disposing of his entire plant to such as wanted, because of Abbas Pasha's stud! "When gone he said to the England's minister, that only Arabs of the Desert could breed and grow Arab horses." I had gotten this from Major General W. Tweedie, C.S.I., for

---

495   The Civil War: The Blockade Runners and Raiders; Time-Life Books, Alexandria, Virginia, 1983, pages 92- 95
496   Ibid.
497   Ibid.
498   "Famous Old Mulberry Has Historic Past," by James Henry Rice, Jr.; The Camden Chronicle, July 6, 1928.
499   Ibid.
500   Ibid.

many years H.B.M.'s Consul General at Baghdad," Randolph Huntington to T.C., June 2, 1903.[501] However, the horse in question was a gift to Jefferson Davis from Edwin DeLeon, when he returned from Egypt. The was delivered by Haggi Mohammed and Hassan Dealers in Cairo, Egypt.[502]

> "Pedigree of the White Horse"
> (Presented by Edwin DeLeon to
> Jefferson Davis)
> Translation
>
> We the undersigned, Haggi Mohammed and Hassan Aga declare and attest that the White Horse, Saglani Ghadrani who has the   mark on his left   is the son of an Avezy horse and of the mare Saglanis Ghadranie was born the property of the Scheck Bedani, Son of Abdallah Beduin of Avezy in the year 1267 and in the month of Cahread, and in 1871 was sold to the late Abbas Pacha (Vice Roy of Egypt) and in the month of Ramadhan 1273 was presented to the late Al Hami Pacha (Son of the Vice Roy) to the Scheriff of Mecca, and in the month of Rabi Awel 1275, on return of the Pilgrims the same horse was brought back to Cairo by Mohammed Effendi, who in the Month of Mohabrani 1276 exchanged him for a Mare.
>
> (Signed)
>
> Haggi Mohammed
> Hassan Aga
>
> We the undersigned also attest that the said horse is Saglani Ghadrani.
> Sevonato, Horse Broker
> Siep Saad   )
> Mphalli Ahmed   )   Of Prince's Stables
> Yuself   )
>
> Cairo in Egypt
>   y th
> Jan. 18, 1861
>
> Accompanying the slip of paper with the information given above, is an advertisement of the sale of horses from the stable of Prince Al-Hami-Pacha, with the penciled statement at the top of the broadside: "The white horse, Saglani Ghadrani came out of this stable 4 years ago- having been presented to the Scheriff of Mecca at that time by Prince Al Hami Pacha". The advertisement is dated: Alexandrie (Egypte) le 14 Octobre 1860.

[503]

---

[501] "Arabian Blood for Stamina: Keene Richards Own Accounts of his Two Desert Expeditions and his Arabian Importations;" The Horse magazine, November- December Issue 1935.

[502] "Edwin DeLeon Thesis," Helen Kohn Henning, May 28, 1928, p. 50. (With permission from the South Caroliniana Library, Columbia, S.C.)

[503] Ibid.

In 1861, Edwin DeLeon left briefly to go to England before traveling to Nassau as a Confederate Agent. He arranged for a "splendid, white steed" to travel to Nassau.[504] The steed was named "Saglani Ghadrani," and was an important gift from the Viceroy (Khedive) Mohammed Said.[505] This individual played an important significance in Jefferson Davis's past, as it was this Viceroy through DeLeon, that Davis had purchased camels in 1856 for the army.[506] DeLeon left the horse in Nassau before running the blockade in the Confederacy. Davis enlisted the help of Fraser and Company to help transport the animal in the summer of 1862, but not until late 1863 was arrangements made with Thomas E. Taylor, famed captain of the ship Banshee.[507]

In 1863, Thomas Taylor went to England in search of establishing the risky business of blockade running using a supercargo vessel.[508] Taylor's first ship, the Dispatch, proved to be fatal due to the craftsmanship.[509] The Banshee was built in Liverpool, England, by Jones, Quiggin, and Company.[510] The Banshee was a "paddleboat boat, made for the business of cargo, made out of steel (the first of its kind) weighed 217 tons, considered fast for those times, consumed twenty tons of coal a day, and the speed was eleven knots".[511]

In a letter from London, the following was said, "At Queenstown, March 5, I saw a beautiful steamer, called the Banshee, from Liverpool, on her way to run the blockade. She was as straight as an arrow, about 160 feet long, raking masts and funnels, sits very low in the water, was said to be very fast, is constructed of steel plates, and in ever particular is a perfect beauty. I only hope that some of our blockaders will catch her. Soon, I feel that the English government will soon take steps to prevent any more of that kind of craft leaving England for the benefit of the rebels."[512]

On the first trip to Nassau, the ship was cranky and unsafe, but the ship made Wilmington. The ship, which was painted black, was lowered to the rails, and repainted white, as the color black was a dangerous color, and the crew wore white.[513] Everything done before the remodel came down and was redone. The ship made seven trips, with the pilot making L700 to L800 per trip.[514]

The white horse was in Nassau, and someone located it and contacted Louis Heilger from New Orleans, acting as a Confederate agent in Nassau, and he arranged transport for the horse to America.[515] Heilger inquired to Thomas E. Taylor about shipping the horse to Wilmington. Thomas Taylor was considered one of the top

---

[504] "The Papers of Jefferson Davis," Volume 10, pages 325-326.
[505] Ibid.
[506] Ibid.
[507] Ibid.
[508] "Famous Old Mulberry Has Historic Past," by James Henry Rice, Jr.; The Camden Chronicle, July 6, 1928.
[509] Ibid.
[510] "Mind Creek Battlefield: Blockade Runners." Website: http://www.minecreek.org/blockade-runners/color-plate-commentary.html.
[511] "Blockade Running;" Thomas E. Taylor's Narrative of his Personal Experiences in the Civil War.
[512] "A Private Letter," Lowell Daily Citizen and News, March 30, 1863, Liverpool, England.
[513] "Blockade Running;" Thomas E. Taylor's Narrative of his Personal Experiences in the Civil War.
[514] Ibid.
[515] "Running the Blockade: A Personal Narrative of Adventures, Risks, and Escapes During the American Civil War." By Thomas E. Taylor, Second edition, 1896.

blockade runners for the Confederacy.[516] Nassau was closer to the coast of South Carolina and Georgia than Bermuda at five hundred miles away in the South Atlantic.[517]

Thomas Taylor made the voyage aboard the Banshee, despite hardships. The major hardship was he was told his ship would be quarantined, and the horse probably would be destroyed. Taylor at once telegraphed Richmond, and the reply was to go deliver the horse at Wilmington and then port the ship.[518] Taylor was told by a health officer to quarantine the ship, but as the ship got closer to a wharf, many of the crew jumped on shore and disappeared. The decision was made not to go ahead and quarantine the horse.[519]

The journey was not boring at all. The ship upon reaching the area near Wilmington came under attack from the Yankees firing at all vessels running the blockade trying to stop ships. The trip in was quiet as on the third day passing the same ships in quarantine, the ship steamed up the river.[520] Crews on other ships quarantined did not like the fact that the Banshee was disregarding the quarantine and sneaking by.[521] On this trip with the white horse, the smell of land got the horse to neighing, and at this point, jackets were placed over the horse's head to keep quiet.[522] However, the neighing had been heard from a Yankee cruiser nearby, and firing began. Luckily, across the way at Fort Fisher, Colonel Lamb saw what was going on and began to fire shells at the Yankee cruiser and over the ship.[523] The trip was very eventful but worthwhile. Avoiding the quarantine, the earning gained an extra L20,000 to L30,000, and saved them from Yankee prison and our beloved ship, the Banshee, from being destroyed.[524]

Ah, the story continues. The horse arrived on October 9, 1863 in Wilmington.[525] A month later, November 11, 1863, the Banshee had a narrow escape going to Fort Fisher. Several shots were fired at the Banshee, one was a shot in her hull, inches above the water line and some distance from the wheel house. The bullet still lodged and left to remain in her hull. Her formats were cut with grape, and her rigging badly damaged. At one point, one of the blockaders were thirty yards from the Banshee, trying to hail her to stop. However, the courage of those on board, and ship, persevered under the commander of the Banshee to cause defiance and elude her capture. The vessel and cargo, all arrived safely into port early in the morning in Wilmington, North Carolina.[526]

Jefferson Davis did not pick up the horse till November, and found his prize to be "a handsome, small horse … and will not admit that he is vicious, although he bites and kicks at everybody, because he eats bread out of his hand" (according to William Preston).[527] While riding with Burton Harrison one evening, the Arabian became

---

516 Ibid.
517 "Confederate Finance and Supply," http://www.cincinnaticwrt.org/data/ccwrt_history/talks/clan.
518 "Running the Blockade: A Personal Narrative of Adventures, Risks, and Escapes During the American Civil War," by Thomas E. Taylor, Second Edition, 1896.
519 Ibid.
520 Ibid.
521 Ibid.
522 Ibid.
523 Ibid.
524 Ibid.
525 "The Papers of Jefferson Davis," Volume 10, pages 325 to 326.
526 "Narrow Escape of the Steamer Banshee," Charleston Mercury, November 11, 1863.
527 "The Papers of Jefferson Davis," Volume 10, pages 325-326.

restless and back over a precipice. Davis fell off halfway down the twenty-foot drop and was struck in the legs and back by the horse's hooves.[528] Soon thereafter, the Arabian was sent to General James Chesnut's Plantation in Camden, South Carolina. The horse arrived in May 1, 1864, when President Davis's man, Stephen, brought his master's Arabian to Mulberry for safekeeping.[529]

In March 1865, the Arabian was lost to a Yankee raiding party, when a Negro boy told them about a white horse near the swamp. That boy was the only boy to leave with the Yankees and as far as we know never returned. In the column, "The Rebel Yell," a Yankee soldier rode the stallion through Camden, and said the following: "You're too fine to ride in these parts, and we'll send you to Old Abe," as he removed the saddle and patted the horse on his rear.[530]

In a letter from Mr. Miller Williams, Fort Smith, Arkansas, dated March 1, 1928, the following was written: "Just before Sherman passed through South Carolina, a small detachment of a mixed nature left Columbia for the mountains of North Carolina, and a discussion came about before starting as to its composition. Aunt Mary Chesnut wanted General Chesnut (Uncle Jimmy) to send the Arab along with Mr. Daniel Blake and myself, the only two whites of the party, the remainder was composed of eleven thoroughbred's two-year old's and nine young Negro men, and one old faithful servant of the Blakes. The latter and Mr. Blake drove on the wagon seat box that was afterwards told me contained quite a sum of gold from the Bank of Columbia. Uncle James thought it safer to send the Arab along with the other thoroughbreds under the care of Adam Team, the Hermitage Owner, to a point about forty miles south of Camden in the river swamp, where it was unlikely the Federal troops would dare to penetrate in small scouting squads. This was done and all the entire group of animals were captured there by a detachment of Potter's men. One of the Negro attendants (latter identified as a young boy and the only one left with the Yankees) deserted the horse camp and informed the Federals of their whereabouts. But for this, the animals would have been perfectly safe, as this squad was the only one that reached this lonely swamp at any time during the war. Uncle James regretted that he had not let me take the horse to North Carolina. It was fortunate that none of the gold, said to be near $1,000,000 and none of the colts with Mr. Blake's outfit were lost. Our route was by Newberry, Laurens, Greenville, and Flat Rock to the hiding place in Buncombe County, North Carolina.

Nothing was ever heard of the Arab to this day. It may have been possible that the party who captured the animals were not aware of the ownership or history. Two racehorses, May Queen and Hark, were recovered by the Canteys, as they were trained on the race track."[531] A story that has been passed down is that on certain times, people have seen a ghost of a white horse wondering the lands of Mulberry. Could this be the ghost of Saglani Ghadrani, Jefferson Davis's Arabian?

---

[528] Ibid.
[529] "Mary Chesnut's Illustrated Diary- Mulberry Boxed Set, Volume 1, Mary Chesnut's Dairy from Dixie," 2011, page 301.
[530] 'The Rebel Yell,' New York Tribune, March 23, 1865.
[531] "Edwin DeLeon Thesis," Helen Kohn Henning, May 1928, pages 50-52, permission by the Caroliniana Library, Columbia, South Carolina.

The State Survivor's Association

In 1866, a group of men led by Kershaw District's own General Joseph B. Kershaw met in Columbia, South Carolina, to discuss the possibility of helping those soldiers and families from the war. These were made up of ex-confederates and soldiers, and led by such well-known Brigadier Generals Joseph Kershaw, Bonham, Conner, and Kennedy.[532] This meeting took place just before the eighteenth of September and held at the Nickerson's Hotel on a Tuesday evening. Upon calling the meeting to order, General Kershaw was selected chairman, with Captain. C. Holmes selected secretary.[533]

Upon taking the floor, General Kershaw made the following address in his own eloquent and informative style: "None of you can fall to comprehend the difficulties which embarrass me when I attempt to greet you on this occasion in suitable terms. There is no heart in this assembly that does not throb in sympathy with the emotions, which I must feel, but may not utter, when for the first time since you laid down your arms and ceased to be soldiers, your old commander addresses you as friends, and citizens, partners of the feeling hopes, and trials of the past, bound together by a common cause, common dangers, toils, and sufferings, nothing remains to us of them but the glorious memories of the buried past, the dissolvable ties of interest and affection, which it has engendered and the proud consciousness of duties faithfully performed. In this spirit, you have been invited to assemble, to cherish the memory of our dead companions, to provide for the necessities of their widowed and orphaned families, to administer relief to our maimed, helpless, and indigent associates, to preserve the history of their crops, and its members, and to commingle in occasional, friendly, and social reunions. To these objects, your consideration is now invited."[534]

The following was then read, submitted, and adopted:

> "Therefore, be it resolved, that we, the survivors of the South Carolina Brigades, commanded at different periods by Brigadier Generals M.L. Bonham, J.B. Kershaw, James Conner, and John D. Kennedy, conceiving it to be our duty to endeavor to relieve the wants of our indigent comrades, and the widows and orphans of our lamented dead, and also actuated by the desire of preserving a true and faithful record of all services of our command, do invite all who were

---

[532] The Daily Constitutionalist, September 18, 1866.
[533] Ibid.
[534] Ibid.

members at any time of the said brigade, and whose military record is clear, to unite with us in forming an association for that purpose."[535]

The next meeting was set and a committee, General J. B. Kershaw, General James Conner, General John D. Kennedy, Colonel William Wallace, Colonel Stackhouse, Colonel D. Wyatt Aiken, and Captain C.R. Holmes, selected to write the constitution for submission at the next meeting in December, and thanks to Thomas S. Nickerson for the use of this fine hall.[536] R.N. Lawrence was selected treasurer.

The following is a list of ex-Confederates, who enrolled at this meeting:

J. B. Kershaw	P.H B. Shuler	Charles Bocsenen
M. L. Bonham	E. McClarkson	J. D. S.
William Wallace	J. H. Clarkson	G. Dickerson
E. T. Stackhouse	D. H. Crawford	J. D. Roberts
James Williams	Richard O'Neal	W. P. Hix
D. Wyatt Aiken	J. G. Murchison	J. F. Duren
R. P. Todd	J. A. Crawford	J. R. Price
W. F. McMaster	J. J. Goodwin	J. Huffman
William Elliot	A. C. Davis	L. Campbell
James D. McCutchen	H. L. Kenzie	T. P. Purse
R. R. Clyburn	G. Bruns	David Jones
R. N. Lowrance	G. M. Scott	W. P. Price
W. D. Peck	W. A. Templeton	S. T. McCaughlin
W. F. Nance	B. C. Pollock	F. L. McKenzie
W. Z. Leitner	M. A. Shelton	S. W. Rowan
S. L. Leapheart	S. Martin	W. H. Stork
W. L. DePass	S. Busshart	M. McKee
B. M. Tolbert	P. Brown	W. K. Evans
C. R. Holmes	C. Kirk	John Martin
William Hood	W.C. McGregor	A. Whisnant
M. J. Hough	Aiken Anderson	S.P. Simmons
J. W. Hurst	W. J. Keller	W. M. Dwight
Dubose Engleton	W.S. Mullins	R.A. Fair
E. S. Brooks	J. H. Brooks	

On November 18, 1869, another meeting took place to officially organize and put an organization together called the State Survivor's Association. What happened from 1866 to this point is not known. Each district will be responsible for developing and organizing a survivor's association in their respected area. Again, Camden's own Joseph Kershaw was called to chair this meeting, which was called to order by Colonel McCrady. Messengers T.P. Lowndes and Pieree Bacot were requested to act as secretaries.

---

535 Ibid.
536 Ibid.

On motion of Mr. T.G. Barker, the delegates present to come forward and register their names: Kershaw County had as their delegates: J.B. Kershaw, W.L. DePass, and William Clyburn. Lancaster County had as their delegate: B.J. Witherspoon. J. Jonathan Lucas was one of the representatives from Darlington County. Lucas was from the Bethune area.

The following officers from the sister societies were present: Z. Davis, President South Carolina Rangers' Charitable Association; Alfred Rhett, President Monumental Association First South Carolina Regulars; A.J. Mimms, Charleston Rifleman Society; G.L. Buist, Palmetto Guard Charitable Association; George II. Walter, Washington Artillery Society.

On the motion of Major Barker, it was:

> Resolved, that survivors in good standing, who have not been regularly appointed, be requested to represent their respective district. It was also resolved that the officers of the District Association be invited to enroll their names as members of the Convention.

A letter from General John S. Preston, endorsing the project of forming the association, and tendering his approval and best wishes for its success, was read, and ordered to be preserved with the minutes.

On motion, a committee of five, consisting of messengers, E.W. McCrady, James Conner, John Bratton, William Wallace, and W.F. McMaster were appointed to draft a constitution and nominate officers for the association, and the meeting then adjourned until four o'clock.

At four o'clock, the convention reassembled, the committee appointed to draft a constitution reported and nominated as officers the following gentlemen:

President - Lieutenant General Wade Hampton

First Vice - President, Lieutenant General R.H. Anderson

Second Vice President - Brigadier General J.B. Kershaw

Third Vice President - Brigadier General S. McGowan

Fourth Vice Present - Major T.G. Barker

Secretary - Colonel A.C. Haskell

Treasurer - Captain W.K. Bachman

The report of the committee was unanimously adopted.

The Secretaries of the Convention were authorized to have one thousand copies of the constitution and minutes of the meeting printed and distributed among the district associations, and this too was adopted.

General Conner stated that the Charleston District Association would bear the expense of printing the above.

On motion of Colonel McMaster, it was:

> Resolved, that the Executive Committee be instructed to assess the District Associations a sum not less than fifty dollars each for defraying the current expenses of the year, and that the secretary be instructed to notify them of the fact.

On motion, the presiding officer of the convention was requested to appoint the executive committee. The following was then made:

> Executive Committee — Colonel Edward McCrady, Colonel W.N. Wallace, General E. Capers, Colonel J.H. Rion, General James Conner, Colonel C.J. Walker, Colonel J. McCutcheon.

Major Barker stated that he had been requested by the Ladies in charge of the Widow's Home to make an appeal on behalf of the institution, and he urged the delegates to use all in their power to aid this worthy work. General Conner introduced the following:

> Resolved. That this Convention cordially recommend the Confederate Widow's Home, of the City of Charleston, to the favorable attention of the Survivors' Association throughout the state, and that the members now in attendance pledge themselves on their return to their homes to use their best efforts to obtain contributions to so noble a charity. This was adopted.

Mr. William Elliott introduced the following resolution:

> Resolved. That the thanks of this convention be tendered to the Survivors' Association of Charleston District for the zealous and successful efforts on behalf of the cause which had today called us together.

In the evening, the members of the Convention were entertained with a supper at the Mills' House. The Survivors' Association of Charleston, with their invited guests, to the number of about two hundred, did full justice to a bounteous collation, prepared by the host Parker, in great style that only he could do.

After the removal of the cloth, Colonel McCrady, the chairman of the meeting, in an eloquent speech, extended a welcome to the guests of the association, and in obedience to a general call General Kershaw replied for a few appropriate remarks.

The first toast of the evening, "Old South Carolina," was responded to by Major T.G. Barker and Honorable James B. Campbell.

The second toast was proposed by Mr. George Bryan, "Robert E. Lee," which was ably and eloquently responded to by Mr. F.W. McMaster of Columbia.

The next toast, "Wade Hampton," had the effect of bringing the entire company to their feet with three rousing cheers. Major Barker was called upon and responded with a glowing tribute to the distinguished soldier.

Colonel Rutledge next gave "The Memory of our Departed Comrades, the Confederate Dead." Alluding in touching terms to their patriotism and devotion to country. The toast was drunk standing and in silence.

Colonel P. C. Gaillard proposed "The Army of Northern Virginia," and the toast was received with a good old rebel hurrah.

Colonel William Wallace made an eloquent response.

By General Conner, "The Army of the West," responded to by Captain William Elliot.

By Colonel Z. Davis, "Sumter," responded by Colonel Alfred Rhett.

By Captain F.W. Dawson, "The Women of the War."

And so the evening passed in pleasant reunion, and amid the reminiscence of the campaigns of war. [537]

---

[537] The State Survivors' Association: Organization and Election of Officers, The Charleston Courier, November 19, 1869.

The Kershaw County Survivors' Association

The first meeting of the Survivors' Meeting took place at town hall about a week ago on a Monday. General J.B. Kershaw was called to the chair and James N. Davis was requested to serve as secretary.

The Chairman then explained the object of the meeting, and that in his opinion delegates should be sent to the meeting on December 18 in Charleston; several delegates were then selected: General J.B. Kershaw, General J.D. Kennedy, Captain W.Z. Leitner, Captain W.L. DePass, J.G. Moffit, W. Clyburn, Dove Segars, A.A. Moore, J.M. Davis, W.M. Shannon, John Doby, and William Whitaker.

On motion of Captain DePass, the meeting then organized under the name "Survivors' Association of Kershaw District." General J.B. Kershaw, President; Generals J.D. Kennedy, Captain W.L. DePass, Captain W.Z. Leitner, Vice-Presidents; J. M. Davis, Secretary, and A.A. Moore, Treasurer.

On motion of Colonel W.M. Shannon, a committee of seven was appointed to draft a constitution and bylaws for the government of this association to report at the meeting to be held on Dec 20. The Committee consisted of W.M. Shannon, J.D. Kennedy, W.Z. Leitner, W.L. DePass, S. Baruch, S. Lorick, and A.A. Moore.

On motion of the chairman, Colonel Shannon was requested to deliver a public address at seven o'clock of the evening of Dec 20. Colonel Shannon signified his cheerful acceptance of the appointment.

On motion of T. H. Clark, it was:

> Resolved that a supper be provided for the member of the association and its guests, after the address, and make necessary arrangements. The committee consisted of T.H. Clark, Dr. A.W. Burnet, Allen Deas, J.T. Hay, W. Whitaker, J.G. Moffit, James R. Arrants, S. Lorrick, John Doby, and Dr. C.J. Shannon.

On motion of W.L. DePass, those present wishing to join the association were requested to enroll their names with the secretary. The motion was adopted.

The meeting was then adjourned.

J.B. Kershaw, President.

J.M. Davis, Secretary[538]

---

[538] Survivor's Association, The Journal, Camden, S.C., November 11, 1869.

The Kershaw County Survivors' Association met on December 20, 1869 in the town hall, for the purpose of agreeing on a constitution. This meeting was called to order by the president, Colonel Shannon, Chairman of the committee to draft a constitution, proceeded to report and submit a constitution. After the reading of the constitution, on motion of General Chesnut but it was decided to vote, but afterwards the motion was amended, upon the suggestion of Colonel Shannon, to decide upon each clause and section separately. The Title was then taken up, and after some discussion, the preference was given to the words District or County, upon the suggestion of the president, it was agreed to take a middle course, and make no use of either term, to make the name of the association, "The Survivors' Association of Kershaw."

The constitution as submitted was taken up by Articles and Section, and adopted, with an amendment to 1st Section, of Article 3, upon motion of Dr. E.M. Boykin, to add a chaplain to the list of officers, there enumerated. W.Z. Leitner moved that two hundred copies of the Constitution with a list of the members of the association, for distribution among themselves, which the motion was carried. Colonel Shannon moved for ballot for vice-president and proposed General Chesnut. Dr. Boykin proposed the name of Reverend John Johnson for chaplain. A motion was then made and carried, to put into the hands of the existing officers, the duty of nominating candidates temporarily, to allow them to confer for that purpose; after consulting, the names of the following gentlemen were proposed and accepted:

>
> Vice-President - General James Chesnut
>
> Chaplain - Reverend John Johnson
>
> Committee on Application - Colonel E.M. Boykin, W.H.R. Workman, R.H. Pegues, John Kershaw, John T. Davis
>
> Committee on Records - Colonel W.M. Shannon, General James Chesnut, Reverend John Johnson, W.Z. Leitner,
>
> and E.M. Boykin.
>
> Committee on Charity - Dr. A.A. Moore, Dr. A.W. Burnet, Dr. S. Baruch, Dr. C.J. Shannon, and Dr. B. Matheson
>
> Committee on Employment- J.M. Davis, W.L. DePass, J.R. Goodale, J.D. Kennedy, and J.D. Dunlap.

Colonel Shannon offered the name of Lieutenant General R.H. Anderson, for honorary membership of the association, and upon a motion, General Anderson was unanimously elected. Upon suggestion of the chair, a motion was made and adopted that a notice be published in the *Camden Journal* for six months, asking for all persons who had any documents or records bearing upon the history of the late war, to turn them over to the association, and the secretary be instructed to attend to said publication. Being no further business, the meeting was adjourned to Jan 1, next.

At half-past seven in the evening, Colonel Shannon delivered a stirring address to a large and enthusiastic audience of ladies and gentlemen.

After the address, the members of the association, and their guests adjourned at Jones Hall, and sat down to a bounteous collection prepared by that well-known caterer, J.W. Rodgers, assisted by his better half.

The appetites of the feasters being appeased; the chairman, J.B. Kershaw, read the following first regular toast:

> The day we celebrate. Responded to by Colonel W.M. Shannon.
> Our honored Dead. Responded by General J.D. Kennedy.
> The Lost Cause. Responded by Captain T.H. Clarke.
> General Robert E. Lee. Responded by Major W.Z. Leitner.
> Our State. Responded by Colonel E. M. Boykin.

After the toasts, the punch having been freely circulated, various sentiments were offered, and responded to in a suitable manner. In fact, so harmonious and friendly a meeting, we have seldom witnessed. Midnight caught most of the revelers on their way homeward. This ended the first celebration given under the auspices of the "Survivors' Association of Kershaw."[539]

From the Kershaw Survivor's Association, the path led to the development of the United Confederate Veterans around the year 1890. The name of the camp was Dick Kirkland Camp, which later was changed to Richard Kirkland Camp. Soon thereafter, as Confederate Veterans began to die off more rapidly, sons of these soldiers came together to form the Sons of Confederate Soldiers. Today the local Sons of Confederate Chapter is called "The Joseph Brevard Kershaw Camp #82."

Prepared for the Survivors' Association
Roll of Company 7th of the State of South Carolina
By Dove Segars

Name	Date Entered	Age Entered	Rank	Promotions
Dove Segars	14 Nov 1861	27	2nd Lieutenant, Elected	Captain of Company F, May 27, 1862
Willam McSween	14 Nov 1861	35	2nd Sergeant	
John Ervin Horton	14 Nov 1861		4th Sergeant	
Henry Dickerson Tiller	14 Nov 1861	17	3rd Sergeant	
Andrew W. Raley	14 Nov 1861	32	Private	
Gilliam Preston King	14 Nov 1861	22	Private	
Stephen L. Gardner	14 Nov 1861	18	Corporal	
James Frank Kelly	1 May 1862	39	Private	
Sampson Hough	14 Nov 1861	28	Private	
Henry Pate	10 Jan 1863	43	Private	

---

[539] Meeting of the Survivor's Association, The Journal, Camden, S.C., December 23, 1869.

Stephen Franklin Phillips	14 Dec 1861	20	Private	
James Hubbard McCaskill	14 Dec 1861	18	Private	
Thomas David Gardner	14 Dec 1861	20	Private	
James Ervin Sowell	12 June 1862	24	Private	
James Hubbard McCaskill	14 Dec 1861	19	Private	
Thomas David Gardner	14 Dec 1861	20	Private	
James Ervin Sowell	12 June 1862	24	Private	
Benjamin James Turner	14 Nov 1861	36	Private	
Stephen Thomas Folsom	14 Nov 1861	20	Private	
Thomas Powell Duren	14 Nov 1861	22	Private	
James Stanley Horton	14 Nov 1861	19	Private	
Joseph West	14 Nov 1861	30	Private	
Redick Raley	25 Feb 1863	21	Private	
James Reddick Bone	14 Nov 1861	44	Private	
William Williamson Bone	1 Nov 1862	21	Private	
James Bruce	14 Nov 1861	42	Private	
Reddick E. Barnes	14 Nov 1861	22	Private	
William Barnes	8 Mar 1863	18	Private	
Neil James Bennett	21 Oct 1864	18	Private	
Robert Jefferson Bell	9 Jan 1862	21	Private	
George Patney Blackman	9 Feb 1864	18	Private	
James Cato	9 Dec 1861	37	Private	
William Thomas Cato	13 Sept 1863	17	Private	
William Cato	2 Nov 1864	43	Private	
John Wilson Caston	14 Nov 1861	18	Private	
Thomas Richardson Cantey	5 Jan 1864	30	Private	
John Henry Culpepper	15 Mar 1864	16	Private	
Thomas Ripley Copeland	25 Mar 1864	18	Private	
Lovick Clanton	27 Sept 1864	17	Private	
Benjamin Campbell	21 Oct 1864	17	Private	
James Campbell	24 Nov 1864	16	Private	
Harbin Thomas Davis	14 Nov 1861	16	Private	
Jessie Dickson	12 July 1863	33	Private	
William Elliott	24 Oct 1864	28	Private	
William Wesley Folsom	14 July 1862	18	Private	
John James Folsom	25 Mar 1864	18	Private	
Daniel Whitfield Gardner	23 Mar 1862	28	Private	
William Jefferson Gardner	17 Mar 1862	37	Private	
Miles L. Gardner	12 Apr 1862	25	Private	
William Nero Gee	17 Mar 1862	28	Private	

Nathan William Gibson	29 Apr 1864	17	Private	
James Hall	14 Nov 1861	22	Private	
William Ellison Hall	17 Mar 1862	27	Private	
Jacob Riley Hall	17 Mar 1862	22	Private	
Joseph Hall	26 Nov 1861	27	Private	
Thomas Reese Holland	26 Nov 1861	27	Private	
James Holland	25 Oct 1864	41	Private	
Thomas Holland	25 Oct 1864	44	Private	
James Emanuel Herron	18 Mar 1862	21	Private	
George Samuel Herron	14 Nov 1861	18	Private	
Ranson Horton	--------	46	Private	
Thomas R. Horton	2 Mar 1854	27	Private	
James Hopkins	14 Nov 1861	30	Private	
Lewis Hopkins	1 Jan 1864	18	Private	
Malcolm Hopkins	1 Sept 1862	36	Private	
Labon Carraway Hough	29 July 1863	18	Private	
Isaac Shepard Hough	17 Feb 1864	29	Private	
Hiram Francis Hollis	19 Mar 1864	18	Private	
Jesse Manuel Haggood	20 Mar 1862	17	Private	
Jesse Hornsby	23 Mar 1864	16	Private	
G. W. Lafayette Hollaman	6 Dec 1864	28	Private	
J. L. Hogan	-------	-------	-------	
Moody Ingram	2 Sept 1862	37	Private	
Richard T. Jones	-------	-------	-------	
John Todd Jones	1 Jan 1864	34	Private	
Nathaniel William Jones	14 Nov 1861	16	Private	
Samuel Newton Jones	1 Nov 1862	19	Private	
Columbus Alexander Jamison	27 Fev 1864	16	Private	
George King	14 Nov 1861	18	Private	
George Kennington	28 Apr 1864	35	Private	
Charles Wesley McCaskill	14 Nov 1861	20	Private	
William Patterson McCaskill	1 Mar 1864	18	Private	
William McLendon	14 Nov 1861	22	Private	
Elias McLendon	7 Oct 1863	19	Private	
Gillis McLendon	13 Mar 1864	18	Private	
Angus McGougan	14 Nov 1861	27	Private	
Archibald McGougan	3 Apr 1863	24	Private	
John McGougan	18 Mar 1862	25	Private	
Redick Mosley	1 Jan 1864	18	Private	
Robert Peele Miller	9 Feb 1864	24	Private	

Henry James Munn	21 Oct 1864	18	Private	
Benjamin Daniel McCoy	29 Apr 1864	17	Private	
John Thomas Newman	14 Nov 1861	19	Private	
John Hamilton Newman	14 Nov 1861	21	Private	
Burwell Wiley Newman	14 Nov 1861	16	Private	
Milberry Wainright Newman	17 Apr 1862	23	Private	
Henry Newsome	17 Feb 1864	18	Private	
Hubbard Norris	12 Apr 1864	45	Private	
Curtis Outlaw	6 Mar 1864	28	Private	
Robert J. Phillips	1 Mar 1862	21	Private	
Charles Ingram Phillips	1 Apr 1863	37	Private	
George Washington Phillips	1 Mar 1862	29	Private	
W. Riley Phillips	24 Dec 1864	44	Private	
Levi Pate, Jr.	1 Mar 1864	22	Private	
Chapman Pate	9 Feb 1864	37	Private	
Dove Raley	14 Mar 1863	18	Private	
William Raley	29 Aug 1863	41	Private	
William Columbus Ratcliff	14 Nov 1861	21	Private	
James Robinson	1 Mar 1864	18	Private	
Hilton Robinson	2 Nov 1864	39	Private	
Musco B. Raines	9 Mar 1864	17	Private	
John Smith	14 Nov 1861	41	Private	
Edward Martin Surles	15 Mar 1862	24	Private	
George Nelson Shoemake	17 Jan 1862	34	Private	
Lilly Thomas Stroud	1 July 1863	18	Private	
John M. Stroud	13 Sept 1863	17	Private	
Charles Spencer Stokes	6 Mar 1864	17	Private	
Timothy Scott	26 Mar 1864	14	Private	
James Frederick Sutton	1 Apr 1864	16	Private	
Wiley Sowell	16 Apr 1864	18	Private	
James Sutt--	21 Apr 1864	18	Private	
J. Dunky---	19 May 1864	18	Private	
Benjamin Danie Turner	5 July 1862	28	Private	
Robert J. Turner	14 Nov 1861	25	Private	
William Black Thompson	14 July 1862	36	Private	
Henry Thompson	28 Apr 1864	17	Private	
Joseph James -----	26 Jan 1864	31	Private	
Thomas Sumter--	23 Oct 1864	18	Private	
Jesse Ellis Watkins	-----	---	-----	
James Jackson Watkins	------	---	------	
F. Watkins	-------	----	-------	

Notes from Dove Segars:

J.D. Shaw - enlisted May 19, 1864 by Lieutenant A. W. Raley. Killed at Tiller's Ferry, South Carolina, July 4, 1891.

Jessie Hornsby was mustered in by Major T.W. Radcliff on the March 1864, until June 15, 1864, as he was very sick on the march from Malvern Hill to Petersburg, and he supposedly fell in the hands of the enemy, and died, as he had not been heard from up to this date - April 10, 1869.

S.F. Phillips was mustered in by R.B. Waddle at Camden, South Carolina, Nov 14, 1861. Transferred to Company F, 7th SC Battalion. He served until August 21, 1862, when he was killed in the corge on the Weldon Ralirod Road. He was appointed sergeant a few days before his death for his bravery and promptness to duty.

George Samuel Herron was mustered in by R. B. Waddle at Camden, South Carolina, Nov 14, 1861. August 21, 1863, he lost a leg in the charge on the Weldon Railroad, and fell in the hands of the enemy and died date unknown.

William McSween was enlisted by R.B. Waddle on Nov 14, 1861. Wounded in the Battle of Drury's Bluff, May 16, 1864, and died from wounds, June 2, 1864.

Ransom Horton was enlisted by Lieutenant R.B. Wadlle, at Camden, South Carolina on Nov 14, 1861, He was discharged April 1862, and rejoined the battalion at Camp Cantey, March 14, 1863, by Lieutenant H.D. Tiller. He was killed in the corge on the Weldon Railroad, August 21, 1864.

W.L. Warren enlisted at Battery Marshall, Sept 11, 1863. He died in the hospital at Petersburg, Virginia, June 29, 1864, of typhoid fever.

E. West enlisted Jan 19, 1863 by Captain L.W.R. Blair. He was killed in the Battle of Drury's Bluff, May 16, 1864, by being shot in the head.

Lewis Hopkins enlisted Jan 1, 1864 at Battery Marshall by Lieutenant McSween. He was severely wounded by shell on June 1864 and died the same day of wounds received in the trenches near Petersburg.

Jessie M. Hagood enlisted at Fort Johnson, March 20, 1864, by Lieutenant H.D. Tiller. He was killed in a skirmish June 16, 1864. Petersburg, Virginia.

W.L. Herron enlisted September 11, 1863, Battery Marshall, by Lieutenant H.D. Tiller. He died in a hospital at Petersburg, Virginia, June 29, 1864, of typhoid fever.

Dove Raley enlisted March 14, 1863, Camp Caney, by Lieutenant H.D. Tiller. He died in a hospital near Petersburg, Virginia, August 31, 1864, of typhoid fever.

G.N. Shoemake enlisted March 11, 1862, Tiller's Ferry, by S. B. Lucas. He died in Chesterfield District, South Carolina, August 26, 1864.

Lieutenant J.E. Horton enlisted November 14, 1861, Camden, South Carolina, by Lieutenant R.B. Waddle. He died at the home of Lewis Sowell in Kershaw District, November 1, 1862, of typhoid fever.

S.J. Folsom enlisted Camden, South Carolina, November 14, 1861, by Lieutenant R.B. Waddle. He was appointed corporal July 18, 1862. He was killed at Pocataglio, South Carolina, October 22, 1862, after being shot through the heart.

James Bruce enlisted November 14, 1861, Camden, South Carolina, by Lieutenant R.B. Waddle. He was wounded at Pocatalogo, South Carolina, October 22, 1862, and died December 5, 1862, at McPherson Hospital. Wounded in the hip joint by a minnie ball.

John W. Caston enlisted November 14, 1861, Camden, South Carolina, by Lieutenant R.B. Waddell. He died September 10, 1864, at the residence of his father, in Lancaster, South Carolina, of typhoid fever.

James Hall enlisted November 14, 1861, in Camden, South Carolina by Lieutenant R.B. Waddle. He was killed at Pocataglio, South Carolina, on October 22, 1862, He was shot through the left breast, and died instantly.

J.W. Horton enlisted March 23, 1863, Tiller's Ferry, by Lieutenant S.B. Lucas. He died at Battery Marshall, South Carolina, on September 7, 1863, of typhoid fever.

John McGougan enlisted March 18, 1862, Tiller's Ferry, by Lieutenant S.B. Lucas. He was wounded at Pocataglio, South Carolina, and died of wounds, October 24, 1862, at McPherson Hospital.

M.W. Newman enlisted April 17, 1862, Camp Chesnut, Colleton District, by Captain L.W.R. Blair. He died at the residence of S.P. Murchinson, Kershaw District, South Carolina, August 24, 1862, of typhoid fever.

R.J. Turner enlisted November 14, 1861, Camden, South Carolina by Lieutenant R.B. Waddell. He was wounded at Pocataglio, South Carolina, in the left shoulder, October 22, 1862, and discharged October 1863.

M.L. Gardner replaced R.J. Bell on 1 January 1864, by command of Brigadier General Ripley.

Richard L. Jones transferred by command of the Secretary of War, August 8, 1864.

List of Deceased Soldiers Company F, 7th S.C. Battalion:

William McSween	Joseph Hall	Wiley Lansley Warren
James Ervin Horton	William Thomas	Cato Dove Raley
Benjamin James Turner	Reddin E. Barnes	George Nelson Shoemake
Stephen Thomas Folsom	Moody Ingram	Charles Spenser Stokes
James Bruce	Lewis Hopkins	James Hall
John Nelson Caston	Levi Pate, Jr.	John McGougan
James Wyatt Horton	Richard Edward West	Stephen Franklin Phillips
Milberry Wainright Newman	Jesse Manuel Hagood	Ransom Horton
George Samuel Herron	Jessie Hornsby	

One Confederate Veteran organization was the Camp Angus McLaurin. This camp was in the Bethune area. No real roll found.

Another Confederate Veteran Organization was the Hanging Rock Camp #738, Kershaw, South Carolina.

Hanging Rock Camp # 738

April 22, 1899 Roll

J. V. Welsh	Company D	1st S.C. Regiment	Commander of Camp
J. Q. McManus	Sergeant Major	1st S.C. Regiment Infantry	Adjutant of Camp
C.C. Horton	Company C	Hampton's Legion	
B. A. Hilton	Company B	Lucas Battalion Heavy Artillery	

J. W. Huntley		North Carolina State Troops	
Frank Blakeney	Company D	Lieutenant- 40th Alabama Volunteers	
N. H. Bowers	Company H	2nd S.C. Volunteers	
B. N. Jones	Company H	4th S.C. Cavalry	
D.J. Davis	Company G	2nd SC	
William Horton	Company H	2nd SC Infantry	
W.J. Horton	Company C	Hampton Legion Cavalry	
J. T. Cauthen	-------	DePass Battery	
L.C. Hough	Company F	7th SC Battery	
Eli Knight	Company C	26th SC Regiment	
J.S. Hinson	Company E	12th SC Regiment	
W.R. Gardner	-------	7th SC Battalion	
P.M. Blakeney	-------	-------	
C.W. Horton	-------	-------	
G.W. Gardner	-------	Waites Battery	
W.A. Ingram	Company E	5th SC Battalion	
E.D. Williams	Company F	7th NC Regiment	
Dr. C.C. Welsh	Assistant Surgeon	DePass Regiment	
J. E. Jones	-------	2nd SC Regiment	
W.A. Barfield	-------	-------	
W.J. Jones	Company D	7th SC Battalion	
W.F. Rutledge	Company D	7th SC Battalion	
V.D. Brown	-------	-------	
S.J. Benton	Captain Company K	2nd S.C. Volunteers	
W.D. Ingram	-------	-------	
John M. Stroud	------	------	
Robert Lowry	Company H	2nd SC Volunteers	
J. W. Boone	Company D	7th SC Battalion	
N.J. Bennett	Company F	7th SC Battalion	
B.M. Jones	Company D	5th SC Battalion	
L.J. Stroud	Company F	7th SC Battalion	
M. L. HInson	Company H	2nd SC Volunteers	
R.A. Criminger	Company E	12th SC Volunteers	
L. D. Ogburn	Company D	8th SC Volunteers	
John Boone	Company G	2nd Volunteers	
W.J. Boone	Company G	2nd Volunteers	
Isaac Gardner	-------	-------	
J. R. Sowell	-------	-------	

Roll of March 14, 1900

James V. Welsh	Commander
L.C. Hough	1st Lieutenant
Bob Jones	2nd Lieutenant
T.C. Horton	3rd Lieutenant
J. W. Denton	4th Lieutenant
J. Q. McManus	Adjutant
B.A. Hilton	Treasurer
W.H. Sowell	Sergeant Major
D. J. Davis	Chaplain
S.J. Benton	Quartermaster
W.M. Horton	-------
W.J. Boone	Color Bearer
E.D. Williams	1st Color Bearer
N. H. Bowers	2nd Color Bearer
Mrs. P.V. Boone	Sponsor
Alex Brown	-------
G.W. Gardner	-------
Isaac Gardner	--------
John Boone	-------
James Boone	-------

Roll of March 30, 1901

Rank in U.C.V.

J.V. Welsh	Private	1st S.C.V	Commander
John B. Boone	Private	2nd S.C.V. Company G	Quartermaster
J.E. Jones	Private	2nd S.C.C. Company G	Private
C.C. Horton	Private	Hampton's Legion	4th Lieutenant
J.T. Cauthen	Private	2nd S.C.V. Company G	Treasurer
W. J. Jones	Sergeant	7th S.C. Battalion Company G	Private
L.C. Hough	Private	7th S.C. Battalion Company F	1st Lieutenant
R.J. Lowry	Private	2nd S.C. V. Company H	Private
B.N. Jones	Private	4th Regiment Cavalry	Adjutant
J.Q. McManus	Sergeant-Major	1st S.C. Infantry	Commissary
B. M. Jones	Private	5th Battalion S.C.V.	Sergeant- Major
S.J. Deason	Captain	2nd S.C.V. Company G	2nd Lieutenant
Dice Davis	Private	7th Battalion S.C.V.	3rd Lieutenant
J. M. Bowers	Private	2nd S.C.V. Company G	Private
S. D. Johnson	Private	2nd S.C.V. Company G.	Private

J. H. W. Stevens	Private	4th Regiment S.C. Calvary Company H	Private
L. O. Jones	Private	7th SC Battalion S.C.V. 3rd	Lieutenant
James Boone	Private	7th Battalion S.C.V.	Private
W.J. Boone	Private	2nd S.C.V. Company G	Private
N. Bowers	Private	2nd S.C. V. Company H	Private

Roll of March 29, 1902

S. J. Benton	Quartermaster
B.A. Hilton	1st Lieutenant Commander
L.C. Hough	Captain and Commander
Martin Cauthen	Surgeon
C.C. Horton	2nd Lieutenant Commander
T.C. Horton	4th Lieutenant Commander
Lewis Gardner	Commissary
J. V. Welsh	Treasurer
J. Q. McManus	3rd Lieutenant Commander
W.F. Rutledge	------------------------------
W. Mack Horton	Assistant Surgeon
J. H. W. Stevens	------------------------------
J. B Witherspoon	Chaplain
N.J. Bennett	------------------------
B.N. Jones	Adjutant
J.T. Cauthen	Sergeant- Major
W.H. Sowell	Officer of the Day
J. W. Huntley	Color Sergeant
J. E. Jones	Vidette
Eli Knight	1st Color Guard
B.M. Jones	2nd Color Guard
Mrs. J. Q. McManus	Sponsor

Roll of 1908

L.C. Hough

J.B. Baker -6 Regiment Butler's Brigade Cavalry

B.A. Hilton

W.J. Jones

W.H. Sowell

B.M. Jones

G.W. Gardner

N. Bennett

B.H. Jones

Delegates to the U.C.V. Reunion, Dallas, Texas, April 22 to 25, 1902

J.Q. McManus

Colonel L.C. Hough

Mrs. J.Q. McManus

Another Confederate Veteran Organization is the Richard Kirkland Camp # 704, Camden, South Carolina.

Roll April 23, 1898

C.C. Haile	Captain and Commander
D.M. Bethune	1st Lieutenant
W. Whitaker	2nd Lieutenant
J. L. Haile	3rd Lieutenant
E.E. Sill	Adjutant
James L. Villipique	Quartermaster
W.R. McCreight	Commissary
A. A. Moore	Surgeon
W.W. Mills	Chaplain
Joel Hough	Secretary, Treasurer, Sergeant-at-Arms
W.F. Russell	--------------------------------
W.S. Marshal	Color Sergeant
John Boone	Vidette
T. B. Denton	1st Color Guard
R.J. Hall	2nd Color Guard

Allen Deas	J. E. Alexander	H. C. Salmond
W.D. Trantham	John W. Rose	B.D. Turner
W.J. Fletcher	N.W. Jones	J. B. Arrants
John Albert	J. J. Rush	J. J. Bell
Thomas Whitaker	J. M. Legrand	Simeon Stokes
W.G. Huckabee	W.P. Dubose	W.A. Ancrum
H. K. DuBose	J. R. DeLoache	J. B. Phelps
William C. Roberts	J. W. Hyatt	L. L. Clyburn
J. B. Steadman	R.C. Brown	Stephen Self
J. C. Boulware	W.F. Reed	E.E. Stokes
W.T. Marshall	A.D. Kennedy	C. J. Shannon
J. D. McCaskill	N.A. Bethune	J. D. McLaurin
T.P. Sanders	A. P. Kirby	W.J. Boone

James Boone	C.L. Moseley	J. Player
E.B. Cantey	James Catoe	William Brown
J. J. Kelly	D.H. Kelly	J. W. Floyd
John Green	Thomas Barefoot	William Gladden
G.W. Watts	L. J. Watts	L. P. Powers
J. G. Rowell	S.A. Branham	W.J. Arrants
James Robertson	W.J.T. Bateman	W.C. Ratcliffe
C. W. Hyatt	A.J. Munn	A.C. Outen
T.H. Davis	T.W.B. Smith	D.A. Baker
G. H. Coates	J. R. Raley	G.W. Moseley
John A. Faulkenberry	R. Moseley	J. R. Hall
J. M. Hall	W.E. Hall	H. C. West
R.J. Turner	Duncan Ray	Hiram Nettles
W. J. Young	E.G. Ward	G. W. Self
W.F. Self	J. D. Stewart	J. S. Cunningham
Moses Hough	J. E. Douglass	R. Douglass
John Outlaw	Isaac Gay	Robert Parham
Joel Hough, Sr.	Amos Hough	William Ray
C.B. Cureton	W.C. Brown	Henry Smith
T.C. Roseborough	Joseph West	W.A. Addison
A.J. McDowell	A. M. Dunn	William Branham
E. Hays	John Ervin	J. H. Isbell
N. Ray	G. L. Dixon	J. C. Truesdel
John M. Perry	J. O. Shaylor	J. C. Rollings
A. H. Boykin	R. J. Hyatt	R. Player
John A. Rabon	J. H. Williamson	E. Hunter
D. E. Stevenson	A. Medlin	A. C. Medlin
James T. Truesdel	G. S. Rhame	J. T. Cottrall
B. H. Boykin	John Boykin	T.G. Coates
Sam Boykin	W. Geisenheimer (added July 16, 1898)	

March 14, 1902 Officers

James L. Haile	Captain and Commander
E.E. Sill	1st Lieutenant and Commander
N.A. Bethune	2nd Lieutenant and Commander
Joel Hough	3rd Lieutenant and Commander
H.C. Salmond	Adjutant and Treasurer
James I. Villipigue	Quartermaster
J. C. Rollings	Commissary
Dr. A.A. Moore	Surgeon
Reverend W. W. Mills	Chaplain

W. F. Russell	Officer of the Day
John Boone	Vidette
Thomas Whitaker	1st Color Guard
J. A. Alexander	2nd Color Guard

Delegates attending Dallas, Texas, April 22 to April 25, 1902 for the U. C. V. Twelfth Annual Reunion

Captain L.L. Clyburn

Captain J.C. Rowlings

Roll for May 12, 1904

W. A. Ancrum	Commander
E. E. Sill	1st Lieutenant
Joel Hough, Sr.	2nd Lieutenant
W. F. Russell	3rd Lieutenant
H. C. Salmond	Adjutant
J. I. Villipigue	Quartermaster
J. C. Rollings	Commissary
A. A. Moore	Surgeon
Reverend W. W. Mills	Chaplain
Thomas B. Denton	Sergeant-Major
Thomas Whitaker	1st Color Guard
J. E. Alexander	2nd Color Guard
John Boone	Vidette

Comrades

Anderson, J.M.	Arrants, John	Alexander, George
Brailsford, A.M.	Bass, S.M.	Boone, James
Boone, W.	Bowen, C.P.	Boykin, A.H.
Branham, H.	Cantey, E.B.	Clyburn, L.L.
DeSaussure, D.L., Dr.	Deas, Allen	DeLoache, J.R.
Dubose, H.K.	Gordon, Reverend W.R.	Haile, J. L.
Jackson, George	Kennedy, A.M.	Jackson, T. J.
Lollis, W. T.	McManus, Joseph	McDowell, W.D.
Moore, S.M.	Munn, H. J.	Phelps, John
Pierce, Benjamin	Player, H.C.	Sanders, T. P.
Reed, W.F.	Self, Stephen	Steedman, J.B.
Stewart, Chap	Trantham, W.D.	Thompson, W.K.
Turner, S.B.	Whitaker, William	Williams, J.C.P.
Williamson, J.H.	Wilson, James	

In 1923, the group had sixteen members on roll with W.F. Russell being Commander. This group met annually.

April 13, 1926 Roll

Bennett, N.J.	Bethune, N.A.	Brailsford, A.M.
Branham, William	Brasington, J.S.	Brown, T.N.
Brown, N.M.	Connell, J.F.	Cunningham, N.A.
DeLoache, J.R.	Faile, Nathan	Gardner, Isaac
Hinson, Reubin	Holland, Isaac	Jones, B.M.
Jones, W.J.	King, G.B.	McKenzie, A.P.
Moseley, G.W.	Murchison, D.P.C.	Nettles, Hiram
Rose, J.N.	Russel, W.F.	Shannon, C.J.
Sinclair, James	Stewart, T.A.	Stewart, C.J.
Terry, William H.	Turner, S.B.	Watts, L.W.

The Ladies Aid Society
(The Confederate Monuments, Other Monuments, and Memorial Days)

THE LADIES AID SOCIETY STARTED on or before 1861. No exact date has been located. The year 1861 is being used as the start date and articles found in the newspaper at that time.

In the Journal, May 16, 1872, the following was found:

> Memorial Day - Decoration of the Soldier's Graves - Incidents of the Occasion
>
> The ladies were out in force on Friday afternoon at the cemetery, to present their annual tribute of love to the memory of the Confederate Dead, who repose in our midst. Many gentlemen were also in attendance.
>
> The proceedings were begun in prayer offered by Reverend A.J. Stokes, which was appropriate for the occasion.

Honorable W.Z. Leitner was then called upon and delivered an address as follows:

> He alluded to the cause of assembling here this afternoon: to pour out the lactation of grateful hearts upon the graves of our heroic dead. The Confederate soldier was a man of peculiar characteristics, highest, and noblest of which was his devotion to duty; (He then narrated certain incidents from life which illustrated their extreme devotion to duty) this devotion was stimulated by the noble women of the South; that the greatest struggles are not those of the battlefield, but those of the human heart, which were fought in the silence of the closet and in the secret of the night watches; that the cause for which we fought is not dead; the glorious cause of constitutional liberty was staked in the issue; it was a part and parcel of our existence; that the Southerners were a peculiar people, noted for the grandeur of their moral character, and the purity of their social nature; it is our duty to promote the interest of the cause for which we fought, by preserving our identity as a people, and the best way of effecting this end is to cherish memories such as these, and by paying such tribute as we do today, and by teaching our children's children to revere the memory, and emulate the virtues of the Confederate Dead.

After this short but eloquent address, the ladies proceeded to the work of decorating the graves of the soldiers, a sad and mournful duty, which they well performed.

We have thought of the propriety of having an Association among the ladies, the object of which should be to have a systematic way of attending to the decoration and care taken of the graves of our soldiers. The plan works well in other places. The annual contribution could be put down to fifty cents, a sum so low that everyone could well afford to belong to the Association, and much might be done in the relief of worthy distressed widows and orphans of deceased soldiers.

The following poem is to commemorate the occasion of Memorial Day.

> We gather round your graves today,
> Our loving tribute here to pay;
> Ye rest in peace, our martyr band,
> Who died to save our Southern Land.
>
> Dying e're yet our flag was furled,
> While still he bring a gazing world,
> Its starry cross was lifted high,
> In triumph, mostly our sunny day.
>
> Tis drooping now, forever furled,
> In blood and death, its bright stars hurled,
> But oh! How proudly this we tell,
> The South, its folds are fought and fell.
>
> And woman's deathless love will shed,
> Forever over our precious dead,
> The bitter tear of grief and war,
> While bending over each bed so low.
>
> A mother's love in anguish deep,
> Where her boy lay in dreamless sleep,
> Upon Virginia's blood-stained field,
> He fell, that Mother's home to shield.
>
> Another lends her orphan boy,
> Her pride and her best earthly joy,
> Where rest within the soldier's grave,
> His here father, true and brave.

She bids him emulate his sire,
Fills his young soul with holy ere,
To do and dare all for the right,
Which served that father's blade so bright.

So now, on the sad tenth of May,
Loved ones and comrades fondly lay,
Their annual gift, these flowers sweet,
On each low grave, as here we meet.

And ever may our hero band,
Be honored thus throughout the land,
And a whole mourning people pay.
Their tribute on Memorial Day.

On April 28, 1874, the Ladies Memorial Association of Camden, South Carolina, was organized.[540] This association agreed "to form an organization from that of a soldier to be known as 'The Ladies Memorial Association,'" in charge of the graves so that they "will be cared for because of that, forming a day to be called 'Memorial Day,' to be observed on May 10."[541] Enough time will be given to allow those who wish to observe with us at this particular time of honor. This organization shall have a president, secretary, and treasurer, selecting annually. Dues shall be three dollars. C.M. Miller will be appointed to carry out the duties of this organization. Meetings held at the Presbyterian Church Lecture Room.

On April 23, 1874, the following were elected:

President - Mrs. Alfred Doby
Vice-Presidents - Mrs. T.W. Salmond
Miss C.M. Boykin
Treasurer - Mrs. Witherspoon
Secretary - Miss A.H. Boykin
Committees - Miss McDowell
Mrs. Villipigue
Mrs. Green

---

[540] Ladies Memorial Association of Camden, South Carolina, 1874-1894; John D. Kennedy Collection, Camden Archives and Museum, Camden, South Carolina
[541] Ibid.

On Sunday, April 13, 1874, the soldiers' graves were decorated, prayer was given by Pastor Hay and Mrs. Davis gave an appropriate address.

The following was in *The Kershaw Gazette*, May 20, 1874.

Memorial Day

Is among the hallowed days of the year, and especially so to those who cherish the sacred memory of the "loved and lost" of Carolina's gallant sons; the young and brave who fought, tried, and died in her holy cause. The ceremony of May 11 will be among the embalmed memories of the citizens of Camden, whose deed rest is the cemetery and on distant fields — noble souls? Who, at their country's call, "rushed to glory, and the grave."

It is a beautiful ceremony, adopted by the fair daughters of our land, to decorate with "flowers, sweet flowers, that neither spin nor toll," whose little lives are one perpetual smile, the sod where softly lie and sweetly sleep the forms of their loved ones — fathers, husbands, and the heart's fond idol; men who in arms excelled — stern, patriots, resilient champions to vindicate the honor of the State — men toward whom,

> "When mustered to the gathering horn,
> The northern chieftain curled his lip with scorn,
> And when they fainted in their forced retreat,
> Tracked the snow-drifts with their bleeding feet."

Beautiful, indeed, in the custom to deck with emblematic flowers the chambers of out dead, "when spring comes laughing in with flowers and fragrance floats from every tree." This pleasant but sad memory was honored by a large concourse of citizens on Monday afternoon of last week, who assembled at the cemetery at six o'clock. Meeting in front of the entrance, they were formed in procession under the direction of Major W.Z. Leitner, acting as marshal, and preceded by the Camden Cornet Band, were marched to the stand, which had been erected near the homes of the departed. Prayer was offered by Reverend S.H. Hay, an appropriate ode sung by a choir of ladies and gentlemen, and an interesting address delivered by Captain James M. Davis, who had been by the Ladies Memorial Association for that purpose.

Among others, the following is one of the beautiful odes sung on the occasion and rendered with pleasing effect:

> Beautiful feet with maidenly trend.
> Offerings being to the gallant dead.
> Footsteps light press the sacred sod,
> Of souls untimely ascended to God,
> Bring Spring flowers in fragrant perfume,
> And, offer sweet prayers for a merciful doom.

Beautiful hands, ye deck the graves
Above the dust of the Southern Brave;
Here was extinguished their manly are,
Bring Spring flowers, the laurel and rose,
And deck your defenders place of repose.

Beautiful eyes, the tears we shed
Are brighter than diamonds to those who bled;
Spurned is the cause they fell to save
But little they'll care if ye love their graves.
Bring Spring flowers with tears and praise,
And chant over the tombs your grateful lays.

Beautiful tribute at valor's shrine,
Wreaths that fond ones lovingly twines;
Those whom they cherished wit heart, hand, and eyes
Will bring Spring flowers and bow the head,
And pray for the noble Confederate Dead.

The display of floral offerings by the ladies were abundant and rich in beauty—gathered from the numerous parteries of our citizens; while the delicate "field flowers, that so meetly seem man's frailty to portray," breathed forth their votive fragrance to hallow the score. To the graves beneath these fragrant flowers will wander our tenderest thoughts, and when these flowers are dead, the leaves all faded, and odors fled, even the memories of the tenants of death's narrow house will be green in our hearts; for each year's returning Spring will be mighty to restore those sacred emblems of the love borne for "the gallant Confederate dead," and again will the fair hands of lovely women.

"Cover the hearts that have beaten so high,
Beaten with hopes that were doomed but to die,
Hearts that have burned in the heat of the fray,
Hearts that have yearned for the homes far away."

After the address and the singing of the odes, with music by the band, the benediction was pronounced by Reverend Mr. Miles, and the assembled crowd dispersed, leaving a few fond ones still lingering at the graves.

April 23, 1875 brought one change at secretary as Mrs. A.H. Boykin, declined to accept, while the others were reelected by motion. Mrs. McDonald was elected in her place. Colonel Shannon gave an address entitled, "The Joys, Sad Music of the Choral Band, along with a Multitude of Lively Tributes." In during this, this has helped this organization keep the memories of the lost cause alive, and its heroes who slumber with it, the dying soon to be in the arms of the day, a benison upon past efforts, and to this key preservation for the future.

The new slate of officers are as follows:

President - Mrs. Alfred E. Doby
Vice-President - Mrs. T.W. Salmond
2nd Vice-President - Miss C.M. Boykin
Treasurer - Mrs. J.K. Witherspoon
Secretary - Mrs. McDonald

May 2, 1876 brought the resignation of Mrs. Alfred Doby as president. In her place, Miss C.M. Boykin was elected.

Slate of Officers:

Mrs. C.M. Boykin, President
Mrs. James Davis, Vice President
Miss Reynolds, 2nd Vice President
Miss McDowell, Secretary
Mrs. McCurry, Treasurer (replaced Mrs. Witherspoon who resigned)

1878

The orator for this group at the time, May 10, 1878, was the eloquent General James Chesnut. The following address was before the Memorial Association of Camden. He was introduced by Colonel E.B. Cantey.

"Ladies of the Memorial Association of Camden - and you, my Friends:

> With pure hearts, and elevated minds with wreaths, and garlands, and with sweet remembrance of worthy heroes, who gave their lives to uphold the good cause of their country, we come this day to do honor to the Confederate Dead.

"Your purpose, my friends, does honour to you as well. The feelings which prompt you lies deep down in the human heart. It is old as humanity itself. Egyptian pyramids and obelisks - Asiatic mausoleums - Grecian sarcophagi - Roman cenotaphs, tombs and monuments — in short, the practice of all nations, from the earliest times down to our demonstration today, attest its antiquity and its universality. It seems to be an injection of Nature. But in honoring the dead, we ought to seek to honour virtue. Otherwise, our efforts would be deceitful, empty and vain. In trying, therefore, to do proper homage to the memory of the comrades who have gone before us, we will honour the virtues which were conspicuous in them, and which will enable humanity.

"What a touching spectacle is this day before us! In every part of the land we behold our Mother-State bowing her majestic head in sorrow over the graves of her sons. But no tear of shame falls from her eye. An honest pride mixed with grief are the component elements of her mourning. At her behest, her hero-sons died in a righteous cause. Yes, my friends! It was a most noble cause. It would be out of time and place, and worse than useless to re-argue that cause. But it is our duty to affirm it now, and ever when occasion requires. It is our justification before high Heaven, and the tribunals of the earth.

"That a state had the right peaceably to withdraw from the union was, before our period, unquestioned. It was claimed by States, and conceded by statesmen. The necessity and the wisdom of the act were alone debatable. That the federal government had the right to coerce the State; to pin it by bayonets to the union was an idea repudiated even by Alexander Hamilton. As we have no other tribunal left us now, we must remit the question to the verdict of posterity. Laudari a viro laudato.

"Perhaps it may not be amiss on this occasion to read before your stanzas written on the fly leaf of a translation of Homer and sent by the late Earl Derby to General R.E. Lee, to show what verdict will probably be. It is a voice coming across the waters, and anticipates, I think, the voice of posterity.

> "The grave old bard who never dies,
> Receive him in our native tongue;
> I send thee, but with weeping eyes,
> The story that he sung.
>
> The Troy has fallen—thy dear land
> Is married beneath the spoiler's heel;
> I cannot trust my trembling hand
> To write the grief I feel.
>
> Oh home of tears! But let her bear
> This blazon to the end of time;
> No nation rose so white and fair,
> None felt so pure of crime —
>
> A widow's moan, the orphan's wail
> Are round thee; but in truth be strong;
> Eternal right, tho all thing fall,
> Can never be made wrong.
> In angel heart, an angel mouth
> (Whose Homer's) could alone for me.
> Hymn forth the great Confederate South;
> Virginia first — then Lee.

"Desiring to avoid all topics purely political, I would like, notwithstanding, to correct a grave popular error. It has been affirmed, and widely believed that South Carolina began the war, which culminated in the late gigantic 'War Between the States.' This I hold to be an error. It will be remembered that the State passed its ordinance of succession on the twentieth day of December 1860. At that time and after it, Fort Sumter and Castle Pinckney were not occupied by Federal Forces but were rightfully in the possession of the State. The right of eminent domain in the territory on which they rested was in the State. The Federal government, however, through its President, claimed property in the structures and their sites. This claim was admitted by the State, but she could act under the changed affairs, concede absolute jurisdiction over them to be in the United States. This would have been an abandonment of sovereignty over a part of her territory — which would have been suicidal. Therefore, on the twenty-first of December 1860, the State appointed three commissioners to proceed to Washington, and treat with the government there in relation to all claims, with power on a fair adjustment to bind the State for the payment of the last dollar and treat for the continuance of peace and amity between this commonwealth and the government at Washington.

"Before their appointment, and before secession, but in anticipation of it, however, our members of Congress then in that city, on the ninth of December 1860, had come to an understanding with the Executive branch of the Federal government, that neither party should change the relative military status in the harbor of Charleston, until South Carolina should have an opportunity through accredited agents to treat with the government at Washington on all the points at issue — to order that collision might be prevented, and peace preserved. On or about the twenty-fifth of the same month, our commissioners arrived in Washington, but before they could communicate with the government, there, the understanding between the parties was violated, and the understood promise of the Federal executive broken. The military status of the parties in the harbor was changed, but not by South Carolina or any of her people. On the night of the twenty-sixth of December 1860, Major Anderson, the Federal officer, in command at Fort Moultrie, spiked his guns, burned their carriages, made preparation for the destruction of the fort, and transferred his entire force with munitions of war into Fort Sumter — an unoccupied fortress within the limits of a power, then foreign, and almost in the very heart of its metropolis. This was an armed and hostile invasion of an alien State; peace with his government and was an act of war. It was the beginning of that great struggle we sought persistently to avoid. Without this invasion, a peaceful solution of the question might have been attained, but with it unrepudiated, as the United States knew fully well, such solution was impossible. Notwithstanding this act of war, so anxious was the State to avoid bloodshed and arrest further acts of hostility, she refrained from attacking the fort, and suffered her commissioners to remain in Washington, still hoping to restore the previous condition of affairs in the harbor and to obtain by negotiation a peaceful settlement of all issues with the government there. But all was in vain. Again, on the ninth of January 1861, before any violence had been done by the State or its citizens, the *Star of the West*, a Federal vessel containing armed men with provisions and munitions of war, appeared in our waters to reinforce Major Anderson, who had already invaded the State, although he was permitted to obtain from the City of Charleston, whatever provisions he needed for his garrison. We fired on this vessel as it was our right and duty to do and turned her uninjured back to sea. Still anxious to avoid hostilities, refraining yet from acts of violence, the State determined to make another effort, and, on the eleventh day of January 1861, she sent a special envoy to Washington with full powers to treat for peace, and for a full and equitable settlement of all matters in dispute, and what was the result? A refusal to treat with the State. Subsequently vessels of war — monitors with all their great armature and huge 'blacksmithery' vexing the bosom of the ocean — appeared off the bar, to supply and reinforce Major Anderson by force, and ready to run in, when wind and water should favor, and, if need be, to bombard the city, and reduce it to submissive or ashes. Of all this we had notice. Upon this last notified exhibition of a purpose to subjugate the State, the manhood of the county, supported by conscience right, could no longer forbear. Honor and safety forbade it. Still, to avoid unnecessary bloodshed, and proposing terms most courteous and honorable, time and again, we demanded the surrender of our fort. Still all was in vain. In the supreme peril of that moment, there was nothing left for us but positimously to surrender up the State, and city without a blow, or to attack the fort and endeavor to expel the invader from our soil. We chose the latter, and the bombardment of the fort followed.

"Then was witnessed one of the most sublime spectacles that ever filled the human eye. First one signal shell ascended in the darkness of the hour, like a globe of fire kissing through its parabolic path until it fell and exploded on the fort. Immediately, thousands of similar missiles from the circle of our batteries illumined the sky—all having the same destiny and the same end. If it were possible to be, it seemed as if myriads of lesser suns had left their spheres to hold high revelry in the harbor of Charleston, and all with concentric movement on the bead of that devoted fort. All the rest you know. If the assault was grand, persistent and irrestable with professional justice, we must admit that the defense was stubborn, heroic, and full of fortitude.

"The recital of the few facts stated above prove that the war waged on the part of the State was defensive, and that all the evils resulting there from must justly be laid at the door of the Federal power. This truth will survive. Not numbers, nor arms, nor force can crush it. Though its voice may be gentle, it will pierce beyond the din of a thousand battles, and be heard amidst the uproar of blind ignorance, or of conscious wrong seeking to cover its own inequity.

"When the State was thus invaded — her city beleaguered — but autonomy denied – her liberty and existence threatened — she called upon her sons to rise, to strip for the fight, and rally to her standard. And what an uprising was there! It seemed as if some God had struck the earth, and every living soul upon it sprang up responsive to the blow, having a divine call which all obeyed.

"We read with admiration of the spirit of the Spartan mother, when she sent forth to the fight, her son armed with javelin and shield, of the Roman matron gathering her jewels around her, and giving them as fit presents to the State, but no Grecian or Roman mother ever exhibited greater and more persistent devotion and heroism than did our Confederate Women. How many thousands of Carolina Cornelias have we seen bringing their jewel boys and with a mother's pride deliver them up, with a smile, and a tear and a prayer, into the bloody hands of the Meloch of war. And have we not seen these noble youths with the light of battle in their eyes, pressing to the front? And, if we were permitted to call the long roll of honor, how many would be able to answer, "Here?" Alas! Too many absent, but thank heaven, they can all be accounted for.

"Every man who rallied to that standard was a patriot. Every patriot became a soldier, and every soldier a hero. Nor was the enthusiasm evanescent. In the forefront of battle — amid the hardships of the bivouac in the suffering of the hospital—for four long years, without an ally, and against overwhelming odds, did this fervor last. Every man had offered his all. Love and devotion to his country were burning deep down on the altar of his soul and kept him true to the last.

"The leading virtues of the Confederate soldiers always seemed to me to be devotion to their cause, constancy, courage, endurance, and fortitude. They possessed the élan of the French and Irish, with the steadiness of the German and Briton. Their valor never suffered the slightest eclipse, whether the field they contested was lost or won Their bravery took new honor from the fight. Allow me to read here a few verses descriptive of the Confederate private:

> Only a private! His jacket of gray
> Is stained by the smoke and the dust;
> As Bayard he is brave, as Rupert he is gay,
> Reckless as Murnt in heat of the fray,
> In God his only trust.
>
> Only a private! To march and to fight,
> To suffer, and starve, and be strong;
> With knowledge enough, to know that the might
> Of justice and truth, and freedom, and right,
> In the end must crush out the wrong.
>
> Only a private! No ribbon or star
> Shall gild with false glory his name!
> No honors for him in braid or in bar
> His cross of the Legion is only a scar,
> And his wounds are his role of fame.
>
> Only a private! One more hero slain
> On the field lies silent and chill,
> And in the far South and wife prays in vain
> One clasp of the hand she shall ne'er clasp again,
> One kiss from the lips that are still.
>
> Only a private! Then let him sleep,
> He will need no tablet nor stone,
> For the grasses and vines o'er his grave will creep,
> And at night the stars through the clouds will peep,
> And watch him who lies there alone.

> Only a martyr! Who fought and who fell
> Unknown and unmarked in the strife,
> But still, as he lies in his lonely cell,
> Angels and Scraphs the legend will tell —
> Such a death is eternal life —"

"This State sent forth to the common cause a body of men as true and noble as ever shook the earth with the tramp of war; and this country furnished her full quota, both in number and quality. Yes, my comrades, the virtues I have mentioned shone forth conspicuously in you. When 'The Bars and the Stars,' sacred emblem of our cause, was to be pressed forward to victory and planted within the lines of the enemy, you were ever in the forefront of battle. You were never in the rear until the rear became a post of duty and of honor; and then you guarded and protected the honor of that sacred through 'falling flag' until it was furled in blood. Your names are now and ever shall be household names in this land.

"You observe that fortitude appears last in my list of Confederate virtues, but it is not the least. The excitement of battle tends to banish all remembrance of hardships, and to depress all thoughts of suffering and apprehension of danger and death that may have existed before. Under such circumstances, the mind becomes exalted in the completion of duty performed, of glorious victory achieved, and the hope of well-earned renown. Then again, the hardships of camp, whether in tents or bivouac, were always alleviated gaiety of a gallant soldier. But fortitude is required most where fewest alleviations are found. The excitement of battle over – no comrade near — no voice to cheer – no friendly hand to give the last cool draught, it may be, to the wounded and dying man—these test to the fullest the heroism of the sufferer. Under all these trials we know that the Confederate soldier stood the test. If he had to die, he died cheerfully, thinking sweetly of his home, and for the independence of his native land. Again, come with me to some of our innumerable hospitals where —

> "Anguish tended the sick busiest from couch to couch;
> And over them triumphant Death his dart
> Shook, but delayed to strike, tho oft involved
> With vows as their child good and final hope."

"Yes, here, all the other virtues having been elsewhere displayed, patience, cheerfulness, faith — all born of divine fortitude — were characteristics of our men.

And here again the Confederate Women come to the front. With coflagging zeal, by day and night, our women devoted themselves to the comfort and welfare of our suffering comrades. Their angel faces, refulgent with the light of heavenly charity, illumined the gloom, and they purified the atmosphere of those other Laxar houses of woe. With delicate touch, they smoothed and cooled the burning pillow; with soft hands, they bathed and dressed the aching wounds; with gentle voice, they soothed the irritation and wiped the death damp from the brow of dying heroes, and bending over couches, caught, and reported the last breath of departing spirits as they whispered messages of love to those they left behind and far away. Sacred deputies of a merciful God! What more can I say for them? The blessings of that some good being attend them and theirs forever is the prayer of every surviving Confederate.

"Look now on those nameless graves. Behold a sad spectacle — but not without its moral. Though we know not the names of the tenants, they were nonetheless our brothers, and will this day be honored at your hands for they, too, gave their all to the common cause. 'To be nameless in worthy deeds exceeds an infamous history.' The good Samaritan lives more honored without a name than Judas Iscariot with one. Who knows whether the best of men be known? Or whether there be no more remarkable persons forgot than any that stand in the known account of time?

"The greater part must be content to be as though they had not been—to be found in the Register of God, not in the record of man. There is no aptidete against the opium of time. Our fathers find their graves in our memories, and sadly tell us how we may be buried in our survivors. Grave stones tell the truth if at all scarce forty years — generations pass while some trees stand—and cold families last not three oaks. Still man is a noble animal splendid in ashes and pompous in the grave solemnizing navities and deaths with equal lustre—not omitting ceremonies of bravery in the infamy of his nature.

"If the spirits of our departed brothers take cognizance of earthly things, they must be filled with joy when they see that the meekest, purest, rarest, yet, most sublime of Christian virtues — charity — with her sisters, mercy and gratitude, yet survives with active ministratess on earth through you.

"Friends, all — let us turn now to another them. When we returned from the war through forests of houseless chimneys and sat amid the charred ruins of our own houses, we did not permit black despair to settle beside us on our broken hearthstones. But with a resolution born of conscious duty, fostered and guided by hope, and under the inspiration and help of our wives, we went to work to rebuild our shattered altars, and to gather up and utilize our scattered fortunes. I will not remind you of the tyrannies and oppressions inflicted upon us by the iron hand of power — such as few if any civilized people ever suffered before. We have experienced the truth of a political axiom — that misrule may be more desolating the war. At length, however, we have been redeemed by the virtues of our own people, and metaphorically speaking, we have ascended our Pisgah from which, though afar off, we can see the promised land. Some of you may be permitted to enter, Many, I hope, will. But those who do not will be comforted by the assurance that posterity certainly will.

"It is true that no deep wound ever healed without a scar — but heal it must, or end in death. We have entered now on a new era, and though we may carry into in our scale, we must adapt ourselves to it. Again, we all the inhabitant of a common country with like interest and destiny.

When the head of peace was stretched to us across the bloody chism, we took it, and baying accepted the situation, we will keep the faith. We will look to the future, and as far as true and honest men can, forget the past — except its sacred memories and it spotless glories, which we will strive to make immortal."

Memorial Day, May 10, 1879 -
Programme of Ceremonies for Next Saturday
The Camden Journal - May 8, 1879
Gather the old, with locks silver sprinkled,

> Gather the youth, with fair brows unwrinkled;
> Even the lambs of the flock should be there,
> All of the brave, the noble, the fair.
> This is the day we give to the dead.

The Annual Memorial Ceremonies will be observed at the Cemetery on Saturday, May 10, at o'clock, p.m.

It is requested that the streets be closed at this hour, so that all may unite in these services.

Ladies and children are especially desired to bring with them memorial tributes of laurels and flowers.

The Association, proposing to erect a Memorial Tablet to those noble sons of our country asleep in other hallowed resting places, urgently appeals for aid. Boxes will be placed at the gates and at Memorial Tree for the reception of contributions.

> Order of Procession
> Major E.E. Sill, Marshall
> The procession will form on Broad Street,
> The right resting on DeKalb.
>
> Infantry - Colonel E.B. Cantey in command.
>
> Citizens on foot.
>
> Survivors
>
> Artillery- Captain J.R. Goodale
>
> Cavalry—Senior Captain in command.
>
> Visitors requested to dismount beyond the gates of the Cemetery,
> the entrance of horses and vehicles being strictly prohibited.
>
> The services will open at the graves of the Unknown.
>
> Prayer - Reverend J.O. Wilson
>
> Ode - Professor Evans and Choir
>
> Decoration of Graves by 20 Misses
>
> The Procession will then march to Memorial Tree.
>
> Ode - Professor Evans and Choir
>
> Address—General J.D. Kennedy
>
> Ode- Professor Evans and Choir
>
> Benediction—Reverend J.O. Wilson
>
> Decoration of Graves in Private Enclosures by Executive Committee.

(One note is the wonder where the Memorial Tree stood in Quaker Cemetery grounds)

In 1880, the officers were President C.M. Boykin, Vice-President Miss Reynolds, 2nd Vice-President Miss James Davis, Secretary Miss McDonald, Treasurer Mrs. McDonald, E.J. Cureton, committees, Mrs. James Villipigue, Mrs. C.M. McDonald, Mrs. A.E. Doby, Mrs. E. Cureton, Mrs. A.M. Kennedy.

In 1880, Major Sill and Colonel E.J. Cureton gave the program.

In 1881, Dr. A.A. Moore gave the program. Resigned as president was Mrs. C.M. Boykin, and Mrs. McDowell as secretary.

The new officers were President Miss L. McDowell, Vice President Mrs. Doby, 2nd Vice President Mrs. James Davis, Secretary Mrs. H.A. Boykin, Treasurer Mrs. McCurry.

Memorial Day was celebrated at the cemetery with the citizens at five o'clock in the afternoon, survivors present and standing with honor, and then all moved to the graves for the service. The Reverend M.F. Lamar read a poem by Mrs. Poston of Virginia. The choir sang "Let the Dead and the Beautiful Rest," and graves were covered with beautiful flowers. Reverend Wm Lamar did the prayer, benediction, and the audience dismissed by the singing of the doxology.

In 1882, the citizens of Camden assembled at the cemetery on May 10, for decorating the graves of "Our Confederate Dead." Reverend Wm Pale did the prayer, General Kennedy then introduced Major W.Z. Leitner, who read an original ode that was highly appreciative. Reverend Wm Dantzler did the benediction, with many little girls preselected to decorate the graves with flowers (a laurel wreath upon each grave).

Officers elected were President A.E. Doby, Vice President Mrs. James Davis, 2nd Vice President Miss Emma Reynolds, Secretary Mrs. J.D. Kennedy, and Treasurer Mrs. McCurry.

In 1883, the same was re-elected. A working committee was formed with Mrs. Herman Baum being selected chairman of the executive committee.

Arrangements were made and placed at the cornerstone of the Confederate Monument in the center of the square.

Memorial Day, the tenth, the corner stone of the Confederate Monument was laid with Masonic Honors by the Grand Master General J.D. Kennedy and the secretary, Charles Ingoldsby. The ceremony concluded, the soldier's graves were decorated with laurel wreaths, and flowers were placed by the children. The monument unveiling was to be held the June 20, with General Wade Hampton, being the guest orator.

Old Camden was never more honored than on June 20, 1883, the day set apart for the unveiling of the Confederate Monument. Nearly everyone in the county and in the state, was represented by visitors, who came to our historic town. Governor Hampton was chosen as the one mist worthy to deliver the oration on this day.

Governor Hampton, General Butler, and other distinguished guests were here. Military companies from nearly every county took part in this ceremony. The procession was formed at one o'clock, near the market on Broad Street, and marched through Dekalb, Littleton, and Laurens Streets to the monument, which is located at the intersection of Broad and Laurens Street. After prayer by Rev. L.H. Hay, Governor Hampton was introduced by Colonel E.M. Boykin, and delivered an eloquent and instructive address. Six young ladies, daughters of soldiers, who had been killed in the war, were selected to unveil the monument. Those being Elise Doby, Marie and Bessie Kirkland, Rebecca Nelson, Miss Cantey, and Mrs. Stephen Richards (née Lily McKain). They were escorted from the stand to the Monument by Colonel E.M. Boykin, Colonel E.B. Cantey, Major E.E. Sill, and John DeSaussure. It was unveiled amid sounds of artillery, shouts of the assembly, estimated at five thousand people. The old town out did itself in hospitality, and the day will never be forgotten as the most glorious in its annals.

In 1884, the citizens met at the cemetery, May 10, for Memorial Day. Wreaths were placed and flowers laid on the graves of the fallen soldiers. Near this day, Sadie Kennedy von Treskow penciled in that her mother died.

In 1885, Memorial Day was observed on the Monday the eleventh following the tenth, as the tenth was on a Sunday. The citizens and vicinity decorated the soldier's graves with wreaths and flowers.

In 1886, the election had Miss Sa? McDonald, President (Mrs. Alfred Doby resigned), Mrs. Samuel Davis, Vice-President; Mrs. E.E. Sill, 2nd Vice-President; Miss Lila Davis, Treasurer; and Miss F.O. DeSaussure, secretary. Memorial preparation occurred with Reverend Samuel Stoney giving the opening prayer and benediction. Reverend W. W. Mills made an address. "Reverend William Capers, D.D." read an ode.

Memorial Day was held on the tenth as usual, on a Monday afternoon to honor our Confederate Dead. The attendance was much larger than usual, and a deeper interest manifested on this occasion. The program consisted of the surviving Confederate Soldiers, fifty in number, forming a line at the gate. The escort was provided by the Kershaw Guard. Captain Shannon moved down to the stand. The services were opened as planned by Reverend Stoney, the choir sang "Concord of Great Sounds" with that patriotic hymn "Shall We Meet Beyond the River." As planned, Rev. Dr. William Capers read a poem. Reverend W.W. Mills, then introduced and delivered his address. The choir sang another song "*In the Sweet Bye and Bye.*" The graves were then decorated.

In 1887, at six p.m., the citizens arrived at the cemetery at the gate of the cemetery, with flowers and wreaths in hand to decorate the fallen and honored soldiers. The lineup at the gate was as follows: Kershaw Concert Band, children of the town in two columns, survivors with their escort, the Kershaw Guards, under Colonel William Shannon, citizens, prayer by Reverend Stoney, hymn sung "In the Happy Eden," rendered by Miss Thompson, and others. Mrs. T.H. Clarke introduced the speaker, Mr. Thomas J. Kirkland, another hymn "Oh Think of the Throne Over There," and then the placing of the flowers and wreaths on the graves.

On April 30, 1888, Mrs. Samuel Davis became President, Vice-President was Mrs. Edward Sill, Secretary Miss F.O. DeSaussure, and Treasurer, Miss Lila Davis. Memorial Day occurred on May 10, 1888, as planned. The Reverend John Kershaw of Sumter, Sumter South Carolina, had been requested to make the annual address; however, illness prevented him to do so. A few devoted ladies prepared for the cemetery the laurel wreaths and flowers for the graves of our heroic soldiers, as a token of love and gratitude to those who died in their country's service.

During the April 29, 1889, meeting, words were said along with a prayer, and in the minute book a blank page, in memory of Mrs. Jimmie Davis. The officers elected were: President Mrs. E.E. Sill, Vice-President Miss E.C. Reynolds, Secretary Miss F.A. DeSaussure, Treasurer Miss A.E. Davis.

Memorial Day was celebrated in the usual fashion. Citizens assembled at six o'clock with the ladies of the association. The survivors formed the procession headed by the Kershaw Cornet Band, and the children of the town bearded garlands and marched to the stand. Opening prayer was done by Dr. E.J. Maynardie, the address was done beautifully by Reverend John Kershaw, which was highly appreciated by his listeners. After an overture by the band, the benediction was pronounced by Reverend W.W. Mills. The committees, and children then proceeded to the decoration of the graves of our Confederate Dead.

On April 28, 1890, committees were appointed to take charge of the decorations on May 10. The officers elected for the year were President Mrs. E.E. Sill, Vice-President Miss E.C. Reynolds, Secretary and Treasurer

Miss Marie Kirkland. Memorial Day came on May 10. The ladies of the association formed a procession with the children of the town, and together with the survivors marched from the gate of the cemetery to the stand, where an immense concourse had assembled. The pray was done by W.W. Mills, General John Doby Kennedy introduced the speaker, who happened to be the Honorable W.D. Trantham. Trantham delivered a most beautiful address, which recalled many tender memories of the past. After an overture from the Kershaw Cornet Band, the benediction was pronounced, and the committees, along with the children, proceeded to the sad but sweet task of decorating the graves of those who died for our "Lost Cause."

On April 27, 1891, the meeting began with the report of funds on hand and expenditures from the past year. Officers elected were President Miss Kate A. Villipigue, Vice-President Miss E.C. Reynolds, and Secretary-Treasurer Miss Marie A. Kirkland. The anniversary of the year fell on Sunday, so Memorial Day was planned on Monday the eleventh. More reverence and activities seemed planned than in the past in several years. A new awakening was sensed with the memories throughout the whole Southland and the principles for which our heroes fought and died are held more sacred as time moved on. Those in attendance listened to a beautiful and patriotic address from the Reverend M.L. Carlisle, in which he reminded us of the undying renown that belongs to our soldiers, urging that we continue to honor and cherish their memory. Reverend W. Carlisle, father of the orator, delivered the prayer and benediction. Then, the graves were decorated by the children and committees, appointed. Music was kindly furnished by the Kershaw Cornet Band.

April 25, 1892, reports of the Secretary and Treasurer were read. The officers elected were President Mrs. P.H. Nelson Jr., Vice-President Mrs. James Haile, and Secretary-Treasurer Miss A.E. Davis. (She was the daughter of Bishop Davis, and sister-in-law of the niece of General James Chesnut, CSA, Mrs. Ester Serena Reynolds Davis. Memorial Day came on the tenth, and Mr. B.B. Clarke delivered the address, after a prayer by Reverend W. Carlisle. The Kershaw Cornet Band kindly furnished the music, and the shortening line of survivors marched to the stand. The graves were decorated by the ladies of the association and the children.

On April 24, 1893, the treasure was absent from home, records from the previous treasurer had been transferred to her care. Showed a sort of ten dollars upon close examination on hand. Most member present paid their annual subscriptions. Those funds collected should be used as a nucleus for erecting a suitable headstone at the graves of the unknown soldiers, and the secretary should endeavor to secure all possible information about them. Also, agreed upon the offices of treasurer and secretary should be separated. The election had President Mrs. P.H. Nelson, Jr., Vice-President Mrs. James Haile, Treasurer Mrs. Herman Baum, and Secretary Miss A.E. Davis. Memorial Day arrived on the tenth, and with it the gathering at the graves of the heroic soldiers in solemn memorial. The survivors of their comrades in arms, young men and maidens, old men, women, and children in greater numbers than before came. Proceeded by the Kershaw Cornet Band, who kindly lent their aid, the procession marched to the stand, where after a prayer by Reverend W. Carlisle, General John D. Kennedy introduced the orator of the day, Reverend James M. Stoney. Mr. Stoney "impressed upon us the principles on which so much had been sacrificed, and reminded us that only by being faithful to the memory of those who fought and died for their country could we inherit their virtues, concluding by instructing the women, their daughters, and granddaughters, the Holy duty of keeping the Lost Cause ever reverently dear to

Southern Hearts." After the benediction, the graves were decorated with laurel and placed by the ladies of the association and the children.

This society became the United Daughters of Confederates group known as John Doby Kennedy Chapter around 1896.

A list of things through the years:

In the Minute Book 1906 – 1912:

March 4, 1907 - A resolution concerning the death of Mrs. Harriet Dubose Kennedy, widow of General John D. Kennedy.

In the Minute Book 1921 – 1930:

- Oct 1921 - The most interesting feature of the afternoon was the presentation of the Flag of the Kirkwood Rangers, which was given to the Chapter by Mr. John Boykin for the Boykin Family. This flag was made by the nuns of Columbia and presented to the company on the eve of their departure to Virginia in 1861. Colonel William M. Boykin, commanding. The cloth of which it is made is of a dress of Governor Pickens's wife, who was Miss Lucy Hollman or Holcohlme of Columbia. Under a large star in the center is a medallion, which was blessed by the Pope. It was in Virginia four years and was brought home by Captain James Doby, who was in command of the company at the time of the surrender at Appomattox. It was given to Colonel E.M. Boykin by Captain Doby after the war. The flag was enthusiastically admired by the chapter. For the present, the flag will be kept at the Camden Library. The Chapter gave a vote of thanks to Mr. Boykin and the Boykin family and the secretary was instructed to write the note.
- Oct 1922 - Miss Leila Shannon, Chapter Historian, made an interesting talk on the Jefferson Davis Highway - Camden is one of the few towns in South Carolina on this highway and our local chapter voted unanimously to stand back of Miss Shannon, who was appointed chairman of a committee to be appointed later by the president to push forward the work of erecting a suitable maker on the national highway.
- Nov 1922 - Eleven stones were purchased to mark the graves of soldiers.
- March 1923 - The committee, of which Mrs. F. Leslie Zap is chairman, was authorized to buy a State Flag, five by eight feet, as Mrs. Richards, the superintendent thought that the most desirable size. The Chapter also decided to have the flag of the Kirkwood Rangers framed and hung in the Camden Library and the members agreed to pay twenty-five cents each to defray the expense of twenty-five to thirty dollars. The chapter has willed to keep it in Camden to be seen by and to inspire the descendants of the men who fought so gallantly to defend it. It will be an historical and decorative way an addition to our public library.
- May 1923 - Miss Leila Shannon gave an interesting talk and appeal for the Jefferson Davis Marker to be placed in Camden. Miss Deica Lamar West of Texas, general chairman of the enterprise is a guest of Miss Shannon and hopes to make the efforts of this highway ocean to ocean, and become, when completed, the greatest memorial any organization ever built.

- June 1923 - NO Meeting due to the tragedy of the Cleveland School Fire.
- Nov 1923 - Miss Leila Shannon as State Chairman is proud of the fact that the Jefferson Davis Highway has been marked through South Carolina and Mrs. Dunn as Chapter Chairman feels sure that the boulder with a handsome bronze plate bearing the name of Jefferson Davis will be placed in front of Hampton Park within the next month.
- June 1924 - The Committee reported everything was ready for the presentation of the boulder, marking the Jefferson Davis Highway, to the city, the exercises to be the following afternoon, June 3. Mrs. W.B. DeLoach suggested that Dickerson's Monument be decorated for Memorial Day but the suggestion was tabled to next May.
- Oct 1924 - The Chapter decided to give two pictures to the school, one of Lee and Jackson and one of Jefferson Davis, also to give one of Lee and Jackson to the Library. The committee reported that the flag under which the Kirkwood Rangers went out in SIXTY-ONE (1861) had been framed and placed in the library, and a motion was made and carried to try to get the pictures of Camden's six generals and present to the school.
- Nov 1924 - Mrs. H.G. Carrison made a plea for the children's honor roll to be placed in the Memorial Hall at Stone Mountain. The membership fee is one dollar and places upon honorable record the name of the girl or boy and his or her Confederate Ancestor. The money goes to the completion of the Stone Mountain Memorial.
- Feb 1925 - The Chapter was asked to put a Confederate Flag in each room of the grammer school. The committee on the flag proposition consists of Mrs. E.E. Sill, Mrs. F. Leslie Zemp, and Miss Ella Zemp. In February, we honor the birthdays of Albert Sidney Johnston, on the second, Joseph E. Johnston on the third, J.E.B. Stuart on the sixth. Also, a call to try to put pictures of Confederate Generals in the schools.
- April 1925 - The large flag, given in trust to the Chapter by the old Memorial Association, will not be loaned again as the sentiment that clusters around it enhances its value. It has more material value to the chapter. Purchased are flags of Southern Cross, the Battle Flag of the Confederacy.
- Sept 1925 - Mr. T.J. Kirkland was the chairman for Kershaw County for the sale of Confederate Memorial coins. The pictures of generals are now framed to be presented by the chapter to the Camden Schools. Two sets will be made and to be delivered. That committee composed of Mrs. Francis Proctor, Mrs. G.E. Taylor, and Mrs. L.A. Wittkowsky.
- Jan 1924 – Blaney High School will receive pictures of Camden's six generals. Sent and was acknowledge five dollars for Christmas at the Confederate Soldier's Home in Columbia. Upon the death of Silas B. Turner, a wreath was sent to the home.
- Nov 1929 - The memorial committee sent a beautiful floral offering to the late Mr. Neil Bethune, who was a gallant Confederate Veteran.

In the Minute Book 1930 to 1939:

- An Annual Dinner held for Confederate Veterans at the Bethesda Presbyterian Church with the following Veterans in attendance:
- I.F. Holland, D.P.C. Murchison, G.E. Watts, B.M. Jones, A.S. McKenzie, and G.S. King.
- The family of Jas. W. Boone of Westville received a marker for a grave at DeKalb Church Cemetery.
- Motion made and carried that the fountain be restored and placed in some suitable place, majority though Hampton Park a suitable place - Feb 1933.
- Mrs. Proctor, Chairman of the Fountain Committee, reported that Hampton Square had been selected for the fountain. It was voted by the Chapter to place it there. A vote of thanks was given to Mrs. Proctor was given for this splendid piece of work. (April Meeting)
- May Meeting - Mrs. Proctor reported that the city was ready to erect the fountain.
- June Meeting - A map of "The Jefferson Davis Highway" was to be presented to the Chamber of Commerce and the Camden Library. Mentioned gifts to Veterans and to the shut-ins.
- Oct 1936 - Mrs. Proctor reported the fountain was unfinished. Mrs. Proctor, Mrs. Dunn, and Mrs. Rhame was asked to see the Mayor and have him finish the fountain. A note of thanks was read from Mrs. Morrison, Librarian, for the picture of the Jefferson Davis Highway. Mrs. Proctor showed the chapter the relics of the U.D.C. Voted to ask Mrs. Richards if they could use the picture of the generals at the school house. Also, that they send the flag to the Relic Room in Columbia.
- Nov 2, 1936 - Mrs. Proctor reported that three pictures of generals showed them in their Confederate uniform.
- Nov 7, 1939 - Mrs. Baum and Mrs. Burns told of the funeral held for Mr. King in Bethune.

In *the Camden Chronicle*, January 22, 1915, the following was put in to show the humor of the soldiers:

Humor of the Soldiers
How Reb's Ready Humor Got Him
Good "East" in War Time

The following was read by Mrs. W.D. Trantham at a meeting of the UDC in 1909.

The unfailing humor of the Confederate Soldier was wonderful. It was irresponsible. No danger, no hardship, no deprivation, however great, could check it. Every old soldier can recall scores of anecdotes and smart sayings of his comrades; and by his will, on occasion, retell them by the hour - with unalloyed enjoyment to his hearers and to himself. An incident illustrative of his humor and innate modesty of the participates, occurred while Longstreet's Corps was on its way from Virginia to North Georgia to help our Bragg. The few railroads between Richmond and Chattanooga were taxed to their full capacity to transport so many men six to eight hundred miles as quickly as the exigency required. As was common in the war times, many men would ride on top of the cars, preferring the smoke, rain, and cold to being packed like sardines in the boxes below. When the train bearing the Second South Carolina Regiment reached Marietta, Georgia, the ladies, as was their custom whenever opportunity occurred, were out in great force with every good thing that could cheer the boys and tempt their appetites, that needed no tempting. The soldiers, poor fellows, were hungry indeed. Three days had elapsed since they left their camp along the line of the Rappahannock, and during that time they had received very scanty rations of the hardest kind of hard-tack; and fortunate was he who had a chance to wash his face at all. Those boys had learned in the hard school of experience what it was to fight and starve and grow brave and strong.

1904 Confederate Reunion at Camden, South Carolina

The "X" marks Jessie Arthur. [542]

---

[542] Photographs Courtesy of Camden Archives and Museum, Camden, South Carolina.

188 | William Guerry Felder

1914 Confederate Reunion in Bethune, South Carolina

Kershaw Counties Six Brigadier Generals

The only County to have so many in the State and
possibly the United States from this Era.

The Tribute was paid May 10, 1911 at the Memorial to the Six Confederate Generals

REPORTER BONNEY TELLS OF CAMDEN and his beloved Charleston. He shares with us that Camden is very similar to Charleston. Camden, being next to Charleston, and the oldest inland town, has just as much history as Charleston. The appearance of Camden is different from the quaintenance of Charleston, because of the unique atmosphere in Camden. Camden, like Charleston, is suffering, how to preserve the history of Camden and still bring in new, progressive methods without an overabundance of commercialism. This task is a noble one for fellow Camdenites. Camden is such a small community to have such an array of talent and have supplied so many officers of such high rank and merit to Southern Armies that can only excite our Southern pride. It is a record unequaled in any state, South or North.

The Monument to the Six Brigadier Generals at Rectory Square

Brigadier General Joseph Brevard Kershaw

Kershaw was born January 5, 1822 in Camden, South Carolina. His background of education was tailored to the legal profession. He went to the academy in Camden, probably under the discipline of Mr. Hatfield, and to the Cokesbury Conference School in Abbeville, S.C. Then in his teens studied under John M. DeSaussure. He was admitted to the Bar in 1843. He practiced in Camden with John P. Dickerson, before going to the Mexican War of 1847, serving as a lieutenant of Company C, Palmetto Regiment. He became ill and was sent home. He was a member of the legislature from 1852 to 1856, and in 1860, participated in the convention that enacted the ordinance of succession.[543] He was one of three from Kershaw District to sign the Ordinance of Succession. The other two was T.J. Withers and James A. Chesnut, Jr. He was very active in the church, specifically the Grace Episcopal Church, becoming a vestryman and a warden, and then a secretary for the Theological Seminary. In 1844, he married Lucretia Douglass, the daughter of James K. Douglas, as successful merchant in Camden.

In February 1861, he was commissioned colonel of the Second South Carolina Regiment, leaving in April 1861, to go to Virginia. His command was part of the regiment of the brigade of General Bonham at Blackburn's Ford and later in the battle of First Manassas. In February 1862, he was promoted to brigadier general to succeed General Bonham. His participation included the Yorktown campaign, the Seven Day's campaign, before being in Richmond, and in fighting at Sharpsburg. Then, he was at Fredericksburg, where he was placed in command after General Cobb was wounded. Other places in led his troops was at Chancellorsville, at Gettysburg, at Chickamauga, at Chattanooga, at Knoxville, in the Wilderness, at Spotsylvania Court House, and at Cold Harbor.[544]

He was then promoted to be major general and, after taking part in the Petersburg battles, was ordered to the support of Early in the Shenandoah Valley. Later, he was sent back to Richmond serving the north of the James Rivers before the fall of the city. His last battle was a Sailor's Creek, where he was captured by Ewell and the majority of his command. He was held as prisoner of war at Fort Warren until August 12, 1865.[545]

Upon his return back to South Carolina, he continued his practice of law, and in the same year was elected to the Senate, making president of that body. In 1874, he was the Democratic candidate for Congress in his

---

[543] "Portrait of General Kershaw Placed in Richmond Museum," The State Newspaper, Columbia, February, 1940.
[544] Ibid.
[545] Ibid.

district, and three years later was elected to the position of Judge of the Fifth Circuit. He served on the bench until 1893, when he resigned because of ill health and resumed his law practice. In February 1894, he was commissioned as postmaster, but he died on April 12.[546] Being a past State Grand Master of the Masonic Kershaw Lodge No. 29, he was buried with masonic honors at Quaker Cemetery.

His obituary was in *The State* newspaper, May 5,1894, and *The State* newspaper, April 15, 1894.

In Memory of Kershaw

The memorial meeting of at which the citizens of Kershaw county were called together to pass a resolution on the death of General J.B. Kershaw was held on the 28. Major A.D. Kennedy was requested to act as Chairman and Dr. John W. Corbett acted as secretary.

"We have assembled this day my fellow citizens, as you have been made aware to do honor to the memory of our deceased friend and fellow citizen, General J.B. Kershaw, who departed this life on the 12th day of April at his home in Camden. I esteem it an honor to preside over a meeting if this character not only because it is a representative gathering, but because of his its avowed subject, that is, to pass appropriate resolutions upon the life and character of our distinguished dead. This meeting bears testimony to the love and respect we have for Carolina's noble son. General Kershaw will go in and out from amongst us no more. He has crossed over the river and now rests under the shade of the trees with those grand old heroes, Lee, Jackson, and a host of others, who have gone on before; his life's work is done, he rests from his labours but his influence of that life must go resounding though the ages. General Kershaw was in all essentials, a great man, and his modesty alone, kept him from reaching the highest principles of fame. He was a great soldier, a pure man and upright judge, and the crowning glory of all a humble follower of the Lord Jesus Christ, his faith, especially in the latter part of his life, in a kind over ruling Providence, was beautiful and subtle. He was the friend of the near and his many deeds of charity will never be known 'kept to himself and his God; for his right hand did not know what his left hand did. It was my privilege to know him all my life; he was my father's neighbor for many years, and when a boy and then a youth, I was frequently to his home; then and there I learned to honor and respect him; beautiful in his home life, kind, considerate, and loving to all about him. His watch word was duty - duty to God, duty to his country. Well, may we mourn the departure of such a man, a loss to our community, our State, and our country. South Carolina never had a more devoted man. May the story of his life be impressed upon the minds of the youth of the State as a model South Carolinian, and one in whose steps they should follow.

The Greenville News Newspaper had: "The knightly old soldier has gone to rest as he should have chosen, with universal love of his people surrounding him, with sounds of sorrow filling the air of the State he loved so well, with all the strife and difference forgotten in one common impulse of mourning for so good a life ended, a pride in a life so well and nobly lived."

Mr. Trantham told the interesting coincidence that his meeting was held on the thirty-third anniversary of the day when Colonel Kershaw met the Flat Rocks Guards, Captain Haile, and the Lancaster Invincible and

---

[546] Ibid.

Captain McManus at Hobkirk Hill, and went with them on a train to the seat of war. General Kershaw was, at the time, the Colonel of the first division of the first corps of that celebrated Army of Virginia.

His burial was held at the Episcopal Church at four in the afternoon. Some of the people present was Governor Tillman, Secretary of State Tindal, Superintendent of Education Mayfield, and Treasurer Bates came over in the morning train. Some came from Sumter and others from Columbia. His remains lay at the church being guarded by the Survivors.

The service was conducted by the rector, Reverend J.M. Stoney, after which the casket was carried to the hearse by grandsons of the General, who then turned over the remains to the senior pallbearers, General J. D. Kennedy, Colonel E. B. Cantey, Major E.E. Sill, Captain William Clyburn, Mr. Alfred Brevard, Mr. G.G. Young, Dr. A.A. Moore, and Captain James I. Villepigue. The procession moved in the following order down Laurens to Broad street and down Broad to the Quaker Cemetery:

Kershaw Lodge No. 29, A.F.M.
The hearse with senior pall bearers on each side.
Survivors
State Officials
The Family and General Public

The procession was in charge by Major L. Haile and marched to muffled drums. As the cortege moved down Broad Street, it was noticed that all places of business were closed, but the sidewalks were full of citizens of the town and country, both male and female, and of both races. It had been arranged to have all the bells tolled but was not done as a special request was made.

There were in the procession seventy vehicles and several hundred on foot, besides many other who went to the cemetery by other routes to avoid the crowd.

One dispatch that was sent came from Wade Hampton. He said, "My sincerest sympathy is given, but for illness I should go Saturday."

**Reports of Brig. Gen. J.B. Kershaw, C.S. Army,
Commanding Brigade of Operations, September 12-18.
SEPTEMBER 3-20, 1862. The Maryland Campaign.
O.R.-- SERIES I--VOLUME XIX/1 [S# 27]**

HDQRS. KERSHAW'S BRIGADE, *McCaw's' DIVISION,*
September 25, 1862.

Maj. JAMES M. GOGGIN,
Assistant Adjutant-General.
MAJOR: On the morning of the twelfth instant I was directed, with Barksdale's Mississippi Brigade and my own (South Carolina), to move from Brownsville and occupy the Maryland Heights, taking the road by Solomon's

Gap to the summit of Elk Ridge, and thence, along the ridge, to the point which overlooks and commands Harper's Ferry. At an early hour, the command was in motion and reached the gap without opposition. At this point, however, the pickets of the enemy were discovered, and it became necessary to approach the position carefully, with skirmishers thrown well to the right and left. This being done, the enemy withdrew his picket after a few scattering shots. Reaching the summit of the mountain, skirmishers were thrown well down the mountain to my right, while the column filed to the left along the ridge. Captain Cuthbert, Second South Carolina Regiment, commanding the skirmishers on the right, soon encountered a volley from about three companies of cavalry, but upon the fire being returned the enemy left with some loss. About a mile farther on, Major Bradley, Mississippi Regiment, commanding skirmishers, reported an abatis across the line of march, from which he was fired upon by a picket. An abatis, abattis, or abbattis is a field fortification consisting of an obstacle formed (in the modern era) of the branches of trees laid in a row, with the sharpened tops directed outwards, towards the enemy. The trees are usually interlaced or tied with wire. Abatis are used alone or in combination with wire entanglements and other obstacles. Directing him to press forward and ascertain the force in front, he soon overcame the obstacle without further resistance. Leaving then the path, which, at that point, passed down the mountain to the right, we filed along the crags on the ridge. The natural obstacles were so great that we only reached a position about a mile from the point of the mountain at six o'clock p.m. Here an abatis was discovered, extending across the mountain, flanked on either side by a ledge of precipitous rocks. A sharp skirmish ensued, which satisfied me that the enemy occupied the position in force. I therefore directed Major Bradley to retire his skirmishers, and deployed my brigade in two lines, extending across the entire practicable ground on the summit of the mountain, the Eighth Regiment, Colonel Henagan, on the right, and the Seventh, Colonel Aiken, on the left, constituting the first line; the Third Regiment, Colonel Nance, in rear of the Eighth, and the Second Regiment, Colonel Kennedy, in rear of the Seventh, constituting the second line; General Barksdale's brigade immediately in rear. These dispositions being made, the approach of night prevented further operations; the commands rested on their arms in the position indicated until the morning of the thirteenth, when I moved forward my first line to the attack. Early in the advance, the Eighth Regiment encountered a ledge of rock which cut them off from further participation in the attack; but Colonel Aiken moved briskly forward, under a heavy fire of musketry, surmounted the difficult abatis, and drove the enemy from his position in about twenty minutes. The enemy is stated by prisoners to have been 1,200 strong at this point. They retired about 400 yards, to a much stronger position, a similar abatis, behind which was a breastwork of logs, extending across the mountain, flanked, as before, by precipitous ledges of rock.

I had, at the commencement of the attack, directed General Barksdale to form his brigade down the face of the mountain to my left, in prolongation of the two lines on the summit, it having appeared the night before that the enemy's skirmishers, occupied a part of that face of the mountain. I now directed General Barksdale to advance his command, and attack the enemy in flank and rear, while I pressed him in front.

Again, I moved forward the Seventh and Eighth Regiments. Reaching the abatis, a most obstinate resistance was encountered, and a fierce fire kept up, at about one hundred yards distance, for some time. Our loss was heavy, and I found it necessary to send in Colonel Nance's Third Regiment to support the attack. They, too, were stoutly resisted. General Barksdale then sent me word that he had, with great labor, overcome the difficulties of the route and had reached the desired position, but that he could not bring his men to the crest of the mountain without encountering our fire, as he was in rear of the enemy. I sent to direct our fire to cease, hoping that we might capture the whole force if General Barksdale could get up. Before this order was extended, the right company of Colonel Fisher's regiment, Barksdale's brigade, fired into a body of the enemy's sharpshooters lodged in the rocks above them, and their whole line broke into a perfect rout, escaping down the mountain sides to their rear. This took place at 10:30 a.m. General Barksdale was directed to occupy the point of the mountain, which he did without encountering anything more than a picket of the enemy, which he soon disposed of. In their retreat, the enemy abandoned and spiked three heavy guns, which were in position on the lower slope of the mountain toward Harper's Ferry, and left considerable commissary stores, ammunition, and a number of tents near the same place. The guns were left by me, as it was impossible to remove them without further time. Lieutenant Colonel McElroy was directed to destroy all the stores, which he could not remove when he left his position.

The next day, through the exertions of Major McLaws's assistant quartermaster, a road was opened, and four Parrott guns brought up the mountain and placed in position — two pieces Read's battery, commanded by Captain Read, and two pieces Captain Carlton's battery, commanded by Captain Carlton. As the major-general commanding was present on Sunday and witnessed the constancy and efficiency of the fire of these guns, it is not necessary for me to refer further to it.

Sunday night I received orders to withdraw the command from the mountain and proceed to Brownsville, to meet the enemy in that direction, leaving Lieutenant Colonel McElroy's Thirteenth Mississippi Regiment and Read's two pieces of artillery. We left the mountain at daylight Monday morning. In this engagement, our loss was heavy, but three of my regiments were engaged, the ground not admitting of the employment of a larger number. The Seventh and Eighth Regiments exhausted their ammunition, and the Third Regiment had but a few rounds left when the place was carried. Prisoners were taken from three different regiments of the enemy, one of which was represented to number 1,000 men. Many of the enemy were left dead on the field, but from the statement of prisoners and the indications in the rear, it is certain that they removed the most of their dead and wounded during the action. The conduct of the whole command, contending as they were against the most formidable natural obstacles, without water, which could not be obtained nearer than the foot of the mountain, and encountering an enemy most strongly posted and superior in numbers to all that could be brought into position against him, is worthy of the highest commendation. To General Barksdale, I am much indebted for his hearty co-operation and valuable assistance. Dr. T.W. Salmond and the medical staff of the brigade were assiduous in the discharge of their duties, under great difficulties, as their ambulances and stores could not be brought upon the mountain. I am much indebted to Major Bradley, of the Mississippi Regiment, for his brave and efficient handling of our advanced skirmishers. Col. D. Wyatt Aiken, and his officers and men, who bore the brunt of the battle and suffered the greatest loss, are particularly deserving of mention. Of all the regiments engaged, it is worthy of mention that not one man went to the rear uninjured during the engagement. My thanks are especially due to Captain Holmes, assistant adjutant-general; Lieutenant Dwight, acting adjutant and inspector-general, and Lieutenant Doby, aide-de-camp, for most efficient and intelligent discharge of the staff duties on the field. I regret to say that

Lieutenant Dwight was seriously injured by a fall from the rocks while communicating a message to General Barksdale.

I have the honor to be, respectfully, your obedient servant,
J.B. KERSHAW,
[Brigadier-General].

HDQRS. KERSHAW'S BRIGADE, *McLAWS' DIVISION,*
Near Winchester, Va., October 9, 1862.

MAJOR: In obedience to orders from division headquarters, I have the honor to transmit a report of the operations of my command at the battle of Sharpsburg:

Owing to the exigencies of the service, my command was without their usual supply of subsistence from Monday morning, September 13, until the night of the seventeenth. They were also under arms or marching nearly the whole of the nights of Monday and Tuesday, arriving at Sharpsburg at daylight on Wednesday morning, September 17. As a consequence, many had become exhausted and fallen out on the wayside, and all were worn and jaded.

About nine o'clock we were ordered forward to the relief of General Jackson's forces, then engaged on the left, in the wood in rear of the church. The Georgia and Mississippi brigades were formed in a plowed field to the right and rear of the wood; my brigade in their rear in the same field. The enemy was discovered in the wood, advancing toward its right face, where some of our guns had been abandoned before our arrival. Perceiving this, Major-General McLaws directed me to occupy that part of the wood in advance of them while our lines were being formed. For this purpose, I ordered forward, at double-quick, Colonel Kennedy's Second South Carolina Regiment to march by a flank to the extreme point of the wood; then by the front to enter it. Before the head of the regiment had reached the point, and when entangled in a rail fence, the enemy opened fire upon them from a point not more than sixty yards distant. They promptly faced to the front and returned the fire so rapidly as to drive the enemy almost immediately. At the same time the brigades of Cobb and Barksdale, now on their left, advanced to their support. I then hurried up my three-remaining regiment — the Eighth, Lieutenant Colonel [A. J.] Hoole; Seventh, Colonel [D. W.] Aiken, and Third, Colonel Nance — and conducted them to the right of Colonel Kennedy, who by this time had advanced beyond the wood and to the left of the church, driving the enemy. I then ordered Read's battery to a position on the hill to the right of the wood and sent in Colonel Manning, who reported to me on the field, with Walker's brigade, to the right of my brigade. Our troops made constant progress for some time along the whole line, driving in column after column of the enemy. Colonel Aiken's regiment approached within thirty yards of one of the batteries, driving the men from the guns, and only gave way when enfiladed by a new battery placed in position near them, leaving Major White dead and one-half their men killed or wounded upon the field. About this time, the enemy was heavily re-enforced, and our line fell back to the wood, which was never afterward taken from us. Read's battery, having suffered greatly in the loss of men and horses, was withdrawn, by my order, when the infantry fell back. The lines were reorganized behind the fences, near where they entered the fight, and their exhausted cartridge-boxes replenished.

Later in the day we moved to the left of General Early's command, which occupied the wood to the left of the church, where we remained until ordered to move across the river on Thursday night, September 18. I deem it proper to state that I left two companies on picket in front of our lines when we marched under command of Captain Hance, of the Third Regiment, with instructions to remain until relieved by the cavalry.

After daylight next morning, Captain Hance, not having been relieved, perceived the enemy advancing in line of battle, and brought off his men in safety and good order, passing the cavalry pickets some distance in his rear.

I cannot too highly commend to your notice the gallant conduct of the troops of my command.

The Eighth Regiment carried in but forty-five men rank and file, and lost twenty-three officers and men.

The Second Regiment was the first to attack and drive the enemy. Colonel Kennedy was painfully wounded in the first charge and was sent by myself from the field. After our lines were first driven back, under command of Major [Franklin] Gaillard, they rallied and broke fresh line of battle that attempted to follow them.

The Third Regiment, led by its efficient commander, twice changed front on the field in magnificent order, and, after twice driving the enemy, retired with the precision of troops on review.

The Seventh, led by Colonel Aiken, trailed their progress to the cannon's mouth with the blood of their bravest, and, when borne back by resistless force, rallied the remnant left under command of Capt. John S. Hard, the senior surviving officer. Colonel Aiken was most dangerously wounded, and every officer and man in the color company either killed or wounded, and their total loss 140 out of 268 men carried in. The colors of this regiment, shot from the staff, formed the winding-sheet of the last man of the color company at the extreme point reached by our troops that day. Major White, whose death we lament, was a most gallant and accomplished officer of elevated character and noble principles. No better or braver soldier survives him.

Read's battery performed the most important service in a position of great danger. Second Lieut. Samuel B. Parkman was killed on the field, gallantly discharging his duty. One gun was disabled and abandoned, and so many horses as to render it necessary to bring off their pieces severally. The acts of individual heroism performed on this memorable day are so numerous that regimental commanders have not attempted to particularize them.

I am, as usual, greatly indebted to Captain Holmes, assistant adjutant-general, and Lieutenant Doby, an aide-de-camp, of my staff, for intelligent and efficient assistance in carrying orders to all parts of the field. They were everywhere exposed, with characteristic courage.

Privates Baum and Deas, orderlies, were also with me in the field, bearing themselves with courage and intelligence. The latter had his horse shot in three places. I have already transmitted a statement of our losses.

I am, major, very respectfully, your obedient servant,

J. B. KERSHAW,

Brigadier-General, Commanding.

Report of Brig. Gen. Joseph B. Kershaw, C. S. Army, Commanding Brigade.
APRIL 27-MAY 6, 1863 — The Chancellorsville Campaign.
O.R.-- SERIES I--VOLUME XXV/1 [S# 39]

HDQRS. KERSHAW'S BRIG., *Massaponax, Va., May* 20, 1863.

Maj. JAMES M. GOGGIN,
Assistant Adjutant-General

MAJOR: I have the honor to submit the following report of the operations of my command during the recent engagements in this vicinity:

At 7.30 o'clock, April 29, the firing of artillery and small-arms along the river announced an attack, and in a few minutes more my command was moved to the front. Arrived at Lee's Hill, I displayed my troops in the trenches and in reserve near the three points, as directed by the major-general commanding.

With little variation, we remained in that position until midnight of the thirtieth, when, under the direction of the major-general commanding: I moved to Major-General Anderson's position on the Plank Road, where we arrived about daylight, and were placed in the trenches extending to the right of the Turnpike Road, and covering the way from Emory's Mills to the Plank Road. About noon I received an order from the major-general commanding, through Major [E.L.] Costin, assistant inspector-general, to move up the Turnpike Road to the front, but not to cut the line of General Jackson's march, then occupying the Plank Road. Arrived at that road, the march was delayed by General Jackson's columns until I received an order through Major Costin to hasten to the front. Having all the troops on the way, I moved at once to a position a half-mile beyond Zoar Church, and, under direction of the major-general commanding, formed a second line of battle to the left of the turnpike, in support of Generals Semmes and Mahone, then both engaged with the enemy, who, however, was soon repulsed. The whole line was then advanced to the heights in front of Chancellorsville, where we bivouacked at nightfall.

The next day (May 2), I formed line of battle on the front line, extending from Semmes's left to the Plank road, and through the thirteen companies in the dense wood in my front, under Maj. D.B. Miller, of James' battalion [Third South Carolina Battalion], who, during the day, under orders from the major-general commanding, was directed to press the enemy continually, to keep him in position.

The next day a similar force was sent out, under the command of Capt. G. B. Cuthbert, Second South Carolina Regiment, with similar orders. Early in the day, Captain Cuthbert was wounded in two places, and has since died. He was succeeded by Maj. F. Gaillard of the same regiment. About nine a.m. the whole line advanced to the attack of Chancellorsville, and by eleven o'clock our troops were in possession of that position, the skirmishers only having been engaged. Moving over to the Turnpike Road to form a new front, under orders from the major-general commanding, I was directed by General R. E. Lee, in the presence of the major-general commanding, to move with General Mahone toward Fredericksburg, to check the advance of a column of the enemy reported coming up from that point, along the Plank road. Arriving at the intrenchments near Zoar Church, the major-general commanding came up, and directed the march to Salem Church. Upon our arrival, the enemy was shelling that position, then held by Wilcox's brigade. My brigade was formed to the right of Wilcox, along a crossroad running out in the direction of the Spotsylvania road. General Wofford's brigade formed on my right. I formed a second line 100 paces in rear of my left, composed of the Second South Carolina Regiment, Colonel [J.D.] Kennedy, and James's battalion, Lieutenant-Colonel [W. G.] Rice. The line had scarcely been formed before the enemy vigorously attacked the front of General Wilcox and the troops to his left. The Third South Carolina Regiment and part of James's battalion became engaged, but Wilcox's brigade soon repulsed the enemy.

The next day, the line of battle of the enemy was discovered in our front, extending along a road from the toll-gate to a house about a half mile from the Plank Road where a battery was placed in position. From that point, the line extended at an obtuse angle down Hazel Run and facing that stream. Late in the evening, my brigade was wheeled to the left, nearly at right angles to our former line of battle. General Wofford formed on my right, and we were ordered at a signal (the firing of three guns in rapid succession in the direction of Fredericksburg) to attack the enemy. About six p.m. the signal was given, and we moved on continuously, with skirmishers in front, commanded by Capt. Stewart Harrison, Seventh South Carolina Regiment. Having to march through a dense thicket of tangled brushwood and fences, harassed by a constant fire of shell and canister from the battery in our front, and another far to our left, which nearly enfiladed our lines, and having to oblique constantly to the right to maintain communications with Wofford's brigade, our progress was necessarily slow and difficult. Upon emerging from the woods into the open ground, I had the satisfaction to find my line in perfect order, and moved rapidly forward, directing the colors of the Seventh Regiment (the directing battalion, the second in line) immediately upon the battery in front. Simultaneously with our debouching from the wood, the enemy fled precipitately. Night having overtaken us by the time we reached the ground lately held by the enemy, I moved by the left flank to the toll-gate, on the Plank Road, and communicated with General McLaws. I dispatched Lieutenant [R.S.] Brown, Second South Carolina Regiment, and ten men down the Plank Road to ascertain the position of the enemy, and, if possible, to communicate with the troops of Major-General Anderson. General Wilcox soon arrived with a portion of his brigade, and Captain [G.B.] Lamar, aide-de-camp, from General McLaws, with information that the enemy had retreated toward Banks' Ford, and I was directed to press them in that direction, changing front over that advance. General Wilcox sent out his regiment toward Banks' Ford, and in a short time the enemy opened a fire of musketry on his skirmishers. I immediately advanced my regiment to a point some 300 yards in front of the woods occupied by the enemy, where I found General Wilcox's troops in position. At the suggestion of General Wilcox, I halted here while Captain [B.C.] Manly's battery was brought into position, and, under the direction of General Wilcox, who was perfectly acquainted with the ground, with great accuracy and rapidity shelled the woods along the river and the ford for about half all hour. At the expiration of the time, with General Wilcox's regiments and the Seventh, Third, and Fifteenth Regiments, we thoroughly brushed the woods and hills about Banks' Ford but found no enemy except straggling prisoners.

Near four o'clock in the morning, I halted, and gave the troops the rest they so much needed. Our pickets on the right were fired into afterward, but the camps were not disturbed.

After sunrise in the morning, I sent a detachment, under Major [F.] Gaillard, as far as the red house, on the River Road, and occupied other troops in gathering arms and accouterments abandoned by the enemy. At this point they collected over 800 stands of arms. About noon I received orders to proceed to the junction of the Mine Road and the River Road, near United States Ford, and take position. I was accompanied by the major-general commanding, and arrived about 2:30 p.m., relieving the troops under the command of General Heth at that place. Soon after I got into position, a severe storm of rain came up, which continued into the next day. Late in the afternoon, General Semmes came up and took position on my left. That night a working party and guard were detached from my brigade to report to Captain [S.R.] Johnston, of the Engineers, to erect works on the River road.

The next morning General McLaws directed an advance of the entire line of skirmishers, and it was soon ascertained that there was no enemy left on the south bank of the Rappahannock.

This morning (Wednesday, sixth), there was a furious engagement between Colonel Alexander's artillery and a number of the enemy's guns on the other side of the river, from the effects of which Col. J. D. Kennedy, Second South Carolina Regiment, who supported Colonel Alexander, by judicious selection of his ground, managed to shield his men. In the afternoon, I returned to my former camp.

I gratefully acknowledge the hand of Almighty God in the success which attends all the operations of this command and the unprecedentedly small sacrifice of life with which it was achieved.

Among the dead we mourn the death of Capt. G.B. Cuthbert, Second South Carolina Regiment, and Captain [C. W.] Boyd, Fifteenth South Carolina Regiment, both young men of the brightest promise; both of commanding talents, finished education, enlarged by foreign travel, elevated social position, and most attractive personal characteristics. None more gallant, none more patriotic, none more devoted represent the chivalry of the South; together they fell before Chancellorsville, *par nobile fratrum.*

On the morning of May 2, Colonel [John W.] Henagan, with the Eighth South Carolina Regiment, was ordered to report to General Jackson, and remained detached until the seventh instant. For an account of the operations of his command, I respectfully refer to the report of that officer, which accompanies this.

During this series of engagements, the Fifteenth Regiment was commanded by Lieutenant-Colonel [Joseph F.] Gist; the Seventh Regiment by Colonel [Elbert] Bland; the Third Regiment by Major [R.C.] Maffett; the Second Regiment by Colonel Kennedy; James' battalion by Lieutenant-Colonel [W.G.] Rice; the Eighth Regiment by Colonel Henagan.

The conduct of officers and men generally has never been more satisfactory to me during any engagement of the war. The good conduct of the men cannot be surpassed.

A number of prisoners were taken by this brigade, but no accurate account taken of them. Lieutenant [R.S.] Brown, with the scouting party above mentioned, not only succeeded in communicating with General Wright, Anderson's division, but brought in sixty prisoners. Colonel Henagan reports taking eighty-four prisoners. I estimated that near Chancellorsville the brigade took fifty; about Salem Church and Banks' Ford 100; Colonel Henagan, at United States Ford, 100. Total, 250. A number of arms besides those enumerated above were captured and sent off, and five horses, which had been turned over in pursuance of orders.

For particular mention of individuals, I respectfully refer to the reports of regimental commanders. To Captain [Charles R.] Holmes, assistant adjutant-general, Lieut. A.E. Doby, aide-de-camp, and Lieut. W.M. Dwight, acting assistant inspector-general, I am again indebted for the most valuable services on the field.

During these operations, the troops were daily supplied with subsistence through the untiring and energetic efforts of Captain [Frederick L.] Smith, acting brigade commissary, and Martin, commissary sergeant. The capacity of the command to perform the labors assigned them I consider in great part due to this regular supply of subsistence.

A list of the casualties of the command is herewith appended.

Through the efficient services of Surg. T.W. Salmond and the other medical officers of the command, our wounded have never been so well cared for in the field.

I have the honor to be, major, respectfully, your obedient servant,

J.B. KERSHAW,
Brigadier-General, Commanding.

Report of Brig. Gen. J.B. Kershaw, C.S. Army, commanding brigade, McLaws' division
JUNE 3-AUGUST 1, 1863 --The Gettysburg Campaign.
O.R.-- SERIES I--VOLUME XXVII/2 [S# 44]

HEADQUARTERS KERSHAW'S BRIGADE,
Near Chattanooga, October 1, 1863.

Maj. J.M. GOGGIN,
Assistant Adjutant-General.

MAJOR: I have the honor to report the operations of my command from the commencement of the march from Culpeper Court-House until the return of the army to that place.

Tuesday, June **16.**--The brigade marched to Sperryville.

17th.--To Mud Run, in Fauquier County. These two days were excessively hot, and on the 17th many cases of sunstroke occurred. At Gaines' Cross-Roads, the wagons were sent by the way of Front Royal. Rice's battalion was detached as a guard to the division train.

18th.--Marched to Piedmont.

19th.--To Ashby's Gap, where Rice's battalion rejoined the command.

20th.--Crossed the Shenandoah River at Berry's Ford.

21st.--Recrossed, and took position in line of battle near Paris, to resist a threatened attack of the enemy.

22nd.--Returned to camp on western side of the river.

23rd.--Obtained 503 new arms from Winchester.

24th.--Marched to Summit Point.

25th.--To Martinsburg.

26*th*.--Crossed Potomac River; encamped near Williamsport.

27th.--Marched by the way of Hagerstown, Middleburg, and Green-castle, and encamped 5 miles from Chambersburg.

28*th*.--Marched through Chambersburg, and encamped 1 mile beyond.

Remained in camp until the 30th, when we marched to Fayetteville.

July 1.--Anderson's and Johnson's divisions and General Ewell's wagon train occupied the road until 4 p.m., when we marched to a point on the Gettysburg road, some 2 miles from that place, going into camp at 12 p.m.

The command was ordered to move at 4 o'clock on the morning of the 2nd, but did not leave camp until about sunrise. We reached the hill overlooking Gettysburg, with only a slight detention from trains in the way, and moved to the right of the Third Corps, and were halted until about noon. We were then directed to move under cover of the hills toward the right, with a view to flanking the enemy in that direction if cover could be found to conceal the movement. Arriving at the hill beyond the hotel, at the stone bridge on the Fairfield road, the column was halted while Generals Longstreet and McLaws reconnoitered the route. After some little delay, the major-general commanding returned, and directed a countermarch, and the command was marched to the left, beyond the point at which we had before halted, and thence, under cover of the woods, to the right of our line of battle. Arriving at the school-house, on the road leading across the Emmitsburg road by the peach orchard, then in possession of the enemy, the lieutenant-general commanding directed me to advance my brigade and attack the enemy at that point, turn his flank, and extend along the cross-road, with my left resting toward the Emmitsburg road. At the same time, a battery of artillery was moved along the road parallel with my line of march. About 3 p.m. the head of my column came into the open field in front of a stone wall, and in view of the enemy. I immediately filed to the right along and in front of the wall and formed line of battle under cover of my skirmishers, then engaged with those of the enemy, these extending along the Emmitsburg road.

In the meantime, examining the position of the enemy, I found him to be in superior force in the orchard, supported by artillery, with a main line of battle entrenched in the rear and extending to and upon the rocky mountain to his left far beyond the point at which his flank had supposed to rest. To carry out my instructions, would have been, if successful in driving him from the orchard, to present my own right and rear to a large portion of his line of battle. I therefore communicated the position of things to the major-general commanding and placed my line in position under cover of the stone wall. Along this wall the division was then formed, Semmes in reserve to me and Barksdale on my left, supported by Wofford, in reserve. Artillery was also placed along the wall to my right, and Colonel De Saussure's Fifteenth South Carolina Regiment was thrown beyond it to protect it. Hood's division was then moving in our rear toward our right, to gain the enemy's left flank, and I was directed to commence the attack so soon as General Hood became engaged, swinging around toward the peach orchard, and at the same time establishing connection with Hood, on my right, and co-operating with him. It was understood he was to sweep down the enemy's line in a direction perpendicular to our then line of battle. I was told that Barksdale would move with me and conform to my movement.

These directions I received in various messages from the lieutenant-general and the major-general commanding, and in part by personal communication with them. In my center front was a stone house, and to the left of it a stone barn, both about 500 yards from our line, and on a line with the crest of the orchard hill. Along the front of the orchard, and on the face looking toward the stone house, the enemy's infantry was posted. Two batteries of artillery were in position, the one in rear of the orchard, near the crest of the hill, and the other some 200 yards farther back, in the direction of the rocky mountain. Behind the stone house, on the left, was a morass; on the right, a stone wall running parallel with our line of battle. Beyond the morass some 200 yards was a stony hill, covered with heavy timber and thick undergrowth, extending some distance toward the enemy's main line, and inclining to our left, and in rear of the orchard and the batteries described. Beyond the stone wall, and in a line with the stony hill, was a heavy forest, extending far to our right. From the morass, a small stream ran through this wood along the base of the mountain toward the right. Between the stony hill and this forest was an interval of about 100 yards, which was only sparsely covered with scrubby undergrowth, through which a small road ran in the direction of the mountain. Looking down this road from the stone house, a large wheat-field was seen. In rear of the wheat-field, and between that and the mountain, was the enemy's main line of battle, posted behind a stone wall.

Under my instructions, I determined to move upon the stony hill, so as to strike it with my center, and thus attack the orchard on its left rear. Accordingly, about 4 o'clock, when I received orders to advance, I moved at once in this direction, gradually changing front to the left. The numerous fences in the way, the stone building and barn, and the morass, and a raking fire of grape and canister, rendered it difficult to retain the line in good order; but, notwithstanding these obstacles, I brought my center to the point intended. In order to restore the line of the directing battalion (the Seventh South Carolina), as soon as we reached the cover of the hill, I moved it a few paces by the right flank. Unfortunately, this order given only to Colonel [D. Wyatt] Aiken, was extended along the left of the line, and checked its advance.

Before reaching this point, I had extended an order to Colonel Kennedy, commanding Second South Carolina Regiment (my left center regiment), then moving in magnificent style, to charge the battery in their front, being the second battery mentioned above, and which most annoyed us, leaving Barksdale to deal with that at the orchard.

Meanwhile, to aid this attack, I changed the direction of the Seventh Regiment (Colonel Aiken) and the Third (Major [R.C.] Maffett) to the left, so as to occupy the rocky hill and wood, and opened fire on the battery. Barksdale had not yet appeared, but came up soon after, and cleared the orchard, with the assistance of the fire of my Eighth South Carolina (Colonel [John W.] Henagan), on my left, and James' battalion (Lieutenant-Colonel [W.G.] Rice), the next in order of battle. This brigade then moved so far to the left as no longer to afford me any assistance.

In a few minutes after my line halted, the enemy advanced across the wheat-field in two lines of battle, with a very small interval between the lines, in such a manner as to take the Seventh South Carolina in flank. I changed the direction of the right wing of the regiment, under Lieutenant-Colonel [Elbert] Bland, to meet the attack, and hurried back to General Semmes, then some 150 yards in my right rear, to bring him up to meet the attack on my right, and also to bring forward my right regiment (Fifteenth South Carolina, Colonel De Saussure), which, separated from the command by the artillery at the time of the advance, was now cut off by Semmes' brigade. Its gallant and accomplished commander had just fallen when I reached it, and it was under the command of Major [William M.] Gist. General Semmes promptly responded to my call, and put his brigade in motion toward the right, preparatory to moving to the front. I hastened back to the Seventh Regiment, and reached it just as the enemy, having arrived at a point about 200 yards from us, poured in a volley and advanced to the charge. The Seventh received him handsomely, and long kept him in check in their front. One regiment of Semmes' brigade came at a double-quick as far as the ravine in our rear, and for a time checked him in their front. There was still an interval of 100 yards between this regiment and the right of the Seventh, and into this the enemy was forcing his way, causing the Seventh to swing back more and more, still fighting at a distance not exceeding 30 paces, until the two wings were doubled on each other, or nearly so.

Finding that the battery on my left had been silenced, I sent for the Second South Carolina Regiment to come to the right, but by this time the enemy had swung around and lapped my whole line at close quarters, and the fighting was general and desperate. At length, the Seventh South Carolina gave way, and I directed Colonel Aiken to reform them at the stone wall, some 200 yards in my right rear. I fell back to the Third Regiment, then hotly engaged on the crest of the stony hill, and gradually swung around its right as the enemy made progress around our flank. Semmes' advanced regiment had given way. One of his regiments mingled with the Third, and, among the rocks and trees, within a few feet of each other, a desperate conflict ensued. The enemy could make no progress in front, but slowly extended around my right. Separated from view of my left wing by the hill and wood, all of my staff being with that wing, the position of the Fifteenth Regiment being unknown, and the Seventh being in the rear, I feared the brave men about me would be surrounded by the large force pressing around them, and ordered the Third Regiment and the [Fiftieth?] Georgia Regiment with them to fall back to the stone house, whither I followed them.

On emerging from the wood, I saw Wofford coming in in splendid style.

My left wing had held the enemy in check along their front and lost no ground. The enemy gave way at Wofford's advance, and, with him, the whole of my left wing advanced to the charge, sweeping the enemy before them, without a moment's stand, across the stone wall, beyond the wheat-field, up to the foot of the mountain. At the same time, my Fifteenth Regiment, and part of Semmes' brigade, pressed forward on the right to the same point. Going back to the stone wall near my rear, I found Colonel Aiken in position, and at the stone building found the Third South Carolina and the regiment of Semmes' brigade. I moved them up to the stone wall, and, finding that Wofford's men were coming out, I retained them at that point to check any attempt of the enemy to advance.

It was now near nightfall, and the operations of the day were over. Gathering all my regiments, with Semmes' brigade, behind the wall, and placing pickets well to the front, I commenced the melancholy task of looking up my numerous dead and wounded. It was a sad list. First among the dead was the brave and able officer, Col. W.D. De Saussure, the senior colonel of the brigade, whom I had been pleased to regard as my successor in command should any casualty create a vacancy. His loss to his regiment is irreparable; to his State and the country not to be estimated. Major [D. McD.] McLeod, of the Eighth South Carolina Regiment, a gallant and estimable officer, was mortally wounded. Col. John D. Kennedy, of the Second South Carolina Regiment, was severely wounded while gallantly leading his command to the charge. Lieutenant-Colonel [F.] Gaillard conducted the regiment through its subsequent operations. Lieutenant-Colonel Bland, of the Seventh South Carolina Regiment, while commanding the right wing of the regiment with his usual courage and ability, was severely wounded, as was also Maj. D.B. Miller, James' battalion [Third Battalion South Carolina Infantry]. A long list of brave and efficient officers sealed their devotion to the glorious cause with their blood, each of whom merits special mention did the proper limits of this report admit it.

All the officers and men of the command behaved most admirably and are entitled to the gratitude of the country. I am especially indebted to the members of my staff--Captain [C.R.] Holmes, assistant adjutant-general; Lieutenant [Alfred E.] Doby, an aide-de-camp, and Lieutenant [W.M.] Dwight, acting assistant inspector-general--for most efficient services on the field under the most difficult circumstances.

About dark, I was ordered to move my brigade to the left, to the peach orchard, where I remained until noon of the next day, when I was ordered to return to the stone wall. An hour later, I was directed to return to the wall where I had first formed line of battle. Hood's division, then commanded by General Law, was engaged with the enemy's cavalry in his front, his line being formed across our right flank. Lieutenant-General Longstreet directed me to move to the right, so as to connect with Hood's left, retaining my then front. This I did and remained in that position until the night of the 4th, when, about midnight, I moved with the army, via Franklin, to Monterey. On the 6th, marched through Hagerstown, via Waterloo, and encamped near Funkstown.

On the 10th. I was directed to proceed, with my own and Semmes' brigades, and a section of [J. C.] Fraser's battery to the bridge across the Antietam, near Macauley's, and defend that position, the enemy having appeared in force on the other side. Some unimportant skirmishing occurred here, and next morning I rejoined the division, near the Saint James' College.

We remained in line of battle, with the enemy in front, until the night of the 13th, when we marched to Falling Waters, and re-crossed the Potomac on the 14th.

March was continued next day to Bunker Hill, where we rested until the 18th, when we resumed the march for Culpeper Court-House, via Millwood, Front Royal, Chester Gap, and Gaines' Cross-Roads, arriving at 10 a.m. on the 24th.

I cannot close this report without expressing my thanks to Maj. W. D. Peck, assistant quartermaster, and Maj. Joseph Kennedy, acting commissary of subsistence, of the brigade staff, and all the regimental officers of their departments, for their assiduous and efficient exertions during this important campaign.

The reports of regimental commanders accompany this. The casualties have already been reported.

I am, major, very respectfully, your obedient servant,

J.B. KERSHAW,

Brigadier-General, Commanding.

Richard Kirkland, The Humane Hero of Fredericksburg
By
General J.B. Kershaw.

(The following incident, originally published in the Charleston News and Courier, deserves a place in our records, and we cheerfully comply with requests to publish it which have come from various quarters.)

Camden, S.C., January 2nd, 1880.

To the Editor of the News and Courier:

Your Columbia correspondent referred to the incident narrated here, telling the story as 'twas told him, and inviting corrections. As such a deed should be recorded in the rigid simplicity of actual truth, I take the liberty of sending you for publication an accurate account of a transaction every feature of which is indelibly impressed upon my memory.

**Yours very truly,
J. B. Kershaw.**

Richard Kirkland was the son of John Kirkland, an estimable citizen of Kershaw county, a plain, substantial farmer of the olden time. In 1861, he entered as a private in Captain J.D. Kennedy's company (E) of the Second South Carolina volunteers, in which company he was a sergeant in December 1861.

The day after the sanguinary battle of Fredericksburg, Kershaw's brigade occupied the road at the foot of Marye's hill and the ground about Marye's house, the scene of their desperate defense of the day before. One hundred and fifty yards in front of the road, the stone facing of which constituted the famous stone wall, lay Syke's division of regulars, U.S.A., between whom and our troops a murderous skirmish occupied the whole day, fatal to many who heedlessly exposed themselves, even for a moment. The ground between the lines was bridged with the wounded dead and dying Federals, victims of the many desperate and gallant assaults of that column of 30,000 brave men hurled vainly against that impregnable position.

All that day those wounded men rent the air with their groans and their agonizing cries of "Water! water!" In the afternoon, the General sat in the north room, upstairs, of Mrs. Stevens' house, in front of the road, surveying the field, when Kirkland came up. With an expression of indignant remonstrance pervading his person, his manner and the tone of his voice, he said:

"General! I can't stand this."

"What is the matter, Sergeant?" asked the general.

He replied, "All night and all day I have heard those poor people crying for water, and I can stand it no longer. I come to ask permission to go and give them water."

The general regarded him for a moment with feelings of profound admiration, and said: "Kirkland, don't you know that you would get a bullet through your head the moment you stepped over the wall?"

"Yes, sir," he said, "I know that, but if you will let me, I am willing to try it."

After a pause, the General said, "Kirkland, I ought not to allow you to run a risk, but the sentiment which actuates you is so noble that I will not refuse your request, trusting that God may protect you. You may go." The sergeant's eye lighted up with pleasure. He said, "Thank you, sir," and ran rapidly down stairs. The general heard him pause for a moment, and then return, bounding two steps at a time. He thought the sergeant's heart had failed him. He was mistaken.

The sergeant stopped at the door and said: "General, can I show a white handkerchief?" The general slowly shook his head, saying emphatically, "No, Kirkland, you can't do that." "All right," he said, "I'll take the chances," and ran down with a bright smile on his handsome countenance.

With profound anxiety he was watched as he stepped over the wall on his errand of mercy — Christ-like mercy. Unharmed he reached the nearest sufferer. He knelt beside him, tenderly raised the drooping head, rested it gently upon his own noble breast, and poured the precious life-giving fluid down the fever-scorched throat. This done, he laid him tenderly down, placed his knapsack under his head, straightened out his broken limb, spread his overcoat over him, replaced his empty canteen with a full one, and turned to another sufferer. By this time his purpose was well understood on both sides, and all danger was over. From all parts of the field arose fresh cries of "Water, water; for God's sake, water!" More piteous still the mute appeal of some who could only feebly lift a hand to say, here, too, is life and suffering.

For an hour and a half did, this ministering angel pursued his labor of mercy, nor ceased to go and return until he relieved all the wounded on that part of the field. He returned to his post wholly unhurt. Who shall say how sweet his rest that winter's night beneath the cold stars!

Little remains to be told. Sergeant Kirkland distinguished himself in battle at Gettysburg and was promoted lieutenant. At Chickamauga, he fell on the field of battle, in the hour of victory. He was but a youth when called away and had never formed those ties from which might have resulted in a posterity to enjoy his fame and bless his country, but he has bequeathed to the American youth — yea, to the world — an example which dignifies our common humanity.

In a letter from Frank J. Hughes to Mrs. DeLoach, dated May 3, 1930, from Rock Hill, South Carolina, the following was written:

> "I belonged to General Kershaw. My mother was named Sally. My mother had a sister named Phyllis, and one named Agnes. Grace was the cook. I was the carriage boy. I drove the children to school until the school got burned down. One man was named Old Daddy Billy. Miss had a daughter names Camilla, one named Mattie Young, a school teacher. One boy was name Sandy, one daughter name was Miss Ellen. I was on the State House - me, and the Missus, General Kershaw - when Fort Sumter was blowed up on Thursday morning. Next Thursday, Marse George went off to the Army. I wanted to go with him but he said, 'No, Frank, you stay here and take care of the Ms. and the children and take care of everything.' I was so glad when the young lady told me Colonel Kershaw was your grandfather.

I had a sister names Patience, one sister named Lucy. When we hid the corn and mule but the Yankees didn't take the mules, nothing but the corn. Old General Kershaw fought the Revolutionary War. My grandfather was killed with him."

Frank J. Hughes died May 18, 1931, in the city of Rock Hill. He was eighty-one years old. He was born in Camden, South Carolina. His parents were Sherman and Sarah Hughes, both born in Camden, South Carolina. His wife was Ellen. He was buried near Rock Hill. He was a farmer by occupation and died of heart disease. (South Carolina Death certificate 8868)

Found at the Longstreet Museum in Russellville, Tennessee. Being one of Longstreet's commanders, General Kershaw stayed nearby at the plantation of the Taylor family, located about a half mile from the Longstreet's Headquarters. Mr. Taylor had an office building that General Kershaw used when in Tennessee. That office building became his civil war headquarters. Ironically, the plans for battle in Mossy Creek, Dandridge, and Fair Garden were developed in winter camp for Longstreet by Kershaw and his staff in this building. The building is 18 by 21 and moved to the site about 2008 to make room for an industrial park on the Taylor Plantation.[547]

James Chesnut. Jr.

James Chesnut, Jr.'s parents were James Chesnut, born at Princeton in 1792, and Mary Cox, daughter of Colonel John and Esther Cox. James Jr.'s birth date was January 18, 1815, in Camden, South Carolina, and died February 1, 1885, at Sarsfield, Camden, South Carolina. He was married to Miss Mary Boykin Miller, daughter of Stephen Decatur Miller, April 23, 1840. Stephen Miller was governor of South Carolina in 1830, United States Senator in 1832. His second wife was Mary Boykin. Governor Miller graduated S.C. College in 1808. James, Jr. entered Princeton's Sophomore

---

[547] Sent to me by Tracy Barfield, Tennessee

class in November 1832, and graduated in 1835. He studied law in Charleston, South Carolina, in the office of James Louis Petigru, and was admitted to the bar in 1839. He was a member of the South Carolina Assembly 1840- 1846, and 1850-1852. He was a member of the South Carolina Senate 1852-1858. He was president of the South Carolina Senate in 1856-1857. He became a U.S. Senator from 1859-1860. He was filling the expired term and was elected in 1859 for six years. He resigned November 10, 1860, to come back home and serve his beloved South Carolina. He was Brigadier General in 1863 and was a Colonel before that and Aide for Staff President Davis 1861. He was a trustee of a S.C. College. After the war, he returned to his home in Camden, South Carolina. In 1868, he was a member of the National Democratic Convention that nominated Seymour and Blair.[548]

During his days as a senator in Washington, he debated with Sumner on the slavery issue. Four months after John Brown's raid, he engaged his fiery opponent in one of the most notable debates ever to ring out in the Senate on the issue which split this nation.

During the war, he served as an aide-de-camp to General Beauregard at the battles of First Manassas and Fort Sumter. He attained the rank of Brigadier General in 1864 and given command of the South Carolina Reserves.[549]

The following is the obituary of General James Chesnut:

> The announcement of the death of General James Chesnut, which occurred at his residence in Kirkwood on last Sunday afternoon about three o'clock, was received with profound sorrow throughout the entire State, especially here in his native county, where he had spent a long and useful life. General Chesnut had not enjoyed good health for over a year previously to his death but had been confined to his home but a short time previous to the sad event.

We shall leave to other and more capable hands the duty of paying tribute to the many noble traits of character displayed by this illustrious gentleman through a long and useful life. *The News and Courier* gives the following brief sketch of General Chesnut's life:

> General Chesnut was born near Camden, South Carolina, in 1815. He graduated at Princeton College and upon return home began the practice of law at Camden. From 1842 to 1852, he was a member of the lower house of the Legislature. From 1854 to 1858, he was a member of the Senate, and was president of that body when he was elected to the Senate of the United States, which he entered during the second session of the Thirty-Fifth Congress. Resigning his seat in Congress, he was elected a member of the Secession Convention, in which capacity he voted for succession. During the military operations which resulted in the fall of Fort Sumter, He was an aid on General Beauregard's staff, and together with General S.D. Lee,

---

[548] Princeton University General Biographical Catalogue 1746- 1916, Chesnut Family Folder, Camden Archives and Museum, Camden, S.C.
[549] Chestnut Family Folder, Camden Archives and Museum, Camden, S.C.

was sent by General Beauregard to demand surrender of the fort, which demand had been anticipated, however by the informal action of Senator Wigfall of Texas. As a member of the Council of State, which was organized immediately after the Act of Secession, General Chesnut was one of Governor Pickens's confidential and most trusted advisors. Upon the assembling of the Provisional Congress of the Confederate States, at Montgomery, he was appointed a delegate to that body, which position he filled until the organization of the permanent government. During the first military campaign in Virginia, he was again a member of General Beauregard's staff, and received honorable mention in that officer's report of the battle of Manassas. Appointed soon afterwards a special aide on the Staff of President Davis, General Chesnut held the closet personal and official relations with the President until appointed brigadier general in 1864. On his staff was the following: Edward H. Barnwell, age thirty from Charleston and the rank of Captain; Isaac Hayne, age twenty-four from Charleston and a Lieutenant; R.H. Hill, a Captain from Tennessee; H.N. Ogden, a Captain from New Orleans; J.G. Brown, captain.

After the war closed, he retired to private life and devoted himself to the care of his father's estate, the maintenance of which required nearly his undivided attention. During this period, however, he was elected to represent the people of this county in the Taxpayer's Convention of 1871 and 1874, in the latter of which he took an active part in all the proceedings, besides holding the important position of chairman of the committee. To him, all resolutions were referred before discussion. He also gave his whole influence on the support of the movement in 1876, which resulted in the overthrow of the Reconstruction Government in South Carolina. Since that time, he has lived in retirement, and has borne no part in politics of the State. In manner General Chesnut was dignified but courteous, and though somewhat reserved, was kind and gentle to everyone who was brought into association with him. He whole moral character was of that high standard which caused him to be both enjoyed and respected by all men. A careful reader and student in all departments of mental culture, he was finest in testifying in questions of law and government and his views upon such questions are characterized by thoroughness of litigation and sound judgement. He was a marked man in his own community and in the State, and his counsel was eagerly sought by his fellow citizens in all matters of public moment. The brief announcement of his death will be received with sincere sorrow and regret by his many friends throughout the whole country.

The funeral services took place at the late residence of the deceased on Tuesday morning at eleven o'clock; Reverend J.M. Stoney of the Episcopal church officiating. The Court of Sessions was adjourned on Monday evening until Wednesday morning in respect to the memory of the deceased. The following gentleman was pallbearers: Governor M.L. Bonham, Mr. John McRae, Major E.E. Sill, Mr. R.M. Kennedy, Mr. George G. Young, Mr. W. Whitaker, Mr. T.J. Kirkland, Mr. A.H. Boykin, Dr. E.M. Boykin, Captain J.I. Villepique.

The remains were interred in the private family burying ground in Knights Hill, about six miles above Camden.

On his Tombstone, the following was carved in:

James Chesnut

Son of

James Chesnut and Mary Cox, His wife

Of Mulberry, South Carolina

Born January 18, 1815

Died February 1, 1885

President of the Senate of South Carolina – 1856

United States Senator - 1858

Member of the Secession Convention - 1860

Staff Officer at the Fall of Fort Sumter - 1861

Delegate to the Confederate Congress - 1861

Chief of the Military Department of South Carolina - 1862

Aide de Camp to President Davis - 1863

Brigadier General CSA 1864 - 1865

In Coelo quieo

Zachary Cantey Deas

Zachary Deas was the son of Colonel James Sutherland Deas and Margaret Chesnut of Camden, South Carolina, with her brother being James Chesnut, Jr. He was educated in Columbia, South Carolina, and in Caudebec, France. In 1835, his parents and he moved to Mobile, Alabama, when the times to buy land and prosper was ready to be had for those who wanted to settle there. Deas became a cotton broker and acquired great wealth. Deas saw action in the Mexican War, and when the Civil War broke out, he enlisted with the Alabama Volunteers. He fought in several battles and was wounded several times. His first duty was an aide-de-camp to General J.E. Johnston. In the fall of 1861, he was commissioned as a colonel. Major Robert B. Armestead help him organize and recruit the 22nd Alabama Infantry. He equipped them himself with Enfield Rifles at a cost of $28, 000 in gold. However, he was reimbursed by the government in Confederate Bonds.

On April 6 and 7, 1862, he led his brigade at Shiloh. In that battle, his officers above him fell, and himself got wounded, but he recovered in time to march through Kentucky with General Bragg. Deas took over the command of Gladden's brigade, when General Gladden got wounded at Shiloh. He was commissioned Brigadier General on December 13, 1862. In the Battle of Murfreesboro from December 31, 1862 to January succeeded General Garder. He led his brigade in the battles of Chickamauga, September 19-20, 1863, the battle of Missionary Ridge, November 25, 1863, and in the battles and skirmishes against General Sherman from Dalton to Atlanta and Jonesboro. Against Sherman, Deas' troops struck his flank so hard that Deas' soldiers routed him and captured seventeen pieces of artillery.[550] He went to Nashville with General Hood and took part in the battles of Franklin and Nashville, November 30 and December 15-16, 1864. After the battle in Nashville, he was transferred to the East to assist in opposing Sherman's March through the Carolinas. At Raleigh, he got ill, and relinquished his command to Colonel H.T. Toulmin.

When the war ended, he moved to New York City, and became prosperous in the cotton trade. He became a cotton broker, and a prominent member of the stock exchange. However, as his life was quiet in Mobil, Alabama, so was his life in New York City.

General Zachary Deas was born October 25, 1819, in Camden, and died in New York City on March 6, 1882. His widow lived passed the year of 1926. Both are buried at Woodlawn Cemetery, New York City.

The following is a report submitted by Colonel Z.C. Deas, Twenty-Second Alabama Infantry, Commanding First Brigade.

Headquarters 1st Brigade, Wither's Division, Army of the Mississippi,
Mobile, Alabama, April 25, 1862

Captain: I have the honor to report that on the morning of April 6, this brigade - composed of the First Louisiana Infantry, Colonel D.W. Adams; Twenty-first Alabama, Lieutenant Colonel S.W. Cayce; Twenty-second Alabama, Colonel Z.C. Deas; Twenty-fifth Alabama, Colonel J.Q. Loomis; Twenty-sixth Alabama, Colonel Coltart, and Robertson's Battery, Captain F.H. Robertson - under command of Brigadier-General Gladden, moved out of camp, marching in line of battle, and shortly after seven o'clock came upon the enemy, when the engagement commenced. One of their batteries was playing upon us with effect, but in a short time, Robertson's Battery was brought on our side, which soon silenced theirs. We then charged, driving the enemy flying through their camp. In this charge, several colors were captured.

Just before this charge was made, General Gladden, while gloriously sustaining the reputation won in Mexico at the head of the immortal Palmetto Regiment, received a wound from a cannon-ball, which proved fatal.

Beyond this camp, the brigade (now under command of Colonel Adams) was halted, and after a time a battery stationed near their next camp opened upon us, which was responded to by Robertson's, and after a sharp contest silenced.

Orders were now received to move forward in support of General Chalmers, and while here the gallant Adams, when encouraging his men by reckless daring and apparent contempt of the missiles of death flying think around him, received a severe wound in the head.

The command of the brigade now devolved upon me. Without instructions, with a staff officer, or oven one of my own regiment mounted to assist me, I moved forward to aid where I could, and before proceeding

---

[550] "Camden Boasts Six Civil War Generals," by Raymond, Robert; Charleston News and Courier, Jan 13, 1964.

far came up with General Breckinridge, who was warmly engaged on my right. I immediately advanced to his assistance. The fire here was very severe, and I sent back for the Twenty-sixth Alabama to come up (which they failed to do), and for a battery, which were brought up promptly, and with this assistance, after a hard and long continued struggle, we succeeded in driving the enemy back.

At this point, General Bragg came up and ordered me to change direction, obliquing to the left. In a short time, I came upon the enemy again, drawn up some distance in front of another camp, and after a short but very sharp engagement, drove them before me, pursuing them to their camp, where I assisted in capturing a large number.

Here, in the hot pursuit, the Twenty-first and Twenty-fifth Alabama became separated from me in the woods, and before I had had time to find them, I received an order from General Withers to form on the extreme left, where I remained until night came on, and then attempted to get back to the camp I had left, but got into a different one. My men being now completely exhausted, and not having had anything to eat since morning, I encamped for the night.

On inspection, I found I had under my command only the First Louisiana Infantry and the Twenty-second Alabama, numbering respectively, 101 and 123 men, with about an average of fifteen rounds of ammunition, although both regiments had replenished during the day.

At daylight on the morning of the seventh, I sent Captain R.J. Hill to hunt for General Withers' division, and to get information. He soon returned and reported that the enemy was advancing. I immediately marched over and formed on the left of the division commanded by Colonel Russell. Under his orders we advanced but perceiving the enemy's skirmishes on our left and rear, fell back to our first position. While here the enemy opened upon us with artillery, when we moved beyond the crest of a hill, and I placed my command in support of a battery, where I remained until I received orders from General Bragg to attack on my left. While marching to this attack, I was joined by the Fourth Kentucky, and with these fragments of regiments, numbering together less than 500, I attacked two brigades; but after continuing this unequal contest for nearly half an hour, and nearly one-half of my command had been killed or wounded, I gave the order to fall back, which was done in good order.

I now formed and moved forward again, with the remnant of my brigade (now reduced to about sixty men), in the last attack under General Beauregard. Here my second horse was killed, and I (having been wounded some time previously) was unable to march.

The indomitable courage and perseverance of the officers and men of this brigade: the willingness and gallantry with which they advanced to the attack when called upon, after having endured almost superhuman fatigues in the desperate and long continued struggles of Sunday and Monday, are deserving of the highest encomiums, Where so many acted nobly it might appear invidious to particularize, but impartiality compels me to record as first in the fight the First Louisiana Infantry and Twenty-Second Alabama.

I wish to call the attention of my superiors to such field officers as especially distinguished themselves under my immediate supervision for their coolness and gallant bearing under the hottest fire. Lieutenant Colonel John C. Marrast, Twenty-Second Alabama; Majors F.H. Farrar, First Louisiana Infantry, and George D. Johnson, Twenty-fifth Alabama; and to Adjutant Kent, First Louisiana; Adjutant Stout, Twenty-fifth Alabama; Adjutant

Travis and Sergeant-Major Nott, Twenty-second Alabama, acting as aides, for their gallantry and bravery in extending my orders.

This report is written without having received any of the regimental reports, and without being able to consult with any of the officers, which will account for my not mentioning all the officers of this brigade who distinguished themselves on the field of Shiloh. For this information, I will respectfully refer to regimental reports, and to refer to the document for killed, wounded, and missing.

I am, Captain, very respectfully, your obedient servant,

Z.C. Deas

Colonel, Commanding First Brigade, Wither's Division.[551]

Brigadier General John Doby Kennedy

On February 22, 1909, the General Assembly was presented a portrait of General Kennedy to the Senate. In accepting this presentation, Senator Hough of Camden made appropriate remarks touching upon the life of this noble Carolinian. Resolutions were ordered spread upon the journal. Senator Mauldin recalled the days of the sixties when General Kennedy fought for this state's rights. His reference to General Kennedy to his work in time of peace and during and after the reconstruction period.

Governor Ansel gave a message on this occasion which included the following:

> "Gentlemen: The family of the late General John D. Kennedy of Camden, South Carolina, have presented to the State of South Carolina a portrait of this distinguished citizen, soldier, and statesman, who was able, honored, and beloved by all who knew him.

General Kennedy was born in Camden, South Carolina, on the fifth of January in 1840, and died in his native town on the fourteenth of April 1896. He served the State and the United States faithfully and well, having been elected lieutenant governor of South Carolina in 1880, serving for two years in that capacity. He was appointed consul general from the United States to Shanghai, China, 1886, and served for several years in that position.

I take pleasure in presenting to you this portrait in the name of the family, I will ask that it be placed in the senate chamber, where he so ably presided over the senate for South Carolina for two years."

In commenting upon the life of General Kennedy, Mr. Mauldin said:

---

551 War of the Rebellion, Official Records of the Union and Confederate States, Series I, Volume 10, Part 1- Reports, page 538-539.

William Guerry Felder

"Mr. President: I rise to second the resolution of the senator from Kershaw County, accepting the portrait of General John D. Kennedy. Mr. President, and senators, I had the privilege of knowing General Kennedy well and pleasantly in the years that are gone, full of memories and history. In this young manhood, as a brave and loyal citizen, he responded to the call of his State, and as a daring and intrepid soldier illuminated the record of his native State upon the field of battle, commanding one of the first regiments in the Confederate army. In the fateful Reconstruction period, when our great state lay prone and prostrate her vitals preyed upon by a horde of adventurers and traitors, he again rendered active and distinguished services to his people. Attractive, genial, and warm-hearted in his personality, he held his friends to an unusual degree in all the relations of life, public and private.

As presiding officer of this senate in the past, his service is remembered by the fairness, courtesy, and impartiality that characterized it. I regard it as a privilege, Mr. President, to embrace this opportunity to pay a simple tribute to a friend, a soldier, and a valued public servant, and I am sure I voice the sentiment of this senate in returning thanks to the family of General Kennedy for presenting to the State this splendid portrait. They may be assured that will be properly placed and grace the walls of this chamber, where at one time he so gracefully presided."

John Doby Kennedy was born in Camden January 5, 1840. His parents were Anthony MacMillan Kennedy and Sarah Doby. He was trained in the best school of Camden and entered the South Carolina College at the early age of fifteen years old, distinguishing himself in a class of brainy men. He was married quite young, his wife being Miss Elizabeth Cunningham of Camden. He was admitted to the bar on reaching his twenty-first year of age. He was made captain of the Camden Light Infantry, the first company raised for military service in 1860-1861 in Kershaw County, which company formed a part of the famous Second Regiment, commanded by Colonel J.B. Kershaw. This was one of four companies that stepped forward on the beach of Morris Island, April 1861, when their commander called for volunteers to go to Virginia. From Richmond, the regiment went to Manassas and participated in the first great fight of the war, assisting greatly in retrieving the fortunes of the day, and converting defeat into an almost unperilled rout. In 1862, when the command volunteered for the war, Captain Kennedy was elected colonel of the regiment, the former colonel being made brigadier general (J. B. Kershaw) at the same time. From that time until 1864, Colonel Kennedy shared in the fortunes of that noble body of soldiers composing the Army of Northern Virginia and added many laurels to his crown of fame. In the summer of 1864, when Kershaw succeeded McLaws in the command of the first division of Longstreet's corps, Kennedy was made brigadier general by promotion, and served in that capacity until the close of hostilities. Longstreet's corps was ordered to Tennessee to reinforce Bragg, and after the great battle of Chickamauga, when Longstreet was ordered to Knoxville, Tennessee, General Kennedy's command, at the earnest request of Governor Magrath, was detached from the rest of the corps, and came to South Carolina in time to confront Sherman on his march to the sea, and oppose his invasion until after Bentonville; the army of General Johnston was surrendered at Greensboro, North Carolina, in April 1865.

General Kennedy bore upon his body the marks of his country's service, being six times severely wounded in battle, and not less than fifteen times was he struck by bullets, but he never failed to return to the post of duty at the first moment he was able, and his skill and gallantry were often made the subjects of favorable mention by his superior officers.

In December 1865, he was elected to Congress from his district but owing to the fact he would not take the ironclad oath he was unable to obtain his seat. He was a delegate to the National Democratic Convention, which met in St. Louis in 1876, and a member of the State executive committee of the Democratic party the same year. He was present at every meeting of that committee, shared as a member of that committee the trying ordeal through which the Wallace house passed when it took possession of the State house. He was a member of the house of representatives from Kershaw County in 1878 and 1879 and was elected Lieutenant Governor of the State in November 1880, with General Hagood as governor. During Cleveland's first administration, General Kennedy was appointed consul general to Shanghai, China, in which capacity he served with distinction and ability, and such was the esteem in which he was held by the diplomatic corps colleagues and the Chinese officials, that when he was rumored to be displaced by President Harrison, a most earnest endorsement of General Kennedy, and request for his retention was forwarded to Washington but the demands of the party triumphed over merit and popularity.

General Kennedy married a second time, his wife being Miss Harriet Boykin. General Kennedy was physically a splendid specimen of manhood. Of noble, handsome presence and courteous to a fault and magnanimous and forgiving in disposition. He was an orator of high order, and an advocate of extraordinary power. A citizen of great patriotic power and, above all, an earnest, humbling, trusting Christian.

General Kennedy loved his State with a devotion that knew no bounds and was prepared always with his means and his life, if necessary, to promote and defend her interests. After his return from China, he resumed the practice of law and had built up a fine practice at the time of his death, April 14, 1896. The portrait that was presented to the State by his excellency, Governor Ansel, through the legislature, was given by his children. Today, that portrait still hangs in the South Carolina Senate Chambers. One can see this portrait of the left side of the Senate speakers' seat facing the front. What honor has this been showing the life and times of General John Doby Kennedy.[552]

In May 1897, the following statement was found concerning the monument of General John D. Kennedy. "Probably the handsomest monument in this section has just been erected to the memory of the late John D. Kennedy in our cemetery. The style of the monument is entirely new, of Italian marble being a massive tablet set upon two bases, one of which is beautifully moulded. On the face of the tablet is a heavy scroll upon which is the inscription, while on the top and extending over the scroll is a sheaf of wheat most elegantly carved. It bears the following inscription, cut in incised mounted letters, which are plain but handsome, and in keeping with the rest of the work:

John Doby Kennedy – 1849 - 1896.

And now abideth faith, hope, and charity, these three:

---

[552] "The Portrait of General Kennedy," The State newspaper, Columbia, S.C., February 22, 1909.

but the greatest of these is charity.

The monument was imported from Italy.[553]

The following is the obituary of John D. Kennedy.

Gone to Join Kershaw
The Death of General John D. Kennedy, C. S. A. in Camden

The sudden end of a noble and distinguished Career - A Brigadier at twenty-four, he had been wounded six times and struck fifteen times by spent balls—After the War, he served his State nobly in redeeming it from the Carpetbagger and Scalawag, and later he served the nation ably as its representative at Shanghai, China- He was active and useful citizen to the last.

Camden, April 14 - The announcement of the death of General John D. Kennedy, which occurred at the home in Kirkwood, a suburb of Camden, this morning at twenty minutes to one o'clock, has cast a gloom of profound sorrow over this entire community, and will be received with sincere regret throughout South Carolina.

General Kennedy was at his law office yesterday looking after his law business until about five o'clock in the afternoon, when he went home, apparently perfectly well. A few minutes before his death, he called Mrs. Kennedy and told her he was feeling badly. He then got up to take something to try to relieve himself, when he was seized with apoplexy, and died in about ten minutes.

Thus, a noble life is ended. A great big heart is stilled. The bosom of Mother Earth must be opened to receive the remains of a loving friend, a devoted husband, a kind father, a useful and patriotic citizen. His death will be sadly mourned by scores of friends throughout South Carolina.

General Kennedy was the foremost man in Kershaw County. He enjoyed a good law practice and was ready to serve the best interests of his home and country.

After his return to Camden, from Shanghai, China, in the fall of 1889, he devoted his time to the practice of law, and never inspired to any public office.

He was a gallant soldier and took special interest in organizing Camp Richard Kirkland, United Confederate Veterans. The old veterans in this county loved General Kennedy with an unwavering devotion, and his heart always beat in profound love for them.

The funeral services will take place tomorrow morning.

---

[553] "Great Men's Monuments. One Mutilated by Relic Hunters. Other Just Erected," The State newspaper, Columbia, S.C., May 17, 1897.

General John D. Kennedy

On wings that are swifter than the wind was flashed yesterday the sad tidings of the sudden death of this distinguished citizen, patriot, and soldier, at his home in Camden. Only last Sunday this paper gave to the world his warm and generous tribute to this lifelong friend and former commander, General Joseph B. Kershaw, reviewing his war record and commending his example, not in terms of extravagant eulogy, but in those just and discriminating appreciation. Hardly had their author read the printed record of events in which he himself bore no mean part before the summons came to him, almost as "in the twinkling of an eye, to cross over the river and rest under the shade of the trees" along with his friend and fellow townsman, and with all the great history of those who with him followed the starry cross of the Southern Confederacy on many a hard fought field until it was folded, nevermore to be unfurled as a nation's standard, at Appomattox and Bentonville.

It is a melancholy duty we owe to the memory of such and one to place on record some brief recital of a career that has been remarkable in many respects from it vicissitudes and for the manhood with which they were met. Attaining to the years of manhood when the war drums were throbbing and men's hearts responding to their stern alarums, a very large part of General Kennedy's life was passed in fighting the battles of this country or in assisting to guide his State through the years of reconstruction that were, if possible, more trying than the four years of actual war, demanding greater wisdom in counsel, more sustained self-restraint and larger powers of endurance on the part of an outraged and indignant people. That is both protracted emergencies he should have carried himself bravely, unselfishly and with distinction is the sufficient proof that he deserves the encomiums of those in whose interests he labored. That in the ripe prime of his maturity he should have been snatched away by death's resistless hand is the sufficient reason why the State should morn over what appears to be his untimely taking off.

John D. Kennedy was born in Camden, South Carolina, on January 5, 1840. Trained at the local academy, taught for many years by Mr. Leslie McCandless, he entered the South Carolina College at the early age of sixteen, remaining there until the fall of 1857, when he married Miss Elizabeth Cunningham and proceeded to the study of law, intending to make that his profession. Admitted to the Bar immediately on reaching his twenty-first year, he was at once called to don his uniform and come to Morris Island as captain of the Camden Light Infantry, itself a company of the 2nd regiment, commanded by Colonel J.B. Kershaw. This was one of the four companies of that famous regiment that stepped forward on the beach of Morris Island when their commander called for volunteers to go to Virginia. From Richmond, the regiment went to Manassas Junction and participated in the first great fight of the war, assisting largely in retrieving the fortunes of the day and in converting defeat into an almost unparalleled rout. At the reorganization in 1862, when the command volunteered for the war, Kennedy was elected colonel of the regiment, its former colonel being made brigadier general at the same time. From that time until 1864, Kennedy shared in the fortunes of that noble body of soldiery composing of the Army of Northern Virginia and added numerous laurels to his crown of fame. In the summer of that year, when Kershaw succeeded McLaws as the command of the first division of Longstreet's corps. Kennedy was made brigadier general by promotion and served in that capacity to the close of hostilities. Soon after his promotion, Longstreet's crop was ordered to Tennessee to reinforce Bragg, and after

Chickamauga, where his brigade covered itself with glory, when Longstreet was ordered to Knoxville. Kennedy and his command, at the urgent request of Governor Magrath, were detached from the rest of the corps and came to South Carolina in time to confront Sherman on his march to the sea and oppose his invasion until after Averysboro and Bentonville, the army of General Johnston. Unreadable line - kindly in manner, generous to a fault, an orator of high order, an advocate of extraordinary power, a citizen of great public spirit, and above all, an earnest, humble, trusting Christian. In this faith, he lived and died, having finished his course, and have fought a good fight.[554]

James Cantey

The Cantey House

The Story of the Cantey Family, Including Winter Cantey, James Cantey's half-brother.

The story of James Cantey goes back to his days in Camden, South Carolina. He was born in Camden, South Carolina, on December 30, 1818, and he died June 30, 1874, at Fort Mitchell, his home from 1849. He was the son of John Cantey. He went to the South Carolina College and graduated December 1838. Some of his classmates were Dixon Barnes, E.M. Boykin, W.D. Desaussure, Samuel H. Hay, E.A. Salmond, and J. Witherspoon.[555] He had a brilliant career in Camden. He practiced law at Camden, served two terms in the South Carolina Legislature, and he volunteered for the Mexican War, in which he served as Captain of the Palmetto Regiment of South Carolina.[556]

---

[554] In a scrapbook in the possession of Mrs. E. N. McDowell, Copy in the files of the Civil War at the Camden Archives and Museum, Camden, S.C.
[555] The Charleston Courier, Charleston, S.C., December 19, 1838.
[556] The Sunday Ledger-Enquirer Civil War Edition, Columbus, Georgia, April 16, 1961.

The Mexican War brought out the first struggle in James's life. It was in the Battle of Churubusco on August 27, 1847, that harm came upon Adjutant James Cantey. He was shot through the jaw and face, while another Camdenite, Lieutenant Colonel Dickerson, died.[557] But there is more to this story that is handed down through the Cantey family. Believing that James Cantey was dead, bodies were thrown out among the dead, and a pile of solders placed upon him. James's body servant, Sam, found him and discovered that there was a faintless beat of life in his master's body, and told the commanding officer immediately. Orders were told to removed Cantey from the pile, and it was then that his body servant picked up James in his arms and nursed him back to the living. During his service in Mexico, Cantey was both 1st Lieutenant and Adjutant of the Palmetto Regiment, and elected Captain of Company C. He was mustered out of service in Mobil, Alabama, in June 1848.[558] Two servants left with James, one servant was Sam Kirkland, and the other one, Winter, still very youthful and was sent back from the battlefield.[559] Sam Kirkland was offered freedom but refused this great gift to remain serving the white folks on the plantation. Sam's intention was to carry James back to South Carolina but stopped in Russell County, Alabama. Because of James Cantey's efforts, he was given two silver pitchers, which was given to him by William Burrous as a remainder of the faithful act given by this black and the memory forever etched in his children's and descendants' minds.[560]

Winter Cantey grew up as a trusted servant by James' mother in Camden, South Carolina, where he was sent back and forth many times to Russell County (Fort Mitchell) with large amounts of money, horses, mares, colts, and Negroes.[561] Trouble was happening on the plantation in Russell County, and James', urging on by his father and others, moved to Russell County about 1849 to deal with plantation problems, and overseers in the area.[562] Winter Cantey was actually treated as member of the family and not a slave. He grew up with James Cantey and was taught to read and write.

Soon afterwards, James Cantey married Martha Elizabeth Benton, born July 10, 1839 and passed away February 18, 1928. She was the daughter of Colonel Lemuel Benton of the Russell County area. From this marriage were three children, Sam, John, and Mary. James and Martha Elizabeth resided in the old Benton house on the part considered the old Government Military Reservation, and part of Colonel Cromwell's estate.[563] The house is now gone but the only thing remaining is an oak tree brought back home from Mobile, Alabama, in the fall of 1864.

On July 27, 1861, James Cantey was appointed colonel of the 15th Alabama Infantry.[564] He was appointed Brigadier General on January 8, 1863, with his successor for colonel being W.C. Oates.[565] In November and December of 1862, he was with Ewell's Division of Trimble's Division, listed as a field officer. In November,

---

[557] The Charleston News and Courier, Charleston, S.C., February 10, 1892.
[558] "The History of Russell County, Alabama," Russell County Historical Commission, F-66., 1982.
[559] Article 10, CanteyMyers Collection, On the internet; with permission of Emory A. Cantey, Jr.
[560] Ibid.
[561] Ibid.
[562] Ibid.
[563] "The History of Russell County, Alabama," Russell County Historical Commission, F-66., 1982.
[564] Service record.
[565] Ibid.

he was on leave for thirty days and in December thirty-one days sick leave at home.[566] The regiment consisting of seven companies were encamped at Fort Mitchell, near the home and plantation of James Cantey, now Colonel.[567] James Cantey was described as a chivalrous and high-toned gentleman, and one no truer and braver.[568] Governor Moore of Alabama would be purchasing to supply the regiment with a complete compliment of arms to take the place of the 400 double barrel shotguns, many recruits had upon joining. Some of the needed arms were purchased by a Mr. Edgar G. Dawson, Esquire, now major of the regiment.[569]

In the Atlanta Campaign, James Cantey's Division consisted of the following: The first brigade had the 1st, 2nd, 4th, 9th, and the 29th Arkansas. The Second brigade had 1st, 17th, 26th, 29th, and 37th Alabama. Also on the list was the Alabama Sharpshooters under Major J.S. Moreland.

During the war, Winter Cantey went with James to the war. James sent Winter back to check on things and see how the family was during. As James left, Sam and the other slaves found themselves as the only protection at Fort Mitchell and the Cantey home. James Cantey heard of the Yankees coming through the area and sent Winter to go and protect the family. During this time, General Wilson's Raiders were passing through and, though their path was on the edge of Russell County, a boy guided them to the Cantey plantation.[570] This boy wanted the Cantey boy's pony, Planet, who was the desire of every slave in the neighborhood to have. With the group of raiders, the worst of the lot of stragglers followed to take and destroy what they could. As the group was heard coming on the plantation and nearing the house, Winter Cantey went to meet them. Mrs. Cantey soon followed to confront those soldiers. As Mrs. Cantey arrived near, two slaves came to be with her, and the Cantey nurse, Dinah.[571] As soon as the soldiers came to the stop, the slave boy ran into the stable, saddled the pony, Planet, and rode to the back of the house. Dinah could not hold back her thoughts and said loudly, "Look at dat nigger on dem chilluns' pony!"[572] Peggy Coffield was a fourteen-year-old girl from the quarters and came to Mrs. Cantey. Mrs. Cantey slipped her some valuable papers telling her to save them, and she disappeared as the soldiers came toward them.[573] The house and premises were searched by the soldiers. While the soldiers were looking, Winter stood in the front yard pleading that they stop and have pity on this helpless woman and her children but the search continued. The soldiers then approached Winter demanding the whereabouts of the money, silver, and any valuables on the place. At one point, a pistol was placed to his forehead and he was threatened. Again, Winter did not give in. Then, the soldiers either tried to hang him by his neck or his fingers. Some reports say his neck, while others say his fingers. Whatever the reason, these soldiers tried to lift him up several times to get him to tell him where the valuables were hidden. However, to no avail, as Winter had hidden the silver pitchers in a hole not far from where he was being hung. In an e-mail from form Mr. Emory A. Cantey, he mentioned his grandmother telling him of Winter's fingers. They were very long. The longest

---

566 Ibid.
567 "Colonel James Cantey's Alabama Regiment," Macon Telegraph, Macon Georgia, July 26, 1861
568 Ibid.
569 Ibid.
570 "Russell County in Retrospect,", Walker, Annie Kendrick, 1950, Dietz Press, Richmond, pages 250 – 253.
571 Ibid.
572 Ibid.
573 Ibid.

she has ever seen. Then, these soldiers approached Mrs. Cantey and demanded the information from her. The two slaves beside her, the soldiers demanded Mrs. Cantey give then her diamond rings for her life. The nurse, Dinah, then sprung into action and pulled a large gold ring and threw it in their faces. Torches were lit to burn the house, specifically the baseboards around the dining room, but the commanding officer rushed in and demanded his soldiers to stop this pillage. Winter had been the one to come back on James's orders to protect and do what was necessary. Winter hid the valuables in a hole in the yard.

As the soldiers were leaving the property, Winter and Dinah followed. They wanted the children's pony back. They had followed for two miles begging for the pony. One of the soldiers demanded that Winter leave or be killed. However, the disturbance was noticed by the commanding officer and he came back and told the officer to give back the pony as they really didn't need it anyway. Moments later, Winter and Dinah could be seen walking Planet home. The Cantey boys were forever happy and grateful to have their pony back.[574]

At fifty-four years of age, General James Cantey died at his home in Russell County, Alabama. He came to Alabama in about 1845 and became a planter. His father had asked him to come to Alabama and live. He came back to Camden and finally arrived in 1849 for good. His record consists of his being wounded, almost fatal, in the Mexican war, to becoming a Colonel and later promoted to Brigadier General in the War Between the States. He went to Virginia and fought in the following campaigns: For his gallantry and his ability displayed in battle in the Valley Campaign under Stonewell Jackson, he received his promotion to Brigadier General and went to the Mobile area, and under General Johnston in the famed Sherman's March to the Sea. Under Johnston, Cantey's regiment went from Resaca down to the ill-starred expedition in Tennessee.[575] He is buried on the plantation of the Crowell Cemetery. His plantation is now a National Cemetery for Veterans, with the main road being called the General James Cantey Boulevard. His wife remarried, and she is buried beside him.

After a visit in 2013 to Columbus, Georgia and Russel County, other details came to light about Winter Cantey. In the 1870s, he ran a school on the Cantey Plantation to teach children from the plantation and neighboring plantations. His daughter became a well-known teacher and even to this day, a scholarship is given in her memory because of her teaching and devotion to the community. Winter and his wife Fannie were buried in Porterdale Cemetery, Columbus County, Georgia. Winter Cantey was born June on 10, 1830, in Camden, South Carolina and died on October 10, 1913 in Columbus, Georgia. Fannie Cantey was born on May 12, 1840 in Camden, South Carolina and died on December 21, 1921 in Columbus, Georgia. In the April 6, 2011 issue of the *Columbus Times*, there was a grave dedication honoring his life of such a heroic slave by members of the Columbus Black History Museum and the Lizzie Rutherford Chapter 60 of the United Daughters of the Confederacy.

Winter and Fannie Cantey

Permission from the Alabama Digital Collections, Alabama Archives

---

574 Ibid.
575 "Death of General James Cantey," Augusta Chronicle, Augusta, Georgia, July 8, 1874.

Obituary of Winter Cantey:

Winter Cantey Died Yesterday
Body Servant of the Late General Cantey Goes to His Reward

Winter Cantey, colored, aged eighty-four, died at the home of his son-in-law, Gus Pitts, on Eighteenth Street and Fifth Avenue, yesterday morning, after an illness of about three weeks. The deceased was the body servant of the late General Cantey, of Fort Mitchell, Russell County, Alabama. He was born in Camden, South Carolina, and went to Russell County with General Cantey during the 50s and remained with him and the family all his life. When General Cantey started to the Mexican War, it was at first his intention to take Winter with him, but the latter was only about ten years old, and was left behind because his youth. When the General went to the Civil War, he took his body servant with him, but did not keep him there long, sending him back home to look after and take care of affairs there, which he did in a faithful manner as could have been done.

All during the war, and after, during the trying days of the reconstruction, Winter Cantey remained with the Cantey family and worked with and for them just as he had always done, and at no time did he show the least inclination to turn against the white people of the South, always voting the democratic ticket.

A member of the Cantey family, to which Winter, as a slave, belonged, declared that he was not only intelligent, but that he was always and under all circumstances perfectly honest and reliable; that many and many a time he had been entrusted to attend to business requiring sound judgement and ability, also inviting his honesty and integrity, and that always he proved himself to be worthy of the trust imposed in him.

Winter Cantey was educated, becoming a veterinary surgeon of wide reputation, and did quite large and successful practice, He was especially successful in the treatment of horses.

He had ten children and all were educated in Booker Washington's school, and those who knew them said they led quiet and useful lives.

His funeral took place on a Sunday afternoon from his daughter's home and be buried in the Negro cemetery.[576]

Fannie Cantey Obituary

Former Slave Dies at Age of Eighty-Four

Fannie Cantey, aged about eighty-four years old, died at the home of her daughter, Mamie Pitts, in the city on Wednesday, and her funeral took place on Friday, December 23, 1921. The deceased was one of the family servants during the slavery days of the late General Cantey, of Russell County. She was born in Camden, South Carolina, and came to this section with her husband, Winter Cantey, body servant of General Cantey, when the latter moved to Russell County before the Civil War. She was a seamstress for General Cantey's mother. Winter

---

[576] "Winter Cantey Died Yesterday," Columbus Enquirer, Columbus, Georgia, October 11, 1913.

Cantey, her husband, was during his lifetime, well known throughout this section as a veterinarian, and a was well thought of by white people generally. This couple reared ten children, all of whom have been noted for their good behavior and all of whom are doing well for people in their section.[577]

Letters from James Cantey to his Wife and Family[578]

Bernard, Louisiana, Nov 28, 1860

"I hear of no news except the difficulties of the times, the banks have all closed their discounts, no money in circulation, a general suspension of business, and everything seems at a standstill. Cotton can't be sold, and no one is wise enough to see the end of the crisis. The general opinion seems to be that a succession of the Southern States is inevitable. The deed is done. The end of the American Union is irrevocably sealed. I was much surprised to see the Western people so much excited upon the subject of succession. It is beyond the settled purpose not to submit to the Black Republican rule, and although there are many opposed to separate secession, yet they will acquiesce in the most effective resistance that may be proposed …"

Richmond, Aug 21, 1861

"We leave tomorrow for Manassas, and the men are noisy with delight at the prospect of getting into active service, they are much improved in looks and drill, and present now a very fine appearance, they are the most orderly, quiet, and tractable men I ever knew, and have won a good name for their deportment."

"Tell the Colonel (Samuel Benton) and Alec to send me all the recruits they can get and set all my friends to do the same. I want 300 men more to fill the companies to 100 men and to organize the remainder into an artillery company, which the President says I can do."

Pageland, Near Manassas, August 26, 1861

(Letter from General Cantey to Colonel Samuel Benton, his father-in-law)

"We have been upon the move ever since we left Richmond, last night we reached this place, and probably we may be stationary for several days. We're under the command of General Johnston in whom, to my surprise, I have the pleasure of meeting an old friend and comrade in the Mexican War. Our encampment, Pageland, is eight miles from Manassas on the extreme left and most advanced post in that direction. I am near and with the 11th North Carolina Regiment under Colonel Kirkland. His regiment had and is suffering from sickness. They have measles, mumps, typhoid fever, and diarrhea. It is a terrible sight to see the poor fellows. Out of 1100 men, the Colonel tells me he has not 300 men fit for duty. I fear that a terrible ordeal is ahead of us …"

"As to future plans of operation, I can say nothing, for nothing is known, our troops are advancing slowly toward the Potomac, and the enemy preparing to defend the Capitol. A thousand rumors of fights and skirmishes

---

577 "Former Slave Dies at Age of Eighty-Four," Columbus Daily Enquirer, Columbus, Georgia, December 23, 1921.
578 The Sunday Ledger- Inquirer Civil War Edition, Columbus, Georgia, April 16, 1961.

come in daily but reliance can't be placed in them. Our camp is in view and only one mile distant from the Battlefield, which is to be the next no one knows …"

"You must all try to get up another uniform for the Cantey Rifles by the end of October, also shoes and blankets. Sent word to John Burch and all other friends of the Company and Regiment, and I should like people of Russell County to uniform all the men that come from that county …."

Camp near Winchester, May 27, 1862

"Since we joined Jackson, we have been marching from 15 to 20 miles every day with no wagons or other encumbrances except our arms, not even a blanket to cover with. Our marching has proved quite a success. We surprised a portion of General Bank's Army on the evening of the twenty-third and took the whole party after a sharp fight of about two hours, with an immense number of prisoners, arms, ammunition, quartermaster, and commissary store. Our loss in killed and wounded but slight. On the 25, we met the whole army of Banks at Winchester. After a very severe struggle, we whipped out completely, killing and wounding a good many and taking some 2,000 prisoners. It was a perfect rout. We chased them in a few miles of the Potomac, when from exhaustion of eighteen miles pursuit our troops were compelled to halt and rest. The enemy is reported as having crossed over the river. They lost over 200 wagons with a large amount of sorts of stores. Banks is said to have had over 35,000 men and our force was less than 20,000. Our loss was much less than was expected. They burnt a great many of their stores and attempted to fire the town of Winchester … I have a great hope the complete rout of Banks army here will have the effect of relieving Richmond, if General Johnston can thrash them there and Beauregard at Corinth. I hope it will tend to shorten the war. We will wait here a day or two to shore up the men and rest them, and then push on for the banks of the Potomac, and I hope cross over and take war into their country."

"General Jackson is a perfect rusher, a man of great energy and force of will, and if the president does not old him back, he will be into Maryland and perhaps Pennsylvania in a short time."

The contrast between our army and the Federals is very great; they are the best equipped troops I ever saw, supplied with not only conveniences but every luxury. Our soldiers got every sort of thing you can imagine …

John Bordenave Villipique

John B. Villipigue was born in Camden on July 2, 1830. Being of French descent, his life was especially a tribute to those whose parents immigrated to America, specifically to South Carolina, and to the community of Camden, South Carolina. He graduated from the United States Military Academy in 1854, and for seven years was a lieutenant in the Second Dragoons, serving on the frontier in Kansas and Nebraska. In 1855, he took part in the Sioux expedition, which contained a march to Fort Lookout, Dakota, and on into Utah territory campaigns, 1857-1858. After attending the Carlisle Cavalry School, he was on duty in Utah until he resigned in 1861 to enter the Confederate service.[579]

---

[579] "Paper Carries Sketch of Native Confederate Hero," The Camden Chronicle, Camden, South Carolina, July 8, 1949

While in service, he received a commission as captain of artillery and, soon thereafter, was promoted to colonel in the provisional army, and then assigned to the 36th Georgia regiment. His heroic efforts in the defense of Fort MacRae in the Pensacola harbor attracted much attention to his superiors. There at the Pensacola during of the heaviest bombardments, John Villipigue was severely wounded.[580]

The attention received was from General Bragg, as he was appointed on his staff as chief of engineers and artillery. He was in command for a time at the Pensacola, then was transferred to Mobile. In 1862, he was appointed to the status of brigadier general, and assigned to the Fort Pillow on the Mississippi. General Beauregard described as "the most energetic young officer" at his command. Brigadier General Villipigue held open batteries week after week, keeping back superior land and naval forces, until he was forced to retire. Upon which, he blew up the forications and brought away his command in safety.[581]

Under General van Dorn in Mississippi, he was given command of the army at Corinth. In the battle of Corinth, he was distinguished both in the attack and in the protection of the retreating troops. Soon thereafter, this campaign, he became seriously ill and died at Fort Hudson on November 9, 1862.[582]

One interesting note was that a Bible belonging to General Bragg had the following inscription.

> John B. Villipigue, Carlisle Barracks, November 7 — and this message
> To General Bragg,
> May God bless and crown your efforts with success. In a different hand.
> JPV Nov 4, 1864

This was a Polylott Bible, and apparently this Bible was probably given to General Bragg by his family as General Villipigue died in 1862. [583]

---

[580] Ibid.
[581] Ibid.
[582] Ibid.
[583] This Bible is at the Confederate Memorial Hall of New Orleans and was on loan through May, 2002. Email sent to Camden Archives February 1, 2002 by Doug Harvey. In file of Villipigue at Camden Archives and Museum, Camden, S.C.

The Estate of General John B. Villipigue[584]
In Account with I.P. Carr

By Greenbacks	$ 50.00
By One Mare	500.00
By Saddle	75.00
By Saddle Blanket	10.00
By One Horse (appraised)	400.00
By One Small Mare	375.00
	$ 1410.00
Debts	
Major Le Baron's Account	225.00
To Pay Mississippi Bill	41.68
To Pay by Harry	300.00
	567.18
	$ 842.82

Mobile, November 14, 1862

Estate of General Villepigue

    To C. Be'roujon City Sexton

Mahogany Coffin	$ 50.00
Lining with Zinc	110.00
Hearse and Attendance three times 15.00	
Candles and Fuel for Guards	3.00
Box and Packing in Coal	20.00
Two Hacks from Haydon's Stable to Railroad	12.00
	210.00
Credited by Thomas M. LeBaron 12.00	
	$ 198.00

Paid by C. Be'roujon

To the Honorable Secretary of War of the Confederate States,

Sir:

I beg to place the name of my son, John B. Villipigue, of Camden, South Carolina, before you, as an applicant for office in the cavalry service of the Confederate States.

---

[584] Villipigue Family Folder, Camden Archives and Museum, Camden, S.C.

He is a Graduate of West Point Academy. He was honored as the second best in his class - was then immediately commissioned as a Lieutenant of Calvary and has been in that service now seven years. He was stationed all the winter past at Fort Crittenden in Utah Territory, and has but recently heard of the difficulties and political dissonance of his native state from the late Union. During his absence, the Governor of South Carolina has been pleased to appoint him to the office of Captain of Cavalry in the enlisted troops of South Carolina. But as this is only a temporary service, and he desires a permanent military service in the Government of the Confederate States.

I have just received a letter from him dated Fort Crittenden, 15 February, in which he says that it is a desperate undertaking, but that he will leave the Post and resign the Commission and leave there just as soon as it is possible and hope to be here in six weeks from the date of this letter.

With great respect,

March 9, 1861
Camden, South Carolina

Extracts of the following:[585]

Headquarters Army of Pensacola
Near Pensacola, Florida
January 27. 1862

General Orders
No. 5

On being relieved by Colonel Jones of his command, at Fort McRae, Colonel J.B. Villepigue will report to the Commanding General for staff duty.

By command of

Major General B. Bragg,
George G. Garner,
Assistant Adjutant General

Colonel Villipigue
Through General Gladden

---

[585] Ibid. All Extracts from family folder. Also, some letters from his time in the Northern Territory about the Cheyenne and Kiowah Indians, from West Point, and others.

Headquarters Department of Alabama and West Florida
Near Pensacola, Florida
January 27, 1862

General Orders
No. 23

Colonel J. B. Villipigue, 31st Regiment Georgia Volunteers is announced as Chief of Artillery and Engineers on the Staff of the Commanding General in place of Captain W. R. Boggs, C. S. Engineers resigned.

By Command of

Major General Bragg,
George G. Garner
Assistant Adjutant General

Colonel Villipigue
Through General Gladden

The Southern Commission Claims of Kershaw County

THESE WERE CLAIMS THAT WERE filed against the Federal Government when the Yankees and stragglers came through the county and caused destruction. These were either barred and disallowed or accepted and paid to these individuals.

The first one filed was by J.C. Gibson. His claim consisted that the following were destroyed:

Two Horses valued at 400 dollars
800 lbs. of bacon @25cents lb. 200 dollars
100 bushels corn @ 2.00 per bushel 200 dollars
80 lbs. lard @ 25 cents per lb. 20 dollars
5 bushel of peas @ 2 dollars bushel 10 dollars
100 lbs. flour @ 6 cents lb. 6 dollars
4-gallon sorghum @ 1 dollar 4 dollars
1000 lbs. fodder @ 1.50 15 dollars
2 saddles 10 dollars each 20 dollars
Clothing 100 dollars
7 bushels meal @ 2 dollars bushel 14 dollars

Totals 989 dollars

This was disallowed because he had done business with Confederates during the war supplying fodder, harness, axes, chains, etc. during the war.

Thomas R. Sessions

His claim was for the taking of goods at his store by the U.S. Army. In that report, he lived at Fair Oaks in Kershaw County, South Carolina, and that he was the overseer on that plantation. He did admit that he was conscripted as a soldier and sent to Georgetown, South Carolina to guard and prevent the landing of Union gunboats or any small boats that may want to run up into the river in September 1864. However, he found a person underage for conscription and paid him in Confederate money one hundred dollars per month to substitute and he came home.

Supplies furnished the U.S. Army includes the following:

Four mules 800 dollars
Two horse 400 dollars
30 hogs 300 dollars
2 saddles 30 dollars
500 lbs. Flour 30 dollars
Signed February 21, 1865 by an officer of the U.S. Army

All disallowed because he sold wood and beef to the Confederacy and served as a soldier on Company D, 5th Battalion in Captain Thompson's battalion and his names appears on a roll of C.C. Haile in the State Troop. Also, he had a son that was in the Confederate Army.

Sessions made the following statement that also cost him his claim:

"When the war began, I think perhaps I wanted the South to whip the North, but after the war had been going on for a long time, felt that it might as well have been hurried up and wanted the North to whip the South. At first, everybody said the North would not dare to fight the South, but I got tired of expecting the South to whip the North, and I wanted the North to whip the South. What I hated most was that my Negroes was set free and my property burnt and taken from me. All that I had was gone, and I thought of that more than I did the Union or the Confederacy."

Joseph C. McWillie

He was represented by William M. Shannon, as he was lunatic about fifty-five years old being at the Pennsylvania Lunatic Asylum in Philadelphia, where he had been for more than thirty years. William M. Shannon was the brother-in-law and on a committee for this person and estate since 1851. He was the owner of a plantation of over 3000 acres. His property was taken by Sherman's army. Those things taken consisted of the following:

500 bushels of corn
20,000 lbs. of fodder
5500 lbs. of bacon
200 lbs. of lard
50 bushels Sweet Potatoes
40 hogs
Two cows and calves

Six sacks of salt

13 choice mules

Two axes

Eight Pairs of gears

Shannon put in a figure of 4,600.50 dollars. What was allowed was 2,733.50 dollars.

Other things said was that McWillie's Plantation was given him by his grandfather, Joseph Cunningham. The overseer was Crayton Williams and his employer was Wm. Shannon. Crayton Williams was born in North Carolina and seventy-eight years old. He had his own farm and was a farmer by occupation. He was down by the river at one point during the day when Sherman's troops came through at the light of day. He was not there as there were so many soldiers on so many places in the area. All he knew that the officer was a colonel and had silver eagles on his shoulder straps. He didn't know his name. The soldiers came early morning on the twenty-third of February. He was in the plantation house. The plantation was on the road to Camden which was 22 miles away and 6 miles from Peay's Ferry. Many U.S. Army troops were in the area. Williams did find out the General Logan was in charge and the different regiments consisted of the following: 14th, 15th, 18th, and 20th Army Corp. At the house with Williams were his wife and several children under the age of fourteen. The amount was paid on August 14, 1876.

Hugh Young

Hugh Young lived on a farm in Kershaw County and had four sons and one nephew in the Confederate Army. His sons went and volunteered despite his objections, except the youngest, who was forced to serve. He stated that during the war he was subjected by ridicule by soldiers and civilians for not supporting the cause. Reflections from the hearing told that, though he consistently said he was loyal to the Union, he never gave aid to them for the cause. He further stated that because of his stand, "people would require a retraction or I might be hung by certain citizens in the area." During and even after the war, he was threatened to be run out on a rail. He even objected when the rebels took his youngest son despite his wishes and his own, although the rebels admitted he was too young for the campaign. Three months later, he was dead. He believed that the Southern States had no reason to leave the Union. He was a magistrate in the 1840s and believed strongly in the United States and resigned in 1861 with the reason that he could not support the Confederacy. Despite his sons being in the Confederacy, he felt no reason for knowing their advancement or where they might be. All he wished for was the restoration of the Union. He was sixty-eight years of age and resided at Granny Quarter's Creek, ten miles from Camden. He did take the Oath of Allegiance to show his support of the United States. He was appointed to the voter registration board in the third precinct of Kershaw County in 1866 and in 1867 in August. Though he refused to give a cow to the Confederate Commissary, one was taken from his farm in 1864. He did send food to his sons, but no money or equipment to use. He admitted he didn't vote for the succession in 1860 and felt loyal to the Union and its cause. He was opposed to slavery and had no slaves, though he could afford to have them. His farm contained 200 acres. Union soldiers came on his place the 25th and 26th of February. The only persons present were his wife, his granddaughter, Temperance O. Young, his daughter, Sarah R. Herald, and a colored person, Nelson Love. Present for the Union was Captain Wheeler and a Lieutenant Frank Skifflin. About twenty Union Soldiers came that morning, the 25th. Young was told that being over a thousand miles from home, they desperately needed horses and any provisions needed being in the enemy's country. As the soldiers approached, one took out their pistol and demanded all the gold and silver Young had on him. Young told him that he had neither and a group of his men entered his house and took many articles, too many to mention on the petition to name. These soldiers left and after a couple of hours, a larger group came back. This group of fifty mounted soldiers had Captain Wheeler with them. The soldiers searched all around the farm - the barn, corn cribs, gathered fodder for the horses, and took food from the table. Three loads of fodder and corn were taken in ¾ wagons, with each taking three hours each.

About ten in the morning, on the 26, Lieutenant Frank Skifflin, came back with about 20 or 30 soldiers, and ordered them to take the buggy and filled it with flour, mill, bacon, and potatoes pulling the buggy to the camp with their own horses. Their camp was three miles from the Young property. About fifteen miles away, a skirmish took place between a portion of the Union army and Wheeler's Confederate Cavalry.

Next came some witness. The first was Robert J. Turner. He testified that he was a farmer in the Granny Quarter's section, twelve miles from Hugh Young's place. He was home from being in the Confederacy on furlough as he was wounded. Young told him that he was not in favor of succession and in favor of the Union. He told Robert Turner, that he was a Union man and always had been one, "and I don't care who knows it. I am willing to die one, and I wish the man who started this succession were in hell." He married one of Young's nieces. He even heard rebels say that Young should be dealt with for his support of the Union. "However, I never saw him give aid to the Union, though he had many Union friends."

The next witness was John R. Pace, who had a farm about three miles from Hugh Young. He was forty-nine years old. Again, Pace said Hugh Young told him many times that he was a Union man. Nelson Love was the next witness. He was colored and born a slave. He was thirty-seven years old and ten miles from Camden on Granny Quarter's Creek. He worked for Young before, during, and after the war. He heard Young say many times he was against the rebellion and sorry for his sons to be in the Confederate Army. During the war, Love lived one mile from Young. Love said, "Adam Taylor and my brother, Jessie Love, both colored, were present when the union soldiers came and got the goods. Some good taken went to camp seven miles away." Nelson's brother Jessie went with the soldiers and has never returned.

The next witness was the sixty-five years old cousin of Hugh Young, Fleming Young. He lived two and half miles from Hugh Young. Flemming said his cousin continually talked of this like of the Union and detestation of the war, and especially those who caused the rebellion. Many of his neighbors knew that he was loyal to the Union. Those people being J.R. Pace, Joseph Mickle, John Mickle, Willis Mickle, and Henry Thorne, Jackson Reid, L.L Clyburn, John Drakeford. Those said to be Union men were Jackson Reid, John Drakeford, Richard Drakeford, John R. Pace, Henry Thorne. In town, many citizens knew Hugh was a Union man. Those being General J.B. Kershaw, T.W. Pegues, E.E. Sill, Joseph Nettles, James B. Cureton, John M. DeSaussure, and Captain W.L. DePass. At one point, at the farm of William M. Shannon, he ordered his Negroes to hang Hugh

Young, but they refused. Other Union men were Flemming Young, Hiram Wheat, John Young Sr., Senator John Young Jr., James Clark, John Munn, Daniel Munn, and Charles Perkins, now deceased.

Young's petition included the following:

1 wagon with harness and gear for three mules 150 dollars

Two mules 500 dollars

1000 lbs. of Bacon 250 dollars

3 barrels of Flour 45 dollars

200 bushels corn 400 dollars

1000 lbs. of Fodder 15 dollars

100 bushels sweet potatoes 100 dollars

3 saddles 60 dollars

1 mare 100 dollars

Not accepted

Church Records

LOCAL CHURCH RECORDS ARE A great source of finding out information from this period. Minutes were taken and some deaths noted. The following is a list of what was found and the church where it was found:

Antioch Baptist Church -

Nancy Holland- February 21, 1862

J.L. Holland- July 1, 1862

Harmon Arrants, Jr.- February 19, 1862

William Mosley- March 9, 1962

Billy McLeod- April 19, 1862

Johannes Arrants - September 19, 1862 - He fell in the Battle of Sharpsburg in the State of Maryland. He was a good soldier in the cause of the South and of Jesus Christ.

Washington Myers - December 18, 1862 - He died from disease contracted while in camp. He was a member of Captain E.M. Boykin's Company of Wateree Mounted Rifle men of Kershaw District.

John Myers- January 9, 1862- He died at Hardeeville, South Carolina, while serving his country as a soldier of Sumter County. He was a member of Captain W.L. DePass Company of O.L.A. He was not only a Soldier of the Confederacy, but a Soldier of the Cause of Christ.

J.D. Rodgers - May 18, 1864 - He died in the Howard Grove Hospital, Richmond, Virginia, of a wound received on the sixteenth in the Battle of Drury's Bluff. He has been in service some two years and a half as a soldier of the Confederate States. He was a member of the Captain B. S. Lucas, Company A, 7th S.C. Battalion when he died. He was a soldier of the cross of Christ.

Angus McLeod - June 21, 1864 - He was a member of Captain W.L. DePass Company, and had been in Service at Hardeeville some four months as a Soldier of the Confederate States. He was a Soldier of the Cross of Christ.

Henry Moonyham - September 23, 1864 - He died of disease contracted while in the service of the South. He was not only a Soldier of the South but also of the cross of Christ. He was a member of Captain A. Mosley Company and was in service nearly three years, was a member of Company, 20 regiment S.C.V.

J.D. Davis - March 1, 1865 - He was a deacon of the church. He was a member of Captain A. Mosley Company, and died at Florence, South Carolina of typhoid pneumonia, while in Confederate service. He had been in service about a month, and was on his way to Virginia in General Hardee's Command. He was not only a Soldier of his country but a soldier of the Cross of Christ. He was eighteen years old.

Frederick McCaskill - June 20, 1865 - He died of disease contracted while in camp. His death was caused by the calamity of war.

John Boykin - July 1, 1865 - Died of disease contracted while in camp.

Grace Episcopal Church

Brigadier General John B. Villipigue - Buried November 18, 1862 by Reverend T.F. Davis. Jr. His staff and guard of soldiers accompanied the remains from Port Hudson, Louisiana to Camden, South Carolina A very large attendance of the funeral.

Lieutenant Henry W. DeSaussure was buried November 19, 1862, by Reverend S.E. Elliott.

Charles H. Peck was buried the 2nd Sunday after Trinity, June 14, 1863, by Reverend T.F. Davis Jr.

William H. Lewis - He was a private in Nelson's Battalion of Infantry. Was buried the fifth Sunday after Easter, May 1, 1864, by Reverend T.F. Davis Jr.

Sergeant Edward G. Williams - buried August 20, 1864, by Reverend T.F. Davis. He was in Company D, 1st Regiment S.C. Regular Infantry. He was killed by one of the enemy's shells near Fort Moultrie, Sullivan's Island.

Lieutenant Colonel P.H. Nelson - August 29, 1865- His remains were recovered and re-enterred at the cemetery in Camden. Service read by Reverend John Johnson. He was commanding the 7th S.C. Battalion and killed in the attack upon enemy's lines in from front of Petersburg, Virginia, June 24, 1864

Thomas C. Haile - February 5, 1889 - Age 41 - Buried in the Camden Cemetery

Zack Cantey - February 21, 1889 - Age 61 - Buried in the Camden Cemetery.

Junius Davis - March 15, 1889 - age 41 - Buried in the Camden Cemetery.

Other notes of importance to the times in the minutes written by ministers.

June 4, 1862 by T. F. Davis, Jr., Rector: Many families from the Low Country are now residing here. Refugees from their homes, which are occupied, or threatened, by the enemy. Our little church is crowded from this cause. Services are better attended than usual doing this war, but no other manifestations of religious feeling. Persons to be confirmed from our own flock very few.

Seminary broken up and students enlisted in the Army.

1863 – August - Confirmation held when one young man, a son of the bishop (Adjutant James M. Davis) at home on furlough from severe wounds in battle, was admitted to the rite; a solemn and affecting scene.

The church was crowded with refugees; more applications for pews than can be met. More funerals than usual this year. Death is becoming almost a familiar thing.

The church bell has been returned, having been found of no use for the casting cannon, and will soon peal forth its familiar notes again.

No election of vestry this year or last owing to absence of so many men in the Army.

My belief is that these trying times of War have deepened genuine piety where it existed and have given rise to some few new cases of it where it did not exist; but only a few; the majority go pretty much as before.

1864 - February 8 - The number of Communicants yesterday white and coloured was about 118. The collection (to be applied to the Free Market of Charleston, where the poor are suffering greatly) amounted to $1,253.15, several Charlestonians now residing here contributing largely.

1865 - February 24 - Sherman's Army entered Camden. They burned the old Cornwallis House, the Railroad depots, and the block of buildings immediately opposite the church (East side of Broad Street between DeKalb and Rutledge). God's mercy in answer to our earnest prayers prevented worse Evils.

March 11 - In the night, the Seminary buildings (two stories and brick) on the lot purchased for a new church (located on the west side of Broad street between Laurens and DeKalb, almost opposite the Bishop Davis's House) were totally consumed by fire, the act of incendiaries.

April 17 - General Potter's forces took procession of the town but departed the next morning having done very little damage. God, Our Heavenly Father, watched over us again.

May 12 - The currency of the country at this date is in an utterly ruinous condition. Church collections are large, but valueless.

The spirit of the people, and of the returning soldiers, is dreadfully depressed. We feel manifold and complicated evils; and with good grounds fear worse. The future is marked with lines of terrible darkness and danger to us. Yet, we are not much sanctified. Public anxieties drink up far too much and several confess that prayer and faith alone support them. Spiritual consolations are not sufficiently resorted to; and we must trust that results, in the long run, will be good and beneficial and will justify and explain God's sharp controversy with us now.

Spring. The failure of the Confederate Cause now induced still further evils and anxieties throughout the Southern States, and in none more severely than in the State of South Carolina. The losses of mere church property were estimated at over a million dollars; while those of individuals were ruinous to themselves and disastrous to the Diocese.

November 12. Written by Bishop T. F. Davis. This Parish was called upon to mourn the loss of death of its valued and beloved minister, the Reverend Thomas F. Davis, Jr., who died after a weeks' illness - age 37 and 9 months, who died after eleven years of zealous ministry in this Parish. His labours were not confined to this Parish as he had done much missionary work throughout the Diocese. Blessed are the dead that died in the Lord.

From January 1856 to December 1865

Baptisms	25 coloured	104 whites
Confirmations	8 coloured	102 whites plus 24 Soldiers confirmed during visits to the coast
Marriages	5 coloured	23 whites
Burials	8 coloured	85 whites. More than half were children under 8 years old

Coloured were always listed as servants of (Owner) or free Coloured

Coloured Sunday School was conducted in the church every Sunday by Reverend T.F. Davis Jr. and/or Bishop Davis.

Eight hundred out of 1000 voters had volunteered. Between 1861- 1862, 80 percent of the entire white population above the age of eighteen had enlisted. Older and younger males organized into Beats to control the slaves.

There are two letters in Historic Camden, Volume II, which describes the Yankee invasion and what was done. The following are those letters:

"The next day — Oh, day of terrors! — they were in our midst. Its horrors are never to be forgotten, but I am not to tell of that, but of the servants in this hour of supreme temptation. The long line of soldiers marched down the street, were disbanded at the corner, and in an incredibly short time swarmed everywhere. They were in every yard, in every house, but ours. What restrained them? We have never known, nor why we were so spared. Of course, they were in the yard, asking the servants to cook for them, tempting, threatening, cursing, swearing, shouting, singing, but never crossing our threshold; and as the morning passed, I went out on the upper piazza for a moment to find out what was going on below us in the street and well remember the comfort of seeing the cheery faces and hearing the undaunted voice of our opposite neighbor: 'What are they doing to you over there?' They are running about my house like ants in an anthill, and immediately several closely cropped heads and blur shoulders were thrust out of her window, and a jeering laugh greeted her Sally."

A Look Back at Sherman's Visit in Camden through the Eyes of Miss. A.E. Davis

"COLUMBIA, CAMDEN, CHERAW—ALL THE CENTRAL part of the State had become a sort of store house for the valuables of the low country, and vacant rooms, outhouses and attics were filled with goods and cotton; these were at once objects of cupidity or vengeance. Doors and windows were broken open, boxes were smashed, goods thrown in the streets; all portable articles, such as silver and gold, hastily selected by the soldiers; pockets and knapsacks rapidly and unblushingly filled, in the presence of the owners; and what they could not carry away were given to the Negroes, who were told it was their wages for long wage less years. The crowds increased continually on the streets and spread the tale of the Yankee generosity and unlimited looting. They will give you just what you please. They will tell you to help yourself, etc., etc.

"It was now getting towards the afternoon, and the younger servants, wearing with carrying their babies — three in number, yet afraid to put them out of their arms, brought them into my mother's room and begged to lay them down on pillows under her high old-fashioned bedstead, fully persuaded that now they would be secure where 'Miss' was - then flew down the main street to see. Again, and again they went and returned to the house laden with their spoils. 'The soldiers gave them to us. Mayn't we put them in the parlor for fear they will take them back again?' Evidently this was not time for a moral lesson and permission was given. The room became a museum of the most useless things to them: Portraits, engravings, mirrors, a miniature, china, glass, books- everything that took their fancy; and we were invited to take what we pleased!

"And so, at last night came, with its terrible yells, its uncertainty, its burning houses, its darkness, unless the lurid glare of the fires could be called light. It was with great difficulty that they could burn houses, for we had had a week of incessant rain, and that alone we believed saved us from the fate of Columbia. As it was, reading was easy in the tiniest pocket testament; and we knew not what was happening to our friends, or what would happen to us the next moment.[586]

"On Friday morning, February 24, we were not expecting them, when suddenly we heard rapid firing on Laurens Street, and we saw a company of cavalry dashing by. There seemed to be no order but they rode as for life into every yard, up to every door. Throwing the reins on their horse's neck a party of them dismounted at

---

[586] Historic Camden, Volume II, Kirkland and Kennedy, The State Company, Columbia, S.C., 1926, p. 167- 168. (An extract from a paper," Slavery as I Knew It," Miss A. E. Davis, daughter of Bishop Davis, read before the Camden Historical Society in 1905, and in the second volume of South Carolina Women in the Confederacy.)

our back door, rushed into the house —from room to room — upstairs and downstairs and into the basement. In wild haste, they broke open doors and drawers and desks, calling for silver, for watches, for wine, and arms. They seemed wild with the lust for booty, and so afraid that others would get ahead of them that they sometimes overlooked valuable items. We gathered in our breakfast room, our mother and we four girls — and I think my mother aged in those few hours and her hair grew grayer. One rough soldier as he dashed by her, said, "Old woman, don't look so freighted, we are not going to kill you." I looked at the agony of her face and that moment stamped upon my memory. That party of soldiers had soon ransacked our house, taking all the silver and jewelry, they could find, towels, knives, etc. Then in hot haste they ran off for the next house. Party after party came and went disappointed that they were not the first. A wagon was brought to the door of the smokehouse and the year's supply of meat carried off. Of it all, I remember one joint alone was left. Everything eatable, that they could lay their hands upon was taken. It was said that they timed their entrance into town just as dinners were being prepared. Our faithful cook tried in vain to smuggle something into the house for us, but it did not matter, we were too frightened to want anything. Slowly, the day crept upon us and we dreaded the night. In my mother's room upstairs we gathered with doors left open, we dared not lock them, and knew we were surrounded by thousands of hostile lawless soldiers, and as utterly cut off from friends as though miles away. Each household met the same ordeal alone. For almost twenty-five hours, there was no communication with even the nearest neighbor.

"Our cook, Mary, did not desert us but sat with us around the fire through all the long night. We saw the flames of burning houses, stores, mills and cotton in every direction, and heard the shouts and yells of drunken soldiers and Negroes on Broad Street, where high carnival was held. The stores were broken open, the contents taken, given to the Negroes, or thrown in the streets.

"From time to time, we threw ourselves on the bed for a little sleep, and I remember when all was quiet Ella and I heard our good Mary come to our bedside, fall upon her knee and pray so earnestly for 'Missis and her children.' It was comforting to feel that the fervent prayer of that righteous one was going to God for us. Slowly the dawn came, and again the party after party of soldiers came searching for valuables. About ten o'clock a knock — the very first — was heard, at the front door. My mother opened the door and an officer stood there. He was Lieutenant McQueen of Howard's Command (15th Illinois Infantry — He protected the homes of Bishop Davis, Mrs. Reynolds, Mr. R.M. Kennedy, and others), and said he brought messages from Dr. William Reynolds, and uncle in Columbia, and had promised to protect us. Through the effects of Lieutenant McQueen, the house, which my uncle's family occupied in Columbia, had been saved from the general conflagration, and for weeks and months forty homeless ones found shelter there.

"Lieutenant McQueen said he was sorry his regiment had not reached Camden the day before that he might have given us a guard. From that time, we were unmolested. He or his ranking officer, Captain King, came and went throughout the day, and when Lieutenant McQueen was obliged to go elsewhere, he left his belt and pistols on the hall table and said, if we were disturbed, to show them and say they was his and he was in charge. A troop of fifteen, soon after, dashed up the avenue and, dismounting, came into the piazza and hall demanding 'wine and watches. 'Mother showed the belt and pistols and gave the lieutenant's message. Forthwith the leader turned and said; 'Come, boys, we can do nothing here.' Lieutenant McQueen, at my uncle's request, had gone to Mrs. Caper's on DeKalb Street to inquire for his (Dr. Reynolds) sister-in-law, Mrs. Capers Jr., who, with her children, had fled from Columbia as the army entered the city, making the journey in an open wagon that cold, rainy day. She reached her mother-in-law in Camden, who was very ill and lived only a few days. Arrangements had been made for her burial but were interrupted by the coming of the enemy, and they were preparing to bury her in the garden when Lieutenant McQueen offered his horse for the hearse. He and Mr. Thomas Davis, rector of Grace Church, carried her to the cemetery and laid the weary Christian to her rest.

"From house to house Lieutenant McQueen went carrying comfort and aid. Late in the day (Saturday, the 25), he and Captain King came to say they were ordered out, and that night not a soldier would be left. They were young men and could not refrain from twitting us about 'our boys.' Lieutenant McQueen said, 'Your boys are going to meet us [587] at the river, now they say will meet us at Lynches Creek.' Ella replied, 'I hope they will,' and went off laughing.

"The next day, there was a skirmish at Lynches Creek and the brave lieutenant was wounded and captured and it would have fared ill with him but for letters my uncle, Dr. Porter, and my mother had given him. We sent him what we could of luxuries for the sick, and when later he was brought to the hospital in Camden, he was well cared for. My uncle and Dr. Porter came over from Columbia and arranged to carry him to Chester where he was exchanged. He recovered and returned to his home in Elgin, Illinois. We have heard from him from time to time, and a few winters ago, he was in Southern Pines, North Carolina, and expected to visit Camden but was prevented."

---

[587] Ibid, pages 170-173.

The Story of the Cockade

DALTON KENNEDY, SR., FATHER OF well-known historian Mrs. Sadie von Tresckow, a beloved teacher, Captain Charles Peck, who was headmaster of the Camden Academy, a semi-military school from 1859-1863. The Academy was in the Western brick building of the Old Orphan Society School, which stood east of Bethesda Presbyterian Church, where the Dunn residence was dismantled and where the late Leslie McCandless presided with a rod for bad boys. In 1886, the academy building served as the Camden High School, when "Miss Sadie" was a pupil under Professors Schoenburg and A.C. More, who later became president of the University of South Carolina.

The boys of Captain Peck's Academy wore uniforms and were drilled. The war fever was very strong, and even these small boys and Captain Peck, though a Northerner, was an ardent sympathizer with the South. His cadets escorted to the train the first contingent of Kershaw County Volunteers enroute to Fort Sumter on April 1862. John Doby Kennedy, later a brigadier general, was their captain. A throng of citizens, wearing palmetto cockades upon their hats, followed the procession as all were headed to the train depot. Palmetto Cockades were badges made of little rosettes fashioned of dried palmetto leaves.

When two days later, the Lancaster Greys, a company captained by J.D. Wylie, hiking to Camden, to board the train. They, too, cheered and were greeted on their way. They had marched the distance of forty miles in one day. Camden was decked out in bunting, and the newly adopted Confederate Flag was flying from the Old Market Hall Steeple.

The town was the chief inland port of entry since it had the only important railway connections to Charleston. During the month of April, other companies of Confederate soldiers boarded the train at Camden and were given similar escorts. They were the DeKalb Rifle Guards under Captain T.L. Boykin, and the Flat Rock Guards under Captain C.C. Haile.

A Lancaster soldier styled Camden - the Cockade Town, and wrote the following stanza:

> When death's dark stream we ferry over,
> A time that surely shall come,
> In Heaven itself we ask no more,
> Than just a Camden welcome.

Professor Charles Peck died in Camden in 1863 and is buried in Quaker Cemetery. The town gave him his burial plot, but no stone to mark his grave. When this was written, a stone had just been placed to honor his grave and memory. The only marker till then was a fringe tree referred to as Grandfather's Greybeard. When Miss Sadie informed Claude W. Brown of Florence Memorial Company, he made a marker for Captain Peck, and presented it to Camden and to the United Daughters of the Confederacy, which Miss Sadie was president. The Peck stone had the following inscribed:

> Captain Charles A.H. Peck
> Beloved Commandant, Camden
> Academy, 1859
> Died 1863
> Northerner, but Southerner Sympathizer
> Plot Given by Citizens

The Peck lot is diagonally across from the Cantey obelisk on Magnolia Avenue in the cemetery. Cantey was a Mexican War Hero, whose monument was given by the citizens of Camden and Kershaw County. It was to be erected on Monument Square opposite another hero of the Mexican War, Colonel James Polk Dickerson. However, Lieutenant Cantey's mother requested that the Cantey monument be put on a Cantey Lot in Quaker Cemetery.

Source: In file folder marked Kershaw County 1861-1865, Civil War.

Josephine Noel - Confederate Spy Courtesy from the
Camden Archives and Museum, Camden, S.C.

Camden's Spy - Josephine Noel
By Elizabeth P. Hough[588]

THE CITIZENS OF CAMDEN LEARNED of Josephine Noel, a Confederate agent, courier, dispatcher, and a spy, was buried in the town cemetery (Quaker Cemetery) in 1915.

Josephine Lovett was born in New York and orphaned at an early age. She was adopted by Charlotte and Thomas B. Ridder, a wealthy New York City tobacco dealer. The couple gave Josephine the best education and social advantages that one could give.

On November 25, 1856, just after her twenty-first birthday, Josephine was fashionably wed to Robert Brown. Robert's father, John Potts Brown, owned a prosperous shipping and channeling business in Wilmington, North Carolina, and New York, where he served as the first president of the New York Corn Exchange.

Josephine's Confederate leanings began with her in-laws, who were avid Southerners and close friends of Virginia Tunstall of North Carolina and her husband, U.S. Senator Clement Claiborne Clay of Alabama. The Browns and the Clays were so close that the Browns named their first son after Senator Clay. Letters from the Browns saved by Mrs. Clay reveal that Josephine called Senator Clay "My dear Uncle Clem," and Robert addressed Mrs. Clay as "Auntie," closing with "Your devoted son."

Robert and Josephine were living on a farm in Eden Prairie, Minnesota Territory, with their two children when Senator Clay's doctor advised "a change in climate." He said that the "quietude and rest" in Minnesota would alleviate Senator Clay's severe asthma attacks, so the Clays bought real estate there, to which they still held title for several years after the War Between the States.

By June 15, 1861, the Clays had left Minnesota. Robert's mother in Allemance, Minnesota, was writing to Clay in Richmond, Virginia. She exposed sympathy for the Confederate cause and added that "various Southern friends in Minnesota were discussing the wisdom of going South." President Jefferson Davis asked Senator Clay to be his Secretary of War, but Clay settled in as a Confederate senator.

Sometime before February 5, 1861, Josephine and Robert left Minnesota. The U.S. Marshall in New York received a telegram that stated: "Arrest Robert Brown, 118 Second Avenue, N.Y. and commit him to

---

[588] Elizabeth P. Hough was the historian for over thirty years with John Doby Kennedy Chapter United Daughter's of the Confederacy in Camden, S.C. She was extraordinary in researching and compiling historical information. The community lost a tremendous person. She will be missed by all who knew her, her work, but most of all, her dedication to tell the true story of Camden and the period of the War Between the States.

Fort Lafayette." When the marshal arrived at the address, Robert could not be found. He was serving in the Confederate Army as an aide-de-camp to an old Wilmington family friend, General John H. Winder, who oversaw all camps for Union prisoners.

After the Battle of Seven Pines, Robert wrote Mrs. Clay about accompanying General Winder:

"…squad after squad of Yankee prisoners were brought up to Longstreet under guards buoyant with victory, and, as each reached headquarters the reserve force would send up a yell of delight that split the air. One little, brave band of fifty-five South Carolinians brought in one hundred and sixty-five, live Yankees and a Captain who they had taken. The excitement was intense!"

Josephine was being watched. When Robert's father gained permission for her and her two children to leave New York and join Robert in Richmond, U.S. Major General John A. Dix of Fort Monroe received an October 20, 1862, warning: "This woman is in full sympathy with the rebellion and willing to do anything to further its interests." Josephine was detained for over a month in Norfolk before she could enter Richmond.

Josephine did not remain with Robert for a very long. She began shuttling their children with friends and family members in Richmond, Wilmington, and New York. Marylanders had rioted and fired on Massachusetts troops passing through Baltimore to answer President Abraham Lincoln's call for quelling the Southern rebellion. Confederate sympathizers and spies in Maryland had a network of taverns along the stagecoach line from Richmond. These taverns did double duty for couriers of the Confederacy Secret Service. The ability to get messages to the proper destination was so erratic that couriers were in great demand.

Robert's letter to Mrs. Clay on December 26, 1863, made a critic reference to Josephine:

"Josie has returned, came to me the morning before Christmas Day, having accomplished all she hoped for. My wife is a great woman."

In another letter, Robert wrote: "Josie is smart, pretty and afraid of nothing!" In June of 1864, Robert, a lieutenant, was transferred from Richmond to Anderson, Georgia, as aide-de-camp to Captain Henry Wirz. After three months there, he received disability leave. Wirz was tried and hanged in Washington, D.C., after the War for alleged mistreatment of Union POWs.

The Raid at St. Albans, Vermont

During the summer of 1864, Davis chose Mr. Clay to head a special commission to Canada. The objective was to stir up unrest near the U.S. border so that Lincoln would have to divert troops from closing in on Richmond. The Confederate Secret Service's attempt to free Confederate prisoners at Camp Douglas in Chicago failed, but twenty-one of Colonel John Hunt Morgan's former raiders succeeded in robbing three banks close to the border at St. Albans, Vermont, resulting in several Union detachments being sent to guard the Canadian border. Canadian courts declared the robberies "nor crimes but acts of war." The Canadian public agreed when the raiders testified that they "were just presenting a sample of the tribulations imposed upon Southerners by Lincoln's invaders."

Josephine had become a trusted agent and courier for Robert's father and for Clay's clandestine Canadian operations. She received traveling expenses for her trips between Richmond, New York, and various places in Canada on a regular basis. Josephine carried dispatches, and her cavalry boots were filled with quinine and other drugs that were scarce in the Confederacy. She was mentioned in consular reports, and by George N. Sanders, a Confederate espionage operator. Josephine was never caught.

On January 12, 1865, Robert's father in New York wrote Clay in Canada:

"Outside of the present movements, I'd do nothing — rather wait and see what is developed. Jo will explain what I do not write."

Sometimes to get messages through, "personals were published in *The New York Daily News* and *The Richmond Inquirer* above semi-coded names. Robert's father used his initials in reverse: B.P.J."

In January, Confederate Secretary of State Judah P. Benjamin informed Clay's brother that Clay's summary reports of the eight-month Canadian mission was finished to give to Davis. So secret were these reports that Clay carried them in an oilcloth sack around his neck. After a shipwreck, Clay arrived in Richmond, and help Davis pack as the capitol was being evacuated. Clay's brother, a colonel on General Kirby Smith's staff, had written Clay this succinct, disheartening message:

"The little successes in North Carolina bode no decided repulse, still less defeat of the enemy.

They are only the flickerings of the expiring lamp."

Upon Lincoln's assassination, federal authorities charged Clay and Davis with involvement. Both were imprisoned in Fort Monroe — Clay for a year, and Davis for two years.

Around the end of November 1865, Robert's mother wrote to Mrs. Clay: "Since your beloved husband's martyrdom, my prayers and tears have been given for him." She added: "Poor Rob has had the eternal ill-will of Mrs. Ridder because he was a rebel. She is doing all in her power to separate Josie and the children from him."

In December of that year, Josephine poured out her heart to Mrs. Clay, concerning her difficulties with Robert. She planned to try once more to have patience with him and asked Mrs. Clay what could be done in Washington to forward Robert's pardon and Mr. Clay's parole. Robert refused to leave Montreal or to take the Oath of Allegiance to the United States, as long as Clay was held prisoner, so Josephine joined him there.

For the next five years, they seemed to be working on their marriage. They had two more children, Vaughn Morgan Brown and Robert Wells Brown Jr., who was born in 1870. The family moved to Mayesville, South Carolina, where Robert raised corn, potatoes, and rice, and planned to build and run a gristmill and a sawmill. However, Josephine divorced Robert in 1873.

On July 18, 1874, Josephine married a Mr. Noel of Riversdale, New York, who died a few years later. On May 14, 1878, Robert's sister had written Mrs. Clay that:

'Josie and the children are spending the summer in the Adirondacks, where she is keeping a boarding house. Mr. Noel is in England in very poor health."

Josephine lived out her declining years in Camden, which became the halfway point for northern tourists on their annual migration from New York to Miami in the late 1890s. The tourists would spend part or all of the winter enjoying hunting season, horse racing, polo, golf, and social life at the various resort hotels and tourist boarding houses. Josephine's son-in-law, K.G. Whistler, and her son, Clement Clay Brown, were members of the town's polo team. Brown was also a Camden policeman for twenty years. Whistler worked as a landscape gardener and trained polo ponies and players. He also assisted his wife, Lottie, in converting several famous homes into accommodations for tourists.

Josephine died in 1915. Her obituary in the Camden newspaper summed up her life in a tantalizing manner.

> She was a beautiful woman of a charming personality …. She and her first husband was closely identified with the most stirring period of the South's history, having personal friendships with some of the most prominent men and women of that time. These pages of her life would read like the most thrilling romance had their written record been preserved for posterity.

Her descendants have two heirlooms, a Ridder pitcher and a gold-headed cane engraved "T.R.B. - 1812." Although Josephine never wrote her memoirs, her mentor, Mrs. Clay, did, and her courage, stamina, and indomitable spirit are reminiscent of Josephine's.

The Body Servants from Kershaw County

During the first of the war, many soldiers took a servant with them to act as a cook, butler, valet, or to do many things for his master or the master's son. In the spring of 1862, the rules changed and only the officers could have a servant. Kershaw District was no exception. However, the exact number may never be known. The Kershaw District has many plantations, some of which came in many sizes. The plantation could be considered anything from one acre to over three-hundred acres.

Those that have been identified are:

Toney Thompson	Owner Mr. James Dunlap- went to war with Ned Edward Dunlap
Sam Clyburn	Owner T.J. Clyburn
Weary Clyburn	Owner Frank Clyburn
Lawrence Chesnut	Owner- James Chesnut
Washington Drakeford	Owner- William Drakeford- went to war with Joseph Drakeford
William Henry Boykin	Owner- W.L. Kirkland
Daniel Johnson	Owner- Captain J.D. Kennedy
Robert Murphy	Owner- Joe Huckabee
Ellison Haile/Hale	Owner- Captain C.C. Haile
Edward Doby	Owner- Alfred English Doby
Sam Kirkland	Owner- James Cantey
James Lang	Owners- James Dickerson, General Beauregard
Hiram Blair	Owner- L.W.R. Blair
Wyatt Cunningham	Owner- Dr. Thomas McDowell
George Cureton	Owner- James Doby

Sometimes the only record found is an obituary of the person that tells his story, a story that his descendants can be humbled by, and in their family heritage, something they can be proud of. These people did serve a function that should be noted and appreciated and told. But the question that must be asked is who were these men that served their masters, and what did these men mean to their masters? They were like family. A family that each could count on and trust. This was a life that they only knew, serving one. Remember this is just a time a history. This is a history that has evolved to today's society. Think of where your family has come from and reflect how far they have come. This society is made up of many races, nationalities, and opinions. These things are what makes America great. The distance each has traveled through their ancestors is a journey that should be shared within their respective families.

Toney Thompson

(*The Camden Chronicle* - December 2, 1910 - Obituary)
Death of a Good Old Colored Man
Quietly and unobtrusively as he lived, there passed away, on Saturday night last, Old Toney Thompson, a fine example of the faithful anti-bellum servant.

He was raised by Mr. James Dunlap, of Lafayette Hall, and always spoke of his "Masser and Misses," with the greatest love and respect. He acted as a body servant to Ned Dunlap throughout the war, and his love and faithfulness toward "his folks," as he called them ceased only with his death, his identity being shown by a yearly pilgrimage to the Quaker Cemetery, where the Dunlaps lie buried, where unasked and without remuneration, since all the family have moved from Camden, he would put their enclosure in order. True to the light, which God had given him, he was an affectionate husband and father (the tears and sorrows arising from his wife's death a few weeks preceding his death), an earnest member and leader of the Methodist Church, and an honest, steady worker.

Well, may the rising generation look upon him as a model and example to their race.

In the 1910 Kershaw County Census, he was sixty-four years of age, his wife is Louisa at sixty-three years of age, his sons, Johnie is twenty-two, and Jerry is eleven. They were living in the DeKalb Township.

Daniel Johnson

(*The Camden Chronicle* - June 22, 1927)
Old Time Negro Died
Winnsboro, June 18. Daniel Johnson, one of Winnsboro's highly respected negroes, died here Sunday night at one o'clock, after a short illness. He was owned by General Kennedy during slavery times, and was with his master during the Civil War, serving in the capacity of orderly. He was a court janitor in Winnsboro for many years and was respected by all who knew him for his honesty and integrity. His death is regretted in the community, where he has lived practically since the close of the war. He was in his eighty-second year of age.

Ellison Haile/Hale

The only official record of Ellison can be found in the service record of Captain C.C. Haile. In that is a hospital record that can't be disputed;

Elison - Servant of Captain Haile, Company G, 2nd Regiment, SC. He was in Chimborazo Hospital, No. 9, Richmond, Virginia. He was admitted March 14, 1862, and on March 17, left with his master, Captain Haile.

Winter Cantey and Sam Kirkland

Much confusion has been made about Winter. The first was that it was Winter, who went with James Cantey to war with Mexico. Winter was with the Cantey family, and with his son, but Winter did not go to Mexico as previously stated. It was Sam Kirkland, who went with James Cantey to Mexico. It was Sam, who after James had been shot and presumed dead, walked over to the pile of bodies, James Cantey's body was at the bottom, and felt his hands and all. He noticed that he wasn't dead at all and went to the officer in charge and told him of his discovery. The officer sent men to see and soon, they uncovered the fact that James Cantey was not dead all but in serious condition. Sam nursed James back to health, and soon they traveled to Alabama. To be more specific, Fort Mitchell, Russell County, Alabama. James's father, John Cantey, was there. James's mother was in Camden, South Carolina, and went back and forth to Alabama. Read more about Winter Cantey in the section on James Cantey.

Robert Murphy

(*The Camden Chronicle* - July 1924)

Death of an Old Negro

Robert Murphy, an old colored man of the West Wateree section, died last Saturday at his home near the plantation of Mr. Robert Mickle. The old man was around ninety years old, and may be more, as there were no accurate records kept of his age. He was born a slave, and took part in the War Between the States, also took part in the red-shirt activities following the war, and always voted a Democratic ticket. The burial was held on Sunday, being buried by his white friends.

His death certificate (SC 13105 - Kershaw County), told about him that he died July 5, 1924, he was a farmer, and that his parents were Joe and Eliza Murphy. He was a widow, and he was buried at Mt. Joshua Church. His wife was Catherine and she was born about 1834 and died December 23, 1906. Both are buried at Mt. Joshua Methodist Church. He did have a Confederate Pension. In that pension, the following should be noted. He was a cook under Joe Huckabee, who was in Company D, 15th SC, under Captain Thomas Warren, and served from 1861 to 1865. He was residing at Longtown, South Carolina, in Kershaw County. W.J. Spradley and Henry Truesdale witnessed his pension and knew he had served in the war. This pension was sent in April 16, 1923 and approved by N.A. Bethune, Chairman of Honor, Kershaw County on April 16, 1923.

William Boykin

(*The Camden Chronicle* - June 27, 1924)

"Uncle William" Boykin, probably the oldest resident of this county, died at his home, just north of Camden, on the Liberty Hill Road last Thursday, and his funeral was held on Friday at Mt. Moriah Church.

Uncle William was ninety-two years old at the time of his death, and except for a few years spent in Mississippi in early life, he had been a citizen of this county. He was a born a slave, and served throughout the war with his master, going to Mississippi. He was one of the few Confederate Pensioners of his race. He was the brother of the late Reverend Monroe Boykin, founder of Mt. Moriah Baptist Church, and has numerous relatives that resided in and near Camden. His wife died less than a year ago and has several surviving children.

According to his death certificate (11031 in Kershaw County), he was ninety-seven years old, dying on June 19, 1924. No parents listed. He was buried in Camden. His wife was Betsy, and she died December 2, 1923. (Death Certificate number 19555 - Kershaw County) She is also buried in Camden. Her parents were Charles Rhodes and Mary Ann Boykin.

His Confederate pension is as follows:

Camden, SC
April 20, 1923
William Boykin, who was the body servant of Dr. Tom Boykin, of Portland, Alabama, served as body servant with him, in Captain Colby's Company, in the Western Army. After serving two years in the Western Army, Dr. Tom Boykin was transferred to General James Cantey's Brigade, and they were mustered out in that service. Dr. Tom Boykin and William Boykin, his body servant, were in the battle of Selma, Alabama, and captured by General Wilson's Army. The troops, after taking Selma, all got whiskey, and the whole brigade was under the influence of whiskey, and they roused banks, and divided equally all the gold and silver, with the Union Troops. William was sent to serve as body a body guard for one of the Colonels of the Union forces, and this colonel gave him fifty dollars in gold, and he managed to escape by swimming the Alabama River, and going back to his mistress, with a note from her husband, and he found them in a constitute condition, and divided this gold with his mistress.

This was validated by Thomas J. Kirkland, through the statement of Mrs. Hunter R. Boykin, and hope William will get approved.

"Under the act of 1923, I served the Confederate States in the War Between the States

Captain Goldsbyn. I went into service in 1861 and served until surrender in 1865. I reside in Camden, SC. In Kershaw County, S.C.

The witness to this was H. R. Boykin, and approved by N. A. Bethune, Chairman Board of Honor, Kershaw County, May 7, 1923."

Jim Lang

His lineage dates to the Thomas Lang Plantation. His father, James Lang, was a valet and remembered Lafayette in 1825. His father lived to the age of ninety or more. He was also one of the infamous slaves who gave testimony in the trials in 1816. His son, Jim, acted as a body servant for Colonel J.P. Dickerson in the Mexican War. He brought home not only the body of his Colonel Dickerson, but the body of Colonel Pierce Butler. Both had fallen closely in the battle in Mexico. During the Civil War, he was a hostler under General Beauregard. He told of his attending upon the Federal General Prentiss, who was captured at the Battle of Shiloh, and detained at General Beauregard's tent.

Source: Historic Camden, Part Two, Nineteenth Century, by Kirkland, Thomas J. and Kennedy, Robert M., The State Printing Company, Columbia, S.C. 1926.

Weary Clyburn

He was born into slavery on the Thomas L. Clyburn plantation. His father was Phillip Blair, the age of his master's two older sons. Frank Clyburn left home to go to Lightwood Knot Springs near Columbia, and Weary left and followed. Weary served with Frank throughout the war, twice saving his life, and both surviving the conflict, Weary left and went to live in Monroe, North Carolina. There, he met and married Viney Moore in December 1867. Weary came back to Kershaw to the founding of Kershaw, and soon Weary soon got arrested. Weary served time for burning the town's dispensary. He also became a well-known fiddler at parties and as a house painter. In 1892, he was cooling off in a window, after a strenuous bout of fiddling when someone shot him. However, he made it home to Monroe. In Monroe, North Carolina, he received a Confederate Pension for his service. In his old age, he had remarried to someone named Eliza, and had one daughter Mattie Clyburn Rice. Mrs. Rice, after spending time in the north, went to the Archives in North Carolina to learn of her father. Even though a petition had been filed for a gravestone, it was refused by the Federal Government. Only after being convinced of his service and bravery, did a gravestone arrived. The day was proclaimed Weary Clyburn Day in Monroe, and in the state. This occurred in 2008.

Source: Kershaw News Era, Aug 12, 2008, Kershaw, S.C.

Wyatt Cunningham

Wyatt's facts are found in his North Carolina Confederate Pension of 1931. His pension was filed in Union County, North Carolina. He was applying under the C.S. 5168 J, Class B. The following was written as his statement:

"On this the 23rd day of July, 1931, personally appeared before me, O.L. Richardson, C.S.C. in and for the State and County aforesaid, Wyatt Cunningham, colored, age 105 years, and a resident at Monroe Post Office, in said County and State, and who, being duly sworn, makes the following declaration in order to obtain the pension under the provisions of Consolidated Statutes of North Carolina, Section 5168J, Class B, (Colored Servants); Chapter 96 of the public laws of 1927; That he is the identical Wyatt Cunningham, colored, who was drafted into the service of the armies of the Confederacy as a wagoneer hauling supplies under the direction of the duly constituted officers and soldiers of the Confederacy, the companies and regiments are unknown to the affluent, to various railway terminals in the State of South Carolina, including Winnsboro, Camden, Ridgeway, and others for delivery at Charleston; that applicant began to perform these duties and to serve the armies of the Confederacy about the ---- day of January, 1862; and that while in the said service at Rocky Mount Ferry on the Catawba River, in the state of South Carolina, on or about the ---- day of March, 1865, he received a wound as follows: a wound inflicted by a bullet from the gun of a Federal soldier, inflicted in the middle calf of the left leg and tearing away the muscles and laming applicant; that the applicant's master was Dr. Thomas McDowell of Liberty Hill, South Carolina.

"He further states that he is, and has been for more than twelve months, immediately preceding this application, a bonafide resident of the State of North Carolina, that he holds no office of any kind and draws no salary; he owns no property nor has disposed of property valued at as much as $2000.00 in any way since

1885, that he is not now receiving aid from the State of North Carolina nor any agency hereof but is supported by his daughter with whom he resides."

He signed his mark. His application was approved this July 23, 1831 in Union County.

In June 1932, he was one of four body servants going from Monroe to Richmond, Virginia, to the National Reunion. Those four was Wyatt Cunningham, age 105, George Cureton, Lewis McGill, and Ned Bird (*The Charlotte Observer*, June 21, 1932).

Wyatt's death certificate in North Carolina gives the following information: He was born March 12, 1825 in Camden, South Carolina, and died November 10, 1933, his father's name is Jack Cunningham, and his mother's name is Harriet Cunningham. His wife's name is Mollie McWain. He is buried in Ebenezer Cemetery in Monroe, Union County, North Carolina.[589]

Source: Confederate Pension of North Carolina.

George Cureton

He was a slave of James Doby. He went in with his master in the 4th South Carolina Cavalry, and then transferred to the 7th. He moved to Union County, North Carolina in 1900. He was born in Liberty Hill, South Carolina between 1830 and 1835.

His death certificate has some interesting facts. He was born in 1841, and died September 5, 1934, in Jackson, Union County, North Carolina. His father was Allen Cureton, and his mother was Lucy Cureton. His spouse was Nannie Cureton.[590]

Jeff Sanders

He was a free slave and served in the war. He was born in Chesterfield, South Carolina in the Lynches Creek area. He was born about 1839 and died in November 4, 1832 in Union County, North Carolina. He was ninety-three and a widow. His father was Chad Lunderbark, and his mother was Angleina Harpens.[591]

Henry Boykin

One story that must be told is that of Henry Boykin. He was not a body servant, but rather a slave. The story was handed down that when General Sherman's troops, went through South Carolina, the soldiers came across Henry in the woods near his home, and thought he was a Confederate Soldier. He was going to be killed, until his mother ran out of the house, and pleaded with the Yankees, telling them that Henry was not a soldier and

---

[589] "North Carolina, Deaths, 1931-1994," index, *FamilySearch* (https://familysearch.org/ark:/61903/1:1:FPNM-6K6: accessed 23 May 2015), Wyatt Cunningham, 10 Nov 1933; citing Monroe, Monroe Twp., Union, North Carolina, 305, State Department of Archives and History, Raleigh; FHL microfilm 1,943,076.

[590] "North Carolina, Deaths, 1931-1994," index, *FamilySearch* (https://familysearch.org/ark:/61903/1:1:FG3V-575: accessed 23 May 2015), George Cureton, 05 Sep 1934; citing Jackson, Union, North Carolina, cn190, State Department of Archives and History, Raleigh; FHL microfilm 1,943,091.

[591] "North Carolina, Deaths, 1931-1994," index, *FamilySearch* (https://familysearch.org/ark:/61903/1:1:FP6B-DRS: accessed 25 May 2015), Jeff Sanders, 04 Nov 1932; citing Monroe, Union, North Carolina, can 198, State Department of Archives and History, Raleigh; FHL microfilm 1,943,062.

not a white man, and, despite his appearance (he looked white), was colored. His dates were 1841- 1926. (Sent to me by Cheyenne Turner, his descendent.)

Frederick Douglass remarked:

> There are at present many coloured men in the Confederate Army doing duty, not only as cooks, servants, and labourers, but real soldiers, having muskets on their shoulders, and bullets in their pockets.

Soldiers of the War Between the States Buried in Quaker and Beth-El Cemeteries in Camden.

George Gilman Alexander
Dr. Isaac Henry Alexander
Thomas J. Ancrum
William Alexander Ancrum
J.D. Anderson
J.B. Arrants
James Robert Arrants
James W. Arrants
Jessie Arthur
George W. Barnes
L.W.R. Blair
James Phillip Boswell
Alexander Hamilton Boykin
Alexander Hamilton Boykin 2nd
Burrell Henry Boykin
Burrell F. Boykin
E. Miller Boykin
Dr. Edward M. Boykin
Samuel Boykin
Samuel Francis Boykin
Thomas L. Boykin
W. Franklin Boykin
J.L. Brasington
Alfred Brevard
William C. Brown
Dr. Andrew W. Burnet
Cornelous Benton Burns
Isaac W. Burns

John Cantey
John Manning Cantey
Richard M. Cantey
Thomas R. Cantey
Zack Cantey
W.H. Capell
John Capers
Sidney W. Capers
T.H. Clarke
S.C. Clyburn
Reuben Collins
George Crosby
Everard Belton Cureton
James B. Cureton
Reverend Frederick Bruce Davis
James Moore Davis
Junius Davis
The Rt. Rev. T.F. Davis
Allen Deas
Dr. Lynch Horry Deas
James Elliot DeLoache
Jacob Depass
William Lambert DePass
Dr. Daniel Louis DeSaussure
Henry W. DeSaussure
Dr. John McPherson DeSaussure
Dr. Louis McPherson DeSaussure
Alfred English Doby

James H. Burns
Edward Brevard Cantey
James Cantey
E.B. Dunlap
Joseph Doby Dunlap
Thomas Samuel Dunlap
W. Clarkson Gerald
John R. Goodale
Joseph Goodale
William Baker Gordon
John T. Graham
Columbus Cureton Haile
James Lenoir Haile
Thomas Cureton Haile
Frank Hammond
James Thornwell Hay
Dr. H.F. Hodgson
Joel Hough
Dr. Edwin C. Hughes
J.M. Ingram
W.L. Johnson
Alexander Dalton Kennedy
Joseph Doby Kennedy
Joseph Brevard Kershaw
Richard R. Kirkland
D.C. Kirkley
S.B. Latham
J. Marcellus Legrand
R.T. Lewis
Arthur Parker Lining
S. Lorick
W.R. Malone
Robert Man
Brown Manning
Reverend Benjamin Faneul Perry
F. Butler Phelps
Francis Lambert Phelps
John Player
H. Columbus Player
George Sinkler Rhame

Edward Cassels Dubose
Henry Kershaw Dubose
Wiles Dubose
G.M. Mathis
Dr. John McCaa
C.J. McDowall
Charles J. McDowall
John McDowall
John Witherspoon McDowall
William Douglas McDowall
H. McKagen
Henry G. McKagen
J.M. McKagen
J.W.P. McKagen
John McKain
John J. McKain
William McKain
Reverend E.J. Meynardie
Reverend William Wilson Mills
Dr. A.A. Moore
C.L. Moseley
Patrick Henry Nelson
Hiram Nettles
Jessie S. Nettles
John T. Nettles
Joseph Nettles
William Nettles
E. Ariovistus Niles
Edward E. Niles
Benjamin McCoy Pearce
Charles A. H. Peck
Ben Perkins
Benjamin Elias Perkins
Roger Griswold Perkins
Lewis Vaughan
James I. Villipigue
John Bordenave Villipique
Paul F. Villipigue
Thomas J. Warren
James J. Watkins

L. William Rochelle
Wardlaw F. Russell
Dr. Thomas Whitaker Salmond
Thomas Polk Sanders
Joel A. Shrock
Dr. C.J. Shannon Jr.
Charles J. Shannon
William McCreight Shannon
Charles W. Sieloff
Edward E. Sill
J. M. Smyrl
Thomas J. Smyrl
William R. Taylor
James W. Thompson
Dr. George Rogers Clark Todd
W. D. Trantham
Henry Truesdale
J.T. Truesdale
S.B. Turner
William F. Turner

John Whitaker
Lawrence L. Whitaker
William Whitaker
Albertus S. White
David Roberson Williams
Edwin S. Williams
Morton W. Wilson
Samuel McCartney Wilson
Thomas J. Wilson
Thomas M. Wilson
W. Randolph Withers
Thomas Jefferson Withers
James Witherspoon
William Clark Workman
George Gilham Young
George Graham Young
James Young
J.F. "Jessie" Young
Dr. Francis Leslie Zemp

Those in Battlefields Elsewhere and in Unknown Graves

Douglas Ancrum
C.T. Billings
John Boykin
Henry Cantey
John Chesnut
James Cureton
Francis Devine
W.T. Dutton
Charles Fisher
Ruben Gerald

M.S. LeGrand
Boykin McCaa
Adam McWillie
Columbus Minton
Burwell Salmond
Allison Shannon
Charles Shannon
Chesnut Whitaker
Duncan Whitaker
John Whitherspoon

Edward Lang

In the Beth-El Cemetery, the Jewish Cemetery, there are three Confederate Graves:

Herman Baum

William Geisenheimer

B. Mendel Smith

The Unknown Confederate Soldier's Plot

In Quaker Cemetery, lies a section of Twenty- Two Unknown. Some of these may be known from March 1865, several were buried in the local city cemetery (now known as Quaker Cemetery) and probably no one came to dig up the body and take them home.

Those are:

John Bradkins, Company D, 1st SC Battalion, of asthma, on March 12.
H. Cook, Johnson's Artillery, of Typhoid Fever, March 12.
A.D. Shaus, Company H, 1st S. C. Battalion, on March 14.
W.C. Wilburn, Company H, 1st S.C. Artillery, of Pneumonia, March 21.
B. Chance, Company G, 32nd Georgia Regulars, of Pneumonia, March 23.
T W. Tucker, Company M., 1st Georgia, "Softening of the Brain" on March 25.
H. Willis, Company I, 5th Georgia Reserves, Chronic Diarrhoea, March 30.
E.T. Teel, Company B. 32nd Georgia Regiment, March 31.

Stories from the War by
Camden Confederates,
Camden People, and
Kershaw County Descendants.

Camden During February 1865

By Bessie Clarke Whitaker as told to Bertie Zemp

In February, the year of 1865, the alarm was given that Sherman was fast marching upon us. In fact, he was expected in Columbia any day, and we knew what would be the fate of our beloved city. It struck terror to our hearts. My mother's home was just thirty miles from Columbia directly in the path that Sherman would take to march on to Camden.

My mother, an old lady, and her three daughters, lived alone. She could not make up her mind that her daughters should be left alone without protection to the mercy of those awful brutes, so she begged, and implored that we leave, and go across to Liberty Hill. We never dreamed the Yankees would go there. After much weeping, we consented to go just to satisfy her.

That night a mighty fire was seen, the light of which illumined the whole southern heavens. We knew too well the meaning of it all. Now was the time to leave. As dark came on the next evening, leaving our loved ones in good care, we silently stole away from the dear home. Each mounted-on horseback, as we had to ride through the woods.

We first went to one of my mother's plantations, a distance of three miles. I never knew what grief and sorrow were before. One sister was so distressed that she said she must get back to Mother and the old home, even if she would be murdered on the road.

In the dead hour of the night, she mounted her horse, and rode through the woods alone. She arrived safely at home for a girl of sixteen.

With us that night was two of our girlfriends, and a gentleman, a neighbor who was badly lamed. That night there was no sleep. We could see fires all around. Just before day, some of the Negroes came running with the cry, "Oh, my God, Marse Jim, the Yankees right here." We ran with all our might and, in short time, reached the swamp. After waiting a short time, we went on the cane brake right on the two-river bank. You can imagine our plight, as it had been raining for some time. The old river flat came slowly down to the us across. We could very plainly see the artillery just above us crossing the river. The roads were rough and rocky, and with their many baggage wagons, and the noise was terrific. It sent terror in our hearts, and for the fear of being seen, we all lay flat in the old flat, and in some way, the old man got us across. Another run for our lives. This time through swamps, cane brakes, and woods, trying to keep as far from the road as possible.

Through the day, we saw many fires. The Yankees burning as they traveled through. One very large blazed, we knew from the direction, was the elegant mansion of Colonel Nick Peay, one of our neighbors. A party of drunken soldiers found in his wine cellar, a quantity of rare old liquor. They got hastily drunk, and fifty, or more, were burned in the house.

We had traveled that day some good many miles. We were hungry, thirsty, and tired, not to mention very scared. Wet to our waist, as we had two or three plunges in small streams. As dark came on us, we were wondering where we should camp, when we spied a light gleaming not so far away. Some of us thought, we should be brave, and try to get a little nearer the road to find out in whose house the light was. A colored girl told us the name of the lady, and we sent, and asked her to come to the road. In a few minutes, she was there, and to our surprise, we found she was an old friend, and delighted to take us in her home. She was lonely and frightened. All alone with her old mother and three babies.

We were too nervous and frightened to sleep that night. We sat up and talked until early daylight, when we lay down in our clothes. We were soon awakened by the sound of a bugle. Goodness! How soon we all got together! From the upstairs window, the road could be seen for quite a distance, so Mrs. W. stationed a colored girl at each window to give the alarm at the first Blue Coat she saw.

We were sitting on the piazza, when galloping horses were heard at first. Raising our eyes, we saw eight or ten at the door. In the twinkle of an eye, they were down and all through the house, hunting silver, and taking anything of value they could find. They spied a very handsome sword hanging on the wall, which Mrs. W. had very carelessly forgotten to hide. He buckled it around his waist, and told us to get used to things, as we would probably see thousands of Blue Coats before night. And indeed we did. They simply poured in from sunrise until sunset. Sherman's whole army of thirty thousand, or more, and the ugliest set of men I ever he held, all with sandy, red hair, and washed out blue eyes.

Right here I must say, General Sherman behaved like a gentleman. After refreshing himself a little, he asked to see the lady of the house. When Mrs. W. came, he told her to have no fear at all, that she and her family were perfectly safe, that he had put a guard around the house, and if we were molested by word or look, just report it to him, and he would have them court martialed immediately. Later, he asked if some of the ladies, wouldn't give him some music on the piano. You must know that he didn't get any music from us. Again, he sent word that had two Confederate prisoners, if the ladies would like, he would send them in. Oh! You may be sure we glad to see those dear men. We almost fell on our knees and worshipped them. One was Dr. Kinloch, and the other Swinton Bissell. Bissell was a young man, wounded in the leg, and walking on crutches. Both was from Charleston.

We rested that night, feeling very safe. In front of the house were large, open fields, where thousands of tents were pitched. The camp fires were indeed too beautiful to describe.

By dawn the next morning, the bugle sounded, and everything was astir. Tents were taken down, and all begun to move. Our prisoners were taken away from us. A little later, a tap at the door with General Sherman's compliments, asking if he would be allowed to serve the ladies with breakfast. We politely declined.

It took them most of the morning to get away. Then came what we dreaded most — the stragglers. They were the ones that did the most harm. Between times, we would rush out to where the tents had stood to see what we could find. We returned with a handful of flour, a little meal, and sometimes a slice of bacon, or a spoonful of coffee. We were delighted to get it, as we have starved for several days. We were afraid to cook in daylight, as we knew the stragglers would take our food away from us. We waited till night time expecting to have a royal feast. The old Dutch oven was brought into the sitting room, we all got busy, and in the shortest time, our feast was ready. That being a big oven of biscuits, fried bacon, and a pot of coffee. Just as things were ready, horses' feet were heard rapidly approaching the house. They were quickly at the door, and the men told us they were Wheeler's men, and was almost starved. We kept a few biscuits for the children and gave the soldiers everything else. After eating all they gave a loud shout and told us they were Yankees.

Next morning, we saw two men on miserable looking horses waving handkerchiefs and approaching the house. They turned out to be our two prisoners, Dr. Kinloch and Mr. Bissell. There were several days before we could return home as the famous Sherman freshet was at its height.

Our own horse suffered as did Mrs. W's. Father, being a large slave holder, killed a great many hogs to feed his hands. This meat was all nicely hidden in a large cave back of our house by two of our most trusted servants. At the same time, several large trunks of beautiful bed and table linens were hidden. One old servant, at the point of a pistol, lost his nerve, and betrayed us, so, of course, the other old man, who was always ready with a lie on his lips said, "Our provision of all kinds was hidden under the basement by taking up the flooring." These, we saved, and our silver. Mother and the girls buried the silver in the dead of night, under a large spreading chestnut tree, and some of it in the Irish potatoes' patch, which we covered over with straw. They pierced all day with their bayonets, but they never found the silver.

The Capture of Joseph Brevard Kershaw

THIS STORY WAS WRITTEN BY Major General Joseph B. Kershaw in year the 1876 of his accounts of his surrender and his capture by Major General George A. Custer, and written after the Lieutenant Colonel Custer died at the Battle of Little Big Horn.

The Late Major General Custer

Ever since the heart rending intelligence of the massacre of the gallant and chivalrous Custer and his brave comrades reached me, I have felt the impulse to record an event in my military career, so creditable to that distinguished officer, that it cannot fail to interest those who value his memory.

On the morning of Wednesday, April 5, 1865, the Confederate troops from Richmond united with those retiring before Sheridan, who led the advance of the Union Army from Petersburg, near Amelia Courthouse. Sheridan held the direct road from Amelia in our front and rendered it necessary that we should make a detour of some miles during the night, which brought us to Amelia Springs about sunrise on the sixth. Halting for a few minutes for refreshments, sorely needed, the march was resumed about eleven a.m., and brought my division about noon to the point where the wagon road turned abruptly to our right rear, leading to Appomattox. At this point, we found the line of march threatened by the Union Cavalry. And, to cover the road, my command was halted until the wagon train, artillery, etc., had passed. Here we were actively engaged in repulsing the charge of the cavalry, which continued in desperate efforts to break the line and reach the train, for several hours. When the last of the wagons had passed this point, and Gordon's advance arrived, covering the rear of the train, I resumed the line of march by a direct road parallel and to the left of that upon the trains moved, Gordon still following the wagon road. Arriving at Sailor's Creek, I posted the Mississippi brigade (Humphreys) on the hill to cover the passage of the creek, and moved on to the heights beyond, where I overtook Curtis Lee and his division (the naval brigade and local troops from Richmond), and was informed by him that General R.H. Anderson was in front, had encountered the enemy in his path, and was then engaged with him.

We then formed line, faced the rear, to hold the Union forces, then pressing upon the Mississippians, in check. My division formed to the right (as we then faced) and Lee's to the left of the road. We had scarcely formed in this order before the Mississippians were forced to retreat across Sailor's Creek and rejoin me. We artillery, two batteries (12 pieces) as well as I can remember, put in position on the opposite hill, some five hundred yards distant, whose missiles of death soon crashed through and over our rank. It was not long before columns of infantry poured over the Creek under a murderous fire and filed to our left, while other columns pressed upon our front and right, until the whole line was engaged in a desperate struggle. General Anderson sent me word that if I could hold the position for half an hour. He thought he could open a way — to which I returned an encouraging answer.

The flower of the Union army was upon us. Hancock's and Wright's splendid corps in my front — and Custer and Merit's cavalry holding Anderson at bay — riding into his lines, and over all obstacles with the utmost gallantry, and a reckless determination. My own command held the ground firmly, fiercely and sternly —with a calm never surpassed even by those veterans and of a hundred battlefields, while the Naval brigade to my left fought with a sort of rollicking enthusiasm— due not only to their splendid courage, but also to the novelty of their position and their recent release from gunboats and the monotony of siege service as heavy artillery. For about an hour and a half of the best and closest fighting of the war, the situation remained seemingly unchanged. But no word came from Anderson — broken, killed, captured or dispersed, his entire command had melted away.

The wings of Sheridan's infantry united to his cavalry to the right and left of us the circle of fire was complete. At length my right gave back, and a fire from the rear announced Anderson's fate. I have the order to fall back, firing, and slowly moved with the retreating line, through the dense woods as near as I could guess toward Appomattox. Not far had we progressed when one of my men informed me that the struggle was useless — that most of my men had surrendered. Riding a few rods in the direction we were moving, I arrived at the edge of an open space, across which in precise and orderly array, was formed one of Custer's brigades. Towards whom were running, with uplifted hands, from all parts of the wood, the men of my command, as fast as they reached the open ground, and comprehend the situation. Riding back to the skirmish line, I ordered them to cease firing, explained the situation, and gave the words "Sauve Qui Peut." Turning to my staff, I dismissed them with orders to escape if they could. I remained where they left me, watching their receding forms as they galloped through the woods, with feelings, which may be imagined, but cannot be expressed.

Soon, I found myself surrounded by some thirty of my brave comrades, including General Dubose and General Sims of Georgia and Major Costier of my staff. I asked the later why he had not gone. He said sadly, "General, I have followed your fortunes too long to leave you now." When further pressed to save himself, he said, "I have no home to return to — I prefer to share your fate." Poor fellow, and gallant, generous gentleman — he did not return to his home afterwards, on the Eastern shore of Virginia, when I trust that the few remaining years of his bright young life were crowned with the honor and peace he so richly merited.

Finding myself responsible for not only myself but also for these faithful comrades, who seemed determined to stand by me to the end, I endeavored to escape with them. Riding slowly through the woods in the direction my staff had taken, I had not progressed far when I met a cavalryman, riding jauntily along from the opposite direction, and following him some twenty or more disarmed Confederates, evidently his prisoners. I halted him and ordered him to dismount and give his horse to General Dubose, who had lost his. He was reluctant to comply with this request that I turned to one of my men and told him to enforce the order. At that moment, some of his prisoners called out to me, "General!" and made a significant gesture of caution pointing to this rear. There, not more than eighty yards off, was a body of the Federal Infantry. "Stop a moment," I said to the

Cavalryman, who was about to dismount. "Are those your troops?" "Yes, sir" he said. "Whose command do you belong to?" I asked. "To Custer's Cavalry." "Corporal Lanham of the 2nd Ohio Cavalry" — touching his hat in a soldierly salute, said, 'I, Corporal, I am Major General Kershaw. This is Major Costier of my Division Staff. This is General Dubose, and this Brigadier General Sims, and these are my men, and they are armed as you see. If I surrender this party, will you pledge your honor as a soldier, that we shall be conducted to General Custer's headquarters without molestation or insult?" "I will," said he emphatically and proudly. "Where are Custer's headquarters?" I asked. "They are with the Light Battery near there," said he, pointing in the direction, when, during the engagement, I had perceived a very annoying series of rifle shells coming from my right rear. "The General will be there tonight," he added. "Then, lead the way, Corporal," said I, and we rode away together.

Emerging from the wood into the open ground, we passed along the line of a regiment of Union Cavalry. We had not preceded far, before a smart, brusque young officer galloped across the field, and joined our party. "Who is it you have there, Corporal?" He asked. "General Kershaw," said Lanham. This officer addressed me: "I see you have a sword by your side?" said he. "Yes," I replied." "I will trouble you for it," said he. I then turned to Lanham and said, "Corporal, I surrendered to you upon pledge of honor that I should be conducted to General Custer's headquarters without molestation or insult, and I call upon you to redeem your pledge." He replied, "General, I did make you this promise, and this gentleman has no right to your sword, but he is my superior officer, and I cannot protect you." I then handed my sword to the officer after obtaining his name and charging Lanham to remember it. He was a Lt. R… of the 8th Illinois Cavalry. Our cortege then proceeded to the point indicated as Headquarters. There was but little to be seen suggesting the importance of the locality. The distinguished cavalry leader was nowhere to be seen. There was no tent spread, not even a fly, and no staff. A single young officer, sitting on the carriage of one of two guns, a section of light battery receiving a communication from Corporal Lanham, and immediately stepped forward with a smile, half of pleasure, and half of sympathy; and addressed me with that courtesy which always characterizes the true gentleman. He introduced himself as Lieutenant Woodruff, and invited us to dismount, saying that was headquarters, that the General would be there at night, and in the meantime, he would take pleasure in entertaining us. Our youthful host, scarcely more than two and twenty, did the honors in a manner that made us for the time forget many of our troubles. In the saddle, on the march, or in battle for two days and a night, without refreshment of any sort for many hours, the memory of young Woodruff's hospitality lingers yet with me, as a pleasing episode of those eventful days of the "Falling Flag."

Let me digress here, to record an incident worthy of mention. The next morning when Woodruff was preparing for the field, I took occasion to express to him my grateful sense of his courtesy and kindness, and taking off my spurs, a splendid pair which I had worn since the first Manassas, where they were captured, I begged him to accept them in memory of our meeting. Warmly thanking me, he pressed my hand kindly adieu, mounted his horse, and rode away with his battery. Ten years later, I received a small package by Express, and with it a note creditable to the writer and to humanity. With this note came my spurs as bright and untarnished as ever to the eye, but infinitely more valuable for the rich sentiment expressed by the writer that lends them a lustre brighter, more precious than gold. I need not say that they are treasured in my household.

To my return to my narrative — very soon after my arrival at — headquarters, my friends, General Corse, and Barton, Brigadiers of Pickett's Division, were brought in as prisoners, from whom I heard the fate of Anderson's command, and Colonel Frank Huger of the Artillery, who with his entire command, battalion, guns, horse and caissons, had also been captured.

It appears that when General Anderson had halted to resist Custer's impetuous dashes upon our line of march, Mahone had moved on, leaving an interval of more than a mile, Huger, wholly unaware that this interval existed, moved on and was gobbled up by the wily Custer, who completed his day's work by occupying the road and holding it against Anderson's advance.

When the sun had gone down, and the shadows of evening settled peacefully upon the scene, lately so worried by the strife of contending armies, a cavalcade rode briskly forward to the spot where we rested. A spare, lithe, and sinewy figure about the medium height, bright, dark blue eyes, ever restless, a florid complexion, brown wavy curls, high cheek bones, and aquiline nose, firm-set teeth, a jaunty close-fitting cavalry jacket, large top boots, Spanish spurs, golden aiguillette's — a serviceable sabre, a quick, nervous energetic movement, and an air of hauteur, telling of the habit of command, announced the redoubtable Custer, whose name had become familiar to this foe, as to his friends. He was met by Lieutenant Woodruff, who introduced us: "Why, General," said Custer, taking my hand with a kindly smile, somewhat tinged with humor, "I am glad to see you here. I feel as if I ought to know you." "Yes," said I. "General, we have met very often, but not under circumstances favorable to the cultivating of an acquaintance." This little passage of pleasantry made us quite at home immediately, and very soon the conversation became free and general, and kindly around the camp fire. With a soldier's hospitality, we were made to feel welcome by our host, and not withstanding our misfortunes, enjoyed not a little, the camp luxuries of coffee, sugar, condensed milk, hard-tack, broiled ham, etc. Spread before us upon a tent fly, converted into a table cloth, around which we all sat upon the ground — Custer and his Rebel Guests.

After supper, we smoked and talked over many subjects of interest to all of us, dwelling, however, almost wholly upon the past. The future, to us, was not inviting, and our host, with true delicacy of feeling, avoiding the subject. We slept, beneath the stars, Custer sharing his blankets with me. Very soon he was asleep, and I lay watching the glittering hosts of heaven as they moved in their wonted spheres, calmly, peacefully, majestically in the sky, seemingly unmindful and uncaring of human misery. We lay in the midst of Custer's squadron, thousands of men and horses — lay around us in easy call, but as the last notes of the bugle sounded "Tattoo" and "Taps," "Silence reigned supreme" unbroken, save by the snorting or stamping of a horse, or the coughing of some wakeful soldier.

That night, as I lay watching the cold, insensate stars, I buried all my banners. I bowed by soul in submission and tried to say, "Thy will be done," from henceforth be mine the task as far as I may, to staunch my country's bleeding wounds." Nature, at last asserted herself, and I slept. When I awoke, the sun shone brightly, and all was bustle and activity. Our host was already up and gave me a cheery greeting as I arose and joined him, standing near the fire. He wore an air of thought upon his face, betokening the work of the day that lay before him — and received and sent many communications.

Whilst at breakfast, one after another, some thirty troopers rode up within a few rods, each dismounting, and aligning himself, and holding his horse by the bridle. Each carried a Confederate Battle Flag, except my captor of the previous day, whom I recognized in the ranks, and he bore two of our flags. He also, as he caught my eye and bowed, pointed to my own sabre worn at his belt with an air of pride and pleasure. My curiosity was greatly excited by this group, and I asked Custer what it meant. "That," said he, "is my escort for the day. It is my custom after a battle to select for my escort a sort of garde du honeur, bearing, for the time, the trophies which they have taken from the enemy. These men are selected as the captors of the flags which they bear." I counted them. There were thirty-one captured banners, representing thirty-one of our regiments, killed, captured, or dispersed the day before. It was not comforting to think of. Lanham's possession of my sword was easily accounted for. I had told Custer of the conduct of the officer who had taken it and requested that Lanham should have it. He said nothing in reply, but nonetheless, had done the right thing. My Lanham's descendants wield that sword in defense of their country, whenever called upon, as honestly as its old master sought to do his duty, according to the dictates of his conscientious convictions. By the time our repast was concluded, Custer's whole division was drawn up in columns of squadrons, in full view of us, a spectacle, to a soldier's eye, full of interest. Finally, the General turned to me and said, "You will remain here a few moments when horses will be brought for you and your companions, and you will be conducted to Burkesville, where you find General Grant. Good-bye." He shook my hand, mounted a magnificent charger and rode proudly away, followed at a round gallop by his splendid escort, bearing the "falling flags." As he neared his conquering legions, cheer after cheer greeted his approach, bugles sounded and sabers flashed as they saluted. The proud cavalcade filed through the open ranks, and moved to the front leading that magnificent column, riding in splendid array. Me thought, No Rom Hector had ever more noble triumph. I saw Custer no more. True child of glory, he courted her smiles where dangers were thickest. "Life's fitful fever ended." He lay enshrined in her arms — sword in hand and armour on — his back to the sod, his feet to the foe, and his eyes fixed on the heavens."

> On Fame's eternal camping ground
> his silent tent is spread
> and glory guards with solemn round
> the bivouac of the dead"

Signed J.B. Kershaw
Major General
Confederate States Army

A Reminiscence of the War

By Mrs. Elizabeth Kennedy Doby
The State Newspaper - March 7, 1906

THURSDAY, THE TWENTY-FOURTH OF FEBRUARY 1865, was a memorable day in the annals of our old, historic town, for on that day the Yankees came into it several thousand strong, under the command, if I remember correctly, of General Howard. Ever since the taking of Columbia, we had been expecting them, but not in the way they entered it, for instead, of coming across the country, they crossed at Chesnut's Ferry, on the Wateree, and came into town via Hobkirk Hill. As company after company of bluecoats with a long train of wagons, the commanding general with his staff, all on fine horses, filed by, our hearts were filled with consternation and fright, for we knew not fate awaited us, taking as precedence their behavior in other places. As they passed on down the street my uncle, Mr. James Dunlap, who was mayor of the town, came out of the residence, Lafayette Hall, and, standing on the pavement with a flag of truce in his hand, waved it, thus making the column halt. He went forward, asking to speak to the general commanding the troops, upon which a fine-looking and handsomely dressed soldier dismounted from an elegant caparisoned horse and heard what my uncle's request was, which was that he would protect the helpless women and children. Much he kept his promise, as we shall see further on, as he allowed his men to do as they pleased. The Yankees took possession of the large public square in the very pretty and desirable part of the town and soon they were putting the torch to different buildings, notably the two depots, the freight and passenger, then the fine bridge across the Wateree, and the Cornwallis House, a building of colonial times where Lord Cornwallis had stayed when he took possession of Camden, a piece of vandalism which we all greatly regretted and the destruction of this old mansion was caused, they said, because we had some of their prisoners confined there. The Yankees rode all over the town and Kirkwood, a beautiful little village just above Camden, on horseback and muleback, going into our yards and houses, but they did not fire any private residences. Why? We never knew. The stores, warehouses, market, and public hall they destroyed. In some of these warehouses were stored furniture, pictures, and books belonging to Charleston and Beaufort refugees, who sent them up to the Camden merchants for safekeeping: also, casks of fine old wine which were broken up and distributed to Yankees and Negroes indiscriminately.

It was a harrowing sight to see the Negro women and children passing by with these handsome pictures, tables, chairs, and other articles of furniture in the down pouring rain, to the injury of these things to valuable to the refugees, who had suffered so heavily. After the Yankees left us, the mayor issued an order that all the articles taken during the raid should be returned to the warehouse of Dr. James Young, where they were inspected and claimed by their rightful owners. All Thursday and Thursday night, we were kept in a state of suspense, lest our houses should be burned, which feeling was kept alive by the Negroes rushing in all the time with a report that this house and the other were on fire, when there was not a word of truth in the rumor.

Recollections of a Southern Girl

By Harriet DuBose Lang
Daughter of General Joseph Brevard and Lucretia Douglass Kershaw

We lived in a long, rambling house overshadowed by great oak and sycamore trees, with a yard covered with a carpet of green grass. There were four of us children, one boy, the eldest, and three girls. Our father and mother were devoted to each other, and to us, so naturally we were very happy children. We have always resided in the quaint old town of Camden, which was founded by one of our ancestors, and the county bears his name. My father was a prominent and successful lawyer, looked up to and loved by all who knew him.

Just before the war, we owned quite a number of slaves, as did many Southerners at that time. Our old cook, Judy, our Mammy Carolina, a seamstress, a washer-woman, two butlers, one hostler, and our three small maids were our help. My sister Mary at the beginning of the war was about thirteen years of age; I came next, age eleven, and Charlotte the baby, nine years of age. The little maids, Mary Ann, Eliza, and Jinnie, were about the same age as their mistresses. We swore by them, and would fight for them any day, and they were as loyal to us. Mammy was our best friend and comfort next to Mother. My greatest terror when a child was the thought, "Suppose Mammy should die?" I would wake up in the night with the dreadful thought, and sob, and pray for Mammy.

My father, soon after the succession, formed a regiment of his countrymen, and went to the front. Oh, those sad days! My dear mother was almost heartbroken at parting from her loved one but bore herself bravely for his sake. I recall our trip to Charleston to be with Father as long as possible. We, with many other officer's families, boarded at the Charleston Hotel, where we daily looked for the opening of hostilities. Early in April 1861, the first gun was fired by Anderson from Fort Sumter.

The dawn was ushered in by the dread sound of the booming cannon. Soon the guests at the Hotel were aroused, and men, women, and children were wildly rushing about. My dear mother called us to her, and many, and heart felt were the prayers she sent up to "Our Father in Heaven" for the safety of our earthly father, and for success for our arms. We soon gathered on the roof of the hotel, which was flat on top, and being very high, was a good observatory. Here we watched the Battle of Fort Sumter. The firing continued as I remember, until quite later in the afternoon, when Anderson raised the white flag. Our people were wild with excitement, and everyone thought that war would soon end, and our dear ones be at home again. Our bands played "Dixie" and

"The Bonnie Blue Flag" to enthusiastic crowds, and every face beamed happily. It is well we cannot look into the future, or else our men could not have had courage to fight those bloody battle; our women and children to endure the hardships they suffered during the years to follow these events recorded.

Soon after the Battle of Fort Sumter, the Ladies of Charleston presented my father with a beautiful silk flag for his regiment. The presentation took place on the upper piazza of the Charleston Hotel. The streets were crowded with citizens and soldiers, to witness the presentation of the flag, and to hear the speech my father was to make, thanking the ladies in the name of his regiment for the lovely flag. He turned around to the group of his officers and handed the flag to a young aide, selecting him as his color bearer. In planting the flagstaff firmly on the floor, to emphasize his remarks, the staff broke. A groan came from all sides of the great crowd assembled. They considered it an omen of disaster. This young color bearer carried this flag gallantly until the First Battle of Manassas, when he was shot to death. When his body was sent to his home for burial, his casket was draped in the beautiful flag he carried so faithfully.

Soon thereafter, my father's regiment was ordered to Virginia to take part in those dreadful battles which were soon to follow. All the men, and even boys of fifteen volunteered for service. Mothers, wives, and sweethearts gave up their best loved for the struggle for liberty. We were too young to appreciate or realize what it really meant. During the days to come, Mother scarcely ever smiled, but she tried to be cheerful for the sake of the children. Women had to manage their own affairs with the assistance of some trusted slave. Our old man was Uncle Ben. Mother gave him a gun and told him, "Now, that your master is away, I look to you to protect us." Many a night, Uncle Ben slept in a room in our house, on the watch for us. The town was left with only old man and small boys, and women and children at the mercy of the Negroes.

Their behavior was truly beautiful. I believe where masters were kind and considerate to their slaves, they repaid them by loyalty and love. We found it so. No fear or distrust ever entered our heads. We loved them, they loved us, and to this day the same love exists. We were very wild children, and I am afraid great tom boys: we climbed trees, rode horseback, went bathing in the creek not far from our home, and in fact did almost anything a boy would do, and we thought, did it just as well. We gathered in mother's living room, the four of us, and our little maids, and a small darky boy (my brother's protégé, called "Pop Skull", on account of a long bulging head). Here, we vied with each other to entertain and amuse Mother, and make her laugh. Brother was always the most successful. When he brought forth a smile or laugh, the whole crowd would be wild with joy. Even the little Negroes would add their share of fun to make Miss laugh. The old-time darky has almost passed away, and I scarcely know what manner of being a new "colored person" belongs to — so full of airs and graces and affections. The heart that old time Negroes had is entirely lacking in this new creation. We sang, danced, and romped together, and forgot that we were of a different race. No game was complete unless our maids had a hand in it.

Our woodland was out in the country five or six miles. Here were large hickory trees, which in the autumn was loaded with nuts. We often begged for a wagon ride to gather these treasures, and together with several little friends by our old coachmen "Jake" (whom we nicknamed "Sulky" on account of his disposition), we would go for a day's pleasure in the woods, such singing, such laughing, such merry jests we had. A lunch under the trees, then tires, but happy, a sweet drive home with the soft moonbeams to light us our way. Home again, where

Mother welcomed us in her own sweet way, and after supper, we crawled into our little trundle beds, and were soon dreaming of hickory-nuts, wagon rides, and moonbeams.

About a mile from our home, through a shady wood, lived a plain respectable family called Thomas. The father was a cooper and made tubs, churns, and buckets for the townspeople. The mother was a tailoress and seamstress. There were several girls or young women in the family, and nothing pleased us so much on Saturdays or holidays, as to gather our companions, and with a trusty servant, to walk over to the farm of Mr. Thomas. We always met with a hearty welcome and the best cheer the house afforded. After resting a few moments, we would beg the girls to carry us huckle-berry hunting, for they knew where the largest and best berries grew. Away we would go, each with a basket or bucket; and soon the blue, juicy berries would tumble into our hands, each trying to outdo the other in gathering them. When tired, we sat under the tree listening to the song of the swamp, of the sparrow, and the sighting of the wind through the tall pine trees, fanning our cheeks with our sun-bonnets, laughing and chatting merrily all the while. Then the word of command would come from our favorite guide Pat, "Come, gals, let's be a waddling," and away we would go across a branch, on a single board, feeling very brave after getting to our journey's end. On the other side of the branch rose a steep hill, on top of which grew a patch of violets, iris, and rocky roses. This spot we called Brother's Flower Garden, for he discovered it. On we went until we came to a long, low building, known as Mr. D's summer house for Negro children.

As we came near, we saw in front of the door what we though a very interesting sight. An old Negro lady, the caretaker, stood over a large pot which bubbled over a wood fire; around her were gathered fifteen or twenty little darkies, from three to nine years of age, waiting for their dinner, which forth a savory odor. These little darkies were all clean, and well clad, and looked happy and contented. They were spending the summer in the sand-hills, as the Negro quarter was in an unhealthy place. After talking to the old women for a while, we crossed a field, and were soon at Mrs. Malone's house. She always had lots of pretty young chickens and little pigs, and we passed many happy hours, looking around the place and admiring her pets. Mrs. M. was famous for her fried squirrel, sweet potatoes roasted in the ashes, and buttermilk, and she never she never failed to treat us when we called on her.

You must not think we did nothing but play, Oh, we went to school and studied, too. Someday I will tell you about our school and our games. Those were happy days to us, though the war cloud was spread all over our land, and fierce battles raged, and dear ones fell. "Children will be children."

During the first year or two of the war, people managed to get on very well, for many had saved supplies, such as sugar, coffee and tea, to last for a short while. These supplies soon gave out, and then a cup of coffee or tea was an unheard-of thing; sugar could not be obtained at all. I am not speaking of everybody but only those I knew well enough to know how they lived.

Planters made corn, flour, bacon, lard, molasses, and peas, etc., in quantities sufficient to supply their families and selves, but families of professional men, such as my father, suffered much for the necessities of life. Our Confederate money could scarcely buy anything, A pair of shoes (homemade) cost hundreds of dollars, provisions were as dear, and the supply was limited. You could not get supplies for love or money. I will give you a bill of fare which we lived on for, it seems to me, weeks and months; corn, bread, hominy, and milk for breakfast: Corn bread and cow peas, boiled without salt or bacon, for dinner. Corn bread and milk for supper. Imagine, if you can, a dish of peas with noting to season them! Our fare was so meager that we did not even go to the table but sat around the fire munching dry bread and drinking our milk. Sometimes we enjoyed it; at others, we put aside with poor appetite. I remember one day at school, I had a piece of corn bread for lunch. After looking at the bread for a while, I threw it out the window and thought no more about it. The next day I was sitting at my desk feeling very hungry. I happened to cast my eyes out of the window, and there on the ground was the bread that I had thrown away the day before. I looked at the bread with longing eyes, my hunger increasing every minute. Finally, I asked permission to go out, and went quickly up to where the bread lay. It had rained a little the night before, which dampened the bread somewhat, and there were a few ants crawling on it; but, oh, the bread did look so good! I stooped down, picked up the bread, carefully brushed the ants off, and soon that bread was devoured, and I was feeling much better. Sorghum, a syrup boiled from sugar cane, was very nice and much enjoyed when we could get it. Many people parched meal, okra seed, or hickory, and used it as a substitute for coffee, with sorghum as a sweetening. The country people called this long sweetening. These substitutes were all poor. A cousin of mine invented a substitute for meat, which I will give to you. It was not very nice or at all nourishing but had a little taste. Here it is—Take corn meal, salt, a little grease, pepper, and onion, mix with water and bake. Sometimes we had supplies and fared better, and then we would get out, and hard times again. My mother wasted away under these hardships and was so frail at the close of the war that I could lift her up. She never complained and tried bravely to keep her children and servants in provisions, for we had no farm, only a house and lot in town. In summer, we had our gardens and fruit, so fared much better than in winter. Some of our neighbors lived very comfortably, but what I write about is our condition. Many others who had no plantation fared in the same way, although I think that our condition was rather worse than any that I knew about. We did not complain; therefore, our friends could not know how we suffered. I am not ashamed to confess how poor we were, for was not our support and stay fighting for his home and country?

The southern girl during the war wore homespun dresses, and wheat straw and palmetto hats made by her own hand, and very pretty hats they were. Our Negro women spun and wove the cloth which they wore; and we learned during those days to dye the cloth very pretty colors: gray, blue, green, and brown. I have seen a lovely plaid homespun, white with just two threads of green forming the plaid. It was a cool, pretty spring dress. I remember a gray homespun worn by my cousin, made in princess style, with large buttons, covered with the material fastening it down the front. It was a dress any lady might have worn.

Our hats were made from palmetto, corn shucks, rye, and wheat straw. The girls plaited this, and then was sewed and pressed in a shape on a block. We usually made these hats in the shape of flats, and for trimming made ornaments of palmetto, or bunches of wheat and rye. They were quite becoming to a fresh young face. Oh, but the shoes we wore! When I think of those clumsy, pegged shoes, with soles so thick and hard, and they would not bend, I wonder how we ever walked or danced! Bet we did both. We knit our own stockings. I don't mean we children, but our women. They were made from cotton with black silk. We would dye our stockings or wear them white.

The candles we were made from tallow, wax, and china berries, which were combined in some mysterious way and poured into candle molds. We used more fat lightwood for lights than anything else. Even in summer, a pine fire lit up our parlors, and we often danced by this light, which was quite bright, though a trifle warm.

I must tell you of a dear little spinning wheel my mother had made for me, for I was very fond of spinning, and made my task every day during our summer holidays. Then I would go to the reel and put my thread into hanks. I tried to keep pace with our Negro women in spinning. I never learned to weave cloth, but guess if the war had lasted much longer, I would have learned that, too.

The war time girl had not candy, soda water, ice cream, etc., like you girls have. No, we did not know the taste of these dainties. There was an old man in town who made very nice sassafras and peppermint candy, but our pennies were few and far between, and it was not often that we indulged in such luxuries. When we got unusually hungry for something good, we would get Mother's recipe book, *The Carolina Housewife*, and read all the good recipes we could find. I must say this was rather tantalizing to a hungry set of children. A biscuit would have been good for us, if we could have gotten one. Sometimes we had them, but these occasions were red letter days.

While this was going on at home, my father and friends were in Virginia fighting many hard battles, and gaining many victories, and sometimes getting defeated. After each battle, there was an anxious waiting for news, and paper were eagerly scanned for accounts of battle, and names of wounded and dead. Then we gathered in our little church, or at our fireside, and earnest prayers would be sent up for our dear ones. In times of trouble, God seems very near to his children! Our dear father surely had a charmed life. While friends and kinsman fell wounded or dead, he passed through battle after battle unscathed. During the entire war, he was never touched by a bullet, although on one occasion his horse was shot from under him. He was always at the head of his troops and fought in all those terrible battles in Virginia. He was promoted to brigadier general, and afterwards to major general. Months would go by, and he could not get off to see us. Sometimes a year would pass away without a sight of his dear face. Then, we would grow desperate. One night I was lying in bed with Mother, talking about Father. Finally, I said: "Mother, I am going to write to General Longstreet, and ask him to let Father come home." After coming to that conclusion, I fell asleep. A day or two after this, I did write to General Longstreet, and after waiting for some time, received an answer from the general, written by himself. I felt very proud to think that a man so occupied as the general was, should have taken the trouble to write a little girl. He spoke so highly of my father and of his services to his country that we were much gratified.

He said: "I cannot possibly spare your father at this time, but as soon as he can be spared, I will let him come home to see his little girl." We lived on this promise for about a month, and then to our great joy, our Father was with us for a while. All clouds, all trouble seemed to fly when he was with us. He would look after our comfort and make provision for us during his absence, which would soon come. How wives lived during those days, I cannot think! The uncertainty, the dread, the suspense, and awful separation! Somehow, they lived through it. My mother was a little past thirty — too young, I think, to have such heavy burdens on her, and on one to help or sympathize with her. Our old Mammy was her greatest comfort during those sad days. One-day Mammy came into my mother's room and found her on her knees by her bedside praying and weeping bitterly. She came up to the bed, knelt beside my mother, put her arms around her and wept with her. I have heard my mother say that she was never more touched in her life than by this act. We were too young to be a comfort to her in just that protecting way that she needed. Dear old Mammy! She has gone to her rest, but her kind deeds and loving care are still remembered by us, and her memory is sacred to the children she nursed and loved!

About twenty miles from our home, there lived a wealthy farmer, from whom my mother sometimes was able to get provisions and sorghum. He was a friend of my father, though a plain country farmer. On one of his visits to town, he asked my mother if my sister Charlotte and I could not back with him and spend a week. After much persuasion, my mother consented. That afternoon my sister, my maid, Eliza, and I got in Captain K's carriage, and away we went for a week's visit, Mother and sister, Mary, promising to come for us at the end of that time. Captain K had a wife and one- granddaughter living with him. We were soon perfectly at home in the old farmhouse. I shall never forget the pleasures of that visit; everything was so new and strange. This was our first visit to the country, and everything was delightful. Mrs. K. was a notable housewife and took pride in showing us her weaving room and all the beautiful homespun she had stored away. Such fried chicken, hot biscuits, and fresh butter beans I have seldom tasted. We rode horseback to the post office and to see the neighbors, and would come in with ravenous appetites, and did full justice, by emptying dishes prepared for us. The days were not long enough for all the delights, and at night, we went to our beds tired out, and with a vague feeling of homesickness stealing over us. Finally, our tired eyes would close, and we would soon be in the land of dreams. It was during the Indian Summer that we paid this visit. The moon shone brilliantly, and the captain kept his hands working until quite late at night, gathering corn. One night, after we had gone upstairs to bed, we heard coming across the fields, the song of the Negroes as they loaded the wagons with corn. It sounded very sweet but plaintative. I could scarcely keep back my tears, and my heart swelled as I listened to the weird sound floating to us through the soft night air. We happened to be there one Sunday. The church was about five or six miles from the K's. After breakfast, some of us got into the carriage, while others rode horseback to the meeting house. All the neighborhood gathered there, each family bringing a basket of dinner. The preacher, a plain country man, got very much wrought up and prayed and exhorted until the whole congregation was in tears. Finally, he called on the sinners to come forward and kneel at the altar, where they wept and prayed. This was all new to me. I had never seen anything like it before. After a time, the congregation was dismissed, and had a recess. They gathered around the spring chatting and eating their luncheon. Our party was invited to dine at a neighbor's house, where a bountiful dinner was served — the chief dishes being chicken pot pie, hot biscuit, apple pie, and buttermilk. After this meal, we went back to the church, where we had an evening service, then home again through the autumn evening, to a hot supper, comfortable bed, and dreams of home. The happy days sped swiftly, and soon our visit was ended. Mother and Sister Mary came for us, and, after spending a night and day, we bid good-bye to our kind farmer friends, and were on our way homeward. This was the last we ever saw of this family. War made sad havoc with them. When Sherman passed through that region, he made his headquarters at the captain's; when the raid was over, the once prosperous farmer had to go where the horses were fed, and gather up corn for his family to eat. According to Union records, Union soldiers stayed at this plantation (Captain Wiley Kelly) for only two to three days. But another story has come to light concerning this plantation. This article was in *The Camden Chronicle*, April 13, 1900.

A Treasure Unearthed

During the Civil War, from 1861 to 1865, many and various plans were adopted on searching for family relics, valuables, gold and silver, from the Yankees, who were coming through South Carolina. Often these hiding places were found and the family left poor and sad. It would make interesting reading to relate here some of the methods used by the folks at home in deceiving the shrewd Yankees as to where the hidden treasures were. But the purpose of this article is to tell of the burial of a treasure by Captain Wiley Kelly during those times, and who, in his haste, forgot to mark the spot where the gold and valuables were buried, and never in his life could find the place, though search after search was made, and hole after hole dug in the swamp of Lynches River. Finally, it became a burden on the old gentleman's mind, and his mental equilibrium became unbalanced. He passed away on December 25, 1873. (*The Camden Journal*, Jan 1, 1874)

Captain Kelly was a prominent citizen of Kershaw County, and a wealthy planter, owning most of the land in eastern Kershaw. His relatives are numerous, Mr. Parrot McNeese, of our town, a great grandson, and Mr. Alex Kelly, of Timmonsville, a grandson, and other relatives in Bishopville and in the west.

Captain Kelly is known to have buried about $500 in gold, several diamond rings, and valuable papers. He also had some money given him for safe keeping by the Bank of Camden. Captain Kelly had no warning of the approach of the Yankees on that dark, dreary night, and had but few minutes to gather his gold and fix it in a pot. He sprang into the saddle of a spirited horse and dashed down the road across Kelly's Bridge, and turned into the swamp on the left, where he dismounted and buried it with a hoe carried for that purpose. In his excitement, he neglected to mark the spots. The Yankees made his place their camping ground for several weeks, and when they left he went for the gold, which he never could find, nor other parties from all over the county.

On or about the first of March of this year (1900), a well-known lady of that community was walking behind a wagon on the road that leads to the left from the bridge, when she noticed that one of the wheels had struck a piece of iron outside of the rut and upon further investigation found the treasure that was buried years ago, gold, rings, and all.

One evening a crowd of girls (our friends) proposed that we should get up by five o'clock the next morning and go out to the creek I told you of and take a bath. We eagerly consented. We were to meet at that early hour near our homes, at a central corner, each girl promising to be there on time. When I got up, I found my sisters not inclined to get up just yet. Nothing daunted I started out, but on reaching the rendezvous, found only one girl there. We concluded that we would let the laziness of the others spoil our fun but would go the Thomas farm and get one of the girls to go with us. Happily, we jogged along until we reached the farm, where disappointment awaited us. The girls were too busy at that hour and could not be spared. We gritted our teeth and determined not to be out done. We were very much frightened at the idea of going into the dark, silent woods alone, but did not confess it to each other. We bravely marched into the pine forest, and after going for about half a mile, came upon a swamp that enclosed our bathing place. We looked all around to see that no runaway Negroes were near, then undressed, and walking on the pine log that led to the stream, we cautiously let ourselves dive into the clear, cool water, catching our breaths, and grasping each other in pure terror. We went on a little farther, dipping into the water now and again, each time looking around to see if any eyes were upon us, fearing to make a sound, even the water dripping from us into the stream terrifying is beyond measure. When we had worked ourselves to a high pitch of excitement, we chanced to hear a weird, dismal sound penetrating the swamp, and filling it with its mournful cries, which reverberated through the lonely place. This was too much for us; we simply flew to the place where we had left our clothes, flung them on, and without looking to right or left, we ran breathless to the Thomas house. Oh, no, we did not tell them we were afraid or had not enjoyed our bath! The sound we heard was only an owl, but it frightened us so that we never ventured into those woods again unless well attended. When we reached home, we found that one of our Negroes had died that morning, and we were sure the owl had come to tell us of her death. The Negroes are very superstitious and think that, if a screech owl cries, it means certain death. The southern children who were white were superstitious too from a long association with their nurses. We would sit with eyes wide open, and cold chills running down our backs, listening, never doubting a word of the story, and 'specting to see a spirit every time we had to go alone in the dark. It took me years to overcome my fears of ghosts and goblins.

One summer during the war, Mother went to Virginia to spend a month or two with Father, taking Charlotte with her. Mary and I spent the time with our Aunt Ella, who kindly took charge of us during Mother's absence. There were several cousins, girls and boys near our own age, in the house with us, and we should have been very happy. Mary, I think, enjoyed herself much more than I did. I was so homesick and missed Mother and Charlotte so much that I could not enter always in the amusements and pleasures of the others. I would sit in a little closet and think of them and picture what they were doing. I am afraid many tears were shed in that little closet. After a time, the girls would come and rout me out from my hiding place, and away we would go. Sometimes it would be to coax Maum Daphne to make us some sweet biscuit, sometimes to gather vegetables, and make a pot of okra and tomato soup; often to get Uncle Edmund to tell us a story. (Uncle Edmund was the carriage driver.)

Aunt Ella's husband was a doctor and a dear old gentleman. He had a plantation of a few miles from town called Hard Scramble, perhaps because the hills were hard to scramble up, or perhaps it was a scramble to make a living on the sandy soil. At any rate, on several occasions, we had a pleasant day's outing at Hard Scramble. The old-fashioned carriage, which went by the name of Cooter, was ordered out, and the crowd of girls, and perhaps a boy or two, would climb up the high steps to the carriage, the door closed, and away Uncle Jim would drive us, a merry crew singing song after song: "Old blind horse come tearing out of the wilderness …," "Shell corn, Fort Sumter's gone." "Maryland," and so forth until the woods rang again. After a short time, the old plantation with its rows of Negro cabins, is in sight, and soon we are at the gate and surrounded by a crowd of Negroes, large and small. We scatter over the place visiting the Negro women, running down the hill to the old grist mill, fishing in the clear brook, where the sun shines on the pebbles making them look like gold; finally, off to the shoes and stocking, and with dresses held up, with shrieks of delight, we wade up and down the cool, sparkling stream. Nothing can equal the delights of wading in a brook! After a time, we are forced by the pangs of hunger to leave the water and return to the quarters, where Aunt Charlotte, a fat comfortable Mama, has prepared for our enjoyment a huge pot of gumbo and rice, a dish she well knew how to cook. The hungry children soon are contentedly devouring this dainty and have not time for words until the last mouthful has disappeared. More fun and frolic after this meal is eaten; then Uncle Jim warns us it is time to go home, and reluctantly we bid the Negroes good-bye, and are speeding home again with song and laughter.

Now while we children were enjoying life as children do, our brave soldier boys were fighting against great odds. Hungry, half-clad, they fought bravely on. Our hospitals were filled with sick and wounded. In our town, the poor fellows were looked after as well as our small means would allow. We had, at that time, a good cow which furnished us with milk and butter. The poor fellows at the hospital soon found their way to our door, where our mother gladly filled their canteens with fresh buttermilk, and when we had it, with hot corn bread to go with the buttermilk. About this time, there were rumors of the raid of the dread Sherman. Our hearts quailed within us. Steps were taken to place what valuables we had in places of safety. We knew not where to turn or what to do. Our kind doctor advised Mother to send her valuables up to Lynches' Creek, where he thought they would be safe. Our wagon was soon loaded with things, and old Jake sent off to hide in the woods until the raid was over. The doctor took our silver and jewels along with his own and carried them to the home of Captain Kelly. In the dead of night, they dug up the basement floor in the captain's cellar, dug a great hole, and buried our treasures. It was a valuable deposit, being the silver and jewelry of five sisters. One of the sisters was the doctor's wife. This mission had to be done very secretly as the Negroes were not to be trusted.

One morning we were on our front piazza; looking up, we saw a soldier being pursued by half a dozen others on horseback, firing pistols every minute. The pursued soldier all of a sudden just disappeared. I cannot see how he escaped. The pursuers soon alighted and were filling the house of a neighbor over the way. Then we realized that Sherman's raid was on. Our yard was filled with raiders in a few minutes. My mother went to the back door to meet them (the children following with curiosity). One big fellow was the first to approach. Our Dear Mother was white and trembling as she met this giant, but found the courage to ask him would he come in. To our amazement, he hesitated, looked down at himself and said, "Well, I aren't fit to come in where ladies are!" This disarmed us and gave us courage. In the meantime, the crowd in the yard were killing our chickens, drawing water from the well, and making themselves at home. Our servants were pressed into service and made to cook for our visitors. We had no dinner that day. They asked for the keys of our store room and went to make a raid. They opened the door and found only a peck of meal and a few pounds of bacon, they locked the door and mercifully left us our scanty store, which was much needed. The entire day was one of excitement and anxiety. We had in our yard a large, fat gobbler, which we had been treasuring. When the raiders left, having caught our chickens, we children ran out and caught the turkey, before it could be stolen, and carried it upstairs, and locked it in a room. Later, we killed it. The fate of our gobbler will be told herein after. First, one group of Yankees and then another were coming in all day. Very tired and faint from hunger, we sat, waiting. We knew not for what. One bunch of Yankee came in during the day demanding food. A dish of rice boiled with bacon was all we had to offer them. After they had eaten, there was a small portion left, which was set aside. Toward evening my poor little stomach ached for food. I thought of the rice which was left until I could stand it no longer. I got it out, and without once thinking of by whom it was left, fell to and made quite a hearty meal. I could not induce my younger sister to taste it, she being more squeamish than I.

During Sherman's raid in Columbia, when the city was in flames and women and children were fleeing for their lives, a certain Captain McKenzie of Sherman's army did many noble deeds for the stricken southern people. There lived across the street from us a family, who had relatives living in Columbia, and it was for this family that Captain McKenzie was instrumental in saving their home during the great fire. With his own hands, he assisted Dr. R. in putting out the fire on his roof. Dr. R. sent a message to his relatives in Camden and advised them to seek protection from this brave captain. They passed the word to my mother — the captain and his headquarters at the hotel. Summoning on one of her trusted slaves, my mother handed him a note, telling him to deliver it to Captain McKenzie. The answer to this note was delivered by the captain himself. He was kind enough to visit our home, and to assure my mother of his protection. He said that no one should molest her. After his visit, he threw his overcoat on the lounge in the dining room and left. In the meantime, we had killed our turkey, roasted it, and were just about to eat it, when on looking toward the big window at the end of the room, to our terror, we saw two villainous Yankees on horseback, peering through the window into the room. In a trice, we picked up a dish of turkey and shoved it as far back under the sideboard as we could get it and resumed our seats. We had scarcely taken our seats when the two half-drunk men blundered in. To say we were frightened does not express our feelings. These bullies had found out whose family lived at the house. They flourished their riding whips over Mother's head, almost in her face, in a most threatening manner. They said, "By rights, the house should be burned down." My mother sat as quickly as she could, then said, "Your captain has offered me his protection. He has been here and has left his coat on the sofa." It was a gorgeous affair of blue broadcloth, gilt braid, and brass buttons. I wish you could have seen the change that came over these creatures! In a moment they fairly cringed and left much subdued. After they went, we got out the dish of turkey and resumed our feast. Night came at last, a night of terror. No rest and no sleep. We dared not go to bed. The whole town as far as we could see was in flames. Wherever cotton or commissary stores were housed, these were set on fire, and the flames spread to surrounding buildings. Stores were thrown open, goods thrown into the streets to be trampled on by horses. Negroes were told to go and help themselves from stores. If they hesitated, they were urged on at that point by the bayonet. From an upstairs window, our little family watched the destruction of our town. All night could be seen crowds of Negroes carrying huge bundles of loot on their heads. About nine o'clock on that awful night, we were sitting around the fire when we heard a loud noise at the front. Our hearts stood still with fear, but finally we got courage enough to go to the door. It proved to be the two drunk men who had visited us during the day. They were very solicitous as to our comfort and tried to ride their horses up their steps to inquire if we needed their help. You may rest assured they were not allowed to enter the house.

My brother, a lad of sixteen years of age, was with his father in Virginia. Mother and her three little girls were left unprotected during all that stormy time. Sherman's entire army did not pass through Camden. After leaving Columbia, a part of the army passed through Winnsboro, while the other part came through our time. The road for miles along the route of the army was a scene of desolation and destruction. The road was strewn from Camden to Lynches Creek, and all along the route, with dead fowls, pigs, and food of all kinds, which our people needed sorely. The wagon train that was sent to Lynches Creek for safety, fell into the handle of the raiding party. Nothing was saved. Sometime after the raid, our kind doctor went up to see for himself, fearing the worst. I am thankful to say those things buried under Captain Kelly's house was saved and returned to their owners. Poor Captain Kelly suffered great losses at this time. All his provisions, horses, and stock were taken. During this raid, the soldiers would open a man's smokehouse, take what they wanted, then open barrels of molasses, flour, meat, and pour the contents on the ground floor of the smoke house, making such a mess of it that it was of no use to the poor farmers. Starvation stared us in the face.

After Sherman's raid, our people settled down once more for a quiet life. Not for long were we to be felt in peace and quiet. In the wake of Sherman were bummers from our own army, who committed many depredations. They stole and terrorized the country as they passed through. Fortunately, their stay was short.

We did not enjoy peace for long, for another raid was expected, that from Potter's raid. Our silver had just been brought home. We knew not where to hide it or what to do with it. As this time, we had two sick Negroes in the yard. It was our custom to read to the them when sick. Several days before the raid was expected, one sister was sent to read to the sick, one to watch while Mother and I took the silver, put it in a crocus sack, and, as we sat quietly as possible, dropped it into the well. The other servants were sent off on errands, so no one saw us when we hid the silver. We girls gathered our few treasures together and gave them to our little maids for safe keeping. One afternoon, I was sitting on the top of the woodshed, reading "Guy Mannering," when I heard the sound of shouting, yelling, and singing in the distance, gradually getting nearer and nearer. The shouting of a great crowd! I got down quickly to where old Mammy was standing. She was crying. I said, "Mammy, what is the matter?" She said, "Damn Yankees is coming and will carry me off!" I begged her, "Mammy, please go to bed and pretend you are sick, and then they will not take you!" Soon the town was thrown into a state of great excitement. From our backyard, we watched the approach of his army. Soldiers on horseback, wagons drawn by four mules, men, women, and children on foot — a motley crowd. As this raid passed through the country, the Negroes from the plantations were carried off in wagons from the farms. By the time they reached Camden, a vast crowd was collected. All were screaming and shouting lustily, singing as they went, "Hang Jeff Davis on a Sour Apple Tree as We Go Marching On!" It was truly terrifying. They camped in a grove and in lots just back of our house. In less time than it takes to write this, there was not a fence standing, and camp fires were soon burning. Our yard, being so near, was run over by the raiders. Our cooks and servants cooking all night for them, our well bucket going up and down continually. The rabble soon made themselves very much at home. Just about dark, a soldier came to our door, a sergeant, and asked my mother for milk. She took his canteen and filled it with nice, rich milk, fresh from our little cow. In exchange for the milk, he handed her a crisp bill, the first greenback I had ever seen. Mother refused to take pay for the milk. The soldier then said," No one shall molest you this night. You can go to bed. I shall guard this house." All night long, true to his word, the soldier kept guard over us. One good deed deserves another.

Potter must have heard that Wheeler's Cavalry was on the way, for very early next morning, the camp was astir, wagons and horses ready for the march. As we watched these preparations for departure, we noticed queer doings in the servant's quarters. Our old bodyguard, Uncle Ben, stood in his room packing his belongings in a large bag, while his daughter, our beloved Mary Ann, assisted him. Mother said, "Ben, what are you doing?" The old man said, "Well, Missis, day all is going, I thought I must go to." Then, my Mother stood up and told them all that they were free and could go if they wanted to. It must have hurt her to see Uncle Ben leaving, for he had taken care of us ever since father left us. Then, the greatest blow of all fell. One of the women had a little son named "Sumter." One morning just after the Battle of Fort Sumter, Amelia sent me word, by one of the little maids: "Tell Miss Harriet, I have a little nigger boy for her." I named him Sumter. We all loved this child and petting him. He was treated as our own. He came to Mother, where we were watching the departure of the raiders, and she took him up in her arms. To our amazement, Amelia, the mother, came on the piazza, where we were standing, went up to the child, who was clinging to my Mother, and tore him out of her arms. We did not realize what was happening. Soon, we saw that Amelia was going off with my little Sumter. He screamed and cried for me, calling my name. I was powerless to help him. The child was desperate, fought and scratched his mother, and broke from her two or three times, running back to me. It was a sad sight. As Amelia went with the child, our neighbors joined with us in sympathy, and many tears fell for the child. I was indeed heart broken. The passed in some ways, the town quiet after the departure of the enemy. Towards evening, to our great surprise, Amelia, with Eliza and Sumter, her two children, came back. She failed to join Potter. The army had crossed the river before she could join them. She came home, but Mother would not allow her to stay in the yard after she behaved to badly in the morning. Eliza and Sumter stayed with us for some time but joined their mother later. That was the last I ever saw of the child. I heard many years later that he met with a tragic death.

News traveled very slowly in those days, letters taking weeks to reach their destination; railroad tracks and telegraph lines out of commission, destroyed by the enemy. Rumors of Lee's surrender drifted in. We could not or would not believe that such a terrible disaster had really happened. Soon, bands of soldiers drifted in on the way to their homes, confirming the reports of the surrender. A ragged, weary body of men, returning, after years of hard fighting and privations of every kind, to their ruined homes and farms, to begin anew the struggle for a living. Nothing to look forward to, no stock and no money. Labor at a premium with slaves feeling their freedoms, so they refused to work. The entire South in poverty. These weary ones often stopped at our hospital for rest on their homeward journey. One afternoon as I was walking up the street on which we lived, I saw, sitting on the carriage block before one of the houses, a poor sick soldier. He was evidently very ill; in fact, he was having a hemorrhage from his lungs. I could not stand the sight or the thought of this fellow's sufferings. I ran as fast as I could back home, and begged Mother please to send her buggy to take this man to the hospital. Always ready to do a kind deed, my mother sent for the soldier and he was carried to the hospital. I could not rest for thinking of this poor boy, lonely and suffering. My next request was for the boy to be brought to our home to be nursed by us. To my joy, dear mother consented, and the young artillery man was duly installed on our poor, but hospitable home. The guest room was prepared for him, and the best the house afforded offered him. He was a beautiful boy. Secretly, I fell in love with him, and would lay little offerings of flowers in his room. His heart was not for me. He cared for my elder sister. We took care of him until he was strong enough to go on his journey. While he was with us, we asked him to try to get our silver from the well. It had been lying there ever since Potter's raid. It puzzled us to know just how to get about taking the silver out. Finally, we took the pothooks from the kitchen, tied them on a rope, and after several attempts, up came the crocus sack. The silver was bruised and black, otherwise intact. Our soldier boy left us after a time, going down the river in a small boat, to his home in Georgetown. I have often wondered about this boy. We never heard from him after he left us.

The refugees from Charleston and Beaufort, who had been with us during the war, returned to their homes, homes destroyed by shot and shell. These former wealthy people, the best in the land, were reduced to poverty.

Their homes gone, their slaves freed, and their household goods stolen. What had they to go home to? Nothing remained to the South but a wonderful courage and bravery to build up their beloved South land.

My father was at Sailor's Creek on the dreadful day when Lee surrendered; my brother, a lad, was with him. Father was with Longstreet. He was taken prisoner along with my brother at the same time. He was taken before General Custer and treated with the greatest courtesy. He gave up his beautiful spurs and sword, a heartbroken soldier, to his captor. After that awful day, Custer invited my father to stay the night with him, sharing his food and his bed. Still left was my mother's silver. This she generously gave for the trousseau and so forth. The silver, which was all battered from having been thrown into the well, and blackened by contact with the water, was boxed up and sent to Baltimore to be sold. In due time, the silver was sold, the money received, and the trousseau purchased. A grand, old time supper was served, with champagne and wine. A real "before the war" feast, nothing lacking from turkey oysters and so forth, to jellies, syllabub, Charlotte Russe, and cakes of all descriptions.

After several months, my mother received a box from Baltimore containing the entire set of silver, beautifully done over, as good as new, and sent to her as a gift. The silver had been bought by a company and returned to my mother from these gentlemen. NO names were mentioned, so we did not know who to thank for so generous a gift. This silver has been handed down to the children, who will prize it most highly.

Just after the war, the South was put under martial rule. Camden is laid off in blocks, with wide streets and parks. In the park near our home, soldiers encamped. I well remember the bugles sounding revelry at dawn and taps at evening time. Then next we had the Freedom's Bureau, where all differences between whites and blacks were settled. Fortunately for us, the captain in charge was a just man who usually adjusted matters impartially. Next came the notorious Carpet Baggers and the Scalawags. The South was overrun by these creatures. The Negroes was promised wonderful things, each man was promised forty acres and a mule. One day a gentleman riding over his plantation, saw a Negro measuring off land. He asked him, "What are you doing?" He answered, "I am measuring off my forty acres." The white men had few privileges, and the polls was practically closed to the whites. Our legislature was composed of blacks and carpetbaggers and scalawags. Our farmers trying to make a living were heavily taxed. Every bale of cotton of cotton was taxed five dollars, and no cotton could be sold until the tax was paid. Things went on in this way until 1876, when the entire state rose as to one man and put General Wade Hampton in the Governor's seat.

An Account of the Experiences of the Family of the Reverend and Mrs. Trapier During and After the War Between the States.

"Transcription reprinted by permission from the South Carolina Historical Society"

YOU ASK ME TO GIVE you some account of our family during and since the war and I will do so, as it will give you some idea of the situation of thousands of others, like our own.

At the commencement of the war, we numbered twelve (my husband and myself and ten children) of these all were girls, except three and one of these is a little boy of nine years of age. Our eldest son, our comfort and stay, always delicate from childhood, but brave of spirit and strong in faith, entered the army at the age off eighteen. Our hearts sank within us as we thought of the sufferings and trials thenceforth to be the lot of one so delicately nurtured so fondly cherished. Little did we know how fearfully were those forebodings to be realized. The first year of the war, we never saw him, but he bore up wonderfully under the hardships, fatigues and want of food which he constantly endured. And our hearts were cheered by letters full of ardent patriotism, constant hope, and patient endurance. Winning by his gentlemanly deportment and faithful discharge of his duties the unqualified approval of his commander and the affectionate esteem of his fellow soldiers. At the end of that time constant exposure brought on the fever of the climate and he returned home feeble and emaciated, but we nursed him with the tenderest care, and home joys and home sympathies acted like a charm and he returned to camp brave and hopeful as ever.

In the meantime, our second son pursued his studies at home and aided his father in every possible way, until the third year of the war when, at the age of seventeen, he too entered the army.

My husband, as you know, is a clergyman. He came to our present home advanced in years and broken down in constitution by twenty-five years of laborious ministerial duty. As professor in the theological seminary of our church in this Diocese, he received a salary of $1500. We owned the house we lived in and the income from our other property amounted to about $2000. So that at the commencement of the war, our large family were able with economy to live comfortably. We knew that this could not last, but we knew the cause to be a righteous one and we gave ourselves to it, expecting and prepared to suffer.

My children seemed born patriots, descended on the father's side from those who had distinguished themselves in the first revolution and on the mother's side from those who had driven out of France during the Reign of Terror, had become broken-hearted by oppression and suffering. The love of liberty and independence seemed a part of their nature. You will not wonder that they gave themselves heart and soul to the work. The chamber of my grown daughters was soon stripped of the carpet from the floor and the curtains from the bed, and even a part of their warm winter, covering went to minister to the comfort of the poor suffering soldiers. They knit at even their meals to supply stockings for our army. I had then four sweet little girls. They called themselves "Us Four," and everyone knew them by that name. Well do I remember the delight with which they packed their first box for the hospital. They earned money by making little fancy articles, and with this they purchased comforts for the hospitals then crowded with the sick and dying.

During the first year of the war, these children earned in this way between 50 and 60 dollars. The second year of the war, our income from the Theological Seminary was withdrawn for a time as its exercises were discontinued, because of the enlisting of all the Students in the Army and everything advanced in price- But success then waited on our banners and we began cheerfully to deny ourselves many of the comforts we had been accustomed to from childhood, we were at no expense for education, my eldest daughter instructing the younger sisters and their little brother. My husband worked daily in the garden and thus supplied us with many little comforts. He tried at one time to teach a boy's school. But his strength failed, and after three months, he was obliged to give it up. Providentially at the next meeting of our Diocesan Convention, it was generously resolved to continue the salaries of the professors, and our income became again more nearly adequate to our expenses. The third year of the war, the taxes became enormous, eating up our entire income, and obliging us to live on our capital. Our younger brother. then Rector of St. Phillips Church died this year, worn out by incessant labours for his flock *and* for the sick, the wounded and dying at the hospitals. His family (a wife and two children) came to us and are with us now. Our capital was invested largely in Confederate and as the only currancy was in Confederate notes, which were at a great discount. We were sinking more and more of our means. Still we never dreamed of the failure of our glorious Cause, and we therefore willingly and cheerfully submitted to increased privations. Tea and sugar and butter were luxuries reserved for sickness.

Often have we been without fresh meat for months, and dessert or sweet things of any kind. I have seen the little children sit down with all of us to a dinner of a shred of bacon, hominy or rice, with some preparation of corn, and get up hungry but without a murmur — yea with smiling faces assuring us that they would be only the more healthy for going without sweet things for their Country's sake, and sometimes they would amuse themselves with descriptions of the wonderful things they would enjoy when *peace* and independence were attained. Alas this year a great sorrow came upon them: The little band of "Us Four" was broken - Our Lillie, the darling of our hearts, sickened and died. Weeks of suffering and anguish, nights of burning fever, had appointed her. God bless the warm Southern hearts that helped us in this dark hour out of their own scanty store: So generously, so unweariedly: Little cups of sugar, papers of tea, a few spoonfuls of arrowroot, little supplies of milk, pats of butter garnished with sweet flowers, would bring a faint smile on her wan face. Especially would we cherish with ever-fresh gratitude the readings with which a gentleman, twelve miles from us, an entire stranger, offered us the free use of his private ice house, into which he had collected with great trouble for the use of his own family and of sick and wounded soldiers, that most refreshing and rarest of comforts in the then condition of our Confederacy - Nor can we forget the kindness of neighbours, who knowing that we had no means of sending for it placed their own servants and horses at our disposal, thereby affording to our dear child the very relish she had been longing for most, and relished most highly.

How hard it was to give her up! She had been with us in all our struggles. How sorely we should miss her when the hour of triumph came! Short sighted affection! Her Heavenly Father knew better. Gradually He reconciled her to the parting. At first it was "Pray for me, Mamma, that I may be better. How can I give you all up? How can I go to the far distant land?" But towards the last a great change came over her. "I want to die. Pray for me that I may continue His forever and daily increase in His Holy Spirit more and more, until I come to His Heavenly Kingdom …" To that "better Country" she has gone, and now that we have no other Country and labour awaits those that remain, we know that "He doeth all things well."

I now pass to the last year of the war. Our pecuniary embarrassments were greatly increased. No clothing could be procured but at an enormous expense. Early in the war we received from Europe through the kindness of a friend, a box containing clothing and the materials for making it up, which proved the greatest possible help to our large family. But this was now nearly exhausted, and the servants were greatly in need. I made coats of carpet for the women and managed to get a suit apiece for the men. My own younger children went without shoes so soon as the weather was warm enough. Dark clouds now gathered round us. Instead of hearing of victories, the tidings were often of defeat. From the moment of General Joseph E. Johnston's removal from the command of the army of the West, our doom seemed sealed. As soon as Sherman got into the interior, the difficulty of procuring food for our armies became more and more serious—Our men, however, had learned endurance—They could have borne personal privations. But now a merciless horde was let loose upon the defenseless wives and children of our soldiers. Daily accounts were reaching them of these fearful raids, which left behind nothing but starvation desolation and dishonour! Ah, little do you know the love, the veneration the Southern soldier feels for women! Throughout this war, she has been his guardian-angel, his tender nurse, her prayers strengthened him in his weakness, her sympathy soothing him in his sorrows, her patient example nerving him to self-denial and endurance, her voice encouraging him to deeds of noble daring- Now these loved ones were to be exposed, alone and helpless, to the insults of lawless ruffians, to the lusts of brutal Negroes – can it be wondered that his heart failed him, that his spirit was crushed? Outnumbered by many thousands, food failing, should he persevere in a struggle which must end in defeat, or should he flee to the protection of all he had now to live for? Up to this time our family had not been visited by any of these fearful raiders. But about the month of January, rumours came of their approach. About the same time, we learned that our eldest son Theodore was ill in Columbia. After an examination by the Board of Surgeons there he was sent home on a furlough of sixty days. He had been sick a long time, but had endured, it patiently till a violent cold brought on a fever with derangement of the liver, spleen and stomach. We were shocked by his emaciation. But we nursed him tenderly and he recovered slowly not *as* on previous occasions of illness, for now the buoyancy of hope was gone.

About the thirteenth of February we heard of the evacuation of Charleston, then of the advance of the enemy upon Columbia. All day on the twentieth we could hear the booming of the cannon and the night of the twenty-first the sky was lighted up by the blaze from the conflagration of that beautiful but ill-fated city, the smoke from which obscured the declining sun of the following day- With sad hearts we began to prepare for our turn, our suffering from the same ruthless savages, who had thus sacked and destroyed our capital.

Hastily we gathered together what we valued most and set ourselves to conceal these in the dead of the night, and night after night, when all others were asleep did my husband and son and nephew, steal out, as if on dark deed intent to secure what of right was theirs, or entrusted to them and groping their way, with scarcely tight enough to see where they were, endeavoured to hide in the ground the silver and jewels which they knew would be tempting to the cupidity of the marauders, who were to be soon among us- Especially had they to be cautious as the Negroes, it was known, were on the look out to appropriate to themselves, or discover to the enemy what would else have escaped the closest search of the latter. We lived on the outskirts of the town of Camden, and unfortunately next to a family of Jews of very bad character. They kept a grocery store in the town where they had large quantities of liquor. This they had been wagoning in open day to their yard and burying in a large pit within sight and with the help of the Negroes. Thus, a new and horrible danger added to our fearful anticipations.

The question pressing most heavily upon us was as to what was to be done with our son. He was feeble. If he stayed he might be carried off as a prisoner or shot. There was no hospital here for him to go — and as it was expected that the enemy would approach in one direction, and perhaps not in very large force, it was determined, on *the* advice of military men that he should go out on horseback and conceal himself in the woods until the advancing army should have passed by. One of our slaves, a boy who had been brought up with him and who he trusted would prove faithful, was to accompany him *and* take charge of the provisions for themselves *and* horses, but what a change from the tender nursing of mother and sisters to cold and rain, privation and fatigue and harrowing anxiety about us. Poor boy! I remember well how worn and sad he looked when he threw himself on the bed beside me *and* exclaimed, "How I should like to rest here for a year!" Alas he had not rested an hour when the servants came rushing in crying out. "The Yankees are in the town!" He jumped up and we all ran down stairs with him. His father was out on one of the horses trying to find out in what direction they were coming, but the other horse was soon saddled. The haversack and blankets were placed on it, and with one hurried kiss and a "God bless you," he went towards the stable. His faithful nurse followed him. And on his return, she said. "Poor fellow! He was so weak he had to be helped on the horse." He left word for his father that he would wait in an adjoining wood for the boy with the provisions. In about half an hour, his father returned and reported that the Yankees were in Camden. Hurrying the boy off, he joined him in the wood. Here after making such arrangements as he could for our sons comfort his father with a heavy heart parted from him commending him to his God and to the care of the servant who seemed to be greatly alarmed. What a sad circle gathered round the fire that evening! Before we retired to bed, however, we were somewhat relieved by hearing that the report of the enemy's being in the town was false, they were still a few miles distant. The next morning everything seemed tranquil. My little Edith was, however, quite sick and several of us were in the chamber with her, when about two o'clock, one of the little girls going to the window, exclaimed, "Why here is Teedy (Theodore) coming back!" "No", said another, "that man has a blue coat." "The Yankees! The Yankees!" we ail cried out. The children rushed down stairs to their papa, while I stayed a few, moments to soothe the sick child, who became very much agitated. When one reached the parlor, I found my sister (Mrs. Dehon), my four grown daughters, my niece and the younger children assembled. Not the slightest symptom of fear or agitation appeared. Several armed men were in the room, demanding weapons. "By what authority do you demand arms of women and children?" said my eldest daughter. "By authority, madam, of the United States," said the officer, apparently a sergeant in command. "I have seen" he added, "many Confederate women, who would as soon shoot a Yankee as eat a dinner." Just then, my husband came in. He had been taken at the gate, to which he had gone to meet the first of this troop, and they had at first spoken of taking him to the General. But after whispering together for a while, they had told him he must come with them into the house and give up whatever arms were there. He had told them he had no arms about him, meaning on his person, and they now accused him of lying, when they found there were arms in the house. He repelled the accusation indignantly, but they persisted in it more and more rudely. When all the weapons of every sort that we had were produced they took them to the front of the house and broke the barrels of the guns by striking them on the post of the piazza, excepting a very superior double-barrel gun of my nephew's which the sergeant took a fancy to and carried off. This is the way. They said, "We do with the arms of rebels. We were now all assembled in the piazza, ten helpless women and children. My husband standing bare-headed on the steps, his gray hairs and noble, dignified and fearless mien our only earthly protection- crowds of soldiers, mostly on horseback without any order and apparently under no control came pouring in. One Man as he looked up *and* saw so many young girls said in a tone of peculiarly impertinent inquiry, "Seminary?" "No," said I, "a private house." "Very nice place" said the fellow, "should like to live here myself." "Yes." added another. "Very good-looking girls, too." An officer as he rode by inquired of my husband how many men there were in Camden? "You do not expect me to answer that question, do you?" said my husband. "No," said the officer and, "if you were to I should not believe you." "You seem to take me for a Secessionist," said my husband. "And I am neither ashamed nor afraid to say that so I have been and so I am. But I am a clergyman with ten helpless females under my care. I ask a guard for their protection." "You should have thought of that, was the reply, "four years ago" and bidding his men to follow him, he rode off, leaving us to the tender mercies of any who might come after him. As he rode off with most of his squad, one of them lingering a little behind came up to my husband and presented his musket, demanded Mr. T's watch. "If you take it," said my husband, "you will be stealing, for l heard your captain just now bid you go with him. "Say that again," exclaimed the fellow, "and I'll blow your brains out."- Whereupon he seized the watch and went off. Men were now surrounding the house, coming in at the back of it and in front, calling aloud for wine and whiskey. My husband assured them we had no whiskey, as we had not been able to procure any for some time, even as medicine, and the only wine in the house was for the Holy Communion. One of the officers insisted on our bringing this; we broke and poured out of the window one of the only two bottles we had, and gave him the other, which he drank the most of and gave the rest to one of his men. They demanded the key to the cellar, saying they didn't believe we had so little and that they would search for themselves. They crowded accordingly into the basement of the house, where we had a pit, in which we used to put ice. They evidently suspected that we had silver there, for they thrust their bayonets down as deep as they could into the sand at the bottom of it and did in fact come within a few inches of a box containing the chief part of our silver which as we have since learned from our son he had buried there under the side of the same pit. At the same time, others in the yard were chasing the pigs, wringing off the necks of the chickens and turning out the cow (which in consequence we lost as also most of our poultry) and doing in short every sort of mischief. It was now near dinner time, all the morning I had been alternately with the family, witnessing these scenes, or with the sick child, soothing her and availing myself of the solitude of the chamber to commit scenes, or with the sick child, soothing her and availing myself of the solitude of the chamber to commit them all to the care of Him without whom not a sparrow falleth to the ground. About this time, the information of the abundance of liquor, next door, began to spread. The inferior officers let the men know that they could wet an abundance of it, and with buckets and cans and jugs and tubs, they crowded over to the house of this Jew. This gave us a brief respite, and we availed ourselves of it to eat a few mouthfuls of dinner knowing that we should need all the strength we could get.

We had hardly finished before the current set in again for our house, now more violently than ever. They now clamoured for provisions coming in at the basement. They dashed right through the windows, shivering not only the panes of glass but kicking to pieces the sashes and even the venetian blinds. They evidently were expecting to find in so large a house, an abundant supply and when on entering the store room they saw only 4 hams, a Vi barrel of rice and a couple of barrels of corn. They suspected us of concealing the bulk of our food. Our seamstress remonstrated with them about taking from a clergyman with a large family the little that remained to him. I too reminded them who had said, "If thine enemy hunger feed him." Some of them seemed abashed and a young lad said he couldn't bear it as his mother had taught him differently. They took nothing from the store room. "We'll send the commissary's wagon for this tomorrow morning," said one of them. We congratulated ourselves that our chief supply of corn (about 75 bushels), which we had put into bins in a room adjoining the stable was thus far undetected. A systematic search was now commenced by them for silver and jewelry. Beginning in the lower rooms, they now ransacked every sideboard, press, bureau, trunk and drawer. The silver forks and spoons used at dinner and taken into the pantry to be washed were soon pocketed. We had asked some of the men for a guard, and we have every reason to believe that the set who at this time were rifling us had orders to keep out others, in order that they might carry on their depredations more methodically and thoroughly. For while they were about this, one or two were stationed at the doors, warned off others, and another calling himself a lieutenant, conducted the movements of the rest. They threatened to break open the locks if the keys were not instantly forth-coming, and one of them, betraying with what practices he was familiar, said, "If I only had a piece of wire, I could open every lock in your house." "I don't doubt it," replied my husband and the man smiled with satisfaction at his recognition of his accomplishment in roguery. Wherever they went, they were accompanied by my husband and daughters and niece, and sometimes me, though they quailed beneath the steady gaze, the flashing eye, and curling lip of these brave, because innocent and patriotic Southern girls thus they saw on the center table in our drawing room two very handsome bibles in morocco cases richly gilt. These they took up, but laid down again, while the eyes of those in the room were upon them, but when the light was carried out (it was now night), they whisked off the Bibles and when we next looked both the books were gone. As they were going into one of the rooms, "This," said my husband, *"is* the chamber of one of my daughters." "What of that?" said one of them. "Do you think a woman's room is better than any other?" And in they rushed opening every draw tumbling up the dresses and which were in it and making offensive remarks on them as they threw them on the floor. They did the same in all the chambers- In my sister's room, they insisted upon her opening her desk from which they took all the Confederate money they found and some pictures of value. They made my niece open her dressing case and carried off from it all it contained. "We're only taking this to the quartermaster," said one of them, as he gathered his spoils into his handkerchief. "You'll have it all back again tomorrow. "You must think us very simple," said my husband. The man smiled and now Gen'l Sherman we see by the papers avows that such were his orders. At length they had gone through all the rooms, except the one where my sick child was in bed already exceedingly nervous with agitation at what she knew was going on, as the men drew near to the door of that room, my husband remonstrated, but they persisted in their purpose and would go in. As they were about to take up the bed clothes, he renewed his endeavor to dissuade them- But one of them said, "You can take her up" and the men were lifting the covering when the poor child became violently agitated and on my husband's exclaiming, "Don't you see how the child is troubled?" As she burst into tears. one of them relented, and said to the others, "Well, let her alone. "They went however over every other part of that chamber, all round the bed, and peeped under it, and drew out a trunk which was there and opened it. In another trunk, they saw a cap of my sons. "Whose is this?" asked one of them. We told him. "Your son is in the Artillery," he remarked.

"A bullet for him," he added as he put the cap on his own head. It was now night. The last room was searched. The ruffians, at length, were thirty out of the house. The house was quiet, and the sick child slept. I was alone, but as I gazed from my window at the camp-fires near to us and knew that hordes of drunken revellers were at that time filling our kitchen and out-houses, my heart sank within me at the thought of the appalling night before us. My young daughters so delicately nurtured, so tenderly cherished! I pleaded with intense earnestness that their Heavenly Father would spread His sheltering wings around them. Descending after a while into the parlour, I found them all collected, hovering over a little fire, as we did not dare to go out of doors to bring in more fuel. They were talking over the events of the day, when suddenly there was a tramp of footsteps, the doors were thrown open and in rushed several armed men. One who seemed to be in command turned to the others and said, "Guards, stand at the doors!" They lowered their muskets and obeyed. My husband was at that moment in another room, soothing the younger children, but he came in on hearing the noise, and all the grown people of our household were thus assembled. The officer inquired if such was the case and on our replying in the affirmative, the fellow threw himself with an insolent air into a chair, saying, "Well, we are Northern Vandals. We know you have silver and jewelry. We intend to have it, and if you don't hand it up, we will search your persons and bum your house." Of course, we began immediately to take of our finger rings, earrings and broaches, they insisted that we had other valuables elsewhere, whereupon one of my daughters said, "I have a few coins upstairs." "Go to your room then," said the ruffian," and one of my men shall go with you as a guard." My husband at my suggestion remonstrated against her going alone with the soldier and with difficulty obtained leave to follow her under charge of another of these men. During their absence, the remaining one employed himself in lecturing us upon the sin of secession but was so intoxicated that he had at times to support himself by holding on to the back of a chair. On the return of those who had gone with my daughter, they demanded who next was ready, and my sister went to her room attended in like manner by one of the banditti, and her valuables left from the previous inspection of her room, were now seized. They then asked my husband if he hadn't any watches. He told them his had *been* stolen by one of their men a few hours before. "Soldiers don't steal," said the inquirer. "They confiscate. But haven't you any more watches?" On my husband replying there was an old one a family relic in his study the most villainous looking of the creatures, a young man of peculiarly forbidding countenance and coarse and rude beyond even the others bade my husband show him the way. He made him open every drawer of his escritoire, from which he took whatever was of the least pecuniary value, among other things a seal. As he took it up, my husband said, "that was the seal of my great-grandfather." "Isn't it gold?" was the only inquiry. and on being told that it was, he coolly put it into his pocket. As he was coming out, he said, "You're a clergyman, you tell me. I was once a minister's son. but now I'm a prodigal." Alas what a history those few words reveal: When this man came back into the room where the rest of us were, they resumed their demands for silver and jewelry. They renewed their threat to search our persons and as I had on their entrance unclasped a broach to which I attached peculiar value. I now told them frankly I had it on and would hand it to them as soon as I could find it They became very impatient and violent, saying we had plenty of jewelry still. The "prodigal" taking the candle from the table said, 'Here's the torch," and at the same time taking out his watch and holding it in his hand, he added, "We give you five minutes. Let's have the rest of your jewelry, or we will either search you or burn your house. Now is your day of salvation."

These last words of blasphemy he uttered with a laugh of scoffing and a look of fearful audacity, winking to the officer who professed to be a pious Baptist and had boasted repeatedly that he was "as good *as* anybody else." At this crisis, we rose in a body. declared that rather than submit to be searched, we would let the house be burned, and with one consent, we moved toward the door. They asked, "what we were after." "Going for blankets," said my sister. "to protect us from the weather," as it was cold and rainy. This decision seemed to startle them, as they had (according to what we afterwards learned) permission to burn only uninhabited houses. Just then, I found the broach. and as I handed it to one of them, remarked that it was a wedding gift and contained the hair of my father, a bishop of the Church to which I belonged. He tried to get out the hair but not succeeding asked, "What are these things?" "Pearls," I said, with which it was set. Whereupon he quietly pocketed it. As we were on our way again towards the door, the pious Baptist, reeling with liquor, began to assume the air of protector, and "They shan't burn your house. They must march over my dead body first," and turning to his associates remarked, "Well, they're honest." Whereupon he opened one of the doors and they marched out. What a relief to listen to their retreating footsteps. God had indeed proven Himself the Hearer of Prayer and under the shelter of His wings, we were protected. They betook themselves to the Kitchen where they became so beastly drunk, that profound slumber soon overpowered them all and thus did the restraining power of God keep us in safety during the long hours of that horrible night: - The frightened servant girls ran to us for protection and slept all night in our nursery. Never shall I forget that night! We separated into two parties, one keeping watch in the parlors, the other in the room of the sick child. The little children huddled together, wrapped in blankets, on the floor, forgot their sorrow in uneasy slumbers. It was raining incessantly, *and* as our fires burned out and we did not dare to go for more wood, those of us who were in the parlor suffered from cold. The poor children had gone supper less to bed. I would have given anything for a cup of tea or coffee. Of the latter we had a little, but unfortunately the milk curdled. Our lights failed, but fortunately we made a discovery of a little flower-trellis. This we broke into small fragments, and the flame we thus kindled gave us a little light and warmth. Towards morning at my husband's persuasion, while he watched I threw myself on the bed and slept from sheer exhaustion. I awoke at daylight *and* hastened to the window- not a vestige of the enemy was to be seen- but flames rising in different parts of the horison, shewed how they were employed. Mills, depots and private dwellings were on fire. About breakfast-time kind inquiries from the neighbours with sad, sad accounts, of robbery insult and drunkenness poured in. How much cause for gratitude! We had been protected from personal violence and injury. Most of our jewelry and silverware had been undiscovered and though our losses were distressing to us, they were nothing compared to those of some others. Our year's supply of corn was yet untouched. Around our family altar, we gathered with thankful hearts, while my husband poured out in fervent prayer our united tribute of praise to Him who had thus far watched over us. About nine and clock, stragglers began to make their appearance in our yard, and as they seemed bent on mischief, asking the servants that "d-d old rebel" (my husband) we persuaded him to stay in the house. Watching them from my chamber windows. we saw them, to our dismay, break open our corn room. One of them had a horse, and as he entered the carriage house and drew out the buggy, we inferred, of course, that he intended to carry off the corn. But after trying to put their horse with our harness *to* the buggy and not succeeding, as some who were there before, had carried away a part of the harness, we heard them breaking the wheels of the buggy, leaving it thus rendered useless to us they returned to the corn room and after remaining in it a few moments came out and to our great joy rode of we advised my husband as soon as they had disappeared to nail up the corn room that its manifestly unprotected condition might not expose it to robbery. This he did. And now came our greatest sorrow? I had thrown myself on the bed for a few minutes to rest, when I saw the Irish girl already mentioned enter the room and looking anxiously at me, whisper something to one of my daughters who started up with an exclamation---I instantly conjectured what had happened. "Theodore has been captured," I said. "Yes," said one of them, William (the servant who had gone with him) is below and is telling his father all about it. We all ran downstairs and what a sad sight greeted us! My poor husband! Bravely and nobly had he borne up through all the scenes so torturing to his Southern spirit, but this last was too much. He was weeping bitterly! Bending before him clasping his knees and sobbing as if his heart would break, sat the poor faithful slave who had just come in. "Oh, sir," said he in disjointed words. "I did all I could for Mas Teeah. We wandered about all night in the rain. No one would take us in. After the middle of the night, I got Mas Teeah to lie down in an old barn, *and* I covered him with both blankets because he was so sick and needed them more than I did. I watched while he slept. The next day, we set out again, but lost our way and about 2 o'clock as we were in an empty house, where we had stopped to dry our clothes, just as we were eating a piece of bread I heard him call out "William the Yankees", and sure enough five soldiers were coming round the corner. He called to me not to shoot but to give up the arms. They then took everything from him, blankets, clothes, food, pocket book, horse, all except the clothes he had on. They did the same to me, taking even too my tooth brush and comb. I told them how sick Mas Teeah was and begged them to let me go with him, but they wouldn't. An officer took him one way while the men carried me another. And, oh, sir, they made me drink about a quart of whiskey and did all they could to make me stay with them. One took me into his buggy, and told me I should do nothing but attend to him, have $10 a month and be free. But I told him I wanted to go home *and* so as soon as I could I got off and I've walked 20 miles today and had to sneek under the house here lest they should catch me again."- This was as well as I can remember, his sad tale. What a stricken group we were! My husband soon recovered composure sufficient for prayer and we all knelt down around him, while he poured out our sorrow to Him, whose ears are ever open into the prayers of his humble servants and commended our sick son to His covenant care, entreating Him that He would raise up friends to him and strengthen and sustain him in his feebleness and imprisonment. We rose comforted and were just leaving the room when someone ran in, crying out, "The stable and corn room are on fire" - Twas too true! The wretches had concealed in the fodder a slow match which was doing its work - My husband rushed out followed by all the children …But what could they do! William still suffering from his intoxication, was the only male, besides my husband on the promises, able to render any aid. Their efforts to extinguish the flames were entirely unsuccessful. The whole pile of buildings was in a few moments one mass of flame. Fences were communicating it to other outbuildings, but with great presence of mind, the female servants under the direction of our daughters broke these down. Flakes, too, were falling on the roof of the piazza of our dwelling-house. But I stationed a servant girl out of my chamber-window with a bucket of water with which she extinguished the flames as fast as they fell. The work of destruction was soon over and, as night closed in, our chief stock of provisions for the rest of the year was a heap of blackened cinders- We remembered the promise of Him who "feedith the young ravens when they cry"- and fully has this promise thus far been fulfilled-

Not a month had elapsed before the sympathy, not of word but of deed replenished our storeroom, if not with abundance, yet with sufficiency- I could fill pages with the misery which these raiders left in their track. Their treatment of the slaves for whose sake the war was professedly entered, was atrocious. A gentleman in our neighborhood assured us that not a female slave on his plantation (with a single exception) was allowed to retain. That which should have been dearer to her than life- This exception, a brave married woman, stood at the door of her house with a log of wood in her hand and said she would dash out the brains of any man who came near her. The raiders left Camden on Sunday Feb 26 and most devoutly did we pray that we might never see another such set of ruffians- But not two months had passed before another wider Gen'l Potter (son of the Bishop of Pennsylvania) was upon us- He brought a large body of Negro troops and his special object was to entice away, or carry off by force, our servants. Fortunately, a body of our militia were in the town *and* another body of our regular army approaching- So that the raiders dared not venture far from their main body nor stay beyond a single night- The next morning, however, numbers of families awoke to find themselves without a single servant- their cooks, chambermaids. washers and men servants all gone, and many a delicate female tenderly nurtured and educated in refinement, was obliged to go into the kitchen and betake herself to the wash tub- But to return to our own family- None of our servants left us- For a month we heard nothing more of Theodore- Our anxiety was intense- At last we learned that he was with Sherman's army, marching rapidly through North Carolina, that the prisoners were on foot and with little to eat- After several more *weeks,* we heard from him from Newberne- What a tale of suffering. Forced marches of from 20 to 30 miles a day, always on foot the latter part of the journey without shoes or stockings, prisoners fare, never a word of comfort or sympathy; but if in his feebleness, he lagged behind. a threat instead to shorten all his troubles quickly. From day to day and week after week no change of clothing! What wonder that he lived in a kind of stupor until all his sorrows and exposures brought on extreme illness and he was taken to a hospital in Newberne. There they cut off his hair and plunged him into a cold bath. Then taking away all his clothing, they left him only a blanket to wrap around him, made him walk thus across the yard to a tent where they laid him on a straw mattrass, to remain there four days with no other covering. There, he was found by some benevolent ladies the spark of life nearly extinct. Such treatment having greatly aggravated the disease (dysentery) from which he had long *been* suffering- The excellent ladies, in the warmth of their true Southern hearts, obtained leave, after great difficulty from the indifference and opposition of those in authority, to take him home and nurse him with the tenderest care. Thus, strikingly were our prayers answered! This account we gained little by little at long intervals, as he recovered strength and had opportunities of writing by private conveyances casually occurring: there being at that time no mails even after the surrender of Lee and Johnston's armies, through which Confederates were allowed to communicate with each other. It is not easy to conceive that painfulness of our suspense as months passed by, leaving us still uncertain whether he was dead or alive. In the meantime, public affairs grew darker and darker. Lee's army, it was rumoured, would be obliged to surrender - At *first* we refused to believe this. But soon accounts reached us of rations being reduced to half a pint of meal a day and of numbers of men deserting for the protection of their families. Soon after the worst was confirmed. Lee's army surrendered. That of Johnston followed, and we knew that we were a subjugated people. All our sufferings for naught! All our hopes crushed! Every day by bitter experiences are we made to feel that liberty and independence for us as a people are gone, perhaps forever. As a family, we are nearly ruined. All our business papers were destroyed by Sherman's raiders. Half of our capital invested in Confederate securities is gone. The other half, chiefly in Rail Road Bonds, even if recovered, will be almost if not quite valueless. So that the house we live in, with the few acres of land around it, is all we know of that remains to us, except the silver we secreted. But we have one another to love and cling to, willing hands to work, brave hearts to endure, and above all a Heavenly Father to look to, who has promised never to forsake the seed of the righteous. And blessed be God that this is our portion! For truly may I say,

> "My boast is not that I deduce my birth
> From loins enthroned and rulers of the earth
> But higher far my proud pretensions rise
> \he child of parents passed into the skies" [592]

---

[592] "An Account of the Experiences of the Family of the Reverend and Mrs. Paul Trapier During and After the War Between the States," by Sarah Dehon Trapier; "Transcription reprinted by permission from the South Carolina Historical Society"

Liberty Hill

When the federal troops came into the village, Liberty Hill was considered one of the wealthiest areas in the county. In the beginning of the war, the drain of manhood and resources hurt the people in the area, and now Sherman and his troops came. In the later part of February 1865, the Yankees camped in and around Liberty Hill, and encamped for over eight days. During this time, destruction and terror fell on the inhabitants. The Wateree River had swollen its banks, pontoon broke when half of the Yankees crossed, forcing the others to cross at Rocky Mount eight miles further down than Peay's Ferry. The buildings that were burned included the Academy, Johnson Brown's tannery, and the homes of Robert B. Cunningham, John S. Cunningham, and James B. Cureton. The others were plundered of their belongings and crops.

The Bloody Battle for Carolinians

100-Year-Old Camden Letter Tells of First Manassas

The following was received from Miss Elizabeth Doby English of Columbia to the editors; July 21, Friday, was the 100th anniversary of the First Battle of Manassas, or Bull Run, as our Northern friends call it. My mother's father was Captain Alfred English Doby. He was aide-de-camp to General J.B. Kershaw and engaged to Miss Elizabeth M. Kennedy of Camden. She saved all of his dozen letters, written from the battlefields of Virginia. The first of them was a vivid description of Manassas.

The Letter
This letter came from Captain Doby to Miss Kennedy, and was written July 25, 1861, in Vienna, Virginia.

My Dearest Lizzie:

Thank God, I have once more the precious privilege of communing with you, after the many hard trials, and dangers of a hard-fought battle. Yes, Lizzie, we have at last had a grand battle, perhaps the largest that was ever fought on this continent, and our exertions, and bravery were crowned with a victory that was only equal to our efforts.

I can almost positively assert that, had it not been for the very opportune time of Colonel Kershaw's command, which consisted of Colonel Cash's regiment, and his own, the day would have been lost, and our army cut to pieces. When he reached the field of battle, we saw hundreds of our men retiring, crying that we were ruined, that the battle was lost, and that nothing could save us from being cut up, if we advanced farther, but onward our gallant colonel leads us, where there was not a single friend to be seen, but only the dense lines of our enemy.

Cunning Fails

We first charged upon the celebrated Ellsworth Zouaves, who finding it impossible to repel us, resorted to cunning to avoid our fury. They fell upon their faces, and groaned, pretending to be either dead, or wounded. Thus, we passed over them, thinking they were really shot down, but when we got some 30 or 40 yards beyond them, they fired upon us from the rear, and they would tumble over again, resorting to the same deception, until our men, finding it out, either killed, or captured, every one of them. The next body we encountered were the regulars, who fought well, but could not stand a charge made on their flank, by General Elzay's command. They became panic-stricken, and an indescribable rout ensued, during which we pursued for several miles, capturing immense quantities of artillery, wagons, guns, stores, horses, and prisoners. I cannot possibly give you the faintest conception of their confusion and fight. The last time we fired upon them with our artillery, created such a panic among them, that, in attempting to cross their artillery and wagons across the bridge, they rushed upon each other so that the bridge was completely blocked up, causing them to abandon everything, except their own personal safety.

Pursuit Ends

Here our pursuit ended, by order of General Beauregard. I have not heard positively the casualties of the day. It is supposed that we lost about 1000 killed and wounded, and the enemy, about 2000 killed and wounded, and as many more prisoners, with several million dollars' worth of property.

Poor little Willie Hardy was killed during the engagement. He was shot down by a concealed for, while gallantly performing his duty. He was shot with a pistol, the ball passing through the neck, severing the main artery, but he lived but a moment. I did not observe him when he fell, on account of his being under cover of the woods, where he was conducting Colonel Preston's regiment, but a friend told me of his death immediately afterwards, upon which I was able to obtain his body. When I found it, all covered with blood, his face disfigured, his eyes rolled in a gaze of death. I momentarily shuddered. I was almost paralyzed. I was almost upon him for a few moments, then, dismounting, put him upon little Swannanoa, which standing near his body, when I found it, but finding that I could not carry his body that way. I took it upon my shoulders and bore it several hundred yards to a place of safety.

Comrade's Blood

Good Heaven's! Lizzie, my back was saturated with his blood! Never had I such feeling before, my own person stained with the blood of my dear little comrade, I covered his body with a few bushes, and again entered battle, not dreaming that I, too might possibly meet, in a few moments, that sad fate. But something above seemed to have thrown an arm of protection around me, and I went through unhurt; one ball passed through my coat, but one did not touch the skin. Poor DePass, I am afraid he is mortally wounded; several others from Camden were also wounded, and one killed. Colonel Hampton's Legion was cut to pieces. Dick Manning was wounded, but not badly. General Beauregard had his horse killed under him by a bomb. General Scott's army was magnificently equipped, one of the finest armies, perhaps, that ever went into battle, but with the manner we dismantled that army beggars all description. We would have pursued to Washington, but General Ewell, who was to have advanced upon the left flank, did not receive the order sent him by Beauregard in time to correspond with the actions of the brigades on the right and center.

Prisoners

Many of our men were held prisoners for some time by the Zouaves, among them Captains Richardson and Hoke, also the renowned Myers Moses, who I am happy to say, stood fire better than I anticipated. The infernal Zouaves came near capturing me, also, but a little piece of strategy, and presence of mind on my part eluded their grasp; in the execution of an order, I was thrown necessarily some distance from the regiment. Zouaves, perceiving this, rushed out from a picket, and drew their guns on me, but one of them, thinking that I was a friend, which was the hand thrown across the nose. I immediately responded by giving their signal, which undoubtedly saved my life. They were subsequently captured and our men saved.

John acted with a great deal of gallantry, receiving one shot in the side, which only penetrated his clothing, and bruised his skin. Zack and Joe also fought well, manifesting bravery and coolness; they were not hurt at all.

Most of the Camden boys fought well. Colonel Kershaw has proved himself an officer of ability, as well as gallantry. I think he ought to be promoted. There are so many incidents that would interest you, but I have not space or time to relate them now. I sent your father a telegram the day after the battle, thinking you all were under a burdensome anxiety about us, but I doubt very much whether he received it. I have not yet received any letter from you by mail and have now given out all hope of hearing from you except through individuals.

I thank God, my darling Lizzie, for your sake, that I was protected from all harm during that disastrous and bloody battle. I doubt not but your constant and earnest prayers in my behalf shielded me from danger. God Bless you, dearest Lizzie, may all your prayers be answered, for they emanate from a heart, pure and chaste in its sentiments, and full of virtue that adorn an angel. Give my love and best wishes to your mother and father and all the family.

I remain as ever,
Yours devotedly,
Alfred

The names mentioned in Doby's letter.
Col. Kershaw- Later General Joseph Brevard Kershaw, Camden, the father of Mrs. L. T. Baker of Columbia.
Col. Cash- Col. E.B.C. Cash. 8th SCV. Camden.
Ellsworth Zouaves
Gen. Elzey- General Arnold Elzey
Gen. Beauregard- Gen. G.T. Beauregard
Willie Hardy- Camden
Col. Preston- Col. J.F. Preston
Swannanoa- Hardy's horse.
DePass- William Lambert DePass, Sr. Later Major, Camden.
Col. Hampton- Wade Hampton, later General.
Dick Manning.
Gen. Scott- General Winfield Scott. Federal General.
Gen. Ewell- General Richard S. Ewell

Capt. Richardson- John S. Richardson, Com. D, 2 SCV

Capt. Hoke- A. D. Hoke, Com. B, 2 SCV

Myers Moses- A Camden man.

John- brother-in-law, John D. Kennedy, later brigadier general.

Zack- William Zack Leitner, later major, a cousin.

Joe- Joseph Dunlap, Camden, cousin.

Father- Anthony MacMillan Kennedy, Camden.

Mother- Mrs. A. M. Kennedy (Sarah Ann Doby)

Source: File Folder Camden Archives, Camden, South Carolina; Kershaw County- Civil War- 1861-1865.

General Sherman Feasted in Kershaw County Home

If the old spirit of General Will Tecumseh Sherman should wander about this section at any time, and should be capable of remembering earthly delights, he would probably pause with nostalgic recollection at the Old Smyrl home in the Flint Hill community. It was there that the general enjoyed a meal of southern country cured ham during his ill-famed march to the sea.

R.L. Smryl, the father of Miss Mamie Smryl, was told the following story about the coming of the Yankees. For some time, the rumors spread about the marauders were coming. The hearing of big guns far off, signaled they were nearing. Those guns sounded like a distant thunder. A squad of blue coated scouts rode into the yard of the Smyrl home, located twelve miles above Camden, on the Liberty Hill Road. The family had its first glimpse of the Yankee Soldiers.

From her early childhood, Miss Smryl remembers the story of the arrival of Sherman himself, with members of his staff, at the plantation home.

A big, bearded man jumped agilely from his horse, threw the reins to a colored boy, and stomped up the front steps. R.L. Smryl described for his children the hollow thump, of the officer's boots, as he strode through the house.

General William Tecumseh Sherman selected the plantation as his temporary headquarters and seemed determined to outdo in savagery the red Indian Chief for whom he was named.

The family was treated to humiliating treatment, while the Yankees plundered the house and premises around it for hidden valuables. Not even the large crock in a food closet, filled with link sausage, and covered with lard to preserve them was spared.

Thinking that gold or silver might be in the crock under the sausage, the Yankees dug down into it with their bayonets, and felt it with their hands in an unrewarded search.

But it was the large ham that the small boy of the family, Robert, remembered, and often told his children, and his grandchildren about. The Yankee took the big ham from a rafter and ordered a slave to prepare it for dinner. Young Robert remembered how the ham sizzled for a delightful brown, and gave forth an enticing aroma, as it was slowly turned on the spit by a grey-headed slave. The Yankees sat around the big fireplace, while the ham was being cooked.

When the hot ham had been placed in the center of the huge table, and the Yankees had gathered around for a feast, young Robert, influenced by the enticing odors, told a grizzled soldier, "I think I'll eat with you."

"Well, who the hell cares," the Yankee replied roughly. Unrebuffed, the boy took a seat at the table with enemy invaders. For years, he remembered vividly the grease-smeared faces of the Yankees, as they stuffed themselves with ham.

The Yankees had with them many heads of livestock, which they had stolen along the line of march. They broke into a large barn on the farm and removed all the corn. They piled the corn in a line along the ground to feed the livestock. The soldiers carried off the mother of a calf, however, the cow was desperate to return to her baby. She broke loose several times, and returned to the home place, as the Yankees were driving her along the line of march. As they drew farther away from the Flint Hill section, the Yankees drew tired of retrieving the straying cow, so they let her stay. That's how the Smryl family happened to have a cow and a calf after the Yankees left. A single rooster, which fled in the woods, was all that was left of the poultry.

Whether the house is still up, one will have to imagine it would be the exact house as the Yankees would have seen when they came through. The covered well with its bucket on a windlass is just as it was when the thirsty Yankees would have drunk from the cooling water. Near it was an herb garden, where the family's species and medicinal herbs were grown.

Missing is the big barn from which the corn was taken by the Yankees. Also, missing is the blacksmith shop, and a commissary, which stood near the house. The house was built in 1852 by Robert Smyrl, grandfather of the Miss Smyrl. The owner was away in the Army of the Confederacy, when Sherman came in 1865. The house was built of lumber from the giant trees of the forest, the wide boards of the house was put together by pegs.

(The article was done by Robert Raymond in the 1950s and in *The Camden Chronicle*.)

Camden Man Relates Stirring Incidents in His Life As A Scout During War Between the States.

Climbed a Tree to Avoid Capture.
The Camden Chronicle, May 22, 1953

THE LATE W.A. ANCRUM OF Camden, father of Thomas A. Ancrum, manager of the Southern Cotton Oil Company, was a scout in the Confederate Army during the War Between the States. In January 1883, he wrote an article for the Weekly News (now the News and Courier) of Charleston, in which he told of some stirring experiences he had while doing duty within the enemy's lines.

By Private W. A. Ancrum of the Second South Carolina Cavalry

Having been urged by friends to contribute to your "Tales of the War," I give you the following reminiscences of some of my experiences as a scout, a task, which entails upon the writer peculiar difficulties, as there was a strong prejudice against this branch of service of the Confederate Soldier, a prejudice founded, I suppose, upon the belief that a life of a scout was only sought as a means of shirking duty.

I also labor under the difficulty of having forgotten the names of most of the citizens with whom we dealt, and from whom we got information, and of the continual use of the ego, mei, mihi, me style of writing, which is absolutely necessary, as there were so few actors in the events, which I am about to describe. In all of which I bore a part.

During the winter of 1862-63, Hampton's Brigade of cavalry was in camp in Culpepper County, Virginia. Scouting parties were continually sent out by the different brigade and regimental commanders, not so much for gaining information, as to harass the enemy by capturing stragglers inside their lines, breaking up their picket posts, and remounting our men with captured horses.

In the early part of June 1863, Col. M.C. Butler, of the Second South Carolina Cavalry, detailed James Dulin, a native of Fauquier County, Virginia, and myself, both of the Boykin Rangers, to carry three dismounted men of our regiment through the lines, and capture horses for them.

The Army of the Potomac was then encamped on Stafford Heights, opposite Fredericksburg, with pickets along the Rappahannock River, to and above the bridge of the Orange and Alexandria Railroad. Crossing the river above them at Waterloo Mills, we rode around Warrenton until we came near the railroad between Catlett's and Bristow Stations, where we usually left our horses in the thicket about two miles from the railroad, in the care of a strong friend of our cause. To cross the railroad required much caution, as besides irregular parties the enemy had regular patrols, which left each station every half hour, and rode to the next, so that they were passing every few minutes. Succeeding after several attempts, we commenced our tramp about dark to a place near Morristown, a village at the intersection of the main road from Fredericksburg to Bealton Station, on the Orange and Alexandria Railroad, and road crossing the Rappahannock at Ellis' Mills, where they were usually an encampment of the enemy, and being far within their lines, there was little difficulty in picking up stragglers. To avoid their scouting parties and lay new picket posts, we made slow time, and arrived at our point of ambuscade only a short time before daylight. Dulin and I went to the road to reconnoiter, but seeing morning, we sat down to wait for light. He, becoming tired, walked out into the road, and I to keep the mosquitos from troubling me, tied my handkerchief around my ears, and trusting to his being on the lookout soon fell asleep, and was aroused by the splash of horse's feet in the branch near which I was lying, and without raising my head, I discovered I was within 20 feet of eighteen of the enemy, who were watering their horses. I concluded not to move, hoping they would pass without seeing me, which they all did, except the last two, one of who cried out, "Captain, there is a man yonder." Before they could unsling their carbines, I was well in the intricate thicket of pine and cedar on the edge of which had been lying, and was not pursued far, according to the usual custom of the enemy, who would not venture into the woods after our fugitive scouts.

I soon met Dulin to be well laughed at for the speed I was making, and to be told that had been almost caught in the same predicament and did not have time to warn me. We made our way to a field on the road where we could better observe the movements of the enemy, knowing that our plans were spoiled at least for a time. We had scarcely taken our positions when we saw one of them galloping across the field on the old road directly to where we were. We took to the trees, and he soon found his fate, for the first intimation he had of our presence was Dulin's hand on his bridle rein. He proved to be an orderly sergeant of the Second Pennsylvannia Cavalry, and he told us he had been detailed to put pickets during the passing of his command, our presence having been reported to the brigade commander. Carrying him back in the woods, we left him in charge of our dismounted contingents and returned to our posts. There was a large force of cavalry passing all day, but the alarm of the morning prevented any straggling. Late in the evening, we returned to our posts of the early morning, and had not long to wait before we saw two stragglers coming up. We took them in without trouble, and one of them proved to be an orderly of Colonel Sir Percy Wyndham, of the New Jersey Regiment of Cavalry, with the mail of the colonel. Having now accomplished Colonel Butler's orders. We concluded that it was best notify General J.B. Stuart of the movements of the enemy and making a forced march to where we had left our horses. I rode on, and reported to General Stuart, giving him, I believe, the first information of the massing of the enemy's cavalry at Rannahannock Bridge, which resulted in the cavalry engagement at Brandy Station a short time afterwards. After making our report, and telling the General how we happened to have been across the river, he astonished me by asking, "How would you like to have a regular detail to scout for me?" which resulted in an order "to all pickets and guards of the cavalry of the Army of Northern Virginia, to allow W.A. Ancrum and J.R. Dulin to pass, they are on special duty for the general commanding." This was a consummation beyond my utmost hopes for the detail of camp life were particular irksome to me, as they were to most of the Confederate soldiers, who, though willing to fight, were very restive under the restrain of discipline.

Returning to the field of my new duty, I met Bill Mickler, the commander of Hampton's scouts, and Tom Butler, a brother of Colonel Butler, afterwards killed at Gettysburg, who was taking the last trip across the river, all of their men having been ordered to return to their commands. Leaving our horses at the same place, we crossed the railroad and made for a rendezvous, a neighborhood of staunch Confederates, when we arrived about ten o'clock p.m. Dividing, Butler and I went to our house, and found that a large party of the enemy had just searched it, and left for that to which Mickler had gone, Double quicking across the field, a distance of three quarters of a mile, to warn him, we stopped for a moment at the well to get some water, and in drawing it, my only pistol fell into the well, and was lost. Our deliberations were cut short by our being halted, and the accent of the customary "Who goes there?" at once told us they were no friend. We posted ourselves behind the fence, and they were behind the barn about twenty steps away. Each party now tried to entice the other forward, but neither responded, and we were now too poorly armed to make the attempt of capturing them, and both sides concluded about the same time to withdraw- a lucky thing for us as we afterward learned they were seven of them, and my scabbard, which I was using as a dummy pistol, would not have proved a very effective weapon against such odds. Hoping against for the safety of Mickler, we carefully advanced to the house, and for there only in time to see him break out the front door, and like a scared buck for the woods. We soon made him recognize us however, and he gave his experience, which was rather startling.

He had been surrounded in the house, and only escaped capture through the ingenuity and coolness of the ladies. One of these, meeting the Yankees at the door, the other two took Mickler into a bedroom, and making him get between the mattresses, one of laid on the bed, shaming a case of illness. After searching the rest of the house, the two officers of the searching party forced themselves into the room against the protests of the other sisters, who begged them earnestly not to disturb the dying inmate of the chamber. They persisted, however, and searched all the room except the bed, one of them, however, giving the pretended patient a severe fright by approaching, and feeling her pulse, which was no doubt beating at a high rate, rapid enough to verify the sage remark from him that it was very high. Then they left, affirming that they knew the man was hid somewhere in the house, as they had seen him go in.

Who, among the Confederate scouts, do not remember most kindly the attentions of "Pap" and his three daughters, whose names I must confess to have forgotten?

We now turn to some woods about three hundred yards from the house, where we stored a supply of blankets. Awaking about daylight, after a good night's rest, we soon saw two of the girls coming to us to consult about our breakfast, Mickler having told them where to find us. We were discussing whether it was safer to go to the house, or to have our meals brought to us, and laughing heartily over our adventures of the night before, when one of the girls, looking up, saw the skirmish line of the enemy about one hundred yards from us. Not needing appeals of "Run, boys, run," we made the other side of the woods, only to find, after several attempts to get out, that the enemy had surrounded us, and were coming through in skirmish line. What to do with ourselves was now the important question?

After passing around and about us, and keeping us in suspense for some time, they finally left, to our great relief, and rode in the direction of an adjoining wood, from which we heard rapid firing, and knew that they had started some of our boys from an ambulance, which we had captured, and hid in the woods, as a sleeping place.

We afterwards found that they had started Dulin, and would have captured him, had not Cedar Creek had been near, by crossing which he escaped them hatless and shoeless. After several hours, we descended from our roost, only to see the enemy returning, and had to clamber up again, this time, all of us in the same tree. This is where we stayed until evening. The pangs of hunger were now very urgent, as we had not eaten anything in over thirty hours. Thinking it safer not to go to the house of any of our friends, it fell to my lot to go got provisions to the house of a strong Union man, a New Jersey settler. At this house, I will not mention, Mickler had his legs broken, and Calhoun Sparks, our color sergeant, was killed the following winter, in an attempt to capture some of the enemy. Obtaining the needed provisions, I returned to my comrades, and after supplying our immediate wants, we concluded to leave the woods, and rest for the night in a sassafras thicket on a ditch bank in a large field. This was a wise precaution, as the enemy were out in full force the next day, driving through the woods. Two of them in gray uniforms rode quite near us in a sweeping canter, and we took them for two brothers of the Black Horse Cavalry, but thinking that they were pursued, and if we halted them, our hiding place would be discovered, we allowed them to pass.

We afterwards learned that they went to a house nearby, shot its owner, and robbed him.

Thinking that a change of quarters was not advisable, we started that night for "Old Ben-----s," a good friend, about eight miles north, and about four miles northeast of Manassas station, where we rested in clover, for several days, at the end of which time we parted.

These are some of the many adventures of a similar kind which show that the life of a scout was full of vicissitudes and dangers, although the excitement of it was captivating. That the scouts of the Second South Carolina Cavalry were good and true men, I know, from my always having felt, when with one of them.

A hurried consultation resulted in each of us taking a different tree as the only means of escape. I resorted to large hickory, which I never could have mounted under ordinary circumstances, but which I managed to scale now, with not only ease to myself, but with wonderful agility. What the cogitations of my comrades were I cannot with certainty tell, but surmise that they were like my own, of the gloomiest description, for we knew that enemy had killed several scouts in cold blood shortly before, one of these being a sixteen-year old brother of Dulin, and they threatened not to take any of us alive. The idea of being shot, as I firmly believe that I would have been if discovered, and of dying like a wounded squirrel, through a fall from my lofty porch, made me think seriously of the past, present, and future. I remember vividly as though it all happened only yesterday, how my mind kept reverting to the sentiment expressing in two lines of a song I had heard only a few days before. Perhaps the ardent wish that I was safe and sound under the parental roof, at a respectful distance from my present dire extremity, made them seem although appropriate to the present occasion.

"Backward, turn backward, old Time, in thy flight, Make me a child again, just for tonight."

Marcus Baum Died with General Jenkins

Venable Dr. Baruch Writes of Incident at the Wilderness, May 6, 1864

Marcus Baum of Camden, orderly to General J.B. Kershaw, was killed by the same volley, which at the Wilderness, May 6, 1864, slew General Micah Jenkins and Captain Doby and wounded General Longstreet. The incident is described in the current issue of *The Confederate Veteran*, Nashville, by Simon Baruch, M.D., of New York City, himself a former resident of Camden. Dr. Baruch was assistant surgeon, Third South Carolina Battalion, Longstreet's Corp, afterward was surgeon to the Thirteenth Mississippi Regiment, and at the close of the war was surgeon in charge of hospitals in Thomasville, North Carolina. Since the war, he has lived in New York City, and achieved international fame as a surgeon and philanthropist.

Dr. Baruch's sketch in The Confederate Veteran is as follows:

> In General Longstreet's book, *From Manassas to Appomattox*, page 564, the following is given: "As the 12th Virginia Regiment marched back to find its place on the other side of the plank road, it was mistaken in the wood for an advance of the enemy, and fire was opened on it from the other regiments of the brigade. The men threw themselves on the ground to let the fire pass. Just then our party of officers (Generals Longstreet, Jenkins, Kershaw, and staff) came up and rode under fire. General Jenkins had not finished the expressions of joyful congregation which I have quoted when he fell mortally wounded. Captain Doby and Orderly Bowen, of Kershaw's staff, were killed. General Kershaw turned to quiet the troops, when Jenkins' Brigade with leveled guns were in the act of returning fire of the supposed enemy concealed in the wood; but as Kershaw's clear voice called out 'F-R-I-E-N-D-S!', the arms were recovered without a shot in return, and the men threw themselves upon their faces. At the moment that Jenkins fell, I received a severe shock from a minnie ball passing through my right shoulder and throat."

Now as to what happened behind the scenes. The morning was well advanced, and the roar of artillery and rattle of musketry, emphasized by an occasional stray shell flying over our heads, were distantly heard at the field hospital, which had just been established. I remember the scene distantly. As I was about to operate on a severely wounded man, Marcus Baum, a handsome fellow, of about twenty-five, attached to the staff of General Kershaw, who was very fond of him, dashed into camp on a white horse covered with foam and with anxious voice begged to know where General Kershaw could be found. "Do you hear the volley, Marcus?" said I. "The General is always in the front. I must go to him at once," cried he. "The General sent me off with a message." Digging the spurs into the flanks of his panting horse, he disappeared from view, while I was vainly trying to explain the impossibility of reaching General Kershaw. The above statement by General Longstreet tells how he fell at the side of his chief, together with the gallant Alfred Doby. All three were from Camden, S.C.

Two hours later, the body of Major General Wadsworth, of the Union Army, was brought to our hospital, and reverently place upon the sod to await transportation through the lines by order of General Lee. A moment later, the white horse of Marcus Baum came trotting into camp, his neck sprinkled with the lifeblood of the gallant rider, who had galloped him to the front to joint his commander. In the confusion of the fight, his body was never recovered. He lies in an unmarked grave on the blood stained soil of the wilderness.

It is but just to chronicle this historic fact and correct the name given by Longstreet as Bowen, which sounds like Brown, as he name was always pronounced. He was a German and a Hebrew. Though exempt from military duty as a foreigner, he enlisted early. No braver man, none truer to the cause, no soldier more loyal to this chief ever breathed than Marcus Baum, of Camden, S.C., special aid to Joseph B. Kershaw, his friend.

In Longstreet's book, *From Manassas to Appomattox*, there is an illustration from the J.B. Lippincott Company, Philadelphia. This illustration shows a man lying on the ground near his escaping horse. He is located on the right side of the picture. This a true likeness of Marcus Baum as I knew him.

The State Newspaper, April 17, 1914, Columbia, South Carolina.

The Confederate Veteran, Volume XXII, April 1914, p. 170.

The following story comes from and was told by Mr. K.S. Villipique.

"When the Federals entered Camden, about three o'clock in the afternoon, I was near the corner of Main and Rutledge Streets. I was then about eleven years old. They came in sight on the hill up Broad Street just above the corner of DeKalb, just above the present Court House. Dr. Thomas Salmond, at the corner of DeKalb and Broad, was firing at them with a pistol. He, Captain Colclough, and a Colonel Boyd took to their horses, and were pursued through town by the Federals, who were firing at them. To get away from this shooting, I went to my home at the corner of King and Market Streets. Soon after I reached home, Captain Devereux came down Market Street at full speed horseback, two mounted Federals after him and firing at him. The two Federals gave up the chase, stopped at our house and threatened to burn it, but was dissuaded by my grandmother. They then went on to the Cornwallis House, which was in full view from our home, standing alone in the midst of an open field. A young Negro woman, Rose Withers, pointed it out to them, and they took her there with them, she is sitting horseback behind one of them. I saw the fire break out, and saw it burn immediately after the Federals went there. It was four p.m. My grandmother said to the Federals: "You will regret burning the old Cornwallis headquarters." They said they did so because government property was in it. The fire lasted a long time — so much meat and tallow stored — for weeks after Sherman's men left, people would get meat out of the ruins, and eat it. Seven Federal prisoners, one an officer, had been taken that morning to the Cornwallis House, which was guarded by Campbell, Alex Matheson, Conway Bell, and Robert Man."[593]

From a letter Captain J. H. Devereux to Miss Kate Meroney, June 3rd, 1906 Florence, S.C., the following was written:

"Well, you want me to say I was a house-burner. My orders were, as shown in the Records of the Rebellion, over the signature of no less a person than General Lee, that all stores should be destroyed, if necessary to keep them from falling into the hands of the enemy. I had witnessed the burning of Columbia, and determined if possible to save Camden by giving them no excuse for firing the Depot of supplies on Main Street, near the Hotel, and moved all the stores to the Cornwallis House, isolated from the town. I had sent away to Hardee's army all stores that could be loaded on the wagons available. On the morning of February 24, the impression prevailed that Sherman would follow Beauregard, and Hampton would follow up the line of railroad towards Charlotte, and that Camden would escape. But Sherman, as he told me after my capture, decided to swing across country to cut off Hardee from Cheraw, and took in Camden in his right wing. Early in the morning of the 24, I had scouted five miles up the Lancaster Road and found no Federal troops. I was certain that Sherman would give us the go by, and returned to town. I had been to the Hotel but a few minutes when I stepped out to see Mrs. Sutherland, who was in great distress at my sending her husband off in charge of the wagons. While trying to quiet her, I heard shots on the street. Stepping to the sidewalk, I saw the body of United States Cavalry, the 29th Missouri, firing down the street at some of our people, who were returning the fire, among them, I think Mr. Shannon and Mr. Hanckle. I learned that Captain Colclough's company had fought them from Hobkirk Hill into town. I gave the order to cease firing, and our men obeyed and threw up their pieces. One near me asked what was my reason. I told them they might kill the women and children, who were running about the street screaming and crying. In the melee, I mounted and rode off, on DeKalb Street, taking a volley without receiving a scratch. I held up to call my wife, who was at a window with the baby in her arms, to lie down on the floor out of range of the guns. My next thought was to destroy the stores, and ordered either John S. Meroney, or someone else set fire to the Cornwallis House—and so you have the story. General Sherman told me next day, after my capture near Hughes (Adam's) Mill, that he had a great mind to have shot me for destroying 600 hogheads of sugar and three million rations. I suggested that

---

[593] Historic Camden, Volume II, 1905, The State Printing Company, Columbia, S.C. p. 166-167.

would not get back the stores and begged him to postpone it, which he did, else I would not be able to prove that your father set fire to his own house to help the Yankees from getting the stores.[594]

---

[594] Ibid, pages 165-166.

Thrilling Experiences as Told by Captain C. C. Haile

The Camden Chronicle, June 5, 1896

DEAR COMRADES OF CAMP RICHARD Kirkland:

I was requested at our last meeting to write my recollections of the Battle of the Crater, July 20, 1861. At that time, I was 1st Lieutenant of Company C, 23rd Regiment, S.C. V., commanded by Colonel H. Benbow, Elliott's Brigade, Bushrod Johnson's Division.

On the day previous to the explosion, we occupied that portion of the line, which was blown up, at a four-gun battery situated on an elevation, at an angle of the breastworks said to be the nearest point to the enemy's lines. We moved to the right the day before just far enough to make room for another regiment, 22nd S.C.V., Colonel Fleming, which occupied the ground that was blown up. Captain Shedd, of Fairfield, one of the officers of the 22nd Regiment, that was blown up, occupied the same position I did the night before the explosion. He was partially hurled on the right edge of the Crater. He crawled out where he had retired to sleep, fell in with our regiment, barefooted, without coat, or hat, remained with us during the battle, rendering all the assistance he could, having lost his company in the explosion. Adjutant Fleming, of the same regiment, also rendered good service, who was a brother of the colonel, who was buried in the explosion.

About dawn of the 30th of July, the explosion occurred, blowing up the battery, and the greater portion of the 23rd Regiment, throwing one or two of the cannons over in front of our line, about fifty feet. The guns were brought back and mounted again. This was accomplished by means of a whidlas(?) (paper not clear) and ropes over a zigzag course, which was dug for the purpose, and so constructed for concealment and protection from the enemy's fire. At the time of the explosion, I had just started off to get some ammunition for the sharpshooters, who had nearly exhausted their supply. The enemy was prepared to make a charge immediately after the explosion doing the excitement and confusion created thereby. We immediately formed line of battle and held the enemy in check. As they attempted to cross the line at the crater, we poured volley after volley into their ranks, and drove them back into the pit, or crater, which was a protection for them for the time, but when our line of mortars in the rear of our position opened on then, throwing shells over us into the crater, they were awfully slaughtered. They were held in check until late in the afternoon. Our regiment caving no field officers for duty that day, Captain Rufus White, of Charleston, was in command. He was wounded early in the early part of the battle, Lieutenant Stone, of Chester, was now in command. He was also wounded. The command of the regiment then devolved on me, I being the next ranking officer. I immediately ordered a charge, as we were exposed to a cross fire, front and back. At that juncture, we were reinforced by General Mahone's Division, just in time to make a spontaneous charge. We charged on the crater and right, and Mahone on the left, where the enemy had entered our lines. We, the 23rd Regiment, lost heavily, including three color bearers. The next day, hostilities were suspended by mutual consent for several hours, to remove and bury the dead. He two armies formed line in front of each other, while a detachment from each was engaged in removing the dead. Some of the officers met and conversed about the battle. The enemy stated, according to official reports, that their loss in killed, wounded, and missing mounted to 5000. Our loss was about one-fourth that number, which statement is verified by history. Company A lost heavily, and was exposed to a crossfire from front and left flank. Only nineteen men reported for duty after the battle. I was ordered by General Johnson to take a surveyor's chain, furnished by one of the staff officers, and measure the dimensions of the crater, and draw a diagram of the same, including the adjoining breastworks, and report to his headquarters. I did as ordered, but do not now remember th exact dimensions which were about 20 feet in diameter, and about 20 or 25 feet deep. There was a lump, or ball of clay, about 5 or 6 feet in diameter that fell in the crater. It was explored all around with minnie balls. The soldiers made quite a number of dirt pipes out of the clay from the crater as relics. I have one here, which I will exhibit, made by myself, with the date of the battle carved upon it: "July 30, 1861, Crater, Petersburg, Va."

The enemy continued to shell the crater every evening for a considerable time after we got in possession of it. Company H, one of the companies of our regiment, which had no commanding officer, occupied that portion of the line on the outside of the breach, with a temporary breastwork thrown up. I was ordered to take command of this company during the time it was stationed at this place. The enemy commenced shelling soon after I took command. I ordered the men not to expose themselves but seek protection as best they could from the shells and cannon balls, as the enemy was out of reach of small arms, and we could affect nothing: I and one of the soldiers should keep on the lookout as sentinels. During the time of shelling one struck the breastworks about a foot or two below the parapet and threw up a portion of the top of the breastworks, which fell upon my head. Another exploded just over and in the rear of where I stood. The firing soon after ceased for the day.

In conclusion, I will read to you the circular address of General Beauregard to the officers and soldiers, who were engaged in this battle; Headquarters, Department to North Carolina, and South Carolina, Virginia.

August 4, 1861

Soldiers! Your commanding General takes great pleasure in expressing his satisfaction at the cool vatorant disciplined bravery displayed by you on the twentieth of July in repelling the advance of the overwhelming forces of the enemy, after the heavy columns had entered the breach during the temporary surprise and confusion cashing upon the explosion of one of the largest mines recorded in military annals.

By your skill and courage, you held the enemy in check until the arrival of Mahone's Brigade of gallant and scar-worn veterans, with whom you then united and aided to drive back the force back with his own works, inflicting upon him one of the greatest disasters of the war, his losses being four times our own. This glorious success conclusively proves that the explosion of the enemy's mine, no matter how formidable under extensive works like those controlling Petersburg, will afford him no protection against disaster and rout, when opposed by a positive and patriotic army.

Signed.

G. T. Beauregard, General

To. C.C. Haile, Lieutenant Commanding, 23d. S. C. Regiment

Dr. George Rodgers Clark Todd

The Brother of Mary Todd Lincoln

GEORGE RODGERS CLARK TODD was born July 4, 1825, in Lexington, Kentucky. He was the youngest child of seven of Robert Smith and Eliza Parker Todd. His mother died of fever the day after he was born. Her mother never got to see a daughter become a wife of a future president, or even a son to become a fine surgeon and physician. He lived three blocks from the Transylvania Medical School. His early years was characterized by the caring of Negro servants, servants on loan from his grandma Parker, or inherited. His education consisted of two sessions a day, 1846, 1847, and a medical thesis in 1848. In 1849, one event occurred to change his life and problems arose. Hannah Todd Stuart married John Todd Stuart, Abe Lincoln's first law partner, and died in 1832 to cholera. Now, in 1849, cholera had returned to Lexington. Many of George's family took ill and died—Uncle James Clark Todd, John Smith Todd, and others too numerous to mention. In the late 1840's and early 1850's, Todd was in the Texas Rangers serving the Rio Grande area. This was confirmed by the Texas Ranger Association in Texas.

When the War Between the States broke out, their family was split, but George went for the Kentucky's own Jefferson Davis, pledging loyalty to the Southern cause. Four of the Todd brothers became officers of the Confederacy- George, Samuel, David, and Alexander. Only Levi Todd went with the Union, and sister Mary Todd was married to Abraham Lincoln. He accepted an appointment as a surgeon and was sent to do medical service in Virginia. There he joined his half-brother Captain David Todd in charge of prison camps. Both brothers were accused of brutality to the Union prisoners after the battle of Bull Run in the summer of 1861. George even kicked the dead bodies of Union solders calling them "Damned Abolitionists." After much complaining to Jefferson Davis, George was sent to the 10th Georgia Volunteers as a surgeon. In December 1862, being encamped at Zoar church near Fredericksburg, Virginia, Todd purchased a keg of French brandy, and failing to share with the other of the regiment, snuck in and shared with the other. George cussed up a storm and demanded a guard to go and find his missing brandy, but no parties were arrested nor the bottle of brandy found. In May 1863, George had the pleasure of working with a capture Union Surgeon Daniel M.

Holt. In Holt's diary, he noted that as he was working with Dr. Todd at the Battle of Salem Church in Virginia, he mentioned he had seen his sister, Mrs. Lincoln, a few days earlier. George's reply," Well, I don't know as I feel better or worse for that. She is a poor, weak-minded woman anyhow." Holt further described Dr. Todd as short, rather inferior looking with an impediment in his speech. In the Camden Confederate, May 1, 1863, noted that Dr. Todd was the brigade surgeon of Kershaw's Brigade in field battle reports near Fredericksburg, Va. He remained there until September 30, 1863, when he was transferred to the General Hospital in Charleston, South Carolina. He was placed in charge of the First South Carolina Hospital in Rikersville, about four miles from Charleston. There, Dr. Todd was said to abuse Union soldiers there, too. So much so, that a Lieutenant Union officer from Kentucky was said to have been thrown by Dr. Todd from his bunk and ordered him bucked and gagged for more than an hour. The next day, the lieutenant died. On August 1864, he was posted to the medical examining board in Charleston. This board approved incoming doctors and surgeons for medical duty and approved doctors for promotions, etc. On December 1864, he was assigned to the Wayside Hospital in Camden, South Carolina. Some 200 patients were said to have been admitted. This Camden Wayside Hospital was started in January 1862. Thereafter, Greenleaf Villa (the Lee house) was used as a Wayside hospital. Before that a large, wooden structure building just north of the old Mills Court House at King and Broad Street was being used. This house could have been the old 21-room McWillie house from the 1840s. When Sherman's troops came to Camden, no mention of Dr. Todd or the patients was mentioned. However, near Cheraw, a buggy belonging to Dr. Todd was found. The Yankees burned it as kindling for the fire to boil coffee. But when General Potter's troops came to Camden, April 15, the sick and wounded numbering three to four hundred was reported by Sergeant W.N. Collins, 54th Mass. Infantry in a letter dated April 15, 1865, to Boston newspapers. No report of the whereabouts or capture of Dr. Todd. During his service as a surgeon, Dr. Todd was noted for his amputating at the hip.

After 1865, Dr. George Todd married Martha Lyles, a lady who he had met while in Camden during the war. Her sister married another Confederate surgeon Edwin Hughes. The house they lived in was the old Reynold's house, named for the builder in 1816. By 1872, the house was sold to Edwin Hughes, and the Todds moved to Barnwell, South Carolina. Both are buried in Quaker Cemetery in Camden. A monument was finally placed on the grave in the 1930s and 1940s. [595]

---

[595] "A Divided Nation, A Divided Family, The Life and Times of a Rebel Surgeon, Dr. George Rodgers Clark Todd, Brother of Mary Todd Lincoln," by Terrance Strater, RN, BS, not dated.

What Makes a Hero?

The Story of Richard Rowland Kirkland
The Angel of Mayre's Height
Chronicle- Independent, December 29, 2014
By W. Guerry Felder

IF YOUR IDEA OF A hero starts with a knight slaying a dragon, a Roman gladiator fighting battles with a sword and suit of armor, or even a soldier fighting in a distant land, then maybe you have the wrong idea of what a hero really is. Is your hero brave and courageous, does he act on his own accord for his or her fellow human life, risking his or her life? Then possibly, you may know and respect the meaning of a hero.

In Kershaw District in August, a baby boy was born. As he grew up, his father made sure he was attuned to Christian values, family love, and service to the family farm. He was shown such qualities as hunting, farming, and in the 1850s, he learned how to use chains for surveying.

Around him were five brothers and a sister. The sister's name was Caroline, and her brother's names were James Allen, Dan, Dick, Billy, and Sam. Their parents were John R. and Mary Vaughn Kirkland. These people made up the Kirkland family, and the hero is Richard Rowland Kirkland. His family came from Farquhar, Virginia, and settled in the Catawba Waters Valley, where streams flowed, falls were present, and steep hills could be seen with giant boulders dotting the landscape. To the Kirkland pioneer, this resembled their beloved homeland in Scotland. This family also came with a mindset to do what they thought was right and absorb the consequences of their actions.

Dan and Billy Kirkland enlisted in the Kirkwood Rangers 7th Cavalry with Billy serving as dispatch under General Lee and General Jackson. Having been elected by the family for overseer duty, James Allen Kirkland stayed during the war and took care of the plantation. Sam Kirkland became wounded and died May 20, 1866.

Richland Rowland Kirkland died on the battlefield September 20, 1863, in Chickamauga, Georgia. What he left from his brief career as a soldier can be told in one mighty episode wartime spectacles and will forever be etched as a humanitarian act that should not be forgotten. Instead, it should measure what we have inside ourselves.

In 1862, Richard Kirkland became sergeant. The following article was found in the Camden Journal dated February 5, 1874. A little background is as follows:

> "The temperature in Fredericksburg, Va., was zero degrees on December 14, 1862. General Cobb and General Kershaw's troops were behind a stone wall on a sunken road. General Cobb fell mortally ill and later died in Martha Steven's house, and then General Kershaw took over. H.P. Hix of Columbia was working on a life-size portrait of Richard Rowland Kirkland and the figures of the famous scene. As Hix was told, this is what he gathered from all the resources: After the gallant charge of the Irish Brigade upon the stone fence behind which a portion of General Kershaw's division of South Carolina was posted, the ground was covered with dead and dying Unionists who, on the repulse and retreat, were left to suffer the untold agonies of a battlefield. It was declared the Irishman made a heroic charge as it had been hopeless and fatal; and whom they had retreated, both armies kept up a murderous sharpshooting upon each other. So fatal was the cruel sport that the federal reports declare 150 Unionists fell in the rifle pits from the fire behind the wall. On the Confederate side, the moment a hand or head was raised above the wall, it was sure to be perforated with a Unionist's bullet. Sergeant R. R. Kirkland, one of the sharpshooters stationed behind the brick wall, is the hero of the incident. He was killed in the battle the following year. He belonged to the Second South Carolina Infantry. The groans of the wounded Federalists lying just over the wall pierced the human heart, and his kindly human nature rebelled against the cruelty of their sufferings. They cried for water and there was no friendly hand to bring it. 'Water! Water! For God's sake, water!' The cries continued hour after hour.

Richard Kirkland resolved to try to relieve the wants of the dying and with that moral and physical heroism, which surmounts all obstacles and dares death for the good of others. Sergeant Richland Rowland Kirkland went to General Kershaw's Headquarters (The Stevens House), and asked the privilege of jumping over the wall and carrying water to the lips of the enemy. General Kershaw refused at first. He told Kirkland that sure death awaited the man who mounted the wall, for the fire was incessant and fatal. Richland Rowland Kirkland declared that he could not bear to hear the groans of anguish which greeted his ears and he would make the attempt to relieve them if the general would give his consent. The appeal was too strong to be ignored and resisted by Kershaw, so he reluctantly gave permission.

The gallant sergeant departed on his mission, assuring his friends that he did not believe he would be killed. A bound and he was over the wall, but he did not even touch the turf before a volley of bullets fired from a hundred different points welcomed him on his mission of mercy. Untouched, he knelt and put his canteen, like a blessed Samaritan, to the lips of a dying soldier and arranged his knapsack for a pillow. The Federals thought he was rifling the dead but when they discovered his noble mission and the firing upon him slacked then ceased, his work went on as it had.

    No firing could be heard. From one to another, he passed his loving work and two great and hostile enemies forgot their animosities in wondering observation and admiration of the hero who braved almost certain death to do a kind act to suffering men. One says that General Kershaw looked out and smiled as his fellow Camdenite performed this act and caused complete silence.

Battle Of Ream's Station

(sic, Battle of Globe Tavern, August 21, 1864)

Haygood's Brigade cut to Pieces
The General's Daring Recovery of a Flag
An Incident that Delighted Col. Rion

Mr. Editor: I will again endeavor to gratify my old comrades and many of my young friends and by giving them another war story, my last. I have in my other war stories endeavored to give due honor to my friends and comrades, the gallant Cols. P.H. Nelson and J.H. Rion, and Capts, Brooks, Segurs(Segars), Clyburn and others of the 7th battalion, to which I had the honor to belong. Now I propose to make special mention of Gen. Johnson Hagood and his gallant brigade.

His general life and war records, I shall leave to be told by older and wiser heads than mine. I shall confine this story to the battle of Ream's Station, sometimes called the Weldon Road. Gen. Hagood has been criticized by a few for the wreck of his brigade on that fatal day. After a full investigation in council of war by several of Gen. Hagood's seniors in rank he was fully vindicated and the mistake was that of Gen. Mahone.

After the crater fight on the 30th of July 1864, on the east of Petersburg, Gen. Grant turned his attention to the southern side of the city. Here the Weldon railroad came into the city. It is the great highway to the South. This road was regarded as a great necessity to Petersburg and Richmond and the Confederacy. To give, it up meant giving up Virginia and retiring to North Carolina. It was important, therefore, for Grant to take it and to the Confederacy to hold it. About the middle of August, Gens. Malone and Hampton were sent by Gen. Lee to defend the road and to head off the Federal advance. Gen. Mahone, on the18th and 19th captured 2,100 prisoners and Gen. Hampton drove into Petersburg a large herd of cattle captured from the enemy.

Among the troops engaged in this feeling expedition of Gen. Mahone was Gen. McGowan's S.C. brigade. When Gen. McGowan returned from the front to report to Gen. Mahone, he was mounted on his old warhorse with hat in hand and answered Gen. Mahone's inquiry as to whether there were any Yankees out there: "Oceans of them, General, oceans" The fire of battle was in Gen. McGowan's eyes, and as they rolled and glistened, Mahone concluded to send for reinforcements.

It was thus on the 20th, Hagood's brigade was ordered from and left the trenches to assist Mahone in retaking the Weldon road which the Yankees had occupied and was about 9 miles south of the city. On Saturday, the 20th, the 7th battalion along with, the brigade was in the trenches on the east of Petersburg, where it had been for three months. Col. Rion was, at that time, in the hospital. His wounded arm had never healed. That day hearing the movement, he came out to see us leave the trenches. The doctors had enjoined upon him not to go with us. He stood with Dr. Hanahan on the banks of the trenches, while the battalion filed past him. The men were pleased to see him and glad also to get out of the trenches, Col. Rion was pleased with the spirit of the men and glad to know they were to meet the enemy on the open field. He gave his men many words of comfort and cheer. But little did he think the next time he saw his faithful battalion it would be reduced to nineteen men.

Through the city we marched to the other side of it, where we met with McGowan's brigade. These we encamped for the night, lying down in a heavy rain. But we enjoyed the best night's sleep we had had in two months. Capt. J.L. Jones, of Liberty Hill, being the senior officer present was in command of the battalion. The next morning by five o'clock, we were marching down the road from the city. The battalion was in front with Capt. Jones and Adjutant W.M. Thomas at its head. We were met by one of Gen. Mahone's aides who directed our line of march to the left of the road where we halted and rested for a few minutes.

Just then Pegram's battery of artillery came down the road at full run. Just to our right and front across the road was an open field. Pegram dashed in to this field and opened a quick fire with all his guns. The enemy's minnie balls and shells aimed at Pegram began to fall about us. Then came, "Attention. Hagood's brigade, forward, march!" and down the road we went at double quick time, passing this battery and forming a line of battle on the road side of the old field. Pegram had already lost all his horses and the most of his men.

It was astonishing what destruction had been done to Pegram's battery in so short a time. As we passed, some of the old artillerymen of the battalion wanted to stop and man the idle guns, but the charge upon the outer lines of the federals had commenced and Hagood's line swept on across the open field towards the enemy in the wood sat the further edge. Slowly at first the enemy gave way. They had butchered Pegram, but now they were in full flight. The 25th Regiment was on the left and the battalion on the right. From the woods came the brave and gallant Gen. Saunders. He was dead, borne on the shoulders of our faithful Alabamians, who had followed their brave commander to his death. Following their dead commander came a squad of stragglers into our lines. Adjutant Thomas endeavored to rally them, and get them to join in with us. But they said they would wait in the road until their brigade came up. One old fellow, however, asked, "What brigade is that?" "Hagood's S. C. brigade," was Adjutant Thomas's reply. "All right," said he "that is good enough for me. Come, on, boys, let's hitch on here. I was born in the old State and I can fight with her." So, they were hitched on to the right of Company D, but I don't remember what ever became of them.

Our battle was only a few minutes. We were again marched forward with skirmishers to the front. We swept through the woods until we came to an open corn field. There we stood in line of battle for several minutes. From where we stood, we could plainly see the enemy entrenched behind the railroad embankment in front of us across the cornfield, and that they had earthworks projecting like forts to the right and to the left of where we were to charge. The enemy's artillery from the front, right and left were playing upon us, killing and wounding our men, tearing off treetops over our heads and cutting down the corn in our front. Gen. Hagood and staff came to us on the right and ordered the right to move just at nine o'clock. Gen. Hagood, seeing the surrounding circumstances were entirely different from what we had been informed, sent his aide, Capt. Martin to Gen. Mahone, who was about a hundred yards in the rear, to ask what to do. Capt. Martin returned with orders from Gen. Mahone to charge them, as he had been informed there was but a light force of the enemy in his (Hagood's) front. Had Gen. Mahone seen it as Gen. Hagood did he might have avoided what followed, this order was final, and there was no alternative for Hagood but to order the advance. Gen. Hagood, in passing the battalion on the right of the line, ordered it to advance at ordinary time until he came back to the right, as he had to go to the left where they were in trouble. All this took time and we were standing still, exposed to their shot and shell and not allowed to return their fire. The command, "Forward," came from Adjutant Thomas to the battalion. With sparkling eye and a cheerful face, he started back to the right. As he passed, Company B, he shook hands with is old friend, Lieut. S. Wade Douglass. Looking him in the face, he said: "Adjutant, we are going to catch it, to-day." His reply was: "Oh, Wade, cheer up. We can't die but once. So long, I will see you again." Scarcely had their hands parted when Lieut. Douglass was struck by a minnie ball and he fell mortally wounded at the adjutant's feet. Thomas called someone and said, "Take care of Wade" and he moved on. Little did one think in five minutes that besides Lieut. Douglass Company B was to number among its dead Capt. Kennedy and Lieuts. Isbell and Robert Kennedy. At this time Hagood came up and the whole line rushed for war. The enemy opened a deadly fire from their batteries just in front of the 21st and 25th regiments and upon which the regiments rushed to their deaths; scarcely one-tenth of their number escaped. Capt. Martin, of the staff, was mortally wounded, and immediately Major Maloney, also of Hagood's staff, was killed. This disposed of the left regiments of the brigade for the day. The others were the 27th on the left, the 11th in the center and the 7th battalion on the right.

It was now ten o'clock. The church bells at Petersburg rang, but that Sunday hour down in the valley of the shadow of death along the railroad those chimes floated on the gentle breeze, as if to remind us of our altars and firesides.

The command was continually given to forward and dress on our colors. The whole line pressed forward amid a murderous fire from the enemy. Men fell at every step, but the brigade closed its gaps. It lost half its number, crossing the first rising ground. When we reached the second rise and were in the flats, the command to halt was given and the order to lay down to be protected as much as possible, until our support came up. But they never came. Here, just at this time and place, your humble scribe received his discharge and carries the missile to this day.

Now, Mr. Editor, the remaining few words I have to say of this terrible carnage of blood is hearsay, but taken from reliable sources, from others more fortunate than myself on that fatal day. Just at this period of the battle, a federal officer rode out from their lines on our left. As the firing ceased, he came into our lines and said to Col. Gaillard of the 27th: "Give up that flag, sir, and surrender. We have you surrounded. There comes a column from the left to your rear to cut off your retreat. I have come here to secure you from further slaughter. You have struggled far enough." The flag was handed over to him. Then he looked towards the battalion. Its line was straight. Its flag was afloat. He asked if the battalion was not in the surrender. But the battalion had not surrendered. Every nerve was stretched, but none quivered. Capt. Segurs (*sic, Captain Dove Segars*), now in charge of the battalion, returned from the right to the left and asked Thomas what was the matter over there on the left. Thomas told him be 27th and the 11th had surrendered to the federal on the horse. Segurs said; "Adjutant we will have to die right here." "We will die," said Thomas, "and let those Yankees see how Carolinians can die." Segurs remarked, "Oh, that Hagood would come up." Just at this time, Gen. Hagood did run up. He said to Thomas: "What is the matter here?" He replied, "The 21st and 27th have surrendered to the federal and he has their colors." Gen. Hagood was then about fifteen paces from the officer. He instantly pulled his pistol and fired at him. Then he rushed at him with pistol in hand, until it seemed to reach his body. "Give up that flag," cried Hagood. "Bang" went the pistol again. The officer fell from his horse and the flag fell from his hands. Hagood seized the horse and mounted it. Capt. Dwight Stoney of his staff grabbed the flag. Hagood shouted: "All save yourselves who can." Gen. Hagood and Stoney safely escaped with the flag through the storm of shot and shell that followed them.

The next day Gen. Lee sought Gen. Hagood and found him sitting alone under a large tree. He was thinking of his noble dead, who lay stretched upon the field, so close that if they were living he could hear him call them. Gen. Lee rode up and saluted him with tears in his eyes and spoke to Gen. Hagood, saying: "Well, General, you have lost your brigade." "Yes," said Gen. Hagood, "I told my men not to charge, but, poor fellows, they would do it, and now they are all gone." "You must not be disheartened," said Gen. Lee. "There are some of them left. Gather them up and take them back to the rear. You will soon recruit up. I will promise you. I will never fight them any more in this war. They have done their share."

As Gen. Hagood desired to be alone with Gen. Lee, he directed the adjutant to gather up the remnant of the brigade and bring them to him. It was easy for him to reorganize the members the battalion, and soon he had nineteen of them and ten of the other regiments. "Fall in here Hagood's brigade," rang out through the woods. But it was so sorry sight to see. When brought them to Hagood, I pressed each one of them by the hand with tears rolling down his cheeks, and told them he knew what they could do, and promise them several weeks of rest and recreation. He turned them over to Thomas to have them rationed and cared for till further orders.

The next day the brigade was sent to Dunlap's farm to rest and recruit up. For several days, the brigade increased from 29 to about 75. It was here that an occurrence took place which delighted Col. Rion to tell. I will tell it and close. One night, Adjutant Thomas was going down the lines to see a friend, and he was passing by a camp fire, I overheard a conversation between some of the soldiers from one of the other regiments. One man insisted that charging breastworks had played out. No one could get him to charge breastwork again. His remarks seemed to have the approval of all present until one man spoke up and said, "Men, that won't do; you have to do it. There is that battalion up yonder. It would charge hell to-morrow morning and there is not a man of you that would not follow them. "In this battle, I closed my career as a humble soldier in behalf of the cause that is not lost!"

Jno. H. Neil.

White Oak, S.C.

"Battle of Ream's Station." *Winnsboro (SC) News and Herald.* May 3, 1905, p. 1 col. 1-4.

I Saw Sherman's Army

Found in the Thompson Folder at the Camden Archives and Museum, Camden, SC.

THE PRODUCE ON THE FARM were plentiful. News in those days seem slow, I was born in 1859, but I heard much about the war, and saw many things. We did hear word that Sherman was approaching Liberty Hill. The first Yankee seen rode his horse up the gate and to the foot of the back steps and demanded who lived there. My grandmother, Charlotte Patterson Thompson, told him what he asked about, and the soldier mentioned something about taking all of our processions. The next day, many soldiers came and overrun the place plundering and taking.

Just before the soldiers came, my grandfather Thompson and Uncle John, just 14 years old, left the home, as did many in the area, to evade capture and stop resistance to their evasion. However, in Lancaster County, they were captured. Their horses, firearms, and their boots taken. A week after the Yankees left, they returned, weary, barefooted, and half-starved. But what they came back to was desolation.

The Yankees had taken all they could and destroyed that they couldn't take. The men stayed for days, and ran rampant, cursing and shouting throughout the house and land. They took the dresses of the women, and some they cut up with swords. They destroyed furniture, and slashed family portraits. All the food was confiscated, or destroyed, and all the animals killed. Soldiers even took delight in shooting the dogs and other animals. A fine pointer, Legare, was killed, and those bodies lined the road. A poor, old hen and two puppies were the only things left on the place. The hen would have been gotten, but she pecked the Yankee so much he gave up. He said being old she was too tough. Days after the departure of the Yankees, one of the servants found an old pony wandering in the woods. We called him Joe Sherman, and he plowed after the war.

In the Camden Chronicle, April 26, 1929, the following was found:

> While digging a clay pit on the farm of Alex West, near Cassatt, laborers unearthed twenty-five bushels of corn in the ear, supposed to have been buried doing the Civil War—found in the column Fifteen Years ago, April 24, 1914.

One Yankee, an officer, offered to exchange references with my mother on behalf of my Father. This was not an uncommon practice. This was done to help the other in case he was wounded or captured. Mother accepted his offer. Their orders were "take what they wanted and destroy the rest." Some of the Negroes left with the Yankees, and some were seized as contraband of war, and forced into service of the nor th. One servant, Old Barlett, and old carriage driver, was threatened with death if he didn't disclose the whereabouts of the family jewelry. He refused and the threat was not carried out. He was even asked in his cabin if he was treated, and he said he was treated well. He was even asked about his clothes, and he told them from his master, and they were good clothes too.

Everyone in the community lost the family silver, jewelry, firearms, and any items worth taking. The Thompson family silver was lost, or at least much of it. My father had sent me a gun that he took off the enemy, and we hid in a tree, but the Yankees found it. The corn was taken away to feed the horses. The small amount of seed potatoes was left. Took all the sorghum molasses in barrels. Then those they could not take, they opened the cocks to the tank and drained it on the ground.

Found in the Rush family folder by John DeWitt Rush.

My grandmother Rush took me out to the barn one day to show where the Yankee soldiers in the Civil War cut through the back side of the log barn to load their wagons with corn, two wagons at a time, one at the front door, and the one in the back, then patched up. The Yankees found the horses and mules hidden in the creek nearby when the Negro slave gave the information reluctantly. The Yankees left one mule and enough corn in the barn to feed both it and the family until a new crop and new mules could be gotten. The family's hearts warmed to the fact that the Chestnut carriage horse bucked and threw off the first Yankee rider that attempted to mount it, who had to be taken away in the wagon ambulance. They hid the silver in the ground. At noon, officers, for the sentinel at the house, was ordered not to admit enlistees, came into the house and asked for refreshments. As Grandmother Young poured the wine, they asked her to drink first. She replied, "Oh, it isn't poisoned." It was the stragglers, however, that gave the most trouble, the camp followers, a bunch of rag muffins that lived off what the army left in its wake plus plundering the helpless families. The Negro slaves wanted to stay on after the freedom edict but gradually the younger ones, members of the Brady and Drakeford families, left to find jobs wherever they could. The older ones stayed on.

Memories of Mrs. U. N. Myers, Sr. 1938

Stories by Grandfather, Hiram Nettles told Me

My grandpa lived on the Stockton plantation, which was owned by Mrs. John D. Kennedy, wife of the future Confederate General. The story occurred sometime after 1856 or 1857. Grandpa was expecting John Kennedy down with a group to hunt, so he was up early to make preparations. His cook, a slave, was an older woman, whose name is now forgotten. Since his appetite was not a good as usual due to the getting up earlier, he declined the bowl of grits, set them down on the floor so the dog could eat them. Shortly afterwards, that dog kicked up his legs and died. I am under the impression that General Kennedy was a lawyer because I am sure that, after the Civil War, he defended Grandpa for caning a Carpetbagger. Anyway, the cook admission to put poison in the grits at the behest of another of the slaves, a man who was taken to and put in jail, and the cook lost her kitchen job.

Another story was told about of the Stockton slaves tapping at the window of an uprising. The man continued to report from time to time until all the ring leaders in the community were known and then a few days before the uprising was planned, all the leaders were arrested and jailed in Camden.

This story embraces the love of Sallie, who fell in love with a naval officer, Phillip A. Stockton. Sallie was at Mrs. Greland's Boarding School in Philadelphia. She danced with Phillip, and in a short time, married secretly. She arrived alone in Camden, then months later her husband arrived and an announcement came. A friend named Barron came with him. Soon afterwards, he resigned his commissioned in the United States Navy, and commissioned a commodore in the Confederate Navy.

Sallie and Phillip had two children living in Camden at the time of the Civil War. Phillip A. Jr. married a Miss Cunningham from the north and lived on the corner of Littleton and Boundary (Chesnut) Streets. Edward C. became an officer in the United States Navy. He opted for the Confederacy and served around Charleston near the end of the war.

The war ended for Grandpa and the rest of the old Kershaw Brigade up near Durham, North Carolina. The heavy fighting ended when the Brigade left the Army of Northern Virginia, which was facing the Federal forces along the Richmond-Petersburg line. When Sherman surfaced in Savannah after his march through Georgia, some South Carolina Troops were ordered back home to help defend the state. The Kershaw brigade passed through Columbia on January 14, 1865, enroute to the defense of Charleston. One lady did not think that our soldiers were demoralized, rather their shouts as they go by gladden my heart. Grandpa must have been one of those shouting soldiers. They soon found out that little to shout for as the resistance to Sherman soon evaporated after Hood's decisive defeats around Atlanta. Hood withdrew into Tennessee thinking Sherman would follow. But Sherman wasted no time thinking of chasing a beaten army, cut the Confederacy in two by striking out on his own to the coast. He arrived before Savannah, December 10, and on the 21st, the city fell. About six weeks later, on February 1, the Federal forces started north through the Carolinas. Columbia was captured February 17, and Charleston was the abandoned the next day. On the twenty-fourth, a detachment arrived in Camden.

Grandpa was now with the Confederate unites retreating before Sherman's advance. Considering the cast difference in the size of the opposing forces, the Federal progress may seem slow, and it was, but not of Confederate resistance. Remember that Sherman was subsisting his troops off the countryside and he was making sure his foragers was cleaning out one area before advancing to a new location. There were many desertions from the defending forces. Those who remained had one goal in mind — unite with Lee, defeat Sherman, and then turn on Grant. About a week after the fall of Columbia General Joseph E. Johnston was belatedly placed in command of what remained of the army, he had turned over to Hood in July 1864. Grandpa retreated north through Ridgeway and Lancaster, Charlotte, Raleigh, and on towards Danville, Virginia, where they were hoping to unite with Lee. This was not to be because the Army of Northern Virginia after abandoning Petersburg and Richmond and starting out for Danville could not evade the Federals and General Lee was forced to surrender his army to Grant on April 9. This left Johnson in a completely hopeless position and so he surrendered to Sherman on April 29. Grandpa was, at that time, in the vicinity of Durham, and they remained in camp until parole arrangements could be made. This took about a week because Sherman's terms to Johnston had been more liberal than Grant's terms to Lee. They were rejected by the Federal government. This was probably caused by the anger that had been created by the murder of President Lincoln on April 14. Whatever the cause it was the 26th before the surrender was concluded.

Grandpa had decided not to accept parole or at least not to sign the necessary papers. This meant getting out of camp unobserved. I have always understood that he talked it over with General Kennedy, but now I am not sure that Kennedy was even there. I do not know who was in command, some say General James Conner, at the surrender, but I am sure that Grandpa said he talked his plan with some officer from Camden and no opposition was offered. His buddy, Jim Brasington, agreed to go with him. They hoarded food for several days, and the night before the parole paper was due to be signed, they slipped away. They traveled by night and slept in the woods by day. Not only did they have to worry about Federal Troops but also local civilians because North Carolina had stood two to one against succession and like Virginia only joined the Confederacy when Lincoln's call for volunteers made it certain that they must either fight for or against the other states from the South. Somewhere they came on a Federal artillery horse that had run away or for some reason left behind. They snagged on to him and took turns riding. Grandpa said, if they heard anyone coming, they would immediately get off the road and hide. It was not very long before "Old Sherman," as they called the horse, caught on and as his ears were sharper than theirs he would on his own leave the road before either of them had heard anything.

The acquisition of the horse gave them even more reason to didge people because he had a big U.S. branded on his hip.

It was a long trip to Camden but finally made it coming in from the north. They found Grandpa's horse somewhere between Gun Swamp and Cool Springs and there Old Sherman stayed. I cannot say why or how, but Grandpa kept the horse instead of Mr. Jim Brasington, and very shortly after returning home he blotted the U.S. Brand with a flat piece of metal that had been heated red hot. The horse must not have been very old during the war because my grandmother remembered him about 1885 when she was in the third grade and living at old "Sandy Hill." Several of the kids would ride him to school sometimes, but she said Grandpa was always careful that the old veteran was not overworked.

In the Battle of the Wilderness (May 1864) during a hand to hand fight, he saw some ten to fifteen yards in front of a flat flask or whiskey bottle which was lying on the ground just ahead of a fallen Yankee. He immediately started to fight his way towards the bottle. As he was getting closer, he noticed, out of his corner of his eye, a Federal soldier about equal distance from the whiskey as he was, and with the same purpose in mind. From the looks that this Yankee flashed at Grandpa from the time to the time as they both fought their ways forward, he appeared to realize that Grandpa was also after the bottle, and it became a race between the two. It seems that the other fellow had less Confederates to handle than Grandpa had Yankees so he won the race. He picked up the bottle and raised it as if to salute to Grandpa. This action was accompanied by what the old man said was an unforgettable sneering smile which riled Grandpa something awful and he made for him but the other fellow was working his way backwards—I guess trying to find a safe place to take a swig. Now normally such an incident would have ended right there with Grandpa losing the whiskey but gaining a nice little side event to tell his grandchildren years later. This affair had a sequel, and it took place the next year in Camden in 1865.

As he told the story, he again saw that sneering smile early one afternoon while on patrol duty on Main Street. As he was ambling along two men in civilian clothes approached. He recognized one as being the Yankee who had beat him to the bottle, but he tried not to show that he remembered the face or that same sneering smile that the man gave to him as they passed. Grandpa continued his patrol until the new shift came on late in the afternoon. He then went to his room and left whatever he wore in the way of a uniform or badge of authority as a policeman and picked up a walking stick that he had made of hickory. With this he went back out on the streets and started looking for the man. Sure, enough they met again as the fellow was either entering or leaving an eating place. Without preliminaries, Grandpa laid onto to him with the stick and as he said, "Beat the hell out of him." Whether he was restrained by cooler heads or finished the job to this satisfaction, I do not recall but afterwards, he returned to his room and went to bed. He was not surprised when there was a knock on his door and it proved to be a sergeant from the local Federal garrison come to arrest him. Grandpa had to dress, and as he was sitting on the side of the bed pulling on his shoes, he reached under the pillow, got his pistol, and ordered the soldier out of his room. He did this simply because he could not let himself be taken by a lone Yankee. A short time later when the sergeant returned with a squad of soldiers, Grandpa considered the odds more equal and went with them peaceably. Bond was arranged for him the next day, but I feel sure he lost his job on the police force.

The trial came up in six or seven weeks in the old courthouse before a Circuit Judge or at least that is as I remember the story. General Kennedy represented Grandpa and asked for some time to prepare his case, and that some of the witnesses needed were not available at that time. The judge denied this request so the prosecution presented its case before lunch, or dinner as they called it. When the court adjourned, the judge ordered Grandpa to be locked up, and with that, General Kennedy object so as this man is an honorable man and had been walking the streets for six or seven weeks till the trial with no desire to run, which may prove he was guilty. The judge agreed not to lock him up. Upon departing the room, the General pulled Grandpa aside, and spoke in a deep voice. "Hiram, this case is going bad for us. This will be your last chance to get away." He told Grandpa there was a horse tied up on the other side of the Wateree River and a man with a boat on the near side to row him across. The main thing was to get away unobserved and to keep moving as fast as he could. They decided it would be better for him not to eat so he went outside and strolled back and forth on King Street. Each time he would go a little further until he was as far as Church Street, where he turned south as if he was going around the block. He continued slowly until he got to Bull Street, and since things were quiet, he took off to the southwest right through the cemetery on to the designated spot on the river, which as I remember was right across from Bettyneck, a Kennedy Plantation. He found the boat and horse as expected and headed out for a location in the vicinity of Blaney, where he had some cousins.

During the war, his sister, Louise, had married Joe Nettles, a brother of the other Louise Nettles, who had been drowned in the Boykin Millpond tragedy. It is very likely that Grandpa stayed with them several weeks or until one night a black man rode in with a warning from General Kennedy that the Yankees were on to his whereabouts, and were sending soldiers to pick him up. He left that night and ended up in Lancaster (or maybe Rock Hill) where he had other cousins on his mother's side - the Riddles. His cousin, Joe Riddle, had served in the same regiment as he so they were very close. Here he remained for several months until his friends could arrange things with the Federal authorities. Finally, on the plea that he was the sole supporter of his widowed mother (his brother John was still a youth) and possibly due to changes in the personnel of the army detachment, the charges against him were dropped and he returned home. [596]

---

[596] Information found in the Nettles Family Folder, Camden Archives and Museum, Camden, S.C.

Some Diaries and Letters of Soldiers

Cornelius TC. Platter
Adjutant
81st Ohio Infantry Volunteers
His diary concerning Kershaw District:

Monday Feby 20th 1865

UP EARLY AND STARTED AT 7 A.M. Marched 22 mile and went in camp at " Muddy Springs" about sun down. We traveled in a north-west direction and were about the same distance from Columbia all day. About 1 P.M. we struck the road traveled by our corps and the rest of the day we marched on a parallel road with the 3d Div [Division] - our teams were in rear of 3d Div [Division] and reached us about 8 A.M. Our route today was through a section of country known as "Sand Hills" which is by far the poorest country I have seen in the Southern Confederacy. Our whole army is under way moving northward - There is no telling where we will halt next.

Tuesday Feby 21st 1865

Left camp at 5 1/2 A.M. our Regt [Regiment] having the advance of everything - Marched northward. Sherman has again "fooled" the enemy - yesterday he threatened Camden and to day [today] he took a course due north leaving Camden in our Rear and right. - Marched 20 miles and encamped in "Dutch Creek" some 3 or 4 mile east of Wainsboro [Winnsboro]. Country [added very] rolling and productive - weather warm and pleasant - in camp early and had a splendid supper of corn cakes "and [unclear: other] good things. - We occupy the extreme right of the army.

Wednesday Feby 22d 1865

Ordered to move at 7 A.M. but as we were in the rear of our Div [Division] it was 10 o'clock when we got under way. - We had to wait for the 1st Div [Division] to pass us. - Just as we were starting heard cannonading in front but did not learn the cause of it. Passed through Poplar Springs - a one horse Country town. Consisting of a store and "Blacksmith Shop." Went into Camp. one mile from Peays Ferry on the Wateree River - distance marched 7 miles. - Saw a great many refugees today - they are in camp near us. - Country very hilly - weather clear and pleasant. Col [Colonel] Adams and St [Sergeant] Pittman had a difficulty just as we were going in camp. - Pittman says he will not remain any longer as a.a.G. - but Col [Colonel] will not relieve him

Thursday Feby 23d 1865

Up early and left at 7 A.M. and crossed Wataree [Wateree] River - a narrow deep stream - Here all the Extra and worthless animals were taken by the Inspector Genls [Generals] and the worthless ones shot. Country very hilly - Passed through Liberty Hill - a small country town which contained some nice country residences - It was nine o'clock before we went into camp and as our trains were in the rear - it was 12 M. before we got our supper. Has been drizzling rain all afternoon. which made it very unpleasant marching. Lieut [Lieutenant] Pittman was relieved as a.a.G. of the Brigade and reported to the Rgt [Regiment] for duty and was assigned to the command of Co [Company] D. Col [Colonel] Adams has not selected another adjutant. Marched 15 miles.

Friday Feby 24th 1865

No orders to be ready to move this morning and consequently when we were ordered to "fall in" at 7 A.M. we were not ready. A great many of the men had to start without eating breakfast. It rained all last night and as our "fly" was leaky we passed an uncomfortable night. It rained nearly all forenoon. Consequently, roads were [unclear: heavy] and marching bad. Our Regt [Regiment] was in the advance of everything to=day [today]. We should have gone to "Flat Rock Church" last night but Gen [General] Hagen who was in the advance yesterday got on the wrong road this side Liberty Hill and Gen [General] Corse followed him. We traveled on the main Camden road untill [until] within 5 miles of Camden. where we changed our direction to the left and [unclear: faced] near the village of Kirkwood where we left the main Camden road. Col [Colonel] Adams with the 12th Ills and Cos of the 66 Ills Infty [Infantry] was ordered to proceed to Camden and take the place if possible - He entered the town without loss. - destroyed a large lot of Commissary stores. R.R depot andc. [et cetera] andc. [et cetera] He skirmished over the battle of "[unclear: Hobkirks] Hill" - Camden is said to be a very beautiful country town - After leaving the Camden road we passed through a level sandy pine country. Saw the finest Southern Residence today I have ever seen - "Cool Springs residence". Quite a number of prisoners were captured to day [today] among them a Rebel Captain a C.S. Col [Colonel] Adams came in from Camden about 7 P M. Has commenced raining again this evening and I fear we will have another wet night. We are in camp in a turpentine camp about 7 miles north of Camden. . We have been hearing rumors of the evacuation of Charleston by the enemy. and I guess the place has been abandoned by them and the "Blue Coats" are occupants of the town. We are now nearing the boundary line between North and South Carolina and unless we change our direction to the east we will in a few days enter North Carolina. It is very uncertain where we will reach the coast. - Distance marched 20 miles. We are on the Cheraw road this eve.

Saturday Feby 25th 1865

Ordered to march at 7 A.M. but it was near 8. before we were under way. The 2d Div [Division] and our Div [Division] have been traveling on the same road for some days. To=day [Today] the 2d Div [Division] had the road and we either had to make a parallel road or march in the rear. Gen [General] Corse [unclear: chose the] former and as we only marched 7 miles we got in camp as soon as the 2d Div. [Division] We marched in a northeast direction all day. on the Cheraw Road. In camp near a turpentine "distillery." Still cloudy and drizzling rain, very sharp thunder and lightening just as we were going to bed.

Sunday Feby 26th 1865

Ordered to be ready to move at 6. A M. but it was a hour later before we broke camp. Marched 7 miles to Lynch' s [sic] Creek. and here we halted several hours. On account of the recent rains the stream was very much swollen and it was found to be impossible to cross the supply and ordinance trains. The creek is more like a swamp than anything else. All the Brigades waded across and the 1st and 3d Brigades trains started and this evening about half of them are "stuck in the mud." The stream is more than half a mile in width and Bumpy my horse fell down with me on crossing and a "ducking" was the consequence -- Col [Colonel] Adams Capt [Captain] Cameron and quite a number of others met with similar luck. The stream is rising very rapidly and there is no telling how soon our wagons will get over. We are [unclear: [deleted:] here without any blankets and it is impossible to send over after them. We sent after our cooks. They succeeded in effecting a crossing. Lt [Lieutenant] Johnson came with them. They had to swim their horses. Lt [Lieutenant] J attempted to recross but he got cracked and about faced and he will spend the night with us -- Our Brigade foragers had quite a spirited little fight with the enemy today. Col [Colonel] Davis 1 Co [Company] received 7. sabre cuts. which were inflicted by the hands of a Lieut [Lieutenant] Col. [Colonel] Our losses 2 wounded. Rebel loss said to be 15 killed -- The foragers certainly deserve great credit for their bravery and gallantry. - The enemy are Cavalry belong to Sutlers command and are just from Richmond. Our direction to day has been north east -- Weather clear and pleasant. Do not think we will soon forget this day. We are ordered to be under arms tomorrow morning at daylight. We are anxious to hear some northern news. It will be at least 10 days before we have communication. Crossed Lynchs Creek at "[unclear: Tellers] bridge."

Monday Feby' 27 65

Slept soundly last night before a huge log fire - under arms at 6 A M. After breakfast went down to the crossing. The 3rd Brigade were pulling their teams out by hand. - They were in the mud water and mire all night. Lieut [Lieutenant] Johnson with several others re - crossed the creek this morning and were all capsized - Spent the day laying around "loose" doing nothing with plenty of help. The creek is still impassable for man and beast. Preparations are being made to build a foot bridge and [unclear: Stream] it is partly built tonight. Water falling fast. A warm pleasant day but it has the appearance of rain. Am ordered to report to Col [Colonel] Adams tomorrow morning as A.A.A.G. of the Brigade. Lt [Lieutenant] Pittman I suppose will be my successor in the Regiment. Retired early.

Tuesday Febry 28th 1865

Up early. Regt [Regiment] under arms at daylight. Reported to Col [Colonel] Adams and entered upon my duties as A.A.A.G. - Lieut [Lieutenant] [unclear: Gillell] and I after various attempts succeeded in crossing the creek to where our teams are parked". When we returned the foot bridge was completed. [Prisoners?]

busy corduroying and bridging the creek. Teams commenced crossing by dusk. Our Brigade wagons had the advance but it was near 11 o'clock before they were all over. We put up a tent and "crawled in" for the night. Has been drizzling rain nearly all day. Lt [Lieutenant] Pittman is Act Adjt [Adjutant] 81st Ohio. No news of any importance only that we will be apt to move some time tomorrow.

Wednesday March 1st, 1865

Slept late. Spent the forenoon in the office. 150 men detailed from the Brigade to report at the creek to build "Corduroy" -- At noon we rec'd [received] orders to be ready to move as the teams were across. - Under way at 2 p.m. Marched 10 mile over a poor pine country in a direction in a direction a little north of east on the Cheraw road and went in camp on Black Creek - Still cloudy and strong appearance of rain Heard today [today] of the capture of Wilmington by Gen [General] Schofield - Troops ordered to be under arms at daylight - There is a probability of our remaining here tomorrow.

Source: ***Hargrett Rare Book and Manuscript Library***, University of Georgia Libraries.

In the Diary of Sergeant James Louis Matthews, Orderly Sergeant

From his descendants, he enlisted in Company F, 12th Indiana Infantry but he joined a month before being mustered out, he became a part of Company E, 59th Indiana Regiment, with Captain William Whitaker commanding.

The following schedule was in this diary in 1865 concerning this area:

> February 23- Crossed the Wateree River on a pontoon bridge. Marched 20 miles and went in camp.
> February 24- Marched 18 miles and threw up works.
> February 25- No marching
> February 26- Marched 10 miles, past a large camp meeting ground, and went in camp. This is the Sabbath Day.
> February 27- In camp near the crossroads at Mrs. Guardner's (Gardner's) Store.
> February 28- Was mustered for pay. No marching today.
> March 1- Marched one mile today. Threw up works in the rear. Camped near the Pedee River.

"***The Civil War Diary of Sergeant James Louis Matthews,***" edited by Roger C. Hackett, Indiana Magazine of History, The Department of History of Indiana University, December 1928, Vol. XXIV, pages 306, 307, and 310.

When Sherman Captured Camden
New York Iowa, Feb 24, 1890
From the Diary of E. P. Burton, Surgeon of Illinois Regiment

To the Postmaster at Camden, S.C., or anyone else who may come in possession of this:

On February 24, 1865, just 25 years ago—I, in the capacity of surgeon of an Illinois regiment, with Sherman's army, visited your beautiful town. As I was looking over the notes in my memorandum book, jotted down at the town, the perhaps foolish fancy took possession of me to send them to you, thinking that possible you might be interesting in looking them over. Perhaps some editor would like these notes for publication.

I don't know the name of the lady that us our dinner, nor in what part of the town she lived, but her husband ran on a railroad and came home each night. We prevented the stragglers from stealing her property. I have persuaded my daughter to copy the accompanying from my Journal, with which you can do as you please.

Yours, most Respectively,
E. P. Burton

Wednesday, February 22, Washington's birthday- We were ordered to start this morning at 7, but the 2nd and 3rd Divisions passed us, so we did not get to moving till half past twelve. Very smoky today. Moved northward on the road from Winnsboro to the Wateree River. Marched about eight miles and camped at Peay's Ferry. There Divisions are here to cross. The country today has been quite hilly---some rocky and some clay. Said to be 500 or 600 rebels in our vicinity today. Two Union soldiers were killed by them today. The creek on which we camped last night is called Dutchman's Creek. The most interesting sight today was the crowds of refuges both black and white. It looks melancholy indeed to see so many women and little children start out without friends and on foot to find a home. Little black children, not over six years, trudging along, and their mothers carrying babies. How I pitied them. Country seems pretty well cultivated about here.

Friday, February 21- Another period of particular interest has passed in the last two days. At noon yesterday we passed the Wateree River. Up two miles passed a pretty town—Liberty Hill. Made a rapid march of ten miles more and camped between 9 and 10 o'clock. Passed a fine country, pretty hilly, but well cultivated, the soil a red clay. Travelled Southeast down the river. Started at 7 and marched all day in the rain. Struck a sandy soil this morning. But the peculiar interest of the day is the capture of Camden. The 12th and 66th Illinois led the division about five miles and entered down. In the suburbs, we passed the old battleground of Camden, the darkies called it Kirkwood. The hill is covered by some most magnificent residences. Camden was a beautiful town, but the soldiers went in for plunder. They gutted all the stores. Seeing a lady looking quite imploringly, I went up to the door. She said she had been wishing to see some officer, and asked me in. She pretended to be a Union lady. Three others and myself took dinner with her. Her husband was on the Railroad. She expected the train in at 5 o'clock. The citizens were well frightened. We scared up a few Johnies and captured three or four. Staid in town but two hours, but the trip is long to be remembered. We got into camp at dark, fifteen miles from last night's camp. We north east of Camden, on the Big Pine Tree creek, at Kershaw's mills. Many of the boys got drunk on wine, and we have left quite a number of stragglers behind. I would love to have lingered around the place of so much historical note. The old house, once the headquarters of Cornwallis, was standing, but used for a warehouse. I did not see it. It was fired and burned by order of the commander.

A Letter from E. N. Yarbrough

E.N. Yarbrough Company F

7th South Carolina Battalion Hagoods Brigade

On Saturday night the 14thof May 1864, our company volunteered to go on picket duty and about 10 or 11 o'clock that night Lieutenant A. W. Raley caught me asleep on my post and he said Ebbin what will I have to do with you? And that woke me up. And I was frightened. He was the largest man that I ever saw. He was right between me and the moon and he looked to be a sight. I just got on my knees, raised my hands, and said Lieutenant, please don't report me, He reached out his hand patted me on the head and said, if you don't tell it, I will not for I would have been shot, he knew it just as I did, but he was a good man. He said here tobacco chew, it put the amber in your eyes so you will not go to sleep anymore tonight. I said Lieutenant I do not need that now for I have had all the sleep that was in me knocked out for the night for I had just past a very dangerous spot in my life and the lieutenant knew that just as well as I did.

Now Sunday the 15th of May 1864

Fell back up the side of the hill just before good light saw a man standing between the two small houses and four of us shot him, he fell, and then the sharpshooting started in real earnest, and I do not know the times I shot or the times I was shot at a plenty here. They could not hit me for I had me a large oak log, but we shot all the same. Finally, all my ammunition gave out. I started for more and they would shoot at me. I would fall down in the brush fill. They would sease firing, get up and go again. They would commence firing at me down in the brush I would go, finally I got up in the Breast Works got my ammunition and went back just as I went out by falling down in the brush when they would shoot until I got back to my log. Then I took my hat put it on my log, Then I took my hat put it on my bayonet held it above the log lying there on my back and they would shoot at my hat. I would shake it at them, they would shoot. Finally, night came and glad was I. I counted the balls in the log for about six feet and there I found 24. I could very easy count them by the moon light. For everywhere they hit the log it had made a bright red spot. Now we were out here 24 hours without anything to eat or drink. Now this was pretty bad.

Monday May 16, 1864

Went into battle had a pretty hot time of it. And the thickest fog I think I ever saw. Has to fall back there and got wounded right arm just above wrist, one bone broken and I thought a scalp on m right side above the hip bone, but you will see different a little later on finally I got over. I was but running away but was just getting away with that was left there to get a way.

When I got in in the Breast works, the captain came to me and said Ebbin, are your wounded? I said yes, Captain. They have got me in my arm and I think a scalp on my right side. He said you had better try and get to the Field Hospital, which I did and had my arm dressed all this till sun up and then I lay down and went to sleep. When I woke up my back was very cold. I called one of the men there to come to me. Which he did. I asked him to examine my back and see what is the matter back there. I said stick your fingers in the holes and let me see how far a part, which I did and here is where I found out it was not a scalp but a plenty bad wound. Then late in the evening word came that all that could walk had better start to Iven's Bluff, or they might have to stay there all night. I thought I could and got up to start and fainted, came to myself and said," Oh, I lay there a while, got up the second time and fainted again." Then I came to myself I said Oh! Oh! Right here I will lie to night. I stretched out, folded my hands and made all preparations a wounded boy could make that far from home but the ambulance driver saw me, he had me taken up, put on the seat with him, and carried me down to the Bluff. There I spent the night right on the bank of the James River and Bluff is 90 feet high.

Thursday 17, May 1864

I was carried up the James River on a boat to Richmond, and when they started with me from the boat, I fainted and when I came to myself was some 50 or 60 yards from the boat under a shade, and there were 3 or 4 ladies around me doing all they could for a wounded boy, and they were sure working doing all that loving hands and loving hearts could for me, and I fainted again. Then, they had a wagon and matress brought, and had me put on the mattress and put on the wagon, and sent up in the city, and put in the Wayside Hospital.

Wednesday 18

Laying there with my left hand over my face, and on my left side right over my head, I saw a small plate with my name on it, how I was wounded, and where from. About 10 o'clock, I felt something about my right side. I looked over my right shoulder, there was a nice-looking lady dressing my side. That made me ashamed when she got through, she came around in front of me, and talked to me, but I could not enjoy her talk for the fix I was in – Black, dirty, and bloody. How in the world could I? She did not seem to care. Finally, she said, "Have you wrote your mother since you got wounded?" I said, "No, I have not. She said she would come back this evening, and write for you. Sure enough she did come and sat there and wrote my mother and said don't you worry about your boy for I am going to take special care of him myself. Then she wanted me to let her have me sent to her home when they would let me leave the Hospital. I said to her that was nice but I wanted to go to my mother then. I was in a fix- Black, dirty, and bloody, and so much pain. I never had the mind to ask her name nor her address. But she did all she could do for me, and I know, with a loving heart could for a wounded boy. I could not enjoy anything she did, but it was in my fault because of the pain I was in.

Saturday, May 21, 1864

They were going to move me. She asked where they were carrying her boy? They told her one thing and did another. When the ambulance got there, she came to me, patted my cheek, and said, "I will see you this evening," but we then lost sight of each other completely by me not getting her address and name.

I was carried to the Jackson Hospital. In here, I spent three weeks. Then I got a furlow (furlough) for home. My clothing was some four or five hundred yards from me. I tried and tried to get someone to go and get them for me but I could not. Finally, I came out of the Hospital bare headed, bare footed, and with the

Thinnest underware on, and I started for my clothing. Don't you know I was a sight to look at that morning? And it seemed if I met one lady I met 500 but I had only resolution in the matter. I never expected to see any of them again, I was going to see my mother. Then, about 10 o'clock, the Doctor put me down on a table, then straightened my fingers, which was then shut fast in my hand from my wound, and I do believe this was as bad as the wound at first, if anything worse, and by 12 o'clock it had thrown me in a fever. Then the Doctor wanted me to stay there some four or five more days longer but I left that evening 23 miles to Petersburg, got there, and I was completely given out, and put in the hospital that Thursday evening, spent the night there. Early Friday morning report came the Yankees were coming and could see them from the top story of the Hospital. There I was with a furlough, and wanting to see my dear mother. This was awful worse than awful going to going to lose one and miss the other. I got to crying and it was real crying too, not any of your snubs either. It was great big boo, whoo's too. The nurse would talk but that done no good. But, the Yankey's did not come in the town. I spent the night there. Early Saturday morning, I left there for Wilmington, got there Sunday night, and left Sunday night, got to Kingsville Monday morning left three in the evening, got to Camden that night. Left Camden Thursday morning, got home about 3 o'clock in the evening. He was sixteen years old when this happened and his home was near Bethune, S.C.[597]

An Interesting Sketch of Wateree Mounted Rifles Company K, South Carolina Cavalry, by One of the Members

In writing a record of the part taken by Company K, 7th regiment South Carolina Cavalry in the struggle for our rights in the war of Secession, the writer of this sketch will try to portray the characters of some of those with whom he was most intimately associat4ed as well as to recall the stirring scenes which tried men's souls. Especially prominent in my memory one very near and dear who just four years ago, March 15, 1864, passed over the river, lamented and beloved by all. We were school boys in 1860 and 1861, our ages ranging from 14 to 16 years. All of us thoroughly enthused with what was going on at that time, and we could not be restrained from sharing some of the martial spirit, which imbued our elders, so after school hours every day several of us (all well mounted) would join in with the Kirkwood Rangers, a fine Cavalry company then being drilled for future services in Virginia. But when the company went into camp preparatory to marching to Virginia, we were ruled out. A year later at the reorganization of the Kirkwood Rangers, Lieutenant E.M. Boykin returned home, and set to work to form a company of boys under 18 years and men over 48 years for our State service. The company was organized in the summer of 1862, and in September we went into active service under the command and care of our beloved and esteemed Captain E.M. Boykin. Our first camp was on Murrell's Inlet on our own coast, our object, to protect some very valuable salt works from marauding parties sent out from the large men of war sailing along our coast. I must mention an incident that occurred here. It was great fun to throw crabs and roasting ears into the salt pans, but on one occasion one of us, W.D. McDowell, paid dearly for his venture by being accidently shot. But noble Spartan that he was, he bore his mishap with the greatest

---

[597] Copied from the Original by Labruce Hopkins, found in the file on Civil War at the Camden Archives and Museum, Camden, S.C.

fortitude exhibiting then, as he did afterwards in Virginia, both on the field of battle and in oft times trying camp life and courage and cheerfulness which made him so valuable as soldier and friend.

Our next move was to Greenville, South Carolina. Before leaving that point, we made quite a dashing raid joining General Vance of North Carolina, we went near Greenville, Tennessee, where the Federals had a garrison 15,000 strong. We drove out 1300 hogs into Asheville, North Carolina. We lost one man, the Yankees attacking us and attempting to rescue the hogs. The Northern troops lost many more. This was one of the many darling encounters with the enemy of which there is no record in history. It was at this little fight that the noble and unselfish character, and cool soldier, was first displayed by Sergeant J.M. Cantey. I was left on the field, and at the imminent risk for my own safety before he returned for me, taking me on his own horse. On our return to Greenville, we were mustered into Confederate service and marched to Virginia, reaching Virginia, just in time to join General Beauregard at Drury's Bluff and Bermuda Hundred, May 16. We then joined the 7th S.C. Cavalry (formerly Holcombe Legion) and were stationed on the north side of the James River, under command of Colonel Alexander Haskell. Now indeed we realized what war is. Our next engagement May 30th at Old Church a few days prior to the general engagements to Cold Harbor. The Old Church fight was fought with disaster to our regiment. Of the eight companies engaged nearly all the officers were wounded and had to retire, every company officer either killed, wounded, or captured. Being left without a commissioned officer, our orderly, J.M. Cantey commanded the company continuously, until the return of Captain David DuBose, who had been severely wounded. I must not omit to mention that at Old Church, we lost among other gallant men one whose memory is very dear to us. I allude to the handsome, chevalier soldier, Tom Boykin, Son of our old Captain and afterwards (Colonel) Lynch Deas was also left on the field wounded, and taken a prisoner first to Washington, and then to Elmira, New Jersey. His hardships while there undermining his constitution so that the was cut off from us a young man. A vacancy now occurring in Company K by the death of Lieutenant Whitaker, Sergeant Cantey was elected a lieutenant. Frequently acting as Captain, I, in the absence of its officers. Lieutenant Cantey now developed great military aptitude and was on more than one occasion complimented for soldierly conduct and coolness in battle.

I recollect on one occasion at the old drill house on Deep Bottom the enemy drove in our skirmish line about daylight, their bullets falling into our camp before were out of our beds, Lieutenant Cantey and myself were sleeping together, and he immediately jumped up ordering the company to fall in quickly with accoutrements and arms, the order was promptly obeyed. We had to double quick about a mile to the breast work, where we were to await the enemy.

With the early day light, we could see them advancing and hear their officers giving orders, the Negro troops being pushed forward by the whole troops in the rear.

Our regiment was in an angle of the breastworks and defended ourselves gallantly though opposed by overwhelming numbers somewhat in disorder, Company K in command of Lieutenant Cantey, and Company H in command of Lieutenant James Haile, were the last to leave the breastworks. These two companies were ordered by their commanding lieutenants to half, retire in line returning the enemy's fire, as we fell back in perfect order. Shortly, after these orders came from headquarters that all officers below captains should be strickly examined, these two young men, Haile and Cantey were excepted who General Gary said he had sufficiently examined on the field.

The following day the enemy falling back, we re-established our advance pickets. While we were skirmishing with the enemy around some houses very near the breastworks, a lady rushed to the door and asked if someone would take her to Richmond, Jones, a member of Company K, dashed up to the door and took her behind him on his horse. The Yankees were so near that we could hear their officer Colonel Spears give his order, "Do not shoot that man," when Jones galloped off with the lady (whom he safely carried to Richmond). You can imagine the cheer that went up from both sides. Perhaps some of you can appreciate his welcome back to the lines accompanied as he was by a bottle of brandy.

As soon as we got behind the siege pieces, skirmishers were thrown out and Colonel Haskell ordered Lieutenant Cantey with the modesty, which was so prominently a characteristic of the boy, as of the man, said to Colonel Haskell, that while perfectly to go he disliked to seem to take the place of ranking officers, but Colonel Haskell answered No! You are my choice. He then promptly went over the breastworks advancing his skirmishers so rapidly that he soon came in contact with the enemy driving them back and capturing a few prisoners. The skirmishers were then drawn in as the enemy were rapidly falling back. I mention this incident to show the estimation in which this young Lieutenant was held by his superior officers.

On the seventh of October, we were aroused about midnight and every man armed with a sabre. This was sufficient to let us know that something unusual was about to happen.

Captain Dubose who had just returned was in command of the squadron, who led the charge. Lieutenant Haile was ordered to take charge of ten picked men of five from each Company H and K and I and meet the enemy with their sabre. We rushed forward, the enemy wheeled and endeavored to rally behind a breastwork but we were too close on them, our men being mixed together. The fifth squad not being properly supported became detached and it was then that our gallant Colonel Haskell, with only a few followers, met General Kantz and his escort Colonel Haskell was severely wounded and left on the field dead.

Lieutenant Cantey was with Colonel Haskell at the time and took from a Yankee cavalry man a sword belt, which had been thrust through by Colonel Haskell's sword leaving the blood stain on it. Lieutenant Cantey preserved the belt intending to present it to Colonel Haskell's son but unfortunately it was lost. The colonel was rescued by the Hampton's Legion, who came to our relief. Lieutenant Cantey continued with the company except when acting as Captain to the company, until we received orders to evacuate dear old Richmond.

He was then placed in command of a small squad acting as the rear guard and was one of the last to leave Richmond having to lead the horses over the foot bridge. He other bridge too far burned to admit of being used after overtaking the regiment Lieutenant Cantey resumed command of Company I and held that position until the surrender at Appomattox. Lieutenant Cantey was most fortunate never to have been wounded. Both Cantey and Haile were promoted to Captains but did not received commission before the surrender.

Lieutenant Cantey came home after the war, and settled down to hard work, such work as was left us to do in our impoverished condition, but through all trials the same honest, unselfish, painstaking, noble, man, and friend to the last as he proved to be while fighting for his country. We mourn him still as a chevalier, "Without fear and without reproach."[598]

Letter from William Kirby to Mr. Benjamin Outlaw

December 27, 1862

Dear Friend, I embrace present opportunity to drop you a few lines to inform you that I am well. This morning hoping this may come safe to hand and reach you all well. I have no news of any interest to write. Times is very??? Still out hear at this time. The Yankis is gone from Fredericksburg and I hope to stay. The wether [sic] is something warmer than it has bin. Our fair is very ruff, we get beef and flour and a little bacon. A nugh to keep us from starving, if they will only give us that much all the time. I wish to say to you that John was sent to the hospital sick before I hear and I have not heard from him since. Abseloem (Absolom Kirby) and Redin is both well and John Turner too and all the Coys formerly. There is some talk of us going to North Carolina, and I hope it may be the case for me. Would get it little nearer home we all cold get to home thirty days and get five hundred dollars county money if we would join the regerlars for five years and go in a fort nite. I don't believe in being grown for four years longer unless I am compeled to be grown. Tell Bently if he is not gone he must write to me and send me all the news of our old times and derect the letters to Richmond, VA, and you must do the same. If you can't write as often as I write to you, you write once and a while. I saw a letter from Richard a few days ago and he was well then, so I remain your friend truly til death.[599]

---

[598] Civil War Folder, Camden Archives and Museum, Camden, S.C.
[599] Letter found in the Outlaw folder, bad spelling and all (corrected in some portions), Camden Archives and Museum, S.C.

Persons Captured at Lynches Creek

Barker, R. M.	Private	Company A, 4th S.C. Mil	Feb 25, 1865
Beard, John	Private	Company A, 14th S.C.Mil	Feb 25, 1865
Birch, James C.	Private	Company A, 4th S.C. Mil	Feb 25, 1865
Brown, J.E.	Private	Company A, 14th S.C. Mil	Feb 25, 1865
Brown, S.E.	Private	Company A, 14th S.C. Mil	Feb 25, 1865
Bunch, J.C.	Private	Company A, 4th SC Mil	Feb 25, 1865
Burke, J.	Private	Company C, 14th SC Mil	Feb 25, 1865
Campbell, E.	Private	Company A, 14thSC Mil	Feb 25, 1865
Canniel, E.	Private	Company A, 14thS.C. Mil	Feb 25, 1865
Carnwell, E.	Private	Company A. 14thS.C. Mil	Feb 25, 1865
Coward, N.M.	Private	Company B, 14thS.C. Mil	Feb 25, 1865
Crim, S.	Citizen		Feb 25, 1865 From Sandy Area of Lexington, S. C. "Samuel"
Dantzler, D.B.	Private	Company E, 14thS.C, Mil	Mar 1, 1865
Dash, L.W.	Private	Company D, 15th SC Mil	Feb 27, 1865
Drummond, James	Private	Company B, 14thSCMil	Feb 25, 1865
Dykes, E.	Private	Company A, 14thS.C. Mil	Feb 25, 1865
Dykes, G.A.	Private	Company A, 14thS.C. Mil	Feb 25, 1865
Elkin, David E.	Private	Company 6th SC Infantry	Feb 23, 1865
Fickling, H.S.	Sergeant	Company A, 14thS.C. Mil	Feb 25, 1865
Fogle, William J.	Citizen		Feb 23, 1865 From Orangeburg County, SC
Fry, Davis	Private	Company D, 15th S.C. Mil	Feb 27, 1865
Gamble, George	Private	Company E, 3rd SC Mil	Feb 25, 1865
Griffen, Silas	Private	Company A, 14thSC Mil	Mar 1, 1865
Harden, J.B.	Private	Company B, 14thSC Mil	Feb 25, 1865
Hay, W.A.	Private	Company B, 14thSC Mil	Feb 26, 1865
Hook, William	Private	Company D, 15th SC Mil	Feb 27, 1865
Horn, J.A.	Private	Company E, 14thSC Mil	Feb 25, 1865
Hunter, Cornelius	Private	Company D, 3rd SC Mil	Feb 25, 1865

Hutto, J.M.	Private	Company A, 14thSC Mil	Feb 25, 1865
Hyatt, George Thomas	Private	Company K, SCV Infantry	Feb 25, 1865
Inabinet, Archibald	Private	Company A, 1st SC Mil	Feb 23, 1865
Jeffcoat, J.	Citizen		Feb 23, 1865
Jeffcoat, J.W.	Private	Company A, 15th SC Mil	Feb 25, 1865
Kemp, James	Private	Company A, 6th SC Mil	Mar 25, 1865
Lancaster, J.C.	Private	Company B, 14thSC Mil	Mar 22, 1865
Lancaster, L.L.	Private	Company B, 14thSC Mil	Feb 25, 1865
Manning, Brown C.	1st Lt.		Feb 27, 1865
Mattox, Samuel	Private	Company D, 15th SCV Infantry	Feb 27, 1865
Maxwell, S.H.	Private		Feb 28, 1865
McLuaige, F.	Private	Company A, 4thSCV Cavalry	Feb 25, 1865
Miller, R.	Private	Company A, 14thSC Mil	Feb 25, 1865
Nix, A.J.	Private	Company B, 14thSC Mil	Feb 25, 1865
Nix, J.F.	Private	Company B, 14thSC Mil	Feb 25, 1865
Pettit, Benjamin F.	Private	Company K, 3rd SCV Infantry	Feb 28, 1865
Petty, Pinckney M.	Private	Company K, 3rd SCV Infantry	Feb 28, 1865
Petty, Thomas M.	Private	Company K, 3rd SCV Infantry	Feb 28, 1865
Plummer, John		Sergeant 14th SCMil	Feb 26, 1865
Plummer, M.	Sergeant	Company B, 14th SC Mil	Feb 26, 1865
Polan, George	Private	Company E, 14th SC Mil	Mar 1, 1865
Pruitt, Benjamin F.	Private	Company K, 3rd SC Mil	Feb 28, 1865
Rast, William R.	Private	Company C, 14th SC Mil	Feb 28, 1865
Rutland, H.	Private	Company B, 14th SC Mil	Feb 25, 1865
Shaver, William	Private	Citizen	Feb 25, 1865
Sherry, M.C.	Private	Company D, 15th SC Mil	Feb 27, 1865
Shull, William	Private	Company D, 15th SC Mil	Feb 27, 1865
Sister, John R.	Private	Company K, 3rd SCV Infantry	Feb 28, 1865
Sox, Samuel	Private	Company D, 15th SC Mil	Feb 27, 1865
Still, Isaac	Private	Company A, 14th SC Mil	Feb 25, 1865
Still, J.B.	Private	Company B, 14th SC Mil	Feb 25, 1865
Still, Thomas E.	Private	Company B, 14th SC Mil	Feb 25, 1865
Stroman, Absalom	Private	Company E, 14th SC Mil	Mar 1, 1865
Templeton, H.B.	Private	Company B, 14th SC Mil	Feb 25, 1865
Tilly, William	Private	Company D, 14th SC Mil	Feb 25, 1865
Trexler, J.J.	Private	Company A, 18th SC Mil	Mar 3, 1865
Wannamaker, William S.		15th SC Mil	Feb 23, 1865
Zimmerman, William	Private	Company C, 14thSC Mil	Feb 28, 1865

Extracted from Service Records

Understanding the makeup of how units began and how during attrition came together

Though no one can detail the many soldiers of the units from Kershaw County, one needs to understand that many came from not only Kershaw County but surrounding counties, and other states as well. Names may not be known but their service should never go unnoticed. Paperwork probably were destroyed or lost, and some reports never sent or received by companies due to injuries, being captured, or even destroyed so the enemy may not have their hands on the records.

List of Units from Camden and Kershaw County

DeKalb Rifle Guards

Gregg's Regiment, Company J.

This unit goes back to the Mexican War as a member of the Palmetto Regiment. Considered the first to board a train in Camden, S.C. April 24, 1861, for Virginia. (Only Company E under Captain Kennedy left earlier for Virginia, departing April 9, 1861.

Camden Volunteers

Company E, 2nd Regiment, SC Volunteers

This company was originally referred to as "The Captain J. D. Kennedy's Company, (Camden Volunteers) 2nd Palmetto Regiment South Carolina Volunteers.

"My Company was accepted by Governor Pickens on the 8th day Jan 1861, by virtue of authority vested in him to accept into the service of the State, South Carolina, ten thousand volunteers to constitute an armed force for said State, by act of General Assembly of said State passed in Dec. 1860, was called into active service on the 9th day April 1861."

John D. Kennedy,
Captain Camden Vols.
2nd Palmetto Regiment, S.C.V.

One should know that the first to enter the battle involved The Camden Volunteers under Captain J. D. Kennedy, who left for Charleston, South Carolina April 9, 1861, to arrive in time to take part in the firing on Fort Sumter, April 12. The DeKalb Rifle Guards under Captain T.L. Boykin left for Virginia on April 24. [601]

This Company became Company E, 2d (Palmetto) Regiment South Carolina Infantry. This unit was called into service April 9, 1861 for twelve months. It was mustered into the Confederate States Service May 22, 1861, and re-organized for the war in May 1862. About April 9, 1865, the 2nd Palmetto Regiment was consolidated with the 20th Regiment South Carolina Infantry and a part of Blanchard's South Carolina Reserves and formed the new 2nd Regiment South Carolina Infantry, which was paroled at Greensboro, N.C., May 2, 1865

Flat Rock Guards

Company G, 2nd SC Volunteers

Originally called 'Captain C. C. Haile's Company, 2 (Palmetto) Regiment South Carolina Volunteers.

"This company was organized on the 16th day of January 1861, by an act of the Legislature of South Carolina, and called into service of Virginia, on the 28th of April 1861, under the command of Colonel J. B. Kershaw, and mustered in service of the Provisional Government on the 22nd of May 1861"

C.C. Haile, Captain

The company became Company G, 2d (Palmetto) Regiment South Carolina Infantry. The regiment was called into state service about April 9, 1861, for twelve months. It was mustered into the Confederate States service May 22, 1861 and re-organized for the war in May 1862. About April 9, 1865, the 2nd (Palmetto) Regiment South Carolina Infantry was consolidated with the 20th Regiment South Carolina Infantry and a part of Blanchard's South Carolina Reserves and formed the new 2nd Regiment South Carolina Infantry, which was paroled at Greensboro, N.C., May 2, 1865.

Kershaw Guards

Company D, 15th Regiment Infantry

Originally Called "Captain T. J. Warren's Company, De Saussure's Regiment South Carolina Regiment. This company became Company D, 15th Regiment South Carolina Infantry. About April 9, 1865, the 15th Regiment South Carolina Infantry was consolidated with the 7th Regiment South Carolina Infantry and a part of Blanchard's South Carolina Reserves and formed the new 7th Regiment South Carolina Infantry, which was paroled at Greensboro, N.C., May 2, 1865.

Kershaw Troop

Company C, 6th Regiment, South Carolina Infantry

The 6th Regiment South Carolina Infantry entered the State service on April 11, 1861, for twelve months and was mustered into the Confederate States service during June and July 1861. Eventually, it was broken up and

---

601 "Military Record of Kershaw Soldiers in not excelled in South Carolina," by R. M. Kennedy, Sr., The Camden Chronicle, August 2, 1946.

a number of men re-enlisted in the Palmetto Regiment South Carolina Sharp Shooters, the 6th Regiment South Carolina Infantry, the 13th Battalion South Carolina Infantry, and the 17th Regiment South Carolina Infantry. In February 1862, the remainder re-enlisted for two years, or the war, and were re-organized inter six companies, which was joined on March 27, 1862 by a company of re-enlisted men from the 9th Regiment South Carolina infantry. These seven companies formed the 1st South Carolina Battalion of Re-Enlisted Volunteers, which was increased to a regiment April 22, 1862, by the addition of three more companies of re-enlisted men from the 9th Regiment South Carolina Infantry, and designated the 6th Regiment South Carolina Infantry. A number of re-enlisted men from the old 5th Regiment South Carolina Infantry, and a few recruits were assigned to the various companies.

Lucas Guards
Company A, 7th Battalion South Carolina Infantry (Enfield Rifles)

Originally Called 'Captain L.W. R. Blair's Company, Nelson's Regiment South Carolina Volunteers.

Company A, 7th Battalion Captain L.W.R. Blair's Company, Nelson's Regiment South Carolina Volunteers, eventually wound up being Company A, 7th Battalion South Carolina Infantry (Enfield Rifles). Organized February 22, 1862, the unit was referred to as Nelson's Battalion, or in some cases just the 7th. Companies A to E was the first five companies organized, with Companies F and G forming in May 25, 1862. The latter two companies forming from soldiers from the first five. Company H was formed as part of the Partisan Rangers on July 14, 1862, serving October 14, 1862.[602] Dove Segars was a part of this battalion, and later Captain of Lucas Rifles

Kershaw Greys
Company D, 7th Battalion South Carolina Infantry (Enfield Rifles)

Originally called "Captain J. L. Jones' Company, 7 Battalion South Carolina Volunteers. The 7th (also known as Nelson's Battalion) was organized February 22, 1862, with five companies, A to E. 22, 1862, with five companies, A to E. Companies F and G were formed May 27, 1862, of men transferred from other companies of the battalion. Company H, which had been organized July 14, 1862, as an independent infantry company of Partisan Rangers, was assigned October 14, 1862.

Company E, 7th Battalion South Carolina Infantry (Enfield Rifles)

This unit was organized February 22, 1862, with five companies, A to E. Companies F and G were formed May 27, 1862, of men transferred from other companies of the battalion. Company H, which has been organized July 14, 1862, as an independent infantry company of Partisan Rangers, was assigned October 14, 1862.

Lucas Rifles

---

[602] Taken from the actual Confederate service record at the bottom of the first card of a soldier in that company.

Company F, 7th Battalion South Carolina Infantry (Enfield Rifles)

Organized February 22, 1862, the unit was referred to as Nelson's Battalion, or in some cases just the 7th. Companies A to E was the first five companies organized, with Companies F and G forming in May 25, 1862. The latter two companies forming from soldiers from the first five. Company H was formed as part of the Partisan Rangers on July 14, 1862, serving October 14, 1862.[603] Dove Segars was a part of this battalion, and later Captain of Lucas Rifles

Moffatt Rifles
Company G, 7th Battalion

The 7th (also known as Nelson's Battalion) was organized February 22, 1862, with five companies, A to E. 22, 1862, with five companies, A to E. Companies F and G were formed May27, 1862, of men transferred from other companies of the battalion. Company H, which had been organized July 14, 1862, as an independent infantry company of Partisan Rangers, was assigned October 14, 1862.

Wateree Mounted Rifles
Company K, 7th Regiment South Carolina Cavalry

Originally called "Captain E. M. Boykin's Company A, Mounted Squadron of Rifles, South Carolina Volunteers."
The 7th Regiment South Carolina Cavalry was formed by the addition of five independent companies to the five companies of the Cavalry Battalion, Holcombe Legion, South Carolina Volunteers by Special Order Number 65, A & L.G.O. dated March 17, 1864.

Kirkwood Rangers
Company H, 7th South Carolina Cavalry Regiment

Captain William Shannon's Company had the following information: This company was successfully designated as Captain William M. Shannon's Company, (The Kirkwoods) South Carolina Cavalry; Captain Doby's Company; Captain's Doby's Company, Cavalry Battalion, Holcombe Legion South Carolina Volunteers; and Company E, Cavalry Battalion, Holcombe Legion South Carolina Volunteers. The Holcombe Legion South Carolina Volunteers, consisting of an infantry regiment and a cavalry battalion, was organized November 21, 1861. The Cavalry Battalion was separated from the Legion and increased to a regiment and designated the 7th Regiment South Carolina Cavalry by Special Order Number 65, A. and L.G.O., dated March 18, 1864, this company becoming Company H of the regiment. [604]

Boykin Rangers
Company A, 2nd South Carolina Cavalry Regiment

Originally called "Captain A. H. Boykin's Company, South Carolina Cavalry"

---

[603] Taken from the actual Confederate service record at the bottom of the first card of a soldier in that company.
[604] Information located at the bottom of a card of a solder in that company.

This Cavalry was formed by the consolidating of the Cavalry Battalion of Hampton's Legion, the 4th Battalion South Carolina Cavalry, and Captain Boykin's and Lipscomb's Companies, South Carolina Cavalry, by Special Order number 196, dated August 22, 1862

DeSaussure Artillery
Company G, Palmetto Battery Light Artillery

This Battalion was formed about November 1861, with three companies, A to C. Seven other companies were added at various times, the last about June 21, 1863. Companies H, I, and K, to begin legally organized, were disbanded by Special Order number 77m A. & I. G. O., dated April 1, 1864. It was known in the field as the Palmetto Battalion Light Artillery, but was designated the 3rd Battalion South Carolina Light Artillery by the A. & I. G. O. It was also known as White's Battalion South Carolina Light Artillery.

Company D, 5th Battalion Reserves (Brown's Battalion)
22d Local Camden Brigade

In 1862, this local militia had elections -Burrell Jones was elected Colonel, William Dixon was First Lieutenant, and W.A. Antrum, elected Mayor. Within this process Beats was developed to protect sections of the city and throughout the county. This brigade became part of the Fifth Brigade with the following regiments- 20, 21, 22, 23, 24 and 44 under the command of Lieutenant Colonel A. H. Boykin, A.D.C., September 4, 1864. Organized in Camden.

The following was a total though incomplete by many statistics:

>Kershaw Troop, Captain E.B. Cantey, Provost Major, succeeded by Captain R.M. Cantey. Enrollment 144, from Kershaw County, 117, casualties 77.
>Lucas Guards, Captain L.W.R. Blair, Provost Major, succeeded by Captain Ben Lucas. Enrollment 104, all from Kershaw County but one, casualties 61.
>Kershaw Greys, Captain John L. Jones. Enrollment 128, all from Kershaw County, casualties 61.
>Company E, 7th Battalion, Captain Burwell E. Boykin, John R. Goodale, 1st Lieutenant. Enrollment 108, 20 from Kershaw County, casualties among Kershaw men were 12 with 5 being captured.
>Lucas Rifles, Captain Dove Segars. Enrollment 140, 80 from Kershaw County, casualties 91. 58 of the men enlisted were under 21 years old with some 16.
>Moffat Rifles, Captain William Clyburn. Enrollment 101, 50 from Kershaw County, and casualties 63.
>Wateree Mounted Rifles, Captain Ed. M. Boykin, who later became colonel. Enrollment 126, 82 from Kershaw County, casualties 32, surrendered 21.
>Kirkwood Rangers, Captain W. M. Shannon, Provost Colonel, succeeded by Captain James Doby, Provost Major. Enrollment 119, 97 from Kershaw County, casualties 24, surrendered 33.

Boykin Rangers, Captain A. H. Boykin, succeeded by Captain John Chesnut. Enrollment 128, 22 from Kershaw County, casualties unknown.

DeSaussure Artillery, Captain W.L. DePass. Enrollment 60, all from Kershaw County, casualties unknown.

Company D, 5th Battalion Reserves, Captain John Thompson, Lieutenant Thomas J. Ancrum. Enrollment 152. This company was organized in 1864, and was composed of boys, old men, furloughed soldiers, or those discharged because of physical disabilities. This company was never in any but local engagements.[605]

---

[605] Ibid.

The Role of Pensions in Kershaw County

IN AN EARLIER CHAPTER ON the Survivor's Association, we learned that their main goal was to help those soldier needs such an illness, loss of a family member, being wounded, or even loss of limb. Now, we shall look at how the South Carolina Government dealt with their role in helping the confederate soldier.

In 1887, the legislature voted to pension all disabled soldiers, who gave their service in the army or the navy.[606] The movement was spearheaded by Major L.L. Coker of Darlington County, asking for help for those soldiers disabled and those veterans needing help.

In 1888, the South Carolina Legislature passed an act to give five dollars to all disabled confederate veterans or their widows.[607] The pension board was at this time in session, and the number of applications far exceeded what figure allowed by the legislature.[608] That figure was over two-hundred dollars when all the applications finished coming in. Later in that year, a bill was introduced and passed to erect a home for those confederate soldiers who were disabled and sailors.[609] The county will be responsible for the selection of five confederate veterans at a meeting.[610] Within this county committee, the selection of indigent and disabled veterans, will occur, where each will receive sixty dollars.[611]

In 1897, an act to exempt soldiers and sailors in the service of the State of South Carolina, or of the Confederate States in the war between the States from taking out the license as a hawker and peddler required by Chapter 43, Volume 1, Revised Statutes, 1893, of South Carolina.[612]

In 1902, Comptroller General Derham gave the figures that Confederate Pensions was two hundred thousand two hundred twenty-seven, serving seven thousand seven hundred fifty. In that number eighty-seven veterans collected one thousand dollars instead of artificial limbs.

In 1912, the following motion led by General Brooks to increase allowances to Confederate Veterans and Widows: "General C. R. Brooks had a bill in preparation to submit to the General Assembly granting a pension

---

[606] Macon Telegraph, December 18, 1887.
[607] Kansas City Star, April 16, 1888.
[608] Ibid.
[609] Critic- Record Newspaper, December 19, 1888.
[610] Ibid.
[611] Ibid.
[612] The Fairfield News and Herald, March 17, 1897, Fairfield, S.C.

of eleven dollars per month to all indigent Confederates who can't pay rent. This information set me wondering if General Brooks was familiar with the distribution of the two hundred fifty thousand pension fund.

In 1916, a bill was drafted to compensate every Confederate Veteran and widow to compensate them for their services rendered. The committee was composed of D.L. McLaurin, of Columbia; B.C. Johnson, of Easley; Alfred Aldrich of Barnwell; W.P. Coker of Fountain Inn; J.M. Hough of Lancaster; J.C. Sellers of Sellers; and John Ahrens of Charleston.[613]

---

[613] "Pensions for All Confederate Veterans' Committee Drafts Bill," The State Newspaper, Columbia, S.C., January 12, 1916.

Kershaw County Pension Records

1888- Soldiers-	Post Office	Filed in 1888	Approved Payment	Amount
William Adam	Camden	Feb 29	April 2	28
John Green	Camden	March 2	April 2	28
John Irvin	Camden	Mar 10	April 2	28
Stephen Self	Camden	Mar 22	April 2	28
Allen G. Ward	Cantey	April 24	April 2	28
J.J. Sutton	Smyrna	April 24	April 2	28
John Mackey	Russell Place	May 22	June 7	18
W.H. Capell	Camden	June 6	June 7	18
William Cook	Smyrna	June 5	June 5	18
W.D. Baskin	Lynchwood	July 17	July 31	13
J.R. Arrants	Camden	July 20	July 31	13
James Sullivan	Lynchwood	July 26	July 31	13
Thomas G. Brown	Camden	Sept 10	Sept 19	3

Widows-

Nancy Williams	Camden	Feb 27	April 2	28
Elvira Honey	Camden	Feb 28	April 2	28
M.A. Pye	Camden	Feb 28	April 2	28
C.L. Cook	Camden	Mar 2	April 2	28
M.T. Moore	Camden	Mar 2	April 2	28
Millie Ammons	Boykin	Mar 2	April 2	28
E.J. Denton	Russell Place	Mar 2	April 2	28
Sallie Boone	Flat Rock	Mar 2	April 2	28
Rebecca Gaskin	Flat Rock	Mar 2	April 2	28
Rhodie Dawkins	Ridgeway	Mar 10	April 2	28
Martha Coates	Flat Rock	Mar 26	April 2	28
S.L. Mobley	Russell Place	Mar 26	April 2	28
Martha Howell	Ridgeway	Mar 22	June 22	28

Nancy McDonald	Camden	April 23	July 31	18
Nancy West	Camden	April 23	April 2	13
Lenorn Kelly	Camden	April 24	April 2	28
M.J. Gardner	Camden	April 24	April 2	28
Elizabeth Suggs	Flat Rock	April 26	April 2	28
Sarah Hays	Camden	April 25	April 25	28
R.G. Nelson	Camden	April 25	April 25	28
M.C. Baskins	Flat Rock	April 25	April 25	28
Caroline Corder	Camden	May 16	May 26	23
M.J. Vincent	Flat Rock	June 13	June 23	18
S.R. Harold	Camden	June 20	June 20	18
Amelia Bowen	Haile's Gold Mine	June 26	July 13	13
Mary Bass	Cantey	Aug 18	Aug 28	8
Mary Irvin	Camden	Aug 20	Aug 28	8
Elizabeth Edwards	Columbia	Aug 30	Sept 19	3[614]

1889 Kershaw County Pensions

Pensions granted under the Act of Congress 1888

Name	Post Office	filed/ granted	Amount
G.W. Frail	Kershaw	Apr 18	23.40
John Ervin	Courthouse	Feb 18	23.40
J.J. Sutton	Smyrna	Feb 13	23.40
William Adam	Courthouse	Feb 13	23.40
Stephen Self	Courthouse	Feb 13	23.40
A.G. Ward	Courthouse	Feb 13	23.40
W.H. Capell	Courthouse	Feb 13	23.40
William Cook	Smyrna	Feb 13	23.40

Widows

Mary Bass	Cantey	March 29	23.40
S.R. Harold	Courthouse	March 29	23.40
Caroline Corder	Courthouse	March 22	23.40
S.L. Mobley	Russell Place	March 22	23.40
Rhodie Dawkins	Courthouse	March 22	23.40
Lenora Kelly	Courthouse	March 13	23.40
Sarah Hays	Courthouse	March 13	23.40

---

[614] South Carolina Deposits and Resolutions, 1888, p. 458-459. South Carolina Archives and History, Columbia, South Carolina, Microfilm number ST- 0788.

Rest of Pensions already granted the year before.

Sarah Hawkins	Courthouse	March 13	23.40
M.H. Cook	Courthouse	March 13	23.40
M.A. Pie (Pye)	Courthouse	March 13	23.40
M.M. Norris	Courthouse	March 13	23.40
T.L. Cook	Courthouse	Feb 18	23.40
Nancy McDonald	Courthouse	Feb 18	23.40
R.J. Pitts	Timrod	Feb 18	23.40
R.G. Nelson	Courthouse	Feb 18	23.40
S.L. Gardner	Timrod	Feb 18	23.40
Emiline Kelly	Courthouse	March 13	23.40
Millie Ammons	Courthouse	Feb 11	23.40
Rebecca Gaskin	West's	Feb 15	23.40
E.K. Doby	Courthouse	Feb 15	23.40
M.J. Gardner	Courthouse	Feb 13	23.40
M.T. Moore	Courthouse	Feb 13	23.40
Elvira Honey	Courthouse	Feb 13	23.40
N.J. Williams	Courthouse	Feb 13	23.40
M.E. Baskin	Courthouse	July 9	23.40
Elizabeth Branham	Courthouse	July 9	23.40
Sally Boone	West's	July 9	23.40
M.J. Vincent	Flat Rock	July 9	23.40
Elizabeth Suggs	West's	July 13	23.40

From Lancaster County from Kershaw getting a pension –

L.E. Horton	Kershaw	March 14	23.40

Disapproved pensions

Soldiers- William D. Baskin

    John Green

    James Sinclair

Widows- W.C. Roach

Members of the Kershaw County Examination Board

A.A. Moore, Md

J.R. Goodale

J.F. Nettles

[615]

---

[615] South Carolina Deposits and Resolutions, 1889, pages 385- 386, 415. South Carolina Archives and History, Columbia, South Carolina, Microfilm number ST- 0789.

1890 Kershaw County Pension Records

Name	Post Office	Total
John Irvin	Courthouse	24.26
J.J. Sutton	Smyrna	24.26
William Adams	Courthouse	24.26
Stephen Self	Courthouse	24.26
A.G. Ward	Courthouse	24.26
William Cook	Smyrna	24.26
Mary Bass	Cantey	24.26
S.R. Harold	Courthouse	24.26
Caroline Corder	Courthouse	24.26
S.L. Mobley	Russell Place	24.26
Rhodie Dawkins	Courthouse	24.26
Lenora Kelly	Courthouse	24.26
Sarah Hays	Courthouse	24.26
Sallie Dawkins	Courthouse	24.26
M.H. Coats	Flat Rock	24.26
M.A. Pie (Pye)	Courthouse	24.26
M.M. Norris	Courthouse	24.26
Nancy McDonald	Courthouse	24.26
R.J. Pitts	Timrod	24.26
R.G. Nelson	Courthouse	24.26
S.L. Gardner	Timrod	24.26
Emeline Kelly	Courthouse	24.26
Millie Ammons	Courthouse	24.26
Martha Howell	Courthouse	24.26
Rebecca Gaskin	West's	24.26
E.K. Doby	Courthouse	24.26
M.J. Gardner	Courthouse	24.26
M.T. Moore	Courthouse	24.26
N.J. West	Courthouse	24.26
Elvira Honie	Courthouse	24.26
N.J. Williams	Courthouse	24.26
M.E. Baskins	Courthouse	24.26
Elizabeth Branham	Courthouse	24.26
Sallie Boone	West's	24.26
M.J. Vincent	Flat Rock	24.26
Elizabeth Suggs	West's	24.26
J.B. Phelps	Courthouse	24.26

L.T. Stroud	Courthouse	24.26
Mary Scott	Tiller's Ferry	24.26
S.H. Cauthen	Kershaw	24.26

Dissapproved Pensions
    G.W. Frail
    T.L. Cook

Kershaw County Board of Pensions
    J.T. Nettles
    J.R. Goodale
    A.A. Moore, M.D.
    616

1891 Kershaw County Pension Record

Name	Post Office	Amount
John Irvin	Courthouse	23.00
J.J. Sutton	Smyrna	23.00
William Adam	Courthouse	23.00
Stephen Self	Courthouse	23.00
A.G. Ward	Courthouse	23.00
W.H. Capell	Courthouse	23.00
William Capell	Courthouse	23.00
Mary Bass	Cantey	23.00
S.R. Harold	Courthouse	23.00
Caroline Corder	Courthouse	23.00
S.L. Mobley	Russell Place	23.00
Rhodie Dawkins	Courthouse	23.00
Lenora Kelly	Courthouse	23.00
Sarah Hays	Courthouse	23.00
Sallie Dawkins	Courthouse	23.00
M.A. Pie (Pye)	Courthouse	23.00
M.M. Norris	Courthouse	23.00
Nancey McDonald	Courthouse	23.00
R.J. Pitts	Timrod	23.00
R.G. Nelson	Courthouse	23.00
S.L. Gardner	Timrod	23.00

---

[616] South Carolina Deposits and Resolutions, 1890, pages 385-386, 415. South Carolina Archives and History, Columbia, South Carolina, Microfilm number ST- 0790.

Emeline Kirby	Courthouse	23.00
Millie Ammons	Courthouse	23.00
Martha Howell	Courthouse	23.00
Rebecca Gaskin	West's	23.00
E.K. Doby	Courthouse	23.00
M.J. Gardner	Courthouse	23.00
M.T. Moore	Courthouse	23.00
N.J. West	Courthouse	23.00
Elvira Honie	Courthouse	23.00
N.J. William	Courthouse	23.00
M.E. Branham	Courthouse	23.00
Elizabeth Branham	Courthouse	23.00
Sally Boone	West's	23.00
M.J. Vincent	Flat Rock	23.00
J.B. Phelps	Courthouse	23.00
Lily T. Stroud	Courthouse	23.00
Mary Scott	Tiller's Ferry	23.00
Sarah A. Cauthen	Kershaw	23.00
Henrietta Gainey	Lynchwood	23.00
Amelia Bowers	Kershaw	23.00
Eliza A. Gardner	Rowland	23.00
P.T. Carraway	Camden	23.00

Disapproved Pensions
    Jane Buzby- Camden
    Eliza Capell- Camden

Kershaw County Examining Board
    J.T. Nettles
    J.R. Goodale
    A.A. Moore, MD.

---

[617] South Carolina Deposits and Resolutions, 1891, pages 30-31, 63, 64. South Carolina Archives and History, Columbia, South Carolina, Microfilm number ST- 0791.

1892 Kershaw County Pension Records

Name	Post Office	Amount
John Irvin	Courthouse	23.00
J.J. Sutton	Smyrna	23.00
William Adam	Courthouse	23.00
Stephen Self	Courthouse	23.00
A.G. Ward	Courthouse	23.00
W.H. Capell	Courthouse	23.00
William Cook	Smyrna	23.00
Mary Bass	Cantey	23.00
Sarah R. Harold	Courthouse	23.00
Caroline Corder	Courthouse	23.00
S.L. Mobley	Russell Place	23.00
Rhodie Dawkin	Courthouse	23.00
Lenora Kelly	Courthouse	23.00
Sarah Hays	Courthouse	23.00
Sallie Dawkins	Courthouse	23.00
M.A. Pie (Pye)	Courthouse	23.00
M.M. Norris	Courthouse	23.00
Nancey McDonald	Courthouse	23.00
R.J. Pitts	Timrod	23.00
S.L. Gardner	Timrod	23.00
R.G. Nelson	Courthouse	23.00
Emiline Kirby	Courthouse	23.00
Millie Ammons	Courthouse	23.00
Martha Howell	Courthouse	23.00
Rebecca Gaskin	West's	23.00
E.K. Doby	Courthouse	23.00
M.J. Gardner	Courthouse	23.00
M.T. Moore	Courthouse	23.00
N.J. West	Courthouse	23.00
Elvira Honie	Courthouse	23.00
N.J. Williams	Courthouse	23.00
M.E. Baskin	Courthouse	23.00
Sallie Boone	West's	23.00
M.J. Vincent	Flat Rock	23.00
J.B. Phelps	Courthouse	23.00
Lillie T. Stroud	Courthouse	23.00
Mary Scott	Tiller's Ferry	23.00

Sarah A. Cauthen	Kershaw	23.00
Henrietta Gainey	Lynchwood	23.00
Amelia Bowers	Kershaw	23.00
Eliza A. Gardner	Rowland	23.00
P.T. Carraway	Camden	23.00
John Green	Camden	23.00

Pension Examining Board

    John T. Nettles

    J.R. Goodale

    A.A. Moore, MD.

1893 Kershaw County Pension Records

Name	Post Office or Area	Total Payment May 15, 1893
John Irvin	Courthouse	22.00
J.J. Sutton	Smyrna	22.00
William Adams	Courthouse	22.00
Stephen Self	Courthouse	22.00
A.G. Ward	Courthouse	22.00
W.H. Capell	Courthouse	22.00
William Cook	Smyrna	22.00
Mary Bass	Cantey	22.00
Sarah R. Harold	Cantey	22.00
Caroline Corder	Cantey	22.00
S.L. Mobley	Russell Place	22.00
Rhodus Dawkins	Courthouse	22.00
Lenora Kelly	Courthouse	22.00
Sarah Hays	Courthouse	22.00
Sallie Dawkins	Courthouse	22.00
M.A. Pie (Pye)	Courthouse	22.00
M.M. Norris	Courthouse	22.00
Nancy McDonald	Courthouse	22.00
R.J. Pitts	Timrod	22.00
R.G. Nelson	Courthouse	22.00
S.L. Nelson	Timrod	22.00
Emeline Kirby	Courthouse	22.00

---

[618] South Carolina Deposits and Resolutions, 1892, pages 31-21, 19. . South Carolina Archives and History, Columbia, South Carolina, Microfilm number ST- 0792.

Millie Ammons	Courthouse	22.00
Martha Gaskin	West's	22.00
E.K. Doby	Courthouse	22.00
M.J. Gardner	Courthouse	22.00
N.J. West	Courthouse	22.00
Elvira Honea (y)	Courthouse	22.00
M.E. Baskin	Courthouse	22.00
Elizabeth Branham	Courthouse	22.00
Sallie Boone	West's	22.00
J.B. Phelps	Courthouse	22.00
Lillie T. Stroud	Courthouse	22.00
May Scott	Tiller's Ferry	22.00
Sarah Cauthen	Kershaw	22.00
Henrietta Gainey	Lynchwood	22.00
Eliza A. Gardner	Rowland	22.00
P.T. Carraway	Camden	22.00
John Green	Camden	22.00
Mary Lee	Camden	22.00
Mary Burg	Tiller's Ferry	22.00[619]
William Adams	Courthouse	22.00
Stephen Self	Courthouse	22.00
A.G. Ward	Courthouse	22.00
W.H. Capell	Courthouse	22.00
William Cook	Smyrna	22.00
Mary Bass	Cantey	22.00
Sarah R. Harold	Cantey	22.00
Caroline Corder	Cantey	22.00
S.L. Mobley	Russell Place	22.00
Rhodus Dawkins	Courthouse	22.00
Lenora Kelly	Courthouse	22.00
Sarah Hays	Courthouse	22.00
Sallie Dawkins	Courthouse	22.00
M.A. Pie (Pye)	Courthouse	22.00
M.M. Norris	Courthouse	22.00
Nancy McDonald	Courthouse	22.00
R.J. Pitts	Timrod	22.00
R.G. Nelson	Courthouse	22.00
S.L. Gardner	Timrod	22.00
Emeline Kirby	Courthouse	22.00
Millie Ammons	Courthouse	22.00

Martha Gaskin	West's	22.00
E.K. Doby	Courthouse	22.00
M.J. Gardner	Courthouse	22.00
N.J. West	Courthouse	22.00
Elvira Honea	Courthouse	22.00
M.E. Baskin	Courthouse	22.00
Elizabeth Branham	Courthouse	22.00
Sallie Boone	West's	22.00
J.B. Phelps	Courthouse	22.00
Lillie T. Stroud	Courthouse	22.00
Mary Scott	Tiller's Ferry	22.00
Sarah Cauthen	Kershaw	22.00
Henrietta Gainey	Lynchwood	22.00
Eliza A. Gardner	Rowland	22.00
P.T. Carraway	Camden	22.00
John Green	Camden	22.00
Mary Lee	Camden	22.00

619

Kershaw County list of Appointments for Artificial Limbs Beneficiary-

Name	Post Office	Paid April 20, 1894
John Irvin	Courthouse	22.00
J.J. Sutton	Smyrna	22.00
William Adams	Courthouse	22.00
Stephen Self	Courthouse	22.00
A.G. Ward	Courthouse	22.00
W.H. Capell	Courthouse	22.00
William Cook	Smyrna	22.00
Mary Bass	Cantey	22.00
Sarah R. Harold	Cantey	22.00
Caroline Corder	Cantey	22.00
S.L. Mobley	Russell Place	22.00
Rhodus Dawkins	Courthouse	22.00
Lenora Kelly	Courthouse	22.00
Sarah Hays	Courthouse	22.00
Sallie Dawkins	Courthouse	22.00
M.A. Pie (Pye)	Courthouse	22.00

---

[619] General Assembly, Joints and Resolution, 1893, pages 448-449. South Carolina Archives and History, Columbia, South Carolina, microfilm number ST 0794.

M.M. Norris	Courthouse	22.00
Nancy McDonald	Courthouse	22.00
R.J. Pitts	Timrod	22.00
R.G. Nelson	Courthouse	22.00
S.L. Gardner	Timrod	22.00
Emeline Kirby	Courthouse	22.00
Millie Ammons	Courthouse	22.00
Martha Howell	Courthouse	22.00
Rebecca Gaskin	West's	22.00
E.K. Doby	Courthouse	22.00
M.J. Gardner	Courthouse	22.00
M.T. Moore	Courthouse	22.00
N.J. West	Courthouse	22.00
Elvira Honea	Courthouse	22.00
N.J. Williams	Courthouse	22.00
M.E. Baskin	Courthouse	22.00
Elizabeth Branham	Courthouse	22.00
Sallie Boone	West's	22.00
J.B. Phelps	Courthouse	22.00
Lillie T. Stroud	Courthouse	22.00
Mary Scott	Tiller's Ferry	22.00
Sarah Cauthen	Kershaw	22.00
Henrietta Gainey	Lynchwood	22.00
Amelia Bowers	Kershaw	22.00
Eliza A. Gardner	Rowland	22.00
P.T. Carraway	Camden	22.00
John Green	Camden	22.00
Mary Lee	Camden	22.00
Mary Burg	Tiller's Ferry	22.00[620]

Kershaw County Artificial Limbs Beneficiary 1894

J.B. Phelps   35.00[621]

---

[620] General Assembly, Joints and Resolution, 1894, pages 32-33. South Carolina Archives and History, Columbia, South Carolina, microfilm number ST 0795.
[621] Ibid, page 444.

1894 Kershaw County Pensions

Name	Post Office	Amount
John Irvin	Courthouse	21.75
J.J. Sutton	Smyrna	21.75
William Adams	Courthouse	21.75
Stephen Self	Courthouse	21.75
A.G. Ward	Courthouse	21.75
William Cook	Smyrna	21.75
Mary Bass	Cantey	21.75
Sarah R. Harold	Cantey	21.75
Caroline Corder	Cantey	21.75
S.L. Mobley	Russell Place	21.75
Rhodus Dawkins	Courthouse	21.75
Lenora Kelly	Courthouse	21.75
Sarah Hays	Courthouse	21.75
Sallie Dawkins	Courthouse	21.75
M.A. Pie (Pye)	Courthouse	21.75
M.M. Norris	Courthouse	21.75
Nancy McDonald	Courthouse	21.75
R.J. Pitts	Timrod	21.75
R.G. Nelson	Courthouse	21.75
S.L. Gardner	Timrod	21.75
Emeline Kirby	Courthouse	21.75
Millie Ammons	Courthouse	21.75
Martha Howell	Courthouse	21.75
Rebecca Gaskin	West's	21.75
E.K. Doby	Courthouse	21.75
M.J. Gardner	Courthouse	21.75
M.T. Moore	Courthouse	21.75
N.J. West	Courthouse	21.75
Elvira Honea	Courthouse	21.75
N.J. Williams	Courthouse	21.75
M.E. Baskin	Courthouse	21.75
Elizabeth Branham	Courthouse	21.75
Sallie Boone	West's	21.75
Lillie T. Stroud	Courthouse	21.75
Mary Scott	Tiller's Ferry	21.75
Sarah Cauthen	Kershaw	21.75
Henrietta Gainey	Lynchwood	21.75

Amelia Bowers	Kershaw	21.75
Eliza A. Gardner	Rowland	21.75
P.T. Carraway	Camden	21.75
John Green	Camden	21.75
Mary Lee	Camden	21.75
Mary Burg	Tiller's Ferry	21.75
Ann Cook	Camden	21.75
E.M. Capell	Camden	21.75[622]

Rejected Pensions

    John E. Outlaw   Camden

    Elizabeth Roach   Westville[623]

Kershaw County Board of Pensions

    Dr. A.A. Moore

    J.A. Goodale

    J.T. Nettles

[624]

1894 Kershaw County Pension

Name	Post Office	Amount
John Irvin	Courthouse	22.00
J.J. Sutton	Smyrna	22.00
William Adams	Courthouse	22.00
Stephen Self	Courthouse	22.00
A.G. Ward	Courthouse	22.00
William Cook	Smyrna	22.00
Mary Bass	Cantey	22.00
Sarah R. Harold	Cantey	22.00
Caroline Corder	Cantey	22.00
S.L. Mobley	Russell Place	22.00
Rhodus Dawkins	Courthouse	22.00
Lenora Kelly	Courthouse	22.00
Sarah Hays	Courthouse	22.00
Sallie Dawkins	Courthouse	22.00
M.A. Pie (Pye)	Courthouse	22.00

---

[622] General Assembly, Joints and Resolution, 1896, pages 460-461. South Carolina Archives and History, Columbia, South Carolina, microfilm number ST 0796.

[623] Ibid, page 496.

[624] Ibid, page 499.

M.M. Norris	Courthouse	22.00
Nancy McDonald	Courthouse	22.00
N.J. Williams	Courthouse	22.00
M.E. Baskin	Courthouse	22.00
Elizabeth Branham	Courthouse	22.00
Sallie Boone	West's	22.00
Lillie T. Stroud	Courthouse	22.00
Mary Scott	Tiller's Ferry	22.00
Sarah Cauthen	Kershaw	22.00
Henrietta Gainey	Lynchwood	22.00
Amelia Bowers	Kershaw	22.00
Eliza A. Gardner	Rowland	22.00
P.T. Carraway	Camden	22.00
John Green	Camden	22.00
Mary Lee	Camden	22.00
Mary Burg	Tiller's Ferry	22.00
Ann Cook	Camden	22.00
E.M. Capell	Camden	22.00
R.J. Pitts	Timrod	22.00
R.G. Nelson	Courthouse	22.00
S.L. Gardner	Timrod	22.00
Emeline Kirby	Courthouse	22.00
Millie Ammons	Courthouse	22.00
Martha Howell	Courthouse	22.00
Rebecca Gaskin	West's	22.00
E.K. Doby	Courthouse	22.00
M.J. Gardner	Courthouse	22.00
M.T. Moore	Courthouse	22.00
N.J. West	Courthouse	22.00
Elvira Honea	Courthouse	22.00

Pension Examining Board

    J.R. Goodale

    J.T. Nettles

    Dr. A.A. Moore

Artificial Limbs to Beneficiaries Compensation

    J.B. Phelps 35.00

---

[625] General Assembly, Joints and Resolution, 1895, pages 32-33, 67, 74. South Carolina Archives and History, Columbia, South Carolina, microfilm number ST 0795.

1896 Kershaw County Pensions

Name	Post Office	Amount
John Irvin	Courthouse	21.75
J.J. Sutton	Smyrna	21.75
William Adam	Courthouse	21.75
Stephen Self	Courthouse	21.75
A.G. Ward	Courthouse	21.75
William Cook	Smyrna	21.75
Mary Bass	Cantey	21.75
Sarah R. Harold	Courthouse	21.75
Carolina Corder	Courthouse	21.75
S.L. Mobley	Russell Place	21.75
Lenora Kelly	Courthouse	21.75
Rhodie Dawkins	Courthouse	21.75
Sarah Hayes	Courthouse	21.75
Sallie Dawkins	Courthouse	21.75
M.A. Pie (Pye)	Courthouse	21.75
M.M. Norris	Courthouse	21.75
Nancey McDonald	Courthouse	21.75
R.J. Pitts	Timrod	21.75
R.G. Nelson	Courthouse	21.75
S.L. Gardner	Timrod	21.75
Emeline Kirby	Courthouse	21.75
Millie Ammons	Courthouse	21.75
Martha Howell	Courthouse	21.75
Rebecca Gaskin	West's	21.75
E.K. Doby	Courthouse	21.75
M.J. Gardner	Courthouse	21.75
M.T. Moore	Courthouse	21.75
N.J. West	Courthouse	21.75
Elvira Honie	Courthouse	21.75
N.J. William	Courthouse	21.75
M.E. Baskin	Courthouse	21.75
Elizabeth Branham	Courthouse	21.75
Sallie Boone	West's	21.75
Lillie T. Stroud	Courthouse	21.75
Mary Scott	Tiller's Ferry	21.75
Sarah A. Cauthen	Kershaw	21.75
Henrietta Gainey	Lynchwood	21.75

Amelia Bowers	Kershaw	21.75
Eliza A. Gardner	Rowland	21.75
P.T. Carraway	Courthouse	21.75
John Green	Courthouse	21.75
Mary Lee	Courthouse	21.75
Ann Cook	Camden	21.75
E.M. Capell	Camden	21.75

Pension Applications Disapproved
  John E. Outlaw- Camden
  Elizabeth C. Roach- Westville

Examining Pension Board
  Dr. A.A. Moore
  J.R. Goodale
  J.T. Nettles
[626]

1897 Kershaw County Pensions

Class B	Post Office	Amount
Stephen Self	Westville	29.10

Class C

John Irvin	Courthouse	19.40
J.J. Sutton	Smyrna	19.40
R. G. Ward	Courthouse	19.40
Benjamin Dixon	Pisgah	19.40
John W. Boone	Westville	19.40
Hiram Addison	Courthouse	19.40
James Reynolds	Courthouse	19.40
Duncan Ray	Dekalb	19.40
Z. Boone	Westville	19.40
D.J. George	Kershaw	19.40
S.J. Yates	Boykin	19.40
J.J. Stokes	Lucknow	19.40
George Jackson	Courthouse	19.40
William Gladden	Courthouse	19.40

---

[626] General Assembly, Joints and Resolution, 1896, pages 460-461. 496, 499. South Carolina Archives and History, Columbia, South Carolina, microfilm number ST 0796.

John Outlaw	Courthouse	19.40
J.T. Jones	Lynchwood	19.40
J.D. Crossland	Courthouse	19.40
W.G. Huckabee	Courthouse	19.40
R.J. Hyatt	Courthouse	19.40
James Taylor	Tiller's Ferry	19.40
George W. Watts	Courthouse	19.40
J.W. Watts	Antioch	19.40
James D. Defee	Camden	19.40

Class C Widows

Mary Bass	Cantey	19.40
Caroline Corder	Courthouse	19.40
S.L. Mobley	Russell Place	19.40
Rhodie Dawkins	Courthouse	19.40
Lenora Kelly	Courthouse	19.40
Sallie Dawkins	Courthouse	19.40
M. A. Pye	Courthouse	19.40
R.J. Pitts	Timrod	19.40
R.J. Nelson	Courthouse	19.40
S.L. Gardner	Timrod	19.40
Millie Ammons	Courthouse	19.40
Rebecca Gaskin	West's	19.40
E.K. Doby	Courthouse	19.40
M.J. Gardner	Courthouse	19.40
M.T. Moore	Courthouse	19.40
N.J. West	Courthouse	19.40
M.C. Baskin	Courthouse	19.40
Elizabeth Branham	Courthouse	19.40
Sallie Boone	West's	19.40
Sarah A. Cauthen	Kershaw	19.40
Hendrietta Gainey	Lynchwood	19.40
Amelia Bowers	Kershaw	19.40
Mary Lee	Courthouse	19.40
Ann Cook	Courthouse	19.40
E.M. Capell	Courthouse	19.40
Rachael Taylor	Kershaw	19.40
Kiziah Hinson	Courthouse	19.40
Mary Craft	Courthouse	19.40
Martha Dinkin	Courthouse	19.40

Mary Ogburn	Westville	19.40
Amanda J. Holland	Courthouse	19.40
Abigail Oxindine	Antioch	19.40
Sarah Jacobs	Ridgeway	19.40
B.D. Branham	Courthouse	19.40
E.C. Roach	Kershaw	19.40

627

1898 Kershaw County Pensions

Class B	Township	Post Office
Henry Hinson	Dekalb	Camden

Class- Number 2

John Boone	Buffalo	Westville
J.T. Jones	Buffalo	Lynchwood
James Taylor	Buffalo	Tiller's Ferry
J.J. Stokes	Buffalo	Lucknow
B.H. Higgins	Buffalo	Lynchwood
A.J. Munn	Buffalo	Abney
W.J. Boone	Buffalo	Westville
Michael Parker	Buffalo	Tiller's Ferry
J.D. Hough	Buffalo	Lynchwood
J.P. Adams	DeKalb	Camden
Wesley Croft	DeKalb	Camden
James Sinclair	DeKalb	Camden
Isaac Moseley	DeKalb	Camden
J.W. Arrants	Dekalb	Antioch
G.W. Watts	DeKalb	Camden
A.G. Ward	Dekalb	Camden
John E. Jones	Flat Rock	Rileys
J.R. Horton	Flat Rock	Westville
A. Matheson	Flat Rock	Lisensby
George Beach	Flat Rock	Flat Rock
Zedekiah Boone	Flat Rock	Westville
Duncan Ray	Flat Rock	DeKalb
Stephen Self	Flat Rock	Westville

---

627 General Assembly, Joints and Resolution, 1897, pages 1246-1248. South Carolina Archives and History, Columbia, South Carolina, microfilm number ST 0797.

J.J. Sutton	Flat Rock	Camden
Hiram Addison	Wateree	Camden
John Outlaw	Wateree	Camden
John Orren	Wateree	Camden
William Gladden	Wateree	Camden
George Jackson	Wateree	Camden
John D. Crossland	Wateree	Camden
Neil Ray	Wateree	Camden
J.H. Williamson	Wateree	Camden
W.C. Roberts	Wateree	Camden
Thomas L. Rosenborough	Wateree	Camden
C.J. Stewart	Wateree	Camden
J.H. True	Wateree	Camden
James D. Dufee	Wateree	Camden
John Green	Wateree	Camden
J.D. Crossland	Wateree	Camden
R.J. Nelson	Dekalb	Camden

Class C, Number 4

Margaret Faulkenbury	Flat Rock	Westville
M.L. BIggart	Flat Rock	Magill
Mary L. Johnson	Flat Rock	Magill
Rebecca Gaskin	Flat Rock	Westville
L.L. Mobley	Flat Rock	Flat Rock
Sarah A. Cauthen	Flat Rock	Kershaw
Lenora Kelly	Wateree	Camden
Rhonda Dawkins	Wateree	Sharp
Ann Cook	Wateree	Sharp
Sarah Jacobs	Wateree	Sharp
Mary Barr	Wateree	Camden
Sallie Dawkins	Wateree	Camden
Sarah Hays	Wateree	Camden
Elizabeth Branham	Wateree	Camden
Carolina Corder	Wateree	Camden
Mary Croft	Wateree	Camden
R.J. Pitts	Buffalo	Abney
S.L. Gardner	Buffalo	Timrod
M.J. Gardner	Buffalo	Camden
M.J. West	Buffalo	Camden
Henrietta Gainey	Buffalo	Lynchburg

Rachael Taylor	Buffalo	Kershaw
Eliza A. Gardner	Buffalo	Abney
Nannie C. Kelly	Buffalo	Lucknow
Millie Ammons	DeKalb	Camden
Elvira Harvey	DeKalb	Camden
Rebecca G. Nelson	DeKalb	Camden
Mary J. Newman	DeKalb	Camden
Mary Outen	DeKalb	Camden
Martha Ann Pie (Pye)	DeKalb	Camden
Mary J. DeKay	DeKalb	Camden
M. R. Young	DeKalb	Camden
Emma S. Nelson	Dekalb	Camden
Mary Lee	DeKalb	Camden
E.C. Roach	Buffalo	Kershaw
Sarah Jacob	Wateree	Ridgeway
Amanda Holland	DeKalb	Camden

628

1899 Kershaw County Pensions

Class A	Township	Post Office
Henry Hinson	DeKalb	Camden

Class B

D.C. Kirkley	DeKalb	Camden
Stephen Self	Flat Rock	Westville

Class C, Number 2

J.W. Arrants	Dekalb	Camden
J.P. Adam	Dekalb	Camden
Hiram Addison	Wateree	Camden
W.H. Addison	Wateree	Camden
R.R. Atkinson	Buffalo	Abney
John Boone	Buffalo	Westville
W.J. Boone	Buffalo	Westville
Wesley Croft	DeKalb	Camden
John D. Crossland	Wateree	Camden

---

[628] General Assembly, Joints and Resolution, 1898, pages 1166-1168. South Carolina Archives and History, Columbia, South Carolina, microfilm number ST 0798.

Hugh Cassidy	Buffalo	Lynchwood
John Irvin	Wateree	Camden
W.J. Fletcher	DeKalb	Flat Rock
W.G. Huckabee	Dekalb	Camden
John Green	Wateree	Camden
T.H. Hunter	Buffalo	Timrod
B.N. Huggins	Buffalo	Lynchwood
(?)T.J. Harton	Flat Rock	
George Jackson	Wateree	Camden
J.T. Jones	Buffalo	Lynchwood
John E. Jones	Dekalb	Kershaw
W.D. Kelly	Wateree	Camden
D.H. Kelly	Wateree	Camden
B.T. Lewis	DeKalb	Camden
Isaac Mosely	DeKalb	Camden
H.J. Munn	Buffalo	Abney
A. Matheson	Flat Rock	Liberty Hill
A.L. McMillen	DeKalb	Camden
John Outlaw	Wateree	Camden
Michael Parker	Buffalo	Tiller's Ferry
R.J. Phillips	Buffalo	Abney
Neil Ray	Wateree	Camden
W.C. Roberts	Wateree	Camden
Thomas L. Rosenborough	Wateree	Camden
Samuel Rosenborough	Wateree	Camden
Duncan Ray	Flat Rock	Kershaw
J.J. Stokes	Buffalo	Lucknow
C.J. Stewart	Wateree	Camden
J.J. Sutton	Wateree	Camden
John Sinclair	DeKalb	Camden
James Taylor	Buffalo	Tiller's Ferry
G.W. Watts	Dekalb	Camden
Allen G. Ward	DeKalb	Camden
J.R. Williams	Wateree	Camden

1901

Class A

Hinson, Henry,	Camden,	Company G, 7th

Class B

Self, Stephen,	DeKalb,	Company D 7th	Lost right arm
Wilson, William,	Lucknow,	20th Regiment	Lost right leg

Class C No 1

Bateman, W J,	Camden,	Company A 7th SCI	Wounded through hip
Boone, W J,	Kershaw,	Company G, 2nd SCI	Arms useless from wound
Green, John,	Bellfield,	Company D, 7th SC Battalion	Shot through left lung
LeGrand, J M,	Camden,	Company E, 2nd SCI	wounded in hand
Sutton, J J,	Camden,	Company E, Company G, 7th SC Battalion	lost left hand
True, James H,	Camden,	Company C, 1st Regiment	Wounded in body
Ward, Allen,	Camden,	Company G, 7th Regiment	Shot in breast

Kershaw County Year 1902

    Transfer from Class C Number 2 to Class C Number 1- J.B. Arrants

Change in roll from last year:

	Class A	**Class B No. 1**	**Class C No. 2**	**Class C No. 3**	**Class C No. 4**	**Class C**	**Total**
On roll 1901	7	2	7	49	15	111	
last Payment	0	0	0	9	2	3	14

Transfer to

Another County	0	0	0	0	0	1	1
Transfer to Class	0	0	0	1	0	0	

Ttal D

Deduction	0	0	0	10	2	4	16

Balance of

1901 Roll	7	2	7	39	13	33	95
New Name Only	0	0	1	20	1	18	42

Transfer to

Other Class	0	0	1	0	0	0	1

---

[629] General Assembly, Joints and Resolution, 1901, pages 271-272. South Carolina Archives and History, South Carolina, microfilm.

Total Additions

| To Roll | 0 | 0 | 2 | 20 | 1 | 18 | 41 |

Person on

| Roll 1902 | 1 | 2 | 9 | 59 | 14 | 51 | 135[630] |

Dead in Class C No 2- R. R. Atkinson, William Bowen, W. J. Fletcher, John T. Jones, W. Knight, F M Mayer, Allen Medlin, Isaac Moseley, H. C. West

Dead in Class C No. 3- Margaret Gardner, Rebecca J. Pitts

    Class C No. 4- E. M. Capell, Martha E. Dawkins, Rachel Taylor[631]

Transfer to another county- Sarah McLemore, Class C No. 4 to Chesterfield[632]

Class C No. 1 1902

| Truesdale, W M, | Flat Rock, | Company 2nd SCV | Wounded in Abdomen in service |

Class C No. 2 1902

Addison, H.,	Camden,	Company H, 7th Regiment	67
Branham, S.A.,	Bellfield,	Company C, 6th SC	63
Brown, R.C.,	Camden,	Company A, 7th Regiment	61
Cunningham, J.S.,	Liberty Hill,	Company E, 2nd SCV	60
Corbett, W.S.,	Tiller's Ferry,	Company C, 19th Volunteers	66
Deas, Lewis,	Abney,	Company I, 17th Regiment	63
Gaskin, John D.,	Westville,	Company G, 7th Battalion	60
Gay, Isaac,	Westville,	Company A, Lucas'	62
Hull, Zimmerman D.,	Lucknow,	Company C, 7th Battalion	70
Hudson, J.W.,	Camden,	Company C, White's Regiment	64
Joyner, W.H.,	Blaney,	Company D, 20th Regiment	60
Kirby, A.P.,	Camden,	Company D, 15th Regiment	62
Langley, W.M.,	Bethune,	Company D, 6th Regiment	62
Nelson, Columbus,	Camden,	Company G,	71
Outlaw, Rozier,	Camden,	Company G, 7th Regiment	61
Outlaw, Angus,	Camden,	Company E, 6th Regiment	64
Player, John,	Camden,	Company H, 7th Cavalry	63
Rowell, J.G.,	Flat Rock,	Company K, 6th Regiment	60

---

[630] General Assembly, Joints and Resolution, 1903, pages 113-115
[631] Ibid.
[632] Ibid

Stokes, W.J.,	Lucknow,	Company D, 7th SC	61
Truesdale, J.C.,	Camden,	Company H, 4thCavalry	68

Class C, No 3 1902

Bass, Mary,	Cantey,	Company C, 6th SC	

Class C, No 4 1902

Atkinson, Sarah A,	Roland,	Company D, 7th Regiment	61
Catoe, Mary E,		Company G, 2nd Regiment	65
Bowen, Sarah,	Blaney,	Company G, Palmetto Regiment	61
DeKay, M.J.,	Camden,	Company D, 3rd Regiment	67
Fletcher, Susan A.,	Westville,	Company G, 2nd Regiment	64
Huckabee, Johanna,	Camden,	Company E, 9th Regiment	64
Hinson, Emma,		Company H, 43 North Carolina	62
Hornsby, Francis A.,	Blaney,	Company D, 15th SC	62
Jacobs, Sarah,	Sharps,	Company C, 15th Regiment	69
Jones, Adeline,	Bethune,	Company F, 7th Regiment	70
Mickle, Jane,	Camden,	Company C, 4thBattalion	60
Matthews, Louisa,	Cantey,	Company E, 12th SC	67
Monroe, H.A.,	Camden,	Company E, 2nd SCV	60
Moore, Martha,	Bethune,	Company E, 19th Battalion	75
Nettles, Mary J.,	Blaney,	Company E, 2nd Regiment	60
Outlaw, Charlotte,	Camden,	Company E, 6th Regiment	68
Peach, Eliza,	Bethune,	Company D, 7th SC	60
Smith, Sallie J.,	Camden,	Company H, 7th SCV	61[633]

Changes in 1903

Dead- Class C- W. G. Huckabee, J. R. McEachen, John E. Outlaw, J.C. Truesdale

    Class C No. 3- Elvira Howle

    Class C No. 4- Joanna Huckabee, Sarah A. Atkinson

    Dropped by County Board- Sarah Bowen (not a widow)

    Transferred to other Counties:

        Class B- William Wilson to Lee County

        Class C No 2- J.W. Arrants, Wiley Bradley, Wesley Croft, J.J. Stokes, W.S. Corbett, Zimmerman Hall, and W.J. Stokes to Lee County

        Class 2 No 4- Harriett Atkinson, Martha, Spradley to Lee County

        Class 2 No 2- John E. Outlaw to Richland County, W C Roberts to Richland

---

[633] Ibid.

County, J.T. Smith to Marlboro County,

    Class C No 3- E.K. Doby to Richland County

    Class C No 4- Martha Moore to Chesterfield County

Transferred to another class:

    Class C No 4 to Class C No 3- Caroline Corder, Henrietta Gainey, Nancy J. Williams, M.J. DeKay

Transferred from another county

    Class C No 2- W.D. Kelly from Fairfield County[634]

Class C No 2 1903

Alexander, J.C.,	Camden,	Company E, 2nd Regiment	61
Albert, John,	Camden,	Company E, 9th Regiment	64
Branham, Hughey,	Camden,	Company H, 6th Regiment	72
Broome, J.W.,	Westville,	Company G, 2nd Regiment	
Baker, H.W.,	Camden,	Company K, 23rd Regiment	67
Baker, D.A.,	Roland,	Company B, 20th Regiment	75
Camell, S.J.,	Sharps,	Company E, 22nd Regiment	65
Isenhour, Daniel,	Camden,	Company C, 2nd Regiment	71
Kelly, Joseph S.,	Camden,	Company A, Wards	81
Moore, James,	Bellfield,	Company C, 6th Regiment	61
Sinclair, James,	Abney,	Company A, 7th Regiment	61
Triminal, R.J.,	Camden,	Company E, 19th Regiment	
Spradley, W.J.,	Camden,	Company D, 15th Regiment	65

Class C, No 3 1903

Corder, Caroline,		Company C, 7th Battalion
DeKay, M.J.,	Camden,	Company D, 3rd Regiment
Gainey, Harriett,	Bethune,	Company E, 21st Regiment
Mims, Mahala,	Roland,	Company A, 7th Regiment
Truesdale, Nancy M.,	Westville,	Company G, 2nd Regiment
Young, Margaret J.,	Roland,	Company G, 2nd Regiment
Williams, Nancy J.,	Camden,	Company G, 7th Regiment

Class C, No 4 1903

Goodale, C.M.,	Camden	Company B, 7th Regiment	60
Shriver(Shiver), Martha,	Camden,	Company G, 20th Regiment	60
Shirley, M.M.,	Camden,	Company A, 7th Regiment	64
Workman, Mary R.	Boykin,	Company H, 1st SC	63[635]

---

[634] General Assembly, Joints and Resolutions,

1904

Dead- Class C No. 2- B.H. Huggins, W.D. Kelly, A.C. Marshall, A. Mathison, John Sinclair, and Angus Outlaw.

Class C No. 4- Eliza Gardner, Nancy Perry, Rachel Taylor, Sarah Jacobs, Adeline Jones, and Jane Parker

Transferred to other counties:

Class C No. 4- W.H. Baker to Richland County, M.M. Shirley to Lee County

Transferred to other classes:

From Class C No 4 to Class C No 3- Rebecca Gaskins

Class C No 1 1904

| Mackey, John, | Heath Springs, | Company I, 12 SCV, | wounded in body in service |

Class C No 2, 1904

| Williams, John C.P., | Camden, | Kirkwood Rangers |

Class C No 3, 1904

| Bennington, Barbary, | Blaney, | Company B, 7th Regiment |
| Gaskin, Rebecca, | Westville, | Company C Witherspoon |

Class C No 4 1904

Evans, Elizabeth,	Blaney,	Company K and Regiment	63
Koon, Sarah,	Blaney,	Company B, PBLA	63
Motley, Tabitha,	Blaney,	Company G, 7th Regiment	60
Niles, Martha,	Camden,	Company E, 2nd Regiment	60
Ross, Martha A.,	Blaney,	Company C, 6th Cavalry	60
Sinclair, Rebecca,	Camden,	Company A 7th Regiment	69

1905 Kershaw County Pensions

Dead

Class A- Stephen Shelf, Class C No 2- Jessie Clyburn, Duncan Ray, J S Cunningham, and Hughey Branham, Class C No 4- Frances Hornsby

Transferred to other counties- Hester Copeland to Laurens County

Transferred from another County- E.N. Dean, Sarah Atkinson, and Martha Spradley from Lee County.

---

635 General Assembly, Joints and Resolutions, 1903
636 General Assembly, Joints and Resolutions, 1904

Class A

| Cottrell, J.T., | Camden, | Company H, 5th Cavalry | Paralyzed |

Class C No A

| Roberts, W.C., | Kershaw, | Company E 12th |

Class C No 2

Gardner, Isaac,	Kershaw,	Company E, 12th
Higgins, Benjamin,	Lugoff,	Company B, 7th
Kinard, A.L.C.,	Lugoff,	Company H 7th
Mahaffey, J.A.,	Bethune,	Company C 6th SC
Parker, John,	Camden,	Company G PBLA
Self, Nancy,	DeKalb,	Company C, 7th

Class C No 4

| Kelly, Ellen C., | Lugoff, | Company B 7th | 62 |
| Pendergrass, F.E., | Camden, | Company C 25th SCV[637] | |

1906 Kershaw County Pension Records

Dead-

    Class C No 1- John Green, W.M. Truesdale, and W.C. Roberts

    Class C No 2- G.S. Rhame and John C. Williams

    Class C No 3- M.J. Newman, M.J. DeKay, Margaret J. Young, Rebecca Gaskins, Sallie Dawkins, and A.S. Wilson.

    Transferred to another County- Joseph Kelly

    Transferred to another county- Mary J. Nettles to Richland County

    Left the State- J.T. Cottrell to Tennessee

    Transferred from another county- Jacob Freeman from Fairfield County.

    Transferred to another class- M.E. Cato from Class C No 4 to Class C No 3.

Class C No 2

Jackson, T.F.,	Lugoff,	Company C 6th Battalion
Kirkland, D.P.,		Kirkwood Rangers
Truesdale, J.R.,	DeKalb,	Company H 1st
Yarborough, Wilson,		Company A 7th

---

[637] General Assembly, Joints and Resolutions, 1906

Class C No 3

Cato, M.E.,	Camden,	Company G 2nd

Class C No 4

Ferrell, M.S.,	Camden,	Company G 2nd	60
Outlaw, A.I.,	Camden,	Company E, 6th	60
Pace, H.C.,	Cantey,	Company Wateree Rifles	63

638

1907 Kershaw County Pensions

Dead-

    Class C No 1- W.J. Broome and J.M. LeGrand

    Class C No 2- John D. Crossland, R.J. Hyatt, George Jackson, and Daniel Isenhour.

    Class C No 4- Estelle McQueen and Martha Spradley.

    Transferred to another county- T.B. Denton and Benjamin Higgins to Richland County, W.H. Joyner to Orangeburg County, Isaac Gardner to York County, and Wilson Yarborough to Lexington County.

    Transferred from another county- J.E. Douglas from Chesterfield County.

Class C No 2

Gunter, A.E.,	Blaney,	Company I 20th
Pearson, J.A.,	Camden,	Company K 15th

Class C No 4

Boone, Bertha J.,	Kershaw,	Company G, Rock Guards	68
Belk, Cordie,	Camden,	Company E 7th	62
Goff, E.F.,	Camden,	Company G 8th	60
Knight, Elizabeth,	Kershaw,	Company F 26th	70
Schrock, Mary E.,	Camden,	Company D 15th SCV	67[639]

1908 Kershaw County Pensions

Dead

Class C No 2- Samuel Bass, James Catoe, Sr., and B.D. Heath.

Class C No 3- Mary Lee, M.T. Moore, and Emma S. Nelson.

---

[638] General Assembly, Joints and Resolutions, 1907
[639] General Assembly, Joints and Resolutions, 1907

Class A Disability Began on Roll

Gardner, James William	Bethune	Company A, 7th	Paralized	1908
Hinson, Henry	Camden	Company G, 7th	Blind	1901
Hyatt, J.W.		Company A, Nelson's	Paralized	

Class C, Number 1

Arrants, J.B.	Camden	Company C, 6th SCI	Wounded in Body	1901
Bateman, W.J.	Camden	Company A, 7th SCI	Wounded through Hip	1903
Freeman, Jacob	Fairfield County	Company E, 9th	Wounded in Shoulder and Thigh	1901
Mackey, John	Health Springs	Company I, 12th	Wounded Back	1904
Mann, H.J.	DeKalb	Company F, 7th	Wounded Leg	1908
Sutton, J.J.	Camden	Company G, 7th SC Battalion	Lost left hand	1903
True, James H.	Camden	Company C, 1st Regiment	Wounded in body	1903
Ward, Allen	Camden	Company G, 7th Regiment	Shot in Breast	1903

Class C, Number 2 on Roll

Anderson, James	Camden	Company A, 4th	1901
Addison, H	Camden	Company H, 7th	1902
Alexander, J.C.	Camden	Company E, 2nd	1903
Albert, John	Camden	Company E, 9th	1903
Anderson, J.A	Camden	Company A, 35th	1908
Boone, John	Westville	Company G, SCI	1901
Branham, S.A.	Bellfield	Company C, 6th SC	1902
Brown, R.C.	Camden	Company A, 7th Regiment	1902
Branham, M.W.	Fairfield County	Company C, 6th	1901
Boone, J.W.	Westville	Company G, 2nd	1903
Baker, D.A.	Roland	Company B, 26th	1903
Connell, S.J.	Sharp	Company E, 22nd	1903
Deas, E.N.	Lee County	Company I, 7th	1901
Deas, Lewis	Abney	Company I, 17th	1902
Douglas, J.E.	Chesterfield County,	Company A, 7th	1902

Pension records in The Camden Chronicle, April 16, 1929

Probate Judge W. L. McDowell has received a check for $10,548 to be disbursed to the Confederate Veterans and widows of Confederate Veterans of Kershaw County. The veterans who will get pensions are:

N.A. Bethune

William Branham

John S. Brasington

G.W. Moseley

D.P.C. Murchinson

Hiram Nettles

William Guerry Felder

W.A. Cunningham
J.R. DeLoache
Isaac Gardner
Isaac F. Holland
B.M. Jones
G.B. King
A.S. McKenzie

J.W. Rose
W.F. Russell
C.J. Shannon
C.J. Stewart
William W. Terry
S.B. Turner
L.W. Watts

Widows are:

R.E. Alexander
Mary J. Anderson
Nannie Benton
C.S. Benton
Y.A.S. Brown
E.J. Brasington
Susan Campbell
Emma Coates
M.C. Cureton
L.S. Dubose
Matilda Easler
Matilda Faile
Harriet P. Floyd
Emma Freeman
Victoria Gardner
Mary J. Gillis
M.S.F. Sinclair
Henrietta M. Sill
Mary A. Smyrl
Julia A Stevens
Ann M. Thorne
Nannie E. Trantham
Sallie E. Truesdale
Susan H. Campbell
Hattie B. Wilson

Eliza Graham
Mary J. Graham
Amanda Hall
Emma HInson
Caroline Hinson
Sarah A. Horton
J.W. Hyatt
Margaret E. Jones
Rebecca C. Jones
Betty B. Kennedy
M.M. Kirkland
Alice McCaskill
Rebecca Marsh
Laura J. Moore
Ella P. Pearce
M.A. Robinson
Sarah West
Rebecca W. White
Harriet Wilson
Bessie Whitaker
Nannie Branham
Ella S. Bell
Mary H. Clyburn
Zimmie D. Dunlap

The Veterans will receive $202.40 each, while the widows will receive $125.00. The Kershaw County Pension Board was made up of N.A. Bethune, W.F. Russell, and B.M. Jones.

Persons Exempt from Military Service in Kershaw County

DeSaussure, D. L.: He was thirty years old. The cause of exemption was that he was treasurer of Kershaw County.

Matthew, John E.: He was forty-four years old. His cause was he was a teacher at an academy in Kershaw County.

Poston, Benjamin: He was forty-two. His cause he was a miller from Lynches Creek.

Poston, Simon- He was thirty-two, his cause he was a Miller from Lynches Creek.

Boswell, J.P.- He was thirty-two, his cause he was the Sheriff of Kershaw County.

Brasington, James L.- He was twenty-six, his cause was he was a fireman from Camden, S.C.

Geralds, Edward J.- He was twenty-one, his cause he was a fireman from Camden, SC.

Goodale, J.R. – He was thirty, and his cause he was a fireman from Camden, S.C.

Arrants, M.J.- He was twenty-three, his cause was he was with the Independent Fire Engine Company of Camden, Camden, S.C.

Love, R.J.- He was thirty-five, his cause was he was with the Independent Fire Engine Company of Camden, Camden, S.C.

Wittkowsky, A- He was thirty-eight, and his cause was he was with the Independent Fire Engine Company of Camden, Camden, S.C.

Collier, F.J. – He was twenty-five, and his cause was he was with the Independent Fire Engine Company of Camden, Camden, S.C.

Wilson, S.M.- He was age thirty-five, and his cause was he was with the Independent Fire Engine Company of Camden, Camden, S.C.

Brown, J.R. – He was age thirty-five, his cause was he was with the Independent Fire Engine Company of Camden, Camden, S.C.

Wilson, P.H. – He was age thirty, his cause was he was with the Independent Fire Engine Company of Camden, Camden, S.C.

Haynes, Augustus M.- He was age twenty-two, his cause was he was with the Independent Fire Engine Company of Camden, Camden, S.C.

Kirby, James D.- He was age thirty-nine, his cause was he was with the Independent Fire Engine Company of Camden, Camden, S.C.

Broyles, O.R.- He was thirty-two, his cause was he was with the Independent Fire Engine Company of Camden, Camden, S.C.

Stuart, Benjamin R.- He was twenty-three, and his cause was he was with the Independent Fire Engine Company of Camden, Camden, S.C.

McSween, John- He was twenty-two, and his cause was he was with the Independent Fire Engine Company of Camden, Camden, S.C.

Nettles, J.T. – He was twenty- three, and his cause was he was with the Independent Fire Engine Company of Camden, Camden, S.C.

Workman, William H.R. – He was fourty- three, and his cause was he was in for seven year's service in state militia in Kershaw County.

Geralds, W. C. – He was thirty-five, and his cause was he was with the Independent Fire Engine Company of Camden, Camden, S.C.

Cohn, William- He was thirty-eight, and his cause was he was with the Independent Fire Engine Company of Camden, Camden, S.C.

Crosby, George- He was thirty-three, and his cause was he was with the Independent Fire Engine Company of Camden, Camden, S.C.

Childers, James- He was twenty , and his cause was he was with the Independent Fire Engine Company of Camden, Camden, S.C.

Goodale, Joseph- He was thirty-three, and he was a fireman in Camden, S.C.

Moore, A.A. – He was thirty-five, and his cause was he was a regular practicing physician in Kershaw County.

Birchmore, T.E.- He was eighteen, he was with the Independent Fire Engine Company of Camden, Camden, S.C.

Moore, T.A. – He was forty-four, and his cause was he was with the Independent Fire Engine Company of Camden, Camden, S.C.

Player, W. Columbus- He was thirty-five, and his cause was he was a member of the Camden Fire Engine Company, Camden, S.C.

Barfield, R.E. – He was twenty-five, and his cause was he was a member of the Camden Fire Engine Company, Camden, S.C.

Davis, T. Bruce- He was twenty-six, and his cause was he was a minister of the Gospel, Camden, S.C.

Jones, Thomas J.- He was thirty-nine, and he was a Fireman Independent of Camden, Camden, S.C.

Wilson, F.J. – He was twenty-nine, and he was a Fireman Independent of Camden, Camden, S.C.

Johnson, John- He was thirty-nine, and he was a Minister of the Gospel.

Man, W.W.- He was eighteen, and he was a Member of the Camden Independent F.E.C., Camden, S.C.

Source: List of Persons Exempt from State Military Duty, South Carolina State Archives, Columbia, S.C.

More Confederate Reunion Pictures.
Taken in the early 1900's
Unknown People

Front Row: 3RD from right- Henry Fleming Boykin (Company H- 7th SC Cavalry)
9th from right- Jim Spradley
9th from left- J. C. Hilton

406 | William Guerry Felder

Our Confederates Can't Speak Anymore

In today's times, our Confederate Society has come under question by forces who for in their own mind feels that the whole War Between the States were squarely the fault on our beloved Confederate South. Remember, it takes at least two to fight but in this case, the beginning of a campaign that took not only the four or so years to survive, but for years afterwards in a period worse than death called Reconstruction.

Even today, two of the most guided groups to educate and make aware of the truths and distortions stand silent. Those groups are the United Daughters of the Confederacy and the Sons of the Confederacy. When the flag was taken down at the Capital building in Columbia, South Carolina, words from these groups lay silent and non-existent.

Today, groups expect all to work together, however only if that cause and rights are always on top. The NAACP is one organization that should be banned as its goals are not only bias but self-seeking. Working together with others is not in their agenda. On the other side, politics will never work with one another.

Today's Confederate is lost in the shuffle, forgotten, thrown away. Soon, other soldiers who fought will soon become a memory—Mexican American War of 1847, the Spanish American War, WW1, WW11 and so on.

These soldiers have faces, families, and friends. Though time has gone by, these family and friends remember. Do you remember?

Their silence is because they are forgotten and can't speak anymore. No one else does either.

Today, a cleansing of the past is taking place. Monuments of anything seem to be targeted and abused and destroyed. Removed from sight as if to say, their lives meant nothing, their leadership meant nothing, and their families had no right to go on. Remember the times and the situations these brave soldiers fought and led men. During their time, these men were respected. We of today should respect their path and their fight.

The following are pictures of Confederates that gave for a worthy cause. Honor and cherish these soldiers.

William Columbus Cauthen

John Zachary Young

Robert T. Owen

Lily Thomas Stroud

(Given by Miles Gardner)

John McKinly Barfield

Robert Kirkley

Amos Hough

Moses Hough

Benjamin H. Burdell

Anderson H. Bowen

Powell McRae Team

John C. West

Isaac Brownhill Alexander

Dove Segars

Simon Baruch

Col. L.C. Hough

Dr. Albertus Adair Moore

Jimmy DeLoach

Two Pictures Dr. William Overton Veal

James Ervin Sowell

Jessie Arthur

John Burdell

Jackson Elijah Hinson

Joseph James Bell

Leslie McCandleless

John Nelson Gamewell

Reverend John Kershaw

Through Many Eyes | 415

W. D. Trantham

Zedakiah (Zed) Boone

Thomas Peter Evans

Thomas Whitaker McCaa

Thomas Jefferson Withers

Lovick William Rochelle Blair

Lewis Lee Clyburn

William Baxter Stinson

Thomas Andrew Cauthen

E. N. Yarborough

G. B. King

Mannes Baum

Isaac "Coot" Gardner

Lewis Gardner

Tristan Burch

C. C. Haile

Floyd Osborn

William "Billy" Crowe Horton

James T. Hall

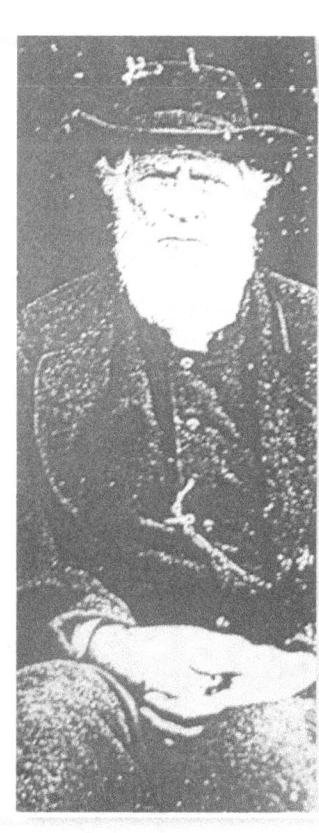
Shelton Benjamin Hall

William Arthur

John, Jessie, and William Arthur

Captain James H. Burns

Reddick Moseley

Two Pictures of Alexander Moseley

George Washington Moseley

Samuel Benjamin Hatfield, Sr.

Private DOVE RAILEY
Co. "P", 7th Batt'n, Enfield Rifles
Killed at Petersburg, Va.,
Aug. 23, 1864

Other Books to Look at:

Historic Camden, Volume 11 by Kirkland and Kennedy

Mary Chesnut's Diary from Dixie and Mary Chesnut's Civil War Photograph Album

A History of Kershaw County, South Carolina by Joan A. Inabinet and L. Glen Inabinet

Long Ago at Liberty Hill: An Historical Sketch by Mary Ellen Cunningham

A History of Lynches Forks and Extended Areas on Big and Little River, South Carolina, by Lon D. Outen.

Kershaw County Cousins, by Charlotte Boykin Salmond Brunson

History and Homes of Liberty Hill, South Carolina, by Louise Johnson.

Stoneboro: An Historical Sketch of a South Carolina Community, by Andrea Deborah VanLandingham Steen

Health Springs, South Carolina, 1752 – 1970, by Andrea Deborah VanLandingham Steen

And Were the Glory of their Times- Artillery: by Hebert O. Chambers, III

And Were the Glory of their Times- Cavalry: by Herbert O. Chambers, III

Steadfast to the Last by Randolph W. Kirkland, Jr.

Broken Fortunes by Randolph W. Kirkland, Jr.

Index

A

Abbas Pasha - 139
Abbeville - 10, 198
Abdullah Beduin -
Abney - 386, 387, 388, 389, 391, 393, 397
Academia and Primary Schools - 94
Academy - 311
Act of April 24, 1863
Act of Congress 1889 - 370
Act of Secession - 214
Adam's Mill (Hughes Mill) - 325
Adam's Run, S.C. - 46, 56
Adams, Colonel - 109, 112, 129, 219, 348, 349
Adams, Colonel D. W. - 219
Adams, J. P. - 386
Adams, Joseph - 89
Adams, W. - 49
Adams, William - 372, 375, 376, 377, 378, 380, 381
Adamson, Miss - 67
Addison, H. T. - 85
Addison, Hiram - 384, 387, 388, 391, 397
Addison, Joseph - 85
Addison, W. A. - 163
Addison, W. H. - 388
Adirondacks - 258
Adkins, W.C. - 87
Adkinson, Ezekiel - 44
Adkinson, Thomas - 44
Advance Piquet - 18
Agnes - 214
Ahrens, John -368
Aiken, Colonel D. Wyatt - 131, 146, 201, 202, 203, 204, 210, 211
Aiken, General - 120, 129
Aiken's Regiment - 203
Alabama - 8, 77, 90, 228, 229, 236, 255, 261, 262
Alabama Archives - 228
Alabama, Carlowville - 77
Alabama Headquarters - 236
Alabama, Mobile - 215, 219, 227

Alabama, Portland - 262
Alabama Regiment - 228
Alabama River - 262
Alabama, Russell County - 227, 229, 230
Alabama Sharpshooters - 228
Alabama Volunteers - 218
Alabama, Poland - 54
Alabamians - 338
Albert, John - 162, 393, 397
Albert, William H. - 41
Alden - 67, 70
Alden, George - 21, 56, 94
Aldrich, Alfred - 368
Alec - 231
Alexander, Colonel - 207
Alexander, Dr. Isaac Henry - 267
Alexander, George - 164
Alexander, George Gilman - 267
Alexander, Isaac Brownhill - 38, 94, 411
Alexander, J. A. - 164
Alexander, J. B. - 34
Alexander, J. E. - 162, 164
Alexander, J.C. - 393, 397
Alexander, L. B. - 68
Alexander, Mary J. - 398
Alexander, Mrs. - 69
Alexander, Mrs. I. B. - 83, 98, 102
Alexander, R.E. -398
Alexander's Artillery - 207
Allen, J. P. - 62
Allen, J. W. - 13, 62, 63
Allen, R. W. - 49
Allen, W. H. - 84
Allen, W. R. - 9, 13
Allen, Wesley - 90
Allemance, Minnesota - 255
Allison, Reverend - 67
Amelia - 277, 295, 296, 298
Amelia Courthouse - 277
Amelia Springs - 277
America - 11, 12, 141, 232, 260

Ammons, H. - 20, 52
Ammons, Millie -369, 371, 372, 374, 379, 377, 380, 382, 383, 385, 388
Ammons, William A. - 20
Ancrum, Douglas - 269
Ancrum, M. - 70
Ancrum, Miss - 98
Ancrum, Miss Lottie - 58
Ancrum, Mrs. T. J. - 65, 67
Ancrum, Thomas A. - 47, 319
Ancrum, Thomas J. - 4, 28, 40, 60, 61, 64, 134, 267, 366
Ancrum, William Alexander - 31, 45, 60, 162, 164, 319, 320, 365
Anderson - 285
Anderson, Aiken - 146
Anderson, George - 256
Anderson, J. A. - 397
Anderson, J. D. - 267
Anderson, J. M. -164
Anderson, James - 397
Anderson, Lieutenant General R. H. - 147, 152, 277, 278, 280, 285
Anderson, Major - 174, 175
Anderson, Major General - 205, 206
Anderson, Mary J. - 398
Anderson, Mrs. William - 61
Anderson, Thomas - 77
Anderson, W. D. - 27, 28, 42, 49, 71, 74, 96
Anderson's Command - 280
Anderson's Division - 207, 209
Angel of Mayre's Heights -333
Anker, Mrs. - 98, 102
Anker, Mrs. J. H. - 98
Ansel, Governor - 221, 223
Antietam - 212
Antioch - 79, 385, 386
Antioch Baptist Church - 59, 60, 79, 242, 243
Antioch Cemetery - 79
Antioch Post Office - 385, 386
Appleton, W. L. - 36
Appomattox - 183, 225, 277, 278, 323, 324, 356
Appomattox Court House - 136
Arkansas - 40, 51, 143
Armestead, Major Robert T. - 218
Army of Georgia -109
Army of Mississippi - 218
Army of Northern Virginia - 149, 200, 222, 225, 320, 343, 344
Army of Potomac - 16, 18, 319
Army of Tennessee - 109
Arrants - 42
Arrants, M. J. - 399
Arrants, B. R. - 63

Arrants, H. - 47
Arrants, Harmon, Jr. - 242, 243
Arrants, J. - 41
Arrants, J. B. -13, 37, 39, 162, 267, 390
Arrants, J. H. - 9, 13
Arrants, James Robert -267, 369
Arrants, James W. - 87, 151, 163, 267, 386, 388, 392, 397
Arrants, Johannes - 242, 243
Arrants, John - 164
Arrants, Joseph - 53
Arrants, Mary - 51
Arrants, Nathan B. - 51, 94
Arrants, William K. - 51
Arthur, Jessie - 54, 187, 267, 413, 426
Arthur, John - 420
Arthur, Mrs. - 98, 130
Arthur, William - 420
Ashby's Gap - 208
Atkinson - 17
Atkinson, C. M. - 84
Atkinson, E. - 65
Atkinson, Harriet - 392
Atkinson, J. E. - 90
Atkinson, R.R. - 388, 394
Atkinson, Sarah A. - 392, 394
Atkinson, T. R. - 44
Atkinson, T.W. - 44
Atkinson, W. H. - 84
Atlanta- 101, 219, 344
Atlantic Campaign -228
Augier, Miss Fannie - 67
Augustine, S. W. - 85
Aunt Charlotte - 292
Aunt Ella - 292
Averysboro - 226

B

Bachman, Captain W. K. - 147
Bachman, Dr. John - 66, 77
Bacon's Company - 18
Bacot, Pieree - 146
Baer, B. M. - 10, 13
Baghdad - 140
Bagley, W. L. - 85
Bailey, G. - 94
Bailey, John - 85
Baker, B.J. - 47
Baker, D.A. - 163, 393, 397
Baker, Daniel - 64
Baker, E. P. - 98

Baker, H.W. - 393
Baker, J.B. - 161
Baker, J.W. - 44
Baker, Mrs. L. T. - 315
Baker, W. H. - 394
Bakers - 95
Ballard, J. F. - 88
Ballard's Farm (Colonel) - 115
Baltimore - 256, 297
Bank of Camden - 15, 73, 77, 79, 82, 96, 104, 105, 291
Bank of Columbia - 143
Bank Officers and Directors - 96
Bank Street - 13
Bank's Ford - 206, 207
Banshee (Ship) - 141, 142
Baptist - 27, 35, 51, 59, 60, 67, 73, 79, 95, 243, 262, 306
Barber, Joseph - 99
Bard, Henry - 22
Barefield, David - 65
Barefield, John - 31, 34
Barefoot, Thomas - 163
Barfield, John McKinley - 409
Barfield, R. E. - 400
Barfield, Samuel - 47
Barfield, Sarah - 315
Barfield, W. A. - 159, 215
Barker - 75
Barker, Major - 147, 148, 149
Barker, J. T. - 65, 91
Barker, R. M. - 359
Barker, T. G. - 147, 148
Barksdale Mississippi Brigade - 200
Barksdale, General - 201, 202, 203, 209, 210
Barnes - 28, 79
Barnes, Dixon - 226
Barnes, Edward - 27, 43, 57, 91, 92
Barnes, A. L. - 44
Barnes, George - 38
Barnes, George W. - 267
Barnes, H.A. - 39
Barnes, Mary A. - 315
Barnes, Reddick E. - 154, 158
Barnes, William - 154
Barns, R. - 88
Barnwell, Edward H. - 217
Barnwell, R. W., Jr. - 60
Barnwell, Reverend - 16
Barnwell, S.C. - 332, 368
Barr, J. W. - 84
Barr, Mary - 387
Barrett - 15
Barron - 343

Barry, Brivet Major General William F. - 109
Bartlett, L. W. - 36
Barton, Brigadier General - 280
Baruch, Dr. Simon - 151, 152, 323, 411
Baruch, H. - 47
Barwick - 40
Baskin, M.C. - 370, 385
Baskin, M.E. - 371, 372, 375, 377, 378, 379, 380, 382, 383
Baskin, William D. - 369, 371, 372, 375
Bass, Henry - 90
Bass, Josephine -315
Bass, Mary - 370, 372, 373, 375, 376, 378, 380, 381, 383, 385, 392
Bass, S. M. - 164
Bass, Samuel -396
Bass, W. - 65
Bass, W.J.C. -38
Bateman, W. J. T. - 163, 390, 397
Bates - 200
Battery Marshall, S.C. - 68, 157, 158
Battle around Knoxville - 76, 198
Battle Around Richmond - 75, 76
Battle Flag of the Confederacy - 184
Battles:
    Battle near Rappahannock - 83
    Battle of Battery Wagner - 68
    Battle of Blue Ridge - 41
    Battle of Boonesboro - 52
    Battle of Bull Run - 331
    Battle of Camden - iv
    Battle of Chancellorsville - 76, 178
    Battle of Chattanooga - 76, 178
    Battle of Chickamauga - 67, 75, 178, 214, 218, 222
    Battle of Churabusco - 227
    Battle of Cold Harbor - 198
    Battle of Corinth - 233
    Battle of Crater - 327, 337, 328
    Battle of Dandridge - 215
    Battle of Drewry's (Drury's) Bluff - 24
    Battle of Fair Garden - 215
    Battle of First Manassas - 3, 13, 45, 48, 216, 217
    Battle of Florida Indians - 9
    Battle of Fort Sumter - 216, 285, 286, 295
    Battle of Franklin - 218
    Battle of Fredericksburg - 51, 59, 213
    Battle of Gettysburg - 63, 75, 76, 178, 214
    Battle of Globe Tavern - 337
    Battle of Hilton Head - 21
    Battle of Hobkirk Hill - 348
    Battle of Little Big Horn - 277
    Battle of Manassas - 17, 18, 27, 33, 48
    Battle of Manassas Plain - 75

Battle of Maryland - 40
Battle of Maryland Heights - 75
Battle of Missionary Ridge - 218, 219
Battle of Morris Island - 63, 68
Battle of Mossy Creek - 215
Battle of Murfreesboro - 218
Battle of Nashville - 218
Battle of Pocataligo - 46, 68
Battle of Ream's Station - 337, 340
Battle of Salem Church - 332
Battle of Second Manassas - 68, 76
Battle of Selma, Alabama - 262
Battle of Seven Pines - 37, 38, 256
Battle of Sharpsburg - 41, 45, 48, 59, 75, 76, 203, 243
Battle of Shiloh - 263
Battle of Valley Campaign - 229
Battle of the Wilderness - 38, 198, 345
Battles and Skirmishes Against General Sherman from Dalton to Atlanta and Jonesboro - 219
Battles of June 28th and 30th - 39
Baum - 204
Baum, Herman - 269
Baum, J. M. and Company - 71
Baum, M. and Brothers - 29, 94
Baum, Mannis - 417
Baum, Marcus - 31, 37, 39, 84, 323, 324
Baum, Mrs. Herman - 180, 182, 185
Baxley, N.D. - 32, 56, 70, 81, 82, 93, 96
Baxley, P. - 44
Be'roujon, C. (City Sexton) - 234
Beach, George - 281
Bealton Station - 320
Beard, John – 359
(Note: Beats became 22nd Regiment) 19, 27, 33, 51, 54, 61, 90, 99, 327, 365, 393
Beat Areas Kershaw County: - 5, 32, 57, 246, 365
Beaufort, S.C. - 58, 283, 296
Beauregard, General -16, 126, 216, 217, 220, 232, 233, 259, 262, 314, 315, 325, 328, 329
Beaver Creek - 78
Beaver Dam Church - 4
Beaver Dam Creek - 115
Beaver, J. R. - 10, 13
Beckham, Dr. B. L - 49
Beckham, S. - 87
Bedon, J. - 39
Beeton, J. - 37
Belk, Cordie - 396
Belk, Joseph - 127, 129
Bell Storehouse - 129
Bell, C. B. - 19
Bell, Catherine -

Bell, Conway - 325
Bell, Ella S. - 398
Bell, J. J. (Joseph James) - 88, 162, 441
Bell, John C. -5
Bell, L. C. - 88
Bell, Mr. - 100, 101
Bell, R. H. - 315
Bell, R. J. - 86, 158
Bell, Robert Jefferson - 154
Bell, S. - 99
Bell, W. H. - 85
Bell, W. R. - 87
Bellfield Area - 390, 391, 393, 397
Belvin, K. D. - 315
Belvin, Sarah - 315
Ben Hur - 139
Benbow, Colonel H. - 327
Benevolent Society - 69, 71, 81
Benjamin, Judah P. - 257
Bennet, Neil James - 154, 159, 161, 162, 165
Bennington, Barbary - 394
Benson, Colonel Samuel - 231
Benson, J. M. - 87
Bently - 357
Benton House (Russell County) - 227
Benton, C.S. -398
Benton, Colonel Lemuel -227
Benton, J. W. - 84
Benton, Martha Elizabeth - 227
Benton, Nannie -398
Benton, Samuel - 35
Benton, Samuel J. - 36, 63, 159, 160, 161
Bentonville- 222, 225, 226
Bermuda - 139, 142
Bermuda Hundred - 355
Bernard, Louisiana - 231
Berry, J.A. - 11
Berry, J.A.W. - 34, 65
Berry's Ford - 208
Bessinger, J. W. - 44
Beteau (Boat) - 103
Beth-El Cemetery (Camden) - 267, 269
Bethesda Presbyterian Church - 185, 251
Bethune, S.C. - 34, 147, 158, 185, 191, 354, 391, 392, 393, 395, 397
Bethune, Daniel M. - 57, 75, 91, 94, 162
Bethune, Neil A. - 162, 163, 165, 184, 261, 262, 397, 398
Bettyneck (Kennedy Plantation) - 346
Bews - 23
Bible Society, Augusta, Georgia - 79
Big Black Creek - 108
Big Lynches Creek -110, 112, 113, 114, 116, 117, 131

Big Pine Tree Creek - 123, 351
Biggart, M. L. -387
Biggs, Lieutenant Colonel Edward- 110
Billings, C. J. - 63
Billings, C. T. - 62, 269
Billings, William M. -28, 65
Birch, Jane C. - 359
Birchmore, T. E. - 400
Bird, Ned - 264
Bird, W. - 63
Birkett (Burkett), Thomas - 65
Bishop Davis' Residence - 127, 245
Bishop of Pennsylvania -308
Bishopville, S.C. - 54, 291
Bissell, M. - 93
Bissell, Swinton - 274, 275
Black Republican Rule - 231
Black Creek, S.C. - 109, 122, 129, 350
Black Horse Cavalry - 322
Black Stock's Depot - 105
Blackburn's Ford - 198
Blackman, W.W. - 87
Blackman, George Patney - 154
Blacksmith, R, R, - 94
Blacksmith Shop - 3, 4, 318, 347
Blacksmith, Wagons, and Carriage Makers - 94
Blackville Hospital -29
Blackwell, B. J. - 87
Blackwell, M.T. - 84
Blackwell, W. - 34
Blair - 24, 30, 163
Blair Company (Captain Francis Blair)- Iv
Blair, General - 119, 120, 121
Blair, Hiram - 265
Blair, L. W. R. - 21, 31, 56, 75, 91, 96, 132, 157, 158, 216, 265, 267, 365, 416
Blair, Phillip - 263
Blair, R. - 69, 71
Blake, David - 14
Blakes- 143
Blakeney, Frank - 159
Blakeney, P. M. -159
Blakeney's Crossroads - 118
Blanchard's SC Reserves - 362
Bland, Colonel Elbert - 207, 210, 211
Blaney- 346, 391, 392, 394, 396
Blaney High School - 184
Blessingh, Lieutenant Colonel Louis Von - 123
Blizzard, E. J. - 84
Blodget, S. H. - 28, 49, 74
Bloomfield, Lieutenant Colonel Ira J. -110
Blue coats - 274, 348

Board of Soldiers Relief -78
Board of Surgeons – 301 \
"Bob" - 83
Bocsenen, Charles - 146
Boggs, Captain W. R.- 236
Bolles, Reverend E. A. - 79
Bompey (horse) - 349
Bone, J. W. - 87
Bone, James Reddick - 154
Bone, William Williamson - 54
Bonham Brigade - 16, 198
Bonham, Brigadier General M.L. -145, 146, 198, 217
Bonney - 197
Bonney, Eli W. - 3, 21, 23, 57, 70, 94, 96, 130
Bonney, Joe - 65
Bonney, Miss - 98
Bonney, Mr. - 102
Bonney, Mrs. - 65
Bonney, Mrs. E. W. - 98, 102
Bonney, Sue - 70, 101
Bonney, U. B. - 87
Bonney, Usher P. - iii, 38, 56, 89
"Bonnie Blue Flag" - 286
Book Seller and Stationary - 94
Booker Washington's School - 230
Boone (Boon) William - 159, 160, 161, 162, 164, 386, 388, 390, 397
Boone (Boon), Zedekiah -384, 386, 415
Boone (Boon), John -159, 160, 162, 164, 386, 388, 397
Boone, Bertha J. - 396
Boone, James -160, 161, 163, 164
Boone, James W. - 159, 185
Boone, John B. - 160
Boone, John W. - 384
Boone, Mrs. P.V. -160
Boone, Sallie - 369, 371, 372, 374, 375, 377, 378, 379, 380, 383, 385
Boone, W. J. - 123, 124, 125, 281, 282, 283
Boonsboro Gap - 40
Bordenave, John - 44
Boston newspaper -332
Boswell, J. A. -32, 33, 71
Boswell, James Phillips - 9, 44, 267, 399
Boswell, L. B. - 65
Boswell, L. M. - 32, 56, 71, 81, 93, 132
Boswell, Mrs. - 98
Bottom Falls, Virginia - 80
Boulware, J. C. -162
Boundary Street (Camden) - 343
Bowen -323, 324
Bowen, Anderson H. - 410
Bowen, C. P. - 44, 164

Bowen, Amelia - 370
Bowen, Frederick - 27, 42, 74, 91, 92
Bowen, P. - 44
Bowen, Sarah - 392
Bowen, William - 10, 13, 39
Bowers, Amelia - 376, 377, 379, 371, 382, 384, 385
Bowers, G. R. - 89
Bowers, J. M. - 160
Bowers, J. T. - 65
Bowers, N. - 161
Bowers, N. H. - 159, 160
Boyd, Captain C. W. - 207
Boyd, Colonel -324
Boykin, S,C,- 3, 130, 369, 3B84, 393
Boykin / Boykin Family - 12, 130, 189
Boykin Millpond Tragedy -376
Boykin Plantation- 136
Boykin Rangers -18, 319, 365, 366
Boykin, Alexander H. - 57, 60, 91, 95, 99, 365, 366
Boykin, Alexander Hamilton, (Jr.) -54, 163, 164, 227
Boykin, Alexaander Hamilton, II - 267
Boykin, Burrell E. -36, 365
Boykin, Captain Burrell -17
Boykin, Burrell Henry -163, 267
Boykin, Captain John - 134
Boykin ,Lt. Colonel A. H. - 365
Boykin, Colonel William M. -183
Boykin, Dr. Edward Mortimer - 38, 40, 46, 47, 48, 55, 77, 111, 152, 153, 180, 217, 226, 354, 365
Boykin, Dr. Tom - 262, 365
Boykin, E. Miller - 267, 354
Boykin, Estate of Burwell - 46
Boykin, Estate of Lemuel - 46
Boykin, H. H. - 19
Boykin, H. R. - 262
Boykin, Henry - 264
Boykin, J. - 97
Boykin, James - 98
Boykin, John -lll, 57, 79, 134, 163, 183, 244, 269
Boykin, Mary - 215
Boykin, Mary Ann - 262
Boykin, Miss C - 69, 70
Boykin, Miss C.M. -169, 172, 179, 180
Boykin, Miss Harriet - 223
Boykin, Miss Mary L.-78
Boykin, Mrs. H, A, -180
Boykin, Mrs. A.H. - 169, 171
Boykin, Mrs. B. - 7, 169
Boykin, Mrs. Edward - 98, 102
Boykin, Mrs. Hamilton - 101
Boykin, Henry Fleming - 267, 401
Boykin, Mrs. Hunter R. - 262

Boykin, Mrs. Lemuel -46
Boykin, Reverend Monroe - 262
Boykin, Sam -163
Boykin, Samuel - 267
Boykin, Samuel Francis - 267
Boykin, Samuel H. - 89
Bpykin, T. E. -10, 13
Boykin, T. S. - 47
Boykin, Thomas Lang - 87, 89, 251, 267, 361, 362
Boykin, Tom - 355
Boykin, W. Franklin - 261
Boykin, W.T. - 47
Boykin, William - 261
Boykin, William Henry -259
Boykin's Mill - 95, 132, 133, 134
Brace, Henry - 75, 91
Bracey, T. W. - 71
Bracey, Washington - 56
Bradby, Corporal -
Bradkins, John - 270
Bradley, C.S. - 85
Bradley, D. T. - 85
Bradley, James - 44
Bradley, John - 51, 52
Bradley, John S. - 95
Bradley, Major - 201, 202
Bradley, T.W. - 36
Bradley, Wiley - 43, 65, 392
Brady family - 342
Bragg - 185
Bragg, General B. - 218, 220, 222, 225, 233, 235, 236
Bragg's Bible, General - 233
Brailsford, A.M. -164, 165
Bramlet, R. H. - 86
Branch Bank (Camden) -96, 130
Brandy Station -320
Branham, B. D. -386
Branham, Elizabeth - 371, 372, 374, 377, 378, 379, 380, 382, 383, 385, 387
Branham, Hughey -163, 393, 394
Branham, M.E. - 374
Branham, M.W. - 397
Branham, Nannie - 398
Branham, S.A. - 163, 391, 397
Branham (Brannon) Warren - 65
Branham, William - 65, 163, 165, 397
Brannon (Brannum)(Brennon) John - 20, 34
Brannon (Brannum), Robert -20, 65
Brannon (Brannum), Samuel - 34
Brannon (Brannun), D - 64
Brannon, E. - 88
Brannon, W. Jr. - 41

Brannon, Warren - 65
Brannon, Wiley - 65
Brannon, William - 64
Brasendon, G. C. - 36
Brasington, E. J. - 398
Brasington, James L. - 267, 399
Brasington, Jim - 344, 345
Brasington, John S. - 165, 397
Brasington, Y. F. - 10, 13
Bratton, John - 147
Breckenridge, John C. - 5
Breckinridge, General - 220
Brevard, Alfred - 22, 39, 200, 267
Brewer's Farm - 116
Bridge, (Railroad Bridge of Orange and Alexandria) - 31
Bristow Station - 320
Broad Street (Camden) - 3, 179, 180, 200, 245, 248, 324, 332
Bronson, Mrs. -69
Brook, C - 124
Brook's Guards-
Brooks, Captain - 62, 357
Brooks, General C.R. - 367, 358
Brooks, E. S. - 146
Brooks, J. H. - 85
Brooks, J. S. - 85
Broome, J.W. - 393
Broome, W. J. - 396
Brother's Flower Garden - 287
Brown - 258, 324
Brown, M.N. (N.M.) - 47, 165
Brown, Alex - 162
Brown, Claude W. -252
Brown, Clement Clay - 258
Brown, Colonel - 134
Brown, E. T. - 85
Brown, George - 44
Brown, H.R. - 49
Brown, J. - 48, 87
Brown, J. E. - 359
Brown, J. G. - 217
Brown, J. S. - 10, 13
Brown, J.J. - 37, 39
Brown, J.R. - 399
Brown, James R. - 49
Brown, Joel H. - 65
Brown, John - 5, 95, 96
Brown, John Potts - 255
Brown, Lieutenant R. S. -
Brown, Lottie - 258
Brown, Miss Lizzie - 89
Brown, Miss M.A. - 101
Brown, Morgan - 257

Brown, Mrs. John - 48, 45
Brown, P. - 146
Brown, R. - 36
Brown, R.C. - 84, 162, 391, 397
Brown, R.S. - 206, 207
Brown, Reverend Manning - 21, 56
Brown, Richard - 44
Brown, Robert - 155
Brown, Robert Wells, Jr. - 257
Brown, Robert's (Mother) - 192
Brown, S.E. - 359
Brown, Samuel J. - 44
Brown, T.N. - 165
Brown, Thomas G. - 369
Brown, V. D. - 159
Brown, Vaughan Morgan -
Brown, W. - 52, 84
Brown, William - 41, 49, 162
Brown, William C. - 27, 163, 267
Brown, Y.A.S. - 398
Brown's Battalion - 133, 134, 365, 366
Brownfield, T. D. - 36
Brownsville - 200, 202
Broyles, O.R. - 400
Bruce, J. G. - 64
Bruce, James - 46, 154, 158
Brun, Joseph G. - 54
Bruns, George - 86, 146
Brunson, David - 44
Bryan, George - 148
Bryant, W. J. - 63
Buchanan, James - 5
Buckley, William - 124
Buff, George - 20
Buffalo Area - 28, 33, 42, 57, 74, 92, 386, 387, 388, 389
Buist, G. L. - 147
Bull Run - 16, 34, 67, 68, 313, 331
Bull Street - 346
Bull, Colonel - 134
Bull, J. - 87
Bullock, William M. - 10, 13, 42
"Bumpy" (Platter's Horse) - 349
Bunch, J. C. - 359
Buncombe County, N.C. - 143
Bunker Hill - 212
Bunn, Captain William S. - 123
Burch, Jesse - 38
Burch, John - 232
Burch, Tristan - 418
Burg, Mary -
Burke, J. - 359
Burkesville - 281

Burnet, Dr. Andrew W. - 151, 152, 267
Burns - 41
Burns, Cornelius Benton - 52, 64, 69, 81, 86, 267
Burns, Henry C. - 7, 8
Burns, Isaac W. - 267
Burns, James H. - 268
Burns, Mrs. - 185
Burnside - 80
Burrous, William - 277
Burton, E. P. - 350, 351
Bush, Jessie D. - 84
Bushnell, M. B. - 124
Bushrod Johnson's Division - 327
Busshart, S. - 146
Butler Guards - 10
Butler, Colonel Pierce - 262
Butler, Jacob W. - 315
Butler, Major General /Colonel M.C. - 107, 123, 126, 130,131, 180, 319, 320, 321
Butler, Tom - 321
Butler's Brigade - 90, 161
Butler's Cavalry - 111, 122
Buzby, Jane - 374

C

C.C. Haile Map of 1894 - 1, 105, 107, 108, 118
Cabinet, Waterooms, and Undertakers - 94
Cairo, Egypt -139
Camden Academy - 251
Camden Archives and Museum - iii, 1, 6, 8, 125, 132, 169, 187, 216, 226, 233, 234, 253, 316, 341, 346, 354, 357
Camden Baptist Church - 51, 67
Camden Bible Society -67
Camden Bridge Company - 91
Camden Cemetery (Quaker Cemetery) - 244
Camden Chronicle - 132, 136, 139, 141, 185 232, 260, 261, 290, 318, 319, 327, 341, 362, 397
Camden Confederate - 18, 21, 22, 26, 27, 28, 29, 30, 31, 32, 33, 35, 36, 38, 39, 40, 42, 43, 45, 46, 48, 49, 51, 54, 55, 56, 57, 58, 59, 60, 61, 62, 63, 65, 66, 67, 68, 69, 71, 72, 81, 82, 83, 84, 86, 87, 88, 89, 90, 98, 101, 132
Camden Cornet Band - 170
Camden Courthouse - 370, 371, 372, 373, 374, 375, 376
Camden Daily Journal - 89, 90, 91, 97, 99
Camden District - 22, 57
Camden Fire Engine Company - 400
Camden High School - 251
Camden Journal- 62, 71, 73, 76, 77, 78, 79, 80, 81, 82, 83, 84, 151, 152, 153, 178, 291, 334
Camden Ladies Aid Society - 48, 50, 55, 56, 58, 65, 66, 67, 78, 81
Camden Library - 185
Camden Light Infantry- 14, 222, 225
Camden Memorial Association - 172
Camden Minuteman Association - 5
Camden Post Office - 83
Camden Road – 106, 108, 110, 111, 112, 113, 122, 123, 348
Camden schools - 94, 184
Camden Tri-Weekly Journal- 102, 103, 104, 105, 137
Camden Volunteers - 9, 29, 32, 34, 45, 49, 50, 68, 361, 362
Camden Wayside Hospital - 332
Camden Weekly Journal - 9
Camden, South Carolina - iii, iv, 3, 4, 5, 6, 7, 8, 9. 10, 12, 13, 14, 15, 16, 17, 18, 19, 21, 22, 23, 27, 29, 30, 31, 32, 33, 34, 35, 36, 37, 38, 39, 40, 42, 43, 45, 47, 48, 49, 50, 51, 54, 55, 56, 57, 58, 59, 60, 61, 62, 63, 65, 66, 67, 68, 69, 71, 72, 73, 74, 75, 76, 77, 78, 103, 104, 105, 106, 108, 109, 110, 111, 112, 113, 120, 121, 122, 123, 125, 126, 127, 128, 129, 130, 132, 134, 135, 136, 137, 139, 143, 157, 158, 162, 170, 180, 183, 187, 197, 198, 199, 213, 215, 216, 217, 218, 219, 221, 222, 224, 225, 226, 248, 249, 251, 252, 253, 255, 258, 260, 261, 262, 263, 313, 314, 315, 316, 317, 319, 323, 324, 325, 332, 334, 341, 343, 344, 345, 346, 347, 348, 350, 351, 354, 357, 361, 365, 369, 370, 376, 377, 378, 379, 381, 382, 384, 385, 386, 387, 388, 389, 390, 391, 392, 393, 394, 395, 396, 397, 399, 400
Camden's Spy -
Camden Tri-Weekly Journal - 102, 103, 104, 105, 137
Camel, S. J. -
Cameron - 349
Camilla - 214
Camps:
    Camp Angus McLaurin - 158
    Camp Boykin - 133, 134
    Camp Camden - 28
    Camp Cantey - 46, 56, 159
    Camp Chesnut (Colleton County) - 158
    Camp Dick (Richard Kirkland) #704 - 224, 327
    Camp Douglass - 256
    Camp Gilbert - 43
    Camp Gist - 22, 27
    Camp Wade Hampton - 27
    Camp Hanging Rock #738 - 158
    Camp Kizey - 80
    Camp Welfare - 132
    Camp White, Sea Shore - 55
Campbell - 325
Campbell, A. - 10, 13
Campbell, Benjamin J. - 41, 47, 154
Campbell, Charlie - 68
Campbell, E. - 359
Campbell, James B. - 148, 154

Campbell, John - 41, 44
Campbell, L. - 146
Campbell, Mrs. M. T. - 94
Campbell, Susan H. - 398
Campbell, William M. - 43
Canada - 256
Canniel, E. - 257, 359
Cannington, G. - 86
Cantey - 43, 67, 114, 172, 175, 189, 267, 268, 269, 270, 272, 273, 274, 275, 276, 277, 278, 280, 285, 288
Cantey 19, 21, 48
Cantey boys - 173, 174
Cantey's Brigade- 262
Cantey Home – 173
Cantey-Myers Collection- 227
Cantey Obelisk - 189
Cantey Plantation - 173, 174
Cantey Rifles - 175
Cantey, E. B. - 18, 28, 30, 34, 35, 36, 37, 48, 50, 126, 127, 132, 137, 138, 151
Cantey, Edward Brevard - 1999
Cantey, Emery A.- 174
Cantey, Fannie - 174, 175
Cantey, Henry – 200
Cantey, J.M. – 355, 356
Cantey, J. N. - 259
Cantey, James - 3, 47, 63, 172, 173, 174, 175, 176, 194, 195, 199
Cantey, James' mother - 173, 175, 189, 195
Cantey, John - 36, 41, 62, 75, 172, 173, 195, 199
Cantey, John Manning - 41, 59, 199
Cantey, Mary - 173
Cantey, Miss - 56, 138
Cantey, Mrs. - 173, 174
Cantey, Mrs. John - 79
Cantey, Richard M. - 51, 199
Cantey, Sam - 173
Cantey, Sergeant (Lieutanant) - 259, 260
Cantey, T. B. - 9
Cantey, Thomas Richardson - 154, 267
Cantey, Willis- iv
Cantey, Winter - 226, 227, 228, 229, 230, 231, 261
Cantey, Zack - iii, 244, 267
Cantey's Pony "Planet" – 228
Cantey Post Office- 370, 372, 373, 375, 376
Cantey's Regiment - 228, 229
Capell, E. M. - 381, 382, 384, 385, 391
Capell, Eliza – 374
Capell, H. - 62
Capell, Hartwell - 63
Capell, J. B. – 91
Capell, J. P. – 20

Capell, John A. - 44
Capell, Sidney B. – 20, 21
Capell, W. H. - 41, 52, 267, 369, 370, 373, 375, 377, 378
Capell, William - 20, 373
Caper, Mrs. - 69, 249
Capers, General E. - 148
Capers, John S. - 136, 267
Capers, Mrs. (Jr.) - 249
Capers, Reverend William, D.D. - 181
Capers, Sidney W. – 267
Captain Alfred Doby – 84, 313
Captain A. H. Boykin's Company, Camden, S.C. - 364
Captain A. Moseley's Company - 244
Captain B. C. Manley's Battery – 206
Captain B. S. Lucas – 63, 84, 88, 293, 365
Captain Boykin's Company - 365
Captain Boykin's Troops - 14
Captain Cantey's Company - 18, 22, 38, 48, 67
Captain Cantey's Mounted Rangers -10
Captain Carlton's Battery- 202
Captain C.C. Hailes' Company-12, 15,16, 18, 64, 162, 199, 251, 259, 260, 327. 362
Captain C. A. Earnest - 122
Captain C. B. Burns – 81, 86
Captain Charles R. Holmes – 145, 146, 208, 212
Captain Colby's Company - 262
Captain Colclough's Company – 127, 129, 134, 325
Captain Conley's Company – 67
Captain Conner – 133, 134
Captain C. W. Boyd- 207
Captain C. W. Ferguson - 136
Captain D. Dixon's Company - 87
Captain DeSausure's Company- 362
Captain Dove Segars – 63, 84, 86, 88, 90, 183, 339
Captain Edward M. Boykins' Company A, Mounted Squadron of Rifles- 66, 77, 243, 364
Captain Calton – 202
Captain Clyburn - 337
Captain Cuthbert – 201, 205
Captain E. W. Dawson - 149
Captain G. B. Lamar- 206
Captain George Elliot – 110
Captain Hance- 204
Captain H. N. Ogden- 214
Captain Holmes – 202, 204
Captain Isaac Hayne – 217
Captain J. D. Kennedy – 8, 9, 14, 16, 18, 84, 133, 222, 224, 225, 259, 361, 362
Captain J. G. Brown- 21783
Captain J. H. Tucker – 83
Captain J. R. Goodale- 179
Captain James W. Davis - 164

Captain James E. Doby – 65, 69, 183, 323
Captain James Doby's Company – 87, 364
Captain James I. Villepigue- 200, 217
Captain James L. Haile- 163
Captain J. C. Rowlings- 164
Captain J. E. Truesdale - 81
Captain J. H. Brooks- 85
Captain J. L. Jones' Company- 63, 86, 88, 90, 99, 363, 365
Captain John Boykin - 134
Captain John Chesnut's Cava;ry – 67, 132
Captain John H. Devereaux – 129, 324, 325
Captain John L, King - 110
Captain John Thompson – 82, 366
Captain John Webb – 87
Captain John W. Headington - 110
Captain Joseph P. Cunningham – 63, 65
Captain Kennedy's Company – 8, 15, 213
Captain L. C. Hough- 161
Captain Levy's Corp – 16
Captain Lipscomb's Company – 365
Captain L. L. Clyburn - 164
Captain Lucas' Company - 68
Captain L. W. R. Blair Company- 157, 158, 363
Captain McCray's Company -
Captain McManus- 200
Captain Owen - 83
Captain Peck's Academy - 251
Captain Perryman's Company – 10
Captain P. P. Gaillard – 84
Captain Read - 203
Captain R. H. Hill- 217
Captain Richardson's Company – 10
Captain S. J. Benton - 159
Captain S.J. Deason- 160
Captain S. R. Johnson- 207
Captain Steen – 86
Captain Team - 153
Captain T. H. Clarke- 153
Captain Thomas Boykin's Company - 10, 68
Captain Thomas E. Taylor - 141
Captain Thompson Battalion – 238
Captain W. C. Vance – 87
Captain W. Courtney - 129
Captain W. D. DePass -129
Captain W. L. DePass Company - 78, 151
Captain White- 124
Captain Wilde - 124
Captain William Clyburn – 63, 90, 99, 104, 200, 365
Captain William Elliot - 149
Captain William C. Ross - 124
Captain William Duncan – 110, 120, 129
Captain William I. Henry – 110

Captain W. K. Bachman - 147
Captain S. Bunn - 123
Captain William Shannon's Company, The Kirkwood, S.C. Cavalry- 111. 136, 181, 364
Captain W.Z. Leitner – 63, 99, 151
Captain William Wallace - 63
Carlisle Barracks - 233
Carlisle Cavalry School - 232
Carlisle, Reverend W. - 188
Carlisle, Reverend M.L. - 182
Carlowville, Alabama - 7
Carlton - 202
Carns, James C. - 124
Carnwell, E. – 359
Carolinas – 344
"Carolina Housewife" - 289
Carpetbagger - 224, 294, 343
Carr, I.P. - 234
Carraway, P. T. - 374, 376, 377, 378, 379, 381, 382, 384
Carrison, Mrs. H. G. - 184
Carson - 13
Cash, Colonel E. B. C. - 313, 315
Cash's Company - 18
Cassatt - 341
Cassels, T. M. - 41
Cassidy, Hugh - 389
Castle Pinckney - 174
Caston, John Nelson - 154, 158
Caston, John Wilson -
Catawba River - 105, 106, 114, 115, 116, 117, 119, 124, 125, 126, 263
Catawba Water Valley - 333
Cater, W. H. - 62
Catlett's Station - 319, 320
Cato, James - 154
Cato, James, Sr. - 396
Cato (Catoe), Mary E. - 392, 395, 396
Cato, Samuel - 32, 34
Cato, William - 28, 42, 64, 74, 92, 154
Cato, William Thomas - 154
Catterson, Colonel Robert F. - 110
Caudebec, France - 218
Cauthan, J. T. - 49
Cauthan, L. M. - 49
Cauthan, Susan - 49
Cauthan, Thomas- 49
Cauthan, W. Columbus - 49, 408
Cauthen, Martin - 161
Cauthen, Mrs. Dr. - 49
Cauthen, S. H. - 373
Cauthen, Sarah A. - 374, 376, 377, 378, 379, 380
Cauthen, Thomas J. - 5, 54, 57, 61, 64, 62, 96, 154, 160, 161

Cauthern (Cauthen), James T. -
Cavins, Lt. Colonel Aden G. - 110
Cayce, Lt. Colonel S. W. - 219
Cedar Creek, Virginia - 322
Central Depot - 14
Central Fairgrounds - 14
Centreville, Virginia - 28
Challes, R. K. - 80
Chalmers, General - 219
Chamber of Commerce - 185
Chambersburg - 209
Chance, B. - 270
Chancellersville, Virginia - 76, 198, 205, 207
Chancellorsville Campaign - 205
Chaney, J. S. - 87
Charleston Courier - 22, 149, 226
Charleston District Association - 147
Charleston Hotel - 10, 11, 285, 286
Charleston Mercury - 18, 84, 142
Charleston Railroad - 120
Charleston Rifleman Society - 147
Charleston Wayside Hospital - 68
Charleston, S.C. - 6, 8, 10, 11, 14, 15, 16, 22, 23, 29, 41, 58, 66, 67, 77, 81, 90, 97, 99, 120, 129, 132, 148, 151, 174, 175, 197, 213, 216, 217, 245, 251, 263, 274, 283, 285, 286, 296, 301, 319, 327, 332, 343, 348, 362, 368
Charlotte, North Carolina - 106, 130, 344
Charlotte Observer - 264
Charlotte Railroad - 114
Charlottesville, Va. - 17
Chattanooga - 76, 80, 131, 185, 195
Chatten, C. L. - 94
Chatten, Mrs. C.L. - 98, 102
Cheatham, Alford - 85
Cheraw - 105, 110, 111, 112, 113, 114, 119, 122, 126, 128, 247, 325, 332, 348
Cheraw Crossing - 106
Cheraw Road - 108, 112, 113, 114, 121, 122, 131, 208, 348, 349, 350
Chesnut Ferry - 208
Chesnut Plantation - 82, 102
Chesnut Street - 343
Chesnut, Ellen Whitaker - 50
Chesnut, James (Colonel) – IV, 7
Chesnut, James, Jr. - 6, 14, 15, 21, 96, 130, 139, 143, 154, 172, 182, 198, 215, 216, 216, 218, 259
Chesnut, James, Sr. - 215, 218
Chesnut, John - 48, 57, 67, 96, 132, 269, 366
Chesnut, Lawrence - 259
Chesnut, Margaret- 218
Chesnut, Mary Boykin Miller - 15, 136, 143
Chesnut, Miss - 55, 60, 61, 65, 66, 67, 69

Chesnut, Mrs. James - 29, 70, 101
Chesnut, Sally - 28, 29, 37, 81, 98, 102
Chesnut's Crossing - 133
Chester - 126, 249, 327
Chester Gap - 212
Chesterfield - 89, 116, 119, 371
Chesterfield County (District) - 115, 157, 393, 396, 397
Chesterfield Court House - 116, 117
Chesterfield road - 118
Chicago - 56
Chickamauga - 67, 75, 198, 214, 218, 222, 226, 333
Chief Commissary of Kershaw District - 81, 93
Chief Enrolling Officer of Kershaw District - 38, 56, 82
Childers, James - 400
Chimborazo Hospital - 260
China - 221, 223, 224
Chipley, William - 81
Chisolm - 98
Christmas, T. H.- 84
Christmas, William - 34, 47, 65, 99
Church Street (Camden)- 346
Churches (Camden and Kershaw County) - 4, 8, 27, 35, 51, 59, 60, 62, 67, 71, 72, 75, 79, 95, 111, 117, 121, 122, 131, 132, 169, 185, 198, 200, 217, 243, 244, 249, 251, 260, 261, 262, 348
Claiborne - 136
Clanton, Dan - 88
Clanton, Loverick - 154
Claremont, S.C. - 133
Clarendon Cavalry - 10
Clark(e), T. H. - 87, 151, 153, 267
Clark, Caleb - 40
Clark, Charles - 44
Clark, Dr. H.H. - 40
Clark, J. B.- 71
Clark, James - 241
Clark's Diary - 60
Clarke, B.B. - 182
Clarke, Mrs. T. H. - 181
Clarkson, J. H. – 146
Clay - 257
Clay, Mrs. – 255, 256, 257, 258
Clay, US Senator Clement Claiborne - 255
Cleveland School Fire - 184
Cleveland, President - 223
Cloud, D. M. - 32
Cloud's House - 124
Clumbers County, Texas - 89
Clune, Lt. Colonel William H. - 110
Clyburn - 8
Clyburn Plantation (Thomas L.) - 263
Clyburn, B. R. - 36

Clyburn, Eliza- 263
Clyburn, Frank - 259, 263
Clyburn, J. H.- 89
Clyburn, J. N. - 85
Clyburn, J. R. - 84
Clyburn, James - 47
Clyburn, Jessie - 394
Clyburn, L. L. (Lewis Lee) - 85, 90, 162, 164, 240, 406
Clyburn, Mary H. - 398
Clyburn, Mattie (Rice) - 263
Clyburn, R. R. - 146
Clyburn, S. F. - 57
Clyburn, S.C. - 85, 267
Clyburn, Sam - 259
Clyburn, Stephen - 27
Clyburn, T. J. – 259
Clyburn, Thomas L. - 263
Clyburn, Weary - 259
Clyburn, William - 22, 46, 55, 62, 63, 88, 90, 92, 99, 104, 147, 151, 200, 339, 365
Clyburn's house- 115
Clyburn's Store - 116, 117, 123
Coats (Coates), D.D. - 5
Coates, Emma - 398
Coates, Gabriel Hartwell- 163
Coates, J. W. - 36
Coates, M. H. - 372
Coates, Martha - 369
Coates, T. G. - 163
Cobb, General - 334, 354
Cobb's Brigade - 203
Cockade - 17, 251
Cockade Town - 9
Cogburn, R. M. - 85
Cohe, Maurice - 62
Cohn, William - 400
Coker, Major L.L. - 367
Coker, W. P. - 368
Cokesbury Conference School, Abbeville - 198
Colclough- 129, 134, 324, 326
Colclough, Colonel - 135
Cold Harbor- 198, 355
Cole -57, 131
Cole, E. D. - 87
Coffield, Peggy - 229
Collector of Tax in Kind - 93
Collen, John - 62
Colleton District - 158
Collier, F. J. -52, 399
Collins, C. - 50
Collins, Reuben - 267
Collins, W. N. (Diary) - 135

Colonel Cash's Regiment - 313
Colonel Cromwell's Estate - 227
Colonel Davis - 349
Colonel Gregg's Regiment - 10
Colonel Hampton's Legion- 314
Colonel John Chesnut's Company - introduction
Colonel Kershaw Command - 313
Colonel Kershaw's Brigade -7, 15
Colonel Preston's Regiment - 314
Colonel Spears - 356
Coltart, Colonel - 219
Columbia Fairgrounds - 21
Columbia Times, Columbus, Georgia - 229
Columbia, S.C. -77, 82, 99, 105, 108, 112, 129, 130, 131, 143, 183, 213, 249, 273, 314, 334, 343, 344, 347, 370
Columbus Black History Museum – 229
Columbus, Georgia -22
Commissary Store- 109, 112, 127, 130, 202, 282, 294, 348
Commissioner of Public Building - 91
Commissioners of Fish Sluices – 27
Commissioners of Free School – 27, 75
Commissioners of Roads- 75, 91
Commissioners of the Poor - 91
Commissioners to approve Public Securities – 75, 91
Committee on Application - 152
Committee on Charity -152
Committee on Employment - 152
Committee on Records -152
Companies:
    Company A -243, 328, 259, 360, 363, 364, 390, 393, 394, 395, 397
    Company B- 36, 62, 84, 86, 90, 124, 158, 270, 339, 359, 360, 393, 394, 395, 397
    Company C- 36, 37, 40, 84, 90, 158, 159, 227, 327, 359, 360, 390, 391, 392, 393, 395, 397
    Company C, Palmetto Regiment- 198, 227
    Company D – 19, 36, 41, 46, 51, 59, 62, 64, 69, 84, 86, 88, 90, 89, 124, 159, 238, 261, 270, 338, 359, 360, 363, 390, 392, 396
    Company D, 5th Battalion- 360, 365
    Company E – 37, 62, 63, 66, 81, 87, 359, 360, 365, 391, 392, 393, 395, 395, 396, 397
    Company F – 36, 46, 63, 75, 86, 87, 88, 90, 124, 153, 157, 158, 159, 161, 350, 352, 364, 392, 397
    Company G – 36, 37, 47, 63, 64, 81, 85, 87, 88, 89, 90, 124, 159, 160, 161, 260, 270, 397
    Company H -270, 328, 355, 356, 363, 364, 391, 392, 393, 395, 397, 401
    Company I- 36, 87, 270, 391, 394, 397
    Company K – 37, 81, 89, 90, 110, 124, 159, 354, 355, 356, 360, 364, 391, 393, 394, 396
Comptroller General- 367

Confederate Agent – 141, 256
Confederate Battle Flag - 281
Confederate Bonds -218
Confederate Commissary -239
Confederate Congress- 12, 14, 28, 217
Confederate Congress Delegate -218
Confederate Espionage operator - 257
Confederate Heritage –introduction
Confederate Memorial Coins - 18
Confederate Pensions - 367
Confederate Quartermaster Agent -93
Confederate Reunion Pictures - 401, 402, 403, 404, 405, 406
    Confederate Reunion, 1904, Camden - 187, 188, 189
    Confederate Reunion, 1914, Bethune - 191, 192, 193, 194, 195, 196
Confederate Secret Service -256
Confederate Soldier's Home, Columbia -184
Confederate State Depository, Camden -81
Confederate States Bible Society -68
Confederate States Engineer's Office - 77 "Confederate Confederate Veteran" Magazine -323, 324
Confederate Tax -30
Confederate War Tax – 60, 92
Confederate Widow's Home of Charleston - 148
Congress -174, 198, 216, 223, 370
Congress of Confederate States -12, 14, 18, 28, 216, 218
Connell, J. F. -165
Connell, S. J. - 397
Conner:
    Conner, Brigadier General James –134, 145, 146, 147, 148, 149, 344. 345
    Conner, Captain- 139
    Conner's Company- 134
    Conner, Colonel- 139
    Conner, Henry W. -70
    Conner, Mrs. 57
    Conner, Mrs. H. W., Jr. -57, 69
Confederate Veterans and Widows- 367, 368
Conwayboro (Conway) -48
Cook, Ann -381, 382, 383, 384, 385, 388
Cook, Benjamin – 28, 42, 74, 75, 92
Cook, C. L. -369
Cook, D. J. - 47
Cook, H. - 270
Cook, J.C. - 15
Cook, M.H. -371
Cook, T. L. – 371, 372
Cook, W. L. – 32, 34
Cook, William – 369, 370, 372, 375, 376, 377, 378, 380, 381, 383
Cool Springs -122, 345
    Cool Springs residence -348

Coonin, S. - 63
Cooper, James D. -46
Cooper, Julius J. -44
Cooper, W. J. – 85
"Cooter" - 292
Copeland - 113
Copeland, G.B P. - 89, 99
Copeland, Hester -394
Copeland, Thomas Ripley - 154
Corbett, Dr. John W. – 199
Corbett, H. – 20, 21
Corbett, H. F.- 20
Corbett, H.H. - 2, 20
Corbett, J. – 20
Corbett, James - 78
Corbett, J. C. -52, 64
Corbett, J. N. - 43
Corbett, W. S. - 391, 392
Corder, Caroline -370, 372, 373, 376, 378, 380, 381, 383, 385, 387, 392, 393
Corder, James - 85
Corinth - 232, 333
Cornwallis- iv, 283, 351
Cornwallis Headquarters - 21, 22, 27, 351
Cornwallis House - 127, 130, 245, 283, 324, 325
Corse, General - 120, 122, 280, 348
Corse's Division - 124
Costier, Major - 278, 279
Costin, Major E. L. - 205
Cotton, J. - 39
Cotton, Jacob - 37
Cotton, John - 85
Cottrall, J. T. -163, 395
Cougar, Mrs. A. F. - 54
Counts, John A. - 44
Courtney, Little Miss Bessie-98
Courtney, Mrs. -97
Courtney, W. -129
Covington, Benjamin - iii
Coward, J. H. - 99
Coward, N.M. - 359
Cox, Colonel John and Ester - 215
Cox, Lt. James -109
Cox, Mary - 215, 218
Coys - 357
Craft, Mary -385
Crammond - 67, 81
Cranton, J. Q. - 51
Crawford, D. H. -146
Crawford, J. A. - 146
Creighton, F. E. - 20, 52
Creighton, H. L. - 52

Crenshaw - 49
Crescent City - 80
Crim, Samuel - 359
Criminger, R.A. - 159
*Croc*kett, John N. – 9
Croft, Mary - 387
Croft, Wesly -386, 388, 392
Cromer, Daniel -20
Crosby, George -52, 64, 267, 400
Crosby, Mrs.- 94
Cross, B. H.- 44
Crossland, John D. -385, 387, 399
Croston (Croxton), J. O. -63
Crowell Cemetery -229
Crowell, Monroe- 33
Crump, T. M. -10, 13
Culpepper County, Virginia - 212, 319
Culpepper Court House -208
Culpepper, John Henry- 154
Cumberland Gap, Tn. - 51
Cunningham, Cornelia - 54
Cunningham, Harriet - 264
Cunningham, J. J. - 51
Cunningham, John S.-163, 311, 391, 394
Cunningham, Jack - 264
Cunningham, Joe- 49
Cunningham, Joseph - 239
Cunningham, Joseph P. -35, 36, 58, 62, 63, 65
Cunningham, Lizzie- 48
Cunningham, Maggie - 48
Cunningham, Mary – 48
Cunningham, Mary Ellen - 423
Cunningham, Miss -343
Cunningham, Miss Elizabeth - 222, 225
Cunningham, Miss M. - 48
Cunningham, Miss S -48
Cunningham, Mollie McWain - 264
Cunningham, Mrs. R. B. -48
Cunningham, N.A. - 165
Cunningham, Robert B. - 28, 42, 48, 57, 64, 74, 92, 311
Cunningham, Robert J. - 42
Cunningham, Sallie - 54
Cunningham, W. A. - 398
Cunningham, W. C. - 33, 64
Cunningham, William - 48
Cunningham, Wyatt - 259, 263. 267
Cureton, Allen - 264
Cureton, C.B. -163
Cureton, E. J. -179, 180
Cureton, Everard Belton - 89, 267
Cureton, George - 259, 269
Cureton, James B. - 38, 70, 75, 87, 91, 240, 267, 269, 311

Cureton, James B., Jr. - 86
Cureton, Lucy - 264
Cureton, M.C. - 398
Cureton, Mrs. - 78
Cureton, Mrs. E. - 179
Cureton, Nannie - 264
Cureton's Mill - 19, 27, 42, 57, 74, 92
Curley, Colonel Thomas - 110
Cusick, Patrick - 13
Custer and Merit - 278
Custer, George A. - 277, 280, 281, 297
Custer's Brigade - 278
Custer's Cavalry - 279
Custer's Headquarters - 279
Cutchbert, G. B. - 36
Cuthbert, G. B. - 201, 205, 207

D

Dabney, Miss - 50
Dallas, Texas - 162, 164
Daniels - 62
Dannelly, Dr. F. Olin (Surgeon) - 58, 66
Dantzler, D. B. -359
Danville Railroad - 80
Danville, Virginia -133, 344
Danzler, Reverend William -180
Darlington -122, 123
Darlington County -106, 147, 367
Darlington Road- 106, 111
Dash, L. W. - 359
Davis, A.C. - 146
Davis, Alfred - 65
Davis, Bishop - 182
Davis, C. W. - 44
Davis, Colonel - 349
Davis, D - 63,
Davis, D. J. -159, 160
Davis, Dice- 160
Davis, E. W. - 47
Davis, Harbin Thomas - 154
Davis, J. A. - 87
Davis, J. D. - 244
Davis, J. J. - 19, 20, 52
Davis, J. R. - 47
Davis, J. W. - 64
Davis, James - 70
Davis, James N./Moore (Captain) -
Davis, Jefferson - 64, 130, 138, 140, 141, 142, 143, 183, 184, 185, 215, 216, 217, 255, 256, 257, 295, 331
Davis, John T. - 10, 13, 152
Davis, Junius - 244, 267

Davis, Miss A. E. - 181, 182, 247
Davis, Miss Lila – 181
Davies, Mrs. – 170, 179, 180, 181
Davis, Mrs. Ester Serena Reynolds - 182
Davis, Mrs. James - 98, 102, 17
Davis, Mrs. Samuel – 181
Davis, Mrs. T. F., Sr.- 98, 102
Davis, Mrs. T. F., Jr. – 98, 102
Davis, Reverend Frederick Bruce - 267
Davis, Reverend S.S. - 75
Davis, Reverend Thomas F, Jr. - 34, 70, 95, 244, 245, 246, 267, 400
Davis, Reverend Thomas F., Sr. - 244, 246, 248, 249
Davis, T. Bruce -400
Davis, T. H. - 163
Davis, Zimmerman (Colonel) - 130, 147, 149
Dawkins, H. - 84
Dawkins, Martha E. - 391
Dawkins, Rhodie - 369, 370, 372, 373, 375, 376, 377, 378, 380, 381, 393, 385, 387
Dawkins, Sallie - 372, 373, 375, 377, 377, 378, 380, 383, 385, 387, 395
Dawson, Edgar G, Esq. - 228
Dawson, F. W. (Captain)- 149
Dawson, Miss - 94
Dawson, Thomas - 65
Deach, Mr. -101
Dean, E. N. - 394
Dean, George - 62, 63
Deas - 204
Deas, Allen - 47, 151, 162, 164, 267
Deas, Dr. Lynch Horry - 27, 71, 75, 93, 96
Deas, E. - 65
Deas, E. N.- 397
Deas, James Sutherland (Colonel) - 218
Deas, Lewis - 391, 397
Deas, Lynch Horry, Jr. - 47, 87, 89, 267, 355
Deas, Meta - 70
Deas, Mrs. - 98, 102
Deas, Zachariah Cantey - 218, 219, 221
Deasch - 98
Deason, S. J. - 160
DeBruhl, Ben - 47
DeBruhl, G. A. - 47
DeBruhl, George- 90
Deep Bottom - 355
DeHay, Zachariah J. - 77
Dehone, Mrs. - 57, 69, 302
DeKalb Church Cemetery - 185
DeKalb Hotel - 30, 31
DeKalb House - 9, 35, 66, 95
DeKalb Post Office-386

DeKalb Rifle Guards - 251, 324, 325, 361, 362
DeKalb Street – 12, 29, 127, 179, 180, 245, 249, 324, 325
DeKalb Township- 260, 384, 386, 387, 388, 389, 390, 395, 397
DeKay, Mary J. - 388, 392, 393, 395
Delaware - 89
DeLeon, Edwin - 139, 140, 141
DeLoache, J.R. - 162, 164, 165, 398
DeLoache, James Elliot – 267
DeLoache, Jimmy - 412
DeLoache, Mrs. - 214
DeLoache, Mrs. W.B. - 184
DeLoache, W. E. - 44
Denoon, Miss Maggie - 94
Dentists - 93
Denton, E. J.- 369
Denton, J. W.- 160
Denton, Thomas B - 162, 164, 396
Denton, W. C. - 65, 88
Department Headquarters of North Carolina- 328
DePass - 31
Depass Battery - 159
DePass Company - 60
DePass, J. E. - 44
DePass, J. S. - 22, 43, 70
DePass, J. W. - 44
DePass, Jacob - 267
DePass, S.C. - 71
DePass, W. D. (Captain) - 129
DePass, William Lambert - 8, 9, 15, 18, 22, 27, 28, 31, 32, 35, 37, 43, 45, 48, 61, 70, 78, 146, 147, 151, 152, 240, 243, 267, 314, 315, 366
Depot, Black Stocks - 105
Depot Railroad - 8, 35, 106, 109, 112, 120, 127, 133, 136, 245, 251, 283, 307, 348
Depot, Richmond – 12, 13, 14
Depot, Soldier's Family - 78
Derby, Earl - 173
Derham (Comptroller General) - 367
DeSaussure - 36
DeSaussure Light Artillery - 42, 43, 45, 365, 366
DeSaussure, Blanding - 48
DeSaussure, Colonel - 18
DeSaussure, D.S.- 74
DeSaussure, Dr. Daniel Louis - 32, 33, 49, 93, 164, 267, 399
DeSaussure, Dr. Lewis- 93, 98
DeSaussure, Eliza H. - 82
DeSaussure, Henry M. - 39, 47
DeSaussure, Henry W. - 244, 267
DeSaussure, John - 136
DeSaussure, John McPherson - 38, 42, 47, 57, 69, 70, 78, 82, 86, 91, 92, 180, 198, 226, 246, 267

DeSaussure, L. - 70
DeSaussure, Louis McPherson - 267
DeSaussure, Lt.Col. Wilmont G.- 99
DeSaussure, Miss Fannie- 66, 67
DeSaussure, Mrs. D. L.- 70
DeSaussure, Mrs. E.O./ E.M. -81
DeSaussure, Mrs. H. - 42, 98, 102
DeSaussure, Mrs. J. - 78
DeSaussure, Mrs. L. - 69
DeSaussure, William D. 59, 61, 64
Devereaux, John H. (Captain) - 81, 93, 129
Devine, F. J. - 10, 13
Devine, Francis "Frank" - 15, 269
Dibrell, Colonel G. G. - 125
Dickerson, G. - 146
Dickerson, James Polk – 227, 252, 260, 262
Dickerson, John P.- 198
Dickerson's Monument - 184
Dickson, Jessie - 154
Dinah (The Cantey Nurse) - 228, 229
Dingle's Mill - 132
Dinkin, Martha - 385
Diocese - 245, 246, 399
Dioceses Convention - 300
District Directory - 91
Dix, U.S. Major John A. - 256
Dixon, Barnes - 226
Dixon, Benjamin - 384
Dixon, G. L. - 99, 163
Dixon, Mrs. William - 48
Dixon, William - 27, 28, 31, 51, 57, 75, 91, 365
Daasch, Willliam - 95
Doby- 302, 323
Doby, Alfred English - 17, 28, 38, 49, 54, 65, 70, 83, 84, 259, 313, 323, 324
Doby, Edward - 259
Doby, Elise - 180
Doby, J. English - 75, 91
Doby, J. W., Jr. - 47
Doby, James - iii, 8, 48, 57, 65, 183, 204, 208, 212, 259, 264, 365
Doby, James A. - 8
Doby, James E.- 66. 70
Doby, James L. - 87
Doby, John - 151
Doby, Joseph William - 32, 33, 54, 56, 73, 77
Doby, Mrs. Alfred English - 69, 98, 169, 172, 179, 181, 182
Doby, Mrs. E. K.(Elizabeth Kennedy) - 101, 283, 313, 370, 371, 372, 374, 377, 378, 379, 380, 382, 383, 385, 393
Doby, Sarah - 222
Doby, Sarah Ann - 316
Douglass - 90

Douglass, Ely - 85
Douglass, Frederick -265
Douglass, George - 54, 94
Douglass, J. E. -163, 396, 397
Douglass, James K. - 198
Douglass, Lucretia - 198, 285
Douglass, Mrs. G.S.- 98, 102
Douglass, R. - 163
Douglass, R. H. - 47
Douglass, S. Wade - 339
Douglass, S.A. - 87
Douglass, Stephen - 5
Douglass' Store (George) - 130
Dowie, R. J. -65
Downs, James L. - 31, 33
Drakeford - 342
Drakeford, J.J. - 9, 35, 36, 81
Drakeford, John - 240
Drakeford, Joseph - 259
Drakeford, R. D. - 42
Drakeford, Richard C.- 28, 54, 64, 127, 240
Drakeford, Washington - 12, 259
Drakeford, William - 12, 259
Dr. R – 294
Drucker, M.- 71, 83
Drucker's corner - 130
Druggists - 94
Drummond, James - 359
Drury's Bluff (also known as Drewry's Bluff) - 84, 85, 157, 243, 355
Dubose, D. - 87
Dubose, D. P. - 47
Dubose, David - 87, 278, 279, 355, 356
Dubose, Edward Cassels - 268
Dubose, General-278, 279
Dubose, Henry Kershaw - 162, 164, 268
Dubose, L. S. - 398
Dubose, Wiles P. - 162, 268
Dufee (not Defee), James D. - 387, 385
Dulin, James R. - 319, 320, 322
Dulin, Mrs. Rice - 30
Duncan, Captain William - 110, 120, 121, 129
Duncan, W.G. - 47
Dunlap - 260
Dunlap, E. B. - 268
Dunlap, Fattle - 70
Dunlap, James D. - 21, 22, 27, 29, 32, 35, 56, 57, 61, 70, 81, 91, 92, 93, 94, 132, 259, 260, 283
Dunlap, Joseph Doby - 9, 35, 36, 92, 93, 152, 268, 316
Dunlap, Miss - 67
Dunlap, Mrs. James - 98, 101, 102
Dunlap, Ned Edward - 259, 260

Dunlap, Thomas Samuel - 268
Dunlap, Zimmie Barfield - 398
Dunlap's Farm - 340
Dunn Residence - 251
Dunn, A. M. - 44, 163
Dunn, Mrs. - 184, 185
Dunn, W. J. - 63
Dunning, R. - 62
Durant, S. P. - 44
Duren, J. F. - 146
Duren, Thomas Powell - 154
Durham, North Carolina - 344
Dusenbury, J. - 87
Dust, George - 85
Dutch Creek - 347
Dutchman's Creek - 106, 108, 110, 112, 121, 351
Dutton, Mrs. Martha - 132
Dutton, William C. - 9, 41, 56
Dutton, William T. - 269
Dwight, W. M. -36, 146, 202, 203, 208, 212,
Dye Plantation (J.R. Dye) - 46, 123
Dye, J. Ross - 46, 57, 92, 96
Dykes, E. - 359
Dykes, G. A. - 359

E

Early, General - 204
Earnestm C. A. (Captain) - 122
Easler, Matilda - 398
Easley - 368
East Bay Street, Charleston, S.C. - 11
East Tennessee - 80, 81
Ebenezer Cemetery, Monroe, N.C. - 264
Eckel, Professor Henry E. - 22, 27
Eden Prairie, Minnesota Territory - 255
Edgeworth's Mills - 115
Edwards, Elizabeth - 370
Edwards, S. B. - 87
Egypt - 130, 139, 140
Eighteen (18) SC Militia -
Eighth (8th) Illinois Cavalry - 279
Eighth Confederate Army - 125
Eighth Regiment - 201, 202, 203, 204, 207, 210, 211
Eighth South Carolina Volunteers - 315
Eighty-Eight (88) Indiana Regiments - 124
Eighty-First (81) Ohio Infantry - 347, 350
Eleventh Battalion - 339
Eleventh (11) North Carolina Regiment - 31
Elgin, Illinois - 249
Eliza - 263, 285, 290, 299
Ella, Aunt - 292

Elzay - 314
Elk Ridge - 201
Elkin, David E. - 359
Elkins, Fletcher - 85
Ella - 248, 249, 292
Ellenburg, M. - 85
Ellerbe's Flour and Grist Mill - 66
Elliot - 44
Elliot, General - 134
Elliot, George (Captain) - 110
Elliot, J. A. - 31, 34
Elliot, Lt. - 49
Elliot, R. E. - 42
Elliot, Reverend S. E. - 244
Elliot, Thomas - 47
Elliot, William - 146, 149, 148, 154
Elliot's Brigade - 327
Ellis' Mills - 320
Ellsworth-Zouaves - 313, 315
Elmira, New Jersey - 355
Elzay, General Arnold - 315
Emmitsburg Road - 209
Emory Mills - 205
Enfield Rifles- 218, 363, 364
England - 139, 141, 258
Engleton, Dubose – 146
English, J. - 91
English, William - 65
English, Miss Elizabeth Doby - 313
English, Thomas - 65
Episcopal Church - 35, 59, 62, 72, 95, 198, 200, 217, 244
Ervin, John - 41, 52, 163, 370
Ervin, Samuel - 52
Estridge, Chapman - 98
Europe - 301
Evans, B. E. - 44
Evans, Elizabeth - 394
Evans, George - 10, 13
Evans, M. - 47
Evans, Professor - 179
Evans, Thomas Peter - 415
Evans, W. K. - 146
Ewell, General Arnold - 198, 209, 314, 315
Ewell's Division- 228
Ewell, Richard S. - 315
Examining Board Camden - 82, 374, 376, 382
Exchange Bank, Columbia - 73

F

Faile, Matilda -398
Faile, Nathan - 165

Fair Garden - 215
Fair Oaks Plantation - 237
Fair, R. A. - 146
Fairfax Courthouse, Virginia - 15, 16, 18
Fairfax, Virginia -18. 34
Fairfield County, S.C. - 132, 327, 393, 395, 397,
Fairfield Road - 209
Falconberry (Faukenberry), W. J. - 17
Falkenberry, A. J. - 64
Falkenberry, J.A. - 89
Falkenberry, John - 63
Falkenberry, Margaret - 387
Falkenberry, W. J. - 17
Falling Waters - 212
Falls Church, Virginia -18
Farin, A. W. - 15
Farmer's Bank - 18
Farrar, F. H. (Major) - 220
Fauquier County, Virginia - 208, 319, 333
Fayetteville, North Carolina - 106, 111, 09
Fenilly's Bridge - 119
Ferguson, C.W. (Captain) - 136
Ferley's Bridge - 117
Ferrel, J.R. - 10, 13
Ferrell, M.S. - 396
Ferrura, F.C. - 87
Fickling, H. S. - 359
Fields, R. H. - 63
Fifteen Illinois Infantry - 248
Fifteen Illinois Mounted Infantry -131
Fifteen SC Infantry - 360, 362
Fifteenth (15) Corps -
Fifteenth (15) Illinois Cavalry - 110, 129
Fifteenth (15) Illinois Fourth Ohio Independent - 129
Fifteenth Alabama Infantry - 227
Fifteenth Georgia Regiment - 211
Fifteenth New York - 106
Fifteenth Regiment - 159
Fifteenth SC Militia - 359, 360
Fifteenth SC Regiment -
Fifth Brigade - 99, 365
Fifth Georgia Reserves – 270
Fifth SC Regimental Infantry - 363
Fifth SC Battalion - 134, 365
Fifth SC Battalion Reserves (Browns' Battalion) - 364, 365
Fifty-four (54) Massachusetts Infantry - 135, 136
Fifty-four (54) Ohio Infantry - 123
Fifty-nine (59) Indiana Regiment- 350
Fifty-six (56) New York - 132
First Alabama - 228
First Brigade - 106, 108, 110, 111, 112, 114, 115, 116, 117, 119, 122, 124, 219, 221, 228, 349

First Division - 110, 113, 114, 115, 116, 121, 122, 200, 225, 347
First Georgia - 270
First Louisiana Infantry - 219, 220
First Michigan - 109
First Missouri - 109
First S.C. Artillery - 270
First SC Battalion - 270, 363
First SC Battalion of Re-enlisted Volunteers - 363
First SC Hospital, Rikersville - 332
First SC Militia - 360
First SC Regiment - 68, 89, 90, 158, 244, 390, 393, 395, 397
First SC Regiment, Company D- 261
First SC Regular Infantry - 160
Fisher, Charles A. - 19, 41, 48, 269
Fitzpatrick, Thomas - 99
Flag of Kirkwood Rangers - iii, 14, 183, 184
Flat Creek - 115
Flat Rock Aid Society - 40, 67
Flat Rock Area - iii, iv, 27, 28, 40, 42, 57, 61, 74, 92, 97, 107, 111, 120, 121, 123, 124, 126, 127, 143, 156, 369, 370, 371, 372, 374, 375, 386, 387, 388, 389, 391
Flat Rock Church - 121, 348
Flat Rock Guards - 17, 19, 28, 35, 40, 42, 51, 199, 251, 362
Flat Rock Ladies Society - 89
Flat Rock Minutemen- 5
Flat Rock Post Office - 108, 112, 369, 370, 371, 372, 374, 375
Flemming, Adjutant - 327
Flemming, Colonel - 327
Fletcher, D. G. - 20, 41, 52
Fletcher, James - 27, 42, 74, 92
Fletcher, John S. - 27, 33
Fletcher, Susan A. - 392
Fletcher, W. J. - 27. 42, 162, 389, 391
Flint Hill - 317, 318
Florence Memorial Company (now Brown's Memorial) -252
Florence Railroad - 120
Florence, S.C. - 120, 126, 132, 244, 325
Florida - 9, 14, 29, 40, 41, 50, 57, 235, 235
Florida War - iv
Flowers, James T. - 44
Floyd, Harriet P. - 398
Floyd, J. W. - 163
Floyd, Lieutenant - 124
Floyd, Osborn - 49, 419
Fogle, William J. - 359
Folsom, John James - 88, 154
Folsom, S. J. - 157
Folsom, Stephen Thomas - 46, 154, 158
Folsom, Tobias - 51
Folsom, William Wesley - 89
Ford, E. J. - 20, 52

Ford. J. W. - 33
Fort Anderson - 104
Fort Crittenden, Utah Territory - 235
Fort Delaware - 89
Fort Fisher - 104, 142
Fort Hudson - 233
Fort Johnson - 157
Fort Lafayette - 256
Fort Lookout, Dakota - 232
Fort Macrae - 233, 235
Fort Mitchell - 230, 226, 227, 228, 261
Fort Monroe - 256, 257
Fort Moultrie- 174, 244
Fort Pillow - 233
Fort Smith, Arkansas - 143
Fort Sumter - 7, 8, 15, 34, 68, 174, 214, 216, 218, 251, 285, 286, 292, 295, 362
Fort Warren - 198
Fort, G. L. (Colonel) - 123
Fortieth (40) Alabama Volunteers - 159
Fortieth (40) Illinois - 110
Forty-eight (48) Indiana Regiment - 123
Forty-second (42) Indiana Regiment - 124
Forty-sixth (46) Illinois -228
Forty- Third (43) Alabama- 90
Fountain Committee - 185
Fountain Inn - 368
Fourteen (14) Corps - 106
Fourteenth (14) Wisconsin - 110
Fourteenth SC Militia - 359, 360
Fourth Arkansas - 228
Fourth (4) Ohio Cavalry - 110
Fourth (4) SC Cavalry - 159, 161, 264, 360, 365
Fourth Division - 108, 109, 112, 114, 121, 122
Fourth SC Regiment - 89, 90, 160
Fourth Kentucky - 220
Fourth Massachusetts - 135
Fourth Regiment- 66, 90
Fourth SC Militia - 359
Frail, G. W. -370, 373
Frails, W. M. - 89
France - 218, 299
Francis, J. H. - 10, 13, 15, 17
Franklin - 212, 219
Franklin, W. N. - 85
Fraser and Company - 141
Fraser's Battery (J.C.) - 212
Fredericksburg - iv, 51, 59, 76, 198, 205, 206, 213, 319, 331, 334, 357
Free Market of Charleston - 245
Freeman, Emma - 398
Freeman, Jacob - 41, 395, 397

Frieks, W. D. S. - 87
Froleich, N. – 34
Front Royal - 208, 212
Fry, Davis - 359
Fulgham, James - 20
Fuller, P.M. - 87
Funderburk, J.J. - 90
Funderburk, W. A. - 90
Funkstown - 212

G

Gadsen County, Florida - 41
Gaillard - 62
Gaillard, Francis-
Gaillard, Major Franklin - 35, 36, 49, 204, 205, 207, 211
Gaillard, P.C. (Colonel) - 149, 339
Gaines' Cross Roads - 208, 212
Gainey, Henrietta - 374, 376, 377, 378, 379, 380, 382, 383, 385, 387, 393
Gainsville, Florida - 14
Galloway, E. L. - 44
Gamble, George - 359
Gamewell, John Nelson - 6, 65, 71, 414
Gamewell, Mrs.- 97
Garden, Elizabeth - 12
Garden's Battery of Light Artillery - 68
Gardner, C. L. - 85
Gardner, Daniel Whitfield - 92, 154
Gardner, Eliza A. - 374, 376, 377, 378, 379, 381, 382, 384, 388, 394,
Gardner, G. W. - 159, 160, 161
Gardner, H. - 85
Gardner, Isaac - 159, 160, 165, 395, 396, 398, 418
Gardner, James - 90
Gardner, James L. - 41, 52
Gardner, James William - 397
Gardner, Jeff - 88
Gardner, Joel - 32, 34
Gardner, L. T. - 10, 13
Gardner, Lewis - 20, 41, 52, 161, 418
Gardner, Margaret J. 370, 371, 372, 374, 375, 377, 378, 380, 382, 383, 387, 391
Gardner, Miles L. - 154, 158
Gardner, R. T. - 41
Gardner, S. L. - 86, 371, 372, 373, 375, 377, 379, 380, 382, 383, 385, 387
Gardner, S.C. - 87
Gardner, Stephen L. - 153
Gardner, T.E. - 63
Gardner, Thomas David - 154
Gardner, Victoria - 398

Gardner, W. R. - 85. 159
Gardner, W. W. - 31, 33
Gardner, William Jefferson - 154
Gardner's Store - 350
Garner - 47
Garner, George G. - 235, 236
Gaskin, E. - 33
Gaskin, G. W. - 85
Gaskin, J. B. - 31, 33
Gaskin, John D. - 391
Gaskin, Martha - 377, 378
Gaskin's Mill (John Gaskins) - 78
Gaskins - 63
Gaskins, John W. - 63, 92, 96
Gaskins, R. - 62
Gaskins, Rebecca - 369, 371, 372, 374, 375, 379, 380, 382, 383, 385, 387, 394, 395
Gaskins, William - 85
Gatewood, Mrs. - 61
Gattis, A. L. - 34
Gattis, J. L. - 31
Gay, C. B. - 85
Gay, Isaac - 163, 391
Gay, L. B. - 44
Gayden, J. - 27
Gayle, Joseph M. - 34, 51, 56, 71, 78, 93, 94
Gayle, Joseph W. - 54
Gayle, Mrs. J. M. - 98, 102
Gee, R. T. - 44
Gee, William Nero - 154
Geisenheimer, William - 163, 269
General Assembly (S.C.) - 221, 361, 367
General Bank's Army - 232
General C. R. Brooks - 367
General Cobb - 198, 334
General Corse - 120, 122, 280, 348
General Edward E. Potter - 132, 133, 135, 295, 296, 308
General G. T. Beauregard - 16, 126, 216, 217, 220, 232, 233, 259, 262, 314, 315, 325, 328, 329, 355
General Gary - 356
General Grant - 281, 337, 344
General Hagen - 348
General Hagood - 223
General Hampton - 146
General Hardee - 126, 244
General Hospital - 17
General Hospital, Charleston, S.C. - 332
General Jackson - 203, 205, 207, 232, 333
General James Cantey Boulevard - 229
General James Cantey Brigade - 262
General Jenkins - 323
General Johnson - 229, 231, 232, 328

General Johnston's Army -222, 226
General Kantz - 356
General Lee - 324, 325, 333, 344
General Longstreet - 56, 212, 289, 323, 324
General Longstreet Book - 323
General Mahone - 205, 280, 328, 337, 338, 339
General Mahone's Division - 328
General McGowan - 147, 337
General Potter's Forces - 143, 245
General Potter's Troops - 135, 332
General Prentiss - 262
General Richard S. Ewell - 198, 314, 315
General Saunders - 338
General Schofield - 350
General Vance - 72, 353
General Wilson's Army - 262
General Wilson's Raiders - 228
George, D. J. - 47
George, Miss S. - 49
Georgetown Road - 113, 135
Georgetown, S.C. - 46, 66, 126, 237, 296
Georgia - 52, 79, 80, 109, 142, 185, 186, 203, 229, 233, 236, 256, 270, 278, 331, 333, 343, 350
Georgia Brigade - 203
Georgia Railroad - 99
Georgia Regiment - 211
Gerald, Edward J. - 399
Gerald, L. C. - 39
Gerald, R. L. - 10, 13, 75
Gerald, Ruben - 269
Gerald, W. C. & Company - 70, 71
Gerald, W. Clarkson - 33, 94, 268
Gerald, W. J., Jr. - 47
Gettysburg - 62, 63, 68, 71, 73, 75, 76, 198, 208, 209, 214, 321
Gettysburg Campaign - 208
Gholson, Judge T. S. -13
Gibson, H. R. - 10, 13
Gibson, J. C. - 237
Gibson, Nathan William - 155
Gilbert, A.A., Jr. - 37, 43
Gilbert, J. R. - 49
Gilbran, Martin - 46
Gillabou, J.C. - 85
Gillard, P.P. (Captain) - 84
Gillis, John - 44
Gillis, Mary J. - 398
Gist, Joseph F. (Lt. Col.) - 207
Gist, William M. (Major) - 210
Gladden, Brigadier General - 218, 219, 235, 236
Gladden, William - 163, 384, 387
Gladden's Brigade - 218

Gladden's Post Office - 115
Glenn, John A. Dr. - 4, 13
Godfrey - 70
Goff, E. F. - 396
Goff, John - 44
Goggin, James M. - 200, 205, 208
Goldsbyn, Captain - 262
Goodale, C.M. - 393
Goodale, John R. - 152, 179, 268, 365, 371, 372, 373, 374, 376, 381, 382, 384, 399
Goodale, Joseph - 268, 400
Gooding, Charles - 32, 35
Goodwin (Goodwyn) - 8, 35, 36, 70, 79
Goodwyn, A. D. -70
Goodwyn, C. M. - 36
Goodwyn, J. J. - 146
Goodwyn, Major -79
Goodwyn, Mrs. A.D. - 56, 69
Goodyin's Store - 28, 42, 74, 92
Gordon, B. F. - 44
Gordon, Reverend W.R. - 164
Gordon, William Baker - 268
Gordon's advance - 277
Gordonsville, Virginia - 14
Government Military Reservation - 227
Governor Picken's wife -183
Governor Pickens - 18, 217, 361
Grace Episcopal Church, Camden -198, 244
Graham, D. - 13
Graham, Eliza - 398
Graham, J. D. - 36
Graham, John T. - 9, 13, 268
Graham, Mary J. - 398
Graham, William - 20
Grain and Lumber Mills - 95
Grand Army of the North - 16
Grandfather's Greybeard - 252
Grandma Parker - 331
Grandmother Rush - 342
Grandmother Young - 342
Granny's Quarter Creek - 239, 240
Grant, Miss - 65
Great Temperance Reform - 74
Green, John - 10, 163, 369, 371, 376, 377, 378, 379, 381, 382, 384, 387, 389, 390, 395
Green, Mrs. - 169
Green-Castle, Virginia - 209
Greenleaf Villa, (Lee House) Camden -130
Greensboro, N.C. - 222, 362
Greenville News Newspaper -199
Greenville, S.C. -10, 143, 355
Greenville, Tennessee - 355

Gregg - 68
Gregory, John A. - 85, 90
Griffin, Silas - 359
Griffin, Stephen - 20, 44, 52, 64
Gum Swamp- iv
Gunter, A. E. - 396

H

Habbersham, Miss - 66
Hackett, Roger C. - 350
Haddrell's Point - 16
Hagerstown - 209, 212
Haggi Muhammed - 140
Haggod, General Johnson - 223, 337, 338. 339, 340
Hagood, Jessie Manuel - 155, 157, 158
Hagood's Brigade - 104, 337, 338, 340
Haile, A. J. - 5, 33
Haile, A. L. - 31
Haile, C.C. Roll - 238
Haile, C.C. Map 1894 - 105, 107, 108, 118
Haile, Columbus Cureton - 1, 5, 12, 14, 15, 16, 18, 19, 28, 57, 61, 64, 75, 91, 94, 162, 199, 51, 259, 260, 268, 327, 362, 418
Haile, Elison - 12, 259, 260
Haile, James Lawrence - 9, 38, 59, 162, 163, 164, 355, 356
Haile, James Lenior - 9, 268
Haile, Mrs. B. - 98
Haile, Mrs. James - 182
Haile, Mrs. Louisa - 101
Haile, Thomas Cureton - 244, 268
Haile's Gold Mine - 370
Haley, J. B. - 84
Hall, Amanda - 398
Hall, J.J. - 88
Hall, J.M. - 163
Hall, James - 20, 46, 155, 158
Hall, James B. - 42
Hall, Jones- 153
Hall, Joseph - 84, 155, 158
Hall, Lafayette - 260, 283
Hall, R. J./Jacob Riley - 53, 88, 155, 162, 163
Hall, Shelton Benjamin- 419
Hall, Temperance- 69, 101
Hall, W. J. - 65
Hall, William Ellison - 155, 163
Hamilton, Alexander - 153
Hamilton, Mrs.- 101
Hammerslough, Mrs.- 59, 95
Hammerslough, S. - 71
Hammond, Asa - 85
Hammond, Frank - 268

Hammond, J.B. - 32, 33, 34
Hammond, John F. - 90
Hammond, P. B. - 33
Hampton Park, Camden, S.C. - 184, 185
Hampton Square, Camden, S.C. - 185
Hampton, General Wade -27, 126, 147, 149, 180, 200, 297, 325, 337
Hampton's Legion - 17, 66, 158, 159, 160, 314, 319, 356, 365
Hampton's Scouts- 321
Hance, Captain - 204
Hanckle -325
Hancock's and Wright Corp- 278
Hanging Rock - 106, 114, 115, 116, 118, 119, 123, 124
Hanging Rock Battlefield- 115
Hanging Rock Camp #738 - 158
Hanging Rock Creek - 115, 116, 117, 124
Hanging Rock Post Office - 115, 117
Hankel, Reverend J. S. - 32
Hankell, Dr. J.J.- 23
Hannahan, Dr.- 62
Hannon Brigade - 135
Hardee, Lieutenant General - 126, 244, 325
Hardee's Army- 325
Hardeeville, S.C. - 78, 243
Harden, J. B.- 359
Hardy, William H. - 17
Hardy, Willie - 314, 315
Hargrett Rare Books and Manuscript Library, University of Georgia Library- 350
Hark (Name of horse) - 143
Harmony College -23
Harold (Herold) , Sarah R. - 240, 375, 376, 377, 379, 380, 381, 383
Harpens, Angleina- 264
Harper's Ferry - 5, 201, 202
Harrell, E.- 65
Harrell, James - 20, 52
Harrell, John - 20
Harris, J. B. - 87
Harris, John - 85
Harris, Robert - 85
Harris, Thomas - 21
Harrison, B.F. - 13
Harrison, Burton - 143
Harrison, Captain Stewart - 206
Harrison, D. - 33, 49
Harrison, John S. - 84
Harrison, President - 223
Harrison, Stewart - 206
Harrison's Crossroads - 119
Harvey, Elvira - 388
Hase, James - 52

Haskell, Alexander C. (Colonel) - 87, 148, 355, 356
Haskell, E.C. - 87
Hassan Dealers - 140
Harton, T.J. - 389
Hatfield, C.R. - 89
Hatfield, Samuel Benjamin, Sr. - 425
Hawkins, P. - 62
Hawkins, Sarah - 371
Hawley, J.- 85
Hawthorne Course (Camden) - 17
Hay- 70
Hay, J.T. - 151
Hay, James Thornwell - 268
Hay, Miss Frances - 55
Hay, Mrs. - 60
Hay, Reverend L.H. - 180
Hay, Reverend Samuel H. - 22, 23, 32, 33, 35, 67, 75, 95, 170, 226
Hay, W.A.- 359
Hayden, Charles-44
Hayes, Emmanuel – 20, 52, 163
Hayes, Joseph- 20, 52
Hayne, Isaac - 217
Haynes, Augustus M. - 399
Haynes, E. J.- 84
Hays, Sarah – 370, 372, 373, 375, 376, 377, 378, 380, 381, 383, 387
Hazel Run, Chancellorsville, Virginia - 206
Hazen, W.B. (General) - 120, 121, 122, 129
Hazzard, J. M. - 85
Headington, John W. (Captain)- 110
Headquarters Department of Alabama and West Florida - 236
Heath Springs, S.C. - 394
Heath, B.D. - 396
Heilger, Louis - 141
Henagan, John W. (Colonel)- 201, 207, 210
Henderson, J.C. - 85
Henderson, M. - 44
Henning, N.P. - 86
Henrico County - 14
Henry, William L. (Captain) - 110
Henson, J. - 38
Herald, Sarah R. - 240
Herbert, S. - 99
Herby, J.- 51
Hermitage (Plantation) - 143
Herron, George Samuel - 155, 157, 158
Herron, James Emmanuel - 155
Herron, W. L. - 157
Hershman, J. T. - 32
Hershman, Mrs. J. T. - 65
Heth, General - 207

Hickory Head - 116
Higgins, B. H. - 386
Higgins, Benjamin - 395, 396
Higgins, John O. - 43, 91
Hill, General B.H. - 67
Hill, J. - 85
Hill, J. M.- 43
Hill, R. J. (Captain) - 220
Hill, R.H.- 217
Hillard Farm - 115
Hillard, A.D. - 49
Hilton, B.A. - 158, 160, 161
Hilton, J. B. -90
Hilton, J.C. 401
Hinson, B. F. - 20
Hinson, Caroline - 398
Hinson, Emma - 392, 398
Hinson, Henry - 386, 388, 389, 397
Hinson, J. E. - 9, 13
Hinson, Jackson Elijah - 413
Hinson, J. S. - 159
Hinson, John - 53
Hinson, Kiziah -386
Hinson, M.L. -159
Hinson, Reubin - 65
Hinson, W. B. - 20
Hinson, W. E. J. - 69
Hix, H.P. - 334
Hix, W. P. - 146
Hobert, Harrison C.(Brevet Brigadier General) -
Hobkirk Hill -
Hocott, Daniel D. - 28, 32, 35, 49, 56, 70, 73, 74, 81, 83, 93, 94, 103, 132
Hocott, Mrs. D.D. - 98, 102
Hocott, Richard - 33, 49, 65, 74
Hocott, W. H. - 28
Hoke, A. D. - 315, 316
Holcombe Legion - 66, 80, 83, 86, 136, 355, 364, 365
Holcombe's Legion Cavalry - 80
Holland, Amanda J. - 386, 388
Holland, Isaac F. - 43, 165, 185, 398
Holland, J. L. - 243
Holland, James - 65, 155
Holland, John - 44, 60
Holland, John C. - 85
Holland, Nancy - 243
Holland, Thomas - 34, 65, 155
Holland, Thomas Rease - 155
Holley, John - 65
Hollis, Hiram Francis - 155
Holloway, J.S. - 62
Holloway, William - 85

Holley, George - 44
Holmes, Charles R. (Captain) - 145, 146, 202, 204, 208, 212
Honey (Honie in Service Records) Elvira - 369, 371, 372, 375, 377, 379, 380, 382, 383
Hood:
    Hood, General - 105, 209, 212, 219, 344
    Hood, William - 146
    Hood's Division - 209, 212
Hook, William - 359
Hoole, Lieutenant Colonel A.J. - 203
Hopkins, James - 46, 155
Hopkins, Lewis - 155, 157, 158
Hopkins, Malcolm - 155
Horn, J. A. - 359
Hornsby, D. - 85
Hornsby, Frances A. - 392, 394
Hornsby, Jessie - 155, 157, 158
Hornsby, Joseph- 52
Hornsby, S.W. - 52, 64, 86
Hornsby, Samuel - 20, 41, 52
Horry District, S.C. - 48
Horton, C. H. - 89
Horton, C. W. -159
Horton, C.C. - 158, 160, 161
Horton, J. R. - 386
Horton, James Stanley - 33, 154
Horton, James Wyatt - 46, 158
Horton, John Ervin - 153, 157, 158
Horton, L. E. - 371
Horton, Ransom - 155, 157, 158
Horton, Sarah A. - 398
Horton, T.C. - 160, 161
Horton, Thomas R. - 155
Horton, W. J. -159
Horton, William -159
Horton, William Crowe- 419
Horton, William Mack -160, 161
Horton's Store - 115
Hough Bridge - 120
Hough Ferry - 113
Hough Rangers - 40
Hough, Amos - 163, 409
Hough, B. - 37, 39
Hough, Elizabeth P. - 255
Hough, Hollis- 20, 53
Hough, Isaac Shepard - 155
Hough, J. M. - 368
Hough, J. W. - 37
Hough, J.D. - 386
Hough, James Stanley -
Hough, Joel - 65, 88, 90, 162, 163, 164, 268
Hough, Laborn Carraway - 85, 155, 159, 160, 161, 162, 411

Hough, M.J. - 146
Hough, Moses - 5, 84, 163, 409
Hough, N - 89
Hough, Sampson - 153
Hough, Senator - 221
Hough, W. - 39
Howard Grove Hospital, Richmond, Virginia - 243
Howard, Major General Oliver O. - 109, 119, 283
Howard, Mrs. H. M. -28
Howard's Command - 248
Howell, Martha -
Howle, Elvira - 392
Howser, General - 129
Huckabee, A.A. - 34
Huckabee, J. J. - 19
Huckabee, J. W. - 86
Huckabee, J.L. - 52
Huckabee, Joe - 259, 261
Huckabee, Johanna - 392
Huckabee, Minton G. - 47
Huckabee, W. B. - 57
Huckabee, W.G. - 162, 385, 389, 392
Hudson - 21
Hudson, J.W. - 391
Huff, Isaac S. - 31
Huff, J. -
Huff, W.C. - 63
Huffman, J. - 146
Huger, Colonel Frank - 280
Huggins, B.H. - 394
Huggins, B.N. - 389
Huggins, T.A. - 87
Hughes, A.F.A. - 46
Hughes, Dr. Edwin C. - 268, 332
Hughes, Ellen - 215
Hughes, Frank J. - 214, 215
Hughes, J. B. - 27, 42
Hughes, Sarah - 215
Hughes, Sherman - 215
Hughes, William E. - 71, 75, 91, 95, 101, 129
Hughes' Mill (known as Adam's Mill) - 78, 325
Hughson, Mrs. Mary A. - 81
Hughson, W. E./L., Jr. - 49, 68, 70, 74, 91, 95
Hull, Zimmerman D. - 391
Humphey's Mississippi Brigade -
Humphries, B.J. - 44
Humphries (Umphries in records), Mrs. - 65
Humphries (Umphries in records), Nathan - 34, 65
Humphries (Umpries in records), Nathaniel - 65
Hunsucker, J. - 85
Hunt Motel - 35
Hunter, A.A. - 53

Hunter, Cornelius - 359
Hunter, E. - 163
Hunter, T.H. - 389
Huntington, Randolph - 140
Huntley, J. W. - 159, 161
Hurst, J. W. - 146
Hutto, J. M. - 360
Hyams, Mrs. - 98, 102
Hyatt, C.W. - 163
Hyatt, George Thomas - 360
Hyatt, J. W. - 162, 397, 398
Hyatt, R. J. - 163, 385, 396
Hyatt, Richard - 96
Hymes, Miss - 67
Hyott, C.W. - 88

I

Inabinet, Archibald - 360
Independent Fire Engine Company of Camden- 399, 400
Ingoldsby, Charles- 180
Ingraham, J.M.- 49, 268
Ingraham, M. - 31
Ingraham, Moody- 34, 155, 158
Ingraham's Mill- 115
Ingraham's Plantation- 124
Ingram, W.A. - 159
Ingram, W.D. - 159
Irby, A.P. - 85
Ireland- 76
Irish Brigade - 334
Irvin, John - 369, 373, 375, 376, 378, 380, 381, 383, 384, 389
Irvin, Mary - 370
Isaac, A. - 36
Isbell - 90, 339
Isbell, J.D. - 34
Isbell, J.H. - 163
Isbell, L.R. - 72
Isenhour, Daniel - 393, 396
Italy - 24
Ives, J.M. - 62

J

J. J. McKain's Store - 29
Jackson - 264
Jackson Hospital, Richmond, Va. - 353
Jackson, D. - 53
Jackson, Douglass - 20
Jackson, George - 164, 384, 387, 389, 396
Jackson, J. - 37, 39
Jackson, T. F. - 395

Jackson, T. J. - 164
Jackson, Stonewell (General) - 184, 199, 203, 205, 207, 229, 232, 333
Jacobs, J. - 36
Jacobs, Sarah - 386, 387, 388, 392, 394
Jake - 286, 293
James Cantey Division - 228
James Dunlap's Store - 29
James Island - 31, 32, 37, 60
James River - 198, 353, 355
James' Battalions - 206
Jamison, Columbus Alexander - 86, 155
Jarret's Hotel - 12, 14
Jeffcoat, J. - 360
Jeffcoat, J.W. - 360
Jefferson Davis Highway Map - 183, 184, 185
Jefferson Davis Highway Marker - 183
Jefferson Davis' Horse - 139, 143
Jeffords, J.J. - 89
Jenkins, General Micah - 84, 139
Jenkins, William R. - 34
Jenks, E.H. - 10
Jenny's Hotel - 79
Jews (Camden) - 302
Jimie, A.S. - 84
Jimme -
Joe - 315, 316
"Joe Sherman" (Name of pony) - 341
John - 315, 316
John Brown's Raid - 216
John Brown's Steam Mill - 10
John Doby Kennedy Chapter - 183
Johnson - 349
Johnson Brown's Tannery - 311
Johnson, A. - 10, 13
Johnson, B.B. - 91
Johnson, B.C. - 368
Johnson, B.F. - 20, 41, 53
Johnson, Daniel David -
Johnson, G.W. - 44
Johnson, George D. (Major) - 220
Johnson, H.B. - 96
Johnson, J.D. (Captain) - 32
Johnson, James P. (Corporal) - 135
Johnson, James W. - 85
Johnson, John -
Johnson, Joseph E. (General) – 328, 344
Johnson, Mrs. W.E. – 48, 61, 66, 75, 97, 101, 152
Johnson, R.B. - 75, 101, 104
Johnson, Reverend John - 152, 244, 400
Johnson, Robert - iii, 69, 70
Johnson, Ruel M. (Major) - 110

Johnson, S.D. - 160
Johnson, Thomas - 86
Johnson, W.B. - 53, 89
Johnson, W.E. - 10, 13, 27, 54, 70, 72, 81, 57, 59
Johnson, W.L. - 268
Johnson, W.M. - 5
Johnson, W.W. - 63
Johnson, William - 65
Johnson, William E., Sr. - 91, 93, 94, 96
Johnson's Artillery Company - 21, 32, 270
Johnston, Albert Sidney - 184
Johnston, Joseph E. - 184
Johnston, Joseph E. (General) - 184, 218, 222, 26, 9, 231, 232, 301, 309
Johnston, Randell - 85
Johnston, S.R. (Captain) - 207
Johnston's Division -
Johnston's Surrender - 136
Jones – 130, 356
Jones, A.D. – 28, 74, 92
Jones, A.D. Jr. – 33, 74, 92
Jones, Adeline – 392, 394
Jones, B. (Colonel) - 4, 18
Jones, B.H. - 162
Jones, B.M. - 159, 160, 161, 165, 185, 398
Jones, B.N. - 159, 160, 161
Jones, Bob - 160
Jones, Burrell - 27, 28, 31, 57, 61, 127, 365
Jones, Calvin - 65
Jones, Daniel - 85
Jones, David - 146
Jones, E.C. - 44
Jones, J. - 28, 49
Jones, J.J. - 88
Jones, James – 38, 59, 93, 136
Jones, James Dargan - 44
Jones, James G. - iii
Jones, James G. Dr. - 4
Jones, Jessie A. - 44
Jones, John E. - 159, 160, 161, 386, 389
Jones, John L. - 22, 28, 29, 31, 62, 63, 86, 88, 90, 99, 235, 338, 363, 365
Jones, John Todd - 155, 385, 386, 389, 391
Jones, L.O. - 85, 161
Jones, Laurence C. - 31
Jones, Margaret E. - 398
Jones, Mrs. A.D. - 48, 55
Jones, Mrs. J.L. - 48
Jones, Mrs. James - 89, 98, 102
Jones, N.W. - 85, 162
Jones, Nathaniel William - 155
Jones, Quiggin, and Company - 141

Jones, Rebecca C. - 398
Jones, Richard L. - 158
Jones, Richard T. - 155
Jones, S.D. (Captain)- 5
Jones, S.I. - 44
Jones, Samuel Newton - 155
Jones, Seaborn- 57
Jones, Theodore - 123
Jones, Thomas I. - 74
Jones, Thomas J. - 88, 400
Jones, W.F. (Corporal) - 80
Jones, W.J. - 159, 160, 161, 165
Jones, William - 85
Jones' Ferry - 127
Jones' Hall - 153
Jordan, B.F. -
Jordan, D. - 41
Jordan, W. - 20
Joseph Brevard Kershaw Camp #82 - 153
Jourdan, W.H. - 53
Journal and Confederate Newspaper- 126, 133
Jowers, J.N. - 89
Joy, Mrs. - 130
Joyner, P.H. - 86
Joyner, W.H. – 391, 396
Judy - 285
Jungbluth, J.H. – 66, 95, 127
Justice, William - 46

K

Kansas - 232
Kantz, General- 356
Keller, W.J. - 146
Kelly, Alex - 291
Kelly, B.P. - 53
Kelly, Captain Wiley (Captain K) – 57, 75, 91, 290, 291, 293, 294
Kelly, D.E. - 58
Kelly, D.H. – 163, 389, 393, 394
Kelly, Ellen C. - 395
Kelly, Emiline – 371, 372, 373, 375
Kelly, J.J. - 163
Kelly, James - 31, 34
Kelly, James Frank - 153
Kelly, John - 34
Kelly, Joseph S. - 393, 395
Kelly, Lenora - 370, 372, 373, 375, 376, 377, 378, 380, 381, 383, 385, 387
Kelly, Mrs. -
Kelly, Nannie C. - 388
Ke93lly, W.D. - 389

Kelly, William M.- 34, 96
Kelly's Bridge – 106, 111, 112
Kelly's Ferry – 108, 112
Kelly's House - 294
Kellytown – 106, 107, 111, 112, 121, 126
Kemp, James - 360
Kemp, K - 20
Kemp, Tia – 20, 21
Kemp, Warren – 20, 53
Kennedy – 70, 81, 90
Kennedy, Alexander Dalton- 162, 199, 268
Kennedy, Allen - 85
Kennedy, Anthony McMillan- 19, 21, 22, 23, 28, 35, 37, 45, 46, 54, 57, 60, 66, 71, 73, 75, 79, 91, 92, 164, 222, 316
Kennedy, Betty B. - 398
Kennedy, Dalton, Sr.- 251
Kennedy, John Doby -8, 9, 14, 15, 16, 18, 27, 29, 31, 33, 35, 36, 46, 60, 63, 69, 70, 79, 83, 84, 98, 133, 145, 146, 151, 152, 153, 179, 180, 182, 183, 200, 201, 203, 204, 206, 207, 210, 211, 221, 222, 223, 224, 225, 226, 251, 259, 260, 316, 339, 343, 344, 346, 361, 362
Kennedy, Joseph (Major)- 212
Kennedy, Joseph Doby - 268
Kennedy, Miss Lou -69
Kennedy, Mrs. A.M. (Sarah Ann Doby) – 69, 95, 98, 102, 179, 222, 316
Kennedy, Mrs. Elizabeth M. - 313
Kennedy, Mrs. Harriet Dubose - 183
Kennedy, Mrs. John D. - 180, 343
Kennedy, Mrs. R.M. – 98, 102
Kennedy, Mrs. William - 56
Kennedy, Robert M. –21, 27, 32, 43, 54, 56, 69, 75, 81, 91, 92, 93, 94, 132, 217, 248, 262, 339
Kennedy, W.M.- 93
Kennedy, W.- 69
Kennedy, William- 21
Kennedy, William Jr.- 71
Kennington, George - 155
Kennington, J.B. - 87
Kennington, Levi - 65
Kent, Adjutant - 220
Kentucky – 218, 331, 332
Kenzie, H.L. - 146
Kerrison, E. - 87
Kershaw Aid Society - 32, 35
Kershaw's Brigade- 7, 15, 17, 67, 76, 200
Kershaw Cadets - 8
Kershaw Concert Band – 181
Kershaw Cornet Band- 181, 182
Kershaw County (Kershaw District) -
Kershaw County Bible Society – 40, 67
Kershaw County Census - 260

Kershaw County List of Artificial Limbs - 378, 379
Kershaw County Pension Examining Board - 371, 373, 374, 381, 398
Kershaw County Pensions Record - 372
Kershaw County Survivor's Association – 151, 152, 153
Kershaw County Tax Collector - 73
Kershaw County Volunteers - 251
Kershaw District Lower Battalion SC Militia Election
Kershaw's Division- 334
Kershaw Gazette – 130, 170
Kershaw Greys - 27, 29, 46, 63
Kershaw Guard - 21, 22, 181, 362
Kershaw Masonic Lodge 29, AFA – 28, 74, 77, 199, 200
Kershaw Mills - 351
Kershaw, Charlotte – 285, 290, 292
Kershaw, John (Reverend) – 72, 152, 181, 414
Kershaw, Joseph B.- iv, 3, 4, 6, 7, 8, 10, 11, 12, 13, 14, 15, 16, 17, 18, 27, 28, 29, 36, 68, 75, 76, 79, 83, 84, 145, 146, 147, 148, 151, 198, 199, 200, 203, 204, 205, 208, 212, 213, 214, 215, 222, 224, 225, 240, 268, 277, 279, 281, 313, 315, 323, 324, 334, 335, 362
Kershaw, Lucretia Douglas – 198, 285
Kershaw, Mary – 285, 290, 292
Kershaw, Mrs. Joseph Kershaw – 70, 98, 102
Kershaw, Old General- 215
Kershaw County- iv, 4, 13, 31, 32, 40, 58, 60, 73, 74, 78, 82, 130, 147, 184, 199, 213, 222, 223, 224, 237, 239, 252, 261, 262, 291, 316, 361, 365, 366, 397, 399, 400
Kershaw County Pension Record- 370, 372, 373, 375, 376, 380, 381, 383, 384, 386, 388, 390, 394, 395, 396, 397
Kershaw District- 4, 5, 6, 16, 17, 21, 32, 38, 41, 42, 45, 50, 51, 56, 57, 64, 68, 69, 72, 77, 78, 81, 82, 83, 89, 90, 102, 105, 126, 145, 151, 157, 158, 198, 243, 259, 333
Kershaw News Era- 263
Kershaw, S.C. – 158, 263, 370, 371, 373, 374, 377, 378, 379, 380, 381, 382, 383, 384, 385, 386, 387, 388, 389, 390, 395, 386
Kershaw, South Carolina Post Office-
Kershaw's Troops-15, 334, 362, 365
Khanoun, Nexie - 139
Khedive – 139, 141
Kilgore- 48
Kilgore, James L. - 68
Kilgore, Jessie - 57
Kilgore, Miss. L.A. - 68
Kilpatrick's Cavalry – 106, 109
KInard, A.L.C. - 395
King – 90
King, Captain John L,- 110, 248, 249
King Street – 324, 332, 346
King, G.S. - 185
King, George – 10, 13, 85, 165, 185

King, George B. – 85, 165, 185, 398, 417
King, Gilliam Preston - 153
King, J.E. - 65
King, M.W. - 47
King, Mrs.-
King's Plantation - 123
Kingsbury Ferry - 115
Kingstree, S.C. - 66
Kingsville, S.C. - 8, 131, 354
Kinloch, Dr. - 274
Kirby, A.P. -
Kirby, Absolom - 20, 53, 64, 86, 357
Kirby, Emeline- 374, 375, 376, 377, 379, 380, 382, 383
Kirby, J.W. - 20, 53, 64
Kirby, James D. - 399
Kirby, John - 34, 85
Kirby, T. - 85
Kirby, William - 357
Kirk, C. - 146
Kirkland - 231
Kirkland, Bessie- 180
Kirkland, Billy - 333. 353
Kirkland, Caroline - 333
Kirkland, D.D. (Colonel) - 5
Kirkland, D.P. - 395
Kirkland, Daniel D. - 38, 75, 91, 333, 353
Kirkland, J.P. - 47
Kirkland, James Allen - 33, 95, 124, 125, 333, 353
Kirkland, James R. - 47
Kirkland, John - 82
Kirkland, John R. – 273, 353
Kirkland, M.M. - 398
Kirkland, Marie – 182
Kirkland, Mary Vaughan- 333, 353
Kirkland, Richard (father) -
Kirkland, Richard Rowland – 7, 10, 13, 213, 214, 268, 333, 334. 353, 354
Kirkland, S.R. - 47
Kirkland, Sam - 87, 227, 259, 261, 333, 353
Kirkland, Thomas J. - 181, 184, 217, 262
Kirkland, W.L. - 259
KIrkley, D.C. - 52, 268, 388
KIrkley, D.M. - 42
Kirkley, Daniel - 20
Kirkley, David -
KIrkley, James M. - 5
KIrkley, Robert - 10, 13, 96, 409
Kirkwood area Camden - 7, 22, 122, 127, 216, 224, 283, 348, 351
Kirkwood Boundary- 8
Kirkwood Cavalry – 38, 56, 66
Kirkwood Ranger's Flag - iii

Kirkwood Rangers, 7th Cavalry – iii, 19, 54, 80, 136, 183, 184, 333, 364, 365, 394, 395
Kirkwood Village- 348
Knight, Eli – 159, 161
Knight, Elizabeth - 396
Knight, W. - 391
Knight's Hill, Camden, S.C. - 217
Knox, Mrs. Jane J. - 96
Knoxville, Tennessee – 76, 198, 222, 226
Koon, Sarah - 394
Koopman and Summers – 21, 56, 70
Koopman, W. - 34

L

Laborde, Dr. – 48, 57
Ladies Aid Association, Camden –55, 59, 65, 66, 101
Ladies Aid Society, Camden – 16, 22, 28, 37, 38, 40, 42, 48, 50, 55, 58, 59, 60, 31, 67, 78, 81, 157
Ladies Aid Society, Flat Rock – 28, 40, 67
Ladies Aid Society, Liberty Hill- 28, 49
Ladies Benevolent Society, Camden – 69, 81
Ladies Hospital, Columbia - 60
Ladies Memorial Association – 169, 170
Ladies of Charleston- 14, 60, 286
Ladies of Columbia - 17
Ladies of Sumter – 11, 12
Lafayette - 262
Lafayette Hall (Stood where the present Court House is now standing) – 260, 283
Lamar, Captain G.B. - 206
Lamar, Reverend M.F. - 180
Lamar, Reverend William - 180
Lamb, Colonel - 142
Lancaster Greys – 8, 9, 251
Lancaster Invincibles – 14, 199
Lancaster Ledger - 9
Lancaster Road - 122, 124, 325
Lancaster, J.C. – 360, 390
Lancaster, L.L. – 360 a
Lancaster, S.C. / Lancaster District – 8, 10, 35, 78, 89, 90, 97, 106, 111, 115, 116, 118, 119, 122, 132, 147, 158, 251,341, 344, 346, 368, 371,
Landsford - 125
Laney, John - 89
Lang, Edward B. – 40, 269
Lang, Estate of T. - 96
Lang, Harriet Dubose - 285
Lang, James – 259, 262
Lang, Mrs (house) - 130
Lang, Mrs. - 65
Lang. Mrs. B.M.

Langley, James - 44
Langley, R. - 85
Langley, William - 391
Lanham, Corporal – 279, 281
Lanier, D.G. - 33
Larkin, William
Latham, S.B. - 268
Latrone, Major - 84
Latta, A. - 71
Latta, A.T. – 21, 71, 94
Latta, R. - 28
Lauren's Square - 9
Lauren's Street, Camden – 180, 200, 245, 247
Laurence - 49
Laurens, S.C. – 143, 394
Law, General - 212
Lawrence, R.N. - 146
Lawyers - 93
Leaphart, S.L. – 36, 146
LeBaron, Thomas M. - 234
Lee County – 392, 394, 397
Lee, A. Markley – 69, 71, 93
Lee, Alexander Y., Jr.- 3
Lee, B. M. – 66, 70
Lee, Mrs. B.M. - 97
Lee, Curtis - 277
Lee, Eliza R. – 70, 89
Lee, General S.D. - 216
Lee, J. - 71
Lee, James S. - 84
Lee, John - 86
Lee, John B. – 38, 87
Lee, Little Miss Fannie B. - 98
Lee, M. - 70
Lee, Mary – 377, 378, 379, 381, 382, 384, 385, 388, 396
Lee, Miss Eliza B. - 69
Lee, Miss. E.K. – 101
Lee, Mrs. J.- 71, 78, 81, 102,
Lee, Mrs. Joseph – 69, 129, 130, 332
Lee, Robert E. – 148, 153, 173, 184, 199, 205, 324, 325, 333, 337, 340, 344
Lee's Army- 309
Lee's Hill – 205
Lee House- 332
Lee's Surrender – 296, 297, 309
Legare (a pointer) - 341
Lege - 70
Legislature – 10, 13, 162
Legrand, J. Marcellus – 268, 390, 396
LeGrande, M.S. - 269
Leitner, Benjamin F. - 50
Leitner, Mrs. Zack - 69

Leitner, William Zachariah – 4, 9, 29, 32, 35, 36, 48, 49, 55, 62, 63, 71, 82, 83, 92, 93, 146, 151, 152, 153, 167, 180, 315, 316
Lemmond, M.L. – 10, 13
Lephart, S.L. - 36
Levi, Chapman - iv
Lewis, B.T. - 389
Lewis, E.S.
Lewis, R.T. – 88, 68
Lewis, William H. – 84, 244
Lewis' Kentucky Brigade Sharpshooters – 133, 134, 135
Lewisville – 34
Lexington, Kentucky- 331
Lexington, SC - 359, 396
Liberty Hill – 28, 33, 42, 48, 49, 54, 57, 62, 74, 92, 101, 106, 108, 111, 112, 113, 114, 120, 121, 122, 126, 263, 264, 273, 311, 338, 341, 348, 351, 389
Liberty Hill Beat Line - 78
Liberty Hill Post Office – 114, 391
Liberty Hill Road – 261, 317
Lick Creek - 115
Lieutenant John A. McQueen – 131 move
Light Artillery Palmetto Battalion – 37, 43, 45, 48, 68, 78, 365
Lightwood Knot Springs Camp – 20, 58, 263
Lincoln, Abraham – 3, 5, 256, 331, 344
Lincoln, Mary Todd – 331, 332
Lining, Arthur Parker- 268
Lippincott, J.B.& Company - 324
Little Lynches Creek – 113, 114, 115, 116, 117, 123, 124, 126, 130
Liverpool, England - 141
Liverpudlian – 139
Lizenby – 42, 92
Lizenby Area -
Lizzie Rutherford Chapter #60 - 229
Lobick, S. - 36
Logan, J. L.- 4
Logan, Major General John A. – 110, 119, 120, 121, 126, 239
Logan, R.L. – 47
Logan, Samuel- 29
Lollis, W.T. - 164
London – 61, 141
Longstreet Museum - 215
Longstreet, General – 56, 80, 84, 209, 212, 215, 222, 226, 256, 289, 292, 323, 324
Longstreet's Corp – 185, 222, 225, 323
Longtown – 40, 119, 121, 261
Longtown Presbyterian Church Cemetery - 132
Loomis, Colonel J.Q. - 219
Lord Cornwallis - 283
Lorick, Soloman – 151, 268
Lousiana – 27, 138, 219, 220, 231, 244

Love, Jessie -
Love, M.C. - 15
Love, Margaret - 81
Love, Nelson - 240
Love, R.J. - 399
Love, R.M. - 63
Lovett, Josephine - 255
Lowndes, T.P. - 146
Lowry, R. - 15
Lowry, Robert J. - 159, 160
Lowry, W. - 15
Lubbers, Major John - 110
Lucas Battalion Heavy Artillery - 158
Lucas Guards – 21, 46, 62, 63
Lucas Rifles -
Lucas, Benjamin Simon – 21, 46, 57, 62, 63, 84, 88, 93, 157, 158, 243, 365
Lucas, J. Jonathon – 147
Lucknow, S.C. – 386, 388, 389, 390, 391, 392
Lucy - 215
Lugoff, S.C. - 395
Lunderbark, Chad - 264
Lyles, J. L. – 44
Lyles, James V. – 20, 22, 54, 71, 73
Lyles, Martha - 332
Lyles, Mrs. James V. – 30, 98
Lyles, W. J. - 15
Lynchburg, Virginia - 20, 21, 52, 53, 56
Lynches Creek –iv, 98, 106, 107, 108, 109, 110, 111, 112, 113, 114, 115, 116, 117.118, 119. 121, 122, 123, 126, 129, 131, 249, 264, 293, 294, 359, 399
Lynches Creek Minuteman- 5
Lynchwood Area - 369, 376, 374, 377, 378, 379, 380, 382, 383, 385, 386, 389
Lyttleton Street, Camden – 180, 343

M

M.Baum and Brother's Store -29
Mackey, Samuel - 90
Macrae, Collin – 92, 94
Macrae, Joel – 92
Magistrates-76, 91
Magnolia Gardens - 29
Mahaffey, William - 63
Mahone, General – 205, 280, 328, 337, 339
Malvern Hill - 157
Man, P.A. – 20
Managers of General Election -
Manassas – 15. 17, 18, 27, 29, 33, 34, 45, 48, 50, 68, 75, 76, 198, 216, 217, 222, 225, 231, 279, 286, 313, 322, 323, 324

Manchester-40, 132
Manget, John -43
Manly's Battery, (Captain B.C.) - 206
Mann, Robert - 65
Manning, Brown- 268
Manning, Brown C.- 260
Manning, Dick- 314, 315
Manning, Governor – 11
Mansion House – 9, 95
Marengo Mills – 106, 111, 122
Marietta, Georgia- 186
Marsh, Alfred - 44
Marsh, Gates - 20
Marsh, James - 20
Marshal and Market Clerk - 93
Marshall, Mr. - 98
Marshall, W.S. - 162
Marshall, W.T. - 162
Marthers, W. (not Marthias, W.) - 39
Marthias, W. – 37
Martin – 89, 208, 338, 339
Martin, John - 146
Martin, P. - 85
Martin, S. - 146
Martin, William H. - 33
Martinsburg - 208
Mary Boykin Chesnut – 15, 136, 215
Maryland – 40, 56, 59, 232, 243, 256, 292
Maryland Campaign - 200
Maryland Heights – 75, 76, 200
Masonic Hall - 127
Masonic Kershaw Lodge #29 – 28, 49
Massaponax, Virginia - 205
Massey, A. - 87
Matheson, Alex – 325, 386, 389
Matheson Storehouse - 129
Matheson, Benjamin H.- 47
Matheson, Benjamin, and Company – 21, 71, 94, 129
Matheson, C., Esquire- 14
Matheson, Dr. B. - 152
Matheson, James D. – iii, 38
Mattox, George - 53
Mattox, Isaac S. – 20, 53
Mattox, James – 20, 41, 53
Mattox, Samuel – 20, 360
Maxwell, J.C. - 36
May Queen (racehorse) - 143
Mayesville – 133, 257
Mayfield, Superintendant of Education - 200
Maynardie,(Meynardie) Reverend E.J. – 8, 14, 18, 71, 181, 268
Mayrant, J.G. - 85
McCaa, J. – 33, 93

McCaa, John Dr. – 54, 71, 268
McCaa, Wlliam Lowndes – 71, 77
McCallum, Reverend B. - 20
McCandless, Leslie – 32, 33, 94, 225, 251
McCandless, Mrs. Fannie – 61, 66, 94, 97, 101
McCants, George - 85
McCants, T.J. - 44
McCaskill, Angus - 57
McCaskill, Charles Wesley – 85, 155
McCaskill, Daniel – 65, 74, 92
McCaskill, Finley – 5, 21, 90
McCaskill, J.D. – 84, 162
McCaskill, James Hubbard - 154
McCaskill, John – 31, 34
McCaskill, William Patterson - 155
McCaskill's Crossroads - 121
McCaughlin, S.T. - 146
McClarin, Angus - 88
McClarin, D. - 88
McClarkson, E. - 146
McClendon, E. - 88
McClester, A. - 65
McCloud, D. – 34
McClure, W. - 27
McCoy, B.T. – 28, 54, 57, 74, 75, 91, 92
McCoy, Benjamin (Captain) - 16
McCoy, Benjamin Daniel - 156
McCoy, Chapman L. – 47, 82
McCrady, Colonel - 146
McCrady, E.W. - 147
McCreight, Mrs. – 94, 97, 101
McCreight, R.J. – 65, 75, 83, 95
McCreight, W.R. - 162
McCreight, Willie - 55
McCulloch, Daniel - 27
McCullough, General Benjamin - 51
McCurry, Mrs. – 172, 180
McCutcheon, Colonel J. -148
McCutchen, James D. - 146
McDonald – 42, 82
McDonald, A. H. -
McDonald, A.J. - 42
McDonald, A.L. – 57, 92
McDonald, Charles A. – 27, 42, 45, 49, 54, 71, 74, 92, 94
McDonald, Donald – 74, 92
McDonald, Miss S - 179, 181
McDonald, Mrs. –98, 102, 171, 172, 179
McDonald, Mrs. C. -
McDonald, Mrs. C.M. - 179
McDonald, Reverend George G.N. - 101
McDow, Mrs. - 48
McDow, Mrs. Robert - 54

McDow, T.F. - 93
McDow, Thomas Dr. – 33, 48
McDowell, A. L. – 75, 91
McDowell, A.A. – 31, 33, 43, 91
McDowell, A.J. – 28, 33, 163
McDowell, Alexander I. - 39
McDowell, C.A. – 12, 56
McDowell, C.J. - 10
McDowell, General - 16
McDowell, George -36
McDowell, James L. – 57, 75, 91
McDowell, M. - 70
McDowell, Miss – 98, 102, 169, 172, 180
McDowell, Miss L. - 180
McDowell, W.D., Jr. - 47
McDowell, W.F.- 77
McDowell, William D. – 69, 75, 82, 91, 94, 164, 354
McDowell, Willie - 65
McDowell's Mill - 120
McElroy, Private/ Lt. Colonel – 131, 202
McEnlow - 129
McEwen, James – 58, 94
McEwen, Miss D.H. – 95, 98
McGinnis, R. - 40
McGougan, Angus – 62. 155
McGougan, Archibald - 155
McGougan, John – 46, 74, 92, 155, 158
McGowan, Brigadier General S. – 147, 337
McGowan, John - 44
McGregor, W.C. - 146
McGrugor, General - 50
McGuire, Henry - 53
McInnis, N.H. - 20
McIntosh, James – 10, 13
McKagen, Henry Green- 8, 9, 59, 69
McKagen, J.W.P. – 10, 13, 27, 34, 268
McKain - 42
McKain, John J. – 9, 21, 22, 28, 32, 34, 268
McKain, Lily - 180
McKain, William – 60, 68, 71, 74, 83, 92, 94, 268
McKain's Drug Store – 29, 127, 130
McKee, M. - 146
McKee, R. - 64
McKenzie, A.P. - 165
McKenzie, A.S. – 185, 398
McKenzie, F.L. - 146
McKinnon, Lauchlin - 27, 34, 42
McKinnon's Old Stand - 78
McLarnon, F. - 21
McLaughlin, Rush - 85
McLaurin, Daniel – 62, 63
McLaurin, J.D. - 162

McLaw's Division – 203, 208
McLaws, Major General – 203, 206, 207, 209, 222, 225
McLeish, Mrs. - 94
McLendon, Elias - 155
McLendon, Gillis - 155
McLendon, William - 155
McLeod - 40
McLeod, Alexander – 28, 42, 74, 92, 95
McLeod, Angus – 64, 243
McLeod, Harriet - 58
McLeod, J.A. – 37, 39
McLeod, J.H. - 35
McLeod, John Nelson – 40, 77
McLeod, Major D. - 211
McLeod, N.A. – 20, 52, 58
McLeod's Crossing - 134
McLernon, J.M. - 28
McManus Bridge 119
McManus, Captain – 10, 14, 200
McManus, J.Q. – 158, 160, 161, 162
McManus, Joseph - 164
McManus, Mrs. J.Q. – 161, 162
McMaster, W.F. – 146, 147, 148
McMillian, Joel - 10
McMullen, A.L. - 47
McNeil, Alex - 87
McNeil, Henry - 85
McNeil, J.Y. - 63
McPherson Hospital – 38, 158
McPherson, Samuel - 17
McQueen, Lieutenant -
McRae, John – 96, 217
McRace, D.- 87
McRae, Harvey -38
McRae, John – 96, 217
McRae, Mrs. - 66
McRae, Mrs. John – 55, 97
McRea, Mrs. - 101
McSween, William – 21, 85, 102, 153, 157, 158
Meanes, S.B. – 10, 13
Mecklenburg, N.C. - 68
Medlin, A. - 163
Medlin, A.C. - 163
Meggs, Stephen - 62
Mehement Ali - 139
Mellon, John - 124
Melrose Mansion - 132
Melton, A.J. - 34
Memorial Days – 167, 168, 169, 170, 178, 180, 181, 182, 184
Memorial Tree - 179
Merchant Tailors- 97
Merony, Bagwell, and Brothers- 94

Merony, John S. – 8, 27, 35, 42, 92, 325
Merony, T.A. - 44
Methodist Church – 67, 79, 95, 260, 261
Methodist Episcopal Church, Camden – 59, 62
Mexican War 1847 - 361
Mexico – iv, 219, 227, 261, 262
Meyer (Myers), Morris - 20
Meyers (Myers), Washington – 47, 51, 243
Mickle, Captain John Belton – 30, 51
Mickle, Captain Joseph - 30
Mickle, J.P. – 10, 13, 47
Mickle, John – 27, 35, 240
Mickle, John B. – 51, 57, 74, 92
Mickle, John L. - 91
Mickle, Joseph – 30, 88, 240
Mickle, Major Joseph - 30
Mickle, Martha Belton - 30
Mickle, Miss Carrie - 57
Mickle, Robert – 30, 98, 261
Mickle, Thomas - 65
Middle East -139
Middleburg - 209
Middleton, D.J. – 10, 13
Milers, S. - 85
Miles, C.R. – 10, 13
Miles, Reverend -171
Militia, Local 22D - 27, 90, 99, 365
Mill Creek - 115
Mill's House - 148
Miller, C.M. -169
Miller, Corporal Andrew -135
Miller, George R. (Captain) -5. 33, 74, 92, 96
Miller, John S. -96
Miller, Major D.B. -205, 212
Miller, Robert Peele -155
Miller, R.G.-57
Miller, Stephen Decatur- 215
Miller, T.B. -44
Millinary and Dressmaking -95
Milling, John Dr. -57, 81
Milling, Miss -57
Mills, Reverend William Wilson- 162, 163, 164, 181, 182, 268
Mimms, A.J. - 147
Mine Road - 207
Minor, James - 85
Mine, R. - 85
Minton, Columbus – 53, 64, 269
Minton, J.B.- 53
Minute Book 1906 – 1912 - 183
Minute Book 1921-1930 - 183
Minute Book 1930-1939 - 185
Minutemen of Kershaw County – 4, 5, 7

Misner, John H. - 124
Mississippi Brigade – 200, 203, 277
Mississippi Regiment – 201, 202, 323
Mississippi River - 80
Mixon, J.S. - 84
Mobley, J.B. - 49
Mobley, Mrs. - 125
Mobley's Plantation - 117
Moffatt Rifles – 46, 55, 63, 364, 365
Moffett, Major R.C. – 207, 210
Moffit, J.G. - 151
Monroe, Alexander - 49
Monroe, George - 49
Montgomery, John - 49
Montgomery, Mrs. - 48
Monument Square, Camden - 132
Monumental Association First S.C. Regulars - 147
Mooner, J.F. - 36
Mooneyham, John – 20, 53
Moore, A.A. (Dr.) – 151, 152, 162, 163, 164, 180, 200, 268, 371, 373, 374, 376, 381, 382, 384, 400, 412
Moore, John (Surgeon) - 119
Moore, S.M. - 164
Mordecai, J. Randolph, Jr. – 37, 43
Morgan, J. - 34
Morgan, W.D. - 34
Morris Island, SC - 8, 34, 63, 68, 84, 222, 225
Morris, John – 20, 53
Morrison, M.W. – 10, 13
Morrison, Mrs. - 185
Mosely, C.L. – 163, 268
Mosely, Craddock – 57, 75, 92
Mosely, George Washington – 163, 165, 397, 421
Mosely, Isaac – 62, 63, 386, 389, 391
Mosely, Reddick- 163, 420
Motley, J.J.- 39
Motley, James – 31, 34
Motley, R.L.- 85
Mount Elon Post Office - 120
Mounted Minutemen (M.M.M.) - 5
Moye, W.L.- 39
Mr. Hatfield
Muddy Creek - 108
Muddy Springs – 106, 110, 112, 119, 347
Mulberry – 7, 136, 143, 218
Mulberry Plantation - 139
Mulholland, John - 87
Mullins, W.S. - 146
Mumm's Quarts - 7
Mungo, C.P. - 34
Mungo, William – 28, 42, 57, 74, 92
Munn, A.J. – 20, 52, 163, 386

Munn, Henry James – 156, 164, 389
Munson's Hill - 18
Murchison, D.P.C. – 165, 185, 397
Murchison, J.G. - 146
Murchison, J.J. - 87
Murchison, S.P. - 158
Murray – 62, 63
Museum of Early Southern Decorative Arts - iii
Myers, John – 78, 243
Myers, T.S. – 21, 94
Myers, W.M.- 36
Myrant, W.R. -

N

Nance, Colonel – 201, 203
Nance, W.F. - 146
Nashville – 219, 323
Nassau – 139, 141, 142
National Cemetery for Veterans - 229
National Democratic Convention – 216, 223
National Reunion for Confederate Veterans - 264
Nebraska - 232
Neil, John H. - 340
Neile, Miss - 67
Nelson, Columbus - 391
Nelson, Emma S. – 388, 396
Nelson, George – 10, 13
Nelson, J.J. – 19, 34, 51, 57
Nelson, John - 27
Nelson, Mrs. J.J. - 30
Nelson, Mrs. P.H., Jr. - 182
Nelson, Patrick Henry –46, 84, 88, 244, 268, 337
Nelson, R.G. – 370, 371, 372, 373, 375, 376, 377, 379, 380, 382, 383, 385
Nelson, Rebecca - 180
Nelson, Rebecca G. – 370, 371, 372, 373, 375, 388
Nelson, S. Warren – 62, 71, 85
Nelson, S.L. - 376
Nelson, Thomas - 47
Nelson's 7th SC Battalion -
Nettles, Hiram – 10, 13, 27, 41, 163, 165, 268, 343, 346, 397
Nettles, J.E. – 87, 96
Nettles, Jessie – 10, 13, 15
Nettles, Jessie S. – 27, 104, 105, 268
Nettles, John T. – 268, 34, 373, 374, 376, 381, 382, 384, 400
Nettles, Joseph – 240, 268, 346
Nettles, Louise - 346
Nettles, Mary J. – 392, 395
Nettles, William - 268
Neuse River - 132
New Bern (New Berne) - 308

New Jersey Regimental Cavalry- 320
New Marker, East Tennessee - 81
New Orleans – 80, 138, 141, 217
New York – 255, 256, 257, 258
New York Corn Exchange - 255
New York Daily News - 257
Newberry District – 73, 143
Newman, Burwell Wiley - 54, 73, 121
Newman, John Hamilton -121
Newman, John Thomas - 121
Newman, Jonathan -38, 43
Newman, Mary J. - 283, 289
Newman, Milberry Wainright - 121, 123
Newman, W.W. - 55
News and Courier Newspaper - 164, 237
Newsome, Henry - 121
Nichol's Ferry - 97
Nickerson, Thomas S. - 33
Nickerson's Hotel - 114
Niles, E. Ariovistus - 14, 201
Niles, Edward E. - 201
Niles, Edward P. - 14, 34, 35, 43, 46
Niles, Martha – 28
Ninth SC Regiment- 363, 392, 393, 397, 401
Ninety -Fourth (94) Ohio Infantry - 99
Ninety-Seventh (97) Indiana - 89
Ninth - 173
Nix, A.J. - 263
Nix, J.F. - 263
Noel, Josephine- 191, 192, 193, 194
Noel, Mr. - 193
Norfolk, Virginia - 17, 192
Norris, George - 56
Norris, Hubbard - 121
Norris, M.M. - 269,270, 272, 273, 274, 275, 276, 277, 278, 279
Norris, N. - 56
North Carolina - 113, 114, 183, 192, 193, 246, 252, 260, 262, 260 (Ashville)
North Carolina Archives - 198
North Carolina Confederate Pensions - 198, 199, 232, 255
North Carolina State Troops - 60, 122
Northern Georgia - 67, 142
Northwestern Railroad - 15
Norton, Rare and Antiquorium Research Library New Orleans - 110
Nott, Sergeant Major - 168
Number 1, 22 Regiment - 21, 31
Number 2, 22 Regiment -21, 24, 27, 32
Number 3, 22 Regiment - 32
Number 4, 22 Regiment - 32
Number 5, 22 Regiment – 32

Number 6, 22 Regiment - 32
Number 7, 22 Regiment - 32
Number 8, 22 Regiment - 31, 32
Nunnery, B. -43

O

O'Neal, Richard -116
Oakes, F.J. - 29, 44, 56, 62, 78
Oates, W.C. - 174
Oath of Allegiance - 183, 193
Odd Fellows - 64
Officers of Court - 76
Officers of the Town of Camden - 77
Ogburn, L.D. -124
Ogburn, Mary - 281
Ogden, H.N. – 165
"Old Abe" - 7, 130, 143
Old Bartlett -servant - 250
Old Ben - 239
Old Camden District - 19
Old Church - 72, 260
Old Daddy Billy - 163
Old Dominion - 15, 21
Old Market Hall Steeple -190
Old Orphan Society School - 189
Old Sherman- horse - 252
Oliver, General - 98
One Hundred Four (104) Illinois Infantry - 99
One Hundred (100) Indiana - 89
One Hundred Fifty- Seven (157) New York - 105
One Hundred Seven (107) Ohio - 107
One Hundred Three (103) Illinois - 89
One Hundred Twelve (112) Illinois - 103
One Hundred Two D (102D) USCT -107
Oppenheim, J.H. and Brothers - 77
Oppenheim, Julius - 59, 60
Oppenheim, Mrs. - 56
Oppenheim, S. - 77
Oppenheimer, Mrs. Joseph - 80, 82
Oppenheimer, Mrs. S. - 101
Orange and Alexander Railroad -- 237
Orange Courthouse, Virginia - 17
Orangeburg County - 289
Orderly of Beat 5 - 69
Ordinance of Succession - 26, 151
Orr - 11
Orren, John - 282
Osteen, William - 33
Ostin, William - 32
Outen, A.C. - 127
Outen, D. - 54

Outen, Mary - 283
Outlaw - 54
Outlaw, A.L. - 289
Outlaw, Angus - 286, 287
Outlaw, B.F. - 73
Outlaw, Benjamin - 261
Outlaw, Bently - 31, 33, 70
Outlaw, Burwell - 31, 33
Outlaw, Charlotte - 285
Outlaw, Curtis - 73, 121
Outlaw, George - 56
Outlaw, J.C. - 71
Outlaw, John - 127, 280, 282, 284
Outlaw, John E. - 23, 47, 277, 280, 286
Outlaw, M.J. - 70
Outlaw, Richard - 71
Outlaw, Rozier - 286
Outlaw, Willey - 55
Outz, J.H. - 71
Owens - 70, 80
Owens, A. - 55
Owens, D. - 40
Owens, E. - 40
Owens, Isaac - 31, 33
Oxindine, Abigail - 281
Oxindine, R. - 36

P

Pace, H.C. - 289
Pace, John R. - 43, 184
Page, Jonathan - 56
Pageland (near Manassas) -177
Pale, Reverend William - 138
Palmetto Battalion - 39
Palmetto Cockades - 190
Palmetto Guard Charitable Association - 117
Palmetto Regiment - 167, 173
Parham, Robert - 127
Paris - 158
Parker - 117
Parker, B. - 55
Parker, E.W. - 72
Parker, Elias - 28, 38, 243
Parker, Emanuel - 9, 21, 28, 63, 75
Parker, Jane - 287
Parker, John - 40, 288
Parker, Michael - 59, 282, 284
Parker, Redding - 23, 59
Parker, William E. - 14, 23
Parkman, 2nd Lieutenant Samuel B. - 155
Parrot Guns - 154

Parsons, E. - 40
Parsons, V. – 40
Pate - 39
Pate, Chapman - 70, 121
Pate, Henry - 32, 120
Pate, Levi, Jr. - 121, 123
Patience - 163
Patterson, Lewis J. - 63, 75, 78, 78
Patterson, R.B. - 54
Patterson, R.C. - 28, 32, 39, 63, 75
Patterson, Reuben - 189
Patterson, W.W. - 34
Patterson, William - 34, 39
Patterson's Plantation - 91, 94, 96
Peach - 60
Peach, David - 81
Peach, Eliza - 286
Peach, William - 70
Peak, C.H. - 31, 33
Peak, Thomas - 56
Pearce, Benjamin McCoy - 201
Pearce, Ella P. - 291
Pearson - 54
Pearson, C.R. - 37
Pearson, J.A. - 289
Peay Colonel Nicholas - 104, 204
Peay, A.E. - 60
Peay, J.E. - 60
Peay, Mrs. Isabella - 82
Peay's Ferry - 85, 87, 89, 90, 91, 96, 97, 98, 99, 100, 101, 105, 183, 233
Peck - 189
Peck, Charles A.H. - 10, 64, 185, 189, 190
Peck, Major W.D. - 161
Peck, Mrs. - 77
Peck, W.P. - 116
Peck's Academy - 10, 13, 18
Pedee River - 93, 101
Pegues, T.W. - 79, 184
Pendergrass, F.E. - 288
Pendleton - 20
Pennsylvania - 10, 178
Pennsylvania Lunatic Asylum, Philadelphia - 183
Pensacola Army Headquarters - 180
Pensacola, Florida - 28, 178, 179, 180, 181
Pensions in Kershaw County - 267
Peoples, Lewis - 79
Peques, R.H. - 14, 18, 118
Perkins, Benjamin Elias - 75, 79, 201.
Perkins, Charles - 78, 184
Perkins, Mrs. Charles - 82
Perkins, Roger Griswold - 201

Perry, A.M. - 34
Perry, Allan - 70
Perry, D.D. -- 22, 39, 44, 74
Perry, J.A.- 14, 33
Perry, J.F. - 34
Perry, John - 28
Perry, John J. - 70
Perry, John M. - 127
Perry, Miss Emily E. - 37, 57, 73
Perry, Nancy - 287
Perry, Pinckney M. - 263
Perry, Reverend Benjamin Faneul -201
Perry, S.G. - 70
Perry, Thomas M. - 263
Perryman, W. - 34
Persons Exempt From Military Service - 292
Petersburg - 74, 83, 122, 151, 186, 206, 242, 243
Petersburg and Danville Railroad - 69
Petigry, James Louis - 164
Pettigrew, George - 55
Pettit, Benjamin F. - 263
Phelps, F. Butler - 201
Phelps, Francis Lambert - 201
Phelps, J.B. - 126, 271, 272, 273, 274, 275, 276, 279
Phelps, John - 128
Phillips, C.G. - 99
Phillips, C.J. - 70
Phillips, Charles Ingram - 121
Phillips, George Washington - 121
Phillips, Lewis - 55
Phillips, R.L. - 70
Phillips, Robert J. - 121, 284
Phillips, Stephen Franklin -- 120, 122, 123
Phillips, W. Riley - 121
Phillips, W.T. - 55
Phyllis - 163
Physicians - 76
Pickens, Governor - 164
Pickens, Mrs. - 2
Pickett, J.R. - 14, 43
Pickett, W.L. - 77
Pickett's Division - 208
Piedmont - 158
Pierce, Benjamin - 128
Pine Tree Church - 97
Pine Tree Meeting House - 87, 91
Pisgah, Sumter County, S.C. - 7, 280
Pittman - 254
Pittman - 255, 256
Pitts, Gus - 176
Pitts, J.C. - 73
Pitts, Mamie - 176

Pitts, Rebecca J. - 269, 270, 272, 273, 274, 275, 276, 277, 278, 279, 281, 283, 285
Planet, Cantey's Pony - 174, 175
Plank Road - 156, 157
Platter, Cornelius T.C. - 204
Player, H. Columbus - 128
Player, John - 72, 127, 201, 286
Player, R. - 127
Player, R.R. - 43
Player, W. Columbus - 293
Plummer, J. - 263
Plummer, M. - 263
Pocotaglio, S.C. - 123
Poe, Brivet Brigadier General, Orlando - 96
Polan, George - 263
Poland - 63
Polk, J.W. - 55
Polley, J. - 55
Pollock, B.C. - 116
Polylott Bible - 179
Pontoon Train Guard - 89
Pope - 2, 141
Pope, Joseph Daniel - 58
Pope, T.W. - 14
Poplar Grove Post Office - 87, 90, 96
Poplar Springs - 87, 91, 92, 97
Pop Skull- 286
Port Hudson, Louisiana - 67, 185
Port Royal, S.C. - 25
Porter, Dr. - 188
Porter's Bridge - 100
Porterdale Cemetery, Columbus, Georgia - 175
Portland, Alabama - 197
Post Commissary, Camden -103
Poston, Benjamin - 292
Poston, Mrs. - 138
Poston, Simon - 292
Potee, Richard - 40
Potomac River - 158, 161, 177, 178
Potter, Brigadier General Edward E.-- 105, 107, 218, 232
Potter's Raid - 108, 114, 136, 218, 219, 295
Potut, J.A. - 70
Powell, W.R. - 34
Powers, L.P. - 127
Powers, Lawrence - 70
Presbyterian Church - 56, 57, 78, 131
Prescott, Benjamin - 106
Prescott, Miss E. - 61
President of S.C. Senate - 165
Preston, Colonel J.F. - 235
Preston, General John S. - 117
Preston, William - 114

Price, Hugh - 54
Price, J.R. - 116
Price, W.P. - 116
Price, William - 56
Prier, Reverend Theodore - 18
Prince Albert - 37
Princeton - 164
Procter, Mrs. Francis - 142
Procter, R.W. - 14, 44
Professor Evans and Choir - 138
Providence Church - 107
Providence Road -106
Provincinal Congress to the United States- 164
Pruitt, Benjamin F. -
Pryor, Roger A. - 10
Pulliam, R.C. - 36
Purse, T.P. - 14
Pye (Pie), M.A. - 369, 371, 372, 373, 375, 376, 377, 378, 380, 381, 383, 385, 388

Q

Quaker Cemetery (also referred to as the City Cemetery) - 47, 67, 179, 199, 200, 252, 255, 260, 267, 270, 332
Queenstown, England -141
Quint, Lieutenant - 129

R

R.M. Kennedy's Store - 29
Rabon, A. - 31, 65
Rabon, John A. - 163
Radcliff's Bridge - iv
Rafting Creek - 135
Railroad bonds - 309
Railroad Depot Camden - 106, 136, 245
Raines, Musco B. - 156
Raleigh, N.C. - 219, 344
Raley, Andrew W. - 5, 21, 153, 157, 352
Raley, B. - 64
Raley, Charles - 57, 92, 96
Raley, Dove - 85, 156, 157, 158
Raley, J.R. -163
Raley, Redick - 154
Raley, William - 88, 156
Randell, B.J. - 85
Randall, Thomas - 98
Randolph, Mrs. - 16
Ransom - 63
Rappahannock River - 83, 186, 207, 319, 320
Rappanhannock Bridge -320
Rast, William R. - 360

Ratcliff, B.J. - 47
Ratcliff, Henry - 28, 42, 74
Ratcliff, W.H. - 47
Ratcliff, W.T. / T.W. - 157
Ratcliffe, W.C.(William Columbus)- 156, 163
Ray, Duncan - 163, 384, 386, 389, 394
Ray, James - 20
Ray, Neil - 163, 387, 389
Ray, William - 163
Raymond, Robert - 318
Read, Captain - 202
Read's Battery - 202, 203, 204
Reardon, G.W. - 43
Receiving and Delivery Agent - 93
Reconstruction Government/Period - 217, 221, 222, 225, 230, 407
Recording Scribe of Grand Division - 77
Recording Scribe of Wateree Division – 77
Records of the Rebellion- 325
Rector of St. Phillips Church - 300
Red Hill Post Office - 106, 111, 121, 122
Redin - 357
Reed, James L. II - 27
Reed, W.F.- 162, 164
Reenatjerna, T. - 93
Regiments -- 7, 18, 30, 99, 120, 124, 129, 201, 202, 206, 211, 220, 222, 239, 263, 281, 323, 339, 340, 365
Reid, Daniel - 84
Reid, Jackson - 240
Relic Room, Columbia, S.C. - 185
Reports of Brigadier General J. B. Kershaw -200, 203, 204, 205, 208, 212
Resaca, Tennessee -229
Revolutionary War - iv, 4, 215
Reynold's House - 332
Reynolds, Dr. William - 248, 249
Reynolds, Emma - 28, 70, 71
Reynolds, Essie - 70
Reynolds, G. - 70
Reynolds, James - 384
Reynolds, Miss - 172, 179
Reynolds, Miss Ella - 69, 70, 71
Reynolds, Miss Emma C. --180, 181, 182
Reynolds, Mrs. - 98, 102, 248
Reynolds, Sallie - 70
Reynolds, W.J. - 47
Rhame, George Sinkler - 163, 268, 395
Rhame, Joseph F. - 43
Rhame, Mrs. - 185
Rhett - 16
Rhett, Alfred - 147, 149
Rhodes, Charles - 262

Rice Creek - 119
Rice, Lieutenant Colonel W.G. - 206, 207, 208, 210
Rice, Mattie Clyburn - 263
Richard - 357
Richards - 14
Richards, J.G. - 33
Richards, John L. - 22
Richards, Mrs. - 183, 185
Richards, Mrs. Stephen - 180
Richardson, John S. - 10, 315, 316
Richardson, O.L. - 263
Richardson, S.M. - 43
Richardson, Samuel W., Sr. - 37
Richbourgh, J.J. - 20
Richland County, S.C. - 55, 392, 393, 394, 395, 396
Richmond Depot - 12
Richmond, Virginia - 10, 11, 12, 14, 16, 33, 38, 47, 50, 52, 53, 58, 59, 75, 76, 97, 142, 185, 198, 222, 225, 231, 232, 243, 255, 256, 257, 260, 264, 277, 337, 343, 344, 349, 353, 356, 357
Richmond-Petersburg Line - 343
Rickersville - 332
Rickerville Hospital - 29
Ridder - 258
Ridder, Mrs. - 257
Ridder, Thomas B, and Charlotte - 255
Riddle, J.H. - 10, 13
Riddle, James - 22
Riddle, Joseph - 346
Riddles - 346
Ridgeway, S.C. - 263, 369, 386, 388
Riley, W.R. - 63
Riley's area Kershaw County - 148
Rio Grande - 331
Rion, Colonel J.H. - 337, 338, 340
Rion, Major - 62, 84
Ripley, Brigadier General - 158
Riversdale, New York -257
Roach, Elizabeth C. - 381, 384, 386, 388
Roach, J.J. - 65
Roach, Mrs. W.C. - 371
Roach, W.C. - 371
Robert's Crossroads - 119
Roberts, D. - 85
Roberts, Henry C. -- 7, 94
Roberts, J.D. -- 146
Roberts, William C. -- 85, 162, 387, 389, 392, 395
Robertson, Captain F. H. - 219
Robertson, D.G. - 19
Robertson, David G. - 34, 75
Robertson, G. - 85
Robertson, J.B. - 85

Robertson, James - 163
Robertson, Robert - 34
Robertson, William K. - 65
Robertson's Battery - 219
Robinson, E.B. -- 87
Robinson, E.G. - 43, 95
Robinson, E.H. - 64
Robinson, Hilton - 156
Robinson, James - 156
Robinson, John - 87
Robinson, L.D. - 64
Robinson, M.A. - 398
Robinson, Mrs. David - 101
Robinson, Samuel - 36
Rochelle, L. William - 269
Rock Hill, S.C. - 214, 215, 346
Rocky Mount - 263, 311, 105, 108, 112, 115, 116, 117, 119
Rocky Mount Creek - 124
Rocky Mount Creek Bridge - 119, 124
Rocky Mount Ferry - 263
Rocky Mount Post Office - 115, 116, 117, 124
Rocky Mount Roads - 112
Rodgers, D.M. Sr. - 32, 37
Rodgers, J.D. - 84, 43
Rodgers, J.W. - 35, 95, 153
Rodgers, Jasper - 85
Rodgers, L.C. - 84
Rodger, Mr. - 30, 31
Rodgers, Mrs. - 66
Rogers, D.M. Sr. -- 43
Rogers, Mrs. - 98, 102
Rogers, Reverend J.E. - 59, 79
Rogers, S.M. - 34
Roland area Kershaw County - 392, 393, 397
Roland Area Post Office - 374, 376
Rollings, J.C. - 163, 164
Rom Hector - 281
Rose, J.A. - 84
Rose, J.N. - 165
Rose, John W. - 162, 398
Roseborough, Samuel - 289
Roseborough, Thomas C./L. -163,389
Ross, Calvin - 65
Ross, J.J. - 47, 65, 92
Ross, Martha A. - 394
Ross, William C. - 65, 124
Ross, W.J. - 31, 34
Rowan, S.W. - 146
Rowell, J.G. - 163, 391
Rowland area Kershaw County - 347, 376, 377, 378, 379, 381, 382, 384
Rugeley's Mill - iv

Rush - 85, 34
Rush, John - 65
Rush, John Jason - 103, 162
Rush, John Dewitt - 342
Rush, William A. - 85
Russell - 130, 220
Russell County, Alabama - 227, 228, 229, 230, 232, 261
Russell, Colonel -221
Russell, Wardlaw F. - 162, 164, 165, 269, 398
Russell, W.T. - 47
Russell's Crossroads- 118
Russell's Place- 97, 113, 120, 123, 369, 370, 37, 373, 375, 376, 377, 378, 380, 381, 383, 385
Russell Place Post Office - 369, 370, 372, 373, 375, 376
Russellville, Tennessee - 215
Rutland, H. - 360
Rutledge Street, Camden, S.C. - 245, 324
Rutledge, Colonel -149
Rutledge, W.F. -159, 161
Ryan, D. - 41
Ryan, D. R. - 63
Ryan, David H. - 58

S

S____, J Dunky -156
Saddlery and Harness - 95
Sagani Ghadrani (White Arabian) -141, 143
Sailor's Creek -198, 277, 297
Saint James College- 212
Salem Church - 205, 207, 332
Salmond, Burwell - 269
Salmond, E.A. - 70, 226
Salmond, Mrs. E.A. - 98
Salmond, Ed - 77
Salmond, Henry C. - 86, 87, 162, 163, 164
Salmond, Louisa - 28, 70
Salmond, Miss - 98, 102
Salmond, Mrs. Ann - 50, 60
Salmond, Mrs. T.W. -17, 169
Salmond, Thomas Whitaker, Dr. - 8, 18, 22, 34, 93, 202, 208, 269, 324
Salmond, Tom -70
Saluda River - 115
Sander's Creek - iv, 78, 120, 122
Sanders, George N. - 257
Sanders, Jeff - 264
Sanders, Thomas Polk - 162, 164, 269
Sand Hills- 347
Sandy - 214, 359
Sandy Area, Lexington, S.C. -359
Sandy Grove Church - 106, 111, 122

Sandy Hill - 345
Sarsfield, Camden, S.C. - 215
Saunder's (Sander's) Creek - 108, 112, 120, 122
Savage Station - 50
Savannah, Georgia - 343, 344
Scalawag - 224, 297
Scarborough, L.W. - 15
Schoenburg, Professor - 251
Scotland - 333
Scott, A. - 84
Scott, G.M. - 146
Scott, General Winfield - 315
Scott, Hasting - 20, 51, 53
Scott, Manning - 20, 41, 53
Scott, Mary - 373, 374, 375, 377, 378, 379, 380, 382, 383
Scott, Timothy - 86, 156
Scriven, R.H. - 87
Scuyler, Robert - 27
Seay, Colonel Abraham - 110
Seay, J. Robert - 38, 39, 40
Secession of the Southern States - 80, 174, 216, 217, 218, 231, 354
Secessionist - 303
Second Brigade - 108, 109, 110, 112, 113, 114, 116, 123, 124, 228
Second Division - 106, 110, 111, 115, 117, 121, 124,
Second Dragons - 232
Second Ohio Cavalry - 279
Second Pennsylvania Cavalry - 320
Second S.C. Cavalry - 125, 319, 322, 364
Second S.C. Infantry/ Regiment – 8, 9, 11, 12, 13, 14, 15, 16, 17, 18, 34, 35, 36, 41, 45, 49, 51, 58, 63, 75, 79, 81, 86, 89, 90, 159, 160, 161, 186, 198, 201, 203, 204, 205, 206, 207, 210, 211, 213, 222, 225, 228, 260, 334, 361, 362, 390, 391, 392, 393, 394, 396, 397
Seep Gand - 112
Segars, Dove - 21, 46, 62, 63, 84, 86, 88, 90, 151, 153, 157, 339, 363, 364, 365, 411
Seibring (Sebring), Mrs. - 97, 98, 101
Seige Train - 90
Self, G.W. - 163
Self, George - 90
Self, Nancy - 395
Self, Stephen - 88, 162, 164, 369, 370, 372, 373, 375, 376, 377, 378, 380, 381, 383, 384, 386, 388, 390
Self, W.F. - 163
Sellers - 368
Sellers, J.C. - 368
Sellers, S.C. - 368
Seminary Buildings, Camden - 245
Seminole War - iv
Semmes, General - 205, 207, 209, 210, 211, 212

Semmes' Brigade - 210, 211, 212
Sessions, Thomas R. - 65, 237, 238
Setzler, J.T. - 47
Seven Day's Campaign - 198
Sevententh Army Corps - 109, 120, 126, 129
Seventh Battalion - 62
Seventh Cavalry - 129, 201
Seventh Corps - 106
Seventh N.C. Regiment - 159
Seventh Ohio Sharpshooters - 109
Seventh SC Regiment - 84, 85, 88, 157, 159, 161, 201, 202, 203, 204, 206, 207, 210, 211, 390, 392, 397, 401
Seventy-Ninth Pennsylvania Infantry - 124
Seventy-Six Ohio - 110
Seymour - 216
Shanghai, China - 221, 223, 224
Shannon - 325
Shannon, Allie - 132
Shannon, Allison - 269
Shannon, Benjamin H. - 72
Shannon, Charles J. - 23, 67, 70, 71, 73, 75, 162, 165, 269, 398
Shannon, Dr. C.J. - 134, 151, 152
Shannon, Dr. C.J., Jr. - 269
Shannon, H. - 70, 71
Shannon, Miss Leila - 183, 184
Shannon, Miss Martha - 132
Shannon, Mrs. William M. - 97
Shannon, S.A.B. - 65
Shannon, Thomas E. - 64, 71, 91, 132
Shannon, William McCreight - iii, 4, 17, 19, 31, 38, 66, 70, 89, 93, 96, 104, 134, 136, 151, 152, 153, 171, 181, 238, 239, 240, 269
Sharp Area of Kershaw County - 387
Sharp, I. P. - 44
Sharp Post Office - 397
Sharpsburg - 40, 41, 45, 56, 59, 75, 76, 198, 203, 243
Shaus, A.D. - 270
Shaver, William - 360
Shaw, J.D. - 157
Shaw, John R. - 57, 75, 91
Shaw, Willie - 37
Shaylor (Shailor), J. - 33
Shaylor, C.H. - 53
Shaylor, J.O. - 163
Shaylor, T.S. - 53
Shedd, Captain - 327
Shedd, J.B. - 64
Shedd, Jessie P. - 53
Shelbyville, Tennessee - 59
Shelton, M.A. - 146
Shenandoah River - 208

Shenandoah Valley - 198
Sheorn, Duncan - 29, 32, 33, 92
Sheorn, J.L. - 71
Sheorn, J.R. - 88
Sheridan - 277
Sheridan's Infantry - 218
Sheriff Barnes - 79
Sherman, William T. - 22, 101, 105, 124, 128, 129, 132, 136, 143, 219, 222, 226, 273, 274, 275, 290, 293, 295, 301, 305, 311, 317, 318, 325, 341, 343, 344, 345, 347, 350
Sherman's Forces (Army) - 105, 126, 128, 130, 131, 132, 238, 239, 245, 264, 274, 293, 294, 308, 325, 332, 341, 351
Sherman's invasion - 130
Sherman's March through the Carolinas - 219, 229
Sherman's Raiders - 293, 295, 309
Sherman's wagons - 130
Sherry, M.C. - 360
Shields, Estate of William - 96
Shiloh - 218, 221, 262
Shingler, C.H. - 64
Shingler's Regiment - 86
Shira, Isaac - 31, 34
Shira, Joseph - 53
Shirley, M.M. - 393
Shirley, Samuel – 85h
Shiver, Isaac - 65
Shiver, C - 19, 21
Shiver, Elizabeth Emma - 3
Shiver, Emma - 3
Shiver, John William- 3, 4
Shiver, John Jr. - 7, 8
Shiver, Lazarus - 4
Shiver, Martha Burkitt - 393
Shiver, Martha Cornelia - 3
Shiver, Samuel - 4, 94
Shiver, Thomas L.- 34, 94
Shiver, William James- 3
Shiver, Zack - 37, 39
Shoemake, George Nelson -156, 157, 158
Shoemaker, F.- 95
Shrewsberry Clock - 11
Shrock, Joel A. - 19, 22, 31, 41, 51, 54, 269
Shrock, Mary E. - 398
Shrock's Mill- 28, 42, 57, 74, 92
Shropshire, James- 40
Shuford, Reverend J.J. - 72
Shuler, P.H.B.- 36, 146
Shull, William - 360
Sieloff, Charles W. - 269
Signal Corps - 129
Sikes, B. - 94
Sikes, William R. - 93, 99

Sill, Edward Elijah - 4, 9, 18, 29, 41, 63, 99, 162, 163, 164, 179, 180, 200, 217, 240, 269
Sill, Henrietta M. - 398
Sill, Miss- 99
Sill, Mrs. Edward E. - 181, 184
Simmons, J.R. - 87
Simmons, S.P. - 146
Simpson, Joseph - 33
Simpson's Station - 113
Sims, Brigadier General - 278, 279
Sinclair, James - 46, 88, 165, 371, 386, 393
Sinclair, John - 389, 394
Sinclair, M.S.F. - 398
Sinclair, Rebecca - 394
Singleton's Creek - 106, 110
Singleton's Plantation - 135
Sioux, expedition - 232
Sister, John R.- 360
Sixth Iowa – 110
Sixth SC Regiment- 37, 59, 89, 212, 359, 360, 362, 363, 391, 392, 393, 394, 395, 396, 397,
Skifflin, Lieutenant Frank - 240
Sligh, T.W. - 90
Slocam, General - 105
Sloman and daughters - 61
Small, A.J. - 87
Small, R. F. - 10, 13
Small, Robert F. - 68
Smith, B. Mendel - 269
Smith, Captain Frederick L. - 208
Smith, Colonel Milo - 110
Smith, D.R. - 46
Smith, G. - 63
Smith, General John E.- 123
Smith, General Kirby - 193
Smith, Henry - 163
Smith, J.A. - 46, 85
Smith, J.T. - 393
Smith, James - 44
Smith, Jessie W.- 20
Smith, John - 10, 13, 156
Smith, John W. - 44
Smith, Mendal - 94
Smith, Sallie J. - 392
Smith, T.H.- 74
Smith, T.W. - 28, 49
Smith, T.W.B. - 163
Smith, W.L. - 63
Smyna Post Office - 369, 373, 370, 375, 376
Smyrl Family - 318
Smyrl House - 317
Smyrl, J.M. - 269

Smyrl, Mary A. - 398
Smyrl, Miss Mamie - 317, 318
Smyrl, Robert L. - 317, 318
Smyrl, Thomas J. - 85, 269
Smyrna area of Kershaw County - 369, 370, 372, 373, 375, 376, 377, 378, 380, 381, 383, 384
Snider, Major William H. - 124
Soldier's Board of Relief - 92
Soldier's Family Depot - 78
Soldier's Rest - 30, 49, 65, 67, 78, 83, 89, 90, 99, 101
Soldier's Wayside Resting Place - 30
Soldiers of the Board of Relief - 27
Solomon's Gap - 200-201
Sommers - 56, 70
Sommers, A. - 19
Sommers, Joseph - 32, 33, 94
Sommers, L.- 28
Sommers, Mrs. - 101
Sons of Confederate Soldiers - iii, 153
Sons of Temperance - 77
Sorrel, G.M.- 56
Sotaers, R. - 71
South Atlantic - 142
South Carolina - iii, iv, 3, 5, 6, 8, 10, 11, 12, 13, 14, 16, 18, 19, 21, 22, 28, 38, 40, 45, 46, 48, 50, 56, 58, 59, 60, 68, 73, 77, 78, 79, 80, 87, 96, 99, 109, 112, 119, 133, 136, 139, 142, 143, 145, 148, 153, 157, 158, 162, 169, 174, 181, 183, 184, 187, 191, 198, 199, 200, 214, 215, 216, 217, 218, 221, 222, 224, 225, 226, 227, 229, 230, 232, 234, 235, 237, 243, 244, 245, 251, 257, 261, 263, 264, 291, 324, 328, 332, 334, 343, 348, 355, 361, 362, 363, 365, 367, 400, 407
South Carolina Assembly - 216
South Carolina Brigades - 145
South Carolina College - 77, 222, 225, 226, 251
South Carolina Death Certificates - 163
South Carolina Legislature - 367
South Carolina Military Academy - 72
South Carolina Rangers - 131
South Carolina Rangers' Charitable Association - 147
South Carolina Regulars -147
South Carolina Reserves- 216
South Carolina Senate - 216, 223
South Carolina State Tax Collector - 68
Southern Commission Claims of Kershaw County - 237
Southern Confederation - 11
Southern Constitutional Equality in the Union - 4
Southern Cotton Oil Company - 319
Southern Cross- 25, 26, 184
Sowell, Gilliam- 28, 42, 51, 57, 74, 75, 91, 92
Sowell, J. A. - 42, 63
Sowell, J. Wiley - 85, 156

Sowell, James Ervin - 154, 413
Sowell, James R. - 31, 33, 96, 159
Sowell, Lewis - 157
Sowell, S. -15
Sowell, W.H. - 159, 161
Sox, Samuel - 360
Sparks, Calhoun - 322
Spears. Colonel - 356
Spears, R.T. - 85
Sperryville - 208
Spotsylvania Court House-86, 198, 206
Spradley, Jim - 401
Spradley, John - 53, 64, 65, 86
Spradley, Martha - 392, 394, 396
Spradley, W.J. - 20, 41, 50, 61, 393
Spring Hill Methodist Church (St Johns) - 79
Spring Hill, Sumter County, S.C. - 3
Springer, R. - 19, 52
St. Albans, Vermont - 256
St.Louis - 80, 223
Stackhouse, Colonel E.T. - 146
Stafford Heights - 319
Stakely, Jacob - 74
Stakely, Mrs. - 98, 102
Stalnacker, B. - 85
Stalnacker, Richard - 85
Stanley, J.D. – 33
Star of the West- 174
State Grand Master - 199
State House, Columbia, S.C. - 214, 223
State Newspaper 198, 283, 324
State Survivor's Association -145, 146
Statesburg, S.C.- 133, 134, 135
Staudemyer, F. - 94
Steadman, J.B. - 162
Steckley, J. - 49
Steedman, J.B. - 164
Steen - 86
Steen, Wilson - 65
Stephen - 143
Stephenson, L.B. - 31, 33, 57, 95
Stephenson, Uriah J. - 89
Stephenson's Store (L.B.) - 61
Steven's House, Fredericksburg, Va. - 334, 213
Stevens, Frank - 44
Stevens, J.W.F./J.H.W.-161
Stevens, Julia A. -398
Stevens, Lieutenant Edward L. -135
Stevenson, D.E. - 163
Steward - 28, 49, 74
Stewart, C.J.- 165, 387, 389, 398
Stewart, Chap-164

Stewart, J.D. - 163
Stewart, Peter- 34
Stewart, T.A. - 165
Stewart, W.G. - 9
Stewart, William - 37, 39
Still, Isaac - 360
Still, J.B. - 360
Still, Thomas E. - 360
Stockton Plantation, Camden - 343
Stockton, Edward C. -75
Stockton, Emma W. - 75
Stockton, Phillip A, Jr. - 251
Stockton, Phillip A.- 251
Stokes, Charles Spencer-73, 122, 123
Stokes, E.E.- 126
Stokes, F.M. - 37
Stokes, John J.- 56, 280, 284
Stokes, Reverend A.J. -130
Stokes, Simeon - 73, 126
Stokes, W.J. - 70, 286
Stokes, W.J.C. - 81
Stokes, W.W.- 14, 43
Stone Mountain Memorial -141
Stone Mountain, Georgia -141
Stone, Lieutenant - 242
Stoney, Captain Dwight - 248, 249
Stoney, Reverend James M. -140, 152, 165
Stoney, Reverend Samuel -139
Stork, W.H. - 116
Stoudemire, G.W. - 40
Stout - 168
Stover, James L. - 31, 32
Strawbridge, R.R. - 14
Strickland, S. - 71
Stroman, Absalom - 263
Strother, D.B. - 72
Stroud Mill - 99
Stroud, John M. - 122, 124
Stroud, L.J. - 124
Stroud, Lily Thomas - 122, 271, 272, 273, 274, 275, 276, 277
Strut, R. - 71
Stuart, Benjamin R. - 292
Stuart, Hannah Todd - 243
Stuart, J.E.B. - 141, 238
Stuart, James - 14
Stuart, John Todd - 243
Stubbs, J.D. - 116
Stuckey, C.C.- 36, 37
Students in the Army - 221
Sturgeon, Thomas - 71
Succession Convention - 164, 165
Suggs, Elizabeth - 268, 270, 271

Sullivan, James - 73, 268
Sullivan's Island - 33, 185
Sulky- 286
Summers- 25
Summerville, S.C.- 22, 105
Summit Point - 158
Sumner, General - 45
Sumner, Senator - 164
Sumter (Sumterville), S.C. - 16, 24, 73, 74, 101, 105, 152, 185, 218
Sumter County (Sumter District), S.C. - 8, 44, 64, 66, 139
Sumter Watchman - 35
Sumter, S. - 41
Surles, Edward Martin - 122
Surrender of Lee and Johnston Armies - 232
Surveyors - 77
Survivor's Association - 267
Survivors of Association of Kershaw District - 118, 119
Sutherfield, J.- 59
Sutherland, J.F.- 60, 77, 78, 82
Sutherland, Mrs. J. - 80, 82, 241
Sutler's Cavalry - 255
Sutt---, James - 122
Sutton, B. - 72
Sutton, G.- 70
Sutton, J.J.- 268, 269, 270, 271, 272, 274, 275, 276, 278, 279, 280, 282, 284, 286, 290
Sutton, James Frederick -122
Sutton, T.G.- 70
Swails, First Lieutenant Stephens-108
Swannanoa (Hardy's) - 234, 235
Swift Creek - 65, 105, 106
Swiss Creek - 107
Sycamore Street- 17
Syke's Division- 162

T

Tan Yards - 78
Tarver, William -77
Tax Collector- 76
Taxpayer's Convention 1871, 1874 -165
Taylor family -163
Taylor, Adam -184
Taylor, George-32, 33
Taylor, James - 280, 282, 284
Taylor, Mrs. G.E. - 142
Taylor, Rachael - 281, 283, 285, 287
Taylor, Thomas E. - 111, 113
Taylor, William R. - 32, 33, 63, 71, 74, 77, 201
Taylor's Crossroads - 95
Taylor's Plantation- 163

Team- 106
Team, Adam -32, 33, 114
Team, James W. - 28, 33, 38, 50, 63, 75, 80
Team, John - 14, 24
Team, Miss Kittie - 61
Teel, E.T.- 202
Temperance Hall- 59, 82
Templeton, H.B. - 263
Templeton, W.A. -116
Tennessee - 46, 52, 61, 67, 163, 165, 170, 172, 175, 251
Tenth Georgia Volunteers - 243
Terebene distillery - 35
Terrell, Richmond R.-75, 91
Terry, William H. - 165
Terry, William W. - 398
Texas - 40, 89, 16, 164, 183, 217, 331
Thames, A.W. - 38
Theological Seminary, Camden - 198, 299, 300
Third U.S.C.T. - 135
Third Brigade - 106, 111, 114, 116, 118, 123, 124
Third Cavalry Division - 118, 119
Third Corp - 209
Third Division - 107, 108, 111, 112, 113, 114, 115, 118, 121
Third New York Artillery - 135
Third Regiment -201, 202, 204, 207, 211
Third S.C. Infantry/Battalion - 39, 156, 157, 160, 40, 323, 360
Thirteenth Michigan -124
Thirteenth Mississippi Regiment - 202, 323
Thirtenth Ohio Infantry -122
Thirtieth Ohio Infantry - 123
Thirty Fifth Congress - 216
Thirty-First Georgia Regiment -236
Thirty-First Missouri -110
Thirty-Second Georgia Regiment -270
Thirty-Second Georgia Regulars - 270
Thirty-Second Missouri - 110
Thirty-Seventh Alabama - 228
Thirty-Seventy Ohio Infantry -123
Thirty-Six Georgia Regiment - 233
Thirty-two U.S.C.T. - 135
Thomas Family - 287
Thomas Farm - 287, 291
Thomas House - 292
Thomas Lang Plantation- 262
Thomas, Davis - 44
Thomas, Jep - 62
Thomas, W.M. - 338, 339, 340
Thomasville, N.C. -323
Thompson Family - 342
Thompson, Charlotte Patterson -341
Thompson, Henry -156

Thompson, J.S. - 49, 64
Thompson, James W. - 269
Thompson, Jerry - 196
Thompson, John - 34, 51, 54, 57, 61, 64, 82, 341, 366,
Thompson, Joseph James- 72, 156
Thompson, Miss -181
Thompson, Mrs. J.S. - 49, 54
Thompson, Thomas Sumter - 156
Thompson, Toney -195
Thompson, W.K. - 127, 128
Thompson, William Black -122
Thorne, Ann M. - 291
Thorne, Henry - 55, 184
Thornton, Mrs. - 50, 80
Tiller, H.A. - 42
Tiller, Henry Dickerson - 74, 120, 122
Tiller, J.J. - 33
Tiller, J.M. - 70
Tiller's Bridge- 85, 87, 91, 256
Tiller's Creek - 103
Tiller's Ferry - 33, 122, 123, 271, 272, 273, 274, 275, 276, 277, 278, 279, 280, 282, 284, 285
Tiller's Ferry Post Office - 373, 374, 375
Tiller's Ferry Road- 98
Tillersville - 96, 97
Tillman, Governor (S.C.) - 152
Tilly, William - 263
Timmonsville, S.C. -215
Timrod Section Kershaw County- 269, 270, 272, 273, 274, 275, 276, 277, 279, 281, 284
Tindale, S.C. Secretary of State -152
Tinkler, L.D. - 71
Tisdale, D. - 55
Tisdale, James -41
Todd, Alexander- 243
Todd, David - 243
Todd, Dr. George Rogers - 201, 243, 244
Todd, Levi - 243
Todd, Mary - 2
Todd, R.P. - 116
Todd, Robert Smith - 243
Todd, Samuel -243
Todd, Uncle James Clark -243
Tolbert, B.M. -116
Tolbert, W.S. - 71
Toulmin, Colonel H.T. -167
Transylvania Medical School -243
Trantham, J.L., Dr.- 9, 28, 31, 50, 77
Trantham, Mrs. W.D.- 142
Trantham, Nannie E. - 291
Trantham, W.D. -126, 128, 140, 152, 201
Trapier - 59, 60

Trapier, Edith - 224
Trapier, Mrs.- 220
Trapier, Reverend - 220, 225(with Mr. T's Watch)
Trapier, Theodore- 223, 224, 230
Trapp, Alan- 70
Travis-168
Treasurer- 29
Tremble's Division-174
Trenholm, George - 67
Trexler, J.J.- 360
Triminal, R.J. - 393
Trotting Park - 14
True, James H. - 387, 390, 397
Truesdale, Henry - 261, 269
Truesdale, J.C. - 392
Truesdale, J.E. - 36, 63
Truesdale, J.R. - 395
Truesdale, J.T. - 31, 269
Truesdale, James J. - 42, 47
Truesdale, Jessie - 35, 57, 91
Truesdale, Nancy M. - 393
Truesdale, S.J. - 31, 33
Truesdale, Sallie E.- 398
Truesdale, W.M. - 391, 395
Truesdel, J.C.- 163
Truesdel, James T. - 33, 163
Truesdell, J.E. - 81
Truesdell, Jessie - 27, 42, 74, 75, 92
Tucker, J.H. - 83
Tucker, T.W. - 270
Tunstall, Virginia- 255
Turnball, John - 87
Turner, Benjamin Daniel -156, 162
Turner, Benjamin James - 154, 158
Turner, Cheyenne - 265
Turner, G. M. - 33
Turner, J.F. - 53
Turner, John W. - 20, 357
Turner, R.D. - 46
Turner, Robert J. - 156, 158, 163
Turner, Silas B.- 164, 165, 184, 69, 398
Turner, W. M. - 10, 13
Turner, W. W. - 20, 21
Turner, William F. - 269
Turnpike road - 205
Tweeddale, Colonel William - 109
Tweedie, Major General W., C.S.I. - 139
Twelfth Illinois -348, 351
Twelfth Indiana - 110
Twelfth Indiana Infantry -350
Twelfth Virginia Regiment- 323
Twelth SC Regiment -90, 159, 392, 395, 397

Twentieth Army Corp Train- 124
Twentieth Army Corps- 239
Twentieth Hagood Battalion- 337
Twentieth SC Battalion - 89, 90, 99, 362, 390, 391, 393, 396
Twentieth SC Infantry -362, 365
Twentieth SC Regiment- 89, 90, 99, 362, 390, 391, 393, 396
Twenty-First Regiment - 339, 340
Twenty- Six Alabama - 219, 220, 228
Twenty-fifth Alabama - 219, 220
Twenty-fifth Ohio -135, 136
Twenty-Fifth SC Regiment - 339, 395
Twenty-First Alabama Infantry - 219
Twenty-First S.C. - 339
Twenty-first Wisconsin Infantry -123
Twenty-ninth Alabama - 228
Twenty-ninth Arkansas - 228
Twenty-Ninth Missouri Cavalry - 325
Twenty-Second Alabama Infantry - 218, 219, 220, 221
Twenty-Second SC Regiment -19, 33, 51, 54, 61, 90, 99, 327, 393, 397
Twenty-Seventh Missouri -110
Twenty-Seventh SC - 67, 248, 327, 339, 340
Twenty-six Alabama - 219, 228
Twenty-Six Iowa -110
Twenty-Six Illinois Infantry -110
Twenty-Six S.C. Regiment -159
Twenty-third SC Regiment- 327, 329
Twenty-two D SC - 27, 90, 99, 365
Tyler - 28, 74
Tyson, W. - 85

U

Umfries (Humphries) , Nathan -32, 34
Uncle Ben - 286, 295
Uncle Edmund - 292
Uncle Jim - 292, 293
Union- 7, 239
Union Army Corps- 109, 125, 240, 277, 278, 324
Union Cavalry - 277
Union Left Wing - 105, 106, 109, 119, 121, 126, 135, 211
Union Right Wing - 72, 106, 109, 119, 121, 126, 134, 211, 325
United Confederate Veterans - 153, 224
United Confederate Veterans Reunions - 162, 164, 187, 191, 264, 401
United Daughters of the Confederacy - 111, 183, 229, 252, 407
United Methodist Church - 67
United States - 139, 174, 197, 221, 239, 257, 303
United States Cavalry - 325
United States Ford - 207

United States Government - 136, 137
United States Marshalls - 255
United States Military Academy - 232
United States Navy - 343
United States Senator - 251, 216, 218
University of South Carolina - 251
University of Virginia - 50
Union County, North Carolina - 263, 64
Upper Division of Kershaw District- 54
Upton, Lieutenant Edward N. -110
Utah - 232
Utah Territory Campaigns (1857-1858) -232, 235

V

Valley Campaign- 229
Van Dorn, General - 233
Vance, General - 72, 355
Vance, W.C. - 87
Vance's Ferry - 136
Vandiver, J.B. - 85
Vaughn, James H. - 38, 74, 95
Vaughn, James M. - 92
Vaughn, Lewis M, - 10, 13, 20, 21, 268
Vaughn, R. H. - 44
Veney, M.S. - 90
Viceroy Khedive Mohammed -141
Viceroy of Egypt - 130, 139, 141
Vicksburg - 80
Vienna, Virginia - 68, 313
Villepigue, F.L. - 40
Villepigue, John Bordenave - 48, 232, 233, 234, 235, 236, 244, 268
Villepigue, James I. -162, 163, 164, 200, 217, 232, 233, 234, 235, 236, 244, 268
Villepigue, James T. - 8, 85
Villepigue, Miss Kate A. - 182
Villepigue, Mr. K.S. -324
Villepigue, Mrs. James -169, 179
Villepigue, P. Bracey - 72
Villepigue, Paul Francis - 268
Villipigue, Paul E. -35
Vincent, Josiah - 88
Vincent, M.J. - 370, 371, 372, 374, 375
Vinson, J. - 33
Virginia - 5, 10, 11, 12, 14, 15, 17, 18, 20, 21, 22, 28, 29, 31, 34, 37, 48, 49, 54, 55, 57, 58, 60, 67, 68, 79, 80, 86, 90, 157, 180, 183, 185, 198, 203, 205, 217, 222, 225, 229, 278, 286, 289, 292, 294, 313, 319, 328, 331, 332, 333, 334, 337, 344, 354, 355, 361, 362
Virginia Regiment - 17, 323
Von Treskow, Sadie Kennedy - 184, 251

Von-Hasselin, A. - 20

W

Waddell, R. B. - 158
Waddill, N. T. - 54
Wade, J.R. - 9
Wadesborough, N.C. - 118
Wadsworth, Major General -324
Wages, Edmond - 55
Wages, William - 55
Waites' Battery, S.C. - 89, 159
Walcutt, Brigadier General Charles C. - 89
Walker, Colonel C.J. -148
Walker, E.P. - 85
Walker's Brigade - 203
Wall, Lieutenant Colonel Hiram W. - 110
Wallace House-223
Wallace, E. - 36
Wallace, Lew - 139
Wallace, William N, -36, 63,146, 147, 148, 149
Walter, George II -147
Walton, J.T. - 85
Walton, John - 85
Wannamaker, William S. -360
War Between the States - iv, 4, 131, 174, 229, 255, 261, 262, 267, 299, 319, 331, 367, 407
War of 1812 - iv, 9, 16, 30, 35
Ward, Allen G. - 369, 370, 372, 373, 375, 376, 377, 378, 380, 381, 383, 386, 389, 390, 397
Ward, E.G. - 163
Ward, John - 54
Ward, R.G. - 394
Wardlaw, Mrs. A.B. - 49
Wardlaw, Mrs. L.W. - 48
Wardlaw, Mrs. S. Watt -54
Wardlaw. S. Watt - 87
Warren, H.F. - 65
Warren, J.O. - 10, 13
Warren, Thomas J. - 8, 9, 18, 19, 21, 29, 31, 40, 41, 48, 55, 58, 59, 62, 64, 68, 71, 73, 261, 268
Warren, W.D. - 41, 53
Warren, Wiley Lansley - 157, 158
Warren, William -20
Warrenton -53, 319
Washington Artillery Society -147
Washington, D.C. - 89, 174, 175, 216, 223, 256, 257, 314, 355
Watches and Jewelry -88, 94
Wateree area -34, 261, 387, 388, 389
Wateree Bridge -106, 127, 283
Wateree Church - 94

Wateree Creek - 116, 125
Wateree Division - 77
Wateree Ferry - iv
Wateree Guards - 27, 28
Wateree Meeting House - 125
Wateree Mounted Rifles (Rifleman) - 40, 45, 46, 48, 55, 72, 243, 354, 364, 365, 396
Wateree River - 27, 78, 103, 106, 107, 108, 110, 111, 112, 113, 114, 115, 116, 118, 119, 120, 121, 127, 132, 283, 311, 346, 347, 348, 350, 351
Wateree Swamp -99
Wateree Trestle - 132
Waterloo and Mills- 319
Waties' Artillery Company - 55
Watkins, F. - 54, 156
Watkins, J.J. - 88
Watkins, James Jackson -156, 268
Watkins, Jessie Ellis- 85, 156
Watkins, John E.- 88
Watkins, Thomas - 65
Watkins, Wiley -32, 34, 65
Watson, James -84
Watson, M. - 65
Watson, W.W. - 20, 41, 53
Watts, Columbus - 20, 54
Watts, E. -41
Watts, Frank W. - 41, 64
Watts, G.E. -185
Watts, George W. - 163, 385, 386, 389
Watts, J.W. - 385
Watts, John - 20, 54
Watts, L. - 37, 39
Watts, L. J. -163
Watts, L. W. - 165, 398
Watts, O.W. - 47
Watts, W.R. - 39
Watts, W.W. -10, 13
Waxhaw, North Carolina - 77
Wayside Hospital, Camden -332
Webb, John - 87
Webb, Samuel - 84
Weekly News - 319
Wehrhan, A.W. - 94
Weinges, C.M.- 71
Weldon railroad -157, 337
Welsh, Dr. C.C. - 159
Welsh, J.V. - 158, 160, 161
Wesberry, J.P. -39
West Florida Headquarters -236
West Indies - 29
West Point Academy -235
West Wateree, Kershaw County - 34, 261

West, Alex - 341
West, C. - 33
West, E. - 157
West, H.C. - 65, 163, 391
West, John C. - 410
West, Joseph A. - 31, 33, 85, 154, 163
West, Matthew C. - 131
West, Mrs. -98
West, Nancy - 370
West, Nancy J. - 370, 372, 374, 375, 377, 378, 379, 380, 382, 383, 385, 387
West, Richard Edward -84, 158
West, Sarah - 398
West, T.G. - 63
West, W.- 63
West. Miss Deica Lamar -183
West's Area Kershaw County -371, 372, 374, 375, 377, 378, 379, 380, 382, 383, 385
West's Crossroads -111, 123
West's Post Office -371, 372, 374, 375
Western Army - 80
Weston, William - 85, 90
Westville, S.C. -381, 384, 386, 387, 388, 391, 392, 393, 394, 397
Wethersby, J.A./ L.A.- 10, 13
Wharton's Tavern - 124
Wheat, Hiram - 241
Wheeler, Captain- 240
Wheeler's Cavalry - 125, 240, 295
Wheeler's men - 275
Wheelright and Ginmaker -95
Whisnant, A. - 146
Whistler, K.G. - 258
Whitaker - 355
Whitaker, Bessie Clarke - 273, 398
Whitaker, Caroline H, Kennedy - 21
Whitaker, Chesnut -18, 269
Whitaker, Duncan- 40, 47, 71, 269
Whitaker, H.- 101
Whitaker, Helen - 58
Whitaker, John- 57, 70, 269
Whitaker, John, Jr. - 21
Whitaker, L. Lawrence - 57, 75, 82, 269
Whitaker, Mrs. H.M. - 56
Whitaker, Mrs. John - 55, 66, 78, 81, 98, 101
Whitaker, Mrs. L.L. - 78, 97
Whitaker, Richard L. -57, 75, 91
Whitaker, Thomas- 162, 164
Whitaker, William -38, 86, 87, 151, 162, 164, 217, 269. 350
White Oak - 119, 125, 340
White Oak Creek - 78, 108, 112, 122
White Oak Station -124

White, Albertus S. - 269
White, Captain -124
White, Captain Rufus- 324
White, Major - 37, 204
White, R.J. - 88
White, Rebecca W. -398
White's Battalion S.C. Light Artillery -365, 391
Widmer, Major John H. -124
Widow's Home -148
Wigfall, Senator - 217
Wightman, Reverend J.T. -95
Wilburn, W.C. - 270
Wilcox Brigade- 206
Wilcox, General - 206
Wilde, Captain - 124
Wilder, W. W. - 36
Wilkinson, T.O.- 90
Williams - 239
Williams Crossroads - 120
Williams Sergeant Edward G.- 244
Williams, A.M. - 87
Williams, A.W.- 20, 52
Williams, B.F. - 20
Williams, Colonel Reuben - 110
Williams, Crayton - 239
Williams, David Roberson- 269
Williams, E.D. -51, 159, 160
Williams, Edwin S. - 269
Williams, G.W.- 86
Williams, J. - 90
Williams, J.B. - 85
Williams, John C.P - 164, 394, 395
Williams, J.N. - 85
Williams, J.R. -389
Williams, James -146
Williams, John - 42, 47
Williams, Miller -149
Williams, N.J. - 371, 372, 375, 379, 380, 382, 393
Williams, Nancy - 369
Williams, R.R. - 31
Williamsburg District - 126
Williamson, G.O. - 84
Williamson, J.H.- 163, 164, 357
Williamsport, Va. - 209
Willis, H. - 270
Wilmington Family- 256
Wilmington, N.C. - 126, 141, 142, 255, 256, 350, 354
Wilson -18
Wilson, A.S. - 395
Wilson, F.J. - 400
Wilson, H.C. - 44
Wilson, Harriet - 398

Wilson, Hattie B.- 398
Wilson, Henry - 20. 53
Wilson, J.M. - 44
Wilson, James - 65, 164
Wilson, Joel - 20, 53
Wilson, John - 63
Wilson, John W. - 90
Wilson, Judge- 44
Wilson, Miss M.- 67
Wilson, Morton W. - 269
Wilson, Paul H. - 20, 53, 64, 399
Wilson, R.R. - 10, 13
Wilson, Reverend J.O. - 179
Wilson, Robert - 44
Wilson, Samuel McCartney -269, 399
Wilson, Samuel T. -44
Wilson, Thomas J. -269
Wilson, Thomas M. - 259
Wilson, William M.- 85, 390, 392
Wilson's Army - 262
Wilson's Raiders - 228
Winchester, Virginia - 41, 203, 208, 232
Winder, General John H. -256
Winder, J.R.- 10, 13
Winnsboro News and Herald -340
Winnsborough, S.C. (Winnsboro) -105, 106, 113, 114, 115, 117, 118, 119, 121, 126, 260, 263, 290, 347, 351
Wirz, Captain Henry - 256
Wither's Division- 219, 220, 221
Withers, General - 220
Withers, Judge Thomas Jefferson - 6, 14, 15, 198, 269, 416
Withers, Rose -324
Withers, William Randolph -72, 269
Witherspoon - 66, 98, 129, 394
Witherspoon, B.J. /J.B. - 147, 161
Witherspoon, H.K. - 47
Witherspoon, J. - 226
Witherspoon, J.H.- 10, 13
Witherspoon, James- 49, 269
Witherspoon, James M. - 54
Witherspoon, J. L. - 32
Witherspoon, John K. - 27,33, 40, 45, 58, 70, 75, 91
Witherspoon, Mrs. - 169
Witherspoon, Mrs. J.K. - 172
Wittkowsly, Mrs. L.A. -184
Wittowsky, Adoph - 38, 399
Wofford, General - 206, 209, 211
Wofford's Brigade - 206, 211
Wolfe, Eugene - 20, 52
Wood, Mason D. - 31, 34, 65
Woodlawn Cemetery, NY - 219
Woodruff, Lieutenant - 279, 280

Woods, Brevet Brigadier General William B. -110
Woods, Brevet Major General Charles A. - 110
Woods, General - 121, 122
Woods, P.C.- 10, 13
Woods, P.E. - 34, 35, 47
Wooten, John - 44
Workman, John J. - 19, 22
Workman, John C.- 21, 75, 91, 96
Workman, May R.- 393
Workman, William Clark - 269
Workman, William H. R. - 67, 71, 75, 82, 152, 400
Worshipful Master- 28, 74
Wright, B.P. - 85
Wright, E.B. - 85
Wright, General -207
Wright, Lieutenant Colonel George W. -110
Wright, W.H. - 10, 13, 15
Wylie, John D. (Captain) - 9, 251
Wyndham, Colonel Sir Percy - 320
Wyrick, L. - 85

Y

Yancy, William Lowndes - 5
Yarborough, Ebbin N. - 85, 352, 417
Yarborough, M.- 31
Yarborough, M.K. -34
Yarborough, Wilson - 28, 42, 47, 395, 396
Yates - 22
Yates, Colonel John B. - 109
Yates, Jessie - 44
Yates, S.J. - 384
Yates, Samuel- 20, 41, 54
Yates, Willie - 54
Yates, Willis - 20
York County - 396
Yorktown Campaign - 198
Young - 46, 123
Young Ladies Tableaux - 65
Young, Allen - 31, 34, 132
Young, Dr. James - 56, 129, 284
Young, E.A. - 90, 91
Young, Fleming - 240, 241
Young, George A. - 18
Young, George Gilliam - 47, 87, 132, 200, 217, 269
Young, George Graham -269
Young, Grandmother - 342
Young, Hugh - 239, 240
Young, J. - 71
Young, J.M. - 85
Young, J.N. - 47
Young, J.W. - 41, 52, 70
Young, James - 48, 269
Young, James A. - 94
Young, Jessie F.- 269
Young, John - 65
Young, John A, - 96
Young, John, Sr. - 240
Young, John Zachary- 408
Young, M.R. - 388
Young, Major General - 132, 135
Young, Margaret J. - 393, 395
Young, Mattie - 214
Young, Mrs. R. - 98, 102
Young, R.W. - 86
Young, Robert - 70
Young, S.H. - 56
Young, Senator John, Jr. - 240
Young, Temperance O. - 240
Young, W.J. - 163
Young's Bridge - 106, 129
Young's Store (Doctor's)- 67
Youngbluth - 67

Z

Zemp - 70
Zemp, Bertie - 273
Zemp, Franncis Leslie - 32, 33, 71, 75, 91, 93, 94, 95, 269
Zemp, Miss Ella -184
Zemp, Mrs. F. Leslie- 183, 184
Zemp's Mill - 130
Zimmerman, William - 360
Zoar Church - 205, 331
Zouaves - 315
Zouaves, Ellsworth - 313

www.ingramcontent.com/pod-product-compliance
Lightning Source LLC
Chambersburg PA
CBHW081426070526
44586CB00020B/2507